MONGOLIA'S Foreign Policy

MONGOLIA'S Foreign Policy

Navigating a Changing World

Alicia Campi

LYNNE RIENNER PUBLISHERS

BOULDER
LONDON

Published in the United States of America in 2019 by
Lynne Rienner Publishers, Inc.
1800 30th Street, Boulder, Colorado 80301
www.rienner.com

and in the United Kingdom by
Lynne Rienner Publishers, Inc.
Gray's Inn House, 127 Clerkenwell Road, London EC1 5DB

Library of Congress Cataloging-in-Publication Data
Names: Campi, Alicia J., author.
Title: Mongolia's foreign policy : navigating a changing world / by Alicia Campi.
Description: Boulder, Colorado : Lynne Rienner Publishers, Inc., [2019] | Includes bibliographical references.
Identifiers: LCCN 2018048638 | ISBN 9781626377820 (hc : alk. paper)
Subjects: LCSH: Mongolia—Foreign relations. | Mongolia—Politics and government—1992– | Mongolia—Economic conditions—21st century. | Natural resources—Mongolia.
Classification: LCC DS798.84 .C36 2019 | DDC 327.517/3—dc23
LC record available at https://lccn.loc.gov/2018048638

British Cataloguing in Publication Data
A Cataloguing in Publication record for this book is available from the British Library.

Printed and bound in the United States of America

The paper used in this publication meets the requirements of the American National Standard for Permanence of Paper for Printed Library Materials Z39.48-1992.

5 4 3 2 1

To my dear friends
Ruth A. Kurzbauer and David N. Cohen,
who have supported me throughout my professional life
and generously edited this book

Contents

Tables and Figures

Tables

Figures

Introduction

This book examines the foreign policy, including the foreign economic policy, of independent Mongolia in the democratic era, which began in 1990. Mongolia, which celebrated its twenty-fifth year of democracy in 2015, has a long, storied history dating back to its founder, Chinggis Khaan,[1] but it only has recaptured the world's attention in the past decade because of its rich mineral resources. The analysis is framed through an integrative approach that emphasizes the Mongolian perspective for researchers and students of Sino-Russo-Mongolian, as well as Northeast Asian and Eurasian, studies. It focuses on geopolitics—the defining of circumstances under which a nation will always act to protect its national interests. While many researchers have attempted to define and explain the policymaking strategies of China, Russia, and Japan, as well as the United States, few have considered the geopolitical strategy of Mongolia.

As Ambassador P. Stobdan has noted, "Mongolia's strategic position at the cross junction of Central Asia, Northeast Asia, Far East, China and Russia attracts major powers towards it."[2] Although Mongolia traditionally has not been a key ally for the United States, it has played a linchpin role in Russian, Chinese, and Japanese strategic views about Northeast Asia for many decades. In the twenty-first century, after the demise of the Soviet Union and the rise of China, Mongolia has become even more prominent in these nations' self-interested calculations and has attracted the keen attention of many other countries. The United States, as the remaining superpower at the end of the Cold War, became involved in Mongolia mainly because this landlocked former Soviet satellite state was seen as an experiment in the simultaneous dismantlement of seventy years of socialism, inculcation of democratic values, and development of a free market economy.

In the 1990s, after decades of isolation from the economic development of most of their Asian neighbors, Mongolian policymakers expected that if they made the necessary economic reforms, their nation would benefit from integration into the booming Asian regional market and the whole of the developed world. Yet, they believed that maintaining national political security was of paramount importance and recognized that abandoning their traditional reliance on one of Mongolia's two border nations for protection was a new and potentially dangerous stratagem. Therefore, Mongolia developed a foreign policy concept labeled the Third Neighbor Policy. This strategy was proposed first by then US Secretary of State James Baker in 1990 as a way for Mongolia to balance the tendency of its border neighbors, China and Russia, to establish control over Mongolia's international and domestic politics and economy.

Over the years, the "Third Neighbor" strategy has become a flexible, multipillared foreign policy that is the rationale for promoting relations with the industrially advanced nations to the West and East, including the United States, Japan, South Korea, the United Kingdom, and Germany, to consolidate best practices and accelerate Mongolia's transition into the global market economy. From 2010 onward, the Third Neighbor Policy has been expanded and reinterpreted both in content and meaning to include cultural and economic partners as diverse as India, Brazil, Kuwait, Turkey, Myanmar, and Iran. Nevertheless, the Mongols always have emphasized that their approach to economic and political security meant that both China and Russia rightly should be accorded top priority in their foreign relations based upon the principle of a balanced, stable, but not necessarily equidistant relationship, and that these border neighbors would be the main trade partners as well as major investors. In 2014 Mongolian policymakers decided to recast the relationship with these two powers under a "neighbor trilateralism" dynamic in order to take advantage of Sino-Russian rapprochement.

Mongolia experienced a tumultuous first decade of democracy in the 1990s in which it had to rely on substantial foreign donor assistance to prop up the transition process. The new millennium saw Mongolia, with foreign expert advice, readjust its macroeconomic plans toward reliance on foreign direct investment (FDI), especially in its mineral sector. In 2012 the World Bank asserted that "Mongolia is at the threshold of a major transformation driven by the exploitation of its vast mineral resources."[3] Its exploding growth rate of 17.3 percent in 2011 and 12.3 percent in 2012 (compared to 6.1 percent in 2010)[4] caught the attention of economic and financial strategists, who wanted to know more about Mongolia's ability to supply key minerals to feed the Chinese economic juggernaut and to expand trade ties with the advanced economies of Japan and South Korea. Mongolia's international image and global presence also increased with the rise of Eurasian continentalism,[5] epitomized by various multilateral, integrative economic and transportation strategies, often labeled Silk Road initiatives, which have accelerated over the last few years. More recently, fluctuating world commodity prices, the slowing Chinese economy, and Mongolia's vacillating legal environment for foreign investors have led to a retrenchment period inside Mongolia and the dimming of international enthusiasm for its actions and minerals. Nowadays, when observers question where the country is heading, they may fail to appreciate the complicated situation Mongolia's democratic political and economic institutions still confront.

I made my first visit to communist Mongolia in 1975, participated in the preliminary discussions in 1985–1986 in Tokyo that led to the establishment of official bilateral diplomatic relations between the United States and Mongolia in 1987, and have been a close observer of Mongolian foreign and domestic affairs during the past thirty years. Posted in Ulaanbaatar in the beginning of 1990 as a US diplomat, I was an eyewitness to the final months of peaceful street demonstrations led by young Mongols, such as the late Sanjaasüreng Zorig and President Tsakhia Elbegdorj. These demonstrations resulted in the fall of the communist government that had been in power for seventy years and the birth of Mongolia's democratic experiment to transform its entire economic and political system. Over the last quarter century, as a diplomat, businesswoman, academic, and commentator, I personally have known every Mongolian president and prime minister, in addition to policymakers in all aspects of civil society and government. This type of deep and well-rounded perspective on Mongolian affairs motivated me to attempt to produce a cogent and multifaceted examination of the formulation and execution of contemporary Mongolian foreign policy, which I call Mongolia's "Wolf Strategy."

During the first decade of change, in the 1990s, I was in and out of the country about fifteen times for research and business projects, and my travel to Mongolia has continued at regular intervals into the new millennium. These experiences have allowed me to develop a comparative viewpoint as a witness to the emergence of the seemingly chaotic democratic society of today's Mongolia from the harsh realities of its collapsed socialist world. The challenge for contemporary researchers on Mongolia is how to find a way to mesh new sources and technology with highly personal accounts to achieve a more accurate analytical context without completely rejecting the old socialist-era research. I believe part of the problem is that many foreign observers and researchers of democratic Mongolia lack real historical understanding of the country, so they fall into the trap of just reporting and analyzing events as they arise—more like commenting on a collection of specific photographs. This kind of analysis fundamentally enlarges Mongolia's problems and minimizes its very real accomplishments. Such a perspective also makes it nearly impossible to predict the country's future behavior because there is little understanding of the fundamental currents underlying Mongolian modern history, including those that created the democratic era and direct its policies.

We in the West have a few key, but little used, Western materials about life in socialist Mongolia. Examples are the memoirs of Britain's first ambassador to Mongolia, Reginald Hibbert, whose *Letters from Mongolia* was written during his posting in 1964–1966, and Daniel Rosenberg's studies of agricultural *negdels* (communes) in the early 1980s.[6] My own first visit to Mongolia was in 1975 during what Mongols called the golden years of Tsedenbal and Brezhnev. I remember only one nearly empty department store and horse carts rather than private autos in the capital. Although I returned to Mongolia as a diplomat in 1990 to seemingly similar economic conditions, the political environment was in fact very much bubbling with enthusiasm for the new changes that Gorbachev's brand of Soviet glasnost and perestroika allowed. As a result, Eastern European–educated Mongols were strongly influenced by the Solidarity movement in Poland.

Mongols, including the politburo, were shocked by the events in Tiananmen in June 1989. They believed the Chinese communist leadership had murdered their own children and colleagues and were determined not to replicate that experience. We know this from deliberations of the Mongolian politburo that were revealed in the memoirs of the last Mongolian communist leader, party general secretary Jamba Batmönkh,[7] who reportedly told his wife, "We few Mongols have not yet come to the point that we will make each other's noses bleed."[8] In large measure, Mongolian demonstrations were well managed by the protesters, and the government, police, and army exercised great discipline in preventing chaos. As a result, Mongolia experienced a tense but peaceful ending to communism without violence, loss of life, or retribution squads. While not well known today, this story stands as a great accomplishment of bravery, persistence, patience, and national reconciliation that should be studied by Mongolia's youth so that they might find lessons to guide them through future difficult periods and as a model of harmony for other societies in conflict. More personal memoirs of democratic and nondemocratic actors in this crucial period must be collected and published. This is a great challenge and should be a nationwide project that Mongolian universities rally behind by encouraging their students of history, political science, and modern sociology to do personal reminiscence-based research.

As for the topic of Mongolia's foreign relations, we have some written sources from the past two decades, especially via online blog interviews. One of the few published books is Morris Rossabi's controversial work, *Modern Mongolia: From Khans to Commissars to Capitalists,*[9] which provides a critical view of Mongolia's US-led development policies in the early 1990s. At the other end of the analytical spectrum is US Ambassador Jonathan Addleton's volume published in Mongolian and English entitled *Mongolia and the United States: A Diplomatic History*[10] that was written to commemorate twenty-five years of US-Mongolian relations. In addition to the publications and media sources, I have utilized personal recollections and private writings of Mongolian leaders and foreign diplomats to humanize my analysis. Among the helpful sources were the personal interviews of some of the US ambassadors to Mongolia, which are being collected by the Association for Diplomatic Studies and Training as part of its Foreign Affairs Oral History Project.[11]

Nevertheless, Mongolian democratic history of the past twenty-five years needs even more diverse materials to provide a better understanding of the process and great economic cost of dissolving the communist structures of the nation. The collapse of the Soviet Union, which provided one-third of Mongolia's budget every year through its COMECOM system, resulted in a very difficult final decade of the twentieth century that included severe food shortages in the cities but no riots or violence. Mongolian policymakers made the decision to establish both a stable free market and a democratic society concurrently—a most difficult and unique path that other former socialist nations making the same transition during the same years did not have the confidence to embrace. To explain this decision-making process, historians need to interview politicians and parliamentarians, some of whom already are retired, and comb through the rich Mongolian newspaper record. However, this record is not yet digitalized in large part, so the publications must be examined in person, for example, at the Montsame photographic services. There also are foreign records and memoirs available in Western languages because the Western donors, particularly the United States, believed Mongolia was a model for other countries to emulate. The US Congress lauded and financially supported the controversial Mongolian model of development. In 1992 the second US ambassador to Mongolia, Joseph Lake, proclaimed, "This is a place where Americans—if we believe what we say about democracy and free enterprise—can affect the future. The Mongolians are now trying to restructure their economy and their government on the basis of the ideas we believe in. If they succeed, this country, as an island of democracy, could be very important to the world."[12]

Ambassador Lake's words can be seen as prophetic because it is irrefutable that Mongolia stands today as the greatest success story in Central Eurasia for ecopolitical reform and development among the nations emerging from the Soviet system. The transition was especially difficult if one understands that Mongolia, unlike Eastern European nations, did not have the underpinnings of a modern nation-state to rediscover and build upon. Mongolia's heritage is that of a nomadic economy of herdsmen loosely controlled externally by a distant Manchu Chinese imperial system for 300 years, domestically governed by a princely class dating back to Chinggis [Genghis] Khaan's Mongolian Empire of the thirteenth century, and a Buddhist lamaist religious government in the early twentieth century headed by a Dalai Lama–like figure. For Mongolia's leaders from the communist-trained Mongolian People's Revolutionary Party (MPRP), as well as the many young democratic movement activists, to embrace a modern constitution in January 1992 with representative parliamentary democracy that has been flexible enough to guide the country through great domestic and global changes is really a modern miracle comparable to the US Founding Fathers' Constitution. Have all the legal ups and downs over the past twenty-five years been correct or effective? Obviously, no. But has the direction the country followed been toward greater human economic and political freedom? The answer is unreservedly yes.

Mongolia's story during the past decades cannot be divorced from the history of Asia, including that of its giant neighbors Russia and China. However, Mongolia is not Russia or China. All three nations have experienced the collapse of old orders swept away by nationalism and revolution in the twentieth century and have been reborn in today's interconnected global world. Many Western nations, along with China and Russia, have forged strong comprehensive bilateral relationships with Mongolia during the past two decades. This fact, together with the great economic and political progress Mongolia has made during the same period, must not be overlooked when discussing present-day challenges. This volume will explain the complicated geopolitical environment the Mongols operate in, historically and today. It will attempt to illustrate the struggles and successes of Mongolian policymakers as they remade their society and government in the post–Cold War world. The role of the foreign community—diplomats, businessmen, nongovernmental experts—and the impact of globalization are also major factors in Mongolia's development strategy. The chapters are arranged in a general chronological manner, highlighting specific critical junctures and trends throughout the democratic era. This book does not claim to cover comprehensively the major domestic events during this same time period, but, because in Mongolia domestic politics and international relations are closely intertwined, many of the key incidents and individuals are included.

Notes

1. Chinggis Khaan is also known as Chinggis Khan, Genghis Khan, or Jenghiz Khan.
2. P. Stobdan, "India and Mongolia: Modi on Ashoka's Path," *IDSA Comment*, Institute for Defence Studies and Analyses, May 13, 2015, https://idsa.in/idsacomments/IndiaandMongolia_pstobdan_130515.
3. World Bank, "The World Bank in Mongolia: Overview," 2012, http://www.worldbank.org/en/country/mongolia/overview.
4. *CIA World Factbook*, http://www.indexmundi.com/g/g.aspx?c=mg&v=66.
5. Enunciated in Kent E. Calder, *The New Continentalism: Energy and Twenty-First-Century Eurasian Geopolitics* (New Haven, CT: Yale University Press, 2012).
6. Reginald Hibbert and Ann Hibbert, *Letters from Mongolia* (London: Radcliffe Press, 2005); Daniel Rosenberg, "Leaders and Leadership Roles in a Mongolian Collective: Two Case Studies," *Mongolian Studies, Journal of the Mongolia Society* 7 (1981–1982): 17–51; Daniel Rosenberg, "The Collectivization of Mongolia's Pastoral Production," *Nomadic Peoples*, no. 9 (September 1981): 23–39.

7. Jambyn Batmunkh, ed. Dojoogin Tsedev, *Khuch Kherkhevch Khereglej Bolohgui* (Ulaanbaatar: Bidnii Mongolchuud, 2001), 21; Jambyn Batmunkh, *There Will Be No Use of Force Under Any Circumstances,* comp. D. Tsedev, trans. R. Baasan (Ulaanbaatar: The Mongolia Society, forthcoming).

8. B. Enkhtuul and R. Oyun, "Ж.Батмөнх агсны гэргий А. Даариймаа: Хань минь багшийнхаа ажлыг хийж байсан бол өнөөдөр амьд сэрүүн байх байлаа" ["Batmönkh's widow A. Daariimaa: If my husband was working as a professor, he would have been alive today"], *Zuunii Medee* [Century News], April 18, 2011, http://www.bolod.mn/modules.php?name=News&nID=54864.

9. Morris Rossabi, *Modern Mongolia: From Khans to Commissars to Capitalists* (Berkeley: University of California Press, 2005).

10. Jonathan S. Addleton, *Mongolia and the United States: A Diplomatic History* (Hong Kong: Hong Kong University Press, 2013).

11. For example, Ambassador Joseph Lake, "Ambassador Joseph E. Lake," interview by Charles Stuart Kennedy, Association for Diplomatic Studies and Training Foreign Affairs Oral History Project, September 5, 1994, http://www.adst.org/OH%20TOCs/Lake,%20Joseph%20E.toc.pdf.

12. Fred Shapiro, "Starting from Scratch," *The New Yorker* (January 20, 1992), 39.

1

A Brief History of Mongolia

In 1990, following in the footsteps of many countries in Eastern Europe, Mongolia began a peaceful transition to democracy and the free market. Now, in the second decade of the twenty-first century, it is a country inextricably committed to its own democratic experiment of representative government, and it is potentially well positioned to become a very wealthy nation through the development of its vast mineral resources. At the same time, it suddenly has embraced its nomadic and imperial heritage, which was denigrated and systematically attacked throughout most of the preceding century. The return to glorification of the nomadic past, somewhat contradictorily, is a response to successful Mongolian globalization and integration into the Asian region during the last twenty-five years as the Mongols seek to establish their own uniqueness. Furthermore, it is stimulated by domestic political reaction to the loss of this same "Mongolness" in the rapid modernization of the capital Ulaanbaatar and, even more, by both the fear of growing Chinese trade monopolization and the impact of Western mining companies on the country.

The ongoing search for Mongolia's heritage at times has been radicalized and reformulated. There has been a psychic return to the romantic notion encapsulated in the "myth of nomadism" as well as a revival of the cult of the founding father, Chinggis Khaan[1]—all harkening back to redefining the Mongolian Empire in the thirteenth and fourteenth centuries. There are many biographies, old and new, of Chinggis Khaan, who created the largest empire in history and realized a European-Asian connection that much larger nations still are striving to recreate. Strife within the ruling family took its toll on the Mongolian Empire, which split into four great parts under Chinggis Khaan's sons. Not many decades after the rule of grandson Kubilai Khan[2] in China, the Mongols abandoned Beijing in 1368 and rode back onto the Mongolian steppe to their old capital of Karakorum to begin 150 years of internecine fighting and constant attacks on the native Chinese dynastic successor, the Ming.

In the seventeenth century the Mongols of Inner Mongolia and then the Khalkha[3] tribes in Eastern Mongolia (now independent Mongolia) lost their fully independent status to the expanding Manchus,[4] Tungusic-speaking forest dwellers who lived in the Manchurian peninsula to the east of the Mongolian plateau. The Khalkha Mongols entered the Manchu Empire in 1691 when their princes swore an oath of allegiance to the Manchu emperor. Their submission was followed by that of the western Mongol tribes and eventually the Tibetans. All these peoples were granted special status within the Manchu Empire and can be viewed as an alliance of subordinate partners rather than conquered nations.

With the establishment of the Qing dynasty (1644–1911) in China, the Khalkha, ruled by their own hereditary princes bound by titles and marriage to the Manchu royal house, were designated a frontier province called Outer Mongolia and governed under the Li Fan Yuan (Board of Dependencies). This deliberate Manchu policy of isolating Outer Mongolia politically and economically from the tribes of Inner Mongolia preserved the unique tribal and nomadic traditions of the Khalkhas. Eventually, heavy taxation and the extravagant lifestyle of the Mongol noble class led to the economic indebtedness of the Outer Mongols to usurious Chinese traders. In the late 1800s Chinese agricultural colonists, who previously had been allowed to populate only Inner Mongolia, moved illegally onto the Mongolian plateau, which caused economic dislocation in the Khalkha steppe economy and engendered a legacy of hatred and fear against the Chinese.

The most important phenomenon in Outer Mongolia during the eighteenth and nineteenth centuries was the development of a Buddhist ecclesiastical establishment comprised of nearly 1,000 Tibetan Buddhist–style lamaseries sustained by strong patronage from the Qing court that stimulated urbanization on a modest scale.[5] Buddhism was organized under the leadership of a personage entitled Jebtsundamba Khutukhtu,[6] whose prestige and power generated a lamaist hierarchy that siphoned off wealth from the political noble class. Manchu policies fostered a mentality of dependency on foreign financial support by both the lamaist and princely rulers. This dependency theme would reoccur in democratic Mongolia. The Buddhist establishment, though immensely popular with the common people, became morally corrupt and economically exploitative through vast estates supported by herding communities, which belonged like serfs to monasteries. As Manchu rule weakened in the late nineteenth century, sporadic and unorganized incidents of popular unrest protesting local conditions grew, aimed at the Buddhist system, Mongol princes, and the Manchu governors (*ambans*).[7]

By the early twentieth century the Manchus no longer saw the Khalkhas as important in resisting tsarist Russia. Both the spreading of the Russian Empire throughout Siberia and the occupation of Korea by the Japanese forced the Qing government to officially modify its immigration policies toward Mongolia to encourage Chinese farmers to settle in the steppe lands after 1906. In the capital of Urga (today's Ulaanbaatar), Manchu officials levied unpopular taxes on livestock, a move that stirred the fires of rebellion. Since the Mongol nobles had pledged loyalty to the ruling Manchu dynastic family, not to China, the disintegration of Qing power at the beginning of the twentieth century encouraged independence sentiment among the Mongols. Understanding how Mongolia first became dominated by the Manchus is key to explaining the dissolution of the relationship in 1911. For Mongols and Tibetans, the demise of the Manchu Qing government on October 10, 1911, did not mean that their superior partner became the Republic of China (ROC). Rather, it meant the empire separated into the ROC, Mongolia, Tibet, and other entities.[8]

A lamaist theocracy with an autonomous[9] government led by Prime Minister Sain Noyan Khan[10] was established with the Eighth Jebtsundamba Khutukhtu[11] (aka the Bogdo Khaan or Bogdo Gegeen and often called Living Buddha) enthroned as emperor on December 29, 1911. In early 1912 many Mongols outside the Khalkha homeland, including those living in Khinggan, Inner Mongolia, Barga, and Hailar in Manchuria, declared their allegiance to the Bogdo Khaan government. However, true Mongolian independence was not to be, since China and tsarist Russia conspired as early as July 1912 to divide the Mongol tribes into their own spheres of influence. Rather, Mongolia embarked on a hundred-year search for a new national identity recognized by the world community. The first decades of the twentieth century were full of civil war in China, a "Great War" in Western Europe, and a Bolshevik Revolution in Russia—all of which influenced Mongolian attempts to create a modern definition of what it meant to be Mongol.

Tentative steps began during the autonomous government throughout the 1910s, when Mongolia secretly approached the United States, Japan, England, France, Germany, and other European powers, as well as Lenin in Moscow, for diplomatic recognition. This author's book, *The Influence of China and Russia on United States–Mongolian Political Relations in the Twentieth Century*, revealed the complicated story of the US government's response to the Mongolian appeal. Ultimately, all the Western powers ignored the approaches; only the Soviet Union responded affirmatively. In early July 1921, a joint army of Mongols and Red Bolsheviks captured Urga to usher in the communist era, but it was only in 1924, upon the death of the Eighth Bogdo Khaan, that the government was reconstituted as a people's republic, the second in world history. The Mongolian People's Republic (MPR) lasted until March 1990, when a successful peaceful democratic revolution swept away seventy years of Soviet-dominated communism.

Western historians have argued the 1911 Mongolian revolution was a nationalistic declaration of independence aimed at the removal of Manchu authority and not a true revolution that intended fundamental change.[12] However, in today's Mongolia, the autonomous decade has been reevaluated and judged as a major element in the overall framework to establish the time line of Mongolian nationhood and has become absolutely essential to understanding recent Mongolian policymaking in the fields of national security and foreign economic policy. The decades of Soviet tutelage established a shaky independent Mongolian identity that was slowly and very reluctantly acknowledged by China and Western governments. At Yalta in February 1945, Churchill and Roosevelt had to agree to Stalin's requirement that the status quo (de facto independence) of the MPR be maintained as the price for the Soviet Union to enter the war against Japan, but it can be argued that the legitimacy of Mongolian independence only became an international reality with the October 20, 1945, independence plebiscite that was monitored by the United Nations. Initially, the ROC's Chiang Kai-shek (aka Jiang Jieshi) accepted this result, although acceptance was retracted when Mao's forces took over the mainland. The People's Republic of China (PRC) was pressured by the Soviet Union to agree to Outer Mongolia's independence, and the Eastern European satellites followed suit. In December 1955 India became the first noncommunist state to recognize Mongolia, and some Western democracies established relations after Mongolia was admitted into the UN in October 1961.

The decades of limited contact with the noncommunist world in the twentieth century meant that the Soviet Union (USSR) was the center of Mongolian foreign relations and the model for foreign as well as domestic development. As Mongolian specialist Alan Sanders has observed, Mongolia's broad foreign policy guidelines were conceived in Moscow, and "Until the end of the 1980s the MPR's international relations were dominated by its ideological bonds and friendship treaties with the USSR and its allies."[13] It was Mikhail Gorbachev's rethinking[14] of the USSR's role in Northeast Asia, which involved the removal of some Soviet troops stationed in Mongolia, that was the catalyst for Mongolia's seeking a more active role internationally. Mongolia was granted permission to move forward on normalizing diplomatic relations with the US during Soviet Foreign Minister Eduard Shevardnadze's January 1986 visit to Mongolia. Ulaanbaatar understood that it was going to have to develop "new thinking" in foreign policy.[15]

Street demonstrations in which students demanded the resignation of all communist Mongolian People's Revolutionary Party (MPRP) politburo members and the right to establish new political parties broke out on December 7, 1989, in western Mongolia's Khovd province. These demonstrations quickly spread to Ulaanbaatar, led by young Mongolians educated in Eastern Europe who were familiar with democratic movements, and united under a loose umbrella organization called the Mongolian Democratic

Union (MDU), which made its first appearance on December 10. These young leaders included Sanjaasüreng Zorig, Tsakhia Elbegdorj, Erdene Bat-Üül, Mendsaikhan Enkhsaikhan, Rinchinnyam Amarjargal, and Bat-Erdene Batbayar (aka Baabar). They would form democratic political parties such as the Democratic Socialist Movement (DSM), New Progressive Union (NPU), Forces of Four, and Democratic Forces, and be involved in building Mongolian democracy to reform the country's political system.[16]

In January 1990 protesters numbering 1,000 met in front of the Lenin Museum in Ulaanbaatar on a plaza renamed Freedom Square. On subsequent weekends ever larger groups of several thousands of silent, well-behaved Mongol demonstrators, often joined by their families and children, would circle through the capital's center, Sükhbaatar Square, in the frigid –30°C cold. In subsequent months popular support for these protests grew in the capital and the provincial cities of Erdenet, Darkhan, and Mörön. The MDU later claimed to have organized protests totaling 60,000 participants from eighty party branches with over 30,000 members.[17]

The young protesters often carried signs in both Cyrillic and the old Mongolian script that had been banned by Stalin in the 1940s. These banners praised Chinggis Khaan, the country's founding father, whose name had been banished by the communist propaganda system. The demonstrators also waved modified national flags, from which the red star symbolizing communism had been removed. The Soviet Union's theory of the "peculiar inertness or stagnation"[18] of Mongols and other Inner Asian nomadic peoples led to its system of denigrating and then destroying the lamaist religious and nomadic economic lifestyle to create a modern Soviet-style state, which had severely damaged the Mongolian psyche. Mongolian political leaders under communism were educated to develop national policies to demean the nomadic economy's cultural value as backward and to dismantle it in favor of creating a sedentary urban workforce in newly established industrial cities. Such socioeconomic policies caused the portion of the population herding animals on communes to fall from over 90 percent in the 1920s to under 30 percent by 1990.

During and after the democratic revolution of 1990, Mongolia had to revisit the issue of its national identity in the globalized world, and most national leaders vowed not to lose its specific Buddhist and nomadic nature as the country modernized. Mongolian society began the campaign to reinternalize its unique heritage and weave it into a modern definition of national identity, national security, and economic policy planning. Defining what it meant to be Mongol moved beyond theoretical discussions by scholars into the offices of Mongolian government policymakers and development economists. In nomadic studies there is the constant question of what the nomadic impact was on the sedentary state and its institutions.[19] In democratic Mongolia, the government linked Mongolian nomadic and religious life to the security of Mongolian culture and civilization by rejecting the old Soviet thesis that the traditional Mongolian nomadic economy and society could not generate a progressive spirit and modern statehood.

Mongolian leaders of all political persuasions, most of whom were educated to be hostile toward nomadism and religion, gradually reembraced their heritage during the democratic protests and wove it into a sometimes romanticized version. In the 1990s, the resurgence of lamaist institutions and the traditional nomadic lifestyle made them "normal" and "legitimate" and thus forces to be considered in formulating Mongolia's domestic and international policies. As a result, Mongolian policymakers explored the "problem of establishing democratic legal institutions on a rural nomadic society with a socialist legacy."[20] They created a new explanation of Mongolia's past to serve as the road map for future generations. This phenomenon is the key to comprehending democratic Mongolia's view of foreign relations and foreign economic policy.

Notes

1. Chinggis Khaan, also known as Chinggis Khan, Genghis Khan, or Jenghiz Khan (c. 1162–August 18, 1227), was born Temüjin. He was the founder and great khan of the Mongolian Empire, which became the largest contiguous empire in history after his death. In 1206 he united the Turkic and Mongol-speaking tribes on the Mongolian plateau, gave them the name Mongol, and took the title of Chinggis. Khaan means "emperor" while Khan means "king." Among his biographies are Harold Lamb, *Genghis Khan: Emperor of All Men* (1927); Rene Grousset, *Conqueror of the World: The Life of Chingis-Khagan* (1944); Paul Ratchnevsky, *Genghis Khan: His Life and Legacy* (1991); John Man, *Genghis Khan: Life, Death, and Resurrection* (2004); and Jack Weatherford, *Genghis Khan and the Making of the Modern World* (2005).

2. Kubilai Khan (1215–1294), also known as Kublai, was the grandson of Chinggis Khaan through his second son, Tolui. His rise to power was contested by his younger brother Ariq Bөke. Although Kubilai eventually defeated his brother, this dispute was the seed of the dissolution of the united Mongolian Empire. Kubilai finished the conquest of southern China and proclaimed the Yuan dynasty in 1271. He expanded Mongolian control into Yunnan and Korea, but his sea invasions of Japan and Indonesia were failures. He moved the empire's capital from Karakorum to Dadu (modern Beijing). See John Man, *Kublai Khan* (New York: Bantam Press, 2007); Morris Rossabi, *Khubilai Khan: His Life and Times* (Berkeley: University of California Press, 1990); "Kublai Khan Biography," *Encyclopedia of World Biography*, http://www.notablebiographies.com/Ki-Lo/Kublai-Khan.html.

3. Khalkha (aka Halh) is the Mongolian ethnic group that comprises the majority (80 percent) of the population of Mongolia, and Khalkha Mongolian is the national literary language of 90 percent of the Mongolian people. The word was first used for the Mongolian people in the second half of the fourteenth century. The Khalkha became divided into North (*Ar*) and South (*Ovor*) Khalkha during the Manchu period (1644–1911). Alan J. K. Sanders, *Historical Dictionary of Mongolia,* 3rd ed. (Lanham, MD: Scarecrow Press, 2010), 91.

4. The Manchu (aka Manzhou, Manj) were a Tungusic nation whose leaders ruled China during the Qing dynasty (1636–1911). They made alliances with the Eastern Mongols (1624) and the Inner Mongols (1636) before conquering the Ming dynasty in China. The Manchus imposed control over Outer (Khalkha) Mongolia in 1691. Over four million people claim Manchu nationality today in north China and Manchuria, but few speak the language. Sanders, *Historical Dictionary,* 123.

5. Alicia J. Campi, "The Rise of Cities in Nomadic Mongolia," in *Mongols from Country to City: Floating Boundaries, Pastoralism and City Life in the Mongol Lands*, ed. Ole Bruun and Li Narangoa (Copenhagen: NIAS Studies in Asian Topics, 2006), 21–55.

6. For the institution of the Jebtsundamba Khutukhtu, see C. R. Bawden, *The Jebtsun Damba Khutukhtus of Urga* (Wiesbaden: O. Harrassowitz, 1961); A. M. Pozdneyev, *Mongolia and the Mongols*, ed. and trans. John R. Krueger (Bloomington: Indiana University Press and The Hague: Mouton and Company, 1971), 364–368, from the Russian text *Mongoliya I Mongoly* (St. Petersburg: Imperial Russian Geographical Society, 1896). This religious personage also was known as the Bogdo Gegeen, Bogdo Khaan, or "Living Buddha." The term *Khutukhtu* means "blessed one" and was a rank given to an incarnation of a high lama according to Tibetan Buddhist religious terminology. All incarnations also were called Gegeen, "the enlightened one."

7. The Manchu term *amban* means "governor" or "high commissioner." This post was occupied by the highest civilian administrative official. In Mongolia there were *ambans* in Urga and Khobdo in North Mongolia. For a discussion of the term and its historical significance, see B. Shirendev, *The History of the Mongolian People's Republic,* trans. William A. Brown and Urgunge Onon (Cambridge: East Asian Research Center and Harvard University Press, 1976), 745 n14.

8. For additional information on interpretations of the breakup of the Manchu Qing Empire, see Henry G. Schwarz, "The Security of Mongolia," *Mongolian Journal of International Affairs*, No. 3 (1996): 68–70, http://www.mongoliajol.info/index.php/MJIA/article/view/431/452.

9. "Autonomous" is traditionally defined as fully in charge of domestic but not foreign affairs, although legally not independent of China.

10. The Sain Noyan Khan (hereditary title) had the personal name of Tyogs-Ochiryn Namnansüren (1878–1919). It is said he was a descendant of the family of Chinggis Khaan. Namnansüren was Mongolian prime minister under the Autonomous Government from 1912 to 1915. He was a member of the delegation sent by the Bogdo Gegeen to St. Petersburg in July 1911 seeking Russian support for his country's independence. He led a delegation again to St. Petersburg from November 1913 to January 1914 in an unsuccessful attempt to obtain Russian backing for a union of Outer and Inner Mongolia. After 1915, his position of prime minister was abolished, and he became minister of the army. See Sanders, *Historical Dictionary,* 153–154. Historian Robert Rupen in *How Mongolia Is Really Ruled* (Stanford: Hoover Institution Press, 1979) has written that he was known for accumulating huge gambling debts and dissolute living in Peking. Morris Rossabi claims these debts motivated the Sain Noyan Khan to lead the anti-Chinese movement. See Morris Rossabi, *China and Inner Asia* (London: Thames and Hudson, 1975), 237. Rossabi and Bawden as well as many other Mongolian historians maintain that the aim of the Sain Noyan Khan government was national independence but not true social revolution.

11. The Eighth Bogdo Gegeen was a Tibetan born in 1869 into the family of an official of the Dalai Lama. Considered a reincarnation of the Seventh Bogdo, his given name was Agvaanluvsanchoyjin-danzanvaanchigbalsambuu. Taken to Mongolia at four years of age, he was beloved by the Mongol common people, but seen by foreigners and Mongolian communists as a drunkard and syphilitic with both male and female lovers as well as a wife. He was made head of state when Mongolia declared its autonomy in 1911. Such was his political power that he was retained as head of state by the communist government in 1921. He died in 1924, after which the communist government disallowed future reincarnations. Ookhnoin Batsaikhan, *Mongolin Suulchiin Ezen Xaan VIII Bogd Jabzandamba, 1911 Oni Yndesnii Xuvisgal* [The Last King of Mongolia Bogdo Jebtsundamba Khutukhtu] (Ulaanbaatar: Admon, 2008); Sanders, *Historical Dictionary,* 27; C. R. Bawden, *The Modern History of Mongolia* (New York: Frederick A. Praeger, 1968), 166–168, 210–216, 232–235.

12. Bawden, *Modern History of Mongolia*, 189.

13. Alan J. K. Sanders, "Foreign Relations and Foreign Policy," in *Mongolia in Transition: Old Patterns, New Challenges,* ed. Ole Bruun and Ole Odgaard (Surrey, England: Curzon Press, Nordic Institute of Asian Studies, 1996), 218.

14. This was epitomized by his 1986 Vladivostok initiative. See Sharad K. Soni, *Mongolia-Russia Relations: Kiakhta to Vladisvostok* (New Delhi: Shipra Publications, 2002), 217–225.

15. First Deputy Foreign Minister D. Yondon's book, *The Big Veto* (ed. Daram Yondon, January 1997, in Mongolian), recounts the fears and pressures on the Mongolian leadership during that period.

16. A list of the new parties can be found in G. Chuluunbaatar, "Renewal of Mongolia's Political System and Its Democratic Development," in *Renovation of Mongolia on the Eve of the XXI Century and Future Development Patterns*, ed. Tsedendamba Batbayar (Ulaanbaatar: Mongolian Development Research Center, 2000), 8.

17. Ibid., 6–7.

18. L. N. Gumilev, *People and Nature of the Great Steppe*, no. 11 (Moscow: Voprosy Istorii, 1987), 84.

19. See, for example, André Wink in *Nomads in the Sedentary World*, ed. Anatoly M. Ikhazanov and André Wink (London: RoutledgeCurzon, 2001), 285–295; B. Sumiya, "Globalization and Mongolian Nomadícs Cultural Heritage," in *Dialogue Among Civilizations: Interaction Between Nomadic and Other Cultures of Central Asia* (Ulaanbaatar: International Institute for the Study of Nomadic Civilizations, UNESCO, August 15–16, 2001), 407–413; David Sneath, "The Rural and the Urban in Pastoral Mongolia," in *Mongols from Country to City: Floating Boundaries, Pastoralism and City Life in the Mongol Lands*, ed. Ole Bruun and Li Narangoa (Copenhagen: NIAS Press, 2006), 140–161.

20. Irina Y. Morozova, *Socialist Revolutions in Asia* (London: Routledge, 2009), 141.

2

The White Horse Democratic Revolution

From the outset of the pro-democracy demonstrations, the Mongolian political leadership appeared to remain committed to finding a political solution instead of a violent one. Mongolian MPRP general secretary and premier Jamba Batmönkh (1984–1990) described the whole tumultuous period and the conflicts within the MPRP politburo over how to handle the political crisis in his autobiography, *There Will Be No Use of Force Under Any Circumstances.*[1] He reported that the politburo already had implemented within Mongolia's one-party structure some of Mikhail Gorbachev's restructuring ideas of the late 1980s and also had the negative example of Chinese actions in Tiananmen in June 1989 to guide it. Although the MDU monitored its demonstrations to avoid violence, rumors and concern mounted over possible government retaliation. A. Jamsranjav, minister for public security at the time, when criticized by party hard-liners for being indecisive in not dispatching the internal security forces, told the politburo, "We do not have strength to defend all the streets of Ulaanbaatar. As for our Ministry, we are ready to defend it. We are responsible for prisons and electro-stations. I do not think that issuing a decree will restore order."[2]

On March 7, 1990, when the government failed to send representatives to talk to a mass of around 100,000 demonstrators in Sükhbaatar Square, the MDU declared a hunger strike in the square and called for the politburo leadership to resign. Premier Batmönkh was asked to sign a decree authorizing the use of force to clear away ten hunger strikers, but he refused. Two nights later the entire foreign diplomatic community (including the Soviets and the Chinese) and the Mongolian people were shocked to hear Batmönkh announce on television that the only way to find a peaceful solution and to stop the hunger strike was for the politburo to resign en masse. After the announcement, the demonstrators and hunger strikers left Sükhbaatar Square. The Mongolian "White Horse" Democratic Revolution had succeeded without a single shot being fired by either side.[3] The democratic revolution had overturned more than a stultified domestic regime; it had terminated seventy years of neocolonial dependence on the Soviet Union in favor of reestablishing Mongolian identity.

On March 21 Batmönkh was relieved from his post as chairman of the Presidium of the People's Great Khural of the MPRP. Mongolia's democratic era officially had begun. Batmönkh later explained, "Some people criticized us, saying that we capitulated. Yes, it was a compromise. But we have to understand who has capitulated to whom. We did not capitulate to a foreign enemy. We did capitulate to the arriving new era and to our younger generation. There was nothing better than that."[4]

The confused MPRP appointed a compromise, seemingly pliable candidate as the new interim MPRP chairman, forty-eight-year-old Punsalmaalag Ochirbat,[5] who was a trained mining engineer, and Dashi Byambasüren[6] as first deputy prime minister. Byambasüren, who had been the MPRP's chief negotiator with the MDU's young demonstrators, visited Washington from April 30 to May 4, 1990, for a successful first round of talks about the future of democratic Mongolia. Although the communist system was still in place, the new political climate was reflected immediately by a warmer relationship with the United States and other Western nations. Batmönkh's remembrances, the accounts of various young Mongolian leaders, and recollections of US embassy officials conclusively indicate that the US embassy played no overt or covert role in inciting or supporting the demonstrators. Rather, the few staffers of the resident Western embassies mainly watched the unfolding of events while occasionally conferring with officials from the Soviet embassy and UN-related organizations.

The MPRP politburo resignation paved the way for the interim government on July 29, 1990, to call a new parliamentary election, in which the MPRP captured 80 percent of the seats. The most important reason for the MPRP victory was that the voters respected the fact that the party had supported the dismantlement of the communist regime and introduced new political freedoms without any bloodshed. Mongolian researchers of the period noted that the legitimacy of the MPRP stemmed from real improvement in living standards throughout the country during the 1970s and 1980s, so that it was associated with prosperity and stability, especially by rural voters. The party also was highly regarded for saving Mongolian sovereignty by preventing China from reclaiming Mongolia after World War II. Because the MPRP had exclusive control over the media and educational system and had orchestrated the change in government without the violence seen in some Eastern European countries, it successfully relabeled itself as the most competent political party to govern during the turmoil of the early democratic years.[7] Finally, the MPRP's immediate willingness to engage

Western countries enabled it to present itself as best able to preserve Mongolia's independence by placing the national interest ahead of party interest during a time of international uncertainty.[8]

The new MPRP government decided to include other parties in its governing coalition because of the unique challenges it faced. This peculiar feature of Mongolian parliamentary democracy—forming a coalition despite the victorious party's possessing a governing majority—was a tactic not practiced in other parliamentary nations. Nevertheless, it would become the Mongolian way during difficult times for the majority party to govern in order to insulate itself from domestic repercussions. The coalition government immediately sought advice and economic assistance from the United States and its allied Asian democracies. Official bilateral diplomatic relations with the United States had only been established in 1987. Even with the collapse of the communist government, there was little US interest in Mongolia. The attitude of the second US ambassador (1990–1993), Joseph Lake, reflected this initial passivity: "Ultimately, from the U.S. perspective, I do not see a U.S. interest in Mongolia—except for a philosophical one." He opined that supporting democracy by promoting the democratic process and the free market in Mongolia was the driving force behind US policy and rejected the notion that Mongolia's central location between Russia and China gave it particular strategic importance:

> I don't think that's a sustainable argument. I think China and Russia both have strategic interests in Mongolia. . . . You could argue there was an American interest in keeping it a neutral ground. I don't argue with that, but it's more a Japanese issue than an American issue per se. Ultimately the American interest is: Can we influence the building of a democratic process?[9]

1992 Democratic Constitution Reorients Mongolia

On May 10, 1990, two sections of the old 1960 communist constitution were amended to permit a presidential system of government, lay the groundwork for political parties, and eliminate the MPRP's monopoly on political power. This revised document abolished the totalitarian regime, rejected the planned economy, and began a comprehensive transition toward a new political system to develop a country that respected human rights, democratic values, a market economy, and the rule of law. These constitutional changes were the foundation for Mongolia's multiparty political system and the initiation of a party formation process that has continued throughout the democratic era. Six parties participated in the 1990 parliamentary election, and by 2000 there were at least twenty-four registered parties. The recurring formation and dissolution of political parties has been a confusing and disruptive feature of Mongolian politics over the past twenty-five years. For example, in the 2016 parliamentary election, twelve parties qualified to participate in the campaign, but only two parties presented candidates in all district contests. Although Mongolian political parties can be differentiated to some extent based on traditional formulas of rightist liberal democratic parties and leftist social democratic parties, ideological lines often are blurred in favor of coalescing around political personalities.

The coalition government recognized that reforming Mongolia's entire political system depended upon the redrafting of the communist-era constitution. Constitutions from France, Great Britain, Japan, Italy, Greece, and Spain were studied. President Ochirbat later claimed that 7,000 organizations and 220,000 suggestions (43 percent incorporated in the final document) were involved in the process.[10] A drafting commission of Mongolian lawyers considered several versions proposed by constitutional scholars from different democratic countries including the United States, Japan, Britain, and France, which resulted in a final document full of ambiguity and inconsistencies. The Mongols, at times unable to differentiate among the legal proposals and unwilling to disappoint foreign donor nations that were providing millions of dollars in economic support, settled on a combined presidential and parliamentary democratic system with its Parliament (Ikh Khural) as the highest organ of state power. Two different drafts were debated by Parliament in a marathon session over seventy-six days.[11] Thirty-five new laws and amendments were eventually adopted, and these became the basis for the revised constitution.[12]

The 1992 constitution, which came into force on February 12, established Mongolia as an independent republic and created a unicameral parliament with seventy-six seats called the State Great Khural. The Parliament enacts and amends laws, determines domestic and foreign policy, ratifies international agreements, and confirms appointments of government officials. However, the powers of the president and the prime minister are not clearly distinguished. Although the president's role is defined as "the Head of State and embodiment of the unity of the people," in hindsight, the presidents, over time and depending upon the individual's personality, began to exercise more extensive power over the government. They can approve the candidate for prime minister, call for the dissolution of the government, propose and veto laws passed by Parliament, and exercise control over foreign policy, including foreign economic policy and appointment of ambassadors. On June 6, 1993, P. Ochirbat won handily over five other political party candidates to become the first elected president under the democratic constitution.

The prime minister is nominated by the president and confirmed by Parliament. The position's powers include choosing cabinet members (subject to Parliament's approval) and managing domestic affairs. However, one distinctive feature in the Mongolian system is that the ruling party or coalition can lose parliamentary votes without having to dissolve the government. Dissolution of the government occurs only upon the resignation of the prime minister, simultaneous resignation of half the cabinet, or a parliamentary vote for dissolution.[13]

An independent judiciary was established with local courts, provincial or appellate courts, and a Supreme Court.[14] The Supreme Court hears appeals from lower courts and cases involving misconduct by high-level officials. Mongolia, which had no history of civil courts, initially did not clarify the civil versus criminal court system. The lack of a strong civil judiciary was a defect that came to haunt Mongolia and its foreign investor community.

New Foreign Policy Orientation Defines Mongolia's Modern Identity

Mongolian democracy and sovereignty were greatly impacted by the collapsed Cold War bipolarity system. The country felt itself adrift, abandoned by its long-term protector, the Soviet Union, which was disintegrating and imploding during 1989–1991. The ideological division between democracy and communism that had lasted most of the twentieth century had ended, but it was not clear what new paradigm would arise—authoritarianism, religious doctrinairism, sectarianism? For Mongols along the entire political spectrum, the answer to the political crisis was seen in nationalism and glorification of Mongolian traditional heritage. However, how nationalism would reconstitute itself and how it could tangibly enhance Mongolia's national security were subjects of intense debate.

During the first year under the democratic system, the Mongolian government, which was under tremendous pressure to stabilize the collapsed economy, reached out to the developed world to replace the assistance that the old Soviet system had provided. In 1980 over 90 percent of Mongolia's trade was with the Soviet Union, and 25 percent of its GNP was directly attributable to Soviet aid. US ambassador to Mongolia Joseph Lake explained, "The severing of this relationship was a critical element in the crisis of change in the 1990s. . . . Soviet imports were not supplements to Mongolian production. In virtually every case there was no Mongolian production."[15] Despite Soviet support, Mongolia in 1990 had the lowest standard of living in the communist world, so the withdrawal of this aid inflicted a high degree of economic trauma. The nation had been receiving many goods including energy via a barter policy or through COMECON, also called the Council for Mutual Economic Assistance (CMEA). Moreover, most of the major infrastructure projects were financed by the Soviet Union in the form of loans. With the CMEA collapse, the Mongols no longer had the socialist world market to rely upon for sales of their animal by-products and copper exports, and they had few Western foreign exchange reserves on which to rely. Soviet soldiers and their arms were totally withdrawn from Mongolia by December

1992.[16] With the withdrawal of the Soviet Union's economic and military support, Mongolia had to face the world alone.

At that time neither the ex-communist MPRP authorities nor the democratic opposition leaders had strong ties to Western countries. The closest relations were with Japan and the United Kingdom, which did not have substantive business links to Mongolia, only limited joint investment operations in animal hair (cashmere and camel hair) textile factories in Ulaanbaatar and no operations at all in the countryside. The Russian and Eastern European businesses in mining and animal by-products collapsed as the communist governments of these countries dissolved. Mongolia's longstanding cultural attachment to India remained strong, but India did not have the capital to provide donor assistance or FDI.

The Mongolian government's bilateral outreach to developed democracies through fewer than fifteen embassies resident in Ulaanbaatar was hampered by the small number of officials who had local language skills. Mongolian embassies were in Moscow and the Eastern European capitals, so the government utilized its missions to the UN in New York and Geneva to quickly expand contacts. Simultaneously, it increased its bilateral embassy staffing in the developed Western countries and instructed the officials to educate themselves in the host country languages. Overseas and in Ulaanbaatar, Mongolian policymakers, many with UN experience, were debating how to recalibrate national domestic and external priorities to respond to the new unipolar world that was emerging from the collapse of the Cold War.

Mongolia recognized that its previous policy of close coordination with its Russian northern neighbor and its cold, even at times hostile, relations with its southern neighbor, China, were no longer operative. China was the closest market for Mongolian products and the place to obtain imported foodstuffs and goods to sustain the faltering economy, so the Mongols immediately accepted the fact that they would have to develop a more balanced and friendly relationship. However, decades of ill will and Soviet-inspired suspicions caused the Mongols to worry about reorienting their foreign policy only toward China. Thus, the government adopted the principle of expanding bilateral relations with Western democracies, and for national security considerations, reached out quickly to the United States, the winner of the Cold War: "These nations have both the means and will to assist former Communist states in their transition to democracy and market economy, so improved relations are vital."[17] Mongolia quickly instituted a new foreign policy concept of seeking closer relations with countries beyond its border neighbors to break the cycle of Mongolia's being a pawn in any "Great Game."

One of the first major foreign policy decisions facing the new government was to define its place in the newly emerging geographical landscape of Asia. As a landlocked country, it recognized that it was a captive of its

Eurasian geography with a history of being wedged not only between two giant neighbors but between two distinct civilizations without being of either culture. As a small people with a difficult location, Mongols had to learn to get along with their dominant and threatening neighbors. The Khalkha tribes in the seventeenth century had allied with the expansionist Manchu Empire to preserve their distinctive nomadic culture, national identity, and lamaist religion. When the Manchu dynasty collapsed in 1911, Mongolia aligned itself with the Russian Bolsheviks out of fear of assimilation by the far more numerous Chinese. Under Soviet protection, it then played the role of a compliant satellite, until the collapse of the Soviet Union caused it again to face a critical juncture that forced it to rethink its strategy for national survival. In 1990, the inspiration of Mongolia's distinct nomadic heritage under the legendary Chinggis Khaan had risen rapidly in the body politic to loom large in the popular political rhetoric. However, the MPRP leaders were uncomfortable with the new Chinggis Khaan–based nationalism that had been exploited by the younger democratic party elements.

As the Mongolian government continued to debate the general outlines of its new foreign policy, Soviet-trained Mongolian scholars maintained that the country's difficult continental climate and the inhospitable geography were conditions that had prevented the influx of Chinese settlers and cultural absorption. However, if Mongolia were going to integrate into the Asian continent in response to the new political conditions of the post–Cold War world, attitudes toward Western countries needed to be quickly revised. The MPRP's Basic Policy Direction adopted in April 1990 voiced the commitment to attract foreign investment, expand relations with Western and Asian countries, and pursue a nonaligned, nuclear-free policy.[18] MPRP and democratic leaders, despite their pronounced differences over internal domestic politics, quickly formed a consensus over an "Open Door" foreign policy to seek foreign connections regardless of political ideology.

Scholars and politicians engaged in theoretical discussions over how to best preserve Mongolian identity, while debate on the streets and inside the government was over how to define Mongolian identity and how this identity could relate to the outside world. Basically, there were two camps. One called for Mongolia to see itself as a Central Asian nation, united with the newly emerging Central Asian republics by its nomadic steppe tribal history and recent seventy years of Soviet Russian governance. The other camp advocated linking Mongolia to the vibrant, modern, and democratized economies of Northeast Asia, even though the country had been cut off from major political and trade relations with most of these countries since the 1920s.

With Central Asia?

The first major official to publicly raise the identity dilemma and suggest that Central Asia was a more natural fit for modern Mongolia was Prime

Minister Byambasüren. Trained as a Soviet-style economist, Byambasüren had been the chief of the State Statistical Office and the Institute of Management and, in 1989, deputy head of the Council of Ministers in the last communist government. His new democratic government, while full of communist-trained bureaucrats, had the unenviable task of revamping the country's external relations through a proactive round of diplomatic visits to Germany, Belgium and France, Russia, and China (the first by a Mongolian leader to China in over thirty years).

Byambasüren argued that Mongolia was located at the crossroads of three great civilizations: Christian Russia, Confucian China, and Muslim Central Asia. This offered Mongolia the potential to build bridges among these civilizations. During the Cold War period, Mongolia was firmly situated inside a Soviet security and trade system that pulled it westward into Europe's Warsaw Pact countries. With the disappearance of the USSR, the five newly independent Central Asian nations in the Commonwealth of Independent States (CIS) in Asia (known in Russian as Srednuyay Aziya) had little experience with modern nation-building, but they were fortunate to have significant energy resources and deep experience in cross-border trade. Byambasüren believed that because of its common Soviet experience, Mongolia should partner with these nations to meet its energy needs and retain a more Western European orientation by utilizing its existing Central Asian and Eastern European connections. Academic and democratic activist B. Baabar also claimed that Mongolia was geographically, historically, and culturally part of Central Asia, and he recommended the country create a Central Asian Security Zone.[19] Advocating a partnership with Turkey, Baabar suggested the two nations could be examples of independent states to the five Central Asian republics, Afghanistan, and Azerbaijan. He believed that Germany and Japan would provide assistance to Mongolia because Germany already had established ties through East Germany and because Japan saw Mongolia as its only ally in Central Asia that could be used to enter the Eastern Siberian and Northern Chinese markets.

As the debate proceeded in the 1990s, another strong proponent of the Central Asia focus for Mongolia was Indian researcher P. Stobdan. He believed that Mongolia, as historically the key country in the Inner Asian region, should logically play the central role in redefining the area after the collapse of the socialist system. Even twenty years later, Stobdan continues to believe that "Mongolia is the geographical pivot of history."[20] He bases this conclusion on four points: (1) The Mongols had played a historical and civilizational role as leader of the Turkic world so now Mongolia should revive its regional geopolitical responsibilities. (2) Because Mongolia's geographical position is at the crossroads of Central Asia, Northeast Asia, the Far East, China, and Russia, it is strategically the most significant country in all of Asia. (3) There is a Mongolian diaspora across Asia with pockets of ethnic groups that could be stabilizers for the Turkic and Iranian cultures. (4)

Mongolia's Buddhist religious background was considered a neutral force for peace by the other religious, cultural, and political actors in the region.[21]

The newly emerging Central Asian states, faced with collapsing economies and civil wars in the early 1990s, also were interested in reducing their dependence on an unstable Russian economy. Wrestling with the challenges and opportunities wrought by the breakup of the Soviet Union, they, like Mongolia, were struggling to define the Soviet experience as it related to their own Eurasian continental identity and to fill their security vacuum. This search for a new synthesis was complex, "deeply rooted like an onion with centuries of different layers"—all influenced by outside actors with their own agendas.[22] Mongolia was a way for the Central Asian republics to reach the large markets in East Asia and approach China, Japan, and even the United States as they sought to find new investor partners for their Caspian oil and gas resources. For Mongolia, the tie to Central Asia's energy resources was a serious developmental aspect not to be ignored because while Mongolia had its own energy resources, they were so poorly developed that the country was totally dependent upon outside imports.

However, Mongolian leaders were concerned that they could not obtain from the Central Asian republics the most modern technology required to make the country self-sustainable. Another important factor was national security. These nations also were landlocked, highly dependent upon Russia, and with ties mainly to the unstable Middle East and only tangentially to Western Europe. Looking toward western Eurasia to find an immediate protector of Mongolian sovereignty appeared dubious. In the early 1990s, former deputy foreign minister Khumba Olzvoy was one of the prime voices arguing that, from the standpoint of developmental strategy, Mongolia should not align itself with the Central Asian countries, but instead deepen its attachment to the Northeast Asia Economic Forum and other subregional organizations. While he saw historical and geographical merit in placing Mongolia in Central or Inner Asia, he laid out the negatives of a Central Asia–centric policy: (1) Central Asia was landlocked and not able to assist Mongolia in overcoming its own landlocked predicament; (2) unlike Mongolia, which had been a sovereign state since 1924, Central Asian countries recently had attained independence and did not have the requisite international experience to help Mongolia; (3) the political and strategic situation in Central Asia was still too unstable; (4) the Central Asian economies were primarily intertwined with Russia; and (5) Central Asian infrastructure was as poorly developed as in Mongolia.[23] Nevertheless, the Central Asia connection deeply touched the nomadic identity of the nation and fit the growing nationalism centered on Chinggis Khaan and his empire.

Another major factor that Mongolia had to consider about aligning itself with Central Asia was the special place held by Kazakhstan.[24] This country was significant for Mongolia not only because it was Mongolia's largest Central Asian trade partner, since it refined Mongolian raw copper, but because it was almost a neighbor (coming within ten kilometers of Mongolian territory). There were 150,000 Kazakhs living in Mongolia's northwestern province of Bayan Ölgii, who constituted about 7.4 percent of Mongolia's population. During the early 1990s, the bilateral relationship was destabilized when Kazakhstan wooed Mongolian Kazakh citizens to voluntarily immigrate or accept contract job assignments. In 1991 about 12,300 Mongolian Kazakhs left, followed by another 26,900 in 1992 and 14,700 in 1993 for a total of over 50,000 Mongolian citizens.[25] However, more than half eventually returned to Mongolia.

With Northeast Asia?

A larger group of Mongolian academics and policymakers argued that Mongolia should align itself unequivocally with Northeast Asia, not Central Asia. Many experienced diplomats took this position out of conviction that most of the nations within Northeast Asia were modern, rich, and dynamic, with strong ties to the remaining superpower, the United States. However, during the socialist period Mongolia was suspicious of and distant from its Northeast Asian regional neighbors. In the 1930s Japan, through its occupation of Manchuria, promoted Pan-Mongolian propaganda, which the Soviet Union saw as a direct threat to its control of Siberia. Stalin thereupon concluded a mutual defense pact with Mongolia that permitted Soviet troops to be stationed in the country. Spying for Japan was used as the pretext for purges among Mongolia's government and military in the 1920s and 1930s. The Japanese attack in eastern Mongolia at Khalkhin Gol (Nomonhan) in 1939, although successfully repulsed, further alienated the older generation of Mongols from Japan. During the communist era, ideological propaganda against the Japanese was very negative in response to Japan's role as a staging area for US troops during the Korean conflict in support of the South Korean government.

However, outreach to Japan began at the end of the communist period. In 1987 Mongolia's foreign minister visited Japan, and in August 1989 Mongolia proposed the creation of a dialogue mechanism in Northeast Asia to discuss cooperation on nonpolitical issues such as economics, science and technology, culture, and education and to promote ecological and humanitarian exchanges.[26] Foreign Minister Olzvoy believed that Mongolia should come "strategically under the economic 'umbrella' of technologically advanced countries like Japan, South Korea, and the United States,"[27] while also improving its relations with the Russian Far East, China's Northeast, and North Korea. He pointed out that Mongolia's eastern area, which was mineral rich, could become integrated with the Tumen River region of Northeast Asia to get access to the sea by developing roads and rail, and thus Mongolia could act as a land bridge between Northeast Asia and Europe. Many Mongolian leaders embraced this concept because it seemed a way to quickly benefit from the success of the Asia Pacific economies.[28] Two decades later, US foreign policy expert Robert Scalapino agreed that Northeast Asia was Mongolia's natural economic territory, a kind of "regional Third Neighbor."[29]

Other Mongols advocated a Northeast Asian–oriented foreign policy mainly for national security reasons since Mongolia's international relations choices were limited by its small population and landlocked geography. Foreign Minister Mangal Dügersüren [30] promoted an open foreign policy to ensure national security by political means and warned that "at the same time Mongolia has to be alert and enterprising in order to avoid marginalization which is a widespread curse for weaker developing countries."[31] He suggested that Mongolia adopt a policy of nonalignment because it was a developing country.[32] He accepted the concept that Mongolia's first priority was friendly relations with its immediate neighbors, but noted that the nation's unique geographical location impelled it to create "vested" interests with other major powers inside the country "to establish in its immediate surrounding a power equation most attuned to its national interest."[33] Concerned that Mongolia not be marginalized, he suggested that its new foreign policy strategy include:

> First, political considerations should clearly be present when choosing partners in projects vital to national security. Second, involvement in disputes, especially those in light of great power politics, should be avoided unless they immediately affect the country's national interest. Third, excessive dependence on any single power should be eschewed. At the same time, it should be made amply clear that friendly attitudes toward all nations and respect for their legitimate interests and rights represent one of the fundamentals of Mongolia's international behavior.[34]

He recommended that special importance be attached to enhancing cooperative relations with Asian countries, including India, South Korea, Singapore, and Thailand, as well as cooperation with Germany, Great Britain, France, Canada, and Australia.

Dügersüren supported Mongolian participation in the political, security, and economic arrangements of the Asia Pacific region, including the Asia-Pacific Multilateral Security Dialogue Mechanism and the Association of Southeast Asian Nations (ASEAN) Regional Forum. He explained that Mongolia's joining regional development programs such as the Tumen River Basin project would promote cooperation in Northeast Asia that would be beneficial to broader Asia Pacific economic structure and security in light of the increasing interaction of China, Japan, Russia, and the United States. Nevertheless, he supported continuation of traditional relations with Central Asian nations and believed that "political, economic and cultural intercourse with ethnic Mongols in contiguous areas and beyond could become a very important part of Mongolia's international cooperation."[35] Mongolian diplomat and scholar Dr. Tsedendamba Batbayar agreed with Dügersüren's concentration on the "power equation" surrounding Mongolia and advised developing more active relations with the United States and Japan. Noting that, in the past, Mongolia had depended on one or the other of its two border neighbors "with apprehension," he believed that "Mongolia looks positively on a new role in the context of Northeast Asia, which can be the bridge to the larger world, and broaden the country's opportunities for security cooperation."[36]

The foreign policy debate continued while the nation's economic crisis deepened in the early 1990s with the contraction of the industrialized economy and food shortages. Nevertheless, Mongolia did not experience any violence or civil strife. This was a markedly different picture from what happened in Russia and some Central Asian and Eastern European nations. Although the question of why the Mongols so stoically persevered through this most difficult period has not been satisfactorily researched, the Mongols themselves have begun to discuss these crucial early years. At a conference in December 2014 on the eve of the celebration of the twenty-fifth anniversary of democracy, Speaker of the Parliament Zandaakhüü Enkhbold reflected that his country had "developed democracy in its own way, and achieved success in becoming a role model for other developing countries pursuing the same goal. This is our achievement."[37]

Perhaps the answer lay in the flexibility inherent in the nomadic mentality, wherein trials must be accepted along with the good, that still lived within the hearts of most citizens; or the calming influence of Buddhist traditions; or the fact that the older generation of Mongols still remembered the "Great Terror" of the 1930s when up to 100,000 people opposing the revolutionary government's Stalinist policies were executed—a decimation of the population that affected almost every Mongol family.[38] It also has been argued that Mongolian leaders had educational and work ties with the most liberal-minded and advanced Eastern European nations such as Poland, Hungary, and Czechoslovakia, which tempered the street protests in the Mongolian cities.[39] Another explanation, which has been labeled "cosmopolitan nationalism," was that the Mongolian leadership "was able to read the external situation and pragmatically shed its ideology" in order to peacefully assure national independence and societal modernization.[40] Regardless of the various explanations, it should be remembered that there was not a dramatic change in the composition of the Soviet era–trained personnel throughout the government. This mainly MPRP-affiliated elite successfully guided the White Horse Democratic Revolution through the next several eventful years.

Notes

1. Batmunkh, *There Will Be No Use of Force*, 32.
2. Ibid., 46.
3. "White Horse" was mentioned by Irina Y. Morozova, *Socialist Revolutions in Asia* (London: Routledge, 2009), 137, when discussing the Mongolian intellectual elite's evaluation of the 1990 democratization process. This term is a reference to the old Mongolian-Tibetan calendar.

4. Batmunkh, *There Will Be No Use of Force*, 53.

5. Punsalmaalag Ochirbat (1942–) was minister of foreign economic relations and supply from 1987 to March 1990 when he was made chairman of the Council of the People's Great Khural. On September 3, 1990, he became the first democratically elected president of Mongolia. He was reelected in June 1993, serving until 1997. See the English translation of his autobiography, *The Time of Heaven*, ed. Peter K. Marsh (Bloomington, IN: The Mongolia Society, 2018) and Alan J. K. Sanders, *Historical Dictionary of Mongolia,* 3rd ed. (Lanham, MD: Scarecrow Press, 2010), 158–159; Jim Hoare and Susan Pares, "Ochirbat," in *A Political and Economic Dictionary of East Asia* (London: Routledge, 2005), 253.

6. Dashi Byambasüren (1942–) was a member of the MPRP's reformist wing. He became the deputy chairman of the Council of Ministers in December 1989 and concurrently chairman of the State Planning and Economic Committee in March 1990. He was Mongolian prime minister from 1990 to 1992. He was elected to the Mongolian Great Khural in 1992. In December 1992 he resigned his seat and the MPRP in opposition to the Jasrai government. In 1993 he founded the World Mongolian Congress and the Mongolian Development Society. In 1994 he founded and was elected leader of the Mongolian Democratic Renewal Party. See Uradyn E. Bulag, *Nationalism and Hybridity in Mongolia* (London: Oxford Press, 1998), 87–88; Sanders, *Historical Dictionary,* 33–35.

7. Tsedendamba Batbayar, *Mongolia's Foreign Policy in the 1990s: New Identity and New Challenges*, Regional Security Issues and Mongolia series, no. 17 (Ulaanbaatar: Institute for Strategic Studies, 2002), 47–48.

8. Statement of Foreign Minister Tserenpil Gombosuren in *The Mongol Messenger,* January 5, 1993.

9. "Ambassador Joseph E. Lake," interview by Charles Stuart Kennedy, Association for Diplomatic Studies and Training Foreign Affairs Oral History Project, September 5, 1994, 8, http://www.adst.org/OH%20TOCs/Lake,%20Joseph%20E.toc.pdf.

10. Ochirbat, *Time of Heaven*, 145–147.

11. G. Chuluunbaatar, "Renewal of Mongolia's Political System and Its Democratic Development," in *Renovation of Mongolia on the Eve of the XXI Century and Future Development Patterns*, ed. Tsedendamba Batbayar (Ulaanbaatar: Mongolian Development Research Center, 2000), 14.

12. For more information on the Mongolian Constitution of 1992, see *ibid.*, 11–16; Alan J. K. Sanders, "Mongolia's New Constitution: Blueprint for Democracy," *Asian Survey* 32, no. 6 (June 1992): 506–520. Text of the constitution can be found at http://www.international.ucla.edu/eas/documents/mon-const.htm; Odgerel Tseveen and Battsetseg Ganbold, "The Mongolian Legal System and Laws: A Brief Overview," *GlobaLex,* NYU Hauser Global Law School (January 2006), http://www.nyulawglobal.org/globalex/Mongolia.html.

13. G. Chuluunbaatar, *Problems of the Contemporary Socio-Political Transformation in Mongolia* (Ulaanbaatar: Institute of Philosophy, Sociology and Law, Mongolian Academy of Sciences, 2009), 9.

14. This judicial structure was established under the Law of the Courts. In 1998 the Mongolian Parliament approved a legal reform program with three types of courts: local courts, appellate courts (provincial and capital), and a Supreme Court. Among the duties of the Supreme Court is the right to examine human rights cases referred by the Constitutional Court or the prosecutor general. The Criminal Code, Criminal Procedures Law, Civil Code, and Executions of Court Decisions Law became effective on January 1, 2001. See Alicia Campi, "Mongolia Confronts Transnational Crime Issues in Its New Democracy," in *East Asian Intelligence and Organised Crime*, ed. Stephan Blancke (Berlin: Verlag Dr. Koster, September 2015), 399–437.

15. Joseph E. Lake, "Perspectives on Early Political Change" (remarks at the Asia Foundation conference on Mongolia's Political and Economic Transition: Challenges and Opportunities, Ulaanbaatar, September 11, 2000), https://asiafoundation.org/resources/pdfs/MongloiaPolEconTransition.pdf.

16. For more information on Soviet forces in Mongolia, see Sergey Radchenko, "Soviet Withdrawal from Mongolia, 1986–1992: A Reassessment," *Journal of Slavic Military Studies* 25, no. 2 (2012): 183–203.

17. Batbayar, *Mongolia's Foreign Policy*, 7.

18. Tom Ginsburg, "Nationalism, Elites, and Mongolia's Rapid Transformation," in *Mongolia in the Twentieth Century: Landlocked Cosmopolitan*, ed. Stephen Kotkin and Bruce A. Elleman (Armonk, NY: M. E. Sharpe, 1999), 251.

19. B. Baabar, "The Central Asian Security Zone," *Mongolian Journal of International Affairs*, no. 2 (1995): 18–32.

20. P. Stobdan, "India and Mongolia: Modi on Ashoka's Path," *IDSA Comment*, Institute for Defence Studies and Analyses, May 13, 2013, http://www.idsa.in/idsacomments/IndiaandMongolia_pstobdan_130515.

21. P. Stobdan, "Mongolia and Asian Security," *Mongolian Journal of International Affairs*, no. 7 (2000): 61, http://www.mongoliajol.info/index.php/MJIA/article/view/140/141.

22. Ibid., 57.

23. Khumba Olzvoy, "A Mongol's View of Economic Development and Cooperation in Northeast Asia," *Mongolian Journal of International Affairs*, no. 3 (1996): 55.

24. Mongolia established diplomatic relations with Kazakhstan on January 22, 1992.

25. Ts. Batbayar, "Mongolia and the New Central Asia," *Mongolian Journal of International Affairs*, no. 3 (1996): 10.

26. Ts. Batbayar and K. Demberel, "Contemporary Mongolian-Russian Relations: Problems and Perspectives," in *The Geopolitical Relations Between Contemporary Mongolia and Neighboring Asian Countries: Democracy, Economy and Security* (Taipei: Mongolian and Tibetan Affairs Commission Conference, September 2003), 329–330.

27. Olzvoy, "A Mongol's View."

28. L. Erdenechuluun, "Mongolia's Strategic Options," in *Northeast Asia Towards 2000: Interdependence and Conflict?* ed. Kyongsoo Lho and Kay Möller (Baden-Baden, Germany: Nomos, 1999), 95, cited in Tsedendamba Batbayar, "Mongolia's New Identity and Security Dilemmas," *Mongolian Journal of International Affairs*, no. 8–9 (2002): 5; Olzvoy, "A Mongol's View," 65–66; Mangal Dügersüren, "Changing Mongolia in a New Environment," *Mongolian Journal of International Affairs*, no. 1 (1994): 21.

29. Robert Scalapino, "The Political Process in Northeast Asia and Mongolia's Challenge" (paper presented at Mongolia-US Bilateral Conference, Mongolia-US Comprehensive Partnership in the Context of North East Asia: Challenges and Opportunities, Washington, DC, February 28, 2005).

30. Foreign minister, 1982–1988.

31. Dügersüren, "Changing Mongolia," 22.

32. "It should always be kept in mind that while the concept of Mongolia's foreign policy is determined by its national interest, the objectives, directions and methods of international behavior are basically influenced by Mongolia's geopolitical situation." Ibid., 21.

33. Ibid.

34. Ibid.

35. Ibid.

36. Batbayar, *Mongolia's Foreign Policy*, 36.

37. "'Democratic Revolution in Mongolia—25' Conference Held," montsame.news.mn, December 5, 2014.

38. For more on the 1930s purges, see Shagdariin Sandag and Harry H. Kendall, *Poisoned Arrows: The Stalin-Choibalsan Mongolian Massacres, 1921–1941* (Boulder, CO: Westview Press, 2000); D. Dashpurev and S. K. Soni, *Reign of Terror in Mongolia, 1920–1990* (New Delhi: South Asian Publishers, 1992).

39. D. Khirghis Munkh-Ochir, "Adrift or Advance? Socioeconomic Aspects of Mongolia-Russia Relations at the Onset of the 21st Century," in *Neighbors Through the Centuries: History and Contemporary Aspects of Bilateral Relations Between Mongolia and Russia*, no. 27 (Ulaanbaatar: Institute for Strategic Studies, 2005), 97.

40. Ginsburg, "Nationalism, Elites, and Mongolia's Rapid Transformation," 250.

3

Searching for a "Third Neighbor"

Russian troop withdrawal from Mongolia was completed on September 15, 1992. The collapse of the Soviet Union fundamentally altered the position of Mongolia in international politics, since Mongolia as a buffer zone between two contending communist superpowers was no longer an operative concept. The reality and dangers associated with the new geopolitical situation led Mongolian policymakers to quickly undertake a methodical analysis of their options in a new international system governed by an asymmetrical, Washington-based power paradigm. It was expected that a new polycentric Eurasian regional architecture would emerge in which Russia, the European Union, China, the Middle East, India, and Japan also would be major players because of their military and/or economic strength. Was Mongolia, in this complex strategic environment, going to play a role in shaping the geopolitical order in Asia like it had during the Mongolian Empire period 800 years prior? Or, would the country that had once been the homeland of a great intercivilizational power become again just a pawn in Sino-Russian rivalry in Asia?

Mongolian leaders recognized that it was necessary to declare their intention to pursue a new foreign policy. As Dr. Tsedendamba Batbayar has explained, "The top priority in Mongolia's next diplomacy was to fill the vacuum in its foreign relations created by the Soviet Union's disintegration."[1] In this climate of crisis and uncertainty there began a debate over formulating a new approach to economic and strategic security for the Mongolian nation. Still, there were historical precedents to guide its foreign policy. N. Tuya, former Mongolian minister of foreign affairs, noted, "Though we are a small nation, geography and history have taught us to attach greater attention than any other small nation would do to our relations with the world's major powers, and to relations between and among major powers."[2]

Mongolia had to consider a number of important factors as a new order emerged in Inner Asia. First and foremost was that Mongolia has a 3,485-kilometer border with Russia and a 4,677-kilometer border with China, so the two border neighbors could not be ignored. Nevertheless, Mongolian strategists believed that across the continent their former historical relations with Turkic civilizations would permit them to revive Mongolia's geopolitical space as a crossroads of Central Asia, Northeast Asia, the Far East, China, and Russia, or possibly even nurture a pan-Mongolism movement that involved Mongol-blooded peoples inside its two giant border neighbors. They understood the country's Buddhist cultural background linked it to India and Tibet to the south more than to the Islamic Turkic or Orthodox civilizations to the west. However, although most policymakers believed that Mongolia's future could not escape its geographical position between Russia and China, they overwhelmingly hoped that any new order in the post–Cold War environment would free Mongolia from choosing one border neighbor over the other.

While China's rise to the position of a major economic power seemed to demand that Mongolia shift from its Russia-centric policies to China-oriented ones, Mongols were for historical and cultural reasons reluctant to side with the Chinese. Mongolia forcibly had deported Chinese miners, traders, and construction workers in the 1920s, 1960s, and 1980s. Although China was a natural trading partner, democratic Mongolia's policy toward China from the very beginning was cautious: there was pressure to continue to limit Chinese political, economic, and cultural influence. Opinion among policymakers, researchers, and average citizens was firm on this question. There was no pro-Chinese clique. Rather, many in the nation believed that Mongolia must play a special role as a moderating political influence on Sino-Russian relations, as well as on relations among the newly emerging states in Eurasia. The challenge was just how to do this.

Democratic Mongolian leaders feared that the Russia arising from the ashes of the Soviet Union would sooner or later try to increase its dominance over Mongolia, as it had done earlier in the twentieth century, so they began to discuss ways to neutralize Russian influence. However, they also were very concerned about demographic and cultural assimilation to China, because Mongolia is geographically linked to the Chinese autonomous regions of Inner Mongolia and Xinjiang. Even though Chinese companies and traders always have been attracted to Mongolia's mineral and livestock resources, concerns over Chinese irredentism among Mongolian political elites and lingering anti-Chinese attitudes in Mongolian society contributed to a hostile climate for Chinese people and businesses in newly democratic Mongolia.

Chinese policies toward its northern neighbor stemmed from the belief that Mongolia's domestic stability directly impacts Chinese internal security and stability. There was and is distrust that Mongolian anti-Chinese elements would support non-Han border peoples' aspirations for political independence. Furthermore, in a more geostrategic vein, China maintains a historical desire to thwart any Mongolian-Russian military alliance. Even during the communist era, China strongly advocated the withdrawal of Russian troops from Mongolia. According to Mongolia scholar Jargalsaikhan Mendee, "Therefore, Chinese policy to Mongolia, on one hand, helps reduce Russian influence on Mongolian politics, economy, and security, while on the other hand, increases overt suspicion about Chinese hidden intentions of take-over and assimilation in Ulaanbaatar."[3]

From the onset of the democratic era, Mongolian political scientists and policymakers were wary of China's potential for monopolizing Mongolia's economy, as the Soviet Union had done. The United States, as the remaining superpower, held similar misgivings. In August 1990, US Secretary of State James Baker made a historic short visit to Ulaanbaatar just as Iraq invaded Kuwait. During a meeting with Mongolian leaders, he stated that they should see the United States as Mongolia's "Third Neighbor." Mongolian sources at the meeting with Baker and Mongolian President Ochirbat reported that discussion over the "Third Neighbor" concept was far-ranging and focused on the whole Western donor community's playing such a role.[4] Baker's public statement initially was perceived as "a rhetorical gesture to support Mongolia's first move toward democracy."[5] However, the Mongolian political establishment grew increasingly enamored of this term, so gradually it became the foundation for Mongolia's democratic era foreign policy and was formalized in its foreign policy legislation.

This strategic concept, called the Third Neighbor Policy,[6] had political, military, cultural, and economic components. It originally meant that another large power, such as the United States, Germany, or Japan, would act as a "Third Neighbor" for Mongolia to counterbalance the traditional roles played by Mongolia's two border neighbors. Mongolia's goal was to find a path forward, particularly in the economic realm, that would not require dependence on and control by either Russia or China. Because the Soviet system was collapsing around them, many Mongolian leaders initially looked at their situation through a political-strategic lens and so concluded that the United States would be *the* "Third Neighbor." They determined that only developing relations with the United States, given its dominant position in the international relations of the post–Cold War world, would meet the national interest of Mongolia.[7] Former Mongolian Minister of Foreign Affairs Luvsan Erdenechuluun[8] noted, "To many Mongolian politicians and government officials, the U.S. would appear as the savior of new Mongolia and 'major pillar' of its national security."[9] Another leading Mongolian strategist opined, "Even though Mongolia is a small country in terms of population, economy, and military, our unique geopolitical position makes the country's political stance very much relevant to almost every country in this region, including the United States."[10]

Early Expectations About the United States as "Third Neighbor"

The United States established diplomatic relations with Mongolia on January 27, 1987. Invited to witness the small ceremony when the first Mongolian ambassador, Genden Nyamdoo, presented his credentials was John Gombojab Hangin, professor of Mongolian Studies at Indiana University and founder/president of The Mongolia Society, who had been active for years in promoting relations between the two countries. US Secretary of State George Shultz at that time noted the occasion was historic because the two countries had been isolated from one another not only by great distance but by human obstacles, yet now there would be normal dialogue between the two peoples, and the opportunity to "expand mutually beneficial trade, and engage in educational and cultural exchanges."[11]

For many decades the United States had not established diplomatic relations because it did not want to offend the ROC government on Taiwan, which continued to claim both Inner and Outer Mongolian territory. The Soviets were concerned that the Americans would use Ulaanbaatar as a listening post situated between the two largest communist countries in the world and so actively discouraged the Mongolians from discussing diplomatic recognition with the United States. With the more open policies of Soviet leader Gorbachev, the Mongols felt they could approach the Americans in 1985 to discuss establishing relations through Japanese intermediaries. As the Cold War was winding down in the latter part of Ronald Reagan's presidency, the two nations finally had the opportunity to regularize diplomatic relations.

The Mongols opened their Washington, DC, embassy in March 1987. The United States, however, waited to open a year-round resident embassy in Ulaanbaatar until June 1989 but with a nonresident ambassador.[12] In this early period the US government had no real economic development strategy for Mongolia but did negotiate cultural and consular accords, which were signed by Secretary James Baker III[13] and Foreign Minister Mangal Dügersüren in Washington in September 1989.[14] Even before the collapse of the communist government, the United States had made the decision to appoint Joseph Lake[15] as full-time resident ambassador. The Department of State expected congressional criticism over the necessity for this posting at a time when only 17 of the 100 accredited ambassadors to Mongolia actually lived in Ulaanbaatar.[16] The additional cost to maintain an ambassador living in Mongolia was $167,000, or almost one-third of the fiscal year (FY) 1990 embassy budget. In his Senate hearing, Lake justified the additional expenditure by noting that, while Ulaanbaatar was possibly the Department of State's most isolated foreign service post, "Clearly, the times have changed. We agree with you that it is important to have the U.S. ambassador resident in Mongolia and we are working to make this happen quickly."[17]

There was a rapid and significant change in the US-Mongolian relationship with the successful March 1990 democratic revolution in Mongolia. A month later, Vice Prime Minister Byambasüren visited the United States, and in July the United States dispatched Lake to prepare for an early August trip to Mongolia by Secretary Baker. This trip, made in the midst of the surprise Iraqi invasion of Kuwait, was severely truncated from five days to less than twelve hours on August 2, 1990.[18] Baker's determination not to postpone the key visit and the Mongols' flexibility in responding to the totally revised schedule initiated a mutually warm outburst of goodwill that dramatically transformed the political landscape for both nations. Baker visited Mongolia again in July 1991 to make up for the aborted original trip. These visits by the US secretary of state raised Mongolia's profile significantly with US policymakers, who were concerned with instability in China and the collapse of the Soviet Union and "threw Mongolia into the arms of the U.S."[19] Ambassador Lake would later claim, "Without [Baker's] interest in and commitment to Mongolia, there would be no U.S.-Mongolia relationship."[20]

Ambassador Lake's year-round residence in Ulaanbaatar symbolized that there would be a new, more dynamic relationship between the two countries. Lake, a communications specialist with experience serving in communist countries, had the expertise to improve embassy communications with the Department of State in Washington, DC. During his three-year tenure, he oversaw the installation of secure communications lines and the establishment of the United States Agency for International Development (USAID) and Peace Corps programs. He later discussed this early period and Mongolia's expectations for its relationship with the United States:

> They were excited to have Americans. They wanted another outlet. They obviously saw us as a counterweight to the traditional Chinese and the Russian role. As change began to take place in Mongolia the U.S. was idealized far beyond our capabilities and reality, as in many of the countries of eastern Europe. Because we had been the evil monster for so long, now we seemed perfect in everything that we did from an economic perspective, political perspective, etc. So to put it mildly, we were welcomed with open arms and the Mongolians were cruelly crushed that we did not do more. In September of 1990, the President actually asked me to arrange for a two hundred and thirty million dollar a year assistance for Mongolia figuring this would replace the Russian assistance.[21]

In 1990 total bilateral trade turnover between the two countries was a mere $900,000, which mostly consisted of exports of animal hair (cashmere goat and wool) and animal by-products such as intestinal casings for sausages. There were almost no US imports reaching Mongolia.[22] Policymakers from both the United States and Mongolia saw strategic advantages in strengthening the bilateral relationship, especially political ties. During the early 1990s many Mongols, including President Ochirbat, believed it was very important to quickly establish a strong working relationship with the United States. He visited the United States in January 1991 to meet with President George H. W. Bush. The two signed a science and technology agreement, and Bush agreed to give Mongolia $8 million in food credits and also issued a waiver opening the door to granting Mongolia most-favored-nation status.[23] Although this state visit launched the beginning of a major American effort to assist Mongolia, the image of Mongolia among the US bureaucracy back in Washington, DC, advanced slowly. Baker's second trip to Mongolia in the summer of 1991 "provided a real boost for the Mongolian process of reform because it was a very clear demonstration by a senior-level American of support for continuation of democratic reforms in Mongolia."[24] Ambassador Lake asserted that there was an incredible "clicking" between Mongolians and Americans.

In that early period American officials dismissed any special claim to the "Third Neighbor" mantle because they viewed Mongolia as a friendly, but minor, nation wedged between significant US rivals, Russia and the PRC. In the State Department, Mongolia was covered by the China-Mongolia desk. Since Mongolia's democratic revolution occurred just after the Tiananmen incident, when US-China relations were much reduced, desk personnel had time to devote to Mongolia. However, after Secretary of State Baker left and the Clinton administration came into office, relations with China improved, and, according to Ambassador Lake, Mongolia received less attention from Washington. Still, Lake was positive that Mongolia was trying to build a new society based on democratic principles and a free market economy "where we as Americans have made a difference."[25] During his tenure, Ambassador Lake never spoke of the United States as a "Third Neighbor." He advised the Mongols to turn to their immediate neighbors, China and Russia, because "Mongolia's long term solution does not lie with the United States. . . . In the long run if Mongolia is to succeed it will have to deal with this reality."[26]

As the 1990s progressed, the official US view on Mongolia became more proactive. Alphonse LaPorta, the US ambassador in Mongolia from 1998 to 2000, saw the American commitment to Mongolia more geostrategically than Lake:

> The main thing that attracted the Washington agencies was really Mongolia's geostrategic position lying between Russia and China. There was a very strong interest, whether during the Bush administration or later in the Clinton years and especially under Madeleine Albright, in seeing Mongolia pursue a steadily independent course to become aligned with Western interests in Asia as opposed to kind of a more Eastward looking interest like Central Asia.[27]

LaPorta recognized that the Mongols were emerging from the Soviet world, but he was unable to interest US and European Sovietologists in

Mongolia. He did attempt to assist the Mongols in integrating into the Asian region by becoming members of the Pacific Basin Economic Council and the ASEAN Regional Forum (ARF). He believed that the Mongolian leadership looked to the United States for real assurance and protection, "because they said only the United States has the power, the interest and commitment to counterbalance"[28] Russia and China. LaPorta admitted to having "almost a mentoring relationship" with Prime Minister (later President) Elbegdorj of Mongolia. "To have such a close relationship on a personal and an intellectual basis with a governing group, not necessarily in the sense of establishing U.S. hegemony, but just helping these guys do the right thing. It was tremendously professionally rewarding."[29] One of the major aspects was in defense cooperation for military education and training to modernize the Mongolian military for international peacekeeping activities.

Mongolia's Concept of National Security and Concept of Foreign Policy of 1994

Mongolia's main foreign policy goals, including its concept of "Third Neighbor," for the post–Cold War period were outlined in two documents adopted by the Mongolian MPRP-dominated Parliament on June 30, 1994—the Concept of National Security and the Concept of Foreign Policy. The Concept of National Security emphasized that Mongolia sought a multipartner or multipillar approach to securing its vital interests. Top priority would be given to balanced relations with its two neighbors, China and Russia, but it would "pursue an open foreign policy." The consensus was that, although specific factors would change over time and exert different stresses on Mongolian national security, "the relations and balance between Russia and China—Mongolia's two big neighbors—have always been the pre-condition of the very existence of Mongolia, and changes in this balance has [*sic*] direct implications."[30]

The two concepts, which had emerged from the national security, intelligence, military, and political establishments, were ratified without public debate. At the time, Mongolia was suffering from extreme economic collapse with widespread milk and meat shortages in the capital and high unemployment with the disappearance of state factories' subsidies and their bankruptcies. The Western donors, led by Japan, Germany, and the United States, were providing funds to keep the government afloat and stabilize the food and power situation, so the concepts' outreach to the Western and Asian democracies reflected an opportunistic effort to placate Mongolia's important donors. Another result of this new strategic thinking was that Mongolian government officials, political scientists, and economists came to support Mongolian integration with the Northeast Asian region as the best chance for the country to develop and prosper as well as to counterbalance China's economic and political influence. Many Mongolian policymakers embraced this thinking because it seemed a way to affiliate with the success of the Asia Pacific economies and to keep the US at a distance. While they did not believe the effects of the Cold War could be quickly swept from the region, some predicted that Mongolia would come under the economic umbrella of the Japanese and South Koreans rather than of the Americans and Western Europeans.[31]

According to foreign policy specialist Migeddorj Batchimeg, democracy provided Mongolia with leverage over its immediate neighbors, Russia and China. Mongols "came to believe that only democracy can give us a real opportunity to develop a relatively balanced relationship with our powerful neighbors. And we believe that this will not only serve for Mongolia's interest, but will also serve for both Russia's and China's interests as well."[32] Unfortunately, in the second half of the 1990s, the Asian economic crisis dashed all hopes of strong "Third Neighbor" roles for Japan or South Korea. In Western Europe, Germany was self-absorbed in its own reunification problems, and the British were downsizing their interests in Mongolia because of the presence of other foreign donors. Thus, for Mongolia, the only realistic choice was the United States as the special "Third Neighbor" since it alone could provide strong economic ties and a market for Mongolian goods as well as strategic security for the Mongols.

National Security Concept of 2010 and Foreign Policy Concept of 2011

Mongolian policymakers fifteen years later decided that the 1994 National Security and Foreign Policy Concepts developed right after the end of its socialist political regime were not completely suitable for the country in the twenty-first century. Seventy Mongolian researchers and policymakers were secretly consulted to update Mongolia's 1994 National Security Concept and Foreign Relations Concept. Their products, the 2010 National Security Concept and 2011 Foreign Policy Concept, were national guiding principles announced to the nation and international community in sections. Revision of the two concepts is significant for two main reasons: (1) Mongolian policymakers believed that the guiding principles enunciated in the concepts of 1994 were outdated because of their link to the collapse of the communist system and so not reflective of the new economic and international challenges facing the nation in the twenty-first century; and (2) the Mongolian government was dissatisfied with the Third Neighbor Policy's results and wanted to reformulate its definition and expectations. Batchimeg noted that the 1994 National Security Concept "played an important role in shaping Mongolia's security and foreign policy, based on its national interests. However, the paper also contained a strong inertia of state-centered thinking inherent from [the] socialist era."[33] Some of its main points still were valid because the fundamental thinking behind Mongolia's view of national security remained unchallenged due to its very unique geopolitical location: "Stable balance of power in the region remains as an important foundation of Mongolia's national security. Any substantial power shift among the major powers in the region directly and deeply affects Mongolia's security."[34]

Mongolia's centuries-long experience of vacillating alliances with and hostility toward China and Russia continued to indicate that good-neighborly and balanced relations with the two neighbors remained the most effective policy. According to Damba Ganbat, director of Mongolia's Strategic Studies Center, "Mongolia's foreign policy's priority was always given to China and Russia, and the statement of fundamental principle of 'balanced relations' with the two neighbors, which was stated in the first National Security Concept, was kept the same way in the new National Security Concepts as well."[35] The 2010 National Security Concept, according to the Mongols, challenged the traditional way of thinking about security by redefining the major components of national security to include security of existence, economic security, domestic security, human security, environmental security, and information security. It emphasized that Mongolia's sovereignty and security were to be ensured by political and diplomatic means and that the country's foreign policy should be open, peaceful, and multipillared. In addition to emphasizing the state's responsibility for the well-being of the nation, the 2010 version highlighted the need for citizen participation in the overall process of security policy, which meant that strengthening democracy through "good governance and civil participation" was necessary for the nation's national security.[36]

The 2011 Foreign Policy Concept expanded upon these general perspectives to enumerate six specific principles or "directions" in priority order:

1. Maintaining friendly relations with the Russian Federation and the People's Republic of China shall be a priority direction of Mongolia's foreign policy activity.
2. The second direction of Mongolia's foreign policy activity shall be developing friendly relations with highly developed countries of the West and the East, such as the United States of America, Japan, and the Federal Republic of Germany.
3. The third direction of Mongolia's foreign policy activity shall be strengthening its position in Asia and securing a constructive participation in the political and economic integration process in the region. Within the framework of this objective greater attention

shall be given to the Asia Pacific region, in particular to Northeast and Central Asia.

4. The fourth direction of Mongolia's foreign policy activity shall be promoting cooperation with the United Nations Organization and its specialized agencies, and with international financial and economic organizations, including the International Monetary Fund (IMF), the World Bank, and the Asian Development Bank.
5. The fifth direction of Mongolia's foreign policy activity will be developing friendly relations with the countries of the former socialist community as well as the newly independent states. Specific mention was made of Poland, Hungary, and the Czech Republic as well as Kazakhstan, the Ukraine, Belarus, Kyrgyzstan, and Uzbekistan, but not the Democratic People's Republic of Korea (North Korea).
6. The sixth direction of Mongolia's foreign policy activity shall be developing friendly relations with developing countries and cooperating with them, as much as possible, in the solution of common objectives.[37]

According to Batchimeg, "In particular, continued benign foreign policy from China, and a stable friendly relationship between Russia and China should be pointed out as the most important external security factors for Mongolia."[38] This 2011 Foreign Policy Concept never refers to "Third Neighbors." In fact, the only mention of neighbors comes in the reference to China and Russia, calling for Mongolia to seek to "promote all-round neighbourly cooperation" with them. The phrase used in references to other nations is "developing friendly relations." The second priority direction cites countries of the West and Asia including the United States, Japan, and Germany. The full text specifically mentions an unusual mix of nations: India, the Republic of Korea, Thailand, Singapore, Turkey, Denmark, the Netherlands, Finland, Austria, Sweden, and Switzerland. Curiously, this list was not updated from the 1994 list to include Canada, Britain, France, or Australia, all of which by 2011 had provided significant donor assistance and/or FDI to Mongolia. The third direction of the 2011 concept indicates that Mongolia will give greater attention to the Asia Pacific region, in particular Northeast and Central Asia, in order to secure "a constructive participation in the political and economic integration process in the region." This direction also includes the promise of greater Mongolian activism in regional Asian affairs: "Mongolia shall take an active part in the process of initiating dialogues and negotiations on the issues of strengthening regional security and creating a collective security mechanism. It will strive to become a member of the Asia Pacific Economic Cooperation forum (APEC)."[39] However, it stipulates that Mongolia will participate in regional integration primarily through bilateral relations with the countries of the region.

Mongolia and the United States: From Acquaintance to Strategic Cooperation

On March 12, 1991, both houses of the US Congress in joint session passed a resolution "to provide maximum assistance to Mongolian reconstruction." A few months later Secretary Baker, on his second visit to Mongolia, spoke before the Mongolian Parliament and proclaimed, "You were the first Asian nation to embrace communism. Today, you have become the first Asian nation to have chosen the road to democracy. . . . In connection with your decision, I would like to say: Mongolia will point others the way towards progress."[40] Baker's visits triggered a phase of rapid development in US-Mongolian relations, concentrated in simultaneously promoting democratic institution-building and creating the political and legal frameworks necessary for the functioning of a private free market economy. The mechanisms of this cooperation consisted of annual coordination meetings of government foreign affairs officials, assistance programs coordinated or funded out of the US embassy, and Peace Corps and other nongovernmental organization (NGO)–building activities. Since 1991, US policies in Mongolia to assist civil society organizations as well as political parties were promulgated through the International Republican Institute (IRI), an arm of the congressionally financed National Endowment for Democracy.[41]

Despite regular exchanges of congressional and official delegations, the next visit to Ulaanbaatar at the secretary of state level did not take place until 1998, when Madeleine Albright, secretary of state under Bill Clinton, spent six hours in the country. Her host was Prime Minister Tsakhia Elbegdorj, a thirty-five-year-old democratic activist who, together with many of his colleagues, utilized the principles of Newt Gingrich's "Contract with America" to construct a "Contract with the Mongolian People"[42] for the leaders of the Democratic Union, and engineered a dramatic win for Democratic coalition forces during the 1996 parliamentary election. Elbegdorj and the US government's policies were in contrast to the "Asian values" argument of such countries as Singapore and China, which promoted economic modernization without free elections or political reform. The United States already had provided Mongolia $80 million in economic aid, mainly for fuel, when Secretary Albright endorsed Mongolia's transition path before Parliament: "Mongolia is a far distance from the United States, but because of your love for democratic values and your commitment to an open economy, in a sense we are neighbors."[43]

The successful democratization of Mongolia, a country in the Sino-Russian geostrategic backyard, attracted significant attention from US administrations as well as the US Congress. The US in the 1990s supported Mongolia's membership in the World Bank, International Monetary Fund, and Asian Development Bank, and urged its ally Japan to lead the International Assistance Group Meetings. The United States valued Mongolia's window on Russia and the PRC and so from the beginning of the democratic era sought to create a stable free market and democratic model that would positively influence the North Asian region. With over twenty years of sustained support from the United States, Mongolia would become the only formerly communist Asian state that simultaneously embraced political and economic transition, thus becoming the successful poster child for US democracy building and application of free market principles.

Aside from political support, the United States gave Mongolia substantial material aid. Starting in 1990, about $16 million was donated annually through USAID in money and wheat (over 100,000 tons) that amounted to $200 million over twenty-five years. After the 1990s, assistance focused on developing and modernizing energy, agriculture, and green technology, especially in the private sector.[44] Thus US-Mongolian relations over thirty years of diplomatic relations developed from modest beginnings in the 1987–1989 socialist era to economic and political patronage and support in the 1990s to comprehensive strategic cooperation in the early decades of the twenty-first century. The energizing principle throughout has been based upon the Third Neighbor Policy.

Still, the dynamics of the United States–Mongolia relationship, particularly in the 1990s, were mainly reactive—responding to developments in a modernizing China and a collapsing Soviet Union. The US focus had changed completely with Mongolia's peaceful democratic revolution and the decision to abandon communism during the concurrent collapse of the Soviet Union's COMECOM (aka Council for Mutual Economic Assistance [CMEA])[45] system in 1990–1991. Although Mongolia from the start of the democratic era was eager to attract US strategic assistance to replace that of its longtime Soviet benefactor and to label the United States its primary "Third Neighbor," the key event for the bilateral relationship came after the September 11, 2001, terrorist attack on the US homeland, when the US government saw the significance of growing military and peacekeeping cooperation with Mongolia. The Mongolian leadership, regardless of political party, recognized that this attack was an opportunity for Mongolia to realize its own goals for the US "Third Neighbor" relationship. Mongolia immediately joined the Coalition of the Willing to go into Iraq and subsequently sent ten rotations of troops there. Moreover, from 2011 Mongolia began to participate in the Sustainable Freedom Operation of the International Security Assistance Force in Afghanistan. All of these Mongolian actions were warmly welcomed by the Bush and Obama administrations.

The American embrace of its role as a "Third Neighbor" for Mongolia continued to evolve in the twenty-first century. Secretary of State Hillary Clinton in 2011 called Mongolia a "new partner"—a term the United States also applied to India, Indonesia, Vietnam, New Zealand, and Malaysia.[46] This term was repeated in congressional testimony by the Department of State's Assistant Secretary of East Asian and Pacific

Affairs, Kurt Campbell—"Mongolia is a reliable, democratic partner with a bright future"—and he encouraged US companies to participate in developing Mongolia's mineral resources.[47]

Japan as Number 1 Asian "Third Neighbor"

The story of Mongolia's "Third Neighbor" foreign policy strategy also is closely interwoven with its bilateral relations with Japan. Mongolia believed it needed Japanese investment to redesign its political and economic system to meet its post–Cold War national security and globalization challenges. It expected that the end of the Cold War meant that politics and military might were no longer vitally essential to sustain national sovereignty, but rather that a strong economic partner could provide protection. Such a view was logical in the context of the early 1990s when the Big and Little Tigers of Asia were militarily weak but economically powerful.[48] Through this strategy, Mongolia was seeking to extricate itself from the geopolitical quagmire of being a Russian buffer against China.[49] In this context, diplomat and foreign policy strategist Dügersüren stated, "Thus the development of active relations with the United States and Japan on the basis of mutual benefit and respect for legitimate interests constitutes a foreign policy objective of a very high priority for us."[50]

When in the summer of 1939 Japan invaded Mongolian territory from Manchuria in the northeast and fought against a joint Mongolian-Soviet force around Khalkhin Gol (Nomonhan), its soldiers were defeated and imprisoned for over fifteen years. During that period, about 16,000 Japanese prisoners worked on forced labor construction projects to build the center of Ulaanbaatar, and 2,000 such prisoners were buried at sixteen different locations in Mongolia.[51] Ultimately, the two countries established diplomatic relations on February 24, 1972. Although contacts developed slowly in the communist period with the establishment of a small permanent Japanese embassy, Japanese investment in the cashmere textile sector became a source of hard currency for the Mongols. The Mongolian side facilitated the repatriation of prisoner remains and permitted the creation of memorials at the cemeteries and visits by Japanese relatives and war veterans to those sites. The bitter animosity that most Asian nations did and often still do feel for Japan because of its World War II military aggression never developed in Mongolia. This factor explained why young Mongolian policymakers could promote a policy of building on the communist-era rudimentary economic relationship to turn Japan into their primary "Third Neighbor" in Northeast Asia.

Mongolia's first prime minister in the democratic reform era, Dash Byambasüren, developed particularly close ties to Japan. In August 1991 he hosted Prime Minister Toshiki Kaifu's visit, the first by a Japanese prime minister and the first by a leader of an industrialized country. Kaifu actively supported Mongolia's transition to democracy and a free market under a strategy, developed with the United States, that called for Japan to take the leading role in coordinating policy and donor assistance. In September 1991 and May 1992, under the joint chairmanship of the government of Japan and the World Bank, Mongolia Assistance Group meetings were held in Tokyo. At the 1992 meeting Prime Minister Byambasüren and First Deputy Prime Minister Davaadorj Ganbold succeeded in obtaining from the participating countries and international organizations commitments of assistance that totaled $320 million to prop up the collapsed Mongolian economy for the 1992–1993 period. Japan's own economic aid to Mongolia in 1990 was slightly over 500 million yen, but in 1991 it rose to 8.4 billion yen, channeled mainly toward satellite telecommunications and railroads.[52] Private people-to-people exchanges also expanded rapidly. Japan quickly became an influential player in Mongolia's economic and cultural sectors but not in security and defense. Its early and generous donor assistance at the beginning of the 1990s cemented the goodwill between the countries and raised Mongolian expectations for significant infusion of Japanese FDI.

It became evident that Japan's FDI at the end of the first decade of democratization, which was only 11.7 percent of the total (down from 23.2 percent in 1995), was very disappointing to the Mongols.[53] Mongolian exports to Japan also fluctuated widely. In 1990 they stood at $7.6 million, in 1995 increased to $46.7 million, while in 1999—reflecting Japan's own domestic economic crisis—plunged to $10.9 million.[54] Meanwhile, Mongolia's trade deficit with Japan grew dramatically. Imports of $9.8 million in 1990 had been close in value to exports but jumped to $45.3 million in 1995 and to $115 million in 1999. The Mongolian government attempted to correct the imbalance by limiting Japanese imports to $73.3 million in 2000.[55] Such economic inconsistencies caused some Mongolian leaders to doubt Japan's ability to be a reliable "Third Neighbor."

India as Democratic and Cultural "Third Neighbor" Model

One cannot analyze the early democratic era in Mongolia without noting the inspirational example of India in Mongolia's view of democracy, of neutrality as a national security strategy, and of cultural-religious ties. The Mongolian political establishment was Soviet-trained and atheistic but included proponents of strong Mongolian-Indian ties in the communist era. The young democratic groups opposing it also considered the "Indian way" as a potential key link for their "Third Neighbor" strategy. Concurrently, with the revival of Buddhism among the Mongolian people and especially their attraction to Tibetan Buddhism under the Dalai Lama, who lives in India, Mongolian leaders had to calculate the impact of this factor on bilateral relations as well.

Indian-Mongolian relations have historical and religious underpinnings dating back to the thirteenth through eighteenth centuries, when Mongol rulers became involved militarily in Tibet and other Indian-influenced territories and embraced Tibetan lamaism with its strong Indian Buddhist features by giving themselves the title of Chakravartin Khan. India's political establishment in contemporary times has attached great strategic importance to Mongolia in terms of India's contentious relations with the PRC. Indian Vice President S. Radhakrishnan visited Mongolia in 1957 and advocated for Mongolia's membership in the United Nations despite Chinese opposition. At the Tenth UN General Assembly, India's permanent representative Krishna Menon proclaimed that "Mongolia was founded neither yesterday nor today, but has existed as an independent State over many centuries. Hence, similarly like any other country, the Mongolian People's Republic has full rights to become a member of United Nations Organization."[56] A few years later Indian Prime Minister Jawaharlal Nehru personally argued for Mongolian UN membership. India also supported Mongolia's membership in the Non-Aligned Movement, despite its Soviet satellite status, while Mongolia during the socialist era supported India's candidacy to become a permanent member of the UN Security Council.

Noting that the demise of communism and the revival of Buddhism added new dimensions to Indo-Mongolian relations, Indian political scientist Phunchok Stobdan has claimed that "the Mongol colour [White Horse] revolution was inspired by Indian wisdom; it chose the Buddhist path for transforming Asia's first Communist state into a democratic society." He argues that it is simplistic and misleading to look at Mongolian-Indian relations only through the prism of both nations' China policies: "Today, the country, located in the remote northeast of Asia, remains the last frontier where Indic cultural imprints remain strong."[57] For India, the cultural bond with Mongolia is its biggest asset, which was illustrated in 2004 when the Indian government conferred an honorary doctorate of letters on Prime Minister Nambar Enkhbayar for his role in promoting democracy and Buddhism in Mongolia. That same year the Indians financed the construction of the first ever Mongolian Buddhist monastery in Bodh Gaya, the Mahabodhi Temple Complex in Bihar. Stobdan has suggested that such actions were key Indian diplomatic moves to reach out to Northeast Asia as well as Mongolia.

Declaring Mongolia a Nuclear-Weapon-Free State

At the dawn of the democratic era, some Mongolian strategists recommended that Mongolia adopt as part of its new foreign policy strategy elements of India's neutralist and non-nuclear weapons policies, which had allowed India to carve out a space between the two superpowers during the Cold War. During the communist era, Mongolia had consistently advocated disarmament and nonproliferation of nuclear weapons. With the end of the Cold War and the loss of a superpower to protect it, Mongolia desired to keep its territory free of nuclear weapons to strengthen its national security by political and diplomatic means. It was believed that clarifying Mongolia's nuclear-weapon-free status at the highest policy level would be important in strengthening mutual confidence and Mongolia's external security environment as well as in linking the country's national security to regional security and stability.[58] Mongolian researcher Mendee further explained Mongolian thinking by asserting that, when China and Russia competed with each other in the Asian region, Mongolia fell into the "geopolitical quagmire" of becoming a Russian buffer state against China, which provided little maneuvering room. However, Mongolia could create its own geopolitical opening when China and Russia become either "cooperative" or "retrenched" (i.e., distracted by their own domestic affairs). During these periods, Mongolia's neutrality and stability became of greater importance for the two large nations as they increased their own economic collaboration or managed other conflicts. This was incentive for both countries to keep Mongolia militarily neutral. Mendee maintains that this geopolitical reality should determine Mongolia's survival strategy and foreign policy behavior.[59]

Within the framework of such strategic positioning, in 1992 Mongolia declared its territory a nuclear-weapon-free zone and took measures to institutionalize this status. It obtained approval from the United Nations General Assembly on December 4, 1998, for its position that Mongolia's nuclear-weapons-free status represented a new international relations approach that would ensure Mongolia's security and serve as a concrete contribution to strengthening the regime of nuclear weapons nonproliferation.[60] In February 2000, the Mongolian Parliament adopted a nuclear-weapon-free status law. The nuclear-free status included a ban on manufacturing, stationing, testing, or transporting nuclear weapons, as well as dumping or disposing of nuclear weapons-grade radioactive material or nuclear waste. However, the government was permitted the use of nuclear energy and technology for peaceful purposes, such as health care, mining, energy production, and scientific research in accordance with the provisions of international law. In addition, the resolution stated that Mongolia would refrain "from joining any military alliance or grouping, or allowing the use of its territory against any other State as well as banning the stationing on its territory of foreign troops and weapons, including nuclear and other weapons of mass destruction."[61] The goal was for Mongolia to pursue its own national interests, develop friendly cooperation with all the countries of the world, and strengthen world peace and security. Oversight and verification of this policy were granted to Mongolia's National Security Council.

This nuclear-weapon-free status was affirmed in 2012 in a joint declaration of all the permanent members of the United Nations Security Council (China, France, the Russian Federation, the United Kingdom, and the

United States), which promised that "as long as Mongolia maintains its nuclear-free status, to respect that status, and not to contribute to any act that violate it."[62] In subsequent years, Mongolia sought unsuccessfully to expand its nuclear-weapon-free policy among other nations to make Northeast Asia a nuclear-weapon-free zone out of the conviction that such a regional commitment would ensure Mongolia's continuing nuclear-weapon-free status as well as increase the role and responsibilities of NGOs and other initiatives toward strengthening regional peace.[63] It is believed that these actions to get its weapon-free status recognized at both the domestic and international level are meaningful for Mongolia because its peaceful foreign policy elevates its prestige on the world stage as more countries formally support Mongolia's status.[64]

Notes

1. Ts. Batbayar and K. Demberel, "Contemporary Mongolian-Russian Relations: Problems and Perspectives," in *The Geopolitical Relations Between Contemporary Mongolia and Neighboring Asian Countries: Democracy, Economy and Security* (Taipei: Mongolian and Tibetan Affairs Commission Conference, September 2003), 333–334.

2. N. Tuya, "Dimensions of Mongolia's National Security" (remarks at the Asia Foundation Conference on Mongolia's Political and Economic Transition: Challenges and Opportunities, Ulaanbaatar, September 13, 2000), https://asiafoundation.org/resources/pdfs/MongoliaPolEconTransition.pdf.

3. Mendee, Jargalsaikhan, "What's Next for American and Japanese Partnerships with Mongolia?" August 20, 2014, unpublished paper presented at the East West Center, https://www.eastwestcenter.org/events/beyond-the-quagmire-the-future-mongolia's-united-states-and-japan-partnerships.

4. Personal communication with the author.

5. Baasanjav Ganbold quoted in "Mongolia's 'Third Neighbor' Foreign Policy," Asia Society, June 23, 2013, http://asiasociety.org/korea/mongolias-third-neighbor-foreign-policy.

6. For further discussion on the Baker statement, see the memoirs of the late Ambassador Olzvoy, who participated in negotiations with Secretary Baker in July 1990. Kh. Olzvoy, "J. Beikeriin Ailchlal xiigeed 'guravdaxi tunsh'—uun asuudald," *Olon Ulsin Xariltsaa, World Affairs* 184 (5), no. 1 (2002): 166–168. For Mongolian analysis of the "Third Neighbor" Policy, see Tsedendamba Batbayar, "Geopolitics and Mongolia's Search for Post-Soviet Identity," *Journal of Eurasian Geography and Economics* 43, no. 4 (June 2002): 323–335.

7. Ts. Batbayar, "The Development of Mongolia's External Relations in the 1990s," in *Renovation of Mongolia on the Eve of the XXI Century and Future Development Patterns*, ed. Ts. Batbayar (Ulaanbaatar: Mongolian Development Research Center, 2000), 80.

8. Luvsan Erdenechuluun was a career diplomat who was Mongolian ambassador to the United Nations (1991–1995) and minister of foreign affairs (2000–2004). He became president of the Human Security Policy Studies Center in 2006 and a member of the Executive Board of the United Nations Educational, Scientific, and Cultural Organization (UNESCO) in 2007.

9. L. Erdenechuluun, "Mongolia's Strategic Options," in *Northeast Asia Towards 2000: Interdependence and Conflict?*, ed. Kyongsoo Lho and Kay Möller. Baden-Baden, Germany: Nomos, 1999), 95.

10. M. Batchimeg, "National Security of Mongolia: Past, Present, Future" (speech presented at Indiana University, November 17, 2010); reprinted in *Mongolian Journal of International Affairs* 10 (2011): 15.

11. "Remarks by Secretary Shultz at US-Mongolian Normalization Ceremony, January 27, 1987," *Mongolia Society Newsletter* (Bloomington, IN), no. 3, February 1987, 4.

12. For details on the early nonpermanent embassy, see Jonathan S. Addleton, *Mongolia and the United States: A Diplomatic History* (Hong Kong: Hong Kong University Press, 2013), 31–35.

13. James Addison Baker III (1930–) was chief of staff to President Ronald Reagan from 1981 to 1984, secretary of the treasury from 1985 to 1988, and secretary of state for President George Bush from 1991 to 1994. He has made several trips to Mongolia after his term as secretary of state and remains involved with Mongolian issues. James A. Baker III, *The Politics of Diplomacy* (New York: G. P. Putnam's Sons, 1995); "James Baker," *NNDB*, http://www.nndb.com/people/331/000023262/.

14. Noted in "Senate Confirmation Hearings for Ambassador-Designate Joseph Lake," Committee on Foreign Relations, May 4, 1990.

15. Joseph E. Lake (1941–) is a career diplomat and information management specialist who was ambassador to Mongolia from 1990 to 1993 and ambassador to Albania from 1994 to 1996. He also served in Bulgaria, Nigeria, Benin, and Taiwan.

16. Afghanistan, Bulgaria, China, Cuba, Czechoslovakia, GDR (East Germany), Hungary, India, Japan, Laos, North Korea, Poland, Romania, USSR, United Kingdom, Vietnam, and Yugoslavia. Lake Confirmation Hearings, "Resident Ambassador," May 1990.

17. Ibid.

18. For Ochirbat's private account of the Baker visit, see Punsalmaagiin Ochirbat, *The Time of Heaven*, ed. Peter K. Marsh (Bloomington, IN: The Mongolia Society, 2018), 313–314.

19. Mark Goleman, "Mongolia and the US: From Acquaintance to Strategic Cooperation," *New Eastern Outlook,* May 5, 2015, http://journal-neo.org/2015/05/31/rus-mongoliya-i-ssha-ot-znakomstva-k-strategicheskomu-sotrudnichestvu/.

20. Joseph Lake, in "U.S.-Mongolia Relations: History and Future Prospects," Roundtable, unpublished proceedings (Washington, DC: October 31, 2005), 24.

21. "Ambassador Joseph E. Lake," interview, 12, http://www.adst.org/OH%20TOCs/Lake,%20Joseph%20E.toc.pdf.

22. The *Mongolian Statistical Yearbook 2000* (Ulaanbaatar: National Statistics Office of Mongolia, 2001), 180, lists no imports from the United States in 2000.

23. For President Ochirbat's description of his trip to Washington, see Ochirbat, *Time of Heaven*, 316–321.

24. Lake interview, 17.

25. Ibid., 29.

26. Ibid., 26–27.

27. Alphonse F. LaPorta, "Ambassador Alphonse F. LaPorta," interview by Charles Stuart Kennedy, Association for Diplomatic Studies and Training Foreign Affairs Oral History Project, February 11, 2004, 165, http://www.adst.org/OH%20TOCs/La%20Porta,%20Alphonse%20F.toc.pdf.

28. Ibid., 166.

29. Ibid., 179.

30. Damba Ganbat, "National Security Concept of Mongolia: Basic Principle," in *Security Outlook of the Asia Pacific Countries and Its Implications for the Defense Sector* (Tokyo: National Institute for Defense Studies, 2000), 92, http://www.nids.mod.go.jp/english/publication/joint_research/series11/pdf/09.pdf.

31. Olzvoy, "A Mongol's View."

32. Batchimeg, "National Security of Mongolia," 13–14.

33. Ibid., 17.

34. Ibid., 16.

35. Ganbat, "National Security Concept," 93.

36. Batchimeg, "National Security of Mongolia," 17.

37. This is an edited version of the text including the first sentence only of each principle. For full version see II.12 a–f on Mongolian Embassy in Vienna website: http://www.embassymon.at/en/concept-foreign-policy.

38. Batchimeg, "National Security of Mongolia," 16.
39. National Foreign Policy Concept 2011, Section 12 (c).
40. Goleman, "Mongolia and the US."
41. The National Endowment for Democracy (NED) is a private, nonprofit foundation dedicated to the growth and strengthening of democratic institutions around the world. Founded in 1983 by President Ronald Reagan, it annually funds about 1,200 grants to support the projects of nongovernmental groups abroad that are working for democratic goals in more than ninety countries. See http://www.ned.org/about/#.
42. The contract called for private property rights, a free press, and foreign investment, and its printing of 350,000 copies made it the most widely distributed document in Mongolian history.
43. Barton Gellman, "'Impressed' Albright Gets a Taste of the New Mongolia," *Washington Post,* May 3, 1998, A28.
44. Goleman, "Mongolia and the US."
45. COMECON, or CMEA, was an economic assistance organization of communist states founded in 1949. Mongolia was first invited in the 1950s as an observer, but it attained full membership in 1962. COMECON's final session took place in Budapest, Hungary, on June 28, 1991, and it disbanded within ninety days. See http://www.britannica.com/eb/article-9054503/Comecon; Robert Bideleux and Ian Jeffries, *A History of Eastern Europe: Crisis and Change* (London: Routledge, 1998).
46. "Remarks," handout, APEC's First Senior Officials Meeting, March 9, 2011.
47. Kurt Campbell, "Testimony Before the U.S. House of Representatives' Committee on Foreign Affairs Subcommittee on Asia and the Pacific," March 9, 2011.
48. Big Tiger: Japan; Little Tigers: Hong Kong, Singapore, South Korea, and Taiwan.
49. Mendee, "What's Next?"
50. M. Dügersüren, "Changing Mongolia in a New Environment," *Mongolian Journal of International Affairs*, no. 1 (1994): 21.
51. There are cemeteries of Japanese captives in Dambadarjaa and in Khujirbulan, both near the capital city; at Sükhbaatar in Selenge province; at Baruunkharaa, Zuunkharaa, Shokhoi, and Tsagaan Bulag in Töv province; and at Nalaikh, Arkhust, Jargalant, Batsumber, Bornuur, and Ukher Chuluu. "Mongolia Monument Honors Prisoners," *Japan Times,* December 11, 2001, http://www.japantimes.co.jp/news/2001/12/11/national/mongolia-monument-honors-prisoners/#.U-kw_PldWCl.
52. These are statistics from the Japanese fiscal year, which is April 1 to March 31. "Regional Situations and Relations with Japan," in *Japanese Bluebook* (Tokyo: Ministry of Foreign Affairs of Japan, 1992–1993), chap. III, section 3-3, http://www.mofa.go.jp/policy/other/bluebook/1992/1992-3-1.htm.
53. Terry McKinley, "The National Development Strategy and Aid Coordination," in *Poverty Reduction in Mongolia,* ed. Keith Griffin (Canberra: Asia Pacific Press, 2003), 140.
54. *Mongolian Statistical Yearbook*, 178.
55. Amounting to 12 percent of total imports. Ibid., 179–180.
56. P. Stobdan, "India and Mongolia: Modi on Ashoka's Path," *IDSA Comment,* Institute for Defence Studies and Analyses, May 13, 2015, www.idsa.in/idsacomments/IndiaandMongolia_pstobdan_130515.
57. Ibid.
58. J. Enkhsaikhan, "Developing Nuclear Landscape in the Asian Heartland: Role of Nuclear-Weapon States," *Mongolian Journal of International Affairs*, no. 11 (2004): 32.
59. "The more militarily neutral policies Mongolia pursues, the less likely the security dilemmas between China and Russia and/or between them and other distant Great Powers escalate." Mendee, "What's Next?"
60. Resolution 53/77D, entitled "Mongolia's International Security and Nuclear-Weapon-Free Status," stated that Mongolia's nuclear-weapon-free status represented a new international relations approach that constituted an important factor for ensuring Mongolia's security, which it considered a concrete contribution to strengthening the regime of nonproliferation of nuclear weapons.

61. Ambassador Od Och, "Declaration by Mongolia Regarding Its Nuclear-Weapon-Free Status," New York, September 17, 2012, http://nautilus.org/wp-content/uploads/2012/09/signed-Mongolian-declaration.pdf. See also "Memorandum from Mongolia Regarding the Consolidation of Its International Security and Nuclear-Weapon-Free Status," (2015 Review Conference of the Parties to the Treaty on the Non-Proliferation of Nuclear Weapons, New York, April 27–May 22, 2015), http://www.un.org/en/ga/search/view_doc.asp?symbol=NPT/CONF.2015/8.

62. "The Joint Declaration of the People's Republic of China, France, the Russian Federation, the United Kingdom of Great Britain and Northern Ireland, and the United States of America on Mongolia's Nuclear-Weapon-Free Status Issued on 17 September 2012," noted in Och, "Declaration by Mongolia."

63. D. Myagmar, executive director of the Global Partnership for the Prevention of Armed Conflict (GPPAC) Northeast Asia, quoted in "Northeast Asian Delegates Gather in Ulaanbaatar to Discuss Regional Issue," *Mongol Messenger,* November 18, 2016.

64. J. Enkhbayar, head of the Parliamentary Standing Committee, remarks reported in GPPAC meeting in ibid.

4

Building a New Economy Through Donor Aid

Mongolia's development prior to 1990 was based on the "noncapitalist way" imposed by the former Soviet Union. As a result, its economy on the periphery of the world socialist system became highly integrated with other centrally planned economies in the Soviet Union and Eastern Europe through the Soviet-led COMECON. At the same time, Mongolia lost its economic and cultural ties with its own Asian region and the rest of the world and became by the end of the 1980s one of the most dependent countries in the world.[1] A March 1991 IMF study titled "The Mongolian People's Republic—Toward a Market Economy"[2] noted that in 1989 Ulaanbaatar held one-fourth of the nation's then 2.1 million people. Mongolian industry was concentrated in the processing of livestock by-products, employing 20 percent of the labor force in various industrial cities. The state farm sector comprised only 4 percent of the economy, about the same as mining; animal husbandry comprised 25 percent; heavy industry represented over 15 percent; and the light industry and food processing sector made up another 15 percent.[3]

Even though Mongolian Prime Minister Byambasüren concluded a new Declaration on Friendship and Good-Neighborly Cooperation and protocol on economic cooperation in Moscow in February 1991, Soviet-era construction projects were withdrawn quickly. Moscow abandoned the Soviet barter system of trading Mongolian copper and other minerals, meat products, leather goods, and carpets for Russian diesel oil and energy-related spare parts in favor of a new hard-currency system, but both sides had no purchasing funds. Mongolia's import of Russian petroleum products in early 1992 was reduced to only 21 percent of needed supplies,[4] resulting in great hardship that winter for the Mongolian people. It was obvious that new sources of energy and consumer goods needed to be found quickly.

The disappearance of Russian financial support in the educational, medical, and industrial sectors in the early 1990s immediately brought about a severe decrease in overall trade and caused spare parts and equipment shortages for all of Mongolia's industrial base. These transitional problems in tandem provoked a severe economic crisis. Mongolia was at sea. It felt abandoned by its longtime Soviet Russian friend, and so policymakers, whether supporters of reform or not, saw no alternative but to turn to Western countries and Asian democracies for immediate financial support and assistance. Mongolia's huge negative economic shock meant that net inflows ceased, supply chains broke, and the favorable terms of trade from underpriced Soviet oil and overpriced payments for Mongolian copper exports terminated. According to one economist, "The combined shock has been estimated at equal to loss of around half of gross national expenditure."[5] The collapse of Soviet funding meant Mongolia's centrally planned economy was faced with the challenge of moving toward economic independence, but it evaded this bitter reality through dependence on international donor aid while the new free market system gradually was installed. In 1991 Mongolia was admitted to the Asian Development Bank (ADB), the International Monetary Fund (IMF), and the World Bank. International donor aid was administered both through direct bilateral assistance and through international organizations—all with the aim of helping Mongolia restructure its economy and political system. During this same period, the concept of NGOs was introduced, and international NGOs of all sizes, working alongside foreign donors, were important influences shaping Mongolia's new economic and social system.

In the communist era, 30 percent of Mongolia's GDP had derived from Soviet assistance, but within a few years this deficit was replaced by international assistance. Western donor aid, while coordinated by the donors at an annual meeting in Tokyo, often was inefficiently allocated and allowed the rise of corruption through lack of defined constraints and benchmarks on the Mongolian government. This problematic coordination and management only encouraged Mongolia's economic dependency. Joseph Lake, US ambassador to Mongolia at the time, commented that by the time of the 1992 parliamentary election, the major foreign donors were very frustrated: "There was a strong feeling that the government was simply looking to the West to replace the massive Soviet assistance program of the past, rather than effectively analyzing its difficulties and trying to overcome them."[6]

Economic activity in Mongolia for centuries had been based on migratory livestock breeding. The Soviets had promoted a policy of moving the economy away from nomadism and toward sedentary industrialization; however, the nomadic economy still had not died out in the modern era. The Soviets labeled the persistence of the traditional economy as the "peculiar inertness or stagnation" of the Mongols due to their bitter struggles for survival.[7] Nomads with their herds were brutally collectivized in the 1930s in a campaign that ultimately failed. A second, more moderate collectivization drive in the 1950s succeeded, and private herding was nearly eliminated. In the mid-1950s, over 90 percent of the population were rural herders, but by 1990 only 33 percent of employment was still in the livestock/agricultural sector.

In the 1960s small industrial cities, developed into provincial (*aimag*) capitals, were created around mining operations and light industrial state factories. The majority of these state enterprises in the early 1990s went bankrupt or were privatized. When the working populations moved away, the populations in almost all provincial capitals greatly withered. Still, from 1992 to 1997 the mining industry produced 30 percent of Mongolia's GDP, and mining exports represented 65.5 percent of the nation's exports.[8] In the early democratic era until 1997, Mongolia suffered from deep recession with the collapse of the command economy, as the country eased price controls, liberalized domestic and international trade, and started the restructuring of the banking and energy sectors. People were forced to leave the failing industrial cities and *aimag* capitals to resume nomadic pastoralism or to move to the one functioning city, Ulaanbaatar, the capital. In 1992–1993, the livestock cooperatives (*negdels*) were the first to be dismantled, and their herds were privatized. This occurred not because the government wanted to give special assistance to the rural population but because privatizing this sector seemed easier than dismantling the socialist-era bankrupt state industrial enterprises. Many Mongols in the first half of the 1990s returned to reliance on the nomadic economy for their livelihoods. This trend was disparaged by the Western experts as "slipping back into primitive subsistence livestock herding."[9] However, it saved the nation from starvation and public unrest since the rural population immediately and on its own without government coordination provided food to impoverished city-dwelling relatives.

Western economic development experts assisting Mongolia in the 1990s did not have a deep understanding of or sympathy for Mongolia's nomadic economy. Rather, they blamed Mongolia's problems on both the nature of this traditional economy and the Soviet-style command economy that was constructed atop it. Foreign economists poured into Mongolia and advised the dismantling of the herding economy as well as the outdated Soviet-created industrial base. Despite no foreign donor aid or Mongolian government funds, livestock herds almost doubled to thirty-four million head by 1999. Unemployed "city boy nomads" moved to the countryside to take up herding, particularly of cashmere goats, which were the most profitable because their hair easily found international markets, especially in China. Nomadic livestock herding became the mainstay during the economic transition to a market economy as private enterprises could not easily move into processing and trade due to a shortage of working capital and investment funds.[10]

The foreign donor community took several years to finally recognize the rural sector's debilitated condition after seventy years of mismanagement and attack under communism. In those early years, hundreds of millions of dollars of foreign donor multilateral and bilateral assistance, including the vast majority of USAID, Japanese aid, and ADB funds, were poured into staving off constant winter heating and electricity crises by keeping Ulaanbaatar's power plants running, providing emergency food aid to the urban communities, and making minimal renovations to Ulaanbaatar's airport. The donors also supported democracy and NGO capacity-building programs within the capital to promote legal, constitutional, and administrative reforms. During that first decade, the reabsorption of so many unemployed from the cities back into the countryside's nomadic life was a phenomenon that finally attracted the attention of the foreign donor and NGO community because the rural economy was blamed by United Nations Development Programme (UNDP) experts for the country's continuing poverty.

Mongolia persistently sought to align its development goals with market economy principles during this difficult transition. In concert with Western advisers, it developed a number of plans to guide its development actions.[11] However, these plans were only spottily implemented because Mongolia had to undertake macroeconomic stabilization policies and structural adjustment reforms, which meant that necessary resources, institutional frameworks, and the legal environment for development policy planning and implementation were absent. Priority was placed on fiscal stabilization in a climate of severe resource constraints, so there was a lack of investment available for development priorities. It was only with Mongolia's accession to the World Trade Organization (WTO) in 1997 that market economy–based trade liberalization and price liberalization policies rose to the forefront. Mongolian economists recognized that Mongolia needed to diversify its economy beyond the sale of raw animal by-products and minerals into tourism and export-oriented production for China and Russia in economic free zones.[12]

Mongolian policymakers felt they had no choice but to accept the recommendations that came with the vital donor assistance, even when they believed the new Western proposals would fail. As the decade advanced, economic observers began to warn that the collapse of the economic base of most of Mongolia's provincial capitals had resulted in spatial inequalities in economic development. Economic growth fueled by donor assistance overwhelmingly was concentrated in Ulaanbaatar, while the rest of the vast country was ignored by donors and the Mongolian government alike. Most donor funds were dedicated to large-scale projects in the energy and mining fields despite rising poverty rates: in 1998, 30 percent went to mining, 27 percent to energy, 19 percent to transport, 8 percent to telecommunications, and only 3 percent to social programs.[13] As the decade proceeded, many in the foreign donor, NGO, and foreign expert communities warned that the results of Western-inspired economic policies were stimulating the development of two distinct ecocultures in Mongolia—one was judged urban and dynamic and the other rural and regressive. Meanwhile, Mongols saw the geographic disintegration of their ex-Soviet planned economy and creation of this bifurcated economy as a severe threat to long-term economic development, territorial integrity, and even independence. The anti-nomadic mentality among the foreign donors intensified at the end of the decade in 1999–2002 with three consecutive years of winter disasters called *dzuds*, when four million head of livestock (especially goats) perished, and agriculture's contribution to GDP declined significantly. Donor and NGO programs and funds to assist people in the countryside had to step in where the Mongolian government did not.

Coordinating and Amassing Official Development Assistance for Mongolia

Mongolia in the first decade of democracy depended upon foreign official development assistance (ODA) provided at the central government level. Donor assistance for Mongolia was actually managed at the macro level by the United States. In 1991 the United States went from zero planned aid for Mongolia at the beginning of the year to over $30 million in assistance.[14] Its program was oriented toward supplying spare parts for Soviet-built systems and technical assistance. Through USAID and assistance from US companies in the energy sector, Ulaanbaatar's central heating system maintained operations during the winter of 1992–1993. However, the crucial ODA factor was that the United States persuaded donor countries, led by Japan and Germany as well as such international organizations as the United Nations, World Bank, and IMF, to provide economic aid to meet the challenges of transforming Mongolia's collapsing socialist economy. This was coordinated by the government of Japan and the World Bank beginning in 1991 at annual Mongolia Assistance Group meetings of donor countries in Tokyo.[15] Eventually, thirty countries and ten international institutions financially supported the Mongols; the major assistance came from Japan, ADB, World Bank, and Germany. Japan was the largest international donor, usually giving $70–$90 million in aid per year. From 1993 to 1997 Japan's assistance totaled $507 million—$261 million in grant aid, $127 million in technical cooperation, and $118 million in loans.[16]

This decade of ODA disbursement of foreign loans and assistance can be divided into three distinct stages. Stage One, from 1990 to 1993, was devoted to stabilizing the collapsing command economy through eliminating food, heating, and electricity shortages and covering the trade deficit. Stage Two, from 1994 to 1995, emphasized medium-term projects for modernizing and reequipping manufacturing enterprises and for conducting feasibility studies.

Stage Three, from 1996 to 2000, was geared toward improving the banking sector and investing in road, rail, and mining projects.[17] Mongolia received long-term low-interest loans from the IMF and World Bank with interest deferred ten years. These loans were "aimed to reach macroeconomic stabilization, to make structural changes in financial and manufacturing sectors, to create working places, to improve infrastructure and to eliminate poverty."[18]

Mongolia, like many other former socialist economies, experienced a painful "transformational recession" in the first few years during its transition to a market economy before recovering as a result of efficiency gains from market-oriented reforms. Real GDP bottomed out in 1993 and then returned to positive rates of growth. By 2000–2001, real GDP had reverted to the level prior to the transition.[19] The positive results from all these policies can be seen when comparing Mongolia's economic progress to that of other new Central Asian nations that emerged from the Soviet orbit to switch from command economies at about the same time. Mongolia in 1991 experienced a GDP of –9.9, which by 1994 had rebounded to +2.1, and its inflation rate of 121.2 percent in 1991 fell to 87.6 percent by 1994. In comparison, Azerbaijan in 1991 had –0.7 GDP, which fell to –21.9 percent in 1994 and a 1991 inflation rate of 105.6 percent that skyrocketed to 1,664.5 percent in 1994. Meanwhile, Kazakhstan had a –13.0 percent GDP in 1991 and –21.0 percent in 1994, and a 1991 inflation rate of 91 percent as opposed to 1,889 percent in 1994.[20]

In the 1990s, 24 percent of Mongolia's GDP was sustained by foreign aid. From 1991 to 2000, total ODA was almost $1.9 billion, an enormous amount of money for a country of only 2.5 million people.[21] During that decade Mongolia was the fifth most aid-dependent developing country in the world. The Western donors and the international NGO community during the transition years urged the Mongolian government to focus priorities on urban economic development, which effectively meant economic development in the capital of Ulaanbaatar. In the 1990s only about 5 percent of all ODA was allocated to agricultural and animal husbandry in the countryside, thus exacerbating the social gulf between the reviving traditional nomadic economy and the Sovietized, Westernized capital city.

The ADB was Mongolia's second largest donor after Japan, providing $54 million in technical assistance and $570 million in loans from 1991 to 2003. The ADB supported Mongolia in six priority sectors: agriculture, finance, revitalization of the public sector, the social sector, urban development, and roads. The World Bank, as Mongolia's third largest donor, provided $300 million of assistance from 1991 to 2003. Fifty-one percent of this assistance was directed toward infrastructure, 23 percent to the financial sector, 12 percent to poverty issues, and 8 percent to deal with private sector and governance issues. In the 2000s, the World Bank focused on the Economic Growth Support and Poverty Reduction Strategy, the Mongolian government's top priority goal, by supporting public sector reform, private sector and social sector development, and infrastructure development (roads and rural electrification).[22]

The major goals of foreign donor and NGO community assistance to Mongolia in its transformation from a command economy to a democratic free market society remained quite consistent during the first fifteen years of the democratic era. Even in the mid-2000s the UNDP declared its funds for Mongolia would be used to further (1) democratic governance, (2) economic transition and poverty reduction, and (3) sustainable natural resource management. Its assistance program aimed to help Mongolia ensure broad-based and sustainable economic growth, equitable distribution of development, and poverty reduction.[23] The ADB consistently emphasized "the promotion of economic growth for job creation and provision of better essential social services for the poor."[24] Donors were reluctant to allocate resources to rural development until Mongolia was hit by the devastating *dzud* of 1999–2000, even though economic studies had already identified growing rural problems.[25]

At the end of the first democratic decade, the rural sector employed nearly 50 percent of the labor force, up from 33 percent at the start of the democratic era.[26] Intimately tied to the traditional nomadic lifestyle, this sector's share of GDP grew from 30 percent in 1990 to 37 percent in 1998. All of this took place despite the total collapse of Mongolia's domestic animal processing industry, the irregular availability of traditional foreign markets in Russia and Eastern Europe for its huge meat resources, serious reversal of rural primary and secondary school attendance rates, devastating successive years of droughts and winter *dzud* disasters, and numerous studies documenting falling productivity and growing poverty among the migratory herdsmen.[27]

Social problems of the period proved the importance of development policy and planning. Critics of the "pure market" policies advocated by the United States and international donor agencies claimed the Mongolian government had failed to meet the social needs of its population. During the first five years of the transition to a market economy (1990–1995), Mongolia experienced widespread poverty in both urban and countryside areas. A household social and economic survey conducted by the National Statistical Office in 1995 found that 36.3 percent of the population was poor. The UNDP and World Bank advised the Mongolian government's National Poverty Alleviation Programme (NPAP) to help rural and urban households establish small businesses within the market economy. The NPAP had a decentralized organizational structure with poverty alleviation councils at the *sum* (county) level and local labor and women's organizations to provide input. From 1994 to 2000, $19 million was contributed by fifteen donors.[28] World Bank support included pastoral risk management, microfinance outreach, a community investment fund, and renovation of rural schools and hospitals. German and New Zealand partners prepared *sum* land use maps, revolving herder community risk funds, hay and fodder development and management, microfinance plans for herders, emergency restocking of livestock, and livestock loss insurance.[29]

Mongolian policymakers continued to endorse policies that were capital and urban oriented. The Mongolian Parliament (Ikh Khural) in its 1996 Resolution on the Concept of Development of Mongolia (a fifteen- to twenty-year perspective) stated that Mongolia's goal was to become an industrialized, export-oriented country based on science and technology. The 1999 Mongolian government paper, within the overall priorities of reducing poverty and fostering democratic governance, outlined medium-term economic and social development strategy through (1) privatization and land reform; (2) structural reform in the banking and financial sector; (3) infrastructure reform including energy, roads, air, and rail; and (4) promotion of export-oriented animal product industries, mining, and tourism.[30] In April 2000, the ADB announced a shift from the large-scale projects it had been funding to an emphasis on poverty alleviation,[31] and the ADB began implementation of the Agriculture Sector Development Program with loans totaling $17 million. Policy objectives included promoting competitive markets for agricultural goods, improving rural financial services, and increasing productivity in extensive livestock production. It established a Green Revolution Program with the Ministry of Agriculture and small NGOs.[32]

In Mongolia's second decade of democracy, foreign investment and trade superseded foreign aid in underpinning economic development. Economic infrastructure and services were the first priority for the remaining ODA, especially provision of an adequate transport infrastructure in the countryside, where the large mining operations were located. The second priority area was education and urban social development. Mongolia's total net ODA as a percentage of gross national income (GNI) steadily decreased from 17 percent in 2001 to about 6 percent in 2010, while total ODA inflows remained relatively stable at about $200–$300 million annually in this same period. In 2010 total grants to Mongolia amounted to $215 million, while gross loans equaled $23.68 million.[33]

China was not a major donor or lender to Mongolia in the 1990s because it concentrated on becoming Mongolia's largest trade and direct investment partner. From 1991 to 1997, only 42.6 million RMB (around $5 million) was given in ODA. The next two years saw aid increase to 30 million RMB per year, but ODA fell to only 1 million RMB in 2000 and 4 million RMB in 2001. Large-scale assistance resumed in 2002–2003 at the level of 50 million RMB per year, mainly for construction of apartments for military personnel.[34] During 2000–2001, China donated an additional 2 million RMB to fight foot and mouth disease and to provide *dzud* assistance.[35] Mongolia began the democratic era with a 28.3 million convertible rubles debt with interest to China carried over from 1958–1960 loans. China provided 130 million RMB in interest-free loans from 1991 to 1994. Additional interest-free loans of 100 million RMB in 1998 and 100 million RMB in 2000 were granted for construction projects and the mining industry.[36] When Chinese President Hu Jintao visited Mongolia in June 2003, he promised to provide a further 300 million RMB in loans for high-efficiency projects in mining and infrastructure development, but in November the Mongolian government declared that it desired concessional loans instead of nonconcessional loans.[37] Six rounds of negotiations over the next two years did not produce a final agreement.[38]

US Assistance

The US government's own USAID strategy throughout the 1990s was pegged to the dual strategic goals of establishing a free market and a democratic society. Although the United States was only the third largest provider, behind Japan and Germany, of foreign donor assistance, all of the aid was given as grants with no loans. It implemented banking reforms, retrained the judiciary, promoted NGO development, pushed for quick privatization of state-owned entities and industries, and championed the establishment of a free press. The USAID program since the mid-1990s had recognized the importance of establishing the foundation for an effective rural civil society with projects directed toward road building and environmental protection/biodiversity, including the Gobi Regional Economic Growth Initiative.[39] In Mongolia it was widely acknowledged that the United States set the agenda for donor ODA planning.

It was the United States that took the lead in devising and supporting programs to accelerate Mongolia's political reforms and to consolidate transition to a sound private free market economy.[40] The US imposed a controversial simultaneous dual development "shock therapy" strategy upon both the Mongols and the donor community. Some analysts believe that Mongolia's subsequent relatively fast recovery was not attributable to geographical, historical, and other noneconomic factors, but rather its prompt recovery of growth was "partly explained by favorable economic and noneconomic initial conditions, the early adoption of appropriate adjustment policies and market-oriented reforms."[41] There was opposition to this "shock therapy" economic formula, particularly from more social democratic–minded Western European countries, and criticism of its effectiveness circulated within both the foreign donor and Mongolian domestic communities.[42] Much of the negative reaction focused on the rise of poverty and the collapse of social services. International financial institutions were criticized for being more interested in restoring macroeconomic stability and reducing the fiscal deficit rather than allocating limited budget resources to poverty reduction and social programs:

> The implementation of this policy has often resulted in undesirable outcomes, with Mongolia experiencing economic contraction, slow growth, unemployment, poverty and inequality as a result. Policy making during the early part of the transition was fragmented and confused, and many of the reforms were unduly hasty and poorly sequenced.[43]

William Bikales, an American financial specialist who from 1993 to 1995 executed the national poverty alleviation strategy under the auspices of the UNDP office in Mongolia, refuted criticism of the dual development strategy. He maintained that critics conflated the shock from the collapse of the old system with the impact of the transition policies. The Mongolian economy and its government structures had been built and sustained in the communist period with massive Soviet financial support—all of which resulted in Mongolia's having a large Soviet-era debt totaling roughly ten times Mongolia's 1990 GDP. The old system could not be maintained in the new democratic era.

> When you look at the criticisms of "shock therapy" in Mongolia you'll find that none of them acknowledge this simple reality. Comparisons with Poland or even Russia, countries that did try "shock therapy," are entirely beside the point. Mongolia was a poor, landlocked developing country whose massive aid from abroad was cut off overnight and which had no trade links with the markets that it suddenly had to sell to. There was no way to avoid a very painful shock.[44]

Bikales claimed that the Mongolian democratic leaders were the ones embracing shock therapy. While not denying that mistakes were made, he claimed the therapy agenda was a Mongolian program and not imposed by international financial institutions.

It is true that the Mongolian political leadership of both parties accepted with pride or perhaps resignation the notion that they were simultaneously developing democratic institutions and installing free market mechanisms as the United States promoted, and so they did not widely oppose the controversial US strategy. However, they likely had no other option than to accede to the American viewpoint. The US advisers and government touted Mongolia's positive attitude and accomplishments as a great success story in the post–Cold War world. This cemented a close political relationship between the two countries and was a major reason behind US willingness to encourage other Western democracies to be active in Mongolian developmental assistance.

The International Republican Institute (IRI), with funding from the US Congress, opened an office in Mongolia in 1990 with the goal of moving the country from one-party authoritarian rule to a multiparty democracy with a vibrant market-based economy. The first free democratic elections had been won by the formerly communist MPRP, but the IRI made no secret of its preference to assist Mongolia's democratic opposition to reformulate its coalition, strengthen its platform, and utilize a modern coordinated strategy for grassroots voter outreach efforts. It developed a close, continuing relationship with leaders of the democratic coalition, including future president Tsakhia Elbegdorj. Therefore, the United States was pleased when the democratic coalition won fifty out of seventy-six seats in the 1996 election, displacing the MPRP-controlled government after seventy-five years. The young democratic leaders then accelerated Mongolia's transition process, including shock therapy under US guidance,[45] but with mixed results.

A very important component of the US assistance program was the Peace Corps, which entered Mongolia in 1991. Early contingents of Volunteers were based in Ulaanbaatar to teach English and computer skills. After a few years, they moved into provincial (*aimag)* capitals in all regions of the country, including remote communities, for projects in education, health, and youth development. Seventy percent of Volunteers were assigned to the English Education and Community Development project component, whose goal was to build capacity in English by training Mongolian English teachers and by directly supporting Mongolian students through individual teaching or co-teaching with Mongolian teachers. Throughout the more than twenty-five years of the program, Volunteers in the community-based health project component have been assisting with community health education, promoting medical English knowledge, facilitating preventive health initiatives, and working with local teachers to educate secondary school students about healthy life skills. They have trained social workers in district children's centers, secondary schools, vocational and training centers, Youth Development Centers, and domestic NGOs and with their Mongolian counterparts have targeted dormitory students and disabled children.[46] Through 2016, over 1,275 Peace Corps Volunteers have worked in Mongolia and raised the profile of the United States throughout the population.

Japanese Assistance

After Japan established diplomatic relations with Mongolia in 1972, it provided assistance worth approximately 6 billion yen by 1990. This assistance included the construction of a cashmere processing factory (5 billion yen), which allowed socialist Mongolia to earn foreign exchange. In 1991 Japan provided emergency assistance to the power sector and became Mongolia's top donor provider. Its assistance priorities were based on mid- to long-term development needs of Mongolia and targeted "infrastructure such as energy, communication and transport (railways, roads), human resource development and institutional building necessary for smooth transition to a market economy, promotion of agriculture and livestock industry, basic needs for living such as education, healthcare, water supply and food aid."[47]

Japan deployed its Japan Overseas Cooperation program, which is similar to the Peace Corps, to assist Mongolia. Since 1992, more than 350 Japanese Volunteers have worked in Mongolia. From 1991 to 2003, Japan provided 36.126 billion yen in loans, 68.810 billion yen in grant aid, and 23.342 billion yen in technical cooperation, or a total of 128.278 billion yen—amounting to almost 70 percent of all bilateral aid to Mongolia.[48] The most consequential infrastructure assistance projects funded by the Japanese included the establishment of the earth station for satellite communications, construction of a cargo reshipment base at the China-Mongolia border, road construction, refurbishment of Ulaanbaatar's fourth thermal power station, provision of urban buses, renovation of school buildings, and provision of diesel generators for rural areas. Other projects include emergency aid, food aid, food production aid, provision of shortwave radios, and human resource training programs. However, the Japanese government admitted that some of its assistance projects were not fully successful because of lack of proper management, financial difficulties, and lack of maintenance budgets. In 2003 alone, Japan provided 3.085 billion yen in grant aid and 1.526 billion yen in technical cooperation for a total of 4.611 billion yen.[49]

Japan, following the USAID model, planned to end its Mongolia grant aid program in 2016, so Japan and Mongolia agreed that the donor-recipient relationship should transition into mutually beneficial economic cooperation. It sent an economic advisory team to the Mongolian government to determine how both sides could collaborate in areas of infrastructure, energy, environment, agriculture, and health care.[50] Also, Japan has continued to deploy emergency teams and provided emergency supplies, such as for the 2013 Mongolian earthquake.

Realigning Donor Aid in Response to the *Dzuds* of the Early 2000s

Only 1 percent of Mongolia is arable; the short growing season of about 100 days results in low crop yields. This explains why Mongols historically have practiced transhumant nomadic herding of animals for their livelihood. Temperatures fluctuate from as low as –50°C in the steppe in winter to 40°C in the Gobi desert in the summer. *Dzud* is a Mongolian term that refers to a range of severe weather conditions, including severe summer droughts and exceptionally cold winters. The common feature is that such disasters obscure or destroy pasture grass and cause significant loss of animals herded by nomadic families. *Dzuds* are a regular occurrence in Mongolia and play an important role in regulating livestock populations, but consecutive *dzuds* from 1999 to 2002 killed about one-quarter of the livestock, nearly ten million head yearly, forcing many people to migrate to urban areas.[51]

These *dzuds* attracted international media coverage and the attention of international relief organizations such as the International Red Cross. In February 2000, an initial appeal was launched to assist the Mongolian Red Cross to provide support in the form of a supplementary food ration of wheat flour and rice, as well as winter boots for herders. As it became apparent that the disaster was going to have more serious food security repercussions, the appeal was extended one month later to assist 35,000 herders over a twelve-month period, including vital support to the Mongolian Red Cross.[52] Its 2001 emergency appeal for "Mongolia Snowfalls" sought to provide humanitarian assistance to 7,000 nomadic herding families and was extended through 2002 to assist an additional 4,400. As the winter of 2002 progressed, similar conditions affected the southwest and western areas of the country, leading to the extension of the relief operation implemented from June to October 2002.[53]

The 1999–2002 *dzuds* were important catalysts for a number of donor-led efforts to provide immediate relief and develop policies to improve pasture livestock management and risk preparedness in local herding communities. The IMF recognized that natural disasters had greatly affected the livelihoods of herders and so recommended that "the government policy priorities should be re-oriented towards those population groups most affected by natural disasters through expanding financial and banking services in rural areas, developing small and middle-size enterprises, stabilization and expansion of agricultural activities."[54] The United Nations Food and Agriculture Organization (FAO) funded two projects in the livestock sector, which utilized $282,000 to improve the livelihoods and food security of pastoral herders[55] and $400,000 for a *dzud* emergency restocking plan.[56] In addition, many foreign countries responded to Mongolian government appeals for *dzud* assistance. The United States, which had offered Mongolia emergency energy assistance back in 1991 and had provided emergency butter and wheat in the mid-1990s, was very active in supplying emergency aid for three successive *dzud* years from 1999 to 2002. During the 1999–2000 *dzud*, output of the agriculture sector, which accounted for 33 percent of GDP, fell by 16.8 percent and increased poverty even further. The overall economy experienced grave difficulties. The national average monthly household income in urban areas stood at 82,000 tugrik, and at 72,000 tugrik in rural areas (equivalent to $50–$60). Social issues came to the forefront, migration to urban areas from rural areas ballooned, and ecological problems worsened, although they were not as severe as the social problems.

However, the lure of millions of relief dollars flowing into Mongolia and the absence of an integrated national development policy and strategy implementation, monitoring, and evaluation systems saw the rise of corruption exploiting this foreign generosity as a cash cow to be milked. A generous $10,000 personal donation by Secretary of State James Baker during the

1999 *dzud* went totally missing.[57] Lack of financial accountability was evident in both democratic coalition and later MPRP governments. Although foreign donors were aware of this problem, there was little mention about this in evaluations of *dzud* relief activities. For example, the World Bank in opaque language in its report *Lessons from the Dzud* noted, "Similarly, when local governments and aid organizations do not effectively communicate and coordinate with each other in disaster response, aid may be mis-allocated or may not be distributed at all."[58] Mongolia experienced other major *dzuds* in 2010 and 2016. While loss of livestock was high, the impact on the economy was not as great as during the 1999–2002 period.[59]

Diminishing ODA in the 2000s

In its March 24, 2000, partnership agreement between the government of Mongolia and the ADB, Mongolia's 2000–2005 strategy was predicated upon point 8—the fact that "poverty is mainly found in urban areas." The agreement's measurement benchmarks in the areas of poverty, human development, and economic conditions never mentioned herders, nomads, or the livestock industry. Nevertheless, economic studies in the early 2000s indicated that, instead of decreasing poverty after a decade of donor assistance, poverty had increased to 36 percent of the Mongolian population, and the herders and *dzuds* were scapegoated for the increase.[60]

The UNDP called for more effective Mongolian government intervention in the economy. Some foreign experts called for the return to livestock collective farms. The UNDP conducted a Lessons Learned exercise after the 1999–2001 winter *dzuds* when more than four million animals were lost. This analysis found a major problem was the lack of preparedness and that much of the *dzud* assistance ($8.23 million in 1999–2000 and $24 million in 2000–2001) came too late. It was recommended that longer-term strategies to revitalize the economy of the countryside be developed. The foreign donor studies did not explore historical studies on the repetitive nature of Mongolian *dzuds*, which traditionally were factored into the calculations of livestock breeders throughout Central Asia.[61] Rather, these studies emphasized research on the stresses on the carrying capacity of the steppe grasslands caused by the successful privatization of herds and the entrance of new "city boy" nomads uneducated in the migratory life cycle. Other scholars argued that much pasture land was underused or not overgrazed,[62] and that the inefficient socialist-style crop farming agricultural techniques and border regional water supply issues had caused just as great negative impacts.

The foreign donor and international NGO community recognized to some extent the importance of the rural sector to Mongolia's economic development. The UNDP and Swedish government issued a 2003 study on the effectiveness of herd restocking strategies on poverty alleviation,[63] and a year later another UNDP research study identified livestock issues related to trade and industry from raw materials to marketing.[64] The European Union's Technical Assistance to the Commonwealth of Independent States (TACIS) program[65] devoted 2.9 million euros to integrating animal production more efficiently into the crop farm sector and to promoting meat exports and improving dairy, wool, and cashmere production and processing.[66] A major rural project was the UNDP/government of Netherlands Sustainable Grassland Management project.[67] It ran for five years (2003–2007) at a cost of $3.1 million, of which only $200,000 was from UNDP monies.[68] It encouraged herders to seek new modes of collaboration different from the *negdel* period's compulsory collectivism and the transition era's individualism by experimenting with registering herding groups as NGOs.[69]

Foreign donor assistance policies in Mongolia attracted growing criticism as it became evident that the gap between rural and urban Mongolia was increasing dramatically.[70] As the gap continued to grow throughout the first decade of the new millennium, discussion focused on whether the foreign donor community and its programs were meeting the goals of its envisaged strategy of development, or, in fact, contributing to the emergence of two distinct socioeconomic cultures and widening the income gap. This debate reemerged when the foreign donors were not supportive of President Nambar Enkhbayar's government plan called Millennium Road, which entailed creation of an east-west road to link the capital with the other *aimag* centers and thus develop local communication and transport in the middle of the country. The donors were always more interested in developing north-south transportation routes through Ulaanbaatar, particularly to the southern border with China. Although donor countries bemoaned the concentration of people in Ulaanbaatar and their move away from the decaying socialist-era industrial cities around the country, their policies and development advice to the Mongolian government did little to support or create infrastructure and communications throughout the country that would lessen the flow of population and budgetary resources to the capital.

The history of donor assistance in Mongolia reveals a long-standing antagonism toward nomadism and ignorance about Mongolia's rural ecology. This was epitomized by the call for Mongolia to give up nomadism and adopt ranching. The unquestioned assumption among twentieth-century economists in the communist and early democratic eras, as well as foreign donor experts and members of the Mongolian government, was that nomads could and should be made into ranchers, which then would mean an end to Mongolia's traditional nomadic lifestyle. In 2000, a UNDP-funded report recommended "the feasibility and desirability of moving towards a ranch-like organization structure for livestock production and reorganization of large-scale crop production businesses into medium-sized family farms."[71] However, the lesson learned in Mongolia's first decade of democracy was that a move from nomadism to ranching could not be supported by the sparse vegetation of Mongolia's environment. Nomadism could only be abandoned if Mongol herdsmen moved from grazing to fodder-fed stock. The unanswerable question became, How can sufficient fodder be grown in a climate so hostile to normal agriculture, particularly since Mongolia has less than 1 percent of its land under cultivation?

Many in the foreign donor and international NGO community never recognized that the rural herders saved the Mongolian urbanites from starvation during the early 1990s when the command economy collapsed, inflation was rampant, and consumables were nonexistent or prohibitively expensive. During those years, Mongolians did not starve because their country cousins fed their fellow citizens. The unemployed from the bankrupt state factories and farms in urban areas returned to the kind of economic activity that is most suitable for the Mongolian environment—migratory livestock raising. The rural sector acted as a great, inexpensive escape valve that prevented real social unrest and solved the immediate need for food.[72] However, foreign donor agencies such as the UNDP denigrated this contribution and saw the return of Mongols to the countryside as a failure of development: "The absence of alternative livelihood opportunities means that dependence on the livestock economy will continue especially for the poorest."[73] While the number of people on the land in the 1990s increased 183 percent, many of the foreign donor agencies were hostile to nomadism and saw Mongolia's rural sector as intrinsically backward and poor, while settled life and industrial work were "modern" and "good."[74] Even the refusal by many experts to use the term "nomadism" out of preference for the phrase "extensive livestock raising" was a conscious denial of the existence and viability of the nomadic lifestyle.[75]

This negative attitude toward livestock utilization was illustrated by the fact that the foreign donors allowed the animal by-products industry and the jobs associated with it to collapse during the 1990s. Although foreign experts agreed that Mongolia's meat and animal hair were not being processed and sold into foreign markets because of lack of modern sanitary production and transport difficulties, there was no World Bank or other seed money to construct a modern slaughterhouse or leather factory. Lack of roads in the countryside and other local infrastructure made costs too prohibitive for private foreign investors. Such private investment gravitated toward mining areas where returns could be enormous, but for regional animal by-product processing factories which create more technically based employment opportunities, substantial FDI in the midterm was minimal. Years of discussion between TACIS and the Mongolian government about utilizing reasonably priced mobile slaughterhouses to solve food safety and transport problems as well as to exploit animal losses during *dzud*s never resulted in funding.

Foreign donor development policy for Mongolia was predicated upon the belief that rural poverty on the steppe was caused by too many herders, who degraded pastureland, and by the severe *dzuds*. The NPAP was established in 1994 to reduce Mongolia's 26.5 percent poor to 10 percent or less by 2000, but in the NPAP's original set of goals, specifically helping nomads or herders was never mentioned.[76] NPAP's midterm evaluation in December 1996 changed course by emphasizing the alleviation of rural poverty through development of small and medium enterprises for processing agricultural products and market animal products, policy reform regarding land tenure, and support for herders' organizations and the restocking of poor families' livestock. However, from $19 million collected by the World Bank for these purposes, by 1999 only $11.1 million, or 59 percent of the funds, had been distributed among 36,400 households, which represented only 19 percent of the estimated 192,000 poor households in the country.[77] This means that very little of the NPAP money reached the herders. Another example of the problem was that in the first decade of transition, a mere 1 percent of all the poverty funds, some $125,866 out of $11.1 million, was allocated for restocking of animals. The UNDP and the Swedish International Development Cooperation Agency (SIDA) in 2004 concluded that Mongol herders could be divided into rich (20 percent), middle income (40 percent), and poor (40 percent). Highest poverty rates were found in *aimag* centers (31.7 percent) and in Ulaanbaatar (28.5 percent).

It should be noted that, when examining the data between "not poor" and "poor" in rural areas, the distinction was not based on educational level, while in urban areas, especially Ulaanbaatar, education was the key factor. The educational component for foreign donors always was significant, even in light of evidence that, for nomads, school-based education was not linked to economic success. Even favorable studies on nomadism in Mongolia sought to "eliminate cultural backwardness of the herders."[78] After years of talking about the failure of Mongolia's public educational system to be responsive to the needs of nomadic children, there still was no change in the content of the curriculum. Vocational education began only in the ninth or tenth grade, as in socialist times, and did not include studying herding techniques. There was great concern among donor groups, international NGOs, and foreign specialists in falling rates of rural school attendance. Responses to the problem centered around rehabilitating rural dormitory school infrastructure and providing enhanced teacher training. It would take years for the donors and the Mongolian educational establishment to understand that the educational content, which was disconnected from the life of a migratory herder, had to be reformed to induce nomadic parents to keep their youngsters in school.

In a December 1996 UNDP/government of Mongolia NPAP Evaluation Mission Team Report and subsequent 1999 Evaluation, the demand for vocational training in animal by-product processing was identified.[79] The UNDP was concerned with economies of scale and so decided to place vocational training facilities regionally instead of in every *aimag*. This inevitably led to some *aimag* capitals', usually those with large-scale mining enterprises, benefiting, while others fell even further behind. The pattern of predominantly funding the modernizing of Ulaanbaatar's educational facilities and ignoring those in the countryside eventually drove Mongols to abandon their traditional home territories and surge into the capital in response to the lure of economic opportunities and better educational opportunities for their children. As a result, in 2016 one-half of Mongolia's population was residing in the Ulaanbaatar region.

Creation of NGOs

Before the 1990s there were domestic organizations such as the Mongolia Trade Union, Mongolian Association of Revolutionary Youth, and the Mongolian Red Cross, which outwardly were somewhat similar to NGOs but actually only advocated ruling-party policy and ideology and functioned under its guidance. By the end of 1992, only seven NGOs were formally registered.[80] US development officials particularly advocated the creation of an effective NGO sector and saw it as a strategic process for Mongolian democracy and free market promotion. They saw international NGOs (INGOs) as key partners in donor efforts to overcome the difficulties of the transition period.[81] The Asia Foundation, Konrad Adenauer Stiftung, Soros Foundation, and International Support Service began their assistance to Mongolia in 1990–1991. Between 1991 and 1996 there were 36 INGOs; this number grew to 95 in the 1997–2002 period and to 116 by 2005.[82]

A key INGO for the United States was the Mongolian Foundation for Open Society under the auspices of the Soros Foundation, which since 1996 has aimed to promote a more open society through education, media, public health, human and women's rights, and legal and economic reforms.[83] Another important US-funded INGO was Mercy Corps, which implemented agricultural and rural programs for the US government. Out of the conviction that communities themselves must control their future development, Mercy Corps in the Gobi regions implemented a rural economic growth program that emphasized agriculture and small business development, rural financial services, and access to accurate market information.[84] Other early INGOs were the International Rotary Club and Amnesty International.

The success of INGOs in Mongolia is associated with Mongolia's Foreign Policy Concept of 1994, wherein Mongolian policymakers indicated the intention to cooperate intensively with international organizations and foundations in cultural and humanitarian spheres in order to integrate the nation into the world community through its multipillar foreign policy. Mongolian citizens embraced the notion of the NGO as a business career so strongly that it was commonly remarked that Mongolia has more NGOs per person than any country in the world! Domestic NGOs mushroomed because most of the projects implemented with foreign countries and INGOs relied on partnering with local NGOs. By the end of 1997 there were 870 NGOs on the books, but, when all were required to reregister with the Ministry of Justice prior to the implementation of a new NGO law, only 280 qualified.[85] The increase in NGOs of all kinds after 1998 was propelled by this law that went into effect in 1999 and helped to create a more favorable legal environment for domestic and international NGOs. Mongolia's NGO law requires that NGO activities be open to the public with free access to their annual reports. However, there were many complaints about the lack of access to such information, including to INGO reports. By the first half of the 2000s, over 80 percent of INGOs were actually national organizations with international operations, not true INGOs.[86]

Seventy-seven percent of the INGOs registered in Mongolia during 1992–1994 were focused on international development and relief. These organizations, which promoted peace, human rights, democracy, and humanitarian issues, opened resident representative or local offices in Mongolia. In 2004, about 32 percent were headquartered in the United States and 14 percent in South Korea. The INGOs varied according to size (large, medium, small) and objective (multipurpose or single purpose).[87] Most INGOs, including the Asia Foundation, Amnesty International, World Vision, and Adventist Development and Relief Agency (ADRA), had multiple funding sources. Some INGOs, such as Save the Children, World Vision, Konrad Adenauer Stiftung, and Amnesty International, had long histories and extensive experience in development aid programming. In the 1990s, twenty-one INGOs had obtained consultative status from the UN Economic and Social Council and thus were utilized to implement UN-funded programs and activities in Mongolia. The larger, multipurpose ones conducted nationwide projects in politics, economy, health care, and charity. The largest one, often utilized by the US government during the decade, was World Vision, which claimed to have reached 500,000 citizens in ten of Mongolia's twenty-one provinces.

Except for Amnesty International, INGOs in Mongolia were mainly developmental organizations that addressed issues of governance, law, economy, education, public awareness, poverty, and natural disasters. The largest expenditures were devoted to relief and poverty alleviation (39 percent), children's rights and welfare (14 percent), education (10 percent), and public health (9 percent).[88] Many Japanese INGOs were active in Mongolia, providing assistance to urban street children and to nomads who had lost their livestock because of *dzuds* and drought since 1999. Other INGOs were religiously affiliated. In Mongolia these included World Vision, the Finnish Lutheran Mission, Norwegian Lutheran Mission, Catholic Church Mission, Help International, ADRA, Global Ministries, and Joint Christian Services (JCS). Some of these stressed programmatic activities such as children's issues and organized orphanages, but others exhibited clear evangelistic motives, which concerned Mongols who traditionally are Buddhist. Such INGOs often work in remote rural areas where other INGOs are not found and so were viewed positively for their rural development activities in areas where the Mongolian government did not allocate resources. According to a nationwide survey, "Mongolians have very strong feelings that foreign religious organizations may have a negative spiritual impact on Mongolian people, especially young ones."[89]

Secular INGOs, such as Save the Children, Mercy Corps, Pact, Cambridge Mongolia Disaster Appeal (CAMDA), Peace Winds Japan, Food for the Hungry, and Vision International viewed relief and development as technical enterprises to alleviate societal problems. Because they have not developed local constituencies like church-based faith organizations, they have not been able to readily solicit local Mongol charitable donations and so remain very reliant on foreign funding. Domestic NGOs, which derived their financial resources mainly from foreign project funding rather than donations from the public, also lacked internal institutional and staff capacities. Local studies revealed many NGOS were not well structured, which detracted from their reputation. Ninety percent of NGO activities were financed by project funding from international and foreign donors.[90] According to one Mongolian scholar, "The negative impact of this financing is that NGOs can become opportunistic, lose their initial motivation, can be in danger of losing their independence and their internal democracy, and develop an unsustainable way of operating by jumping from project to project."[91]

During the 1990s one could not isolate the Mongolian INGO experience from other international trends. In general, INGOs enter a country as agents providing emergency relief to temporarily ameliorate the symptoms of poverty. Many evolve into broader developmental institutions that support community development projects through self-help. As time goes on, some organizations morph into catalysts with distinctive tactics to mitigate poverty in the many countries they cover. Small INGOs often did not employ long-term strategies against poverty, so their results were only transitory. Even within the Mongolian communities, this led to duplication of efforts and a kind of NGO fatigue that led international donors to rethink their concepts of development assistance.

Because the INGO and NGO mandates and financial and legal differences were poorly understood by the Mongolian public and the results of their programs were very uneven or not evident, by the end of the 1990s INGOs had a mixed and distorted reputation. About 70 percent of Mongols viewed INGOs as financially very strong and wealthy but nontransparent. INGOs were required to provide the Ministry of Justice with annual financial reports, but generally organizations only delivered brief reports, not full financial statements. Additionally, the INGOs in Mongolia, like those worldwide, usually were accountable only to their trustees or donors and neglected to disclose success stories and failures to the recipient community or public (often called "downward accountability"). This resulted in false public perceptions about their operations and hid ineffective or illegal actions. Moreover, INGOs controlled their own fund disbursement in Mongolia, so they often bypassed local government channels. This had both positive and negative effects in the country because, in some cases, the INGOs worked in areas the government had neglected, such as sexual abuse and human trafficking, embarrassing local authorities and prioritizing social problems from an international perspective rather than a Mongolian one (LGBT rights are a recent example).

In the early 2000s, the new MPRP-led government, in order to prevent commercial businesses from setting up NGOs for the purpose of illegal tax exemptions, reviewed NGOs, which had grown in strength and number under the 1997 NGO law. In 2013 more than 6,000 NGOs were registered in Mongolia,[92] but civil society experts estimate that only 10–20 percent of them were active.[93] Women monopolize their leadership positions and membership. Most civil society activities are concentrated in the capital, Ulaanbaatar, not in the countryside among the herders and poor. Nevertheless, it is clear that Mongolia psychologically embraced the concept of the NGO, and most people perceive them to be safeguards and watchdogs over the government and society.[94] Mongolian civil society researchers attribute the emergence of NGOs to several factors: (1) passage of the Foreign Policy Concept in 1994 wherein Mongolia sought as a priority to integrate itself into the world community and indicated its desire to cooperate intensively with international organizations and foundations in various spheres; (2) passage by Parliament in 1997 of the Law on NGOs to create a favorable legal environment for domestic and INGOs; and (3) Mongolian governmental difficulty in managing the consequences of natural disasters and poverty that emerged in Mongolia.[95]

A diverse number of domestic NGOs have played a significant role in the efforts to assist Mongolia in addressing the difficulties of the democratic transition in a mineral-rich economy, but they have been slow to shed a spotlight on the nature of and fight against transnational crimes such as money laundering and human trafficking. Domestic NGOs joined forces with internal governmental agencies, such as the General Police Department and the Ministry of Social Welfare, to fight trafficking, but a few international organizations with their greater financial resources and public relations experience were the key to raising societal awareness. Amnesty International;[96] End Child Prostitution, Pornography, and Trafficking of Children for Sexual Purposes (ECPAT); and Asia Foundation have affiliate groups in Mongolia working on international trafficking issues. The Asia Foundation has been an especially strong presence in monitoring and educating Mongolians about human rights violations and crimes.

The Asia Foundation and the Mongolian Student Union started a campaign in 2007 to raise student awareness about human trafficking throughout the country.[97] The Asia Foundation also supports research conducted by the local NGO Centre for Human Rights and Development (CHRD) and the Mongolian Gender Equality Center (MGEC) to increase understanding of trafficking in Mongolia, recommend policy responses, and establish baseline data on the problem.[98]

In 2010 the Asia Foundation with support from the US State Department joined with the Mongolian Women Lawyers Association (MWLA) and ECPAT to advocate for passage of a new law on human trafficking by mobilizing national support in all the provinces, developing educational fact sheets on trafficking, and lobbying parliamentarians and officials. Partnering with the Human Security Policy Studies Center, the Asia Foundation sponsored a national conference on the need for a revised law to combat trafficking. This law ultimately was approved by Parliament in 2012. The drafting and advocacy of a law initiated by an INGO heralded a new model in Mongolia's legislative development process.[99] However, the ultimate success or failure of this law's implementation may rest on whether or not domestic stakeholders are fully committed to fighting this type of crime.

Conclusion

Mongolia began the 1990s with a serious negative economic shock, yet by the end of the decade, it successfully had transitioned from central planning to a market-based economy. The collapse of the USSR and the end of Soviet assistance had a catastrophic impact on Mongolia's economy with a cumulative fall of over 20 percent in real GDP. Mongolia opened a stock exchange in 1991, joined the WTO in 1997, and embarked on an extensive privatization program. Still some economists claimed that because of sluggish growth, despite massive amounts of ODA, Mongolia only regained its 1989 living standards by 2001.[100] The Mongolian economy entered the democratic era with three distinct sectors: (1) the traditional economy, which mainly consisted of animal husbandry and crop production; (2) mining, manufacturing, and construction; and (3) wholesale and retail trade together with transport and communication. The traditional livestock economy was the principal engine of Mongolia's quick recovery during the first decade of democracy, although its share in GDP began to decline in 1999. The trade sector was the other main source of growth during the late 1990s, and by 2001 it had surpassed agriculture as the largest sector. The importance of the mining, manufacturing, and construction sector was more limited during the 1990s. This sector would become dominant after 2000.[101]

The Mongols' "dependency on foreign donors" syndrome of the 1990s likely evolved from a popular mind-set developed in the Manchu Chinese and Soviet eras, which was exacerbated by the crash of the command economy during the early years of democracy. Despite poverty and societal imbalances, by the end of the foreign donor assistance decade, Mongolia had become a stable, if unpredictable, democratic country that had conducted five successful nationwide democratic elections. Donor assistance averaged 16 percent of GDP each year.[102] Bilateral aid together with IMF and World Bank assistance amounted to approximately $1.5 billion during the first fifteen years. This brought Mongolia's 325 percent inflation rate in the early 1990s to single digits by the opening of the twenty-first century and increased per capita annual income from under $600 to $1,800. Some analysts lauded Mongolia as one of Asia's most flourishing democracies, noting that by the late 1990s it was pursuing a policy of almost complete free trade: "Indeed, the democratic regime has been a positive political element of both the commitment to economic liberalism and the coping with adversity."[103]

Despite the poverty, Mongolia at the end of the 1990s could feed its own population. Herds were up about 30 percent from the socialist era with a 180 percent increase in the number of herders. The banking system and monetary economy were extended to the countryside, and herder income and access to consumer goods had substantially increased.[104] Nomadic life, which had been dying in Mongolia in the 1980s, revived considerably, although new ideas for rural development often could not find funds beyond pilot studies.[105] Still, there is no doubt that the 1990s donor assistance decade reinforced the dependency mentality of the Mongolian government and people. Development specialist Bill Bikales explained this syndrome:

> Unhealthy attitudes about debt that developed under the Soviets, when the government borrowed year after year without any even slight concern about repayment, were further reinforced. Borrowing from abroad continued to be a normal part of budgeting, and banks were used over and over to provide loan funds to projects and businesses that the government could not afford to support with its own resources, again with no attention to repayment capacity. Borrowed funds were treated like any other funds, just spent on anything the borrower wanted rather than being invested in projects that were expected to pay enough of a return to allow repayment. Of course the economic and budget situation were so dire for most of the 90s that some funds to finance daily operations of the government were appropriate. But a pattern was created that has lasted even after those conditions changed.[106]

Some foreign experts, epitomized by Keith Griffin, called for fresh thinking about the role of ODA in the transition period. Noting that foreign aid was substituted for domestic tax reform and resulted in the weakening of the Mongolian government's capacity to manage the economy, Griffin warned, "The intent of donors no doubt is benevolent but the effects of aid have been pernicious. Donors have had far too much influence over economic and social policy, . . . and over the entire transition strategy. On balance their advice has been poor, their aid ineffective in promoting growth and reducing poverty and their influence baleful."[107]

At the same time, although foreign and domestic experts decried the emergence of two cultures (urban/modern versus rural/traditional) in Mongolia, they did not focus on the fact that donor funds were overwhelmingly distributed in the capital. Because rural development projects included establishing Ulaanbaatar-based training or distribution centers or required that funds first be allocated to the central government or Ulaanbaatar-based INGO organizations, the amount of monies that actually filtered down to the countryside was very small. All the foreign donors and the development-enhancing institutions they created sought to enhance the life of the average Mongol. Yet, in the main they did not inform themselves about actual rural conditions, nor were they open to creative solutions to challenge their own preconceived ideas. In many cases, code words for development such as poverty or illiteracy were used to destroy empathy for Mongolia's nomadic economy and lifestyle. The donors did not accept the principle of the sustainability of Mongolia's nomadic economy and so did not effectuate successful and profitable plans to modernize this sector. As a result, seeds of greater social instability were sown that were publicly recognized only in the second decade of Mongolia's democracy.

Notes

1. Khumbayn Olzvoy, "Political and Economic Aspects of Mongolia's Transition into a Market Economy," in *Regional Economic Cooperation in Northeast Asia: Proceedings of the Yongpyeong Conference, September 26–28, 1993* (Honolulu: Northeast Asia Economic Forum, Hawaii Asia-Pacific Institute, April 1994), 206.

2. Elizabeth Milne, "The Mongolian People's Republic: Toward a Market Economy" (International Monetary Fund Occasional Paper, March 15, 1991).

3. John W. Mellor, *Mongolia Food Sector Study* (Washington, DC: USAID, November 1992), x, http://pdf.usaid.gov/pdf_docs/pnacb064.pdf.

4. Ts. Batbayar and K. Demberel, "Contemporary Mongolian-Russian Relations, 333.

5. Richard Pomfret, "Transition and Democracy in Mongolia" (CIES Discussion Paper 99/07), Adelaide, Australia, April 1999), 3.

6. Joseph E. Lake, "Perspectives."

7. L. N. Gumilev, *People and Nature of the Great Steppe* (Moscow: Voprosy Istorii, 1987), 84.

8. A. Buyantogs, "Foreign Investment, Loans and Assistance in Mongolian Development," *Mongolian Journal of International Affairs*, no. 7 (2000): 46.

9. Ole Bruun and Ole Odgaard, "A Society and Economy in Transition," in *Mongolia in Transition: Old Patterns, New Challenges*, ed. Ole Bruun and Ole Odgaard (Richmond, UK: Curzon, 1999), 27.

10. Elizabeth Morris and Ole Bruun, *Promoting Employment Opportunities in Rural Mongolia: Past Experience and ILO Approaches* (Bangkok: International Labour Office, 2004), 11.

11. Among them were Development Concept for Mongolia (1996), Master Plan for Mongolia's Population Settlement and Development (1996), Sustainable Development Action Program of Mongolia for the 21st Century (MAP 21) (1998), Mongolia's

Regional Development Concept (2001), and Pole Cities for Regional Development (2003). See Mongolia's national report, *Managing the Transition from the Millennium Development Goals to the Sustainable Development Goals* (Ulaanbaatar: Government of Mongolia, 2015), 4.

12. Buyantogs, "Foreign Investment," 44.

13. Rossabi, *Modern Mongolia*, 92, citing United Nations Development Programme, Mongolia, *Mongolia Update, 1998* (Ulaanbaatar, 1998), 29.

14. "Ambassador Joseph E. Lake," interview by Charles Stuart Kennedy, 13.

15. For an account of the difficulties encountered in organizing the Assistance Group, see ibid., 17–18.

16. Batbayar, *Mongolia's Foreign Policy in the 1990s,* 203.

17. Buyantogs, "Foreign Investment," 48.

18. Ibid.

19. Kevin C. Cheng, "Growth and Recovery in Mongolia During Transition" (IMF Working Paper no. 03/217, November 2003), 4.

20. See Kh. Olzvoy, "A Mongol's View of Economic Development and Cooperation in Northeast Asia," *Mongolian Journal of International Affairs*, no. 3 (1996): 54, Table 2. While these figures show that Mongolia did much better than some of the newly independent states of Central Asia, Olzvoy also acknowledged that Laos and Vietnam did better than Mongolia during the same period.

21. Terry McKinley, "The National Development Strategy and Aid Coordination," in *Poverty Reduction in Mongolia,* ed. Keith Griffin (Canberra: Asia Pacific Press, 2003), 135.

22. *Country Assistance Program for Mongolia* (Tokyo: Ministry of Foreign Affairs of Japan, November 2004), 25, http://www.mofa.go.jp/policy/oda/assistance/pdfs/e_mongolia2004.pdf.

23. UNDP website, "About UNDP Mongolia" and "Current Project-Poverty," 2004.

24. Asian Development Bank, *Country Strategy and Program Update (2004–2006): Mongolia*, August 2003, 2, https://www.adb.org/sites/default/files/institutional-document/32345/files/csp-mon-2003.pdf.

25. McKinley, "National Development Strategy," 137.

26. K. Sundaram, "Human Resource Development and Training in Mongolia: Issues and Options" (unpublished report, International Labour Office East Asia Multidisciplinary Advisory Team, August 2000), 17.

27. Keith Griffin, "Agricultural Involution and Urban-to-Rural Migration in Mongolia" (Department of Economics Working Paper, University of California Riverside, February 2, 2000), http://economics.ucr.edu/papers/papers02/02-02.pdf; Ole Odgaard, "Living Standards and Poverty," in *Mongolia in Transition: Old Patterns, New Challenges*, ed. Ole Bruun and Ole Odgaard (Richmond, UK: Curzon, 1999), 103–134.

28. Andy Batkin, Ts. Bumhorol, Robin Mearns, and Jeremy Swift, *Independent Evaluation of the National Poverty Alleviation Programme and Options Post-2000* (Ulaanbaatar: Government of Mongolia and World Bank, October 1999), 10, http://www.forum.mn/res_mat/Independent%20Evaluation%20of%20the%20Natinoal%20Poverty%20Alleviation.pdf.

29. John Morton, "A Note on Comparing International Experiences of Drought Management in the Pastoral and Agro-Pastoral Livestock Sectors," World Bank, 2002, 4, http://citeseerx.ist.psu.edu/viewdoc/download;jsessionid=496FFD7AA564E7E35392C86D88E920AE?doi=10.1.1.566.6021&rep=rep1&type=pdf; Sabine M. Schmidt, "Pastoral Community Organization, Livelihoods and Biodiversity Conservation in Mongolia's Southern Gobi Region," in *Rangelands of Central Asia: Proceedings of the Conference on Transformations, Issues, and Future Challenges,* RMRS-P-39 (Fort Collins, CO: USDA Forest Service, 2006), 18–29.

30. "Mongolian Government Paper on Social Sector Issues and Strategies, Medium-Term Economic and Social Development Strategy 1999–2000," unpublished paper (Ulaanbaatar: Government of Mongolia, 1999). For an annotated bibliography in English on the topic of poverty in Mongolia, see "Bibliography of Materials Related to Poverty in Mongolia" (2004), http://pdc.ceu.hu/archive/00002470/01/Poverty_Eng_0002.pdf.

31. IMF, "Mongolia: Poverty Reduction Strategy Paper of Government of Mongolia," *Economic Growth Support and Poverty Reduction Strategy* (Washington, DC: IMF, July 3, 2003).

32. The International Fund for Agricultural Development (IFAD) designed a six-year rural poverty alleviation project for Arkhangai, Khubsgol, Bulgan, and Khentii *aimags* for $16.6 million. This multifaceted project aimed to improve livestock and range management, prepared resource maps with seasonal pastures, issued possession certificates, restored wells, set up *dzud* emergency funds, and lent money to herders. Morton, "A Note on Comparing International Experiences," 6–7.

33. "International Support Measures: The Case of Mongolia" (Draft UN Discussion Paper, Vientiane, Lao People's Democratic Republic, February 27, 2013), 1, http://www.unescap.org/sites/default/files/DP3-B.pdf.

34. N. Altantsetseg, "Russian-Mongolian and Sino-Mongolian Relations Since the Nineties," in *The Geopolitical Relations Between Contemporary Mongolia and Neighboring Asian Countries: Democracy, Economy and Security* (Taipei: Mongolian and Tibetan Affairs Commission, 2003), 379.

35. *Montsame* (Ulaanbaatar), March 26, 2001.

36. *Emailnews Daily*, no. 236 (Ulaanbaatar), December 5, 2001; Altantsetseg, "Russian-Mongolian and Sino-Mongolian Relations," 379.

37. According to the Organisation for Economic Co-operation and Development, nonconcessional loans are extended on terms substantially more generous than market loans. The concessionality is achieved either through interest rates below those available on the market or by grace periods, or a combination of these. Concessional loans typically have long grace periods. Nonconcessional loans have the potential for mismanagement that could result in rapid reaccumulation of external debt as well as increased demand for IDA grants, which are allocated on the basis of a country's risk of debt distress.

38. Tsedendamba Batbayar, "Mongolian-Chinese Economic Cooperation as an Important Factor in Northeast Asian Economic Regionalism," ERINA Report no. 64 (July 2005): 40.

39. Managed by Mercy Corps, it had a four-year $18 million project to help herders in Dundgovi, Zavhan, Ovorkhangai, Uvs, Arkhangai, Bayanhongor, Tov, Khubsgol, and Gobisumber provinces to increase herder productivity, improve veterinary services, establish revolving fodder funds, improve management of water sources and supply, increase credit to herders, and stimulate the creation of new rural businesses. Morton, "A Note on Comparing International Experiences," 8.

40. Government of Mongolia/USAID, "Mongolia Country Strategic Plan, 1999–2003" Ulaanbaatar: Government of Mongolia, 1998.

41. Cheng, "Growth and Recovery," 14–15.

42. See Frederick Nixson and Bernard Walters, "The Transition to a Market Economy: Mongolia, 1990–1998," *International Journal of Economic Development* 2, no. 1 (January 2000): 35–66; Keith Griffin, *Poverty and the Transition to a Market Economy in Mongolia* (London: Macmillan, 1995); Morris Rossabi, *Modern Mongolia: From Khans to Commissars to Capitalists* (Berkeley: University of California Press, 2005).

43. Enkhbayar Shagdar, "Neo-Liberal 'Shock Therapy' Policy During the Mongolian Economic Transition" (ERINA Discussion Paper no. 0703e, Niigata, Japan, April 2007), 13; Enkhbayar Shagdar, *Mongolia's Economic Transition and Development Challenges: An Evidence of Poorly Managed Neo-Liberal, Shock Therapy Transition and Economic Destitution* (Riga, Latvia: Lambert Academic Publishing, 2012).

44. Rebecca Empson, "An Interview with Bill Bikales," *Emerging Suspects* (blog), University College London, October 31, 2016, https://blogs.ucl.ac.uk/mongolian-economy/2016/10/31/an-interview-with-bill-bikales/.

45. Mark Green, "Mongolia, 25 Years from Soviet Satellite to Democratic Partner," *IRI Conference on Mongolia's 25 Years of Democracy.*

46. "Peace Corps Director Visits Mongolia to Celebrate 25th Anniversary," Peace Corps Mongolia, August 15, 2016, https://www.peacecorps.gov/news/library/peace-corps-director-visits-mongolia-celebrate-25th-anniversary/.

47. *Country Assistance Program for Mongolia,* Ministry of Foreign Affairs of Japan, 23–24.

48. Ibid., 24.

49. Ibid., 24–25.

50. Japan International Cooperation Agency (JICA), "Major Projects in Mongolia," http://www.jica.go.jp/mongolia/english/activities/activity16.html.

51. "Country Profile—Mongolia," *New Agriculturalist,* May 2009, http://www.new-ag.info/en/country/profile.php?a=732; Patrick Kingsley, "Nomads No More: Why Mongolian Herders Are Moving to the City," *The Guardian,* January 5, 2017.

52. Caroline Nath and Ros Armitage, "A Way of Life Imperiled: Mongolia's Uncertain Future," *In Action* (blog), 2000, http://www.redcross.int/EN/mag/magazine2000_2/Mongolia.html.

53. International Federation of Red Cross and Red Crescent Societies, *Annual Report: Mongolia* (2002), 3, http://www.ifrc.org/docs/appeals/annual02/013902annrep.pdf.

54. IMF, *Economic Growth Support and Poverty Reduction Strategy*, para. 2.18, 29.

55. "Pastoral Risk Management Strategy," FAO project number TCP.MON/0066 A.

56. "Provision of Animal Health Inputs and Animal Feed to Assist the Restoring of Severely-Affected Households in Snowstorm-Affected Areas," FAO project number TCP/MON/00067 E.

57. Reported to the author personally by a Mongol official working at the time in the Mongolian embassy to the United States.

58. María E. Fernández-Gimenez, Batbuyan Batjav, and Batkhishig Baival, *Lessons from the Dzud: Adaptation and Resilience in Mongolian Pastoral Social-Ecological Systems* (Colorado State University and the World Bank, June 2012), 139, http://documents.worldbank.org/curated/en/986161468053662281/pdf/718440WP0P12770201208-01-120revised.pdf.

59. See ibid.; Jonathan Watts, "UN Launches Mongolia $4m Appeal to Clear Up Livestock Killed by Big Freeze," *The Guardian,* February 25, 2010; Charlotte Benson, "*Dzud* Disaster Financing and Response in Mongolia" (paper prepared for World Bank study on Structuring *Dzud* Disaster Preparation, Financing and Response to Increase Resilience of Herder Households to Climatic Risk in Mongolia, May 2011); "The Slow and Deadly *Dzud* in Mongolia," *BBC News,* May 14, 2016, http://www.bbc.com/news/world-asia-35983912; Ankit Panda, "After Brutal *Dzud* Winter, Mongolia Seeks Foreign Aid," *The Diplomat,* February 29, 2016.

60. *Human Development Report Mongolia 2003: Urban-Rural Disparities in Mongolia* (Ulaanbaatar: Government of Mongolia, 2003), http://hdr.undp.org/sites/default/files/mongolia_2003_en.pdf; Keith Griffin, ed., *Poverty Reduction in Mongolia* (Canberra: Asia Pacific Press, 2003).

61. Jacques Legrand, "The Mongolia 'Zud': Facts and Concepts from the Description of a Disaster to the Understanding of the Nomadic Pastoral System," in August 15–16, 2001, *International Symposium on Dialogue Among Civilizations: Interactions Between Nomadic and Other Cultures of Central Asia* (Ulaanbaatar: International Institute of the Study of Nomadic Civilizations, 2002), 14–30.

62. Griffin, *Poverty Reduction,* 70.

63. Three thousand herding families in seven *aimags* were given thousands of head of livestock on credit to restock animals lost in the 1999–2001 *dzuds*. One of the most important conclusions was that investment needs to go beyond restocking to establishing a new animal husbandry environment that included marketing. UNDP/Swedish International Development Agency (SIDA), "Poverty Research, Examination of Effectiveness" (2003).

64. One thousand herders were surveyed in five regions—Zavhan, Ovorkhangai, Khentii and Dornod, Omnogobi, and Selenge. Among the survey's conclusions were that government support was necessary for savings and loans and cooperatives; herders needed increased knowledge to adapt to weather and market changes and to eliminate the mentality that their losses from natural disasters would be solved by outsiders; herders' income was low because there were only a few, inadequate channels for selling

animal raw products; and the *sums*' development must follow diverse models, not just one developmental model, in order for the local administrations to be more responsive to herders' problems. See UNDP/SIDA, "Poverty Research, Options" (2004).

65. TACIS is a foreign and technical assistance program implemented in 1991 by the European Commission to help members of the Commonwealth of Independent States and Mongolia in their transition to democratic market-oriented economies. TACIS has merged into the EuropeAid program.

66. Morton, "A Note on Comparing International Experiences," 8.

67. UNDP project number MON/02/301/A/01/99 (2002).

68. This project was the successor to a study funded by the government of New Zealand and the UNDP in 2002 on "Developing and Piloting a Sustainable Development Model for the Extensive Livestock Industry." The target group consisted of herding households at the *sum* or *bag* level in three of the five major economic regions of the country—Khangai/Khubsgol, Selenge/Onon, Altai, Central/Eastern steppe, and Gobi. Project work concentrated on (1) institution building and pasture management with herding communities of ten to thirty households; (2) supporting the creation of a *bag* executive co-management committee to coordinate grazing plans and resolve disputes; (3) preparing land use plans at the *sum* level.

69. Groups consisted of poor, middle, and wealthy herders, who were offered loans for fodder and veterinary drugs. The major objective of the pilot project was the recognition "of existing possession and use rights of herders over pastoral resources by registering them." Possession rights were granted by the *sum* governor for sixty years, according to a contract under the powers of the Land Law of 1994. Morton, "A Note on Comparing International Experiences," 21.

70. "Balancing Rural and Urban Disparity," UNDP.

71. Government of Mongolia, UNDP, and World Bank, Independent Evaluation of the National Poverty Alleviation Programme and Options Post-2000, mimeo, Ulaanbaatar, 1999.

72. This point of view was supported by Kevin Cheng in his analysis of Mongolia's transition, where he noted that neither education nor employment made a major contribution to Mongolia's early economic growth in the democratic era, but livestock-raising was "a principal engine of Mongolia's quick recovery during the second half of the 1990s, although its share in GDP has been declining since 1999." Cheng, "Growth and Recovery," 4, 10.

73. UNDP website on "Mongolia," Menon, "Strengthening," March 31, 2003.

74. UNDP website on Mongolia, Menon, "Integrating Poverty Reduction Study," July 2001. Recovery and development of the industrial sector is the key to employment, broad-based growth, and poverty reduction.

75. ADB, Program Performance Audit Report on the Agricultural Sector Program (Loan 1409-MON[SF]) in Mongolia, PPA:MON 27536 (November 2002).

76. Batkin et al., *Independent Evaluation*, 65–66.

77. It was not clear how many of these 36,400 households were nomadic, but at least 21,000, or 60 percent of the households, were paid for construction projects not involving herding. Ibid., 46, 53.

78. Herders have to live in severe natural conditions isolated from "civilization," which is the inherent weakness of nomadic culture. L. Naranhuu, D. Shombodon, B. Jandagsuren, S. Amgaa, Ts. Altanbat, UNDP/SIDA, "An Examination of the Effectiveness of Herd Restocking Strategies in Building and Securing the Incomes and the Livelihoods of Herder Households," UNDP/SIDA Poverty Research and Employment Facilitation for Policy Development, MON/01/U01 Project (2003), 77.

79. Income General Funds in 1998 and 1999 were focused on cities, *aimags,* and *sum* centers, and not available to herders, which even the World Bank criticized as shortsighted. Batkin et al., *Independent Evaluation,* 20.

80. G. Chuluunbaatar, "Renewal of Mongolia's Political System and its Democratic Development," in *Renovation of Mongolia on the Eve of the XXI Century and Future Development Patterns*, ed. Tsedendamba Batbayar (Ulaanbaatar: Mongolian Development Research Centre, 2000), 24–25.

81. It should be noted that, with the collapse of the Soviet Union and its satellites' social institutions, INGOs worldwide often flowed into the vacuum to assist donor governments in remaking economies and the public space. D. Byambajav, "NGOs in Mongolia: A Crucial Factor in Mongolian Society and Politics," *Mongolian Journal of International Affairs*, no. 13 (2006): 134 cites Marc Lindenberg and Coralie Bryant, *Going Global: Transforming Relief and Development NGOs* (Boulder, CO: Lynne Rienner [Kumarian Press], 2001).

82 Byambajav, "NGOs in Mongolia," 133.

83. "Brief Introduction," www.soros.org.mn, 2004.

84. Byambajav, "NGOs in Mongolia," 143.

85. Chuluunbaatar, "Renewal," 25.

86. Byambajav, "NGOs in Mongolia," 136.

87. INGOs also had different constraints on their funding. Organizations formed under the umbrella of international political parties and government agencies were legally bound to receive funds only from public entities (e.g., German political foundations and the IRI). Ibid., 137–138.

88. Ibid., 139.

89. Ibid., 144.

90. Asian Development Bank, *Governance: Progress and Challenges in Mongolia* (2004), 68.

91. Danaasuren Vandangombo, "NGOs as Accountability Promoters: In the Mongolian Case" (paper presented at the Sixth Asia Pacific Interdisciplinary Research in Accounting Conference, Sydney, Australia, July 12, 2010), 9, http://apira2010.econ.usyd.edu.au/conference_proceedings/APIRA-2010-166-vanDanGombo-NGOS-as-accountability-promoters-Mongolia.pdf.

92. Reported by Swiss Agency for Development and Cooperation, "Supporting Mongolia's Civil Society Organisations," December 16, 2013, www.swiss-cooperation.admin.ch/mongolia/en/Home/State_Reform_Local_Governance_and_Civic_Participation/Mongolia_s_Civil_Society_NGO_Capacity_Building_Project. *The Directory of Mongolian NGOs* (Ulaanbaatar: Mongolian Foundation for Open Society [Soros Foundation], 2003) listed 2,700 organizations officially registered as of July 2002. At this time there were no NGOs fighting trafficking. Among the NGOs that primarily were devoted to transnational crime issues in this directory, which were still listed in 2013, were (1) Human rights NGOs: Movement for Human Rights and Justice; Human Rights Education Center; Shine; Mongolian National Coordinating Committee of Amnesty International; Mongolian Lawyers Group of Amnesty International; National Center Against Violence; Genden Foundation (victims of political repression); Tsekh; Mongolian Human Rights Center; Mongolian National Center for Human Rights; Center for Human Rights and Development; Mongolian Railway Association for Human Rights; Mongolian Student's Center of International Human Rights Organization; Amnesty International; Association of Freedom and Legal Principle; Eviin Bagana; Human Rights Fund; Global CS Association; Correction and Penitentiary Institutions' Association ICPA of Mongolia; Erdenet Khumuun Center (see 104–109). (2) Legal NGOs: fifty-three organizations and among them Tulga Legal Bureau, Dens Legal Bureau; Public Control; Lawyers Center for Legal Reform; Association for Fighting Against Corruption; Mongolian Association of Criminologists; Mongolian Crime Prevention Foundation; Tugs Javkhaa Center of Legal Information and Awareness; People's Control Association (see 110–113). (3) Anticorruption: Group for Independence of Judges and Lawyers; Juramt Mongol; Citizens' Association Against Corruption; Degjil 21.

93. The Open Society study found ninety-seven, or 2.6% of, NGOs in 2005 working in the field of democracy and human rights (a total of ten) and 20 percent active. See "NGOs in Mongolia," Open Society Forum, 2005, 3, www.forum.mn/res_mat/NGOS_Survey20060314_en.pdf. Meanwhile, Byambajav found only 10 percent active; see Byambajav, "NGOs in Mongolia," 134.

94. Swiss Agency for Development and Cooperation, "Supporting Mongolia's Civil Society Organisations," ibid.

95. Byambajav, "NGOs in Mongolia," 134–135.

96. For an appraisal of Mongolia, see "Mongolia: Amnesty International Submission to the UN Universal Periodic Review" (ninth session of the UPR Working Group, November–December 2010), lib.ohchr.org/HRBodies/UPR/Documents/session9/MN/AI_Amnesty%20International_Revised.pdf.

97. The Asia Foundation, "Mongolia Highlights," June 2007, https://asiafoundation.org/resources/pdfs/1-MGMultistakeholderIV.pdf.

98. Human Rights Development Center, "Combating Human Trafficking in Mongolia: Issues and Opportunities," Ulaanbaatar. ME Consulting (2005).

99. Josh Friedman, "Mongolia Marks Passage of Landmark Anti-Trafficking and Corruption Legislation," Asia Foundation, February 15, 2012, http://asiafoundation.org/2012/02/15/mongolia-marks-passage-of-landmark-anti-trafficking-and-corruption-legislation/.

100. Brian Sturgess, "Investing in Mongolia," *World Economics,* September 2012, http://www.worldeconomics.com /Papers/Investing%20in%20Mongolia_c93dbdb0-1a04-4e33-b331-51c25d21d47a.paper#_ftn5.

101 Cheng, "Growth and Recovery," 4–5.

102. IMF, *Mongolia Selected Issues and Statistical Appendix* (November 2005), 30.

103. Pomfret, "Transition and Democracy in Mongolia," 1.

104. The Agricultural Bank was reorganized and began giving herders loans in August 2001. As of March 2003, 8.7 percent of all Agricultural Bank loans were to herders, even though such loan delivery met only 4%–8% of the demand. "Khan Bank, The Agricultural Bank of Mongolia," John Gutin Robin Young (ed.) January 2005, https://www.marketlinks.org/sites/marketlinks.org/files/resource/files/ML1790_mr_11_khan_bank_the_agricultural_bank_of_mongolia_1_04.pdf.

105. Examples are a yak dairy, alternative sealant products used for rural road development, microenterprises for agriculture inside *gers*, and rough-terrain small mobile slaughterhouses.

106. Empson, "Interview with Bill Bikales."

107. Griffin, *Poverty Reduction*, xvii.

5

China Replaces Russia

Mongolian society did not naturally develop trade markets until permanent Buddhist establishments came into existence in the seventeenth century, and there was no indigenous merchant class. Trade was controlled by tribal leaders who engaged foreigners to conduct mercantile activity. During the Mongolian Empire, Central Asians and Western Europeans such as Marco Polo acted in this role, while in the Manchu Qing period, trade was mainly under the control of Han Chinese itinerant traders. The extreme poverty of Mongolia in the early twentieth century was blamed on the exploitative structure of Chinese-managed trade, which was one of the reasons for Mongols' residual bitterness and suspicion toward the Chinese. Prior to the introduction of socialism, few Mongols were involved in trades or skilled crafts that could be the basis for an urban labor force. In 1924 one Mongolian leader observed that not more than 150 Mongols were engaged in any kind of industrial activity in the whole country.[1] A state monopoly on foreign trade, under the control of Soviet advisers, was established by December 1930, and soon commerce was dominated by Soviet and Eastern European trade. Thus Mongolia emerged from its communist isolation in 1990 with certain national characteristics that were fundamentally different from those of other command economies. One major difference was a high comfort level with foreigners' making its economic policy decisions. In many ways, the story of the Mongolian democratic experiment is intimately connected with Mongolian efforts, successful and failed, to develop the expertise and confidence to assume responsibility for economic as well as foreign affairs policymaking.

The collapse of the COMECON system in 1991 forced Mongolia to fundamentally alter its interactions with the world. It had to seek new trading partners in the increasingly competitive globalized economy. Its accession to the WTO in 1997, supported by the United States, gave Mongolia access to new markets and encouraged trade and FDI. The collapse of the manufacturing sector in the 1990s forced displaced skilled workers to return to herding life, become artisanal miners, or participate in the underground service sector. Many workers left the country individually or under factory labor contracts, especially with South Korea.

Mongols and their government's economic planners did not operate in a vacuum. Their options were impacted and limited by their two large border neighbors as well as by the Western foreign donor community that overwhelmed the feeble Mongolian economy during the 1990s. Mongolia's dependence on foreign donor assistance put its development and security future in the hands of Americans and Europeans to a degree that should have been of concern to national leaders. However, a serious domestic discussion of the impact of ODA on national policy did not take place. This was because other factors, such as the Asian economic crisis, the war on international terrorism, the economic rise of China, instability on the Korean Peninsula, domestic political crises, and even weather-related disasters, limited Mongolia's options. After the fall of the Soviet Union, Mongolian-Russian relations were further strained over disagreements about the amount of Mongolia's Soviet-era debt. Political changes within Russia forced the withdrawal of Soviet troops, advisers, and subsidies from Mongolia by 1992. Although in 1993 the two countries signed a new treaty of friendship and cooperation, Russian financial and technical assistance did not resume, so the dominant role of Russia in the economy receded quickly and remained significant only in sectors such as electricity and diesel fuel.

Sino-Mongol Ties Impacted by Sino-Soviet Relations

Mongolia and China have had rocky ties for over 1,000 years. At the beginning of the twentieth century, the two were part of the dying Manchu Qing Empire, and then both experienced major political revolutions to restore their national sovereignty. These upheavals moved them into the international socialist camp led by the Soviet Union. Mongolian relations with China, republican (ROC) and communist (PRC), ebbed and flowed with Sino-Soviet relations. Many Mongols saw Stalin sympathetically as the man who preserved the independence of Mongolia at the 1945 Yalta conference. The United Nations conducted a plebiscite in Mongolia on October 20, 1945, in which Mongols overwhelmingly voted for independence from China. In January 1946, the ROC government recognized the Mongolian People's Republic, although it rescinded this recognition after Mao Zedong's successful communist revolution.[2]

PRC China and Mongolia today share a 4,677-kilometer border. The two countries established formal diplomatic relations on October 16, 1949, but the course of their bilateral relations during the communist era was, in the main, determined by the Soviet Union. In 1951 they established trade relations, and eleven years later signed a Boundary Treaty and a Sino-Mongolian Treaty on Friendship and Mutual Assistance. In the 1950s, when Sino-Soviet relations were at their closest, tens of thousands of Chinese workers were sent by train to Ulaanbaatar to provide manpower and expertise for construction projects such as the Government Palace, which today houses the president's office and the Mongolian Parliament. China provided some soft loans and assistance grants as well as workers, while Mongolia sent horses to the Chinese army.

The Sino-Soviet split, which Mongolians called the Double Cold War,[3] had a particularly negative impact on Sino-Mongolian economic and political ties. Mongolia was pressured by the Soviet Union to isolate itself from China. From 1960 to 1980 relations were frozen in hostility. During the PRC Cultural Revolution, Chinese Red Guards denounced Mongolia as a neocolony of the Soviet Union, while on the Mongolian southern border there was a massive buildup of Soviet and Mongol troops and missiles. After the death of Mao in 1976, Mongolia doubled the size of its army at the request of Soviet Defense Minister Dmitry Ustinov, and in 1979 Soviet forces in Mongolia reached a peak of 120,000. Tsedendamba Batbayar, one of Mongolia's leading strategic studies researchers, has noted that Mongolia's top leadership during that period played its own "China card" with the Soviets to squeeze out more economic aid.[4] One such project was the development of the huge Erdenet copper deposit in northern Mongolia from 1970 to 1990. The Soviets expended 600 million rubles and were given half ownership. This enterprise became the largest revenue generator for Mongolia, including in the democratic era. Under the leadership of Deng Xiaoping, the basis for the restoration of closer bilateral relations was laid. In 1987, China and Mongolia restored the scientific and technological exchanges that had been suspended for more than twenty years and signed the 1987–1988 Plan for Scientific and Technological Cooperation, but the true breakthrough in Mongolian relations with China was the collapse of the Soviet Union.

New Mongolian-Chinese Economic Relationship in the Democratic Era

China reformulated its overall export strategy toward more Asian-based trade partners after the Western boycott over Tiananmen in June 1989. The importance of reimagining a more integrated Sino-Mongolian relationship was equally important to the Mongols, who were struggling to find economic alternatives to their decades-long dependency upon the Soviet Union. In May 1990, just after the collapse of Mongolia's communist MPRP government, newly elected Mongolian president P. Ochirbat chose to make his initial international visit to China. This was the first time a Mongolian president went first to Beijing, not Moscow, effectively ending two decades of hostility. Although the Chinese were very wary of the democratic movement taking place in Mongolia, they were interested in exploiting the economic vacuum left by the Soviets. In 1991 during the state visit of Chinese President Yang Shangkun to Mongolia, the two governments signed a new trade agreement, replacing the intergovernmental credit trade system with cash trade and guaranteeing Mongolian access to the sea via the Chinese port of Tianjin, and concluded an investment protection agreement. In April 1994 during a visit by Chinese Premier Li Peng, the two nations revised their Treaty on Friendship and Cooperation, which established the political and legal foundations of their revised relationship. This treaty included a mutual pledge not to participate in political-military alliances against each other.[5]

In the 1990s the original burst of bilateral trade was not stimulated by official treaties. Rather, Mongolian and Chinese young entrepreneurs, with permission to travel without a visa for up to one month, would ride trains between Ulaanbaatar and Beijing hauling foodstuffs and clothing items to sell in the Mongolian black market. These businessmen, called smugglers in other societies, did not pay any customs duties and forged links that expanded over time into other sectors. Such underground bilateral trade, which kept Mongolia fed and clothed during the early transition years, was conducted through personal ties and devoid of regulation. Many of today's Mongolian businessmen, including some of great wealth, had their beginnings in such trade, and their propensity for corrupt practices and tax avoidance was forged during those years.

It is also noteworthy to mention that, since 1985, Mongolia and China have developed their border trade with much local autonomy on both sides of the border. Trade through eleven seasonal ports has been conducted between China's Inner Mongolia, Xinjiang Uygur and Ningxia Hui autonomous regions, and Hebei and Jilin provinces with Mongolia's border provinces. In 1990, Mongolia reopened its consulate-general in Hohhot, and in 1996, Mongolia's consulate-general at the railway border crossing of Eren (Chinese Erlien) was established. Border issues between the two countries always have been delicate. In principle, China and Mongolia have no outstanding unresolved border disputes, yet other problems emerged in the 1990s. Because of the scarcity of towns near the borders, rustlers, poachers, smugglers, tax evaders, and illegals became irritants in the bilateral relationship. Both countries were concerned about the smuggling of animal by-products such as cashmere hair without paying duties through the porous southern border, with much revenue lost by both governments. Seventy percent of the Sino-Mongolian border in the 1990s had an iron mesh fence that was inspected daily. In the early 2000s, China reinforced the fence by building a solid two-meter-high barrier with concrete poles to stop illegal crossing by people and animals.[6]

Although modest cultural exchanges between the two countries began in 1951, in Mongolia's democratic era they have slowly intensified under a 1994 Cultural Cooperation Agreement. Chinese Cultural Minister Liu Dezhong led a delegation to Mongolia in 1997, the first visit to Mongolia by

China's cultural minister since the establishment of diplomatic relations. The next year Mongolian Minister of Education Saikhanbileg visited China to sign the 1998–2000 Executive Plan for Sino-Mongolian Cultural Exchanges. This agreement was updated by the 2001–2003 Executive Plan for Cultural Exchanges and Cooperation. China and Mongolia started educational contacts in 1952. These were revived in 1996, when Mongolian Minister of Science and Education Tumur-Ochir visited China, and both sides signed the 1996–2000 Educational Exchanges and Cooperation Program. In 2000, the two countries agreed upon a plan to help Mongolian students study in China via free Chinese scholarships. As a result, between 2002 and 2003 Mongolia sent 180 trainees and students to China, while China dispatched 15 trainees and a teacher,[7] and seventy-seven Chinese private students from Hebei and Inner Mongolia began studying in Mongolia.[8] Another important feature in bilateral ties was that Mongols were permitted to access inexpensive health services in China. In 1999 a Medical Treatment Agreement was signed, and in 2001 alone, 33,000 Mongols utilized this medical travel treatment.[9]

China's focus for its Mongolian relations has always been through the lens of its border provinces of Gansu, Ningxia, Xinjiang, Shanxi, and Inner Mongolia. To meet its own goals for domestic stability, China needs to establish a peaceful environment along its border and, increasingly, to obtain energy, oil and gas, and foodstuffs from the border nations. Thus, in the 1990s, and certainly after the September 11, 2001, terrorist attack in New York City, Central Asian nations and Mongolia were viewed as "crucial geopolitical interests" for China's western development strategy. The Chinese policy that animated its relationship with Mongolia was its "go-out" strategy, formally adopted in 2000, which was the first signal that the Chinese government was prioritizing outward FDI. This policy mandated that Chinese state-owned companies should strengthen their international operations to improve resource allocation and enhance international competitiveness.[10] Also, the PRC State Council incentivized Chinese companies to enter overseas markets by granting financial and foreign exchange assistance.

From 1991 to 1996, Mongolia had a favorable balance of trade with China, but this trend reversed as the decade continued. Mongolia increasingly bought Chinese foodstuffs and consumer goods and exported its raw materials (from cashmere hair to coal) to China for processing. Chinese businesses rapidly poured into the Mongolian market both to provide commodities to fill the void left by the collapse of the Soviet-dominated command economy system and to take advantage of the open economic system for investors established under Western donor guidance. In 2001 Mongolian exports to China grew to 55.7 percent, compared to only 1.7 percent in 1990. Chinese imports in 1990 stood at 21.9 percent compared to 2.4 percent eleven years prior. China also became Mongolia's largest trade volume partner (35.5 percent).[11] According to statistics from China's General Administration of Customs, in 2002 Sino-Mongolian trade volume totaled $363 million, of which Chinese exports accounted for $140 million and imports $223 million. The Mongols claimed that by the end of 2002 there were 825 enterprises with Chinese investment exceeding $281 million.[12]

In the 1990s, FDI in Mongolia amounted in total to about $284 million, which represented less than 4 percent of the country's GDP. Foreign investors from developed economies complained that the Mongolian legal and banking environments were not stable and so "were reluctant to invest substantial amounts given the country's remote location and undeveloped infrastructure."[13] However, Chinese FDI from 1990 to 2001 soared to $136.9 million, while Russian FDI during the same period plummeted to $29.8 million.[14] China became the major investor in Mongolia in 1997.

No other country could match China's economic incentives, trade, and investment in Mongolia. In 2002 the Mongol press reported that there were 260 joint ventures with China, with an investment value of $236 million, compared to Russian investment valued at $31 million and US investment of $50 million. Chinese FDI represented 31 percent of all foreign enterprises and 21 percent of the total FDI in Mongolia.[15] A year later Chinese joint ventures had jumped to 349, and eighty-four additional enterprises were 100 percent Chinese-owned. Most Chinese investment in the 1990s was in animal husbandry and by-products, light industry, construction, agriculture, and the service industry because the Mongolian government deliberately limited Chinese presence in large state industries, including the mineral sector. In the twenty-first century, massive Chinese investment came after mineral sector restrictions were lifted. Of the $3.6 billion in Chinese FDI in the last twenty years, over $1 billion was made in 2011 alone. In 2016, 49 percent (5,951) of foreign-invested companies were Chinese.

In 1997 Sino-Mongolian trade turnover stood at $252 million, an increase of 26.7 percent over the previous year. The reason for the increase was not because of Chinese investment in Mongolia's mineral sector but was due to the decision by both nations to reduce trade surcharges 50 percent to facilitate transportation. By the end of the 1990s, China had taken over the Mongol cashmere goat hair export market, and Mongolian oil was almost exclusively sold to China.[16] Because of Western donor policies pressuring Mongolian officials not to protect or subsidize native industries in the free market, the government did not act to stave off competition from more established Chinese and Inner Mongolian competitors, who quickly bought up unprocessed hides and hairs and drove Mongolian and other foreign animal by-product enterprises out of business. For Mongolia the relationship with China became its top foreign policy priority as trade volume with China, which was only $24 million in 1989, jumped to over $300 million in 2000.[17]

China's economic rise in Mongolia was clearly the result of China's pursuit of nearby diversified Asian markets, Chinese willingness to conduct illegal and poorly regulated cross-border trade and other nontransparent economic practices, and, more recently, its strong need for the raw materials to feed its rapidly growing economy. Ironically, the Chinese takeover of the

Mongolian market also was in large part a consequence of US trade policies toward Mongolia. The US government accorded Mongolia most favored trade (MFT) status when President Ochirbat became the first Mongolian head of state to visit the United States in January 1991. In 1997 MFT status was extended, and Mongolia joined the WTO. These actions caused a boom in the Mongolian apparel industry by giving it access to the US market. In the late 1990s, Chinese companies, whose own US textile quotas were full, started shipping Chinese-made cotton clothing pieces to Mongolia for assembly and reshipment to the United States to avoid US restrictions. In 1992 textiles represented 4.4 percent of Mongolia's GDP. In 1997 this nearly doubled to 8.1 percent, and by the end of this "golden era" in 2004, textiles represented 11.6 percent.[18] By 2003 Mongolian textiles (cashmere and noncashmere) represented 20 percent of all Mongolian exports.[19]

With 98 percent of Mongolia's garment production going to the United States, the industry was "an essentially artificial creation of the global quota system."[20] The eventual US abolition of Chinese quotas in 2005 meant that Chinese companies no longer needed to export through Mongolia to the US market. The textile sector in Mongolia could not compete with low Chinese prices, so Chinese companies closed their FDI operations. The UNDP reported that, in the first four months of 2005, Mongolian garment exports to the United States declined both in value (20 percent) and in volume (40 percent) compared to the same period in 2003,[21] and it was estimated that at least 20,000 full-time workers (mostly women) lost their jobs due to the closure of the Chinese factories. This US-engineered trade policy after 2005 left Mongolia highly dependent upon copper and coal sales for its export revenues and launched Mongolia's mineral era. Equally significant, in 1997 Mongolia adopted a very liberal mining law,[22] ending the exclusion of Chinese FDI in this sector. Gold, oil, and other mineral concessions were opened to the Chinese because of pressure by Western donors on Mongolia to level the playing field for all countries. Chinese FDI without any auctioning or compensation began to flow into exploration licenses sold on the territory of previously discovered deposits. More than 7,000 licenses were distributed for territory covering more than 40 percent of the country.[23]

It is undeniable that the remarkable penetration of Chinese FDI into the Mongolian economy was facilitated by the improvement in Sino-Mongolian political ties. In December 1998, at the invitation of Chinese President Jiang Zemin, Mongolian President N. Bagabandi paid a state visit to Beijing. Their joint communique[24] emphasized the mutual desire to establish neighborly, friendly relations and cooperation into the twenty-first century based on long-term stability. In July 1999 President Jiang paid a reciprocal state visit to Mongolia. Mongolian Prime Minister N. Enkhbayar in January 2002 made an official visit to China, and in June 2003 Chinese President Hu Jintao visited Ulaanbaatar. At that time both sides issued a joint statement pledging to establish a neighborly and mutual-trusting partnership. From 1990 to 2010, over 10,709 foreign companies invested in Mongolia—51 percent were Chinese, while the second largest amount of FDI was 8 percent from Canada (see Figure 5.1).

Chinese domination of Mongolia's economy came with another price tag: it created real domestic unrest in Mongolia because average citizens were concerned about being ethnically and economically colonized by their southern neighbor. Official Mongolian reaction to the growing Chinese FDI in the economy has been mixed. Morris Rossabi conducted personal interviews in July 1998 and found that some policymakers, such as Foreign Minister Rinchinnyam Amarjargal, did not object to Chinese investment in land, industrial, or retail businesses. He noted that Jambaljamts Od, foreign policy adviser to Prime Minister Elbegdorj, believed that China would be a huge market for Mongolian exports, and some older pro-Soviet elites saw no threat from the growing Chinese investment. Rossabi found that, while some democratic reformers were ambivalent about China, they still sent their children to China for education. A Sant Maral Foundation survey in February 1996 found that only 35 percent of the population supported closer ties with China, while 79 percent desired closer links with Russia.[25]

Figure 5.1 Mongolia's Sources of FDI, 1990–2010

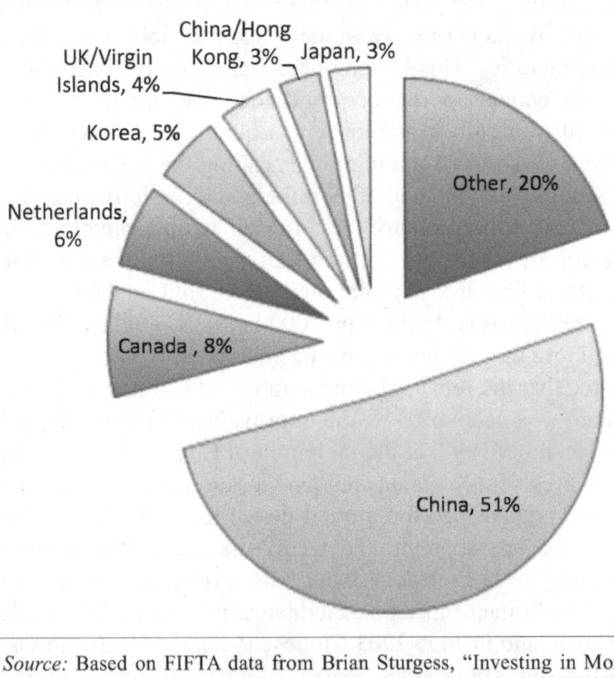

Source: Based on FIFTA data from Brian Sturgess, "Investing in Mongolia," September 2012, Figure 5, https://www.worldeconomics.com/Papers/Investing%20in%20Mongolia_c93dbdb0-1a04-4e33-b331-51c25d21d47a.paper.

Given Chinese monopolization of Mongolia's economy since 2000, government officials have worried about a secret Chinese agenda for Mongolia. In 2016 there were 15,000 to 40,000 Chinese legal and illegal workers, and these numbers were expected to increase with Mongolian mineral exploitation. There has been a well-documented rise in anti-Chinese feelings and attacks. Mongolian politicians of all parties have promoted a Mongolian nationalism that at times is tinged with strong anti-Chinese rhetoric. Although the last twenty years have seen no outstanding border disputes between the two nations and increasingly frequent high-level political exchanges, the legacy of historical warfare and increasing Chinese presence in Mongolia's economy from foodstuff supplier to mineral developer has perpetuated a widespread fear that Mongolia will become "sinified" and lose its language and identity, as has happened in Inner Mongolia (South Mongolia).

SOCO Sells to China, and China Takes Over the Petroleum Sector

Another major factor that increased Chinese dominance in Mongolia's economy was the SOCO affair, which transferred ownership of Mongolia's only producing oil field in the 1990s to China. SOCO was an American-operated oil exploration company headquartered in London that was explicitly given the rights to the field by the Mongolian government, without a transparent bidding process, in order to assure US FDI in this key sector. Thus, the transfer to Chinese hands, the exact opposite of what the Mongols intended to happen, also broke the trust of the Mongols in the reliability of their American investment partners. In fact, this trust has never been fully repaired, and US FDI in Mongolia since then has steadily declined.

Around 1940, Soviet geologists identified the Zuunbayan oil field with reserves estimated at 6.2 million tons in the east Gobi. They built the country's first refinery, Mongolneft, in 1950 with a processing capacity of 400,000 tons, but even during its peak year, the refinery only produced 150,000 tons of petroleum. The Zuunbayan field eventually yielded about four million tons of crude oil, and, combined with Russian crude oil, the refinery supplied up to 20 percent of Mongolia's fuel and lubricants. However, the refinery ceased operations in 1969 due to equipment failure resulting in a well pressure decrease and a fire at the refinery. To date the refining of oil has not resumed. After the Petroleum Authority of Mongolia (PAM)[26] was established in 1990 as a state-owned agency, the government introduced a new petroleum law in 1991 with a Petroleum Program that classified prospective petroleum areas into contract blocks and released them for modified international bidding (Chinese and Russian bids initially were not accepted). This law regulated the operations of Mongolian and foreign entities or individuals involved in the exploration for and the production, processing, transportation, storage, and marketing of petroleum originating in Mongolia.[27] In 1991 PAM began granting foreign exploratory licenses in order to obtain technical and financial assistance from Western companies and intentionally barred Chinese entities from such licenses. However, the trend over the decade was for private Western companies to sell out to Chinese state-owned enterprises (SOEs) with the Mongols powerless to stop it.

Zuunbayan exploration studies first were carried out by British Petroleum and Philips Petroleum in 1990–1993. The initial production sharing contract (PSC) was signed in 1993 with the US company SOCO, which drilled its first exploration well to a depth of 3,000 meters in the Tamtsag Basin a year later. By the end of the 1990s, Mongolian policymakers believed that measurably strengthening strategic ties with the United States was best achieved by developing deeper US investment and economic relations. This was the rationale behind granting, without an open tender, SOCO Mongolia, Inc., a UK-based subsidiary of Snyder Oil of Houston, 100 percent control of Mongolia's national oil company in a production-sharing contract covering 2.8 million acres of the Tamtsag Basin of northeastern Mongolia.

SOCO established a wholly owned subsidiary, SOCO Tamtsag Mongolia (SOTAMO), under president and CEO Ed Story[28] and began work through a Chinese contract drilling company, Huabei Oilfield Services, which was given a pro rata working interest participation of 10 percent in the PSC. Another 5 percent working interest was held by Petrovietnam, the Vietnamese national oil company. Crude oil produced from the pilot production program in 1993–1994 and sold at world prices under a contract with China National United Oil Corporation was trucked under a turnkey contract to a pipeline terminal in Aershan Oilfield in China for refining.[29] Later the Mongols concluded PSC agreements with two other Texas-based US oil companies—Nescor Energy Co. of Austin and Medallion Petroleum of Houston—to work with existing production capacity in the southeast Gobi desert and the northeast Tamtsag basin.[30]

Mongolia's last prime minister in the communist era, D. Byambasüren, claimed that during 1993 the MPRP government

> signed an agreement with the USA, stating that Mongolia will not refine locally drilled oil. When I broached the people who were in charge back then, they replied that they were told to do it that way and followed the order. The American side transferred the contract to Chinese people and left. The Mongolian side, on the other hand, was left unable to change that agreement.[31]

Whether or not this claim is true, the ramification was that in December 2003 the Mongols passed legislation permitting the extension of PSCs. At that time SOCO publicly announced that, with two of its three contracts for PSCs expiring within a year, it needed to extend its contracts in Mongolia because "there would not have been sufficient time to follow-up on the Zuunbayan success we had last year in our first year of adequately exploring this interval."[32] SOTAMO was granted the full five-year extension of its three Zuunbayan licenses. US Deputy Secretary of State Richard L. Armitage, who witnessed the signing of the new contract at the Presidential Palace in Ulaanbaatar on January 31, 2004, asserted that the event symbolized the type of cooperative endeavor that attracted the US foreign direct investment needed in Mongolia. He noted that Story and colleagues had invested $85 million in Mongolia: "They're making a bet that this is going to be a very successful country, and that's the same bet the United States Government has made. We want to be part of that success. And today I think what we witnessed was yet another American company who has made a decision that Mongolia is a place to be, it's a place on the rise, and it's a place of the future."[33]

Story made no secret of the fact that SOCO was discussing the Mongolian project with interested parties. Nevertheless, a year later it came as a complete shock to the Mongolian government when Story announced without prior consultation or warning that SOCO had sold all of its Mongolian interests to Daqing Oilfield Limited Company, a subsidiary of PetroChina, a subsidiary of state-owned China National Offshore Oil Corporation, for $93 million. Since the Mongolian assets were 100 percent in private hands, the sale only required SOCO shareholders' approval.[34] The Mongols believed that SOCO had deliberately deceived them, selling out Mongolian interests to the Chinese, and that the US government's unwilling-ness or inability to stop the sale was an unambiguous sign that the open free market advocated by the Americans could jeopardize the country's national security. This bitter lesson for the Mongols in how private enterprises legally functioned in the globalized marketplace convinced Mongolian policymakers that it was necessary to wall off certain strategic mineral assets from total private ownership. Perhaps more significantly, it left the Mongolian government and business community highly cynical about the United States and severely wounded the bilateral economic relationship. As for the actual PSC contract held by PetroChina, Mongolia could not renationalize the oil tracts without incurring litigation, so it acquiesced to the entrance of the Chinese in its energy sector.

When PetroChina acquired the rights to conduct drilling operations for the next twenty to thirty years from the SOCO sale, it claimed that 40 million of the 177 million barrels of crude oil reserves in its sites were economically recoverable reserves and projected that it could pump 93.3 million barrels of crude oil between 2010 and 2019. The original deal included a promise by the Chinese side to build roads between the Tamtsag fields and Bichigt border crossing point to China by 2011, but, despite increasing exports, no road has yet been built. In 2012, 500 of its 521 drilled wells were operating and produced 410,000 tons of oil—an eleven times increase in production over the previous five years. This crude was carried out in 80 to 100 trucks per day along thirty-one eroded dirt track roads. In 2013 the Mongolian government planned to increase volume up to 660,000 tons, about five million barrels, for export to China.

The American oil company Nescor Energy in 1994–1997 also conducted exploration and appraisal operations in the southeast Gobi under a US Trade Development Agency grant, and in February 1997 the Mongolian government gave Nescor 50 percent rights to these fields, which covered thirteen million acres.[35] The next year a joint venture of Gulf Canada and ROC Oil (Sydney, Australia) acquired all Mongolian rights and assets of Nescor Energy. Its crude was exported into China by truck, pipeline, and train. In January 1999, Gulf Canada withdrew from the joint venture due to an oil price downturn. Later in June 2001, ROC Oil sold its interests to Dongsheng, a subsidiary of China's SINOPEC. This action, along with PetroChina's buyout, enabled China to take full control of Mongolia's oil sector. From 1993 to 2011, FDI totaling over $1.5 billion was made in petroleum exploration in Mongolia, leading it to officially become an oil-producing country in 2010.

Currently, there are only two producing basins in Zuunbayan, including the old SOCO fields, which had exported 2.66 million barrels of oil as of February 29, 2012. The Tamtsag basin in the southwest of the country started production in 1998 and is the most active oil field. Since 2012, out of a total production of 10.58 million barrels of oil, 9.89 million barrels have been exported to China for refining because there still is no in-country refinery. PetroChina has long promised to construct new transmission pipelines from the Tamtsag field, since it now is extracting crude in an area that neighbors Manchurian China that it must transport by tanker trucks to a Chinese refinery across the border. In a move similar to Mongolian threats to use noncompliance/performance clauses in Rio Tinto's Oyu Tolgoi agreement as the reason to reopen negotiations over the entire contract, Mongolian officials threatened in 2013 that "if the company [PetroChina] fails to build road transportation, their permit is not allowed" to continue.[36]

Crude oil production in Mongolia totaled over 2.6 million barrels in 2011. As of 2016, there were thirty exploration blocks in Mongolia covering 531,000 km^2, and PAM has concluded PSCs with fourteen domestic and foreign companies in eighteen exploration blocks. Thirty-three percent of the contractors are Mongolian companies, and 39 percent are Chinese companies.[37] An important but smaller Chinese company now actively exploring in Mongolia is Mongolia Energy Corporation Limited (MEC), a mining and energy development holding company operating in Mongolia and in Xinjiang in northwest China. MEC's exploratory concessions operate in western and southern Mongolia in cooperation with China National Petroleum Corporation (CNPC) Daqing Petroleum. Another Chinese company, Gold BC LL, has been working in Mongolia since 2010.

With so much Chinese investment in the oil sector and with China's being the major customer for Mongolia's exported crude since 1998, the ramifications of such massive Chinese investment became a concern for the Mongolian public. Despite Mongolian sensitivity to Chinese activity, economic planners were willing to let China become a significantly larger supplier of oil products, at least in the short term, to break dependency on more expensive Russian petrol. After expansion upgrades were made to the Zamyn-Uud railroad switch loading yard on the Sino-Mongolian border, monthly petrol imports increased to 20,000 tons. This was an example of the two nations' finding new ways to cooperate despite tensions in the Sino-Mongolian petroleum relationship. In mid-March 2013, Mongolia made an agreement with PetroChina to exchange crude oil drilled in Mongolia with end products processed in the PRC's Inner Mongolia Autonomous Region.

Over 20 percent of Mongolia's imports in 2014 were petroleum products. Mongols have claimed for years that the Russian supply has been interrupted for political reasons, such as in May 2011 prior to parliamentary elections, and that these products have grown increasingly expensive while failing to meet soaring consumer and industrial demand.[38] The government promised to continue to seek cheaper, but higher standard, less polluting sources of fuel, in hopes such policies would reduce consumer prices. Nevertheless, it believes the future of petroleum supply lies in the creation of Mongolian refinery infrastructure. As early as 2009, Dashzeveg Amarsaikhan, then chairman of PAM, stated, "We shall have more leverage once we manage to diversify our sources and reduce captive dependence on one supply source. The Government is clear about this and has been working to achieve that objective. Things will get better once we extract enough oil at home and also have a refinery here."[39] In 1996 President Ochirbat soaked his cashmere *deel* (gown) in the oil drilled from Dornod province and promised that the Mongolian government would build an oil refinery within seven years. This was never realized because the property was legally transferred to other ownership. Former Prime Minister Byambasüren in 2016 voiced the frustration of many Mongols when he complained that officials were not actually interested in building an oil refinery: "The main reason for this is that the government doesn't consider the nation's interests as first priority. They respect foreigners' interests and suck up to them."[40] It would not be until the summer of 2018 that Mongolia, with funds from India, launched construction of a refinery in the southern Dornogovi province that will process 1.5 million tons of crude oil per year. Planned for completion in late 2022, it should meet all of the nation's demand for gasoline, diesel, aviation fuel, and liquefied petroleum gas (LPG).[41]

Explosion of Corruption

In the move to a free market economy, one of the major challenges Mongolia has faced is the growth and spread of corrupt practices throughout the government and society.[42] During the communist era corruption generally was disguised by the communist MPRP party and not discussed openly in the official press. This did not mean that the people were unaware of corruption, only that its extent was not clearly evident—at times minimized and at other times exaggerated. However, as the Cold War receded, government leaders became more willing to confront corruption and incompetence within the law enforcement agencies by strengthening the role of the Ministry of Justice, bolstering the independence of prosecutors, and improving training and evaluation of personnel.[43]

In Mongolia's mineral-resource-dependent economy of today, there is a tendency to consider Mongolian corruption as a twenty-first-century phenomenon stemming from foreign investors interested in Mongolian minerals who collude with Mongolian government officials or rich local entrepreneurs. During the 1990s, the lack of foreign donor attention to growing Mongolian corruption may be seen, for example, in the transcript of a three-day conference in September 2000 in Ulaanbaatar sponsored by the Asia Foundation. The topic was "Mongolia's Political and Economic Transition: Challenges and Opportunities,"[44] yet not one of the prominent presenters mentioned the word "corruption." It would seem from reading such materials that corruption was not a problem in the 1990s. However, this is a basic misunderstanding of how corruption and its toleration grew in democratic Mongolia.

With the fall of communism, the foreign donor community sought to reorganize Mongolia's legal regime to eliminate the old communist system and establish judicial procedures in compliance with democratic institutions. In 1990 the public sector in Mongolia accounted for 90 percent of GDP. The constitution of February 12, 1992, consisted of seventy articles that establish Mongolia as a democratic parliamentary republic. Article 46, supplemented by the 1993 Law on Government Service, established the basic tenets of a civil service system through provisions for merit-based hiring and promotion, performance pay, and position classification and grading. However, legislation often was ambiguously worded, so corruption emerged during the conduct of business or the resolution of legal disputes.[45] The most difficult part of the early reform process was trying to inculcate within the police, justice officials, and judges—the vast majority of whom were products of Soviet education—a democratic and rule-of-law mentality. From the beginning years of democratization, complaints surfaced that political interests were interfering in the effective implementation and application of laws and regulations. Government institutions, staffed by Soviet-trained officials, were highly politicized and lacked professional and technical expertise. Individuals within and outside the government usually were motivated by personal survival concerns as the old command economy fell apart and the new private enterprise system fitfully took shape. As a result, the civil service and ministerial appointment systems became openly politicized in the 1990s. Although these systems were reformed several times during the decades of transition, political interests still continue to plague the hiring process up to the present day.

In the early democratic era, hiring and promotion practices were governed by the spoils system. Political appointees were allowed to hold only two positions in each ministry; yet, according to unofficial estimates, as many as 60 percent of all government personnel, including civil service employees, were terminated and replaced after the parliamentary elections of 1996 and 2000, when the party in power changed. Even after the 2004 parliamentary election, when the same party remained in control, turnover was estimated at between 30 to 40 percent. Staff were, and even today are, often chosen on the basis of political patronage, not skill-based capabilities.[46] Mongolians justified their corrupt actions by pointing to the low salaries paid to government officials. This argument had some validity in the early 1990s when public employees received minimal compensation yet were asked to administer massive ODA dollars and state assets redistribution programs. For example, in 1995 judicial salaries ranged from $33 to $51 per month, which were comparable to those of civil servants but lower than lawyers in private practice.[47] Undoubtedly, the presence of ODA and loosely monitored privatization programs provided opportunities for illegal activities such as favoritism, insider trading, and bribery.

The first wave of corruption entered Mongolia in 1991 when the government instituted a sweeping privatization program. The State Privatization Commission (SPC) was established to oversee the privatization of state-owned enterprises, and the Mongolian Stock Exchange (MSE) was established a few months later to issue stock in these assets. The Foreign Investment Law was ratified in July 1993 and the Securities Law in June 1994. A secondary market in equities emerged in 1995.[48] In the privatization program from May 1991 until the end of 1994, mining, energy, transportation, communications, and water supply companies were excluded. The focus was on the promulgation of a color-coded Voucher Privatization Program for privatization of agricultural lands and livestock, small commercial enterprises under $50,000, and large enterprises through purchase of stock market shares.[49] More than 90 percent of the population received the stock vouchers. A total of 4,483 enterprises were sold with fixed assets valued at 21,628 billion Mongolian tugriks (MNT). However, this scheme was ripe for abuse: politically connected people with access to private capital cheaply bought up vouchers from the poor who needed the money for consumables. There was no audit during the first five years of privatization, and, when an audit of foreign loans finally was conducted, the auditors confirmed that at least $10 million was misused and $190 million of the $650 million was missing.[50] There were many complaints about the system not actually redistributing public assets: "330 companies were created. No more than 1,500 individuals, representing 0.5 per cent of the population, own over 70 per cent of the shares of these 330 companies."[51] Many of Mongolia's present-day large companies and very wealthy businessmen owe their start to the clever manipulation of the privatization program. While foreign donors by no means created corruption, the availability of large sums of assistance money and the poor management of these funds by the donors and their recipients greatly accelerated both the amount and sophistication of the corruption.

One of the major findings in the UNDP's Urban Poverty Pilot Project's analysis of international projects and programs for poverty alleviation was their lack of effectiveness. It was found that many of the poor did not know about the existence of the programs or could not access them. Local district groups were organized, but the allocated money disappeared into the capital's ministries never to be distributed. An example was the ADB's $1.5 million in Green Revolution horticultural money disbursed to the Ministry of Agriculture over several years but not dispensed. An additional problem was that the more money donors gave to relieve poverty in Ulaanbaatar, the more poor Mongols drained out of provincial cities into Ulaanbaatar. Some of the agricultural policies implemented by the foreign donor community and the government of Mongolia were wasteful and even failures. UNDP studies concluded that simply restocking herds without improving the quality and marketability of the animals and their byproducts was not a successful, sustainable strategy. The most shocking example of mismanagement of agricultural funds was buried within the ADB's Program Performance Audit of its 1995–1998 $35 million agricultural loan project. There was no actual official explanation of how funds were spent on its five major loans and the ADB administrative costs. The report concealed the depth of the failure by using generalized terms to rate the success of the thirty-one policy measures under ten policy objects. The audit report noted, "The objectives of ensuring the sustainability of the extensive livestock and establishing agricultural extension systems were not achieved," and "reforms to revitalize agricultural financing and to reduce government interventions in the state emergency fodder reserve failed."[52] The entire wheat farming support program, a main focus of spending, failed totally. Hidden in the analysis was the grudging admission that the ADB had never conducted any prior research on the difficulties of growing wheat in the hostile Mongolian climate.

After the fall of communism, Mongolia had quickly developed a free press, and, because corruption could be examined in the media and used by political parties to vilify each other, the corruption issue assumed great importance both domestically and internationally. There is no doubt that the close ties between business and politics resulted in increased corruption and conflicts of interest. Corruption became a significant concern among the populace, and there was a pervasive feeling that there was no political will to improve public sector accountability.[53] Fear of illegal turnovers of government personnel spurred a mind-set of unprofessionalism and a desire to use government positions for quick self-enrichment or to provide jobs for party loyalists. Although the Mongolian government quadrupled official sector wages from 1996 to 2004 to about $80 per month,[54] the tide of corruption was not halted.

Mongolian law provides criminal penalties for official corruption, but the government did not always implement the law effectively or transparently. The Criminal Code proscribes the acceptance of bribes by officials, provides for fines or imprisonment of up to five years, and outlaws offering bribes to government officials. NGOs alleged that prosecution of the official soliciting a bribe and also the person paying it reduced reporting of official bribery. Limited immunity was given to those paying smaller bribes, which NGOs reported did somewhat lessen the problem.[55] Since parliamentarians are immune from prosecution during their tenure and they held most ministerial posts, those accused of corruption often did not go to trial. Another complication was that prosecution of high-level officials was thought to be political retribution.

The United States pressed Mongolia for years to take action against corrupt practices and had its own donated wheat scandal in 1997, which resulted in the sacking of Mongolia's Ministry of Agriculture state secretary in connection with the disappearance of $500,000 from the proceeds raised by the sale of the wheat.[56] In 2005 President George W. Bush and President N. Enkhbayar linked the two nations' comprehensive partnership to Mongolia's commitment to continued political and economic reform, rule of law, good governance, transparency, and public sector accountability, including Mongolia's ratification of the UN Convention Against Transnational Organized Crime. In their official statements they agreed "to enhance their cooperation against all forms of organized, transnational crime, to include trafficking in people, counterfeiting, money-laundering, and terrorist financing."[57] However, the US reputation for transparency suffered in the early 2000s from both the SOCO affair and the development of the giant copper-gold mine Oyu Tolgoi, which will be discussed in Chapter 6.

Despite new anticorruption initiatives introduced in 2002 and 2003 to strengthen ethical standards among civil servants, the corruption problem only intensified with the entrance of Chinese FDI to establish textile enterprises that took advantage of Mongolia's Most Favored Trade status as well as with the practice of selling and reselling mining licenses by government officials to domestic and foreign investors. The press reported that cheap Chinese imports had overwhelmed new enterprises and that the Chinese, at times through Mongolian agents, had bought majority shares in important enterprises on the national stock exchange.[58] Western scholars also criticized Chinese corruption in Mongolia's privatization process, particularly in the second phase dismantlement of large state enterprises during the Democratic Union coalition government (1996–2000).[59] Chinese investors were said to have paid Mongolians to bid for them at privatization auctions and that Chinese enterprises violated health, safety, and labor laws.

Mongols then and now have been quick to blame Chinese companies for the spread of corruption throughout Mongolian society. This is to deny the reality of corruption and favoritism practiced throughout the communist era as well as the role played by the flow of ODA money into government circles in the 1990s. However, it is also an inescapable fact that Chinese businessmen really did illicitly pay bribes to get licenses to acquire many textile businesses and small mining operations in the 1990s and early 2000s, which accelerated the Chinese monopoly over Mongolian trade. This practice, well documented in other countries,[60] laid the groundwork for the large illegal payments to Mongolian officials by Chinese extractive companies such as China Shenhua Energy Company and PetroChina Daqing Tamtsag, LLC (the joint venture that bought out SOCO). At the end of the 1990s, the Chinese publicly promised large investments in mining assets and a Gobi oil refinery in Zuunbayan and to expand rail and road links between the two countries.[61] Many of these promises were never realized because of Mongolian parliamentary reluctance to implement the bilateral agreements negotiated in a nontransparent manner between the two governments.

The Independent Authority Against Corruption (IAAC) is the principal agency responsible for investigating corruption cases in Mongolia. In July 2006 an anticorruption law was ratified that requires all government officials, parliamentarians, and judges to submit yearly income disclosure statements. From 2007 to 2011, the IAAC referred twenty-one cases of corruption to the General Prosecutor's Office for prosecution and investigated an additional fifty cases. Although there have been questions about the IAAC's political impartiality, the Mongolian public has been supportive of its activities. However, the domestic political scene was roiled by a successful IAAC-initiated corruption-related prosecution of former Mongolian President N. Enkhbayar in 2012. While in a prison hospital awaiting his court appearance, Enkhbayar began a hunger strike, and his severe loss of weight came to the attention of the international community. Amnesty International demanded Mongolian authorities respect his human rights,[62] and UN Secretary-General Ban Ki Moon phoned Mongolian President Tsakhia Elbegdorj to express concern. Enkhbayar eventually was convicted of corruption, sentenced to seven years' imprisonment (three were suspended), and fined for misuse of state properties and of government power.[63] On January 19, 2013, Mongolia's Parliament passed the Law on Preventing Conflict of Interest in Public Service aimed at curbing illegal foreign investment in the mining sector. This law introduced new standards and requirements for public officials, increased transparency and accountability, and created a legal basis for managing and restricting public officials' private interests that conflict with official duties. Anticorruption reformers in Parliament had advocated since 2010 for this legislation as a way to bring Mongolia into further compliance with the United Nations Convention Against Corruption (UNCAC).[64]

Casinos

One idea that captured the imagination of Mongolians was developing casinos as a major revenue generator that would attract gamblers from abroad.

In 1998 a German-Malaysian joint venture casino was opened in Ulaanbaatar's most modern hotel, but by January 1999 the parliament passed legislation banning casinos to prevent corruption and crime. Only a few months later in August, the casino was shut down by the democratic coalition government, which then gave the gambling rights to a Macao-based company. The German group complained that large bribes had been paid by the new company and that money laundering was the purpose for the change of ownership. Later that year, rumors linked this casino deal with the October 2, 1999, death of Mongolian democratic revolution leader S. Zorig.[65] The casino did not reopen, and three Democratic Coalition parliamentarians were eventually jailed for accepting bribes.[66]

The Mongols tried again to open a casino in 2006—timed to mark the 800th anniversary of the Mongolian nation's coronation of Chinggis Khaan. The government of President Enkhbayar awarded in a nontransparent fashion a contract to develop the Zamyn-Uud free economic zone (FEZ) at the Mongolian-Chinese border to a British Virgin Islands–registered company called Western Paradise Co., promising tax breaks and other incentives. Under intense domestic criticism, that deal collapsed. In another compromised bidding process, the government then signed a contract with a mysterious US real estate company with South Korean ties, Winwheel Bullion, LLC, which was registered in Mount Vernon, Missouri,[67] to build the FEZ with a casino complex. Located 563 kilometers northwest of Beijing and across from the Chinese city of Erlian (population 100,000), the Zamyn-Uud FEZ was a development concept at the south border terminus of the Ulaanbaatar Railroad. At that time, approximately 70 percent of Mongolian foreign trade passed through the border town of Zamyn-Uud. The Mongols agreed to provide 104,000 acres of land for a master-planned commercial center. Beginning in the summer of 2006, Winwheel Bullion promised in phase one to develop 2,224 acres with construction of an international airport, hotels, casino, shopping complexes, banks, industrial complexes, sports stadium, theme park, and golf courses. In addition, residential and community infrastructure plans included housing, hospitals, public parks, and a retirement community.[68] The success of the plan depended on attracting visitors, particularly gamblers, from China, which bans casino gambling on its territory except in Macao.

Minister of Industry and Trade B. Jargalsaikhan, governor of the Central Bank of Mongolia O. Chuluunbat, and Minister of Finance N. Bayartsaikhan jointly announced the new plan. Winwheel and the Mongolian side called the contract an important milestone for Mongolia's transition to a free market economy, but the contract had been awarded without a transparent bid and with only vague information about financial arrangements.[69] According to a 2004 USAID report, Zamyn-Uud, population 8,400 plus over 10,000 head of livestock, suffers from a severe lack of water. Winwheel's planners claimed to have found underground water to overcome the scarcity and asserted that they were working with partners to build up the town's electricity supply. The USAID report strongly recommended postponing plans until after feasibility studies were completed. It did agree that the Zamyn-Uud FEZ could "piggyback" on Erlian's prosperity as well as benefit from any pan-Asian highway system and modern telecommunications connections linked to the cross-border railway. In the end, the whole casino proposal was disavowed by the Mongolian government out of concern about bribery from the foreign investment company, so the casino concept has remained dormant for ten years.

After casinos were banned, a law was passed that allowed gambling machines in the country, but a massive influx of slot machines resulted in many Mongols' losing everything due to gambling addiction. Eventually, all these gaming centers also were shut down. Horse racing on a professional race course is another idea that has surfaced from time to time in Mongolia. In 2014 it was reported that a consortium from Kentucky was promoting a plan to develop a horse racing track near the site of the new Khushigt International Airport, fifty-four kilometers south of the capital. Fifty horse trainers from Mongolia were scheduled to visit Hong Kong to study the business. However, the necessary laws to legalize online gambling and lotteries and a second law to allow betting on horses and setting up jockey clubs did not receive parliamentary approval.[70]

The casino concept reemerged in 2015 at a time when Mongolia's economy was spiraling downward. At the outset, the project was intended to attract approximately $500 million in FDI to the country. Two casinos, privately owned and operated, were approved by the cabinet. While the exact locations were not specified, the press speculated that one would be sited in Zamyn-Uud on the Chinese border and the other at the new airport. The target tourist market was Chinese, Japanese, and Russian gamblers, since Mongolian citizens were forbidden to play.[71] Each license fee was pegged at 35 billion MNT (approximately $14 million), and there were estimates that the casinos would generate $124 million in revenue.[72] In a February 11, 2016, cabinet meeting, the ministers voted to repeal the 1999 parliamentary ban on casinos in order to increase financial resources for the state and enhance tourism. As the casino bill languished in Parliament, the government decided to link the project to its national lottery, which had been operated since 2011 by the Singapore-based Monvest Group, led by controversial investor Nixon Yap.[73]

The government concluded an agreement in July 2016 with an Australian company, Frontier Capital Group Ltd., to take over operating the Mongolian National Lottery as a stepping-stone toward exercising its right to develop a casino.[74] Completion of the deal was targeted for March 2016, but Frontier Capital later terminated the agreement.[75] Gambling, particularly casinos, remains very controversial in Mongolia because it represents more than just corruption: "Mongolia is a small country with two neighbors facing money laundering, drug trafficking, and other challenges, so we need to be careful about opening casinos. If illegal activities such as money laundering and drug trafficking begin sprouting up in a small country with a population of only three million people, it will threaten our national security."[76] In addition to the connection of casinos to money laundering, drug trafficking, and other illegal enterprises, they represent for Mongols a fear of foreigners, especially Chinese and Russians, engaging in illegal operations, which is why repeated efforts to establish casinos have so far failed.

Conclusion

Mongolia ratified a Law on Foreign Investment in 1990 and revised it in 1993. Nevertheless, due to being landlocked and having poor infrastructure connectivity, it was not able to generate much FDI, and so Mongolia remained dependent on foreign donor assistance during its first decade of democracy. Although a new mining law in 1996 did stimulate some investment interest in oil exploration and gold mining, it attracted mainly Chinese investors. With the breakup of the Soviet Union and the collapse of its economy, Russian ability to maintain economic ties with Mongolia in the 1990s dramatically decreased. It was not unexpected that China, compared to "Third Neighbor" country investors, had unmatched advantages in the Mongolian market because of proximity, complementarity, and familiarity.[77] A 1993 survey revealed that many ordinary Mongols, particularly small businessmen, feared a Chinese takeover of the country. As the first democratic decade proceeded, new liberal legislation designed to create a favorable FDI environment disproportionately benefited China. In the 1990s, Chinese FDI in Mongolia stood at $66.5 million.[78] This investment was centered around construction, restaurants, fast food, and retail sales via small-scale private investors. When Mongolia entered the Free Trade Organization (FTO) and acquired US free trade status, Chinese FDI moved strongly into Mongolian textile and animal hair enterprises in order to circumvent US quotas imposed on Chinese-made products. In the early 2000s, when these US quotas against China were lifted, FDI in textiles quickly disappeared. The next phase of Chinese FDI, in the form of a large infusion of funds from Chinese SOEs, came when Mongolia opened up its mineral sector in the twenty-first century and China granted soft loans totaling $300 million in 2003 for twenty years at an interest rate of 2 percent.

Mongolian researchers and the media have identified several significant factors to explain Chinese FDI monopolization during the transition period: (1) Most small Chinese investors used their business registration to obtain long-term residence permits rather than to invest in business activities. (2) The low required amount of initial capital to register (1 million tugrik, or less than $100) made joint venture registration easy with no monitoring of actual engagement in that activity. (3) Most Chinese enterprises were small-scale and technologically inferior and involved in acquiring raw materials to export back to China for processing rather than adding value to the exports by developing Mongolian processing centers.[79]

Notes

1. Marshal Choibalsan quoted in *Area Handbook for Mongolia* (Washington, DC: Foreign Area Studies, 1970), 339–340.

2. Mongolian independence was recognized by the ROC on October 3, 2002, by the ROC Ministry of Foreign Affairs. Although it excluded Mongolia from the definition of the "mainland area" for administrative purposes and in 2006 repealed old laws regulating Outer Mongolia, there has not yet been a vote by the National Assembly (as required by the constitution) or via a referendum to eliminate Outer Mongolia from the legal definition of the country. The official status of recognition is currently ambiguous, although economic relations continue to expand.

3. Between the East and West and then between the USSR and PRC. See Luvsan-gombo Molomjamts's foreword in Alicia Campi, *Modern Mongolia-Chinese Strategic Relations Challenges for the New Century*, Regional Security Issues and Mongolia, no. 21 (Ulaanbaatar: Institute for Strategic Studies, 2004), 5.

4. Tsedendamba Batbayar, "Mongolian Perspectives on Northeast Asian Regional Development," in *Politics and Economics in Northeast Asia*, ed. Tsuneo Akaha (New York: St. Martin's Press, 1999), 208–209.

5. Ts. Batbayar, "The Development of Mongolia's External Relations in the 1990s," in *Renovation of Mongolia on the Eve of the XXI Century and Future Development Patterns*, edited by Ts. Batbayar (Ulaanbaatar: Mongolian Development Research Center, 2000), 79.

6. *Montsame,* October 7, 2002.

7. "China-Mongolia Relations," *China Daily*, May 27, 2010, http://www.chinadaily.com.cn/china/2010wentour/2010-05/27/content_9899648.htm.

8. *Montsame,* October 3, 2002.

9. N. Altantsetseg, "Russian-Mongolian and Sino-Mongolia Relations Since the Nineties," in *The Geopolitical Relations Between Contemporary Mongolia and Neighboring Asian Countries: Democracy, Economy and Security* (Taipei: Mongolian and Tibetan Affairs, 2003), 381.

10. In 2004 the National Development and Reform Commission and the Export-Import Bank of China released a statement to encourage overseas investment (and mergers and acquisitions) in specific areas such as resource exploration. See UNCTAD, *World Investment Report 2006: FDI from Developing and Transition Economies: Implications for Development* (New York: UN Conference on Trade and Development, 2006), chap. 6, http://unctad.org/en/Docs/wir2006_en.pdf.

11. Sumio Kuribayashi, "Structural Change and Economic Performance in Mongolia," in *The Geopolitical Relations Between Contemporary Mongolia and Neighboring Asian Countries: Democracy, Economy and Security* (Taipei: Mongolian and Tibetan Affairs, 2003), 79, Table 21.

12. "China-Mongolia Relations."

13. Rossabi, *Modern Mongolia,* 93.

14. L. Erdenechuluun, "The Principal Document of the Friendly Relations" (Ulaanbaatar: Ministry of Foreign Affairs, 2003), 10.

15. *Montsame,* September 19, 2002.

16. Altantsetseg, "Russian-Mongolian and Sino-Mongolia Relations," 374–375.

17. P. Stobdan, "India and Mongolia: Modi on Ashoka's Path," *IDSA Comment*, Institute for Defence Studies and Analyses, May 13, 2015, http://www.idsa.in/idsacomments/IndiaandMongolia_pstobdan_130515.

18. IMF, *Mongolia Selected Issues and Statistical Appendix* (Washington, DC: International Monetary Fund, September 7, 2005), 31.

19. Out of about 100 companies in the noncashmere garment sector, almost all of them were foreign investors mainly from China (37 percent) and South Korea (19 percent) to take advantage of the absence of US quota restrictions.

20. James Brooke, "Down and Almost Out in Mongolia," *New York Times,* December 29, 2004, http://www.nytimes.com/2004/12/29/business/worldbusiness/down-and-almost-out-in-mongolia.html?_r=0.

21. Categories affected by the quota removal—mainly cotton shirts, blouses, and trousers—are 70 percent of the output.

22. For June 5, 1997, text in English, see faolex.fao.org/docs/texts/mon37842.doc.

23. Dorjdari Namkhaijantsan, "EITI in Mongolia 2006–2011: Lessons and Prospects" (PowerPoint presentation for seminar on promoting EITI in Tajikistan, Dushanbe, July 12, 2011), 6–7, http://siteresources.worldbank.org/EXTEXTINDTRAINI/Resources/3634714-1315498215486/Mongolia.pdf.

24. "Mongolian and Chinese Joint Communique" (Ulaanbaatar: Ministry of Foreign Affairs, 1999), 6.

25. Rossabi, *Modern Mongolia,* 231.

26. The Petroleum Law of Mongolia was adopted on January 18, 1991. The PAM's functions include Contracts and Exploration Division: in charge of organizing international biddings and concluding PSCs; Joint Exploration Agreements: all contracts; Exploitation and Production Division: monitoring and supervision of exploitation, development, production, and transportation of oil; Finance and Investment Division: all financial matters of PAM, auditing investment and cost accounting of investors in the oil industry; Supply Coordination Division: ensuring stable and reliable supply of petroleum products; Refining and Technology Division: providing recommendations for the construction of refineries. See "Oil in Mongolia," https://www.petromatadgroup.com/mongolia/oil-in-mongolia/.

27. Ibid.

28. According to his official biography listed by SOCO, Ed Story was one of the founding directors of SOCO International and serves as president and chief executive officer. He has over forty-five years' experience in the oil and gas industry, beginning with Exxon Corporation, where he held various positions, including seven years resident in the Far East. He was formerly the vice president and chief financial officer of Superior Oil Company, a cofounder and vice chairman of Conquest Exploration Company, and a cofounder and president of Snyder Oil Corporation's international subsidiary, which merged its controlled holdings into Cairn Energy, thereby creating the leading South Asian oil and gas company in the UK independent sector. "Board of Directors," https://www.socointernational.com/board-of-directors.

29. "Preliminary Results for the Year Ended 31 December 2003," SOCO International, March 11, 2004, https://www.socointernational.com/news_33.

30. John C. Wu, "The Mineral Industry of Mongolia," US Geological Survey, July 30, 2010, 2, https://minerals.usgs.gov/minerals/pubs/country/1995/9319095.pdf.

31. Byambasüren quoted in Bayarsaikhan Dulguun, "Former PM Speaks About Mongolia's Financial Woes and Forgotten Promises of Politicians," *UB Post,* November 21, 2016.

32. "Preliminary Results."

33. Richard L. Armitage, "Contract Signing Ceremony between SOCO International and the Petroleum Authority of Mongolia," US Department of State Archive, January 31, 2004, http://2001-2009.state.gov/s/d/former/armitage/remarks/29141.htm.

34. "Sale of Mongolian Assets," SOCO International, April 1, 2005, https://www.socointernational.com/news_24.

35. *New Straits Times*, Kuala Lumpur, February 27, 1997.

36. Speaker of Parliament Enkhbold quoted in english.news.mn, April 8, 2013.

37. "Oil in Mongolia."

38. Mining Minister Davaajav Gankhuyag commented, "In order to get rid of petroleum supply from one route (Russia), we are negotiating with third parties that brings some positive results." According to interview with Chairman of Petroleum Authority G. Ulziiburen, "Mongolia and China to Sign Oil for Petroleum Deal," *Montsame,* March 19, 2013, http://covermongolia.blogspot.com/2013/03/southgobi-restarting-production.html.

39. en.mongolianminingjournal.com, October 8, 2009, accessed May 9, 2013.

40. See Dulguun, "Former PM Speaks."

41. "Mongolia Launches Construction of First Oil Refinery with Indian Aid," Reuters, June 22, 2018, https://www.reuters.com/article/mongolia-refinery/mongolia-launches-construction-of-first-oil-refinery-with-indian-aid-idUSL4N1TO1TO.

42. For books in the Mongolian language that analyze corruption, see Zagdin Batsukh, *Khergiin Gazraas Survaljilsan Temdeglel* [The struggle to identify criminal sites] (Ulaanbaatar: Mongolian Police, 2006); Abilgal, *Monkhuun Uzegdel bish* [Bribery: No perception of money] (Ulaanbaatar, 2002).

43. *Mongolia: A Country Study*, 259.

44. The Asia Foundation Conference on Mongolia's Political and Economic Transition: Challenges and Opportunities, Ulaanbaatar, September 11–13, 2000, https://asiafoundation.org/resources/pdfs/MongloiaPolEconTransition.pdf.

45. Michael Aldrich, *The Report: Mongolia 2012* (London: Oxford Business Group, 2012), 236.

46. USAID and Asia Foundation, *Assessment of Corruption in Mongolia: Final Report* (Alexandria, VA: Casals and Associates, August 31, 2005), 12, http://pdf.usaid.gov/pdf_docs/Pnade136.pdf.

47. Cited in Jon S. T. Quah, *Curbing Corruption in Asian Countries: An Impossible Dream?,* Research in Public Policy Analysis and Management, vol. 20 (Bingley, UK: Emerald Group, 2011), chap. 11, 397–438.

48. Maya Och, "Privatization of SOE in Mongolia" (slide presentation, December 6, 2012).

49. For a detailed explanation of the plan, which was highly supported by foreign donors such as the United States and the World Bank, see Cevdet Denizer and Alan Gelb, "Mongolia—Privatization and System Transformation in an Isolated Economy" (Working Paper no. 1063, World Bank, Country Economics Department, December 1992), https://www.researchgate.net/publication/23721596_Mongolia_-_Privatization_and_system_transformation_ in_an_isolated_economy.

50. Rossabi, *Modern Mongolia,* 91–92.

51. Sanjaasurengiin Oyun, "From the Year," quoted in ibid., 51.

52. Since financial data were nonexistent, it was impossible to verify if a specific program really was "successful" or "partly successful," or the extent of any "failure." ADB, "Executive Summary" [Program Performance Audit of its 1995–1998 $35 million agricultural loan project], *Audit Report* (2002), 1.

53. Danaasuren, "NGOs as Accountability Promoters", 16, http://apira2010.econ.usyd.edu.au/conference_proceedings/APIRA-2010-166-vanDanGombo-NGOS-as-accountability-promoters-Mongolia.pdf.

54. This was a rate comparable to those in other transitional democracies. Och, "Privatization of SOE in Mongolia," 13.

55. US Department of State, *Mongolia 2013 Human Rights Report* (Washington DC: 2013), 16. https://www.state.gov/documents/organization/220425.pdf.

56. Richard Pomfret, "Transition and Democracy in Mongolia" (CIES Discussion Paper 99/07, Adelaide, Australia, April 1999), 9n16.

57. "Joint Statement Between Mongolia and the United States of America," White House, Office of the Press Secretary, November 21, 2005, https://georgewbush-whitehouse.archives.gov/news/releases/2005/11/20051121-1.html.

58. Rossabi, *Modern Mongolia*, 231.

59. A prominent critic of the Mongolian privatization process is Morris Rossabi. See Rossabi, *Modern Mongolia*, chap. 4.

60. More than 900 Chinese companies have disclosed a combined total of over $600 billion in illegal payments. "Transparency Matters: Disclosure Payments to Governments by Chinese Extractive Companies," Global Witness, January 15, 2013, https://www.globalwitness.org/en/archive/transparencymatters/.

61. *UB Post,* December 15, 1998; *Mongol Messenger,* December 16, 1998.

62. "Mongolian Authorities Must Respect the Human Rights of Former Mongolian President Following His Arrest," Amnesty International, May 2012, www.amnesty.mn/en/aim-news/amnesty-international-public-statement.

63. He actually spent less than a month in prison and the remainder as a patient in a hospital, until given a presidential pardon one year later.

64. Josh Friedman, "Mongolia Marks Passage."

65. This death is still unsolved. See Conor O'Clery, *May You Live in Interesting Times* (Dublin: Poolbeg Press, 2017), 26; Jennifer L. Hanson, *Nations in Transition: Mongolia* (New York: Facts on File, 2003), 47.

66. "World: Asia-Pacific Mongolian MPs Face Corruption Probe," BBC News, April 12, 1999, http://news.bbc.co.uk/2/hi/asia-pacific/317344.stm.

67. Some years later, Bloomberg reported that this company was founded in 1999 and was headquartered in Newport Beach, California. http://www.bloomberg.com/research/stocks/private/snapshot.asp?privcapId=43967454.

68. "Casino Resort Part of Mongolia Project," Cash at Casinos, April 29, 2006, http://www.cashatcasinos.com/casino_news/3863.php.

69. Investment in the construction of storage facilities, cargo terminals, and hotels in Zamyn-Uud was to be exempt from income tax for an initial five-year term, then granted a 50 percent income tax concession for three subsequent years.

70. Michael Kohn, "Mongolia to Allow Gambling on Horse Races to Tap China," *Financial Review,* April 14, 2014, http://www.afr.com/business/mongolia-to-allow-gambling-on-horse-races-to-tap-china-20140430-ik4a2#ixzz4ZBmpfyzL.

71. Peter Amsel, "Mongolia Casinos to Target Chinese, Russian and Japanese Gamblers," CalvinAyre.com, February 18, 2015.

72. "Mongolia to Approve Draft Law on Casino," business-mongolia.com, February 24, 2015.

73. Led by Malaysian entrepreneur Dr. Nixon Yap, who operated a diversified business empire from Malaysia with holdings across Mainland China, Southeast Asia, and North America. His investments included film studios, agar wood plantations, lottery companies, mining rights, and event organizing. Monvest was deregistered in August 2016.

74. Martin John Williams, "Australian Miner Set to Run Mongolia's Lottery," GamblingCompliance, July 15, 2015, https://gamblingcompliance.com/premium-content/insights_analysis/australian-miner-set-run-mongolia%E2%80%99s-lottery.

75. "Frontier Capital Drops Deal for Lottery Licence in Mongolia," GGRAsia, February 23, 2016.

76. Bayarbat Turmunkh, "Are Casinos the Right Path to Riches?," *UB Post,* November 23, 2016.

77. See a discussion of this by Lincoln Kaye, "Two Mongolias: Faltering Steppes," *Far Eastern Economic Review,* April 9, 1992, 16.

78. Mongolian Ministry of External Relations, *Foreign Policy Blue Book* (Ulaanbaatar: Admon, 2000), 26.

79. Batbayar, "Development of Mongolia's External Relations," 143.

6

Mineral Development: Blessing and Curse

In 2002 Mongolia derived 20 percent of GDP from agriculture/herding, 21 percent from industry, and 58 percent from services. In 2003 Mongolian per capita GDP was $1,800, and the Mongolian population below the poverty line was estimated in UNDP studies to be 36 percent, unchanged for five years. However, there was improvement in employment numbers with the national unemployment rate pegged at 4.6 percent in 2001, although many questioned its accuracy.[1] In 2002–2003, FDI increased due to Canadian investment in gold and copper mines and to Chinese investment in mines, construction, and textiles. The Mongolian countryside was dotted with 30,000 "ninjas"[2] or unauthorized small miners digging or sifting for gold for less than $10 a week. By 2007 ninja numbers would increase to 100,000. However, Western experts believed that the Mongols could not attract the necessary FDI to develop the country's large mineral deposits unless Mongolia's lingering Soviet-era debt to Russia was resolved. The failure to settle this issue had frozen Western companies' access to major capital for a decade because Mongolia's international credit rating in fact was nonexistent.

Mongolia sought an international rating from Moody's to strengthen its long-term strategy of integrating its economy into the global economic and financial system. In this atmosphere, the Mongolian government reached out to former US Secretary of State James A. Baker III, then residing in Houston, for assistance. The story of Mongolia's old Soviet debt and its relationship to the development of Mongolia's South Gobi Oyu Tolgoi (OT) mine, the world's largest copper-gold-silver deposit, is complex, convoluted, and plagued with a history of nontransparency, high-level corruption, and environmental and domestic political controversy. This relationship is behind the continuing problems in Mongolia's mineral sector today.

Solving Mongolia's Soviet Debt

In 1990 the USSR received 78.3 percent of Mongolia's exports, and 77.5 percent of Mongolia's imports came from its northern neighbor. The Soviet Union in 1990 accounted for 77.9 percent of its total trade. That same year, the PRC trade turnover with Mongolia represented only 2.1 percent, with only 1.7 percent of Mongolian exports going to China and only 2.4 percent of its goods imported from China.[3] By 1998, 40 percent of Mongolia's imports were Russian, but only 10 percent of its exports were bound for Russia because of high customs and transit transportation tariffs and lack of solvent Russian partners. Although Mongolian-Russian trade rebounded to $267.7 million in 2002, a 12.4 percent increase over 2001, the trade volume was not comparable to the communist-era level. Mongolian exports to Russia represented only 10.3 percent, and imports from Russia stood at 36.4 percent.[4] There also was a scandal in the Democratic Union government involving then Mongolian Prime Minister Janlav Narantsatsralt, who attempted to sell Mongolia's share of the Erdenet copper venture to a Russian private company for less than a quarter of a million dollars. This scheme was discovered by the Mongolian Parliament, and he was compelled to resign in 1999.[5]

Mongolian debt to Russia had become a major issue between the two countries in the 1990s as bankrupt Russia gradually retreated from the Mongolian market. What was the nature of that debt? It was the accumulated massive credits that the Soviets provided over the preceding decades—in increasing amounts in the 1980s—that financed nearly everything in Mongolia from budget deficits and trade deficits to infrastructure, construction, and rural government facilities. These credits equaled more than 30 percent of GDP in the last years of communism. Mongolian industry had been part of the economic trading bloc system administered under the Soviet Union's Council for Mutual Economic Assistance, known as COMECON. Under its network and rules, factories obtained imports at below world market prices and had guaranteed markets for their goods. With the Soviet Union's fall, this market system for Mongolia and other partner countries collapsed, but the debt remained unpaid.[6]

Russian President Vladimir Putin made a state visit to Mongolia November 13–14, 2000, the first such visit in twenty-six years. In the resulting "Ulaanbaatar Declaration," the issue of Mongolia's debt to Russia (the successor to the USSR) was raised without resolution. The Russians claimed that, in addition to the 600 million ruble investment the Soviets had made in the Erdenet copper enterprise, they had given the Mongols 6 billion rubles in soft loans for capital investment, 670 million rubles in nonrepayable aid, and over 2 billion rubles in loans for trade deficits. Mongolia was third on the list of Russia's debtors, behind Cuba and Syria, and its debt equated to roughly $4,800 for each of Mongolia's 2.4 million inhabitants, which represented over ten times Mongolia's GDP in 2002.[7] With such a huge outstanding debt, Mongolia could not qualify for a viable debt rating from the international agencies assisting major foreign investors and thus could not obtain sufficient capital funds for investment to develop its large mineral deposits or for other costly infrastructure projects. During the 1990s, Mongolia could not find a way to break out of its donor-assistance-dependent economy because it could not relieve the debt burden.

Progress was made on resolving the debt issue during the June 2003 official visit to Moscow of Mongolian Prime Minister Enkhbayar. At the same time, Secretary of State James Baker was in Moscow to give a speech on the importance of Russian-US relations. Baker, who had an illustrious government career as White House chief of staff (1981–1984) and secretary of the treasury (1985–1988) under President Ronald Reagan, and as secretary of state (1989–1992) and White House chief of staff (1992–1993) under President George H. W. Bush, had numerous high-level contacts with many world leaders, including Russian President Putin. Baker was also a Texas lawyer with a background in representing oil and energy companies. During the Clinton presidency (1992–2000), he returned to legal practice at Baker Botts, which had several high-placed Russian mineral and oil clients. In the early 1990s he became an equity partner and senior counselor in the merchant bank Carlyle Group,[8] which had launched Carlyle Asia Partners in 1999, Carlyle's first Asian buyout fund, which generated returns of four times the invested capital. Some press then reported that Baker's own financial stake at Carlyle had grown to $180 million.[9]

During his June 2003 Moscow visit, the Mongolian leadership sought Baker's assistance to broker a nontransparent deal between Mongolian Prime Minister Enkhbayar and President Putin to reduce the Mongolian debt total from $10 billion to $3.5 billion (using the formula of the old Soviet ruble exchange for the dollar). This was a creative way for the Mongols to pay off the Soviet-era debt, which then would allow Mongolia to receive an international credit rating. On the last day of 2003, the Mongols announced that 98 percent of the debt would be considered as an investment and the remaining 2 percent, or at least $250 million, would be repaid by the Mongolian government to Russia—an amount that still represented a quarter of Mongolia's GDP.[10] This payment, to be raised from a government bond sale, appeared to finally settle the 1947–1991 "big debt" of 11.4 billion transferable rubles ($10 billion).

A few weeks later Russian Minister of Foreign Affairs Igor Ivanov flew to Ulaanbaatar to complete the write-off arrangements. He explained that "Russia views Mongolia as one of its main partners in Asia."[11] Noting that this would be the biggest write-off of debt in Russian history, if not in world history, the Russian media reported that the Mongols in exchange would green-light the final transfer of former Soviet shares in its biggest enterprises (including Erdenet) to Russia. All of this debt forgiveness was particularly curious since Russia's own external debt at the beginning of 2004 stood at $185.7 billion.[12] Concurrently, it was announced that a Canadian exploration mining company based in Singapore, Ivanhoe Mines Ltd., whose chief legal counsel was Baker's son, James A. Baker IV,[13] had bought $50 million worth of government debt from Mongolia and received in exchange 100 percent control over the OT copper and gold deposit. Ivanhoe had been operating in OT in a small capacity since 2000, when it paid $5 million to mining giant BHP Billiton PLC to buy the original Mongolian exploration licenses.[14] The fact that Mongolian authorities were not willing to provide details about the monetary arrangements of the debt resolution and any possible connection to Ivanhoe's license to exploit the OT deposit was attacked by some opposition parties, and the suspicious media connected the license to the payment of bribes.[15] Stories circulated that Prime Minister Enkhbayar and President Putin had each received $50 million to buy their cooperation and that Ivanhoe had hired James Baker IV as its lawyer as part of the compensation package to his father.[16] Mongolian sources reported in the local press and in foreign publications such as *Asian Survey* that Mongolia had paid $250 million in cash from its foreign reserves and issued dollar-denominated treasury bills in a deal whose terms were not disclosed.[17] Beyond the political opposition's doubts about the whole matter, there were questions as to whether or not there was in fact any real Soviet-era debt at all, and if it should be repaid: "G. Purevbaatar argued that there was no debt to be settled between Mongolia and Russia and, that if there was, it should have been annulled when the Soviet Union collapsed."[18]

Another report circulated that when Prime Minister Enkhbayar negotiated the debt with the Russians, he was told that Mongolia should put this money into the Mongolian-Russian joint venture Mongolrostsvetmet as part of its capital. Enkhbayar said a decision on the issue would be made later but, when he returned to Mongolia, he never mentioned this proposal publicly. Rather, Enkhbayar asserted that he had persuaded Russia to waive all debt, a claim that likely helped him win the 2005 presidential election. During his four years in office, Enkhbayar never raised this debt issue.[19] In July 2004 a report on the 2003 Russian debt settlement was released by Mongolia's parliamentary review committee. This document declared the matter of Mongolia's pre-1991 Soviet debt to Russia was settled, despite the fact that many questions remained about the agreement's undisclosed details. Secretary Baker's reputation in Mongolia at that time was impacted positively, since he was considered to be the friend of the Mongols who had found a way to resolve the Soviet debt issue, which allowed Mongolia to get an international credit rating. Mongolian policymakers recognized that President George W. Bush had great confidence in Baker, given that in December 2003 he had appointed Baker as his special Iraq envoy to discuss with creditor nations the restructuring of $100 billion in Saddam Hussein's international debts.[20]

The clearest advantage to Mongolia's write-off seemed to be a balancing of massive incoming Chinese FDI with a further strengthening of Mongolia's economic ties with Russia, which was a goal of the Enkhbayar government that was popular among the people. No one could have predicted how Ivanhoe's practices would incur the enmity of successive Mongolian governments and average citizens over the next years, or how this maneuver to solve the debt crisis would have so many negative ramifications, including severely wounding the reputation of James Baker and, by extension, the US government. On October 4, 2005, Moody's "assigned to the government of Mongolia a B1 foreign-currency country ceiling for bonds and notes and assigned the same rating for the government's foreign-currency debt and local-currency debt" with a projection for a stable outlook. These first-ever ratings reflected "the country's containment of relatively high but concessional external debt." The rating agency acknowledged that Mongolia had been able to attract a steady inflow of FDI into the mining and banking sectors while offsetting current account deficits and strengthening the balance of payments.[21] Moody's mentioned other positive factors that went into this strong rating, including a relatively sound legal system and a generally competitive investment regime, and particularly continued improvement in the development of Mongolia's dynamic mining industry. It hedged its prediction by recognizing the fragility of Mongolia's financial system and capital markets and tying the country's economic performance to the favorable external factors of strong Chinese economic growth, high world copper and gold prices, and improvement in Mongolia's balance of payments. This credit rating stimulated new interest by foreign investors in Mongolian minerals, leading to a flood of FDI in this sector.

Ivanhoe and Oyu Tolgoi

All eyes then turned with expectation to see how Ivanhoe would develop the huge reserves in Oyu Tolgoi. A 46,000-square-mile deposit within Khanbogd *sum* in the south Gobi, approximately 235 kilometers east of the Ömnögovi provincial capital Dalanzadgad, OT had been discovered in 2001, based on old Soviet studies dating from the 1940s. Ivanhoe Mines issued its first press statement on July 17, 2001, announcing the discovery of "potentially significant gold, copper and molybdenum mineralization" at OT and asserting that the site ultimately would become one of the world's top three copper-gold mines.[22] Ivanhoe claimed the reserve contained an estimated 40.6 billion pounds of copper and 20.9 million ounces of gold, with an additional inferred resource of 40.6 billion pounds of copper and 25.3 million ounces of gold. By 1994 Ivanhoe's chairman, Robert M. Friedland, an American mining executive known as Toxic Bob[23] because of environmental problems in his Colorado mining project, had dozens of mining exploratory licenses in Mongolia and claimed to have invested more than $60 million in its Mongolian OT and other Gobi operations.[24] Asserting that its investment would help the Mongolian economy by generating 117,000 jobs and paying 46 percent of its pretax profits, or $7 billion, to the state over the contract's thirty-five-year term, Ivanhoe raised Mongolian expectations of huge, quick profits to unsustainable levels.

By 2005 Friedland had staked a huge claim, larger than Greece, in the Gobi Desert. His flamboyant sales campaign that proclaimed that OT could be worth more than $100 billion and his openly contemptuous behavior toward the Mongols in all negotiations soon earned him a very negative reputation in the Mongol media. An example of his dismissive attitude was evident when he told an investor conference about his Mongolian venture: "So we're coming in from outer space and landing at Oyu Tolgoi. . . . And the nice thing about this: there's no people around; the land is flat, there's no tropical jungle; there's no NGOs. We're only 70 km from the Chinese border. It does not snow here. You've got lots of room for waste dumps."[25] Additionally, Ivanhoe's environmental policies did much to galvanize the anti-mining movement inside Mongolia. It was accused of practices at OT that were harmful to the sparse water and grass needed by the herds of the surrounding nomads. These practices were condemned in the media by Mongolian politicians, particularly from the democratic parties, as they repeatedly clashed with the ruling MPRP government on how to develop the country's mineral resources.

The government revised Mongolia's Mineral Law, adopted in 1997 and amended in 2001, in response to domestic pressure that stemmed from the fallout of the OT deal. The proposed amendments increased the minerals royalty to 5 percent from 2.5 percent, increased license fees, reduced tax incentives for mining, and changed the terms and conditions for exploration and resource licenses.[26] One of the main new proposals that was very controversial among the foreign investors required up to 50 percent government ownership of "strategically significant" resources, such as coal, copper, gold, lead, silver, uranium, and zinc, if the exploration was jointly funded in the past by the Mongolian government and private investors, and up to 34 percent if the funds were only from foreign investors. (See Table 6.1 and Figure 6.1.) These amendments were in response to local government pressure to aid domestic companies and to stimulate quicker production and more responsible environmental mining policies.[27]

Under the shadow of the new Mineral Law debate, the Mongols and Ivanhoe began negotiations over a stability agreement for OT's development. The discussions were protracted and difficult with local Gobi leaders' publicly disagreeing with both Ivanhoe and Mongolian central government authorities led by President Enkhbayar and Prime Minister M. Enkhbold. Ivanhoe, angry about the Mineral Law provisions that would deny it 100 percent control over OT, framed the dispute as an effort to maintain a pos-

Table 6.1 Mongolia's Strategic Mineral Deposits

Deposit Name	Mineral Type	Location/Province
1. Tavan Tolgoi	Hard coal	Omnogobi
2. Nariin-Sukhait	Coal	Omnogobi
3. Baganuur	Brown coal	Ulaanbaatar City
4. Shivee Ovoo	Brown coal	Gobisumber
5. Mardai	Uranium	Dornod
6. Dornod	Uranium	Dornod
7. Gurvan Bulag	Uranium	Dornod
8. Tumertei	Iron ore	Selenge
9. Oyu Tolgoi	Copper, molybdenum, gold	Omnogobi
10. Tsagaan Suvarga	Copper, molybdenum	Dornogobi
11. Erdene	Copper, molybdenum	Orkhon
12. Burenkhaan	Phosphorus	Khubsgol
13. Boroo	Gold	Selenge
14. Tumurtein Ovoo	Zinc, lead	Sukhbaatar
15. Asgat	Silver	Bayan-Olgii

itive environment for foreign investment and enlisted the assistance of Secretary Baker in the negotiations.

At the end of March 2005, Baker, accompanied by Mongolian ambassador to the US Ravdan Bold, flew out to Ulaanbaatar "as part of a multifaceted philanthropic and business trip to Asia," and as a legal representative of Ivanhoe, to speak to Mongolian leaders. In a speech to government officials and cabinet ministers widely reported in the Mongolian media, Baker lauded the strategic, economic, and political benefits of FDI and issued a not-very-subtle warning to the Mongols that the whole world was watching the OT negotiations: "It is in Mongolia's interests to be known as a place where an agreement that is made is an agreement that sticks; where the rule of law and sanctity of contract are abiding principles."[28] Baker explained that he believed the Mongolian government recognized the importance of being seen as a country that welcomed foreign investment. Not only did Baker's intervention fail to quell Mongolian concerns about the Ivanhoe agreement, but also the hostile press coverage damaged his credibility and legacy for many Mongols. While President Enkhbayar and Prime Minister Enkhbold praised Baker's past efforts to assist Mongolia, both pointed out that the frank discussions over the stability agreement with Ivanhoe must continue within the context of the new amendments to the Mineral Law.

In April, tensions escalated when 2,000 people, led by S. Ganbaatar, an environmental activist with the Radical Reform Movement, took to the streets to protest against Ivanhoe and the Mongolian government's handling of the OT contract. An effigy of Friedland was burned, eggs were thrown, and protesters occupied the central square in front of the presidential office building in Ulaanbaatar for three weeks.[29] Fifteen hundred pro-government counterprotesters confronted the civic groups representing the poor and

Figure 6.1 Map of Deposits of Strategic Importance

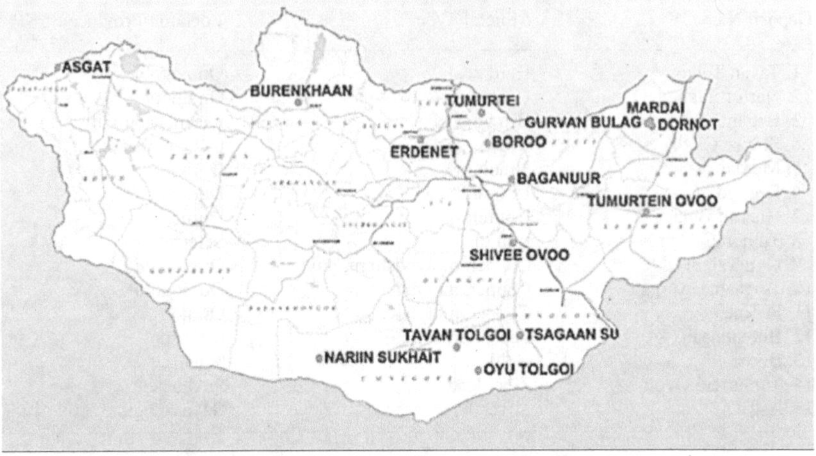

Source: 2011 EITI Reconciliation Document, in Christopher J. Carter, "Mongolia, Mining and Data Interactivity," Asia Pacific Policy Project, March 9, 2014, http://blogs.ubc.ca/maapps/2014/mongolia-and-data-interactivity.

unemployed, and police had to be called in to break up scuffles between rival demonstrators. Protesters demanded that the newly elected government resign if it could not renegotiate more favorable terms from Ivanhoe. They insisted that the government stop giving away Mongolia's wealth, that the Mineral Law be changed to give the state a larger share in any foreign-owned mine, and that Mongolia retain 51 percent ownership of OT, thereby abrogating Ivanhoe's 100 percent ownership rights.

Antigovernment protests expanded to include criticism over the lack of transparency in the original deal that gave OT to Ivanhoe. The MPRP government was in a difficult position since it had just attained power three months before, after a wave of demonstrations. In trying to defuse the protests, Industry and Trade Minister B. Jargalsaikhan promised on national television that the Parliament would renegotiate the terms of a "long-term stability contract" with Ivanhoe and amend laws on mining, taxation, and foreign investment to favor Mongolia.[30] Thereupon, foreign investors, from China to the United States, and their government representatives intensified complaints that the Mongolians were violating international contracts and destabilizing the country's investment environment. However, there were countercalls from Mongolian citizens for the government to strongly reject foreign pressure and the "mob tactics" of Baker and companies like Ivanhoe Mines: "The mining industry is one of Mongolia's tickets to economic prosperity and the government should not squander Mongolia's future to some money-grabbing people and companies whose sole interest lies in their own profits and not in Mongolia's health and wealth."[31]

In May 2006 Parliament approved a "windfall profit tax" on copper and gold exports at a rate of 68 percent when the copper price exceeded $2,600 per metric ton and the gold price was at $500 per troy ounce. Proceeds were to be deposited into Mongolia's Human Development Fund,[32] which was later established in 2008 with the goal of bringing Mongolia's human development status to the same level as that of developed countries by 2020. This law was devised to encourage investment in value-added industries such as smelting copper into concentrate instead of exporting unprocessed ore.[33] In July 2006 a new, more stringent Mineral Law was passed by the Mongolian Parliament. Although amended over twenty times by successive Parliaments, as of 2017 it still remained the nation's blueprint for mineral development. These legislative events further soured the investment picture and halted any real operational progress on OT under Ivanhoe, although new significant gold deposits were identified.

For years the atmosphere between the Mongolian government and Ivanhoe did not measurably improve. A stability agreement was not signed, and there were only very limited mining operations at the OT site, which further damaged the reputation of the company for not honoring its grandiose promises. The foreign investor community also grew increasingly cynical about Mongolia's legal regime and the ability of the government to carry out the terms of its contracts. Mongolian domestic politics were roiled by competing politicians, at times within the same party, who attacked the validity of the original agreement. Friedland continued to make incendiary statements in the press, which made him the most disliked foreign figure in the country. This situation damaged not only Ivanhoe's and Friedland's reputations but also stoked anti–foreign investment feeling throughout Mongolia, while reinforcing the view that American and Western business practices were as dangerous to Mongolia's welfare as Chinese or Russian corrupt deals. As Mongolia's Western FDI remained depressed, Chinese investments continued to grow and monopolize the mineral sector.

Financial experts and Mongolian policymakers, concerned about the unbalanced nature and lack of transparency of Chinese investment and the unattractive FDI climate for Western investors, came to believe that the only answer for Mongolia was to resolve the OT impasse. The British-Australian owned Rio Tinto, a multinational mineral company with extensive operations in China and other Asian markets, began negotiations with Robert Friedland about acquiring a stake in Ivanhoe Mining's OT project. The proposed deal featured Mongolia's regaining a 34 percent stake in OT in exchange for holding a special session of Parliament to repeal the windfall profits tax on copper and gold and to pass revisions to three other laws. Critics saw problems in the proposed shareholders agreement with its exorbitant interest rates, the fact that Mongolian shares were structured to create an illiquid debt instead of an asset, and the absence of any mechanism to protect Mongolia's assets or control adverse behavior by Friedland and

Ivanhoe. Also, Ivanhoe was permitted to charge Mongolia a management fee for its own invested capital.

Despite the difficulties, a deal was finalized in October 2009 under newly elected President Tsakhia Elbegdorj. It included a five-point secret section added by the National Security Council that called for an up-front payment of $225 million by Ivanhoe to the Mongolian government and tax rate changes. In the new shareholders agreement, Rio Tinto, which in 2006 had bought 9.95 percent of Ivanhoe with a $303 million investment, was accepted as a partner by the Mongolian government. It was agreed that Rio Tinto could exercise its option to raise its stake in Ivanhoe to 43.1 percent in a phased investment process worth approximately $2.4 billion.[34]

Since OT was lauded as the country's biggest ever foreign investment project, it was expected that this deal would set a precedent for future foreign mining investments. All sides were optimistic that the underground mining operations finally would move forward, but the project continued to face many difficulties. During the next six years, Rio Tinto step by step increased its percentage of ownership in Ivanhoe Mines in what was labeled a "creeping takeover," and company proceeds were allocated toward completing the first phase of the site's two-phase development plan. However, the new ownership did not adopt significantly different public relations policies to repair the image of OT management and its operations among the local populace. Resistance to the project continued on site. Friedland, even though reduced to a minority holder, persisted in his inflammatory rhetoric, which was negatively reported by the media. Nonetheless, relations with Mongolian officials in the capital improved because Rio Tinto executives provided a buffer. According to Rio Tinto, OT by 2012 had contributed over $2 billion to the Mongolian economy through technology, jobs, and other revenues. Also, Rio Tinto's entrance into Mongolia did raise the profile of the country among international mining investors and ushered in a short golden era.

By 2012 Rio Tinto had increased its initial 9.95 percent stake to 51 percent control of Ivanhoe. That April, Friedland was forced out as CEO,[35] and Kay Priestly, Rio Tinto's CFO of its global copper group with a background at the international tax firm Arthur Andersen, replaced him. Priestly eventually engineered a change of name for the company to Turquoise Hill and started OT open-pit commercial production in 2013. Nonetheless, faced with cost overruns estimated at around $2 billion and the realization that Mongolia's much-heralded 34 percent equity ownership would likely not pay dividends for decades, the government became keen to revisit the agreement terms. Discussions around phase two, a multibillion-dollar underground expansion, provided the opportunity. Prospective lenders like the International Finance Corporation (IFC) and the European Bank for Reconstruction and Development (EBRD) required government sign-off on the phase two financing plan. This provided the Mongols with negotiating leverage to review problematic aspects of the earlier phase one, including cost overruns, tax liability, and management service fees. At that time, Mongolia likely was emboldened by relatively high copper prices and its status as the world's fastest growing economy.

When the OT project became a major issue during the parliamentary election campaign in the spring of 2012, some politicians openly advocated for what foreign observers labeled a more resource-nationalist agenda. The new government led by new Prime Minister Norov Altankhuyag sought renegotiation with Rio Tinto of the ownership split in October 2012.[36] He asserted that, as part of a mining action plan, all investment agreements in the mining and energy sector needed to be reviewed and that the OT agreement should be subject to a full and transparent parliamentary hearing. The legacy of Ivanhoe's arrogance, Rio Tinto's continuing bad public relations inside Mongolia, and the failure to resolve environmental and employment disputes at the local level resulted in a two-and-a-half-year halt in most OT operations that delayed the second-phase expansion of the $5.4 billion underground mine. The Mongolian government raised thirty issues for discussion. Particular concern centered around supposedly deliberate cost overruns (40 percent) of the open-pit operation, which would delay the Mongolian government from profiting from its 34 percent stake.[37] The Mongolian Parliament, reflecting the anger of the public, became closely involved with the negotiations: "Although much time has passed since the project's first stage came into operation, Mongolian people have not yet felt its benefit. People have the right to know when the project will work at a profit and with how much profit. Therefore, the project will be at the attention of parliament, and MPs will often ask about the project."[38] The long work stoppage and continuing wrangling with the Mongolian government over the implementation of the OT agreement caused deep unease among the foreign investor community. At the same time, Turquoise Hill CEO Priestly had another controversial Ivanhoe project, SouthGobi Resources, to manage, which further weakened her position inside Mongolia. She subsequently retired from both Turquoise Hill and Rio Tinto at the end of 2014.

Rio Tinto had thought the lack of production and income from OT would force the Mongolian government to modify its negotiating position, but instead the dispute dragged on for months. Amir Shafaie, a legal analyst with the Natural Resource Governance Institute, has studied how the length of the OT negotiations shifted the bargaining power of the parties:

> Oyu Tolgoi's key lesson for countries in similar situations is that any natural resource deal renegotiation must be thought through strategically and with eyes on both the commodity price cycle and political economy impacts. When circumstances such as price are in the government's favor, it is important for officials to act quickly to achieve the best possible deal while recognizing the limits of negotiating leverage. Waiting or overestimating the government's bargaining position runs the risk that volatile factors such as commodity prices may change in an unfavorable direction.[39]

Commodity price changes and economic and political pressures played a particularly important role because the 33 percent drop in copper prices from October 2012 to January 2015 weakened the Mongolian government's hand and caused Rio Tinto to reject any fiscal changes by giving the impression that it could postpone the development of phase two. The Mongolian government lost more leverage as copper prices collapsed, Chinese demand for copper softened, and Mongolia's economy fell into recession. FDI plunged from $4.45 billion in 2012 to $510 million in 2014, and Mongolia's mining investment attractiveness ranking dropped from the 38th to the 69th percentile, as other foreign investors supported Rio Tinto.[40] By late 2014 new Prime Minister Chimed Saikhanbileg responded to the economic pressure and called for a text message referendum on the new agreement. Yet intransigent Rio Tinto did not obtain a one-sided victory because it too was pressed monetarily to move forward the strained on-and-off negotiations. In the months preceding the revised agreement, copper prices rose 17 percent, which made the timing to begin OT's phase two more attractive. Rio Tinto also was under Chinese pressure to fulfill contracts to supply OT copper to North Chinese factories.

Finally, in May 2015 Rio Tinto and Mongolia agreed on a revised agreement. Rio Tinto announced that it had transferred to Mongolia about $148 million, 2 percent of the overall value of the project. On December 16, 2015, an underground development funding agreement for OT was signed in Ulaanbaatar, and international financial institutions committed to provide $4.4 billion for a second phase of development over the next five to seven years.[41] Shafaie called the new terms of the May 2015 Oyu Tolgoi agreement a victory for each side: For Rio Tinto, the phase one cost overruns were resolved without any admission of fault, and there were no new measures to limit possible cost overruns in phase two. On the tax dispute, a settlement was affixed at $30 million, significantly less than the $127 million initially claimed by Mongolia. Furthermore, the initial agreement's tax stability principles were maintained. Regarding phase two's financing plan, the Mongols accepted in principle a solution that included using the mining licenses as collateral and the option sought by Rio Tinto to use the debt to first repay existing shareholder loans from Rio Tinto. Meanwhile, the government of Mongolia won a reduced management services fee rate of 3 percent (down from 6 percent) of capital costs incurred for phase two.[42]

OT's first-phase open pit currently is in production, but its second phase requires construction of a 200-kilometer tunnel with completion expected in five to seven years. From 2009 to 2014, the OT project's first phase had attracted $7.9 billion in FDI and paid out $1.3 billion in taxes to Mongolia.[43] The second phase's Underground Mine Development and Financing Plan involves funding by international commercial financial institutions and export credit agencies, along with fifteen commercial banks (providing a total of $2.34 billion) led by BNP Paribas.[44] At the 2015 signing ceremony,

Prime Minister Saikhanbileg proclaimed, "Starting today, the OT project becomes a pure business project. The project is no longer a political or government issue,"[45] but phase two development involves overcoming key hurdles, which would lead to further delays. The government and Turquoise Hill agreed to pay Rio Tinto an annual completion support fee equal to 2.5 percent of the amounts drawn, with interest-only payments the first five years and structured on a stepped amortization schedule. Project financing terms must be approved by Parliament, so debate was pushed past the June 2016 elections to avoid becoming embroiled in domestic politics.

With estimated development costs in excess of $7 billion and a more than forty-year mine life, OT is conservatively expected to double Mongolia's annual GDP when it reaches full production. However, the reward for Mongols appears to be far off. Rio Tinto Group's CEO Jean-Sebastien Jacques in 2016 said that Mongolia will not receive any dividend from OT for ten years, until it completes phase two's $5.3 billion underground expansion: "Until we get to a steady state, which is clearly 10 years down the road, we will not pay a dividend to anybody."[46] A new German financial model[47] estimates that the Mongolian government should receive up to $1.1 billion from OT and could earn many hundreds of millions of dollars a year by the 2020s, principally through royalties, value-added tax, income tax, and other revenue streams. It is predicted that the 34 percent direct stake is unlikely to earn any extra revenues until the 2030s unless commodity prices increase dramatically. If such calculations are correct, OT's financial management likely will continue to be a source of animosity for the populace and plague the foreign investment environment.

SouthGobi Resources and Chalco

Ivanhoe under CEO Robert Friedland had spun off its non-OT coal assets in 2006 into a company called SouthGobi Resources, which received a controlling stake in Ovoot Tolgoi coal mine located forty kilometers north of the Chinese border. Friedland called Ovoot Tolgoi, which sold its entire production to Chinese customers, a cash cow and the "beluga caviar of coal." After the Rio Tinto deal to buy into Ivanhoe's OT operation, Friedland and Rio Tinto looked for other investors to monetize their stake in SouthGobi's Ovoot Tolgoi. Ivanhoe approached several Chinese SOE coal miners like Shenhua Group and China National Coal without success. In 2012, at the same time he was being forced out of OT, Friedland found a willing investor for SouthGobi Resources in Aluminum Corp. of China Ltd. (Chalco). Chalco was interested in gaining control of Mongolian coal production as it expanded into other commodities and diversified its revenue stream. Ivanhoe planned to sell 60 percent of its SouthGobi holding for $928 million. Chalco agreed and also proclaimed willingness to purchase as much as 100 percent of SouthGobi's coal for up to two years.[48]

The news of the upcoming sale provoked an uproar in the Mongolian press. Not two weeks later, the Mongolian government, under great parliamentary pressure, suspended SouthGobi's exploration and mining licenses for Ovoot Tolgoi for national security reasons. This sale, which was considered relatively routine in international financial circles, became yet another cause célèbre for both the Mongols and foreign investors that severely impacted the inflow of FDI. By June 30, operations at Ovoot Tolgoi had completely ceased. Foreign observers suggested that the deal was killed not for economic reasons but as "a result of hostility expressed by leading Mongolian politicians and an increasingly uncertain regulatory environment within that country."[49] Foreigners saw the sale as a routine share transaction transferring ownership between two private parties and believed that the Mongols politicized the deal because Chalco was a state-owned entity (SOE). It also was possible that a rival but markedly lower bid by Mongolian Mining (part of the Mongolian private MCS Group) used its governmental connections to oppose the sale.

The foreign community badly miscalculated the domestic political environment the Mongolian government faced as it entered a parliamentary election just two months later, as well as the damage done by Friedland's years of negative publicity and bad faith. Foreign critics labeled the Mongolian reaction as "resource nationalism," which would cause deep uncertainty about the openness of Mongolia's FDI climate and the future of the OT agreement with Rio Tinto. The tone of the criticism was intense: "The deal caused many politicians to express xenophobic concerns about Chinese control over Mongolian mineral assets and it acted as a catalyst speeding up the passage of restrictive legislation in Parliament limiting foreign investment in certain strategic industries including mining."[50] These financial experts did not believe that government would risk a major loss of FDI inflows and economic collapse, particularly when Mongolia's GDP in 2011 had catapulted to 17.5 percent.

While Western attitudes were one-dimensional (perhaps swayed by the hyperbole coming from the Ivanhoe representatives) and tone deaf regarding Mongolian domestic politics and the high anxiety of the average Mongol about further Chinese involvement in the economy, the reaction of Chalco was quite different. It had begun business with Mongolia the previous year when it signed a contract to buy coal from Mongolia's state-owned Erdenes Tavan Tolgoi (ETT). Buying into the coal business was a first for the company, which was facing a difficult aluminum market. Although Chinese analysts believed that the deal could boost Chalco's earnings, there was concern that the company might not manage the political and economic uncertainty of moving into a new industry in a different country.[51] There was recognition that Chalco would have to win over Mongolian officials, but its executives thought that their own government would be able to pressure Mongolian authorities to permit the sale, so they patiently waited throughout the summer for the crisis to dissipate, twice extending the takeover deadline.

However, on May 17, 2012, the MPRP-controlled Parliament, preparing for June elections, pushed through a new Foreign Investment Law that allowed Parliament to regulate large investment in a number of key strategic sectors. These sectors were defined as banking, media and telecommunications, and mining. Ambiguously worded, the law was written especially to limit the ability of companies owned by foreign countries rather than private corporations to invest in these sectors. For example, if privately owned foreign shareholding exceeded 49 percent in any particular company and the amount of the investment at the time exceeded 100 billion MNT (approximately $75 million), then parliamentary approval of the transaction was required. If the foreign ownership came from SOEs, there was no minimum threshold of ownership required because all proposed investments from SOEs required parliamentary approval. Furthermore, if a foreign entity wanted to acquire one-third or more of the shares of an investment in a strategic sector, then the $75 million limit did not apply since cabinet approval for the investment was necessary.[52] Foreign investors and governments reacted with anger and disbelief, but due to the popularity of the new law with the electorate, Mongolian policymakers did not accurately judge the impact the law would have on new FDI.

Since Chalco was an SOE and was seeking a large share in the strategically important sector of coal mining, the criteria in the new law were applicable. SouthGobi Resources, as one of the largest coal producers in Mongolia, owned four major Mongolian projects. The suspension of SouthGobi's licenses meant it had to curtail all its operations throughout the summer and into the third quarter. Potential coal customers were reluctant to enter into new sales contracts given the uncertainty about the company's mining licenses, so SouthGobi's net income plummeted. To solve the issue, it sought international arbitration and claimed that the Mongolian authorities' actions were the equivalent of unlawful expropriation. With no resolution in sight, in early September Chalco decided to drop its offer to purchase a stake in SouthGobi. At the same time, Rio Tinto, which held a 58 percent stake in SouthGobi through its OT agreement with Ivanhoe Mines, now renamed Turquoise Hill, replaced the SouthGobi board of directors with its own officers. Kay Priestly, the chief executive of Turquoise Hill Resources, was named chairman of SouthGobi.[53] However, SouthGobi's troubles were not yet over. In October 2012, Sarah Armstrong, an Australian citizen who was chief legal counsel of SouthGobi Resources, was prevented from leaving Mongolia for several months due to allegations that company management had bribed Mongolian officials. The Mongolian Anti-Corruption Agency shut down and searched the company's headquarters. In May 2013 SouthGobi Resources employee Justin Kapla, a US citizen who had been questioned by this agency for bribing local officials and money laundering, was banned from exiting Mongolia for two years while his case was being investigated. Despite strong pressure from US authorities, he was convicted of tax evasion in January 2015 and sentenced to nearly six years in prison, only to be pardoned by President Elbegdorj the following month.[54] Such cases were viewed as Mongolian retribution for the attempt to sell the company to the Chinese and further alienated the foreign investor community.

The Russian Debt Reappears

Mongolia had been assured in the original 2003 OT agreement with Ivanhoe, brokered by former US Secretary of State James Baker, that its Soviet-era debt had been resolved. However, in 2009 the debt issue was reopened by the Russian side in Moscow during negotiations with two officials from the Mongolian presidential office to finalize preparations for Russian President Dmitri Medvedev's visit to Mongolia that July. Earlier, in January, Russian Prime Minister Putin had met in Moscow with Mongolian President Elbegdorj, who was seeking a $300 million emergency agriculture loan. At that time Putin showed interest in Mongolia's Dornod uranium mine. When the Russian and Mongolian governments thereupon announced a joint venture that covered uranium extraction, Putin believed that Mongolia would commit to exclusive Russian participation in Mongolia's uranium mining sector.

The Mongols on the Medvedev visit preparation team, when discussing the agriculture loan, were told by the Russian presidential office that this loan could not go forward since, under Russian law, no commercial loan could be given to a country that owed Russia money. Russia claimed that Mongolia still had not yet repaid the majority of the $150–$160 million of the "grand debt" accumulated in the post-Soviet era. The shocked Mongolian side replied that they believed all outstanding Mongolian debt to Russia had been waived. They noted Russia previously had stated that it was withholding the agricultural loan only on the grounds that the Mongols must guarantee that commercial banks would repay the money. While in Ulaanbaatar, President Medvedev, accompanied by Sergei Kiriyenko, chief of the Russian state's nuclear energy company, Rosatom, publicly agreed to end the dispute over unpaid Mongolian debt by suggesting the Mongols allow Russia "to move ahead with the Dornod [uranium] deposit," which holds over seven times as much uranium as Russia's total annual production. He then granted the Mongolian government the $300 million loan for agricultural development.[55]

Later, in October 2009, as Rio Tinto was doubling its stake in Ivanhoe Mines under its new agreement, Mongolian and Western media reports claimed that the Russian government was pressuring the Mongols to cede control of their 34 percent stake in OT to Russia's state-owned monopoly Russian Railways (RZD). Russian Deputy Finance Minister Dmitry Pankin noted that Mongolia still owed 180 million rubles to Russia, and he threatened it would formally complain about the debt to members of the Paris Club.[56] Ivanhoe declared that its own shareholders would have to approve any change of ownership and noted that the new OT investment agreement stated that Erdenes-MGL, the Mongolian state-owned partner of Ivanhoe, must be wholly owned and solely controlled by the Mongolian government. In 2010 the debt and its tie to the rights to Mongolia's uranium deposit at Dornod again were raised in an article in *Pravda.*[57] On December 15, *RIA Novosti* reported that an agreement had been concluded by Prime Minister Putin and Mongolian Prime Minister Sukhbaatar Batbold that would drop the threat to complain to the Paris Creditors' Club if the Mongols made a onetime payment of an additional $3.8 million. However, the actual write-off of the debt did not happen until 2016, when the Russian Duma on January 22 approved the ratification bill that was signed by President Putin and affirmed by his Federation Council on January 27.[58] The disposition of Mongolian uranium rights still has not been publicly settled.

Notes

1. This statistic was considered unreliable and likely is as much as four times higher. See Enkhbayar Shagdar, "Unemployment and Impoverishment in Mongolia: A Close Look at the Reality" (ERINA paper, 2003), 2, http://www.academia.edu/6718735/Unemployment_and_Impoverishment_in_Mongolia_A_Close_Look_at_the_Reality.

2. The name *ninja* was used because they wore green plastic pans on their backs, which some thought made them look like Teenage Mutant Ninja Turtles of TV fame.

3. Sumio Kuribayashi, "Structural Change and Economic Performance in Mongolia," in *The Geopolitical Relations Between Contemporary Mongolia and Neighboring Asian Countries: Democracy, Economy and Security* (Taipei: Mongolian and Tibetan Affairs, 2003), 79, Table 21.

4. Ibid., 79.

5. *Mongol Messenger,* March 3, 1999.

6. Empson, "An Interview with Bill Bikales."

7. Joel, "Mongolia Wins Debt Relief (and Russia Does Well, Too)," *Far Outliers* (blog), January 25, 2004, http://faroutliers.blogspot.com/2004/01/.

8. At the end of 2004, during negotiations to solve the Iraq war debt, Carlyle Group described itself as a consortium with a roster of former high-level US and European politicians who have "personal rapport with the stakeholders in the anticipated negotiations" and are able to "reach key decision-makers in the United Nations and in key capitals." See Naomi Klein, "James Baker's Double Life," *The Nation,* October 12, 2004, https://www.thenation.com/article/james-bakers-double-life/.

9. Robert Bryce, "The Man at Their Side," *The Nation,* September 28, 2004, http://www.alternet.org/story/20012/the_man_at_their_side.

10. IMF Mongolia, "Staff Report for the 2005 Article IV Consultation" (Washington, DC: September 1, 2005), 6, https://www.imf.org/external/pubs/ft/scr/2005/cr05396.

11. Citing *Nezavisimaya gazeta* in "Russia Writes Off Mongolian Debt," January 13, 2004, accessed January 3, 2005, http://www.russiajournal.com/node/17010.

12. Throughout 2004 Russia continued to write off the debts owed to it by the poorest countries, including Iraq and Ethiopia. The volume of external debt acquired by Russia since the breakup of the Soviet Union amounted to $39.6 billion, while the debts of the former USSR amounted to $55.9 billion by 2005. "Russia's External Debt Grew by $25Bln in 2004," *MosNews,* April 04, 2005, http://cbonds.com/news/item/310381.

13. James A. Baker IV, also known as Jamie, is a partner at Baker Botts, LLP. In 2016 he was serving there as chairman of the Global Projects Department. His practice has been focused on a variety of international commercial and trade-related matters and commercial transactions, principally in the energy, telecommunications, and financial services industries in the Middle East, Central Asia, Europe, and Russia, and many of those matters have involved negotiations between private concerns and government agencies or state enterprises.

14. "Canadian Miner Buys $50 Million Mongolian Debt," *New York Times,* January 1, 2005, http://www.nytimes.com/2004/01/01/business/canadian-miner-buys-50-million-mongolian-debt.html?_r=0. In other sources it was reported that in May 2000 Ivanhoe entered into an earn-in agreement with BHP Exploration to earn a 100 percent interest in the Oyu Tolgoi property. Ivanhoe earned its 100 percent interest in February 2002 by incurring $3 million in exploration expenditures, paying to BHP Exploration $1 million and delivering to BHP Exploration a $4 million non-interest-bearing promissory note with a one-year term. The earn-in agreement also required Ivanhoe to incur additional exploration expenditures of $3 million by February 2006.

15. *Mongol Messenger,* January 21, 2004; "Opposition Questions Hoopla Around Forgiveness of Soviet-Era Debt," *UB Post,* January 8, 2004.

16. Mongolian government officials participating in the negotiations privately mentioned these details to the author.

17. The *Far Eastern Economic Review* of January 15, 2004, stated, "But the news is tempered by uncertainty about how the debt was repaid. . . . [It is said that] Canadian firm mining firm Ivanhoe, which is exploring for copper and gold in southern Mongolia, agreed to buy $50 million worth of Treasury bonds; a further $50 million worth will be sold domestically, and the remaining $150 million to finance the repayment came from national monetary reserves, the bulk of it foreign exchange reserves." Quoted in Ian Jeffries, *Mongolia: A Guide to Economic and Political Developments* (New York: Routledge, 2007), 66–67.

18. Joel, "Mongolia Wins Debt Relief."

19. Julian Dierkes, "Contract Transparency in Mongolian Mining: Unbundling Contract Transparency in the Extractive Industry: The Case of Mongolia—Part I," *Mongolian Focus* (blog), December 11, 2015, http://blogs.ubc.ca/mongolia/2015/contract-transparency-in-mongolian-mining/.

20. John King, "Bush Appoints Baker Envoy on Iraqi Debt," CNN, December 3, 2003.

21. "Moody's Assigns B1 Rating to Mongolia," Moody's, October 4, 2005.

22. "Tenth Anniversary of First Major Gold and Copper Discovery at Oyu Tolgoi by Ivanhoe Mines Coincides with Period of Peak Construction on Mongolia's Largest Mining Complex," Yahoo!, *Marketwire*, July 17, 2011, https://www.yahoo.com/news/Tenth-Anniversary-of-First-ccn-1681354512.html.

23. The EPA had to spend $200 million to clean up the site. Rossabi, *Modern Mongolia*, 103.

24. Grainger David, "The Great Mongolian Gold Rush: The land of Genghis Khan has the biggest mining find in a very long time. A visit to the core of a frenzy in the middle of nowhere," *Fortune Magazine,* December 22, 2003, http://archive.fortune.com/magazines/fortune/fortune_archive/2003/12/22/356094/index.htm.

25. "Robert Friedland," *New Internationalist,* August 2, 2006, https://newint.org/columns/worldbeaters/2006/08/01/.

26. The law also reduced the tax exemption to 100 percent for the first two years, followed by a 50 percent exemption for the next three years, limited the duration of the exploration licenses to three years with two extensions, and set the duration of resource exploitation licenses to twenty years with two twenty-year extensions.

27. Under the 2001 Mineral Law, companies received the 100 percent tax exemption for the first five years of operation and the 50 percent exemption for the next five years. Mineral resource licenses were issued for 60 years with a possible extension of 40 years for a total of 100 years. Pui-Kwan Tse, "The Mineral Industry of Mongolia," in *2006 Minerals Yearbook: Mongolia* (Washington, DC: US Geological Survey, October 2007), 15.1, http://minerals.usgs.gov/minerals/pubs/country/2006/myb3-2006-mg.pdf.

28. "Ivanhoe Welcomes Mongolian Government's Acceptance of New Initiatives to Facilitate the Completion of a Stability Agreement for Development of Oyu Tolgoi Copper-Gold Project," Ivanhoe press statement, March 23, 2006.

29. Luke Distelhorst, "Civil Movements Burn Effigies, Start Hunger Strike," *UB Post,* April 20, 2006.

30. Ganbat Namjil, "Mongolians protest over Canadian firm," Associated Press, April 12, 2006, http://www.globalgoodnews.com/government-news-a.html?art=1144798812117613.

31. "That the copper and gold mine Ivanhoe Mines wants to exploit is huge might be deduced from the fact that former US Secretary of State, James A. Baker, came to Mongolia to 'talk' to Prime Minister M. Enkhbold and Minister of Trade and Industry, B. Jargalsaikhan. Mr. Baker didn't come with velvet gloves on as he demanded that the government comes to a (favorable, of course) agreement with Ivanhoe Mines, and warned (might I say 'threatened'?) that otherwise all foreign investors would disappear from Mongolia." See "Former US Secretary of State puts pressure on Mongolian government," *Shards of Mongolia* (blog), March 27, 2006, http://shardsofmongolia.blogspot.com/2006/03/former-us-secretary-of-state-puts.html.

32. Part of the country's National Development Strategy, this fund made it legally possible for every citizen of Mongolia to be equally eligible to own a share of the nation's mineral wealth. Initial capital for the fund was drawn from the OT mine project. Additional revenues would come from development of Mongolia's $2 billion Tavan Tolgoi coal deposit and other rich mineral resources. Other sources include income from sale of shares and dividends of state property connected with state-owned mineral deposits; fees for exploration and processing activities in these mining sites; advance payments and loans related to the exploitation of the strategic mining sites; and income from bonds, loan certificates, and savings interest from international and domestic financial markets.

33. The Human Development Fund was expected to provide pension, health, housing, and educational benefits, as well as cash payouts to all citizens, and thus be a mechanism to distribute the wealth obtained from Mongolia's minerals equitably among the populace. Originally, the fund's resources were to be applied for investment and capital repairs, to reduce the budget deficit, and for social welfare systems. However, its use has become embroiled in Mongolia's volatile election politics. See Alicia Campi, "Mongolia's Quest to Balance Human Development in Its Booming Mineral-Based Economy," *Brookings East Asia Commentary,* January 10, 2012.

34. Dan, "Mongolia and Ivanhoe to sign Tuesday Oct. 6 the $3.6 Billion Oyu Tolgoi Copper-Gold mine agreement," *To Mongolia* (blog), October 3, 2009, https://tomongolia.blogspot.com/2009/10/oyu-tolgoi.html.

35. Alistair MacDonald and Carolyn King, "Ivanhoe Mines CEO Quits in Deal with Rio Tinto," *Wall Street Journal*, April 18, 2012, http://www.wsj.com/articles.

36. The new coalition government was petitioned by a group of twenty-four ministers of Parliament who called for the enforcement of a parliamentary resolution that the Mongolian government should own 51 percent of the OT project once foreign partners recouped its startup investment.

37. The 2009 agreement with Rio Tinto stated that the Mongols would not receive any share of the profit until Turquoise Hill (Ivanhoe) recovered all project costs.

38. Davaajav Gankhuyag, Mongolian mining minister, stated that, according to the OT investment agreement and feasibility study, the total initial investment of the OT project was projected to be $5.1 billion, until the launch of first production. However, a group of Mongolian economists and mining experts had assessed that investment had reached $7.1 billion or an overrun of 40 percent, "without good reason," by the end of 2012. B. Ooluun, "OT's Underground Development Slows as Talks Continue," *Montsame,* April 18, 2014.

39. Amir Shafaie, "Rio Tinto, Mongolia, and the Art of Negotiating Amidst Price Volatility," Natural Resource Governance Institute blog, June 24, 2015, https://resourcegovernance.org/blog/rio-tinto-mongolia-and-art-negotiating-amidst-price-volatility.

40. Ibid.

41. B. Khuder, "Minister of Mining reports," *Montsame,* December 18, 2015, http://en.montsame.mn/mining/minister-mining-reports.

42. The fee is still based on uncapped costs; as costs go up so do the fees, meaning there is a perverse incentive by which the manager gains from incurring higher costs. Shafaie warned that this ambiguity as to "sustaining capital" (subject to higher 6 percent fee) could lead to future disputes. Also, Mongolia obtained the cancellation of a regular payment of 2 percent net-smelter value of production, which was a legacy of the buyout of first concession holder BHP. Shafaie, "Rio Tinto."

43. Khuder, "Minister of Mining Reports."

44. Initial senior loans will total $4.4 billion, funded by Export Development Canada, the European Bank for Reconstruction and Development, the International Finance Corporation, the United States' Export-Import Bank, and Australia's Export Finance and Insurance Corporation. *Mongol Messenger,* December 18, 2015.

45. Khuder, "Minister of Mining Reports."

46. Jesse Riseborough, "Rio CEO Says Mongolia Won't Receive Mine Dividend for 10 Years," *Bloomberg*, October 6, 2016, https://www.bloomberg.com/news/articles/2016-10-06/rio-ceo-says-mongolia-won-t-receive-mine-dividend-for-10-years.

47. A Berlin-based consultancy, OpenOil, has developed a methodology to analyze a number of mining and oil and gas projects to develop a public financial management paradigm to upstream modeling of extractive industries on a project-by-project basis. Olumide Abimbola, "Press Release: Mongolian Government Unlikely to Receive Dividends from Oyu Tolgoi Until 2035," OpenOil, October 26, 2016, http://openoil.net/2016/10/26/press-release-mongolian-government-unlikely-to-receive-dividends-from-oyu-tolgoi-until-2035/.

48. Michelle Yun, "Chalco Agrees to Buy SouthGobi Stake to Gain Coal Mines," Bloomberg, April 2, 2012; "Chalco to Buy Coal Miner SouthGobi," *South China Morning Post,* April 3, 2012, http://www.scmp.com/article/997345/chalco-buy-coal-miner-southgobi.

49. Brian Sturgess, "Investing in Mongolia," *World Economics*, September 2012, http://www.worldeconomics.com/Papers/Investing%20in%20Mongolia_c93dbdb0-1a04-4e33-b331-51c25d21d47a.paper.

50. Ibid.

51. Oswald Chen, "Chalco to buy SouthGobi's majority stake," *China Daily Asia,* April 3, 2012, http://www.chinadailyasia.com/news/2012-04/03/content_112879.html.

52. Sturgess, "Investing in Mongolia."

53. "SouthGobi Says Chalco Abandons Bid, Unveils Board Changes," proactive investors, September 4, 2012, https://www.proactiveinvestors.com/companies/news/89246/southgobi-says-chalco-abandons-bid-unveils-board-changes-34213.html.

54. Yuriy Humber, "Mongolia Bars SouthGobi's U.S. Chief from Leaving Country," Bloomberg, February 1, 2013, http://www.bloomberg.com/news/articles/2013-02-01/mongolia-bars-southgobi-s-u-s-chief-from-leaving-country; Maury Glover, "Minnesota Native Pardoned, Released from Mongolian Prison," Fox9.com, February 26, 2015, http://www.fox9.com/news/1564143-story.

55. Dierkes, "Contract transparency."

56. "This informal group of financial officials from 19 of the world's richest countries provides financial services such as debt restructuring, debt relief, and debt cancellation to indebted countries and their creditors. Debtors are often recommended to the Paris Club by the International Monetary Fund after alternative solutions fail." See Dorothy Kosich, "Russian Disinformation Campaign Aimed at Oyu Tolgoi, Mongolian Debt," Mineweb.com, October 15, 2009; *UB Post,* October 13, 2009.

57. Phill Hynes, "The Uranium Shakedown: How Mongolia and Russia Conspired Against Western Investors (Part 2)," *Frontera,* March 29, 2016, https://frontera.net/news/uranium-shakedown-mongolia-russia-conspired-western-investors-part-2/.

58. The signed document stated that the total amount of Mongolia's regulated financial liabilities as of December 14, 2010, was $174.2 million, and 97.8 percent of Mongolia's debt was forgiven, totaling about $170 million. The Mongols made a onetime payment of $3.8 million to settle the entire debt: "Mongolia Fully Repays Big Debt to Russia," *Montsame,* March 2, 2016, http://en.montsame.mn/video/politics/mongolia-fully-repays-big-debt-russia.

7

Resource Nationalism: Boom Days and Collapse

With the resolution of the OT agreement covering Ivanhoe Mining and Rio Tinto in 2009, optimism about foreign investment in Mongolia's mineral sector ran high. It was as if a dam had broken so that new FDI from many different sources could pour into the economy. The US embassy, for example, was openly and perhaps naively positive about Mongolia's future as a mining opportunity for investors: "Observers of Mongolia's investment climate consider passage of this agreement an unambiguously positive sign for foreign investors . . . that it shows Mongolia can say—Yes! to key projects undertaken with foreign involvement and investment." It proclaimed that the OT agreement confirmed the Mongols' commitment to compensating private holders of most strategic deposits and that the government and Parliament were willing to amend laws and regulations to enhance the commercial viability of mining projects: "The positive impact and message of the OT deal for investors should not be underestimated."[1] B. Byambasaikhan, CEO of Erdenes Mongol, LLC, the state-owned Mongol partner of Ivanhoe, reflected positively on the deal: "Mongolian companies all have benefited from Oyu Tolgoi mine, which is fundamental to Mongolian competitiveness at global stage. For instance, GDP of Mongolia, USD 4.5 billion in 2009, has witnessed [a] three-fold increase within [the] last five years thanks to the project."[2]

However, Mongolia's remarkable growth and mining boom went far beyond the OT project. According to World Bank figures, Mongolia attracted over $4.2 billion of FDI between 1992 and 2010, of which 83 percent or $3.52 billion (around $1,100 per capita) came in the last five years of this period. It was in significant measure connected to the development of OT and to the extraction, processing, and delivery of Mongolia's extensive mineral commodities to a number of consuming countries.[3] Data from the Foreign

Investment and Foreign Trade Agency (FIFTA) reveal that between 1990 and 2010, the sector of geological prospecting, oil exploration, and mining accounted for 65.3 percent of all inward investment, while trade and catering services accounted for a further 18.9 percent.[4] In the 1990s the collapse of the USSR and the end of Soviet budgetary assistance had resulted in a cumulative fall of over 20 percent in real GDP and subsequent sluggish growth; living standards, despite over $1 billion in Western donor aid, only regained their 1989 peak by 2001. Privatization of the state industrial and agricultural assets and joining the WTO in 1997, together with Mongolian textile products' surging into the US market, all produced economic momentum, but economists claimed that the real GDP annual growth average of 8 percent between 2002 and 2008 also was affected by high copper prices and new gold production.

The World Bank in 2016 placed Mongolia in the lower middle income country category. One can understand how it attained this status and its close connection to the mineral resource economy by examining various World Bank economic data charts. For example, Mongolia began the democratic era with a GNI per capita of $1,430 in 1990 (using unreliable communist-era data). In the 1990s this was more accurately expressed at a level in the $400s. In 2000 the GNI per capita stood at a meager $470 but, as the economy grew by developing its mineral resources, it jumped to $1,800 by 2008 and then to $4,370 in 2013 before beginning its slide to $3,830 in 2015.[5] The economic contraction continued into the middle of the 2010s, but, if one reviews the last twenty-five years of democracy, there are many positive economic factors that have increased the living standard for the majority of, but by no means all, Mongols.

Mongolia's Mineral Resources

Mongolia has been called the Saudi Arabia of coal with proven reserves of 12.2 billion tons and estimated potential exploitable reserves of around 163.2 billion metric tons (this would make Mongolia the seventh largest world producer of coal).[6] It has the potential to become one of the world's largest coal exporters since it possesses substantial high-quality coking coal reserves, large thermal black coal deposits, as well as lower-quality brown coal deposits.[7] In 1995 the World Bank found that there were sixteen coal mines producing approximately 5.5 million tons a year. Of these, three were the large-scale open-cut mines of Baganuur, Shivee-Ovoo, and Sharyn Gol.[8] The Tavan Tolgoi (TT) deposit, ranked as the world's largest undeveloped coal deposit, is in the South Gobi desert near China's border. It began to be exploited in the mid-2000s and is estimated to hold six billion metric tons of steelmaking coal. State-owned ETT manages the majority of TT's coal mining interests.[9]

Mongolia has been a major exporter of copper since communist times, when it established the Erdenet copper mine in 1974 as a joint 51–49 percent

Mongolian-Russian venture. This is Asia's largest deposit of copper ore and the fourth largest copper mine in the world with 3.3 million tons of reserves. In 2006 Erdenet mined 22.23 million tons of copper and molybdenum ore. In the pre-democratic years, it provided the major share of Mongolia's hard currency; before OT began production, Erdenet accounted for 13.5 percent of Mongolia's GDP and 7 percent of tax revenue.[10] Today Mongolia's largest copper deposit is OT, which is expected to become one of the world's top three copper mines. In 2016, OT was predicted to produce 175,000–195,000 tons of copper and 255,000–285,000 ounces of gold concentrates from its phase one aboveground mine. Its underground phase two shafts hold the bulk of the resources: recoverable copper of twenty-five billion pounds, twelve million ounces of gold, and seventy-eight million ounces of silver over a mine life of forty-one years. Underground production is expected to commence in 2021 with peak production in 2025–2030.[11]

Vast resources of not yet exploited uranium, which are concentrated in the east of Mongolia, were first identified by Soviet geologists. There are two main deposits. The first is Gurvanbulag with resources estimated at 6,900 tons. The Canada-based Western Prospector Group Ltd. and its Mongolian subsidiary, Emeelt Mines, explored the site in the mid-2000s. In March 2009, Western Prospector was taken over by China National Nuclear Corporation (CNNC), a 74 percent subsidiary of CNNC Overseas Uranium Holding Ltd., and in July Mongolian authorities suspended for three months all of the company's uranium exploration licenses for alleged violations of Mongolian laws. The ownership structure of Gurvanbulag was amended to meet the requirements of the Strategic Assets Law, so now the Mongolian government holds 51 percent and CNNC 49 percent, but to date no mining has begun on site. The second site is the Dornod uranium mine in the east of Mongolia, which is estimated to contain 33,000 tons of uranium and was exploited by the Erdes Mining Enterprise, a subsidiary of Priargunsky Industrial Mining and Chemical Union from 1988 to 1995. Russia's Atomredmetzoloto (ARMZ) claims that it spent the equivalent of $600 million (in 2009 dollars) on site exploration and development before railing the ore 480 kilometers to Siberia for refining. The nearby town of Mardai, built in the 1970s to house 10,000 Russian mine workers, now is nonfunctional. In the late 1990s, Canada-based Khan Resources Inc. obtained a 69 percent share in the Dornod project by acquiring controlling interest in Central Asian Uranium Co. (CAUC), a Mongolian stock company set up by World Wide Minerals under the direction of the Mongolian government.

In April 2008 Russia and Mongolia agreed to revive Russia's involvement in Dornod. When in February 2010 Khan Resources recommended that its shareholders accept a full takeover by a Chinese SOE, the Mongolian state-owned holding company MonAtom and the National Atomic Energy Commission proceeded to exclude the Canadians from Dornod. In January 2011 the Russians ratified the establishment of a joint limited liability company with 49 percent ARMZ ownership and 51 percent under Mongolian state-owned MonAtom. Khan Resources then sued the Mongolian government for expropriating its Dornod license and sought $200 million in damages and over $126 million in interest and costs. An arbitration panel in March 2015 awarded $100 million to Khan as compensation for cancellation, but the Mongols protested until a $70 million settlement was agreed upon a year later.[12] Production of uranium at Dornod has not yet resumed.

The Petroleum Authority of Mongolia has estimated that there are four to six billion barrels of recoverable oil in Mongolia. There is a scarcity of exploration data on Mongolia's petroleum potential, but, because of the geologic similarity of Mongolian hydrocarbon basins to adjacent producing Chinese basins, it is believed that there is a high probability of finding substantial petroleum reserves in Mongolia.[13] At present there are thirty petroleum fields, twenty-one of which were established through product-sharing agreements. Of these twenty-one, only three sites are actually productive, while the rest are in the exploratory stage under the direction of fourteen different companies, of which four are Western. These include the Swiss company Manas Petroleum through its subsidiary Gobi Energy Partners, LLC, in the east Gobi Basin; Australian Central Asia Petroleum, LLC; Canadian Shaman, LLC; and Canadian Sunwing Energy.[14] The three oil-producing fields, managed by Chinese majors PetroChina and Sinopec, are Zuunbayan, Tamsag-19, and Tamsag-21, which in 2012 together produced a total of 482,000 tons of crude oil (3.6 million barrels). Their production has increased eleven-fold since 2007. Zuunbayan is in the south of the country not far from Mongolia's giant coal-uranium deposit of TT and its Rio Tinto–controlled OT copper-gold deposit. The other two sites are in the northeast near the Chinese Manchurian border. Among the important Chinese companies now actively exploring in Mongolia is MEC, a mining and energy development holding company operating in Mongolia and Xinjiang in northwestern China. MEC's exploratory concessions are in western and southern Mongolia in cooperation with China's CNPC Daqing Petroleum.[15]

Other increasingly important Mongolian minerals are rare-earth elements, which now are mined almost exclusively in China. Mongolia's rare-earth reserves are estimated up to thirty-one million tons, which means that Mongolia's nearly 17 percent of the world's total ranks second. The country also has sizable reserves of gold, iron ore, molybdenum, tin, tungsten, and phosphates. Mongolia's geographical position just north of populous and resource-hungry China gives it special strategic importance as a regional supplier of mineral commodities. It is evident to the international financial community that the country's continuing and future prosperity is heavily dependent on both commodity prices and the attraction of FDI to mineral extraction.[16] Table 7.1 is an overview compiled by the US Geological Service (USGS) of some of the main minerals in Mongolia.

Mongolia's meteoric rise in growth rate and FDI during 2009–2013 was associated with its dynamic new president Tsakhia Elbegdorj, a long-time Democratic Party politician. He had defeated, on May 25, 2009, the MPRP-backed incumbent president, Enkhbayar, who was negatively associated with the nontransparent OT deal with Ivanhoe Mining, high inflation, lack of capital inflow in financial sectors, and a recession in real estate as well as a post-2008 parliamentary election riot that resulted in several deaths. During the election campaign, Elbegdorj pledged that the country's natural resources would be better utilized to improve the livelihood of the Mongolian people, and he promised to fight corruption, instill judicial reform, and support the nomadic economy.

In his first months as president, Elbegdorj[17] was able to shepherd the new OT shareholders agreement through Parliament, finalize Rio Tinto's participation in the OT operations, and convince Parliament to repeal the Windfall Profits Tax. He oversaw an administration that was perceived as supportive of Western foreign investments because it had successfully managed to amend the Mineral Law to ease FDI regulations in strategic industries such as mining, banking, and telecoms. His foreign policy agenda was openly pro-Western (pro-American, -EU, -Japanese, and –South Korean), and he appeared committed to finding resolutions to outstanding issues

Table 7.1 Main Minerals in Mongolia

Commodity	Reserves	Significance
Oil	2.4 billion barrels	While underexplored, Mongolia's proven reserves are in the east with frontier exploration in the west. Significant reserves of unconventional petroleum (shale gas and shale oil) are also estimated.
Gold	3,290 metric tons	Alluvial gold—off-limits to miners—accounts for over half of reserves, but several larger deposits are in development. Gold is also associated with large copper deposits like Oyu Tolgoi.
Silver	3,493 metric tons	Despite only one producing mine in the north, there are several other silver deposits spread across the country.
Copper	60.7 million metric tons	Mongolia has the world's twelfth largest copper reserves. Oyu Tolgoi will become the world's second largest operating copper mine once the underground phase two expansion is completed in 2020.
Coal	31.7 billion metric tons	Mongolia has the world's fourth largest coal reserves, thermal and coking coals combined. Tavan Tolgoi is the world's largest undeveloped coal mine.
Iron	1.65 billion metric tons	Proven reserves of iron ore are fragmented and spread out nationwide, leading to smaller average deposit sizes and shorter operating lives for mines.

Sources: "Extractive Industries in Mongolia" in *Mongolia Extractive Industries Transparency Initiative: Mongolia Ninth EITI Reconciliation Report 2014* (KPMG Audit, December 2015), chap. 5; *2012 Mongolia Minerals Yearbook* (Washington, DC: US Geological Survey, February 2015).

related to both OT and TT. The Elbegdorj administration also benefited from comparison with that of his predecessor in world economic trends. Since the new Mongolian economy was so heavily based on mineral commodities, it was particularly vulnerable to external shocks, such as the 2008 global financial crisis and any fall in commodity prices. These factors in 2009 caused a sharp fall in government revenues, and real GDP dropped by 1.3 percent. In early 2009, the IMF reached a $236 million stand-by arrangement with Mongolia that allowed the country to weather the crisis, but it did not come in time to save the Enkhbayar administration.[18]

Overview of Mongolia's FDI Mineral-Related Legislation

Mongolian law in many ways was very open to foreign investors in 2009. It did not discriminate against them in favor of Mongolian citizens, and they could invest with as little as $100,000 cash or the equivalent value of capital material. They could own 100 percent of any registered business, with no requirement for a Mongolian joint venture partner. Investment was welcomed in all activities except land ownership (only permitted to citizens but available on thirty- to ninety-year leases), petroleum extraction (oil extraction firms were required to enter into production-sharing contracts with the government), and strategic mineral (especially uranium) deposits. In 2006 the Mongolian government passed a Windfall Profits Tax Law after only six days of debate and no consultation with stakeholders on any of its provisions. This law imposed a 68 percent tax on the profits from gold and copper mining that set price thresholds as to when the highest level would go into effect. Profits were to be placed in a special fund for a combination of social welfare expenditures and a reserve fund. The OT Investment Agreement required amending this law as a precondition to its parliamentary approval since Ivanhoe and Rio Tinto had argued that they would not be able to run a commercially viable OT operation unless the tax was changed. Therefore, Parliament agreed to end this tax on all copper concentrate and gold products by 2011.

The 2006 Mineral Law, which replaced the 1997 law, created the legal concept of strategically important mineral deposits, which gave the government the right to obtain up to either a 34 percent or a 50 percent share in such deposits. The law defined the strategically important deposit as "a mineral concentration where it is possible to maintain production that has a potential impact on national security, economic and social development of the country at national and regional levels or deposits which are producing or have potential of producing above 5% of total GDP per year."[19] However, because Parliament was given the power to determine what is or is not a strategic deposit, this definition has fluctuated over time. When the Mineral Law was adopted, two appendices listed strategically important deposits. The first listed fifteen deposits that already were accepted as strategically important, while the second referred to an additional thirty-nine deposits that required further exploration to determine if any of them qualified for this designation.[20] To date, the government of Mongolia has labeled only its world-class copper and coal reserves and all rare-earth and uranium deposits as strategic. If a mineral deposit is determined to be strategic and if the Mongolian government at some juncture were to utilize public monies for the exploration of that deposit, the government could claim up to 50 percent ownership. If the deposit were explored and developed only with private funds, the government could obtain only up to 34 percent of the equity. State share is determined in each case by an agreement between the government and the private firm; however, Parliament may act to determine the government stake based upon official mineral reserve statistics. Furthermore, all petroleum and mineral licenses (exploration and mining operations) can only be registered to Mongolian entities, so all foreign investors are forced to establish Mongolian corporations.

To facilitate foreign investment and navigate investors through the entire process, Mongolia established a trade organization (FIFTA) in 1998.[21] It was

> charged with implementing policies and legislation with respect to foreign investment, to research possibilities to increase foreign investment, to organize investment promotional activities, to provide investors with relevant information, and to involve foreign investors in project tenders; to provide foreign investors with a complete "One-stop service," to prepare information on foreign investment statistics; to approve and/or disapprove establishment of a business entity with foreign investment or a branch of a foreign legal entity; to terminate, temporarily or completely, the activities of a business entity with foreign investment or a branch of a foreign legal entity; and other rights specified in legislation.[22]

In September 2000, FIFTA was placed under the Ministry of Industry and Trade. Its two major responsibilities were the development of foreign investment projects and the promotion of FDI. FIFTA developed a "One-stop service" center to coordinate assistance to investors who wished to establish business enterprises. This center provided advice on taxes, customs, labor regulations, and other business licensing organizations and issued certificates of incorporation to foreign investment or representative offices. It promised support in post-incorporation issues such as importing capital and equipment, issuing ID cards for investor residency permission and multiple-entry visas, and providing advice about which government entities could assist with solving specific problems. However, FIFTA's record was criticized as spotty and lacking coherence.

Impact of 2009 Laws on Investor Rights

The year 2009 was a pivotal one for mining development in Mongolia. The OT agreement was the big positive story, but the passage of two other key laws impacted domestic politics, foreign investment, and the overall development of the mineral sector in ways that muddled Mongolia's claims to being a competitive and predictable investment environment. New legislation imposed significant controls on uranium mining and its processing, through the creation of the Nuclear Regulatory Authority of Mongolia (NRA), a regulatory agency, and MonAtom to hold assets the government reclaimed from current holders. All uranium exploration and mining licenses were revoked, and all previous holders then had to reregister these licenses with the NRA for a fee. These new licenses included the clause that the Mongolian state has an absolute right to take, without compensation, at least 51 percent of any company that will develop any uranium property. A new uranium-specific licensing and regulatory regime was promulgated for discovering and developing uranium resources.[23] The Law on the Prohibition of Minerals Exploration in Water Basins and Forested Areas, aka The Law with the Long Name, was passed to prohibit mining in water basins and forested areas. This law was imposed because there was popular anger at the environmental damage caused primarily by placer gold mining (mostly in Chinese hands) in forests and watersheds.[24] It revoked mineral exploration and mining licenses for areas within 200 meters of a water or forest resource. Compensation was granted to license holders for their expenses or revenue lost. One area of nontransparency was that the law stated local officials had the discretion to extend the 200-meter minimum limit.

Foreign investors and their governments used inflated rhetoric to condemn these two new laws as nontransparent and potentially expropriatory. They argued that Mongolia was changing its laws suddenly and introducing unpredictability into the investment environment. Domestic and foreign critics complained that the laws were passed without any detailed plans for indemnifying rights holders or allowing public review and comment, and the license holders were not consulted as part of the drafting process. Another major complaint was that greater decisionmaking powers and broad discretion over mining licenses were passed down to local officials. While these changes in the Water Basin Law's licensing and regulatory regime were inconvenient for the foreign investors who preferred negotiating terms with more Westernized central government officials in Ulaanbaatar, they were exactly what Mongolian citizens in the areas affected by environmental degradation were demanding. Mongolian civic groups saw this as local democracy's taking back power from Ulaanbaatar bureaucrats who had been corruptly selling licenses in faraway districts, often with total disregard for local considerations.

Researchers on Mongolian nomads have long recognized that nomadic pastoral society operates "through the building up of relationship networks,"[25] which derive heavily from neighboring cooperation and alliances that weaken over distance. Mining operations in Mongolia were legalized in the distant national capital but had little validity for and connection to the migrating rural population in the mining areas. Nevertheless, foreign-invested companies believed the central government must enforce the terms of the contracts instead of the companies spending their time and capital building up relations with or greasing the palms of the migratory Mongols who shared the same space. Friction between legal reality and customary practice advanced to the point where Mongolian local leaders were rejecting instructions from Mongolian mineral authority officials and greatly frustrating foreign investors. The disconnect between pastoral traditional psychology and modern economic concepts influenced the movement within the Mongolian Parliament to take decisionmaking about new mining licenses out of the hands of Ulaanbaatar-based ministries and include input from the people's political representatives at the local level.

Mongolian politicians feared the growing presence and activities of mining in local communities were triggering local community or herder complaints and grievances that could potentially escalate into conflicts. In January 2011, the Mongolian government announced a trilateral memorandum with trade unions and the employers' union to solve any conflicts and complaints regarding exploitation of the mining resources. The official state news agency, Montsame, said the document was authored by the head of the cabinet secretariat, Ch. Khürelbaatar, the chairman of Mongolia's Trade Unions, and the president of Mongolia's Union of Employers. The memorandum called for the formation of a training program for local governments, businessmen, and state officials to promote citizens' participation to benefit from mining revenue, consult at national and local levels, expand access to opportunities, and peacefully solve any conflicts over the mining resources. Politicians of all parties argued repeatedly over how to exploit mineral resources in response to critics who accused the government of giving away Mongolia's wealth and demanded that foreign investment laws be changed to increase the government's share of all foreign-owned mines. In September 2011, a bloc in Parliament, in opposition to the government, startled international investors by threatening to disregard the long-standing foreign investment agreement with Ivanhoe and Rio Tinto at OT. This situation was only defused when the president and prime minister jointly renounced revoking this contract.[26]

Parliament members, in direct response to the concerns of their constituents, saw the Water and Forest Basin Law's confrontation with foreign investors as politically necessary, and some turned their complaints into a nationalistic outcry against the rapacious acts of the many small Chinese companies involved in illegal gold mining operations. The law was championed by the well-known and controversial nomadic activist Tsetsgee Munkhbayar, a former herdsman turned environmentalist who has been variously called a "resource nationalist,"[27] extremist, or populist. Frustrated by what he said is the mining industry's tendency to ignore land regulations under the protection of national officials, Munkhbayar and others took to violent civil disobedience and intimidation to gain publicity. In a romantic but powerful gesture out of Mongolia's past, Munkhbayar on June 3, 2010, led a group of fifty horsemen into the center of Ulaanbaatar, where they shot arrows at the Government House. After his arrest, Munkhbayar declared, "We are doing what we should do. We have inherited this entire land from our ancestors and must reserve this wholly to our descendants." On September 16, 2013, Munkhbayar with leaders of his Mongolia's Fire Nation (Gal Undesten), an environmental and human rights coalition, organized a mass protest in front of the Mongolian Parliament. Six of the ten arrested protesters, including Munkhbayar, were detained on the charge "group attempt to severely threaten well-being of society." In January 2014, the six were sentenced to twenty-one years and six months in prison.[28]

A more widespread problem was the inconsistency as well as corruption found in the Mongolian judiciary when hearing cases involving foreign investors. The US government found "no concerted, systematic, institutional abuse specifically targeted at foreign investment," but believed that "most problems arose from ignorance of commercial principles rather than antipathy to foreign investment."[29] Although Mongolian law provided for the sanctity of contracts, the concept was not consistently applied. This inconsistency was explained as stemming from the slow transition from Marxist-based jurisprudence to more market-oriented laws and judicial practices, so many observers believed that, with greater training and the retirement of Soviet-era jurists, the entire system would improve.

Despite these destabilizing and negative elements emanating from foreign investment, Mongolian policymakers consistently have understood that FDI was essential to exploiting the extensive mineral deposits across their country. The success of the government's international cooperation framework and arrangements was evidenced by the significant increase in FDI in major development projects. Average annual domestic and foreign investment growth was about 20 percent in 1999–2005, increasing to 54.1 percent in 2006–2012. During this same period, FDI investment increased 10.2 times, and domestic investment multiplied by 7.6 times. According to World Bank data, FDI as a proportion of GDP rose from 5 percent in 2000 to 23 percent by 2010.[30] Simultaneously, Mongolia closely cooperated with international organizations and donor countries to receive $910.6 million in concessional loans during 2006–2012, which was spent on implementation of the nation's Millennium Development Goals.[31] An additional $848.9 million was obtained in donor grants for 429 projects during this same period so that the number of projects and programs under the foreign aid program grew 2.4 times.[32]

The state-owned Mongolian Development Bank was officially launched in October 2011. This government-owned, policy-oriented, for-profit financial institution was created to foster Mongolian economic and infrastructure development by providing long-term financing for large-scale projects consistent with the government's macroeconomic development strategy and

Millennium Development Goals to improve living standards and enhance Mongolia's competitiveness in international markets. Among its strategic sectoral program and startup projects are a state strategy on rail transport, the Sainshand (South Gobi) Industrial Complex, roads around Ulaanbaatar, and energy construction projects. The Mongolian Development Bank issued dollar bonds in various international financial markets and raised $2.4 billion on commercial terms from international financial markets. Although warned at the time by the World Bank and IMF about assuming too much debt, the Mongolian government began a cycle of debt accumulation that was to be repaid starting in 2017.

Another feature of the boom era was the growth of Mongolian firms seeking to acquire equity by listing themselves on overseas exchanges rather than relying on only the Mongolian Stock Exchange. Around thirty firms have shares listed on commodity-rich global exchanges, such as London's Alternative Investments Market and the New York Stock Exchange.[33] While several firms participated in the full listing process, a growing number utilized reverse takeovers as a backdoor means of listing assets abroad. The four largest stocks listed offshore in 2011 were Ivanhoe Mines, Centerra Gold, Mongolian Mining Corporation (an MCS Group subsidiary listed in Hong Kong), and SouthGobi Resources, together holding a combined market value of $23.1 billion, roughly three times Mongolia's 2011 GDP.[34]

Tavan Tolgoi

The other major strategic deposit that captured the imagination of foreign investors because it promises to become even more lucrative for investors and the Mongolian government is the giant coal-uranium deposit known as Tavan Tolgoi (Five Hills) or TT. Located in the South Gobi desert 150 kilometers from OT, in an area without roads or rail for deliveries to the Chinese border 240 kilometers away nor the electric power and water supply necessary to support big mining, TT is the site of the world's largest high-quality coking coal deposit (used in steelmaking), with reserves estimated at 7.5 billion tons. TT was discovered in the 1940s by the Soviets, who continued exploratory drilling and feasibility studies until 1985. Early in the democratic transition, the Anglo-Australian multinational BHP Billiton gained TT exploratory rights, which it relinquished in the mid-1990s. In 2006, Energy Resources, LLC, a Mongolian private company that includes MCS Group, the largest private holding group in Mongolia, and Petrovis, LLC, the largest Mongolian petroleum import company, was granted a thirty-year mining license over one TT section, while the whole of TT was listed in the 2006 Mineral Law as a strategic deposit, which permitted the government to retain ownership. The next year the MPRP government under

President Enkhbayar and Prime Minister Sanjaa Bayar proposed that the state hold 50 percent of TT, Energy Resources keep 14 percent, and the remaining 36 percent be offered to other foreign investors. As a result, in 2007 Erdenes MGL, LLC, was formed as a wholly government-owned company to manage the renationalized Tavan Tolgoi. Energy Resources still held its Ukhaa Khudag section, which has coal reserves of 580 million tons. Erdenes MGL in 2010 formed a new company called Erdenes Tavan Tolgoi (ETT) to hold the licenses and operate in TT.

TT has been divided into three major sections with three different exploitation strategies. Ukhaa Khudag, whose production is sold solely to China, as of 2016 is controlled privately by Mongolian Mining Corporation (MMC), which operates Energy Resources and also holds a thirty-year license for another large coking coal site, Baruun Naran, with reserves of 300 million tons.[35] MMC in 2011 constructed a road from Ukhaa Khudag to the Gashuun Sukhait border crossing with China and by the end of 2014 had completed construction of an 18-megawatt power plant, a water supply system, a coal transport railway, and a three-module processing plant. It also planned to construct a Chinese 1435 mm standard gauge rail spur for direct connection to China's railway network. The two largest sections of TT, East Tsankhi and West Tsankhi, are under the management of the Mongolian government through ETT. East Tsankhi is fully owned by the Mongolian state company ETT, which had a $500 million contract with Australian mining company MacMahon Holdings from 2012 to 2017 to exploit it through a joint venture. This section has experienced a number of work stoppages because of delayed payments to MacMahon, but production, which is all destined for Chinese clients, has averaged three million tons per year, with a total value over five years of $2 billion.

In 2012 the Mongolian government decided on a plan to float 20 percent of ETT's East Tsankhi stake in an initial public offering (IPO) on the Hong Kong, London, and Ulaanbaatar stock exchanges. A further 10 percent of ETT was to be sold to local Mongol companies with 10 percent of the shares to be distributed to every Mongolian citizen. Foreign mining experts, as well as the Mongolian government, stoked unreasonably high expectations for TT:

> TT will be even bigger, and is expected to raise as much as $10 billion. Here is where it gets fun. The government has given each of its three million citizens 538 shares, or 10% of the company. At $10 billion, the shares would be worth $360—or $193,680 per citizen. According to the CIA's *World Factbook*, Mongolia had a total GDP of $11.02 billion in 2010. Per capita income was $3,600. In other words, Mongolians will suddenly be rich.[36]

The Mongols shortlisted BNP Paribas, Deutsche Bank, Goldman Sachs, and Macquarie as advisers on the IPO, but the IPO has been repeatedly postponed as foreign investors wanted the West Tsankhi investment agreement settled. The promise of distributing ETT shares from East Tsankhi to Mongolian citizens simultaneously was used by the government for domestic political purposes to influence the outcome of the 2012 parliamentary elections.

The West Tsankhi section of TT has been functioning as a small coal mine for the Mongolian market since 1967, and ETT in August 2011 began exporting coal to China. In order to obtain FDI for the TT's West Tsankhi, Mongolian officials began negotiations in 2009 with international mining companies. Domestically, they promoted the necessity of FDI in West Tsankhi: "In selecting the strategic investor as partner for the Tavan Tolgoi deposit, an option that will create a conducive environment for development, and also strengthen and balance the political and economic relations of the country will be supported."[37] During this period coal prices were high, and Chinese demand was strong. Fifteen major international mining companies reportedly participated in these discussions. The Indian giant Jindal Steel made several visits to Ulaanbaatar, while the US government supported the proposal of the American company Peabody Energy, the largest private coal company in the world, which opened an office in Ulaanbaatar. Since Japanese steelmakers were keen to diversify their coal sourcing, initial bidders included two Japanese-led groups: a consortium of Itochu-Sumitomo-Marubeni-Sojitz and Mitsui partnered with China's state-run Shenhua Group. Another bid came from South Korea's Korean Resources Corporation together with Russia's state-owned Russian Railways.[38]

There was a great deal of foreign government pressure and nontransparency about the entire process. The Mongolian government in January 2011 required potential foreign bidders for the West Tsankhi to submit initial proposals that included a nonrefundable upfront payment of $1 billion to hold a place for consideration. Other requirements included building a railway for coal transportation; arranging permission to use a seaport; presenting a workable transit plan; building a coal processing plant; and utilizing the most advanced, nonpolluting extraction technology. Since TT is located in an area without the roads and railways needed to quickly and economically deliver coal to markets, some proposals included the offer to construct a new railway connecting Mongolia and Russia (to transport the coal to South Korea and Japan via Russia's Pacific coast) or to ship coal through the existing route from China to Japan. Nine of the potential bidders dropped out, mainly discouraged by the large advance payment. The Mongols privately screened all offers to decide which were qualified to proceed even before launching the official bidding process and shortlisted six companies—Shenhua Group, ArcelorMittal, Russia's Railway Alliance, Peabody Energy, Vale S.A., and Xstrata. The South Korean and Japanese conglomerates were encouraged by the Mongols to partner with other mining giants.

Rumors were rife in July 2011 that the government had awarded the contract to mine West Tsankhi to three of the bidders: China's Shenhua

Group, a Russian-led consortium, and Peabody Energy Corporation, which was surprising since two of the winners did not participate in the call for tenders. Shenhua was selected, but its association with the Japanese company Mitsui was not mentioned in the final result. As for the Russian consortium, it was not on the list of bidding candidates, and it was claimed to not yet exist.[39] When Mongolia's National Security Council[40] rejected this investor list just two months after the winners were announced, it was explained that the losing bidders from Brazil, India, and South Korea raised serious concerns about transparency, while Japan called the whole bidding process "extremely regrettable."[41] ETT officials promised that a final decision would come in 2012. This delay reportedly was supported by Russia to be certain that any new rail spur from TT to China was 50 percent Russian-owned.[42] During the long delay, coal prices began to slide, so the Mongols encouraged ETT to begin mining operations alone in Western Tsankhi.

Two successive Mongolian People's Party (MPP) prime ministers, Sanjaa Bayar (2009) and Sukhbaatar Batbold (2011), concluded agreements to borrow $350 million from the Chinese state-owned aluminum company Chalco to cover future sales of Eastern Tsankhi coal at a very low price. The initial agreement had fixed the price of coal at $70 per ton, but it was later reduced to $47 per ton, in keeping with prevailing global rates. Chalco's CEO visited Mongolia in September 2011 to finalize the deal with Prime Minister Batbayar and pressure ETT to clear the advance payment as soon as possible.[43] However, after the spring 2012 election, a new parliamentary government led by the Democratic Party and Prime Minister Norov Altankhuyag took over the TT process. Altankhuyag tried to amend the Chalco agreement, which only annoyed the Chinese government and led to a temporary halt in coal exports. Mongolian attention turned to confirming the building of a joint power plant project with Japan's Marubeni and dealing with ETT's outstanding debt to Chalco, which then was involved in a different crisis with the Mongols over the purchase of coal-producing SouthGobi Resources from Ivanhoe Mining. The new government emphasized strengthening Mongolia's transport interconnectivity by signing an agreement to develop a China-Mongolia-Russia Economic Corridor.

New conditions set by Mongolia's National Security Council proved unattractive to many foreign companies looking at TT. Peabody Energy dropped out of the bidding pool and closed its Ulaanbaatar office. Mongolia's Russian partners were unhappy because under this new formula their bidder, Ulaanbaatar Railways, would first have to wait until the completion of a Chinese narrow-gauge railway before the building of a Russian-style, wide-gauge railway from TT to the Sainshand industrial zone. The National Security Council had made mandatory a new condition that the investor should export thirty million tons of semiprocessed coal in the first two and a half years to move exports from just raw materials to value-added products. In a trade diversification measure, at least five million tons of semiprocessed products were to be sold to Japan and South Korea. The coal purchase agreement between Chalco and ETT was not implemented because Chalco declared that it did not have to fulfill its responsibilities if the Mongolian government did not provide the TT coal on schedule. Commercial activity at the mine halted repeatedly as a result of financial constraints.

In 2014 Altankhuyag revived the TT bid discussion by contacting the shortlisted companies. The TT terms were amended to permit foreign mining companies to operate within the entire site (the East and West Tsankhi division was dropped) in order to reduce costs for building roads and rail and avoid constructing two washing plants and two power plants. Fifty-one percent of the deposit that earlier belonged to state-owned ETT was to be vested with a private consortium composed of Tavan Tolgoi, LLC, Mongolyn Alt,[44] and Energy Resources. ETT, which continued to hold the mining license, was permitted to enter into an investment and cooperation agreement with an investor on payment of an agreement fee, but ETT's debts of $110 million to Chalco and $280 million to banking institutions would automatically transfer to that investor.[45]

How to move forward with TT had become a key domestic economic issue for the Democratic Party (DP), after Mongolia's GDP had slowed with declining coal sales and FDI had fallen 71 percent in the first three quarters of 2014 compared with the same period the previous year.[46] That November, after political infighting and a flagging economy resulted in a vote of no confidence in Altankhuyag, Chimed Saikhanbileg took over as prime minister for the DP government. Within six weeks foreign investors were excited to hear that Saikhanbileg's government privately had identified a new group of foreign investors for the TT tender without a rebidding process. Without explanation, the Mongols teamed China's Shenhua Energy and Japan's Sumitomo Corporation with MMC's Energy Resources to come up with $4 billion in investment to develop the mine in partnership with the state. Mongolian authorities explained that the winning consortium had agreed to invest, without strings, around $4 billion; promised to assume the remaining $160 million in debt for TT that the Mongolian government owed to Chalco;[47] and pledged to construct new TT railroad spurs that could move the coal to northern as well as southern markets.

Buoyed by this news, foreign observers said that this "investment into Tavan Tolgoi could have a similar impact on Mongolia's $12 billion economy as the initial $6.5 billion investment between 2009 and 2013 into the country's other giant mine, Rio Tinto's Oyu Tolgoi copper-gold mine." There were projections that this $4 billion in FDI could increase to $8 to $12 billion over two or three years.[48] However, greater confusion about the future of TT developed when Erdenes TT's former chief executive officer Yaichil Batsuuri,[49] a DP politician known for his aversion to dependence on Chinese purchases of TT coal, was jailed on embezzlement and corruption charges. This controversial arrest occurred when Erdenes TT was negotiating Shenhua Energy's participation as a TT finalist, which Batsuuri may have opposed. Media reports noted, "Natural-resources deals with China are politically sensitive in Mongolia and have been the backdrop for other controversial corruption charges in the past."[50]

However, four months later in April, just twenty-four hours after Rio Tinto–controlled Turquoise Hills was allowed to proceed with its long-delayed phase two expansion of OT, the Mongolian Parliament canceled the entire TT consortium foreign investment deal, although the previous weekend Prime Minister Saikhanbileg had announced that discussions with Shenhua Energy and Sumitomo Corporation were in their final stages. In late December 2015, coal extraction resumed in TT's Eastern Tsankhi section after a one-year break. During that time, the government had renewed its contract with TTJV, a Chinese company, and settled a contentious labor dispute with on-site workers after their trade union leader publicly set himself on fire to protest the transfer of Mongol workers to TTJV. Still unresolved was $150 million ETT owed to Chalco Group.[51] As of 2017, foreign investment in TT has not proceeded, while the management of the TT tender process is seen as an example of Mongolian bureaucratic bungling and unrealistic expectations.

Mongolian Economic Bubble Bursts

When Mongolia dismantled the country's Stalinist system in 1990 and replaced it with democratic and free market institutions, it seemed to be leveraging its vast mineral resources to achieve quick socioeconomic growth. The development of the huge copper-gold deposit of OT and coal-uranium deposit of TT led to a 17.3 percent growth rate in 2011 and 12.3 percent in 2012. Former US Ambassador Jonathan Addleton noted that, when he arrived in Mongolia in the mid-1990s as USAID director, Mongolian per capita GDP stood at $300, but when he ended his tour as ambassador in 2012 it had risen to $3,000.[52] In an allusion to the successful Asian Tigers of the 1980s (Singapore, Taiwan, South Korea, Hong Kong, and Japan), Mongolia was labeled the Asian Wolf and its mineral-based economy, the Wolf economy. Financial blogs spoke of mining mania, and the Mongolian government itself promoted the idea of foreign mining countries lining up to sign lucrative deals worth $25 billion in investment.[53]

China since the late 1990s had become Mongolia's largest trading partner. In 2014 trade with China accounted for 61.8 percent of the total ($11 billion) or $6.8 billion, while trade with Russia accounted for 14.6 percent or $1.6 billion. This represented a 23.9 percent increase in trade turnover between Mongolia and China.[54] China was the largest source of FDI (49 percent in 2012), followed by Canada (8 percent), the Netherlands, and Luxembourg. Approximately 65.3 percent of Chinese FDI gravitated to the "geological prospecting" oil and mining sector.[55] The reasons for the steep rises and declines in FDI in

Mongolia during the past two decades were connected to world economic commodity trends, Mongolia's vacillating foreign investment policies, foreign government pressures, corruption, and conflicting strategic mineral deposit development plans. Mining companies in an environment of depressed demand for commodities also were struggling with their own massive debt obligations. This factor and the failed TT tendering efforts over the years increased foreign investor reluctance to develop the site.[56] It appeared that the Mongolian mineral resource economy was riding a roller coaster.

Yet, this economic analysis is not sufficient to understand Mongolian policymaking delays and reversals. The next chapter will go into more detail about the overarching Mongolian strategy toward development and national security, beyond market fluctuations and the cyclical nature of the commodities business. Here it is important to point out that underlying the above mentioned economic factors are strong historical and cultural biases that at times have superseded economic best practices and roiled domestic politics in Mongolia's young but vibrant democracy. If one looks at Mongolian coal exports, for example, China at present is the overwhelming buyer, which gives China total control of pricing and volume. The Chinese major coking coal supplier Winsway increased its purchases of Mongolian coal from zero in 2006 up to 6.5 million tons by 2010. So, when in July 2011 Shenhua Energy, China's largest coal-producing company, was offered 40 percent control in the nontransparent TT tender process, the Mongolian public and its parliamentary representatives reacted with political hostility leading to political indecision by the Mongolian government. Additionally, Mongolian policymakers felt burned by the foreign investors on OT, so there was special concern that the same mistake should not be made, even if all the delays were disadvantageous economically. In 2015 Mongolian Ambassador to China Tsedenjav Sükhbaatar explained the circumstances of his country's slow repayment of its TT coal obligations to Chalco: "We know that due to the long negotiation, we have missed the golden era when China's coal price was high. But considering its vast deposits, the world's largest untapped coal mine, we still believe it is necessary to put deliberation as a priority."[57]

President Elbegdorj and the National Security Council feared that Chinese companies possessing mining licenses already held too much market power and the ability to control production and pricing against Mongolia's best interests. They believed that for Mongolia to stay competitive and be less dependent on coal prices, it had to diversify its trade partners, and this could only occur if the country moved forward with infrastructure development. Thus, building railways with Chinese gauge down to the Chinese border, which previously was viewed with fear, was considered an absolute necessity to reduce freight costs and lower Mongolian export prices in the Elbegdorj era. Nonetheless, Mongolian policymakers today still insist that to break China's trade monopoly, construction of Russian-gauge rail spurs connecting north to the Trans-Siberian were equally necessary.

Because constructing the hard rail and road infrastructure to connect with Chinese and Russian railways is so costly, many foreign experts encouraged Mongolia to develop downstream coal processing plants within its own borders to increase value and competitiveness.[58]

To expand domestic mining-related industries, at least some of the large mining projects must proceed, despite local community environmental concerns. However, in the twenty-first century, both Mongolia's often unstable domestic political climate and the falling international demand for coal, especially in the Chinese market, have made it nearly impossible to attract more diversified sources of FDI. According to the World Bank, in 1991 (first year of FDI data) Mongolia attracted only $11,120,000 in FDI. By the end of the first decade of democracy, FDI had increased fivefold to $53.7 million. While this was a significant rise, the baseline was so low that such a statement can be misleading. Figure 7.1 indicates clearly that the jump in Mongolian FDI begins in 2005 ($184.6 million) with the resolution of the Soviet-era debt and the opening development phase of OT under Ivanhoe. Even the 2006 Windfall Profits Tax on gold and copper did not deter the strong growth, which accelerated in 2008 to $844.7 million with the emergence of Rio Tinto in the OT negotiations.

During 2009 there was a significant dip in FDI while the OT negotiations slowly proceeded, but once there was a final agreement, FDI skyrocketed in 2010 and especially in 2011 when it reached $4.7 billion—the year of its maximum—due to 80 percent of capital inflows to the mining sector (see Figure 7.2). The TT tender was in 2011, which likely was the main reason for investor interest in Mongolia. Even in 2012, when the Mongolian economy began a slowdown of coal exports to China, FDI inflow still was very high ($4.5 billion), and it remained stable as a proportion of GDP, amounting to 40 percent. However, in 2014 when the TT deal collapsed, the bottom fell out, and FDI plunged 62.4 percent to only $383.9 million, a level not seen since 2007. The Mongols still have not stopped the downslide. In 2015, FDI was only $195 million,[59] and in 2016 it was not expected to rebound significantly.

Mongolia's real GDP growth rate since the beginning of 2003 has grown between 7 and 10.6 percent for six consecutive years. According to the World Bank, in 2009 the global financial crisis hit Mongolia and for the first time in sixteen years its economy contracted by 1.27 percent. The downturn did not last long because of the infusion of FDI in the country's two major mining deposits of OT and TT. In 2010 Mongolia's GDP registered 6.4 percent real growth, but one year later, in 2011, Mongolia recorded real GDP growth of 17.5 percent, making it the fastest growing economy in Asia and one of the top five economies in the world.[60] Another positive factor was that in early July 2013, Rio Tinto through its partner Turquoise Hill started shipping copper from OT to Chinese customers.

Since 2010, 4,000 mining-related licenses were returned or canceled without compensation. Many of these licenses covered placid deposits

Figure 7.1 Foreign Direct Investment, Net Inflows, 1986–2017 (BoP, current US$)

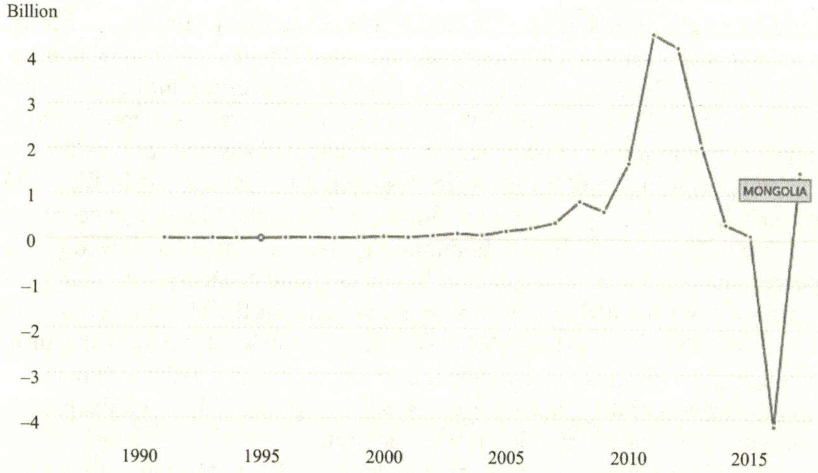

Source: World Bank, https://data.worldbank.org/indicator/BX.KLT.DINV.CD.WD?end=2017&locations=MN&start=1986&view=chart.

Figure 7.2 Mongolia's Annual GDP Growth, 1982–2017

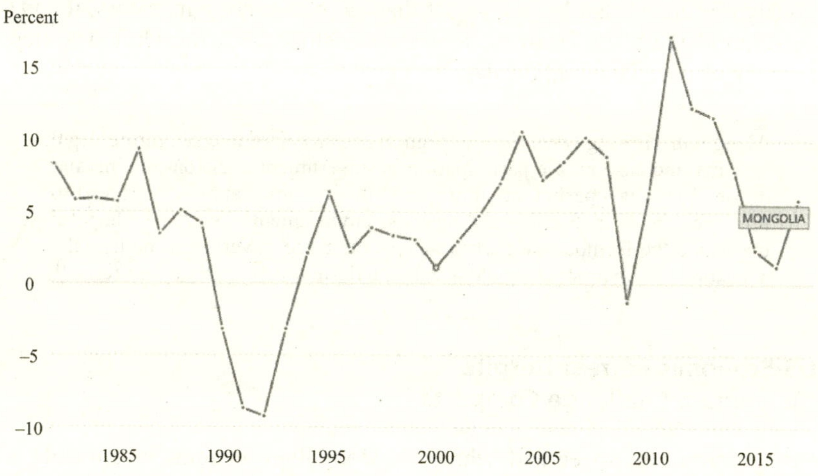

Source: As reported by Mongolia's National Statistics Office and World Bank, 2001–2018.

along river sources and water basins and were banned for environmental pollution reasons by Parliament. In the beginning of 2013, private companies, domestic and foreign-invested, held 2,239 mining exploration licenses over twenty million hectares of land.[61] The Mongolian Mineral Authority, which is responsible for all licensing, indicated that it could cancel another 1,400 licenses by 2014, stop granting new private licenses until 2017,[62] and let mineral exploitation proceed only in the fifteen strategic deposits (such deposits are required to be at least 50 percent state-owned, except for the OT copper-gold project) that were designated by Parliament in the 2006 Mining Law.[63] As a result of these mining policies, the Mongolian economy was brought near to collapse. Economic growth in Mongolia slowed to 1.4 percent in 2015. The Mongolian policymakers and citizenry, although well warned about the dangers of relying so heavily on the mineral sector, did not avoid the crash. Mongolia was able to somewhat cushion the drop through indiscriminate international borrowing, but in 2017, these massive debts started coming due with unknown but potentially very dangerous consequences, including countrywide default.

President Elbegdorj's reelection in June 2013 kept the Mongolian government in the hands of the Democratic Party. Even though the first term of his presidency had seen both boom and early signs of bust in the resource mineral economy and significant restrictions in the mineral legal regime to create a less friendly environment for foreign investors, the world financial community blamed these developments upon the rising nationalism of Parliament and not the pro-Western president. Investors supported his reelection action plan of a transparent governance framework, sustainable economic development through a fair and stable investment climate, and environmentally friendly approach to mining development. They were cautiously optimistic that he would not discriminate among investors, the OT agreement would be retained, and relationships with the United States, Japan, and the EU would deepen:

> Along with fighting corruption, Elbegdorj has promised to enact further legal reforms, increase public participation in government decision-making and boost Mongolia's participation in global institutions that all should lead to improvement of investment and business environment. We are also hopeful that since the Democratic Party rules all the three government bodies, the decision making process should accelerate during the next four year term.[64]

US Economic Retreat Despite Millennium Challenge Compacts

Few predicted the speed with which the Mongolian economy would slide or Elbegdorj's inability to reverse the precipitous fall. Also unforeseen was the retreat of the United States from playing a high-profile role in Mongolia's economy. On the surface, the mainstays of a thriving relationship existed. In 1990 the American-Mongolian Business Council (renamed the North American–Mongolian Business Council) was established. A bilateral trade and investment agreement was signed on July 15, 2005, and a US Chamber of Commerce opened in Ulaanbaatar in 2011. However, the warning signs were evident. When the United States and Mongolia marked the twenty-fifth anniversary of the establishment of diplomatic relations in January 2012, then US ambassador to Mongolia, Jonathan Addleton, stated that, despite the growth in ties over the quarter century, "Ultimately, vibrant commercial relations and growing people-to-people ties are needed to build and sustain bilateral relations between our countries."[65]

The reality was that the US economic position steadily eroded during Mongolia's mineral resource development era. The United States, Mongolia's major partner in promoting democracy and free market reforms for twenty years, was mostly distant and economically disconnected from the mineral boom. In 2013, US investment ranked eighth, while fifteen years previous it had been number one. In 1992 the US imported $6.9 million in Mongolian goods and exported only $2.3 million to Mongolia. By 2003, trade turnover reached $166 million, of which $143 million was in Mongolian exports (90 percent was fabric, cashmere, light industry products, and clothing).[66] In 2013 Mongolian imports were only $20 million (down 53.4 percent from 2012), but US exports to Mongolia were $282 million (down 57.5 percent from 2012) because of aircraft, vehicles, and machinery.[67] Although the nature of the bilateral relations was multifaceted, it was highly influenced by mineral commodity prices and mining legislation beyond Sino-US and Russian-US strategic considerations.

How to reduce the decline in American FDI over the last fifteen years was a problem the Mongols recognized but could not solve. The US position during that period was that it was one of Mongolia's special partners; it accepted the title of Mongolia's "Third Neighbor" and was committed to cooperating with Mongolia to further its democratic progress and international engagement. Although the Department of Commerce and US Trade Representative Office devoted time, funds, and energy through trade promotion seminars and company site visits in both the United States and Mongolia to encourage US companies to invest in Mongolia, the State Department and US embassy through USAID instead emphasized programs promoting economic competitiveness and policy assistance on anticorruption and anti–human trafficking measures. There is an investment incentive agreement between the United States and Mongolia requiring the Mongols to extend national treatment to Overseas Private Investment Corporation (OPIC)–financed projects in Mongolia. For example, mining licenses of firms receiving an OPIC loan may be pledged as collateral to OPIC, a right not normally bestowed on foreign financial entities. The US Export-Import Bank offers programs in Mongolia for short-, medium-, and long-term transactions in the public sector and for short- and medium-term transactions in the private sector.

With the passing of the donor assistance decade and the lack of major American FDI in Mongolia, the US government sought to stay relevant by playing a new economic role in Mongolia through a President George W. Bush–era program, entitled the Millennium Challenge Account, established by the US Congress in 2004. It was administered by the Millennium Challenge Corporation (MCC), an independent agency separate from the State Department and USAID that delivered foreign assistance based on competitive selection, country-led solutions, and country-led implementation. MCC was envisioned as a way to reward countries that had made progress on seventeen independent and transparent policy indicators associated with establishing democratic, free market institutions. The MCC Board required selected low-income countries to identify their priorities for achieving economic growth and poverty reduction. An agreement called a compact was awarded to oversee all aspects of implementation.[68]

After nearly three years of negotiations, the MCC signed a five-year, $285 million compact with the government of Mongolia on October 22, 2007, aimed at reducing poverty and promoting sustainable growth through investments in four projects. At the White House signing ceremony, President Bush welcomed then President Enkhbayar, saying, "The Millennium Challenge Account is an important part of our foreign policy. It's an opportunity for the United States and our taxpayers to help countries that fight corruption, that support market-based economies, and that invest in the health and education of their people." Enkhbayar replied that the two countries shared a commitment to good governance: "Mongolia also appreciates and upholds the principle of aid with accountability and ownership advocated by the government of the United States."[69] Yet, implementation of the compact almost immediately experienced major problems connected to changes in Mongolia's investment laws and negotiations over OT, which caused US investors to be concerned about the sanctity of contracts. The president of Citizens Against Government Waste in Washington singled out Mongolia in March 2008 for strong criticism:

> It is imperative that the United States communicate that future assistance for Mongolia will not go forward without significant reforms. One way to do that is for the MCC to make sure Western investment is being encouraged and property rights are protected. Until it demonstrates a commitment to reducing corruption and respecting the rule of law, Mongolia's MCC grant should be suspended.[70]

Despite such criticism, the MCC grant went forward. Originally, the majority of the MCC funds were to be invested in a $188 million rail project to upgrade Mongolia's only north-south railway, the Ulaanbaatar Railway. Funding was to be utilized for training and other technical assistance to improve its operational, management, maintenance, and regulatory practices, with significant monies devoted to equipment purchases to obtain up to thirty freight locomotives, 150 types of freight wagons, track maintenance machinery, and a modernized signaling and communications system for installation on the mainline track.[71] Much of the equipment was to be manufactured by General Electric. However, the MCC negotiators with no background in Mongolia's political-economic situation ignored the warnings of the US Ambassador to Mongolia Pamela Slutz to first coordinate their plans with the Russians on the governing board of the Ulaanbaatar Railway. Two years after the project was accepted, the Russians vetoed the entire American proposal, which led to the cancellation of the rail project. Two new projects were hastily added through an amendment to the compact in January 2010.

The amended compact included the following five projects: (1) $28 million Property Rights Project to improve the national property land privatization and registration system, privatize and register 52,995 (original target was 75,000) land plots for 1,300 poor herder households, lease approximately 465 tracts of rangeland to herder groups in peri-urban areas, and install 346 wells on leased lands; (2) $39 million Health Project in which 49.7 percent of the target population was screened for diabetes and more than 9,100 girls (ages 11–15) received one dose of human papillomavirus vaccine to prevent cervical cancers; (3) $48 million Vocational Education Project to update curricula, establish a labor market information system, supply new equipment, install and upgrade fifty-four technology labs, modernize 106 practical training sites, and implement professional development programs for vocational instructors that resulted in the graduation of about 12,000 students from MCC-supported educational facilities; (4) $47 million Energy and Environment Project (added by amendment) to increase the adoption of energy-efficient, less-polluting stoves in the *ger* districts to reduce wintertime air pollution in Ulaanbaatar and support the development of renewable energy, including a component for Wind Activity that supported an upgrade to a substation of the first commercially wind-powered electricity generation facility in Mongolia and installation of a training simulator for dispatchers of the National Dispatching Center in Ulaanbaatar; (5) $80 million North-South Road Project (added by amendment) to construct a 176-kilometer road between the towns of Choir and Sainshand in the Gobi, although bridge reconstruction and a second road were dropped for lack of funds and construction time.[72]

When the Mongolian Compact came to a close in September 2013, $269,002,143 of the original budget had been expended, leaving approximately $15.9 million in funds returned to MCC. A subsequent US government audit of the MCC program determined that $43 million was consumed by compact administration, and that several of its programs were poorly organized and wasteful. There was a $12 million budget shortfall on the North-South Road Project due to contractor changes and procurement delays, and the well houses constructed in the Property Rights Project were at times not properly ventilated, resulting in carbon monoxide poisoning.[73] Also, the Health component became very controversial when the Mongolian media raised a furor about the validity of vaccinating young girls, leading parents to withhold consent for the second and third shots in the series. The MCC did not reveal the failure and only admitted: "Assessing the achievement of the ultimate goal of the Health Project, increase of life expectancy of the Mongolian population, is not possible within the time frame of the project or immediately afterwards."[74] Thus, the Millennium Challenge Corporation First Compact, which originally was expected both to positively impact the Mongolian domestic rail transport situation and fuel new US-Mongolian business ties, resulted in neither. Its deliverables were so transitory or tangential to Mongolia's boom/bust economy that most were considered to be failures by the Mongolian people and policymakers.

With the economic footprint of the United States in Mongolia continuing to fade, American officials rationalized that the absence of US investment was due to a lack of transparency and an unstable legal regime in Mongolia. In the US-Mongolia Bilateral Investment Treaty, which had entered into force in 1997, Mongolia and the United States agreed to international law standards for expropriation and compensation for expropriation. US officials advocated that Ulaanbaatar control the country's endemic corruption by adopting a bilateral transparency agreement. Although the two governments signed such an agreement in September 2013,[75] opposition in the Mongolian Parliament to some terms delayed its ratification until December 5, 2014. The US embassy in Ulaanbaatar hailed the significance of the document's ratification as "an important milestone in the US-Mongolia trade relationship," but the transparency agreement ratification received almost no coverage in Mongolia's media beyond official government websites. Credit for the transparency agreement's ratification in the midst of a Mongolian governmental collapse and reorganization went to President Elbegdorj and his Democratic Party for recognizing that it was the key to unlocking Washington's agreement to a Second Millennium Challenge Compact. A week after the transparency agreement was ratified by the Mongolian Parliament, Elbegdorj was phoned by the CEO of the MCC with news that the country had been selected for its efforts to control corruption and enhance "good governance."[76] Elbegdorj replied that Mongolia's selection "demonstrates the United States' significance to bilateral relations of the two countries and democratic development in Mongolia."[77]

Nonetheless, symbolism and high-sounding verbiage did not halt the reality of the deteriorating economic relationship between the two countries. Even though the US company Peabody Energy Corporation in 2014 was shortlisted as a finalist for the development of TT, as soon as Mongolia was selected for the Millennium Challenge Compact Phase II, Ulaanbaatar announced that it had accepted a Mongolian-Japanese-Chinese consortium bid for TT, eliminating all chance for a sizable infusion of American FDI.[78]

US officials from the Department of Commerce and Department of State did not mask their disappointment at this news, and their hopes that a significant role for Peabody Energy would ultimately develop were totally dashed when Peabody left Mongolia several months later. Meanwhile, the MCC had moved slowly into consultations with the Mongolian government because Mongolia's second compact eligibility was in abeyance pending a decision on whether its recent move from lower middle income to upper middle income status excluded it from compact eligibility. When analysis identified a weak macroeconomic environment and policies negatively affecting business, air pollution impacts on health, and lack of access to water and sanitation in poor communities as possible compact targets, the process restarted.[79] The Second Compact was funded in the summer of 2018 at the level of $350 million and focuses on supporting the construction of new groundwater wells, introduction of a modern water purification plant, and construction of a new wastewater recycling plant and pipelines, all to enhance the long-term sustainability of Ulaanbaatar's water supply. These investments will increase the bulk water supply to Ulaanbaatar by more than 80 percent.[80]

Notes

1. US Department of State, Bureau of Economic, Energy, and Business Affairs, *2010 Investment Climate Statement: Mongolia* (Washington, DC: March 10, 2010), 5, https://www.state.gov/e/eb/rls/othr/ics/2010/138766.htm.
2. B. Enkhbat, "More Local Companies to Benefit from OT Underground Development," GoGo Mongolia, November 4, 2015, http://mongolia.gogo.mn/r/149498.
3. Brian Sturgess, "Investing in Mongolia," *World Economics,* September 2012, http://www.worldeconomics.com/Papers/Investing%20in%20Mongolia_c93dbdb0-1a04-4e33-b331-51c25d21d47a.paper#_ftn5.
4. Ibid.
5. "GNI per Capita, Atlas Method (Current US$)," World Bank, https://data.worldbank.org/indicator/NY.GNP.PCAP.CD?end=2017&start=1962.
6. "Mongolia Has 163.2 Billion Tons of Coal Reserve," *Business Mongolia,* September 5, 2011, http://www.businessmongolia.com/mongolia/2011/05/09/mongolia-has-163-2-billion-tons-of-coal-reserve/.
7. "Mongolia and Coal," *SourceWatch*, https://www.sourcewatch.org/index.php/Mongolia_and_coal.
8. World Bank, "Mongolia Energy Sector Review" (World Bank Report no. 14586-MOG, November 3, 1995), 12–14, http://documents.worldbank.org/curated/en/483911468773986690/pdf/multi-page.pdf.
9. "About Us," http://en.tavantolgoi.mn/.
10. Montsame News Agency, *Mongolia* (Ulaanbaatar: 2006), 80, 83. In 2015 profits were said to be only $4.6 million. See Lkhagva Erdene and Sergey Radchenko, "The Mysterious Sale of Mongolia's Erdenet Mine," *The Diplomat,* July 9, 2016, http://thediplomat.com/2016/07/the-mysterious-sale-of-mongolias-erdenet-mine/.
11. Erik Els, "Oyu Tolgoi Copper, Gold Production Drops," *mining.com*, August 2, 2016.
12. "Uranium in Mongolia," World Nuclear Association, April 2016, http://www.world-nuclear.org/information-library/country-profiles/countries-g-n/mongolia.aspx.
13. Petroleum Authority of Mongolia, http://english.pam.gov.mn/home.shtml.
14. *Mongolia Mining Journal*, mongolianminingjournal.com, September 20, 2012.

15. Interview with Chairman of Petroleum Authority G. Ulziiburen, in *Montsame*, March 19, 2013.

16. Sturgess, "Investing in Mongolia."

17. Elbegdorj studied economics at the University of Colorado and has a master's in public administration from Harvard University.

18. Sturgess, "Investing in Mongolia."

19. Quoted in US Department of State, *2010 Investment Climate Statement: Mongolia*.

20. N. Ariuntuya, "Strategy on Strategic Mineral Missing," *Mongolian Mining Journal*, August 8, 2012.

21. FIFTA is a successor entity to the Board of Foreign Investment, which was created in 1996 by the Parliament.

22. "FIFTA," *Invest Mongolia*, https://investmongolia.wordpress.com/category/fifta/.

23. US Department of State, *2010 Investment Climate Statement: Mongolia,* 5–6.

24. Not fully implemented by the government, it was upheld by Mongolia's Supreme Court in October 2011. David Stanway, "Mongolian Court Orders Govt to Enforce Mining Ban," Reuters, October 21, 2011.

25. Jacques Legrand, "Nomadic Pastoral Societies: The Importance of Compromise in Dealing with Tension, Conflict and Security," in *Mongols et Nomades: Société, Histoire, Culture* (Ulaanbaatar: Admon, 2011), 332.

26. Matthew Hill, "Mongolia Reaffirms Oyu Tolgoi Investment Agreement," *Mining Weekly*, October 6, 2011.

27. A characterization made by parliamentarian Ms. Sanjaasuren Oyun, who explained, "He fired guns near mining equipment last year and now says he and his followers may have to take up arms against the government." Quoted in Dexter Roberts, "Mineral-Rich, People-Poor Mongolia Prepares for Flood of Money Next Decade," *Bloomberg News,* July 21, 2011, http://www.bloomberg.com/news/2011-07-21/mineral-rich-people-poor-mongolia-prepares-for-flood-of-money.h.

28. Keith Harmon Snow, "Goldman Prizewinner Gets 21 Years for Resistance to Genocide," *Dissident Voice,* February 6, 2014.

29. US Department of State, *2010 Investment Climate Statement: Mongolia,* 11.

30. Sturgess, "Investing in Mongolia."

31. In 1992 in Rio de Janeiro, Mongolia developed the Sustainable Development Action Program of Mongolia for the 21st Century (MAP 21), the Millennium Declaration, and eight Millennium Development Goals (MDGs) to be achieved by 2015 for implementation of long- and medium-term national development policies, establishment of economic development planning, and development of monitoring and evaluation systems in Mongolia. In September 2000, leaders of 189 UN member nations endorsed these, and the Mongolian Parliament endorsed the Mongolian MDGs in 2005. Mongolia also added in 2008 its own ninth MDG on "Strengthening Human Rights and Fostering Democratic Governance." See http://www.indexmundi.com/mongolia/millennium-development-goals.html.

32. New projects and programs in education, health, social welfare, poverty reduction, gender, infrastructure, governance, and environment grew two to six times for the period in comparison to the previous six years. United Nations Economic and Social Council, "Annex to the Letter Dated 9 April 2015 from the Permanent Representative of Mongolia to the United Nations Addressed to the President of the Economic and Social Council, Executive Summary" (New York: Mongolian Mission to the UN, April 10, 2015), 10, paras. 34–36.

33. Other exchanges are the Australian Stock Exchange, Canada's Toronto Stock Exchange, Canadian National Stock Exchange, the Stock Exchange of Hong Kong, and the Singapore Exchange.

34. Other resource-linked stocks like Mongolia Energy Corporation, Petro Matad, Aspire Mining, and Xanadu Mines (also on the Australian Stock Exchange) and Prophecy Coal Corp. (also on the Toronto Stock Exchange) were represented offshore. "Tapping Offshore: Issuing and Floating Abroad to Finance Growth," Oxford Business Group, 2012.

35. Mongolian Mining Corporation, *Interim Report 2016* (Ulaanbaatar: MMC, 2016), 12, 14, http://www.mmc.mn/uploads/MMC_Interim%20report_2016_Eng.pdf.

36. Christian DeHaemer, "With Erdenes-Tavan Tolgoi's IPO, Mongolians 'Will Suddenly Be Rich,'" *Asia Journal of Mining,* June 9, 2011, http://www.asianmining.com/2011/06/with-erdenes-tavan-tolgois-ipo.html.

37. Recommendation of the National Security Council of Mongolia in April 2010, reported by L. Bolormaa, "Tavan Tolgoi Gets Ready for New Suitor, at Long Last," *Mongolian Mining Journal,* December 2, 2014, http://en.mongolianminingjournal.com/content/58189.shtml.

38. "Update 3: Two Japan-Led Groups to Bid for Tavan Tolgoi Coal Mine," Reuters, January 31, 2011, http://www.reuters.com/article/mongolia-tavan-tolgoi-idUSTOE70U02Q20110131.

39. "O. Tsendsuren: Mongolian and Russian Consortium Doesn't Exist," *Business Mongolia,* July 25, 2011.

40. Among those serving on the National Security Council were newly elected President Elbegdorj, MPP Prime Minister S. Batbold, and MPP Parliament Speaker D. Demberel.

41. Cecilia Jamasmie, "Mongolia Halts Landmark Deal with Foreign Firms over Massive Coal Mine," *mining.com*, April 7, 2015.

42. It was suggested that Russia preferred first to develop coking coal sites in Kyrgyzstan, which financially would be more beneficial. Bolormaa, "Tavan Tolgoi."

43. L. Bolormaa, "At Tide's Ebb," *Mongolian Mining Journal,* October 25, 2013.

44. MAK or Mongolyn Alt is a successful Mongolian mining company with twenty years of experience working with foreign, especially Chinese and Russian, investors. It operates the Shivee Khuren coal mine and Tsagaan Suvarga copper deposit and is developing the Khuut shale deposit and a mega coal liquefaction project based on its Aduunchuluun deposit.

45. Energy Resources, LLC's processing plant at Ukhaa Khudag, has a capacity of fifteen million tons, while that of ETT is planned to have twenty million tons. It will cost $570 million, and its feasibility report has been approved by the Minerals Council. See Bolormaa, "Tavan Tolgoi."

46. Terrence Edwards, "Mongolia's giant Tavan Tolgoi coalmine soon to be under new management," *IntelliNews,* January 14, 2015, http://www.intellinews.com/mongolia-s-giant-tavan-tolgoi-coalmine-soon-to-be-under-new-management-500442965/?archive=bne.

47. For Chalco debt see Infomongolia.com, December 12, 2014.

48. Edwards, "Mongolia's giant coalmine."

49. Batsuuri, a former member of Parliament who also served in Mongolia's foreign service, was head of Erdenes TT from October 2012 to February 2015.

50. "Local company head arrested as foreign executives pardoned," *The Economist,* March 3, 2015.

51. Jamasmie, "Mongolia halts landmark deal."

52. Jonathan Addleton, "The United States and Mongolia: A Diplomatic Perspective" (speech given at the East West Center Washington Office, October 23, 2013), http://www.eastwestcenter.org/vents/the-united-states-and-mongolia-diplomatic-perspective.

53. Jaime FlorCruz, "Mining fuels Mongolia's 'Wolf Economy,'" CNN, May 20, 2011, http://www.cnn.com/2011/WORLD/asiapcf/05/19/mongolia.mining.economy/index.html.

54. It also was a 0.8 percent decrease in trade turnover between Mongolia and Russia. N. Otgonsaikhan, "The Current Situation for Mongolian Foreign Trade and Cooperation with Northeast Asian Countries" (ERINA Report no.127, December 2015), http://www.erina.or.jp/en/wp-content/uploads/2015/02/se12712_tssc.pdf.

55. Zhang Yunbi and Wu Jiao, "China, Mongolia to Boost Ties," *China Daily,* January, 13, 2012, www.chinadaily.com.cn/cndy/2012-01/13/content_14436254.htm; Erdenebat Mungunzul and Taikoo Chang, "Foreign Direct Investment in the Mongolian Mining Sector," *International Journal of u– and e– Service, Science and Technology* 9, no. 3 (2016): 254, http://dx.doi.org/10.14257/ijunesst.2016.9.3.24.

56. Interview with Marius Toime, a project finance partner at Berwin Leighton Paisner's office in Singapore in "Mongolia: A Case Study in Foreign Direct Investment," *Steppe Dispatches,* March 23, 2015, https://steppedispatches.com/2015/03/23/mongolia-a-case-study-in-foreign-direct-investment/.

57. "Neutral Mongolia looks to be economic link," *Global Times,* November 11, 2015.

58. "Mongolia: A Case Study."

59. According to the US Department of State's *2016 Investment Climate Statement: Mongolia*, which was published in August 2016, this figure was inaccurately reported to be $232 million. See p. 1, "Executive Summary," https://www.state.gov/e/eb/rls/othr/ics/2016/eap/254299.htm.

60. "Mongolia's Foreign Direct Investment at a Crossroads," *Unuudur.com*, http://www.unuudur.com/?p=26969.

61. This was a reduction from 2008 when exploration licenses numbered 4,111 over nearly fifty million hectares. B. Ooluun, "Dependence on Foreign Oil Products to Be Reduced," *Mongol Messenger*, March 22, 2013.

62. Told to the author in Ulaanbaatar by Altansukh, the head of the Mineral Authority in June 2012.

63. According to the twenty-seventh resolution, Article 8.1.4 of the Mineral Law of Mongolia. *Law of Mongolia on Minerals Revised* (Ulaanbaatar: July 8, 2006), https://s3.amazonaws.com/rgi-documents/2c242a91b27ecc449f3040515c517d7c1e20c21a.pdf. The Mongolian government is considering adding new deposit sites to this list and in November 2012 started the procedure to add the Khushuut coal mine.

64. "Mongolia's Foreign Direct Investment at a Crossroads."

65. Quoted in Alicia Campi, "Developing U.S.-Mongolian Relations," *Asia-Pacific Bulletin*, no. 113 (May 26, 2011).

66. Imports from the United States were at $23 million in equipment for the mining industry, vehicles, tools, hygiene products, and household goods. See Mark Goleman, "Mongolia and the US: From Acquaintance to Strategic Cooperation," *New Eastern Outlook,* May 31, 2015, http://journal-neo.org/2015/05/31/rus-mongoliya-i-ssha-ot-znakomstva-k-strategicheskomu-sotrudnichestvu/.

67. Office of the US Trade Representative, *Mongolia*, 2013, https://ustr.gov/countries-regions/china-mongolia-taiwan/mongolia.

68. "About MCC," Millennium Challenge Corporation, https://www.mcc.gov/about.

69. Office of the Press Secretary, "President Bush and President Enkhbayar of Mongolia Sign the Millennium Challenge Corporation Compact," October 22, 2007, https://georgewbush-whitehouse.archives.gov/news/releases/2007/10/20071022-3.html.

70. Thomas A. Schatz, "CAGW Expresses Concern with Millennium Challenge Corporation," Citizens Against Government Waste, March 28, 2008, https://www.cagw.org/media/press-releases/cagw-expresses-concern-millennium-challenge-corporation.

71. "Millennium Challenge Compact Between the United States of America Acting Through the Millennium Challenge Corporation and the Government of Mongolia, Annex" October 22, 2007, 2–4, https://www.state.gov/documents/organization/111590.pdf.

72. "Mongolia Compact," Millennium Challenge Corporation, https://www.mcc.gov/where-we-work/program/mongolia-compact.

73. Office of Inspector General, "Audit of the Millennium Challenge Corporation's Funding of Activities in Mongolia" (audit report no. M-000-12-001-P, Washington, DC, March 22, 2012), https://oig.usaid.gov/sites/default/files/audit-reports/m-000-12-001-p.pdf.

74. "Measuring Results of the Mongolia Health Project," Millennium Challenge Corporation, https://www.mcc.gov/resources/doc/summary-measuring-results-of-the-mongolia-health-project.

75. Office of the United States Trade Representative, "United States–Mongolia Transparency Agreement to Enter into Force." January 2017. https://ustr.gov/about-us/policy-offices/press-office/press-releases/2017/january/united-states-mongolia-transparency.

76. *Mongol Messenger,* December 19, 2014. .

77. Infomongolia.com, December 15, 2014. Accessed January 20, 2015.

78. Infomongolia.com, December 23, 2014. Accessed January 20, 2015.

79. Curt Tarnoff, Millennium Challenge Corporation, Congressional Research Service, April 5, 2016, 17, https://fas.org/sgp/crs/row/RL32427.pdf.

80. "Mongolia Water Compact," Millennium Challenge Corporation, https://www.mcc.gov/where-we-work/program/mongolia-water-compact.

8

"Wolf Strategy" Energy Policy: A New Form of Resource Nationalism?

That mineral-rich Mongolia is now part of the new "Great Game" in Eurasia and that the young Mongolian democracy employs its own strategy in that game remain a surprise to foreign observers, although perhaps it should not be. In 2012, 89 percent of Mongolian exports, the vast majority being raw minerals such as coal, went to China.[1] In that year China imported only 8 percent of its coal, with 43 percent coming from Mongolia. In 2012 over 5,000 Chinese firms operated in Mongolia and had a combined investment of around $2.5 billion[2]—$1.4 billion alone invested by PetroChina.[3] Russia, which had subsidized one-third of Mongolia's budget in the communist era and supplied 80 percent of Mongolia's imports in the 1980s, provided only 2 percent of Mongolia's exports in 2011. However, Russian influence over Mongolia stemmed from the fact that Mongolia purchased 91 percent of its diesel and petroleum products from its northern neighbor in 2014[4] and 13 percent of its electrical power (in three western provinces Russian electricity is the only source).[5]

As the second decade of the twenty-first century began, there was the fear that Chinese and Russian construction projects would make transport of Mongolia's mineral exports even more dependent on those two countries. Mongolia was forced into reconfiguring its "Third Neighbor" policy to avoid overdependence on the border neighbors and to attract FDI from the European Union and other Asian nations, such as Japan and South Korea. Mongolian policymakers believed that the key to economic independence was to create a new energy development policy for the nation.

Mongolian researcher Mendee has argued that Mongolia is "a prototype buffer state." Such buffer states in contemporary international relations can choose to (1) institutionalize neutrality; (2) depend upon one of the buffering powers; and/or (3) rely on third powers. In the post–Cold War period, Mongolia has pursued the first and third strategies and decisively rejected the second strategy. Faced with a new set of opportunities as well as challenges confronting a buffer state, it must exploit its available foreign policy options: align with China to capitalize or bandwagon on China's rapidly rising economic power and growth; accommodate Russia's assertive behavior by more linkages to Europe; or embrace linkage with global geopolitics through Japan and other like-minded democracies. Such options would facilitate Mongolia's desire to become an economic corridor, promote its integration within the greater Asian region, and retain its unique heritage: "Mongolia operates under the geopolitical and economic forces of rising China, reactive Japan and Russia, and retrenching America. It strives to preserve its nomadic, democratic, and Buddhist identities while accommodating currents of Western, Chinese, Russian, and Islamic civilizations."[6]

Traditionally, Mongolia has played a significant role in the formulation of Russian, Chinese, and Japanese strategy in Northeast Asia. In the twenty-first-century world of new economic and political realities following the breakup of the Soviet Union and the rise of China, it is logical to assume that Mongolia has become even more prominent in their self-interested calculations as these states pivot and readjust their overall strategies to reflect changing regional dynamics.[7] The Asian region as well as major world powers are paying attention to Mongolia's energy security debate for two reasons. First, because Mongolia increasingly is seen as a supplier of energy resources, its abundant deposits, particularly of coal, are seen as emerging new sources to meet the energy demands of a number of Northeast Asian consumers. The development of Mongolia's own domestic energy scene has broad implications not only for Mongolian energy policymakers but also for potential foreign investors and governments. Therefore, as an emerging energy-exporting nation, how Mongolia manages the development of the industry and trade of its commodities impacts a range of stakeholders. Second, because of Mongolia's geostrategic positioning, the involvement of other countries in its domestic energy scene has attracted attention, which has serious implications for the sovereignty of the country, as it seeks ways to balance both Chinese and Russian interests in Mongolian energy resources. While Russia's status as Mongolia's traditional "big brother" is significant, the emergence of China in Mongolia's energy sector has become increasingly important. Mongolia's close proximity to China, the world's largest coal importer, and the high quality of its coal favor Mongolia as a supplier, but declining Chinese demand will substantially reduce revenues over time. In 2015 Mongolia's coking coal exports to China decreased to 12.7 million tons from 14.7 million in 2014. Since this trend likely will continue, Mongolia will need to look to new markets.

Mongolia is seeking a formula to manage its economic growth and development as it confronts energy security challenges from China and

Russia. It seeks support from its "Third Neighbors" to implement its foreign policy objectives in a world where major powers want a stable geostrategic environment. Mongolia has the opportunity to forge economic linkages so long as it avoids being caught in the region's geopolitical rivalries. The attention of global political and financial investment communities is attracted to Mongolia because they calculate that there is a growing need for key minerals to feed the Chinese economic juggernaut as well as the advanced economies of Japan and South Korea. However, while it is understood that Mongolia has the potential to influence the political, economic, and environmental atmosphere of its region, at present it has limited geostrategic and economic value for its border neighbors and "Third Neighbors" because of the lack of integrative transportation infrastructure that could provide access to its mineral wealth.

Attempts to Avoid the Resource Curse and Foreign Investor Reaction

Mongolia is faced with the following realities as it plans its future economic and strategic security. It is a leading producer of coking coal, copper, iron ore, and crude oil. Its extractive industries accounted for 17 percent of GDP, 26 percent of government revenue, and 89 percent of total exports in 2014. Public debates have centered on the environmental impact of mining, reserving areas for conservation, and the government's role in developing large-scale strategic deposits while improving transparency and public participation in resources management at the local level.[8] Meanwhile, according to the International Energy Agency, energy demand from China is calculated to grow by over 2 percent annually between 2009 and 2035. It predicts that China will make up over 80 percent of the demand growth in coal between 2008 and 2035. Chinese oil imports will grow from 4.3 million barrels a day in 2009 to 12.8 million barrels a day in 2035, and China will need to increase its oil imports from 53 percent of domestic demand to 84 percent by 2035.[9]

Pressure and enticements from China will only increase for Mongolia's mineral resources. Mongolia cannot escape the growing Chinese political and economic clout because China is the major gateway to the Asia Pacific region: "Yet, this option is the least desirable in a country where anti-Chinese sentiments easily override any developmental discourse."[10] On the other hand, the Chinese recognize that Mongolia sits on its northern road to Russia, shares its longest land border, and has strong historical, ethnic, and cultural ties with minority peoples in China's Inner Mongolian, Xinjiang Uyghur, and Tibetan border regions. The question of whether China will play by the established market rules governing trade and investment in Mongolia is intertwined with Mongolia's version of resource nationalism.

Resource nationalist tendencies are of concern not only to regional players but also to US strategic and political interests in Asia. Many Western financial experts have warned Mongolia about the so-called resource curse or Dutch disease wherein quick riches not properly managed are dissipated in corruption, mismanagement, and income inequality. Such comments reveal that most foreign observers do not comprehend that Mongolia has its own design for balancing its two giant neighbors with other nations in the Asian region, or that it has a vision of its place in the world beyond raw economics that motivates its relations with distant nations, including the United States. While some economic commentators have recognized that "there are many counterweights [to Chinese monopoly] available, and the Mongolians are skilled at utilizing them,"[11] they have not explained what these options are or indicated what might be the overarching strategy motivating Mongolian decisionmaking.

One of the main cultural traits of Mongols is that they retain their flexibility to react to conditions by rarely explaining their actions. Instead they cleverly respond to the words and actions of others. Thus, President Elbegdorj, noting that he described his country "as a little pony between two big elephants," often attempted to reassure Western economists that Mongolia wanted to learn from the historical experience of other resource-rich countries. Mongolian delegations during the boom times were sent to such places as Norway, Chile, and Indonesia to research various mineral-based economies and look for best practices to avoid the mineral curse. Despite foreign advice, fact-finding trips, and public statements from Mongolian policymakers, it is clear that Mongolia did not avoid the boom-bust effect of other mineral-based economies. Mongolian foreign economic policy and the domestic legal regime underpinning it since the mid-2000s were not in large measure revised to incorporate the advice of Western financial development specialists. This failure usually was explained by analysts inside and outside Mongolia as the result of intense competition among domestic political parties

> that resulted in a weak bureaucracy, a vulnerable judiciary, and an unstable legal and regulatory environment. In pursuit of short-term and parochial interests, domestic actors delay developmental projects and attempt to shake up the political landscape even before the four-year election cycle to improve their bargaining position. This intensifies mismanagement of resources, bonds, loans, and debts and undermines the democratic political order.[12]

Such observers asserted that, unless domestic political stability, rule of law, and the fight against corruption improve, Mongolia will not be able to penetrate the markets of its neighbors. Many foreign financial experts never questioned their assumptions that twenty-first-century Mongolia must tie itself overwhelmingly to China and that Chinese monopoly over the Mongolian economy could not be avoided. As a result, foreign experts, who were poor at forecasting Mongolian economic behavior, became perplexed when the Mongols did not respond to Chinese or Western investor pressures and grew increasingly hostile to reliance on FDI:

> Economic policies designed to protect Mongolia's sovereign interests and to respond to the expectations of the Mongolian public have discouraged FDI—despite statements from Mongolia's senior politicians that the government is committed to improving the business environment, reigniting foreign direct investment flows, and fostering Mongolian growth.[13]

Much foreign criticism has been directed toward the Mongolian Parliament's debate on what constitutes an appropriate legal and regulatory framework for mining that satisfies domestic expectations that the mining sector should benefit the public. Concerns were raised that the resulting statutes and regulations were "crafted in a manner which incorporates multiple approaches and political imperatives,"[14] not acknowledging that for democracies such a legislative process is totally normal. Western government and private investors believed that Mongolia's mining investment laws were hastily passed, regulations only partially implemented, and statutory commitments promised by the Mongolian government often not fully respected. "Investors may perceive, and have to accept that, the current political process creates an unclear policy environment that may increase investment risk, while Mongolian politicians see the process as yielding the necessary level of political comity."[15]

Mongolia's Version of Resource Nationalism

Mongolia's landlocked status is an obstacle to exporting its vast energy commodities, as exports must go through either Russia or China—the world's largest consumer of energy—in order to find other potential buyers. The country's geostrategic location has fueled the historical rivalry between its neighbors to gain access to continental mineral and energy deposits and has created new challenges for Mongolia's political autonomy. How the country balances its neighbors' vested interests in its energy deposits, in light of complicated trilateral historical political relations, is crucial. Mongolia must be cognizant of how China and Russia could impact Mongolia's energy security. While the role of China as chief customer for Mongolian energy commodities and biggest investor in the development of the country's energy sector creates opportunities for growth, this emerging dependency also brings with it numerous risks. Alongside China's enhanced role in Mongolia's energy sector is evidence of new Russian threats to the nation's political independence in energy-related decisionmaking. The way Mongolia manages these factors will determine the country's future domestic energy security and its role as a regional energy supplier.

When examining Mongolian policymaking on mineral development, we must consider "the ability of Mongolia not to forget strategic against huge economic gains."[16] This is clearly seen in how Mongolia handles its energy security in the face of domestic and regional challenges. Energy planners constantly take national security into consideration when facing obstacles in meeting the increasing demands of domestic consumption, including dependency on foreign energy imports, and huge infrastructure shortcomings. Mongolia's coalition government in 2008 appointed a successful businessman, banker, and mining financial expert, Luvsanvandan Bold, as the country's first ever civilian minister of defense. This move indicated that, for Mongolia, defense should be closely intertwined with mineral development policies.

Mongolia's main economic and political challenges are all linked to ensuring steady growth through the boom and bust mineral cycles likely to impact its resource-dependent economy. In this environment, what is Mongolia's strategy for mineral development, and does it transcend political parties and administrations? The answers are diverse. Some Mongolian military researchers have claimed there is no special strategy, while Ministry of Foreign Affairs and Mineral Authority officials have asserted there definitely is a strategy and cite the 2010 National Security Concept and 2006 Mineral Law with its revisions. The response from Mongolia's intelligence community is not as clear, but a high-ranking Mongolian intelligence official privately has admitted that Mongols know when they sign a mineral contract with a Chinese state-owned company, the Mongols do not have to follow the terms. Yet, when Mongols sign a contract with Russians, they believe that they must fulfill the terms of the contract or they will be punished by the Russians.[17] Mongolia understands that Northeast Asia's economic growth requires secure energy resources and sees its own energy mineral deposits as the motivation for regional players to implement an Infrastructure Linkage Strategy so Mongolia can build up its poor rail and pipeline freight transportation to become a transit corridor. Concurrently, they believe the Asian continent cannot proceed with economic cooperation without ameliorating the Korean Peninsula situation and historical animosities that push countries to increase bilateral defense relations.[18]

Chalco–SouthGobi Resources Controversy Accelerates New Mineral Policies

International financial experts on FDI have long expressed concern that a populist, resource-nationalist streak among Mongolian lawmakers could put mineral operations at risk. But the specific catalyst that precipitated strong mineral protectionist legislation in Mongolia was the attempt in early 2012 by the Aluminum Corporation of China (Chalco) to buy up 58 percent control of the Canadian company Ivanhoe's private Ovoot Tolgoi coal mine operated under the name SouthGobi Resources. Although all Mongolian foreign and domestic observers were certain that no new mining-related legislation could be enacted prior to the June 28 elections, the April announcement by Chalco and SouthGobi Resources of their intention to finalize their deal on July 4 provoked a violent wave of resource nationalist sentiments from both policymakers and citizens. The Ministry of Mining revoked SouthGobi Resources' mining license, and in May Parliament, backed by the MPRP government, passed the Strategic Entities Foreign Investment Law (SEFIL) that stopped the takeover. SEFIL governed foreign investor participation in Mongolia's mining sector and especially limited the activities of foreign SOEs. The provisions were in direct response to voter concerns that Mongolia's sovereignty was being threatened by acquisition of mineral resource rights in legal stock takeovers of Western or Mongolian private firms by Chinese SOEs.

The Chalco bid, after several extensions, finally was withdrawn in early September 2012. Controversy was heightened when in January 2013 a Mongolian judge revoked an additional 106 existing licenses (11 were held by foreigners), licenses that had been obtained in 2008–2009, for nondevelopment of the properties and bribery.[19] These 106 licenses covered territory almost six times larger in surface area than all active mining licenses in Mongolia. Because of the revocation and the fact that the 2012 mining law amendments remained in effect, business confidence was further undermined, and FDI dropped 43 percent throughout the first half of 2013, prior to the presidential election. President Elbegdorj, who was running for reelection, pledged to seek legislative relief for the foreign investor community. However, when two Mongolian senior officials, who were caught in an Elbegdorj-supported crackdown on corruption in the Mineral Resource Authority, brought further negative attention to the sale of mining licenses ahead of the election, this promise was not immediately kept after Elbegdorj won.

In response to an economy that was rapidly contracting due to plunging FDI and vociferous complaints from the FDI community, changes to the 2012 SEFIL were made in November 2013. Mongolia's cabinet secretary called the amendments a "turning point" since the revisions provided more certainty surrounding mining taxes and royalties and eliminated the distinction between foreign and domestic private investors. However, the restrictions on foreign state-owned company investment continued, and all 106 mining licenses remained canceled.[20] Further legal changes were made on July 1, 2014, when Parliament passed thirteen amendments to the Mineral Law of 2006 and simultaneously repealed the prohibition on the granting of new exploration licenses, but Western legal analysts pointed out that vague new categories for mineral deposits had been introduced into the law.[21] The maximum area that could be licensed under a single exploration license was reduced nearly one-third in size, and an exploration license (excepting for radioactive minerals) could be issued for up to twelve years.

Previously, the emphasis had been on any "mineral deposit of strategic importance." This was the classification that allowed the state to claim at least 33 percent ownership in the deposit. The number of these strategic deposits was reduced by the new legislation, but government powers were expanded through a new government agency, the National Geological Office, which is responsible for conducting various geological cartographic surveys and maintaining a national database of mineral resources. The powers of the Ministry of Mining also were broadened to include approval of the procedures for placing mines and mining/concentrating plants into operation. New regulations also were adopted regarding confiscation of licenses and how compensation was to be awarded in a timely fashion. The amendments abolished pre-mining agreements that had been granted for a period of up to three years post-exploration to allow license holders sufficient time to adequately prepare for full-scale mining operations. License holders were required to pay a daily late fee equal to 0.3 percent of the original license fee in the event that they failed to pay license fees on time, and the license could be revoked if payment was more than thirty days late. Previously, fines for violations of the Mineral Law had been in the range of 100,000 to 2,000,000 MNT (approximately \$50–\$1,000). The new changes increased them by ten times. Finally, regarding the 106 revoked licenses, the regulation stated that the Ministry of Mining could reissue them by a competitive tender and that parties participating in the tender must place a deposit equal to at least 30 percent.[22] By the end of 2014, only 18 of the 106 licenses were offered up by the government for tender.

Since then, various Mongolian governments, regardless of political party, have manipulated the mining exploration license issue for domestic political purposes. In October 2016, newly appointed Minister of Environment and Tourism Dulamsuren Oyunkhorol announced the intention of the recently elected MPP government to reestablish the Fund for Air Pollution Reduction in 2017 because of public complaints about increased pollution and evaporation of several rivers and lakes. Therefore, the Ministry of Environment and Tourism suspended the activities of some mining companies working near the rivers and now is preparing a bill on land rehabilitation for submission to Parliament that will outline terms for halting the issuance of additional exploration permits.[23]

Populist Pressure to Revise FDI-Friendly Regime

The firestorm provoked by Chalco's attempted takeover engendered long-lasting effects. General popular distrust, not necessarily xenophobia, of foreign companies that came in to try to make money in Mongolia rose substantially. When things were going well and the commodity cycle was at its apex, "populists were raising their hands and asking, 'Well, why are these foreigners making so much money on this stuff in the ground that's owned by the Mongolian people? Why are any foreigners in the country at all?'"[24] When the projects failed to produce the exaggerated revenues promised because of mismanagement, corruption, and falling world prices, the citizenry was further inflamed by revelations of poor contractual terms that the Mongolian government had negotiated. In June 2012 the Mongolian cabinet and president decided that no new private mining licenses would be distributed for the next five years. Almost one-third of the Parliament in the fall 2012 parliamentary session demanded the renegotiation of the OT investment contract, which once again turned upside down the once favorable Mongolian mineral investment environment for all foreign investors.

Another significant problem was the legacy of bad coal deals made by the Mongols with the Chinese. Mongolia, which entered China's coal market when China's largest coal suppliers, the Australian mining companies, were closed due to floods, exported twenty million tons of coal in 2011, and coal exports became the largest part of the Mongolian economy. When China's economy began to slow in early 2012, Mongolian exports decreased, but when China's coal imports rose again by 40 percent after April 2012, Mongolian exports kept dropping. This was connected to supply price. The inexperienced Mongolian domestic and state-owned mining companies had made agreements with Chinese companies to supply coal at a fixed price, regardless of world market price. From the beginning, coal exports had not been well organized. The Mongolian coal companies had not planned to develop any rail transport infrastructure to handle the coal volume, so transportation costs became too steep. There were no long-term contracts for coal exports to China from Mongolia, so when Mongolian private mining companies, such as Energy Resources, could not mine profitably, they suspended operations for over a year to wait out the price drop, thus breaking their contracts. This unleashed a strong reaction from China, which turned to other countries for coal. Mongolia had been the largest supplier of China's coal imports, reaching 40 percent in 2011, but fell to 17 percent within two years to become the seventh largest supplier:

> We've lost our position in this market because of trying to export coal at higher prices. . . . It's hard to take back our lost position. But stopping coal export until coal prices rise is bad policy. We should export coal for permanently, for the long term. In other words, it's time to conclude an agreement with both China and Russia within the framework of strategic partnership. It is not about negotiating coal prices.[25]

Although the World Bank and Western financial analysts attributed the drop in Mongolian coal exports to China's cooling economy, it is evident that Mongolia's trade downturn to some degree was desired and even manipulated by Mongolian policymakers who were strongly influenced by overwhelmingly anti-Chinese domestic popular opinion. Mongolia, out of concern that overheated economic growth from 2010 to 2013 was both unsustainable and dangerous, sought to reduce coal exports, which made up the bulk of its exports to China. However, this was not the whole story. Mongolia was very anxious about the Chinese monopoly over its overall trade, mineral development, and FDI. Centuries-long historical animosity between the two nations continued into the twenty-first century to become a factor in the way Mongols view their domestic economic development as well as national security. The reality that Mongolia's strong growth rate was directly tied to China, the nation's number one trade partner and investor, was not seen as a fortunate boon but rather a slippery slope that coincided with Chinese desire to overwhelm and incorporate independent Mongolia into Chinese territory—as happened to Inner Mongolia.

In addition to pressuring the Chinese for better prices for less coal product, the Mongolian government in 2013 took a number of steps to diversify its future TT coal customers, especially by giving preferential treatment to Japanese and South Korean investors. This trend accelerated with the reelection of Mongolian President Elbegdorj. At meetings in Tokyo between the two governments on how to implement their economic partnership agreement in early August 2013, Mongolia offered to give Japan privileges in the mining sector and establish stable conditions to extract coal and copper. Discussions included the topics of exempting Japanese private companies from high mineral export taxes and waiving laws and regulations that limited investment in the financial and communications sectors. These special preferential conditions were announced that year when Mongolia's Prime Minister Norov Altankhuyag visited Japan. As for South Korean companies, they were favored as international investors for construction in Mongolia's transportation sector. Samsung C&T Corporation was awarded a $483 million contract in 2013 to build the 267-kilometer Russian broad-gauge railway from the TT coal field to the Chinese border, even though using this gauge added $3 to the cost of each metric ton of delivered coal.[26]

It seems clear that Mongolian policymakers and politicians of all political persuasions wanted to modify the foreign investor climate of the past decade because they saw it as a failure in many ways, despite the years of high economic growth. Opening Mongolia's economy to the outside world during the past twenty years did not prevent the monopolization of the economy by one of the two border neighbors. The Soviet monopoly of communist times had been replaced by that of the Chinese in the democratic era, and this simply is not acceptable or sustainable for Mongolia. Mongols blamed Western financial experts and multilateral organizations for pushing the country to seek economic development regardless of how it could injure the country's sovereignty and national identity and for institutionalizing policies that promoted Chinese interests at Mongolian expense. One Mongolian official responsible for executing Mongolia's mining laws regarding foreign and domestic investment in minerals asserted that Mongolia was growing too fast, and that, if the investment laws were changed to the point of discouraging foreign investors, well, that was not a bad thing.[27]

The Mongolian people were encouraged by Western economic advisers and their own politicians to think that mineral development meant they would become rich quickly. The scandals surrounding FDI led the populace to perceive that the monies realized from the foreign investments were funneled into the hands of foreign businessmen and their own corrupt officials and not into the public's pockets. This impression, whether correct or not, was not countered by sound argumentation to dispel public concern. In fact, the constant drumbeat of criticism by Western observers about Mongolian "corrupt practices" increased the cynicism within Mongolian society and tempered its respect for free markets. This environment eventually caused Mongolian policymakers to create their own resource nationalism strategy, one based primarily on national security objectives and domestic nationalist sentiments, and to modify the unregulated democratic, free market structures of the first years of democracy, even when such actions dried up FDI.

Influence of Russia's Energy Game Plan on Mongolian Mineral Development Strategy

Mongolian public opinion is generally positive toward Russia. It is still considered an important regional player, but some Mongolian researchers remind us that the relationship is complicated. First, Moscow does not want to reduce its influence in Mongolia, whereas Ulaanbaatar does not want to grant it "privileged" status. Second, Russia has been reluctant to support proposals for Mongolia to become an economic corridor between China and Russia because it would rather build natural gas and oil pipelines, railroads, and roads through its Far Eastern territories to develop its own local economies and lower transit risks. Russia does not advocate an increase of Chinese or Western influence in Mongolia, and perhaps would rather see North Korea as the economic corridor to East Asian economies. Third, in the final analysis, Russia and Mongolia are now economic competitors seeking Chinese and East Asian markets for their copper and coal.[28] Nevertheless, it is quite clear that, primarily in reaction to massive Chinese investment in its economy and lack of Mongolian faith in Western laws and practices to stop overwhelming Chinese intrusion, Mongolia since 2006 has emulated many Putin-devised Russian energy security policies and legislation. To better understand Mongolia's thinking, it is necessary to examine Putin's concept of Russia as an energy superpower that exploits energy assets for specific political goals and uses energy companies as instruments of foreign policy.[29]

Putin's actions have three overarching themes: restoring military security, using energy development to obtain security, and rebuilding Russia's greatness.[30] Mongolia understands and to some extent shares these goals but is reluctant to enter into new business deals or projects where Russian elites seek privileged status. Putin's energy and domestic economic policies prove that, for Russia, geopolitical goals outweigh business considerations.[31] For example, he renationalized Russia's energy resources industry because this action guarantees Russia's regional energy supply. Such policies required expanding the state's role in the economy through powerful corporations, termed "national champions," which receive preferential treatment. Because of a revised tax regime, imports of oil, gas, and coal from Central Asia and Caspian countries have become cheaper than developing new Russian fields in Siberia and the Far East.[32] At the same time, Russia's eastward export share of crude and petroleum products, which was only 8 percent in 2008, is expected to reach 22–25 percent in 2030. Gas exports to Asia are expected to grow from almost 0 in 2008 to 19–20 percent in 2030.[33] Russia's energy strategy in the Asia Pacific region is to reassert its major power status, develop Siberia and the Far East region, and integrate with China's economy. Moscow's "Look East" strategy has gained momentum as tensions with Ukraine escalated in 2014, and its eagerness for political and economic partnership with China has risen to counter Western economic pressure. Although China is its key partner, Russia has been attempting to diversify its economic interactions with other Asian states, as well as maintain its former privileged status in Mongolia, Central Asia, and North Korea.

Russia has leveraged its abundant energy resources and energy wealth to restore the Russian economy, consolidate power domestically, and then project it abroad.[34] Putin's plan to use oil and gas exports as a cartel to rebuild Russia was aided by the steep rise in hydrocarbon prices in the early twenty-first century. Andrei Illarionov, a Russian economist at the Cato Institute, has called the Russian model the "resource curse" with its increasing dependency on export revenues and declining growth combined with the "state curse" wherein the quality of institutions managing the mineral wealth is so undermined that the governance system becomes corrupted and political expediency triumphs over economic common sense to create "energy egoism."[35] Energy specialist Anita Orban believes that the primary motive of Russia's energy imperialism is to increase its power and that the most effective means to do this is by expanding its political-economic presence in the energy sphere,[36] while security studies political scientist Pavel Baev analyzes Russian policy as a process of reconstituting the Soviet Empire as an oil and gas cartel by focusing on maximizing control over energy resources and flows.[37]

Published energy strategy pronouncements under Putin have emphasized that energy security is the most important element in Russia's national security.[38] An important element of this strategy was the creation in April 2002 of a list of strategic natural resources, including fossil fuels and mineral deposits above a certain size, that was codified into legislation in February 2004.[39] The Russian state became the developer of "strategic" businesses and forced out the private sector.[40] Foreign-invested deposits were confiscated for "booking" reserves instead of developing them.[41] Windfall taxes imposed on energy profits generated billions of dollars, supposedly to fund energy investment in developing new deposits but were mainly spent for politically popular social benefits and pensions and to build up a Reserve and National Wealth Fund.[42] Such policies later became the blueprint for the Enkhbayar government in Ulaanbaatar to develop its strategic mineral deposit list and 2006 Mineral Law and to distribute wealth funds prior to elections to buy voter goodwill. A final point is that Russia's energy policymaking is not just about producing sufficient domestic energy; it is also about ensuring an exportable surplus that generates revenues.[43] When the Russians saw the stagnation of their major market in Europe in the 2000s, they decided to move more vigorously into the East Asian market to partner with China to develop energy trade. The Eastern Siberia Pacific Ocean pipeline project under Rosneft became the exclusive supplier of crude to China in 2009 and now supplies Mongolia with oil at higher than market prices.[44]

Putin in the middle of the 2000s felt it necessary to reengage with Mongolia, which had become overwhelmed by Chinese investment. In the subsequent ten years he has reinvigorated ties with Russia's former satellite through high-level state visits and more economic and military aid. At the same time, he has not shied away from blatantly interjecting Russia into Mongolian affairs. The most famous example was in May 2011, when he forced the Mongols to include the Russian state-owned Russian Railway Company, which had not even offered a bid, on the shortlist for foreign investors for the giant TT coal mine.[45] His desire to be involved in TT is not just for the strategic reason of not ceding TT's fields to the Americans and Chinese but also because it is evident that, with Russian domestic coal production faltering but Russian coal demand growing, the exploitation of Mongolian coal resources is a cheaper alternative for Russia than finding and extracting coal from costly-to-develop East Siberian deposits. Russia's reaction to China's penetration of Mongolia's economy has been negative, even though Russia and China are today publicly in a cooperative relationship. Russia does not want to lose its privileged status in Mongolia, so it seeks to reassert Russian influence and curb Chinese monopolization of Mongolian trade. Mongolia is considered a rightful part of Russia's sphere of influence in Asia and serves as a buffer to growing Chinese economic and migration penetration north toward East Siberia. Thus, Russia seeks to control Mongolian uranium resources not only to monopolize the market price but also to exclude ownership by China or democratic countries.

Russia, as the supplier of Mongolia's petroleum-based products into the democratic era, has been able to leverage this position by periodically cutting off already purchased diesel and oil supplies to achieve specific Russian objectives. In 2010 Russia still provided 95 percent of Mongolian diesel and petroleum products and 90 percent of imported electric power. Putin in April 2011 turned off diesel supplies because of domestic shortages and tried to strong-arm Mongolian policymakers into allowing new Russian petrol stations.[46] This move soured the relationship between Putin and President Elbegdorj, who lost confidence in Russia as a reliable energy supplier and began to diversify petrol imports toward China. As of 2016, Russia co-owns the trans-Mongolian Ulaanbaatar Railway, Erdenet copper-molybdenum mine, and Mongolrostsvetment fluorspar factory. All three joint enterprises, especially the railway and Erdenet, remain vital to Mongolia's economy, and so Russia retains the ability to be a game-changer for Mongolia's energy strategy and policies.

Mongolia's Energy "Wolf Strategy"

A decade of discussions, parliamentary debate, new laws, rescinded laws, and more debate concluded with the emergence of the Asian Wolf Strategy to handle energy economic development, the China question, and strengthening national security. Policymakers had been studying the economic development experiences of other countries for successes and failures in resource development, but the strategy that emerged during the presidency of Elbegdorj is based upon the revised National Security Concept of 2010. This document states, "The ideological basis of the policy ensuring national security is national patriotism," and "Economic security represents the cornerstone of the independence and sovereignty of Mongolia." It warns about overestimation and blind imitation of civilizations of other nations and the negative side effects of a market economy, modern science, and technology. The key element of the Mongolian Wolf Strategy is centered around Foreign Security Concept provision 3.2.2.2, which indicates that the country should design a strategy whereby the investment of any foreign country does not exceed one-third of overall foreign investment in Mongolia, undertake a policy to restrict investments by foreign state-owned companies, and balance the volume of investments by neighboring and highly developed countries within strategically important sectors.

The strategy does not mean that Mongolia is abandoning its Third Neighbor Policy but rather that it is interested in encouraging more Russian investment in some of Mongolia's mineral resources to curb Chinese economic and political penetration. The Mongols are promoting their nation as a buffer to protect, if possible, the Russian Far East. The return of an activist Russia to being a big player in their economy and politics is not unwelcome, especially if Japanese, Korean, Canadian, and Australian investment does not materialize. While certainly Mongolia does not want to lose its vigorous democracy and free market or return to its Cold War–era satellite status, its policymakers increasingly are thinking that inviting greater Russian FDI and even military assistance is not a bad idea at all since Western nations, including the United States, have so far proven disappointing economic partners.

Furthermore, despite Mongolia's unease in dealing with Russia, its democratic-era government, regardless of which party has been in power, adopted some of the major protectionist points of Putin's energy development policy because it had lost faith in the open free market system advocated by Western financial experts. In 2006 Mongolia amended its liberal Mineral Law to create a government-owned Strategic Deposit List based on deposit size with state control of up to 50 percent, a Putin-devised formula. Mongolian Mineral Authority officials openly stated in 2012 that this list will be revised and expanded in the future. In 2006 the government imposed additional measures, similar to those in Russia, such as a 68 percent windfall tax on gold and copper,[47] and from 2009 to 2012 canceled about 4,000 private mining licenses for environmental violations and another 1,400 for nondevelopment. In April 2010 a moratorium on new mining exploration licenses was imposed.

The goal of this overall energy development–based Wolf Strategy is to rebalance to some extent Chinese trade monopolization of Mongolia's economy by expanding and diversifying the players in the foreign investment field and to tighten foreign ownership regulations through parliamentary legislation with stronger central and local government oversight. Mongolian policymakers have expected to accomplish this goal through renationalizing many existing mineral deposits by confiscating nonperforming or illegally performing mining deposit licenses. The reasons cited for license revocation have been that license holders have caused environmental damage or nondevelopment of sites. These politically correct rationales are offered to avoid international court cases and payment of compensation, such as happened with the uranium site in the Khan Resources case. The Wolf Strategy includes developing strategic mineral deposits under the aegis of large state-owned companies that are given preferential treatment from the government, much like the Russian "national champions" model. However, because Mongolian companies only have limited expertise and manpower, they will need to subcontract much of the extraction activity to favored foreign companies.

The Mongolian government has promised to place tax and concession revenues from the mining sector into its Human Development Fund but, in emulation of Putin, it instead has used the monies to make payouts to the citizenry to influence domestic elections. The government continues to attempt to revise or develop mineral agreements to include demands that foreign investors finance power plants, mineral processing industries to produce value-added products, and domestic rail and road transport infrastructure. Mongolian economic planners expect the growth of domestic mineral production to fall in the near term; however, they are confident they will receive increased revenue from the fewer locally produced, higher-value products. Moreover, while Mongolia still needs to rely on Putin's Russia for its energy supply, it rejects closer energy connections to Russia. It has been actively reducing imports of Russian diesel, oil products, and power by sponsoring quick, homegrown alternatives, even if they are more costly and less efficient because of their small scale. Mongolia today has a conscious policy to diversify its oil imports[48] and eventually refine its own crude. For example, in 2013 it made a swap agreement with China Oil (China National Offshore Oil Corporation) to exchange crude oil drilled in Mongolia for 10,000 tons of petroleum end products processed in Inner Mongolia.

Mongolian Petroleum Authority Chairman G. Ulziiburen promised that the government would continue to seek cheaper sources of fuel in hopes such policies would reduce prices.[49] The results of the petrol diversification policy were quickly evident. In 2012 it imported a total of 1.2 million tons of oil, of which petroleum products comprised 1.1 million tons—64 percent of which was imported from Rosneft. In the first three months of 2013, imports from Rosneft decreased by 30 percent, so in the first quarter of 2013 Mongolia imported 50 percent of its monthly supply from Switzerland's Gunvor Group (fourth largest crude oil trader in the world, which obtains much of its crude oil from the Russian Federation), South Korea's SK Energy, and Hyundai Oilbank, in addition to China, at prices that averaged \$100–\$200 per ton cheaper than Rosneft.[50] Publicly, Mongolian officials claimed that they "do not choose an investor on the basis of its country, but look for the most competitive offer and one that offers the maximum benefit and profit to Mongolia. These are our criteria, nothing else. We work for our national interests and considerations like a company's base country are immaterial. Geopolitical factors do not affect our decisions."[51] In accordance with the Government Action Plan for 2012–2016, construction started on a Mongolian-Japanese joint venture, Darkhan-Petroleum refinery, with annual capacity of at least two million tons in Darkhan-Uul province, about 240 kilometers north of Ulaanbaatar. Although there have been delays in construction, it could be completed before the end of the decade. Additionally, in June 2018 the Mongols in Dornogobi *aimag* began constructing an oil refinery, built with \$1 billion of Indian soft loan financing. Estimated to boost Mongolia's GDP by 10 percent, the refinery will have a processing capacity of 1.5 million tons of crude and is estimated it will produce 560,000 tons of gasoline, 670,000 tons of diesel fuel, and 107,000 tons of liquefied gas per year. Construction is to be completed in late 2022.[52]

The Mongolian government recognized that the above-described mineral sector development strategy would result in a cooling-off period that would slow the pace of FDI. Perhaps less anticipated was that these practices also encouraged favoritism or discriminatory decisionmaking that added volatility to Mongolia's investment climate. Yet, policymakers were not deterred from this strategy because they believed they could develop revenue streams from anticipated higher energy resource prices, "advanced tax payments," and promises of future favors to an often gullible, mineral-seeking foreign investment community. Such a rosy view of energy economics is a result of both Mongolian democratic experience with a very generous foreign donor regime in the 1990s and a history of commodity manipulation techniques perfected over centuries of dealing with Chinese emperors and Russian czars. If Mongolian leaders have made a miscalculation, it was to underestimate the precipitous fall in FDI tied to depressed world mineral prices, the slowing Chinese economy, and the power of the world financial media's continuous negative reporting to destroy the image of Mongolia as a welcoming investment environment. Therefore, they did not predict that the economy would slow to only 1.2 percent GDP growth in 2016.[53]

Effect on Mongolia of Chinese Dragon's "Great Game" or Outgoing Strategic Policy

Mongolia's Wolf Strategy has developed within the parameters of China's own energy strategy, which seeks to support and guarantee the successful attainment of the Chinese national social and economic development goals. Among these goals are to (1) provide support for an average growth rate of 7.5 percent and meet people's energy consumption demands; (2) bring production and consumption of energy in line with population changes, resources, and environment; and (3) enhance security in the energy supply. China's key concerns regarding energy and energy minerals are to increase the overall capacity of energy supply, especially oil, and reduce insecure elements; increase clean energy supply; reduce pressure on resources and the environment; improve energy efficiency and conservation; diversify the energy supply while reducing the risks to ensure energy supply security; strengthen the role of the market in allocating resources while always maintaining the government's strategic leading role as well as its policies in guiding energy development and conservation; and reduce price distortions.[54]

Although it is the second largest energy-producing country in the world next to the United States, China is also the second largest consumer of energy resources, especially of coal, because its energy power policy is based on coal production and usage.[55] A significant factor is that the quality of most of China's coal is poor, and high-quality coking coal—the type that Mongolia has in abundance—must be imported. Furthermore, because of strong economic growth, China's coal reserves are projected to last only a few more decades.[56] Today China's coal industry is the world's largest, but it already is importing a small, but proportionally growing, amount. Although China is trying to decrease its dependence on coal for energy production, 64 percent of its energy consumption in 2015 still was supplied by coal.[57] There are diverse opinions on whether China has a comprehensive energy security strategy, or only a leveraging of bilateral relations through political clout and market advantage out of a desire to build stronger energy ties with Russia.[58] It is clear that Chinese SOEs are utilized as vehicles to improve China's overall energy security and that investment is promoted through high-level political delegations and infusions of capital. Certainly, this approach can be seen in recent Sino-Mongolian relations as well as in Sino-Russian relations. China's energy security model is based on the successful experience of its SOE oil companies throughout the last two decades of globalization. Their "Outgoing Energy Strategy" utilizes SOEs such as CNPC and Sinopec to buy and exploit mineral deposits overseas, the same system China has employed in Mongolia.

In 2011 Mongolia became China's major coal partner because of geographical proximity and the fact that it had the high-quality coal grades needed to supply China's steel mills. There is a vagueness in Beijing about its Mongolian mineral investment strategy. Some experts opine that China is not interested in Mongolian minerals per se but invests in Mongolia only for political reasons out of concern over "terrorists" in Inner Mongolia who might receive assistance from independent Mongolia.[59] There also is the long-standing belief that Mongolia really belongs to China, so it is prudent to strengthen bilateral ties to encourage eventual reunification. Still, other Chinese mineral experts maintain that, of course, the Chinese economy needs Mongolian coal and copper and is bargaining with Mongolian mineral producers in good faith but just making bad deals.[60]

Even assuming that China's mineral acquisition policy in Mongolia is based primarily on national security and "antiterrorist" objectives, there still is evidence that Chinese SOEs have reorganized their Mongolian operations to concentrate more on business functions. There is no doubt that the big beneficiary of Mongolia's open market policies in the 1990s was China, yet their SOEs' penchant for ignoring local politics has brought Chinese FDI to a crisis point. Chalco's bid for control of SouthGobi Resources in April 2012 and the suspension of coal deliveries from TT in early 2013 are examples of how China has permitted its SOE investment strategy to negatively impact bilateral relations. The Chinese Outgoing Energy Strategy seems to be directed by culturally insensitive economists and SOE business executives, not foreign policy specialists on Mongolia who understand

Mongolian mentality, history, and the vagaries of regional geopolitics. If this trend continues, the Chinese will find their economic enterprises in Mongolia increasingly unstable.

Japan's Post-Fukushima Game Plan for Mineral Acquisition in Eurasia

Mongolia's mineral-based Wolf Strategy unexpectedly has been strengthened in the 2010s by Japan's energy challenges after the 2011 Fukushima nuclear accident. "For Mongolia, Japan is the only proximate major power that could potentially serve as an external balancer against a rising China and an alternate source of technology, capital, and markets."[61] Mongolia for years was asking Japan to partner with Russia in building mutually beneficial pipelines and expanding rail routes north to the Pacific to enable Mongolia and Far Eastern Russia to develop access to new trade partners and decrease reliance on the south-to-China transport route. This improved infrastructure in the country would mainly be used to export mining goods.

Resource-scarce Japan has few domestic energy resources and was only 16 percent energy self-sufficient as of 2012.[62] Modern Japanese history has seen a recurring theme: "Securing stable supply of mineral resources is a matter of national importance, namely maintaining and strengthening the industrial competitiveness is, in other words, an imperative issue for Japanese economic security."[63] Although Japan mainly relies on oil for energy, oil's share of total energy consumption declined from about 80 percent in the 1970s to 42 percent in 2010, as Japan gradually closed its oil-fired power stations in favor of nuclear energy. In the first decade of the 2000s, Japan's plan for resource mineral acquisition was one of diversification from heavy reliance on Middle Eastern petrofuels. The government's 2006 Energy Strategy Plan sought to secure a stable supply of oil and natural gas: "The government's goal is to import 40 percent of the country's total crude oil imports from Japanese-owned concessions by 2030, up from the current estimated 19 percent."[64] Nuclear energy for decades was the original preferred replacement solution for petroleum, with natural gas a strong second choice. Japan was forced to recalculate its energy security strategy after the Fukushima Daiichi nuclear power accident in March 2011, a catastrophe that led to the shutdown of all of the country's fifty nuclear reactors.[65] Japan's decision to idle its nuclear reactors left a 30 percent gap in the country's electricity supply that was replaced by imports of liquefied natural gas, oil, and coal. The negative impact of the 2011 Fukushima nuclear disaster resulted in a nationwide loss of faith in Japan's nuclear technology, and Japanese policymakers searched for immediate alternative power sources with natural gas initially the preferred fuel of choice.[66] Japan's liquefied natural gas (LNG) imports swelled, and utilities were pushed to the brink of financial ruin as gas prices surged. To save money, Japan's utilities increasingly switched to cheaper coal.

Domestic coal production in Japan ended in 2002, but coal remained important. At the time of the nuclear accident, coal-fired power plants still were providing about 25 percent of Japan's power. The country's energy dependence on imports rose to 94 percent in 2013 from 80 percent in 2010,[67] while coal imports rose 4.8 percent to a record 114.145 million tons in 2015. Japan has reversed its anti-coal policy and in 2016 planned to build forty-seven domestic coal plants. The country has become the world's top public financer of overseas coal plants, technology, and mining.[68] Japan's interest in Mongolia's mineral resources has economic, geopolitical, and ideological implications. In the first decades of the twenty-first century, Japanese investment in Mongolian minerals was supported by the Ministry of Trade and Industry as a minor part of its diversification and long-term mineral acquisition strategy. Interest in Mongolia had been high in the mid-2000s, but because of failure to turn negotiations into working contracts, after changes in the investment climate, the pursuit of Mongolian mineral joint ventures faltered.

The Japanese power crisis after 2011 and the growing importance of Russia and its plans to upgrade the Northeast Asian transportation network,[69] which would solve Japanese energy resources supply chain questions, all have impacted the approach of Japanese policymakers to Mongolia and its minerals. Although the most generous aid donor to Mongolia over the past three decades, Japan considered Mongolian minerals mainly within the context of Japanese companies' acting as middlemen to sell to established Chinese customers rather than bringing the minerals back long distances to Japan. Some Japanese advisers to Prime Minister Yoshihiku Noda in June 2012 asserted that the Japanese government did not appreciate Mongolian importance within Northeast Asia, so it did not support a trade diversification policy that fully included Mongolian mineral products.[70] In addition, Japanese government officials and businessmen felt they had trouble communicating with Mongols[71] because, although they successfully negotiated mineral agreements, these contracts were seldom implemented.

The Japanese were particularly angry at not being shortlisted for the TT coal project and were uncomfortable with the Mongolian counter suggestion to partner with the Russians. However, after Fukushima, the Japanese did cooperate with the Russians on new pipelines for natural gas and to build new LNG facilities on the Pacific coast until stymied by the economic sanctions imposed on Russia owing to the Ukraine crisis of 2014. The Mongols believed they could manipulate the Japanese into expanding this Russo-Japanese cooperation into Mongolian mineral development, such as participating in Mongolian natural gas and oil extraction.

Japan had become a strategic economic partner for Mongolia in 2010, but it was the administration of Prime Minister Shinzo Abe, in cooperation with Mongolia's activist president, Elbegdorj, that led the countries into a closer energy and economic cooperative relationship. Mongolia saw Japan as an important "Third Neighbor" for technology and investment in rebalancing its trade exports, while Japan coveted Mongolia's abundant resources. Japan was Mongolia's fourth largest trade partner in 2012 as well as its largest assistance donor.[72] Prime Minister Abe on March 30–31, 2013, made his first state visit to Mongolia, while the Mongolian economy was still booming.[73] Declaring that the importance of Mongolia in Japanese foreign policy was increasing, Abe announced a new Japanese initiative labeled *Erch* (meaning "power" or "energy") to intensively develop economic relations. *Erch* had two main purposes: (1) improvement of the investment and business environment for Japanese companies, and (2) bilateral cooperation to be financed with Japanese loans for projects to improve living conditions, build infrastructure, and elevate human resources training. Calling Mongolia an energy giant valuable to Japan's energy security strategy, he declared, "We want to bolster ties with Mongolia with the objective of creating a good makeup of various energy sources."[74] Mongolian Prime Minister Altankhuyag replied that his government sought priority development of their strategic partnership, including providing coal, and of " our official negotiations focused on activating this partnership in all social spheres, especially elevating economic ties to a new level."[75]

Japanese media coverage of the trip analyzed the meaning of the new initiatives with Mongolia from an international geopolitical perspective and suggested that Abe was seeking to check the growing regional influence of China. There was speculation that the trip was an attempt to give a wake-up call to China to counter China's moves to increase its influence in Mongolia and other parts of Asia through a trilateral framework of Japan, Mongolia, and the United States for policy discussions.[76] The Mongolian viewpoint was best summarized by President Elbegdorj, who proclaimed, "It has been said many times that with Mongolia's wealthy resources and Japan's hi-tech, we can develop complementary cooperation, and now it is the time to be realized."[77]

Implementation of the new *Erch* initiative was discussed further that April in Ulaanbaatar in a third round of negotiations over an economic partnership agreement. The Japanese loans offered through *Erch* included a 4.2 billion yen loan to renovate Mongolia's biggest power plant, No. 4 with 580 MW capacity, and loans for construction of a new international airport, major highway overpass, and a feasibility study for an Ulaanbaatar metro by 2020.[78] It was agreed that the Import-Export Bank of Japan would facilitate loans to Mongolian companies to buy mining equipment and that Japanese private companies would provide loan financing for the construction of an oil refinery in Darkhan with the capacity of two million tons per year. Mongolia, which plans to launch an earth reconnaissance communications satellite, obtained Japanese consent to negotiate a memorandum covering a joint program to use a Japanese-made satellite.[79]

Mongolia's proactive soft-balancing diplomacy toward Japan was a key element of its Wolf Strategy. As Mongolia's economy entered a bust phase in 2015, with declining interest from the United States and European Union, Mongolia's "Third Neighbor" policy began to lose momentum. The Japanese option became increasingly critical for Mongolia—"to balance against rising Chinese influence, to consolidate its democratic identity, and to strengthen its political and economic engagement globally and regionally."[80] The EPA and 2015 free trade arrangement permitted Mongolia greater access to Japan's advanced technology and expertise, while Japan focused more on Mongolia's livestock resources and minerals, including rare earths. Still, for Japan, Mongolia's lack of rail and pipeline infrastructure remains a major inhibitor to increasing Japanese FDI or mineral purchases.

The Koreas' Role in Implementing Mongolia's Wolf Strategy

With Russia's fading as a viable trade partner and China's growing monopoly over Mongolia's economy in recent decades, the Mongolian problem still remains how to reach alternative "Third Neighbor" customers for Mongolian minerals. In addition to the challenge of attracting FDI to construct domestic rail, road, and pipe infrastructure, finding a new transit port on the Pacific that could accommodate Mongolian mineral traffic has led Mongolian development experts to look toward the Korean Peninsula as the only reasonable option. Thus, from the beginning of the democratic era until today, Mongolia has been interested in working with both Korean governments on energy and mineral projects.

South Korea (Republic of Korea [ROK]) has limited mineral resources, possessing only 10 percent of the coal and iron deposits on the Korean Peninsula since the vast majority are located in North Korea (Democratic People's Republic of Korea [DPRK]). Yet, South Korea already has become one of the top 10 energy consumers in the world, and the International Energy Agency expects its power needs to increase 37 percent between 2006 and 2020. The ROK is the world's fourth largest oil importer and second largest coal and LNG importer after Japan. All energy imports arrive by sea, with 85 percent from the Middle East, but it is willing to develop Russian oil imports. Nowadays, the ROK focuses on natural gas, bituminous coal, and nuclear power (15 percent), while seeking to reduce its reliance on imported oil. Even after the 2011 nuclear accident in Japan, the ROK continues to see nuclear power as an increasingly important part of its energy strategy despite the necessity of importing all uranium fuel. South Korea's energy strategy is complicated by the North Korean situation, and any conflict or unification scenario would increase energy demand. It is clear that South Korea's desire to acquire Mongolian minerals is intimately connected with and, therefore, stymied by the lack of progress on Northeast Asian transport infrastructure integration and Korean Peninsula instability. Nevertheless, for Mongolia, South Korean technology and FDI are very welcome, and the ROK is seen as a genuinely viable trade partner.

The ROK and Mongolia had a large increase in bilateral trade volume between 1990 and 2015 from $2.7 million to roughly $300 million. Bilateral trade volume of $370 million ($351 million of Korean imports) in 2014 represented a 140-fold increase from $2.71 million in 1990. That same year, Korea's $750 million FDI made it Mongolia's seventh largest investor.[81] It has been a key donor to Mongolia, providing $137 million since 1990 in loans and grants.[82] According to the Trade-Investment Promotion Agency South Korea (KOTRA), in 2015 the ROK was Mongolia's fourth largest trade partner, accounting for 3.6 percent of Mongolia's total trade volume. From 1995 to 2005, minerals, particularly gold, dominated Mongolian exports to South Korea, while the ROK sold transportation and machinery/electrical products, as well as textiles and foodstuffs, to the Mongols.[83] More recently, South Korean–Mongolian trade has been dominated by investment in the construction industry. Major investments began in real estate, telecommunications, and banking but have moved into the mining and educational sectors. The state-owned Korea Resources Corporation, steel-making company Posco, and Korea Electric Power Corporation made an unsuccessful joint bid to develop the TT Western Tsankhi coal field.

In March 2011 a South Korean consortium that included the state-run Korea Rail Network Authority, Daewoo Engineering and Construction, Hyundai Engineering and Construction, and Lotte Engineering and Construction signed a $3 billion preliminary deal to build a 1,040-kilometer railway in Mongolia that could carry TT coal products to Choibalsan City near the border with Russia. Two years later, Samsung C&T was commissioned by the Railway Authority of Mongolia as the sole contractor to implement the $483 million project to build 217 kilometers of the TT–Gashuun Sukhait border rail as well as construct a rolling stock depot.[84] This line will link up to the Russian-gauge main north-south railroad in Mongolia going through Siberia and is expected to be the catalyst for South Korea to acquire Mongolian raw minerals such as coal. Kyeryong Group has become involved in major construction projects for redevelopment of the capital city of Ulaanbaatar and in building a 365-kilometer highway between Ulaanbaatar and the northern border town Altanbulag, site of a Mongolian-Russian free trade zone.[85] Once these domestic rail and road networks are in place, Mongolian minerals will have access north through Russia to Pacific customers, not just to Chinese buyers.

However, for the Mongols the key country on the peninsula in the future will be North Korea. The reason Mongolia pays special attention to its North Korean relationship lies in what it sees as potential access to international markets that cooperation with the DPRK could offer. North Korea since its founding in 1948 has developed its foreign economic relations based on the *juche*,[86] or self-reliance, principle. In North Korea, foreign companies from China, Japan, US, and UK have participated in around twenty-five mining projects connected to substantial mineral deposits, while Chinese FDI has been involved in twenty mining projects since 2003.[87] Most of these deposits presently are unexploited, but if they are developed in the future, they could compete with Mongolia's minerals. China is North Korea's major trading partner and accounts for 90 percent of North Korea's foreign trade—in 2014 this was nearly $7 billion out of an estimated total of $7.6 billion in total foreign trade. Of that $7 billion, roughly $3 billion was in North Korean coal, iron ore, and petroleum exports to China. In January 2016, Chinese imports of North Korean mineral resources were worth $76.9 million.[88]

A Mongolian oil company with ties to North Korea expects to entice foreign investors into North Korea's energy sector with geological data that indicate the presence of oil and gas resources. Mongolian Stock Exchange–listed HBOil JSC is planning to open a data room—a place where interested parties can inspect geological information on underground structures that could indicate the presence of oil and gas fields. HBOil is seeking to exploit onshore oil basins and is in a joint venture with the Korea Oil Exploration Corp. (KOEC), North Korea's state-run oil company, to attract international bids on onshore oil and gas blocks on behalf of KOECII, an international subsidiary of North Korea's state-run oil company.[89]

Finally, the Rajin-Seonbong (aka Rason) region in North Korea has strategic significance as the northernmost year-round ice-free port in Northeast Asia. This site was identified in the United Nations–backed Tumen River Development Project as a potential geostrategic transit point for the shipment of goods to landlocked Northeastern China, Mongolia, and the Russian Far East. The Chinese Chuangli Company contracted to develop Rajin's port number one, reportedly for a period of only ten years, while Russian investors have been offered a forty-nine-year deal to develop the second part of Rajin.[90] In 2013 Russia rebuilt a rail line between Rajin and the small Russian border city of Khasan. Such transportation plans are strongly supported by the Mongolian government because if international rail lines are built to North Korean ports, Mongolia will have an answer to its northern transportation route problem and new access to Asia Pacific markets.[91] In 2009 Mongolia's Ministry of Road and Transportation signed a transit agreement with North Korean authorities to utilize the Rajin Port for export purposes.[92] Already linked by Russian rail, Mongolia is promoting new rail construction to Rajin as a way for its minerals to reach diverse Asian markets.

Summary of Mongolia's Wolf Strategy

It is likely that the major pillars of Mongolia's mineral and energy development Wolf Strategy will continue into the 2020s, regardless of changes in political power. If political and economic events in Northeast Asia warrant, Mongolia has the flexible mentality and track record to readjust individual components. Endowed with an anti-legalistic cultural mind-set from its nomadic ancestors, the nation will continue to approach mining and economic development according to its own vacillating agenda and thus continue to frustrate foreign investment partners who seek stability. To review, the main objectives of the Wolf Strategy are as follows:

- Modify the friendly foreign investment climate in Mongolia of the past decade because Mongolia considers it a failure in many ways.
- Employ a resource nationalism strategy based primarily on national security objectives while maintaining democratic, free market structures.
- Learn from other countries', especially Russia's, successes and failures in resource development. Seemingly listen to all foreign partners' advice and concerns, yet persist in pursuing Mongolia's own agenda.
- Rebalance to some extent Chinese trade monopolization of the Mongolian economy by expanding and diversifying the foreign investment picture, and tighten foreign ownership regulations with oversight through parliamentary legislation.
- Retrench the mineral environment through renationalizing some existing mineral deposits via license review and confiscation, citing environmental damage and nondevelopment to avoid international court cases, despite the likelihood of adding volatility to the investment climate.
- Slow foreign investment and mineral development in general with a five-year cooling-off period lasting to at least 2018.
- Develop revenue streams from anticipated continued high energy resource prices, "advanced tax payments," and promises of future favors; put revenues in a Human Development Fund, but give payouts to the populace at times to influence domestic elections.
- Ask foreign investors to finance power plants and mineral processing industries to produce value-added products; expect increased revenue from these fewer, higher-value products.
- Ask Australia, Japan, and the Koreas to partner with Russia in building pipelines and expanding rail routes north to the Pacific to enable Mongolia to find new trade partners.
- Reduce reliance on Russian diesel, oil products, and power by sponsoring quick homegrown alternatives, even if less profitable.

- These policies will continue through changes of parties and administrations in Mongolia until political and economic events in Northeast Asia make adjustments to the Wolf Strategy necessary.

Notes

1. "Mongolia mics," September 2012, www.tradingeconomics.com/mongolia/balance-of-trade.

2. Zhang Yunbi and Wu Jiao, "China, Mongolia to Boost Ties," *China Daily*, January 13, 2012, http://www.chinadaily.com.cn/cndy/2012-01/13/content_14436254.htm. The figure $2.3 billion was cited by Zhang Xiaoqiang in www.english.news.mn, January 16, 2013.

3. www.english.news.mn, January 16, 2013.

4. Mongolia in 2014 imported 91 percent of its petroleum products from Russia, including gasoline, jet fuel, and diesel. As of 2013, Mongolia imported $1.03 billion worth of refined petroleum products accounting for 67 percent of imports from Russia. In 2011, Mongolia imported 90 percent of its petrol products from Russia. Trade volume between Russia and Mongolia decreased by 2.8 percent as of May 2015. Samantha Brletich, "Mongolia and the New Russian Oil Diplomacy," *Modern Diplomacy,* March 4, 2016.

5. In recent years, the imported electricity price from Russia had risen 30 percent each year. "Should We Keep Importing Electricity?," *UB Post,* November 19, 2014.

6. Jargalsaikhan Mendee, "Mongolia's Dilemma: A Politically Linked, Economically Isolated Small Power," *Open Forum,* April 30, 2015, http://www.theasanforum.org/mongolias-dilemma-a-politically-linked-economically-isolated-small-power/.

7. Ibid.

8. "Mongolia," EITI, https://eiti.org/implementing_country/7.

9. International Energy Agency, *World Energy Outlook* (Paris: IEA, 2010), 98–99.

10. Mendee, "Mongolia's Dilemma."

11. Jaime FlorCruz, "Mining Fuels Mongolia's 'Wolf Economy,'" CNN, May 20, 2011, http://www.cnn.com/2011/WORLD/asiapcf/05/19/mongolia.mining.economy/index.html.

12. Mendee, "Mongolia's Dilemma."

13. US Department of State, *2014 Investment Climate Statement: Mongolia* (Washington, DC: Bureau of Economic and Business Affairs, June 2014), 1, https://www.state.gov/e/eb/rls/othr/ics/2014/231041.htm.

14. Ibid., 2.

15. Ibid.

16. Antoine Maire, "Mongolia at War: Economic Warfare Under Blue Sky" (paper presented at the Tenth International Congress of Mongolists, Ulaanbaatar, August 9–13, 2011).

17. Information in this paragraph was obtained in private conversations this author had with Mongolian officials in various agencies in June 2012.

18. A. Tuvshintugs, "National Perspectives on Linkage Strategy: Mongolian Perspective," in *Political Economy of the Northeast Asian Regionalism: Linkages Between Economic and Security Cooperation* (Seoul: Korea Institute for National Unification, 2006), 488–490.

19. For only 31 of the 106 impacted licenses, about $19 million had already been spent and a further $36 million planned. A report by Independent Mongolian Metals and Mining Research stated that these licensees had no legal recourse or rights to undertake exploration on their existing licenses due to a criminal court case involving corruption. Els, "Mongolia Passes Mining-Friendly Law."

20. "Foreign Investors Cry Foul as Mongolia Revokes Mine Licenses," Reuters, November 7, 2013, http://www.reuters.com/article/mongolia-mining-licenses-idUSL3N0IS33820131107.

21. Such as "mineral resource wealth" (an accumulation of a mineral—the size, form, content, composition, or economic importance of which has not been fully assessed) and "mineral deposit reserve" (a mineral resource—the size, form, content, and mineral composition of which has been determined by exploration work).

22. For a detailed analysis of the amendments to the 2012 law, see Hogan Lovells, "Amendment to the Law of Mongolia on Minerals," *Lexology,* September 15, 2014, http://www.lexology.com/library/detail.aspx?g=e7e4f13e-7114-454a-881f-288825b456eb.

23. "Mongolia Aspires to Become a 'Center of Nomadic Tourism,'" *Mongol Messenger,* October 28, 2016.

24. Michael, "Mongolia: A Case Study in Foreign Direct Investment."

25. From an interview with the director of the administrative board of the Mongolian Coal Association, L. Davaatsedev. B. Anu, "L. Davaatsedev: Stopping Coal Export Until Coal Prices Rise Is Bad Policy," *UB Post,* August 6, 2013.

26. This is because the coal must be transferred to railcars that are suitable for the smaller, internationally accepted gauge used in China. english.news.mn, May 10, 2013.

27. Private discussion with the author in June 2012 in Ulaanbaatar.

28. Mendee, "Mongolia's Dilemma."

29. Putin has said that "Russia enjoys vast energy and mineral resources which serve as a basis to develop its economy as an instrument to implement domestic and foreign policy. The role of the country in international energy markets determines, in many ways, its geopolitical influence." Roman Kupchinsky, "LNG—Russia's New Energy Blackmail Tool," *Eurasia Daily Monitor* 4, no. 77 (April 22, 2009). Category: Eurasia Daily Monitor, Home Page, Energy, Russia.

30. Ibid., 2.

31. Nina Poussenkova, "'They Went East, They Went West . . .': The Global Expansion of Russian Oil Companies," in *Russia's Energy Policies: National, Interregional and Global Levels*, ed. Pami Aalto (Cheltenham, UK: Edward Elgar, 2012), 202.

32. International Energy Agency, *Russia Energy Survey 2002* (Paris: IEA, 2002), 135.

33. Cited in Shinichiro Tabata and Xu Liu, "Russia's Energy Policy in the Far East and East Siberia," in *Russia's Energy Policies: National, Interregional and Global Levels*, ed. Pami Aalto (Cheltenham, UK: Edward Elgar, 2012), 159.

34. Adrian Dellecker and Thomas Gomart, eds., *Russian Energy Security and Foreign Policy* (London: Routledge, 2011), introduction. Putin's 1997 thesis at the University of St. Petersburg was on the role of natural resources in economic development.

35. Andrei Illarionov quoted in Pavel K. Baev, *Russian Energy Policy and Military Power: Putin's Quest for Greatness* (London: Routledge, 2008), 164.

36. "These aims are conditioned by the Russian leaders' perceptions of the country's role in the balance of power and the resources available to the Russian state." See Anita Orban, *Power, Energy and the New Russian Imperialism* (Westport, CT: Praeger Security International, 2008), cited in Pami Aalto, ed., *Russia's Energy Policies,* 12.

37. Baev, *Russian Energy Policy,* 130.

38. *EnergeticheskayastrategiyaRossiina period do 2020 goda [Energy Strategy of Russia up to 2020]*, Pavitel'stvoRossijskoiFederatsiiUkaz 1234, August 28, 2003, and modified in *EnergeticheskayastrategiyaRossiina period do 2030 goda* [*Energy Strategy of Russia up yo 2030*]on November 13, 2009.

39. Alexander Sutyagin, *Monitoring BTS/Bellona* (St. Petersburg, May 6, 2004), www.bellona.ru; Alexander Sutyagin, "Russia: Top Secret Oil," *Energy Bulletin,* April 28, 2004, www.energybulletin.net/stories/2004-04-28/russia-top-secret-oil.

40. Putin put 1,000 enterprises under state ownership via the List of Strategic Enterprises and Strategic Joint Stock Companies. Most were in the defense-industrial complex, but the list also includes state-controlled energy companies including Transneft, Transnefteprodukt, and Gazprom. The list has been revised several times. See Philip Hanson, "The Sustainability of Russia's Energy Power," 6, 40n66. See also "On Approving the List of Strategic Enterprises and Strategic Joint Stock Companies," *VremyaNovostey [News Time],* Moscow, August 6, 2004.

41. Robert E. Ebel, *The Geopolitics of Russian Energy: Looking Back, Looking Forward* (Washington, DC: Center for Strategic and International Studies, 2009), 53.

42. Gaddy and Ickes argue that Russia did not suffer very much from resource curse because of these policies. See Aalto, *Russia's Energy Policies,* 11.

43. Michael Bradshaw, "Russian Energy Dilemmas: Energy Security, Globalization and Climate Change," 208.

44. According to Mongolian Mining Minister Davaajav Ganhuyag, in 2013 the cost of one ton of oil from Rosneft Company was $200–$300 more than from South Korea, Switzerland, or Chinese suppliers. B. Ooluun, *Mongol Messenger,* March 22, 2013.

45. The Mongolian government has promised every Mongol citizen 1,072 shares of common stock in the company that runs TT. This deposit is being developed by the country's largest state-owned coal company, Erdenes TavanTolgoi, LLC, and is thought to hold 6.4 billion metric tons of coal reserves.

46. S. Bold-Erdene, "Own Oil Refinery Only Way Out of Russian Pressure," *Mongolian Mining Journal*, September 12, 2011, http://en.mongolianminingjournal.com/content/16844.shtml.

47. Rescinded January 1, 2011.

48. Mining Minister Davaajav Gankhuyag, a well-known supporter of resource nationalism, explained, "In order to get rid of petroleum supply from one route (Russia), we are negotiating with third parties that brings some positive results."

49. *Montsame,* March 19, 2013.

50. *Mongolian Economy and Finance* (blog), March 18, 2013, mongoliaeconomy.blogspot.com.

51. *Mongolian Mining Journal*, October 8, 2009. Accessed May 9, 2013.

52. E. Altanzul, "Construction of Mongolian First Oil Refinery to Begin," *Montsame,* June 20, 2018.

53. According to ADB, "Mongolia: Economy," https://www.adb.org/countries/mongolia/economy.

54. Que Guanghui, *China's Energy Sector: A Sustainable Strategy* (Beijing: Foreign Language Press, 2007), 16.

55. China's total verified basic reserves of coal are estimated at 114 billion tons. Whole regions of China have their growth tied to coal mines, and the accompanying environmental damage and deaths have led to popular social unrest and desertification. In 2006–2007, the government changed its tax structure to encourage coal imports by abolishing the tax incentive for coal exports and the coal import duty.

56. China's medium- and long-range sustainable development strategy for the energy sector continues mainly to rely on domestic coal supplies and maintaining coal as the energy foundation; accelerating large coal field production; diversifying development of new resources, including more nuclear power; and increasing the import of oil and gas from outside China. China's willingness to import hydrocarbons and energy minerals from Russia is seen in Chinese imports: 2.1 percent of its oil for its energy production in 2000, over 10 percent in 2005 and 2006, and 7.5 percent in 2009. See Tabata and Xu, "Russia's Energy Policy in the Far East and East Siberia," 171.

57. Sophie Yeo, "Analysis: Decline in China's Coal Consumption Accelerates," *Carbon Brief,* February 29, 2016, citing 2015 Chinese government statistics.

58. Testimony of Dean P. Girdis, director of PFC Energy (a global energy strategy firm) in US-China Economic and Security Review Commission, *China's Energy Needs and Strategies* (Washington, DC: US Government Printing Office), 45–46. However, according to the commission, "China has a comprehensive energy security strategy, consisting of demand reduction, diversification, leveraging bilateral relationships with key Middle East suppliers, building stronger ties with Russia, and establishing a market position in Central Asia"; ibid., iii.

59. A well-respected Chinese mineral expert advising the PRC State Council and state-owned enterprises investing in Mongolia explained to the author in a private meeting in June 2012.

60. For example, Zhang Xiaoqiang, deputy director of China's National Development and Reform Commission, on a January 2013 visit to Ulaanbaatar during the third meeting of the China-Mongolia Cooperation Commission on Mineral Resources and Energy,

stated that the two countries should work more closely to jointly develop large-scale mining and construction transportation projects. www.englishnews.mn, January 16, 2013. Accessed February 1, 2013.

61. Mendee, "Mongolia's Dilemma."

62. Japan was the world's largest importer of LNG, second largest importer of coal, and the third largest net importer of oil in 2012. "Japan Energy Profile: Only 16 Percent Energy Self-Sufficient—Analysis," *Eurasia Review* (June 6, 2012), http://www.eurasiareview.com/06062012-japan-energy-profile-only-16-percent-energy-self-sufficient-analysis/.

63. Shuhei Kojima, *Stable Supply of Mineral Resources* (Tokyo: Ministry of Economy, Trade and Industry of Japan, Mineral and Natural Resources Division, July 12, 2002).

64. Energy Information Administration, "Country Analysis Briefs: Japan," June 4, 2012, https://www.eia.gov/beta/international/analysis.php?iso=JPN.

65. Elaine Kurtenbach, "Japan Back to Trade Deficit, $6.5 Billion in July," Associated Press, August 22, 2012.

66. Energy Information Administration, "Country Analysis Briefs: Japan."

67. Greater coal usage violated Japan's 2010 Basic Energy Plan, which called for reducing coal power from 25 percent to 10 percent, although new "clean coal" technologies were being considered to meet environmental targets. "Reactor restarts pivotal to Japan's energy policy, says IEA," *World Nuclear News* (September 22, 2016), http://www.world-nuclear-news.org/Articles/Reactor-restarts-pivotal-to-Japan-s-energy-policy.

68. According to a report by the Natural Resources Defense Council, Oil Change International, and the World Wide Fund for Nature, Japan invested more than $20 billion into coal projects between 2007 and 2014—roughly a quarter of total international support for coal power from Vietnam to India to Chile. They've also put about $5 billion into coal mining projects around the world over the same period. See Darius Dixon, "How Japan Pushes Coal on the World," *Politico*, August 12, 2015, http://www.politico.com/agenda/story/2015/08/japan-exporting-coal-plants-000195.

69. Russia and Japan are cooperating to modernize Russia's fossil fuel power plants and exploring ways to develop a power bridge between Russia and Japan or Eastern Siberia to China. See International Energy Agency, *Russia Energy Survey 2002* (Paris: IEA, 2002), 203, 215, 216.

70. Opinions given to the author in personal interviews in Tokyo, June 2012.

71. Two high-placed Japanese officials in different meetings in Tokyo in June 2012 asked me, "Are Mongolians Asian people?" Another Japanese official who has led several mineral-related negotiating teams to Ulaanbaatar said that the more he is in contact with Mongolians the less he understands them and their goals.

72. "Country Assistance Policy for Mongolia," Japan International Cooperation Agency (JICA), April 2012, https://www.mofa.go.jp/mofaj/gaiko/oda/files/000048303.pdf.

73. Abe assumed the prime ministership for the second time in December 2012. His first term in that position was from 2006 to 2007.

74. Kotaro Ono, "Abe strikes energy deal with Mongolia in a bid to curb China's clout," *Asahi Shimbun,* March 31, 2013, http://livedrifting23.blogspot.com/2013/04/abe-strikes-energy-deal-with-mongolia.html.

75. During that visit, Abe asked the Mongols to support Japan in re the Senkaku/Diaoyu Islands dispute with China. When questioned about the North Korean nuclear situation, Altankhuyag noted that Mongolia had offered to assist in easing tensions between the two Koreas: "As Mongolia has a normal relationship with North Korea, we are ready to help if the sides decide to meet in Ulaanbaatar." *Mongol Messenger,* April 5, 2013.

76. The visit made it clear that Abe was pursuing a diplomatic policy as "part of his strategy to put pressure on Beijing by enhancing ties with democratic countries surrounding China." Hiroshi Tajima, "Japan in Depth: Abe's Mongolia Visit Strategic Move," *The Daily Yomiuri* , March 31, 2013, https://www.questia.com/newspaper/1P3-2931677501/japan-in-depth-abe-s-mongolia-visit-strategic-move.

77. *Mongol Messenger,* April 5, 2013.

78. Japan also pledged new grants for a training and diagnostic hospital, implementation of the bilateral offset credit mechanism for low-carbon development partnership, and improvement of engineering and technical higher educational institutions.

79. *Mongol Messenger,* April 5, 2013.

80. Mendee, "Mongolia's Dilemma."

81. Ts. Sükhbaatar, "Hwang Kyo-ahn: Mongolia and South Korea Are Close Partners in Trade and Investment," BDSec, December 18, 2015, https://www.bdsec.mn/?lang=mn.

82. "Korea and Mongolia," *Eurasia Capital,* June 6, 2011, www.eurasiac.com/korea-and-mongolia.

83. Sh. Enkhbayar, "Recent Trends in Mongolian Foreign Trade with the Countries of Northeast Asia" (ERINA Report no. 96, Tokyo, November 2010), 48.

84. "Samsung C&T Wins $483 Mil. Project to Build Railway in Mongolia," *Korea Economic Daily,* May 8, 2013, http://english.hankyung.com/news/apps/news.view?c1=04&nkey=201305081245301.

85. M. Zoljargal, "Tsast Group partners with Kyeryong Group for redevelopment," *UB Post,* July 7, 2013. http://ubpost.mongolnews.mn/?p=4732.

86. *Juche* is based on the three principles of political independence, economic self-sustenance, and self-reliance in defense.

87. Choi Kyung-soo, "The Mining Industry of North Korea, *Korean Journal of Defense Analysis* 23, no. 2 (June 2011): 212.

88. Shannon Tiezzi, "It's Official: China Is Cracking Down on North Korean Trade," *The Diplomat,* April 6, 2016.

89. Leo Byrne, "Investigation: North Korea makes moves toward oil exploration," in Business Council of Mongolia, *NewsWire*, no. 332 (July 4, 2014), http://www.slideshare.net/ulziimyagmar/04072014-newswire-issue-332.

90. The National Committee on North Korea, "Special Economic Zones in the DPRK," *NCNK Issue Brief*, January 14, 2014, https://www.ncnk.org/sites/default/files/issue-briefs/NCNK_Issue_Brief_DPRK_SEZ.pdf.

91. "North Korea's Ports Mongolia's Gateway," *Bloomberg,* June 19, 2011, http://gulfnews.com/business/shipping/north-korea-s-ports-mongolia-s-gateway-1.823264.

92. Tiezzi, "It's Official."

9

An Economic Corridor for Regional and Continental Integration

Across the Eurasian continent, new and revived regional institutional structures are emerging to cope with twenty-first-century transnational threats and issues. Some of these institutional structures have origins in UN global initiatives that have been slow to develop, while others are attempts to formulate innovative solutions to calcified political and economic challenges. Since the end of the Cold War, interregional and intercontinental linkages have deepened, and such realignments can be catalysts for global transformational changes once "organizational gaps" in Northeast Asia are overcome. The past decade of Middle Eastern instability, which shows no signs of reversing, has led to refocused attention on the importance of geography when calculating energy supplies that drive economic development. On the Eurasian continent such phenomena are leading to shifting political and economic influence for the nation-states that call the region home.

In the past ten years Mongolia has emerged as a rapidly growing mineral-based economy that increasingly is asserting its own voice in international affairs. Traditional bilateral political alliances with its two border neighbors and new bilateral trade and investment ties to "Third Neighbors," such as Japan and the United States, have not been able to meet its needs, so it has embraced a greater role in promoting its vision of Eurasian regional synergy. As a result, in the second decade of the twenty-first century, Mongolia has become active in North-South Korean issues, northern corridor transit routes, border free trade zones, and international peacekeeping operations. It has chosen to work through existing mechanisms such as UN multilateral organizations and international movements, including Davos-organized economic summits and the Community of Democracies Governing Council, and, increasingly, to be willing to create its own regional structures.

In the last decade Mongolia's two giant neighbors and other countries in the Eurasian region have become more serious about pursuing greater transport and pipeline connectivity to promote integration and economic development. For Mongolia to stand outside this trend rather than be a part of the decisionmaking structures would be to doom the Mongols to marginalization and poverty. Infrastructure network development issues in Northeast Asia are fundamental to establishing integrated relations in this mineral-rich region. Mongolia understands that transportation networks have strategic significance for reducing its international isolation, so this chapter explores the latest concepts that Mongolian policymakers are promoting with their border neighbors and other ideas for deeper Mongolian participation in Northeast Asia and Eurasian economic development strategies.

Mongolia wants to take advantage of the broad continentalist trends that have emerged to expand its own role in Eurasia and break out of its landlocked stranglehold. During its seventy years of communism and the early years of its democratic era, it stood back and watched the actions of its two neighbors, China and Russia, as well as those of the developed Northeast Asian economies of Japan and South Korea (supported by the United States), accepting their overwhelming dominance over the Asian continent. This kind of passive foreign economic policy was appropriate for a country in the twentieth century that had to maintain its independence within the Soviet system and later find its way to create a new democratic society in the post–Cold War world. But nowadays Mongolia's goal for its Asian activism is "to strengthen its position in the Asian region, to intensify bilateral relationships with other regional countries, to engage to a dialogue on political, security and economic cooperation of the region and to participate in the regional integration processes."[1]

The issue of transit connections is of major concern to Mongolia because it spends 15–20 percent of its export earnings on transport services, while its two neighbors spend on average less than 6 percent. It has been noted by Mongolian Ambassador to Canada Gotov Dugerjav that, as a landlocked country with a fragile economy, "Mongolia depends on the world market prices of a few export items, such as copper and gold, and the issue of transport may impede the abilities of landlocked countries to fully benefit from the globalization process of international trade and foreign direct investment."[2] It has tried to break out of its isolation by joining many international and regional organizations and today is a member or a participant in the Treaty of Amity and Cooperation in Southeast Asia, the ASEAN Regional Forum, the Pacific Economic Cooperation Council, the Shanghai Cooperation Organization, the Asian Cooperation Dialogue, the Asia-Europe Meeting (ASEM), the Conference on Interaction and Confidence-Building Measures in Asia, the Forum for East Asia–Latin America Cooperation, and the Bali Democracy Forum. Particularly since 2010, Mongolia has found itself at a critical juncture where Eurasian continental integration has been energized by the rise of the Chinese economy and the rapprochement between Mongolia's twentieth-century protector Russia and its traditional nemesis China.

For Mongolia, China is an attractive option to connect with East Asian and Central Asian economies. China is projecting a benign peripheral diplomacy to neutralize the influence of strategic rivals and to attract Mongolia to its regional order. President Xi Jinping repeatedly expressed the importance of a win-win principle in China's neighborhood diplomacy during his state visit to Mongolia in 2014. Xi became the first Chinese leader to publicly enunciate that "China will respect Mongolia's territorial integrity, independence, and developmental choice forever." China tries to convince the Mongols that it has limited economic interest in Mongolia and that its policy is "progressive, tolerant, and particularly accommodative to Mongolia's requests."[3] However, one Mongolian researcher has warned that (1) more Chinese developmental investment will increase the presence of Chinese nationals (mostly male labor), which will incite historic, nationalist, and protectionist backlash; (2) more Chinese FDI will invite more corruption that will trigger public discontent and media outrage if it stokes domestic corruption; and (3) more Chinese influence in Mongolia risks jeopardizing traditional Russian geopolitical and economic interests.[4]

Chinese, Russian, and South Korean Views of Regional Integration

China has viewed Russia as a strategic partner since the mid-1990s. In 2005 China supplied 94 percent of its own energy but expects by 2020 this will drop to 80 percent—the same year that China will become a net coal importer. Russian energy mineral supplies can be brought overland to China through Central Asia and Mongolia. However, there remain significant points of tension between the two powers, including slow Russian development of its resource deposits and transport (pipeline) infrastructure; the unpredictability of Russian decisionmaking and verbal agreements; Sino-Russian traditional rivalry in Central Asia and Mongolia; and attempts by Russia to play off China and Japan. Russia's deliberate inaction and ambiguous energy and export strategies have led the Chinese to look to Kazakhstan and Mongolia for alternative mineral supplies.

With the 2014 Ukraine sanctions' limiting Russia's energy trade partners, China has taken advantage to upgrade its Russian trade relationship. Development of Sino-Russian energy ties is the most important factor today driving the "strategic convergence" of China and Russia.[5] This Chinese policy is most disquieting to Mongolia, which fears encirclement by its border neighbors, and reminds Mongolian policymakers of the times decades ago when these countries made decisions about Mongolia's foreign and economic affairs without consulting the Mongols. China's well-known One Belt, One Road (OBOR) or Belt and Road Initiative (BRI) embraces the trend toward a multipolar world of economic globalization and Eurasian continental cooperation. Announced by Chinese President Xi Jinping in the early fall of 2013,[6] BRI aims at highly efficient allocation of resources and deep integration of markets among the countries along what was the historical Silk Road and the southern maritime route that linked Asia and Europe in previous centuries. The Chinese have claimed that they are creating "an open, inclusive and balanced regional economic cooperation architecture that benefits all" under what China calls its "Five Principles of Peaceful Coexistence."[7] This multilateral concept has many dimensions, but most of the attention has been concentrated on its transit, infrastructure, and financial connectivity projects. Building BRI infrastructure mainly is aimed at promoting economic prosperity and regional economic cooperation, but just as importantly, the concept includes a cultural component that is discussed in the next chapter.

The BRI transportation network initially was planned to incorporate two east-west rail corridors to bypass Russia yet still connect China with major destinations within Central Asia, Western Asia, and Europe. It would traverse regions where natural resources are being extracted with Chinese investment with a rail journey time of six to ten days (twenty days fewer than by road), reducing transportation costs by 30 percent.[8] Japanese carmaker Toyota, which currently ships automobiles manufactured in Japan to Kazakhstan via a sea route that takes seventy days, was interested because the Chinese railway corridor could reduce this delivery time to just fifteen days.[9] However, because much of the Chinese domestic rail system already is near full capacity, China plans to open two more railway routes involving Russia and possibly Mongolia from Xi'an to Rotterdam and from Xi'an to Moscow. Central Chinese factories hope to export petroleum equipment and heavy trucks worth $98 million annually. In addition to the Chinese companies, countries in East and South Asia would be able to utilize these routes to reach markets in Central Asia and Europe, and these rail connections also would enable Central Asian countries to transport their natural resources eastward.

As for Mongolia's northern neighbor, over the past two hundred years Russia has spread Russian language, economic policies, and culture throughout the Central Asian and Siberian Pacific regions. The Soviet period incorporated some 160 different ethnic groups in Eurasia under the communist economic umbrella, which was the first exposure to modern Western civilization for many of the impacted Asian peoples, including the Mongols. Soviet Marxist Leninist ideology overwhelmed native traditions during the twentieth century. With the fall of the USSR in 1990, many of the Turkic-Mongol states reemerged throughout the continent, and the last several decades have seen attempts to remove Russian influences and reassert nativist traditions. Russia remains a great, but reduced, major power in the region as the world's twelfth largest economy, and it has both a tradition and a continuing interest in defining and spreading the Russian ethos to all peoples of Eurasia without the constraints of ideology. While Russia's pivot to Asia includes the important task of creating a Eurasian trading bloc, it also is a way to limit the loss of Russian influence in Central and East Asia and to counterbalance China's rise as a major continental trading partner via a new form of Eurasianism.

Eurasianism, a political movement that emerged in the 1920s, is focused on the geopolitical concept that Russian civilization should not be categorized as European but rather as non-European Orthodox Christian. After the collapse of the Soviet Union, there arose the modified ideology of Neo-Eurasianism that considers Russia to be culturally closer to Asia than to Western Europe.[10] One of its first institutional manifestations came in 1994, when the Russian-controlled Collective Security Treaty Organization (CSTO), which promotes security, military, and paramilitary cooperation, grew out of the framework of the Commonwealth of Independent States (CIS). Reorganized in 1999, CSTO now consists of Russia, Armenia, Belarus, Tajikistan, Kazakhstan, and Kyrgyzstan. An associated movement has been the Russian World project, a type of soft-power public diplomacy that was mentioned for the first time officially in 2001 by Vladimir Putin.[11] This can be viewed as an institution to promote Russian language and culture in the Eurasian region. The Eurasian Economic Union (EEU) is another Russian-dominated vehicle developed in the post–Cold War period to maintain Russian relevance in Eurasia. In theory, Russia's goals for the EEU are congruent with those of the Russian World project, particularly those devoted to the Eurasian neighborhood that center on shared economic strategies.

Putin's EEU, inspired by a suggestion of President Nursultan Nazarbayev of Kazakhstan in March 1994, seeks strengthening economic integration between Europe and Asia through a single comprehensive national alliance in the political, economic, cultural, and security spheres.[12] The EEU Single Economic Space established a single market across the territory of Belarus, Russia, and Kazakhstan in 2014, and in 2015 Armenia and Kyrgyzstan joined, which brought together a market of some 183 million people.[13] The EEU is designed as a bridge between the European Union and China's New Silk Road economic belt to substantially boost Russia's economic superpower image on the world stage. Through the EEU, Russia primarily is seeking to link its European eastern regions to East Asian markets—a goal all the more important after Europe and the United States imposed sanctions on Russia because of the Ukraine crisis. Thus Russia, by embracing the Asian region more broadly because it sees its Far East regions developing into the backbone of a Russian energy-resources-based economy, has decided to recreate the Great Silk Road as a unified transport network by linking its Trans-Siberian railway with the railways of South Korea, North Korea, China, and Europe. The Russians have pressured Mongolia to join both the EEU and CSTO. Mongolia has deflected this since 2008 by joining a series of bilateral joint military exercises that focus on peacekeeping and antiterrorist activities. For Mongolia the appeal of EEU is greater, which is why its DP government in 2015 signed a memorandum of cooperation with it. When the new MPP-controlled government took power in the summer of 2016, discussions immediately resumed on new forms of EEU trade and cooperation.[14] Mongolian Ambassador to the EEU Banzragch Delgermaa announced that a study group was established to develop economic dialogue between the EEU and Mongolia to reduce import duties on Mongolian goods and apply the lessons learned from creating a Vietnam-EEU free trade agreement to Mongolia.[15]

The other major Northeast Asian country calling for a new type of energy and logistics infrastructure across the Eurasian continent is South Korea. In November 2013, shortly after China proposed BRI and a month before she was to meet President Putin in Seoul, President Park Geun-hye announced at a Global Cooperation in the Era of Eurasia conference a South Korean Eurasian Initiative called the "Iron Silk Road Express." She advocated developing a logistics and energy network to not only reduce logistics costs and stimulate global trade but also to stabilize raw materials costs and contribute to the world economy's growth. Saying that establishing logistics and energy networks across the continent would facilitate the formation of a free trade Eurasian economic bloc like the European Union, Park called for abolishing trade barriers by "linking energy infrastructures including electricity grids, gas and oil pipelines, and co-developing China's shale gas and eastern Siberia's petroleum and gas."[16]

Greater Tumen Initiative

Soon after Mongolia's embrace of democracy, a new organizational infrastructure was created in 1992 to promote Northeast Asian integration. Mongolia supported this connectivity concept called the Greater Tumen Initiative (GTI), originally labeled the Tumen River Area Development Programme, that covers the Greater Tumen River basin region from Yanji, China, and eastern Mongolia to Cheongjin, North Korea, to Vladivostok, Russia. A few years later the target zone was expanded to cover the three northeastern provinces of China, the Rajin and Seonbong areas of North Korea, the Maritime Province of Russia, and the Korean East Sea. With a both skilled and low-cost labor pool, the Tumen River basin is at the crossroads of vital trade, transport, and energy routes (see Figure 9.1). Rich in gas, oil, and minerals, the region has easy access to affluent markets and hundreds of millions of Northeast Asian consumers. This is significant to

Figure 9.1 Map of the Greater Tumen River Basin

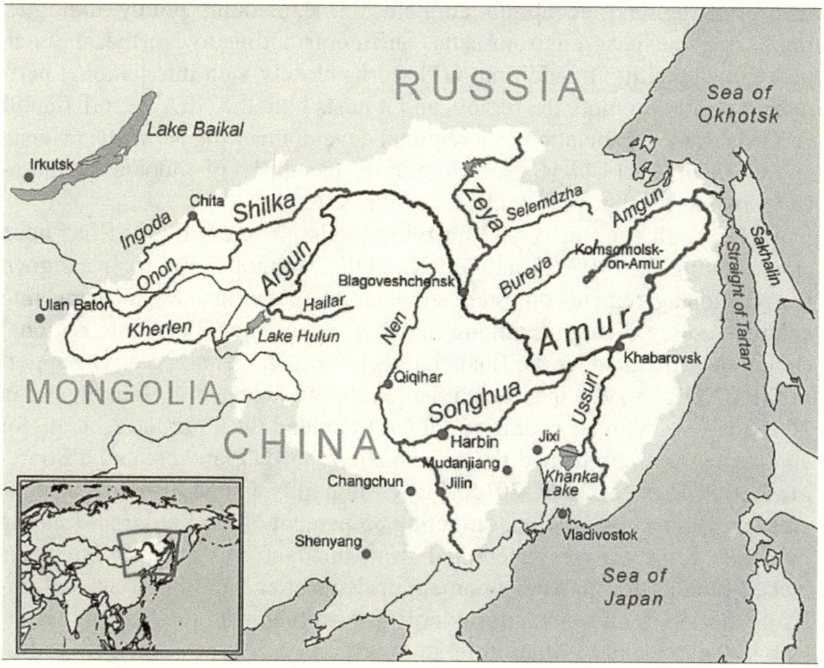

Mongolia because of its high trade turnover with Northeast Asia. In 2009, Mongolia's trade with Northeast Asian countries accounted for 75.1 percent of its total trade, and exports and imports accounted for 77.5 percent and 72.9 percent of the country's total exports and imports, respectively. During the period 1990–2009 this trade pattern was fairly consistent.[17]

The GTI regional cooperation mechanism among the ROK, China, DPRK, Mongolia, and Russian Federation, supported by the United Nations Development Programme (UNDP), was established in 1995 to strengthen economic and technical cooperation to promote greater growth and sustainable development in Northeast Asia (NEA). GTI focuses on the priority areas of transport, trade and investment, agriculture, tourism, and energy, with environment as a crosscutting sector. Increased regional cooperation is projected not only to lead to economic prosperity and sustainable development but also to contribute significantly to regional solidarity and stability. The core decisionmaking institution is GTI's Consultative Commission, which is composed of vice ministers from GTI member governments. The commission's role is to foster support for regional cooperation and development and to promote mutual understanding via annual meetings to discuss key policy issues and cooperation projects and host sessions with strategic partners as well as local governments. The GTI vision is for a partnership for prosperity with the objective of becoming an effective platform for regional economic cooperation, expanding policy dialogue, improving business environments, and contributing to Northeast Asian peace and stability. In addition, GTI works closely with international partners to jointly promote the region, and it hosts both the NEA Export-Import (EXIM) Banks Association as a regional development financing mechanism and the GTI Local Cooperation Committee in support of cooperative initiatives among local governments in Northeast Asia.[18]

Even with such lofty and unifying goals, progress on GTI has been slow moving. In 1995 China, DPRK, ROK, Mongolia, and Russia signed cooperation agreements on establishing an intergovernmental mechanism to enhance policy dialogues among member countries and promote regional economic growth under the financial, technical, and administrative support of the UNDP. In 1998 the Tumen Secretariat was created in Beijing, and in 2005 the five member countries agreed to extend the 1995 agreements for another ten years, renamed the organization the GTI, and created a Strategic Action Plan for 2006–2015.[19] Environment was one of the first focus areas of Tumen cooperation, attracting 85 percent of total program funding by 2004. Slow progress stemmed from the fact that member countries lacked funding for GTI development projects after the Asian financial crisis of the 1990s and intensifying political problems on the Korean Peninsula in the late 2000s. Many foreign experts regarded the Tumen River Initiative as a failure, both as a regional economic scheme and as a mechanism to protect the Tumen River basin's ecosystem. There also was concern about the regional environmental impact on rare species in the river basin's ecosystem and potential devastation from unchecked development.[20]

The most positive area of cooperation was in the energy field. In 2005 the two-component Baseline Study and Capacity Building for Energy Cooperation in NEA project was launched and seemed to engender new integration momentum. The energy focus moved forward via an energy cooperation training program for the DPRK in May–June 2006 in Beijing and in July 2006 in Pyongyang, and a training program for Mongolia in March 2008 in Seoul and in April 2008 in Ulaanbaatar by the Korean Energy Economic Institute. The GTI's tenth Consultative Commission meeting was held in March 2009 in Ulaanbaatar just as Mongolia's resource economy was accelerating but without DPRK participation. The Consultative Commission's focus was on strengthening regional cooperation through organizing an Energy Board, Tourism Board, and Environmental Board.[21] That September the Mongolian Ministry of Mineral Resources and Energy and the UNDP hosted the inaugural meeting of the GTI Energy Board on NEA energy cooperation. The UN Economic and Social Commission for Asia and the Pacific (UNESCAP) and energy experts reviewed GTI energy proposals to be implemented in the next three years and established a GTI Energy Expert Council for 2009–2011.[22]

The transit and energy connectivity momentum that had developed under the GTI rubric came to an abrupt halt with increased military tensions on the Korean Peninsula and strained relations between the DPRK and Japan. North Korea withdrew from the GTI in November 2009. The other member countries continued to be optimistic that China's encouragement would persuade the DPRK to reengage with the GTI process, especially when, in early June 2011, the DPRK and China agreed to establish three special economic zones—Hwanggumpyong Island, Wihwa Island (both on the Yalu River), and the Rason (North Korean) Economic and Trade Zone, which had the potential to spur positive DPRK economic growth:

> Based on the DPRK's close economic ties with China, and its eagerness for economic development, it is assumed that the DPRK would carefully consider the GTI members' proposal to re-engage in the GTI cooperation, which will benefit the promotion of these special economic zones and the DPRK's economic prosperity through the GTI platform.[23]

However, several years without DPRK participation, which blocked implementation of specific GTI rail and port projects, led to a growing pessimistic outlook for the GTI's ever becoming a vehicle for greater regional integration. For South Korea, though, the GTI still represented an important opportunity to actualize the Eurasia Initiative of President Park.

Mongolia, a potential energy mineral resource partner for the ROK, remained willing to link up its poor northeast outbound transportation routes to this Eurasian Initiative in order to find new mineral customers in Northeast Asia to generate more revenue and break the Chinese monopoly over its economy. Since the GTI transportation grid design meshes completely with Mongolia's intention to expand its customer base to new consumers in Korea, Japan, and Europe, it was anticipated that establishing a new cross-border transportation network would strengthen ROK-Mongolian energy cooperation. Mongolian leaders, seemingly inspired by the activism of President Elbegdorj, committed more time and resources to promoting the GTI vision. The fourteenth meeting of the Consultative Committee of the GTI and Northeast Asia Economic Cooperation Forum was held in Ulaanbaatar from October 30 to November 2, 2013. Vice ministers of GTI member nations discussed NEA regional cooperation and development strategy, reaffirmed the significance of the GTI in building regional partnerships for common prosperity, and reviewed transforming its strategic direction into an independent organization by 2016.[24] The focus of the discussions was on the February 2013 GTI study *Integrated Transport Infrastructure and Cross-Border Facilitation Study for the Trans-GTR Transport Corridors*.[25] The emphasis on transport corridors meshed well with Elbegdorj's vision of Mongolia as an economic transit corridor. Prime challenges discussed at this session were how financing institutions could meet NEA private sector demand, and what kinds of channels and mechanisms could be developed to increase regional economic prosperity.

The Northeast Asia Economic Cooperation Forum was held immediately at the conclusion of the GTI meeting with the aim of facilitating dialogue on NEA regional economic cooperation as well as development needs and opportunities. It focused on the legal status of the GTI program and assessed project implementation for transborder transportation passages and simplification of border-crossing procedures. More than 100 delegates from GTI member governments, the business sector, and financing associations attended.[26] Mongolian Deputy Prime Minister Dendev Terbishdagva reported that Mongolia sought to participate more actively in regional economic integration and the infrastructure network.[27] This round of consultation established the NEA EXIM Banks Association, which consists of the EXIM banks of the ROK and China, the Development Bank of Mongolia, and Russia's State Corporation Bank for Development and Foreign Economic Affairs (Vnesheconombank). The NEA EXIM Banks Association's main function is to collaborate with the GTI and member governments in financing suitable economic projects in the region.[28] At this meeting the parties agreed to further develop the GTI into an international organization and organize an Agricultural Sector Board, regularly hold a GTI International Trade and Investment Expo, and set up a strong network among respective policy research institutions. The establishment of the NEA EXIM Banks Association came on the heels of Chinese President Xi's launch of the Asian Infrastructure Investment Bank (AIIB) while on a state visit to Indonesia in October 2013.[29]

By the time of the fifteenth GTI Consultative Committee meeting in Yanbian, Jilin province of China in September 2014, Chinese President Xi Jinping already had announced his BRI Eurasian connectivity concept. GTI did not attract the participation of the North Koreans, although senior commercial officials in the Chinese government as well as UNDP, United Nations Industrial Development Organization, and export-import banks in Northeast Asia attended with those from three other member countries. China suggested "to combine the development of the GTI with China's Silk Road belt strategy to promote GTI regional development at a higher level." Mongolia responded by supporting "cooperation with China and other countries on big projects, especially on energy and railways,"[30] while Chinese and Russian officials sought more promotion of financing channels, infrastructure construction, a tourism center, and enhanced cooperation on bilateral trade by reducing customs formalities.

Because Mongolia's railway today is Russian-gauged, Mongolian policymakers in the first two decades of the democratic era at first chose to only expand this gauge domestically, which would favor mineral products' flowing north into Russia's Trans-Siberian Railway and out to Pacific Rim customers. During the mineral resource boom in the mid-2000s, Parliament began awarding bids for route spur expansion to link large mineral deposits to the main Russian rail system rather than to approve Chinese-gauge rail spurs directly to China. Since Mongolian construction contractors did not have the technical ability to fully handle new construction on their own, they had to partner with foreign expertise and South Korea often was their partner of choice. In a significant move toward regional rail connectivity independent from GTI, a fifty-four-kilometer, double-track rail link that took five years and $340 million to complete opened in September 2013 between Rajin, in North Korea's first SEZ, and the nearby Russian town of Khasan.[31] Rajin had always been a key feature in GTI's transportation network because it meant that South Korean firms could ship exports first to Rajin and transport them elsewhere via Russia. This route also opened a return route for Mongolian exports to reach South Korea.

The opening of this new rail spur was followed on November 13, 2013, by a summit between President Park Guen-hye and President Putin in Seoul. During the summit, Park stated that her rail transportation strategy included Eurasian energy linkage cooperation.[32] The leaders signed a memorandum of understanding (MOU) that called for steel giant POSCO, Hyundai Merchant Marine Co., and Korea Railroad Corp. to participate in the Rajin-Khasan development project. The project was designed to turn North Korea's ice-free northeastern port of Rajin into a logistics hub for sending cargo by rail to and from East Asia and Europe via the Russian Trans-Siberian Railway. RasonKonTrans, a Russian–North Korean joint venture, was to implement the rail and port renovation project. Russian Railways, the same state monopoly with a 50 percent interest in Ulaanbaatar Railway, has a 70 percent stake in this entity, with the DPRK holding the remaining 30 percent. It was expected that, after a due diligence study was conducted in 2014, a South Korean consortium would buy about half the Russian stake in the rail joint venture. However, this indirect investment in North Korea via Russia conflicted with Seoul's ban on new DPRK investments and did not go forward. The partnering of the ROK with Russia on other long-term transportation construction projects, including building a northern routed natural gas pipeline linking Russia and South Korea and creating Arctic shipping routes to reduce shipping distances and time between Asia and Europe, indicated that South Korea was responding to the challenge of developing new transportation links to mineral and energy resources and was willing to move bilaterally, when suddenly the GTI multilateral platform slowed. This Rajin-Khasan development project also fit neatly into President Park's Eurasian Initiative of the Iron Silk Road Express and the GTI plan.

Past prospects to realize the Iron Silk Road Express often were stymied due to strategic concerns. The Korean Railroad Research Institute, the ROK's think tank in the railway sector, researched how to connect trans-Korean and intercontinental rail networks for a borderless Eurasian economic bloc. It concluded that construction of a logistics and transportation system is a key economic issue for the two Koreas, so it recommended that logistic bottlenecks needed to be resolved first to secure a stable and cost-effective transportation route. In the long run, the completion of a trans-Korean rail would lead to the development of a strategic international multimodal transport route connecting to Northeast Asia and Europe.[33] Such railway planning has been central to development plans for North Korean SEZs, which have been predicated upon creating a new rail axis between the two Koreas and then on to Russia, China, and Mongolia. Such an axis concept also correlates closely with the transit ideas embodied in the GTI program.

After a nearly two-year lull in activities, suddenly in 2016 the GTI became very active. Likely this was a reflection of accelerating trilateral cooperation among China, Russia, and Mongolia, especially in the regional transportation infrastructure sector. A Northeast Asia International Conference for Economic Development was cohosted by Niigata prefecture's Northeast Asia International Conference for Economic Development Executive Committee, Niigata City, and the Economic Research Institute for Northeast Asia (ERINA) in January 2016 in Niigata. This prefecture is an observer member of the GTI NEA Local Cooperation Committee. The conference was preceded by four sessions that discussed international cooperation for development finance, transportation and distribution cooperation, the impact of the US Trans-Pacific Partnership on Northeast Asia, and the quarter century of change for China and Russia from a business perspective.[34] The sixteenth GTI Consultative Commission meeting was held in Seoul on April 28. In attendance were the five GTI member states and the representatives of local NEA governments, financial and research institutions, and international organizations.

Mongolia was the site of the first GTI cooperation in the field of agriculture. On March 29, 2016, the Mongolian Economic Cooperation Confederation (MECC) president, Byambatsogt Sandag, visited the GTI Beijing headquarters. The MECC, which is a business development NGO of more than 1,000 members, offered support to the GTI to explore collaboration with similar organizations in the region and cooperation in infrastructure and agriculture.[35] The first working meeting of its Agriculture Committee, co-organized with Mongolia's Ministry of Food and Agriculture, was held in July in Ulaanbaatar. The objective was the initiation of the GTI Regional Agricultural Strategic Action Plan based on the member states' national strategies and the findings of the GTI's *Regional Report on Agricultural Cooperation in the Greater Tumen Region*. The GTI Agriculture Cooperation Strategic Action Plan was to be finalized that November.[36]

In October 2016 the energy project restarted when the first NEA Energy Forum was held back-to-back with the fifth GTI Energy Board Meeting in Seoul. The Korea Energy Economics Institute and the ROK Ministry of Trade, Industry, and Energy cohosted the forum, while various research institutes, the Ministry of Energy of Mongolia, and the GTI Secretariat attended. The experts discussed (1) the current status, opportunities, and challenges of energy trade in NEA; (2) promoting regional cooperation via intraregional energy cooperation projects in NEA; and (3) challenges and the way forward to NEA energy cooperation and the roles of the NEA Energy Forum and GTI.[37] Despite constraints to cooperation among the GTI members, there was renewed interest in utilizing the NEA Energy Forum as a mechanism to expedite energy development and to accelerate energy trade among the NEA countries. Because Mongolia was hosting the eleventh ASEM in Ulaanbaatar in July 2016, the sixth GTI Transport Board Meeting was held in Seoul on July 12, co-organized by the GTI Secretariat and ROK Ministry of Land, Infrastructure, and Transport. At the first meeting of the ASEM Expert Group on Eurasia Transport and Logistics, the board members agreed to implement the GTI Regional Transport Strategy's extension of the Medium-Term Transport Action Plan through 2018. Among the developments discussed was the NEA EXIM Banks Association Logistics Subcommittee's pilot experimental rail transport project of Mudanjiang-Suifenhe-Vladivostok-Donghae-Sakaiminato.[38]

Another significant GTI transport initiative that began in 2016 was the ROK proposal for EuTraLop. This is a platform for coordination of activities by research institutions and international organizations to study the Eurasia transport and logistics network, propose ways to make the Eurasia network more efficient, and contribute to long-term growth on the Eurasian continent. During the meeting hosted by the Korea Transport Institute on October 14 in Jeju, participants reviewed the feasibility and economics of network construction.[39] There were additional GTI meetings in 2016: at Suifenhe City, there was a discussion by the PRC of rail testing; the ninth GTI Tourism Board Meeting[40] was cohosted by the China National Tourism Administration and Arxan municipal government in Arxan, China; and the fifth GTI NEA Tourism Forum was held in Hunchun, in China's Jilin province.

The breadth of renewal of GTI activities in many sectors has silenced, at least temporarily, the question during the past five years of whether or not the GTI framework can be utilized by partner countries as a springboard for new regional cooperation in transportation construction and logistical projects. Research by the GTI has forecasted that for the DPRK the projects will activate the local economy of Rason by restoring some parts of the old railways and increasing cooperation between the DPRK and Russia, as well as improving economic ties with Northeast China and Mongolia. As for Russia, GTI projects should resolve the congestion at Far Eastern ports and modernize and strengthen the Eurasian logistics network of the RZD. Russia's economic and political influence in the DPRK and NEA as a railway and energy power should further increase. The ROK can look forward to easing of political tension on the Korean Peninsula with development around Rajin based on trilateral cooperation among the ROK,

DPRK, and Russia. The projects also will link South Korea more closely to Mongolian and Siberian mineral/energy resources and stimulate greater economic growth. Regarding China, GTI cooperative actions are predicted to promote economic development of the three Northeastern provinces and permit acquisition of energy-related commodities from Russia and the DPRK. For Mongolia, its limitations as a landlocked country could be overcome and economic development accelerated as northern and eastern exits are secured. Even for Japan, especially its western region of Niigata, Tottori, and Kanazawa, GTI integration can be another commercial entry into Northeast China, Russia, Mongolia, and Europe.[41]

Any Northeast Asian railway cooperation model must create an international transport network based on railway infrastructure and a cooperation consultative group mechanism. The GTI plan through the UNDP utilizes the existing international railway cooperation bodies and organizations, does not require establishment of additional international organizations, and thus minimizes the financial burden of manpower and equipment.[42] As the 2013 *Integrated Transport Infrastructure and Cross-Border Facilitation Study for the Trans-GTR Transport Corridors* emphasized, the GTI "must be an organization that comprehensively deliberates on the bilateral and multilateral issues of international railway operation from the perspective of joint benefits in the Northeast Asia regions,"[43] while recognizing that strategies and the standards of railway infrastructures and services in the concerned countries vary significantly. The short-term task is to develop multilateral projects and resolve issues in a timely manner, such as utilizing pilot projects. These would build trust among the partner countries and come to practical solutions for interfacing among the connected routes and customs operations to resolve bottlenecks in each country. Positive results should generate international publicity that will encourage financial partners to participate in costly, but necessary, Northeast Asia railway network expansion. Ultimately, the GTI's long-range goal is to facilitate a Northeast Asia peace project through the Northeast Asia railway cooperation consultative group that would develop into an independent organization. Its key functions would be to promote railway operational improvement, set freight and passenger railway rates, and improve railway routes and signal systems. Such efforts are aimed at maximizing the integrative role of transport passages in a vibrant economic market.[44] If this goal is realized, the benefits to Mongolia will be substantial.

Mongolia's "Steppe Road" or Economic Transit Corridor

During a period of trends that at times strongly limited Mongolia's regional and global developmental choices, Mongolia decided that it must be more proactive in promoting its own ideas for political and economic continental integration to overcome obstacles to its economic progress and to solidify its national security. Mongolia under the Elbegdorj presidency also actively expanded its interregional contacts with other Asian countries to develop additional mechanisms for economic partnership. One example is its accession to the Asia-Pacific Trade Agreement (APTA) in October 2013. The APTA is a preferential trade agreement whose membership is open to all developing East, Southeast, and South Asian member states of the United Nations Economic and Social Commission for Asia and the Pacific (ESCAP). According to Ravi Ratnayake, director of ESCAP's Trade and Investment Division, "Business opportunities arising from preferential trade and investment cooperation under APTA could generate higher incomes from exports and create employment in export-led industries for Mongolian people."[45]

Not satisfied with the GTI process, Mongolia's role in such multilateral platforms, and no longer willing to be left out of Asian continental economic integration in the face of the Eurasian Silk Road transport strategies of China, Russia, and South Korea, the Mongolian government felt it imperative to develop its own proposal to connect to new trade partners by developing rail, road, energy grids, and pipelines in natural gas and oil. Therefore, Mongolia introduced its "Steppe Road" concept in 2014 in Ulaanbaatar, when Mongolian President Elbegdorj hosted separate bilateral summer summits with Chinese President Xi and Russian President Putin.[46] A few weeks later the Mongols claim he obtained the verbal endorsement of the World Bank for the Steppe Road in order to validate the concept within the world economic community.[47] At Central European University in Budapest, Hungary, on October 18, President Elbegdorj explained to a global audience that this Steppe Road would link Russia and China with highways, high-voltage electrical lines, and gas and oil pipelines. He called Mongolia an honest broker in dealing with promotion of peace and security in Northeast Asia by, ironically, evoking the days of the Mongol Empire when his people "actively engaged with nations near and far in Asia, Europe and the Middle East. It was an era when the Mongols strove to establish a new world order—justice, peace and cooperation in their relations with other states and peoples."[48] Later in 2014, at an APEC meeting, Elbegdorj publicly announced that "Mongolia is planning to become the shortest transit line country that connects Asia and Europe [and] . . . strives to have access to the regional infrastructure hub, seaport, by establishing a transit transportation route and efficient logistics system."[49] During the first Mongolia-China Expo in October 2015, Mongolian Minister of Industry Dondogdorj Erdenebat further elaborated on the "economic circulation of Mongolia" and its participation in the China-initiated New Silk Road by creating an "Economic Corridor" through Mongolia. This Mongolia-Russia-China economic corridor was defined as a combination of the Steppe Road with the different Eurasian Silk Road Economic Zone initiatives: "Mongolia wants to determine its role in this New Silk Road that crosses 88 countries of Europe and Asia and covers 40 percent of the world economy."[50]

The Mongolian Steppe Road is intimately bound to the Elbegdorj principle of reconceptualizing Mongolia's geopolitics as a "transit nation" between China and Russia. The transit corridor theory of Mongolia is expressed by the term *zam sudlal* or "roadology" and makes *zam* (road) into both an object of study and a prism through which to view Mongolia in terms of its connectivity to its neighbors and the world.[51] This strategy seeks to elevate Mongolia's regional profile by proposing linkages to the BRI and EEU, while carefully carving out its own space independent from these two initiatives. Mongolia aims to become a northern transit corridor to facilitate trade between its two giant neighbors via rail, road, and pipe and to develop export and transit freight, particularly from Russia to China, to strengthen its north-south Ulaanbaatar Railway's role in the Eurasian transport network.[52]

Mongolia's interest in establishing a rail connectivity corridor has its origin in the multidimensional Transit Mongolia program adopted by the government in May 2008. It included construction of a secondary railway line; railway electrification; construction of Asian Highway Routes AH3 and AH4 in Mongolia; facilitation of transit transport through Mongolian territory; and construction of transport and trade logistics centers and cargo terminals.[53] In October 2012 the Mongolian Parliament passed a resolution authorizing the construction of phases one and two of the country's railway project. However, the overall plan was significantly impacted in October 2013, when Mongolia agreed with China to establish a Mongolian-Russian-Chinese Northern Railway working group to oversee the construction of new road, rail, and pipeline infrastructure connecting the two countries with Russia. Some Mongolian analysts suggested that the way for Mongolia to become a transit corridor was to build a Ж-shaped railroad transportation network with mixed gauges in order to allow Russian and Chinese trains to enter and exit Mongolia without changing train wheels, as was done on a two-kilometer bridge on the Swedish-Finnish border. It was proposed that, when building this railroad network, Mongolia should construct all railway lines from the north with wide gauges and those from the south with narrow gauges. In this way the western rail portion could become Russia's gateway to India through Mongolia and China:

> If we build a safe, fast and cheap international trade transit route, Mongolia will naturally prosper from its fees without having to pay a single penny. Then we will be able to mine our mineral resources for our own needs and process and sell them for maximized profits. The time would eventually come where our neighbors are dependent on us, not the other way around. We would also then be able to seize the opportunity to find the balance between the interests of our two neighboring nations.[54]

In April 2015, Mongolian Minister of Foreign Affairs Lundeg Purevsuren paid an official visit to Beijing for discussions with his Chinese counterpart, Wang Yi, on developing a regional economic zone. At a joint news conference, Purevsuren announced Mongolia's "interest to actively participate in important initiatives to establish an economic corridor linking China and Russia and develop the regional economy and make them integrate with Mongolia's 'Steppe Road' [called Prairie Road by the Chinese] initiative." Foreign Minister Wang replied that the Chinese "are confident that this would bring economic benefit to our three countries and serve as a major boost to the economic advancement of Eurasia as a whole."[55] The Chinese Foreign Ministry's statement on the consultations supported Mongolia's new platform for trilateral cooperation: "The construction of the China-Mongolia-Russia economic corridor would connect China's Silk Road Economic Belt to Russia's transcontinental rail plan and Mongolia's Prairie Road program."[56] Russian media reports on these ministerial discussions emphasized that this platform mirrored Russian President Putin's Eurasian transport corridor initiative to link Moscow and Beijing via high-speed rail and road, and that China was interested in investing $5.2 billion in the first-stage high-speed rail line between Moscow and Kazan.[57]

In the July 2015 summit at Ufa, Russia, the leaders of Mongolia, China, and Russia agreed to Mongolia's proposal for an "Economic Corridor" connecting the Silk Road of China, Steppe Road of Mongolia, and Eurasian Economic Union of Russia. Chinese, Russian, and Mongolian rail authorities confirmed plans to implement railway transit transport cooperation, improve existing railway freight volume, research building of a trilateral transportation logistics company, develop railway transport capacity from Ulan Ude-Naushki to Sukebaatar-Zamyn-Uud-Erenhot to Jining, promote cooperation among railway educational institutions, and support personnel training and scientific research cooperation.

On June 23, 2016, ahead of the Tashkent, Uzbekistan, eleventh meeting of the Shanghai Cooperation Organisation (SCO), there was another trilateral summit among Presidents Xi, Putin, and Elbegdorj. They signed a trilateral economic partnership program to develop an economic corridor consisting of thirty-two proposed projects. President Xi proposed that the three countries prioritize the aligning of China's Silk Road Economic Belt initiative, Russia's development strategies, especially its transcontinental rail plan, and Mongolia's Steppe Road program to spur trilateral cooperation. President Elbegdorj endorsed the economic corridor development plan by promising Mongolia would join China and Russia to advance the construction of transportation infrastructure and strengthen economic cooperation in border regions.[58] The "Economic Corridor" would be comprised of eight corridors, including a railroad connecting Erdenet copper mine with the Russian border, new railroads in western and eastern regions of Mongolia, eastern rail spurs bound for the Far Eastern ports of Russia through Chinese Manchuria, and the main railroad network connecting Moscow and Beijing through Mongolia. A key part of the Tashkent agreement involved cooperation on improving roads and modernizing other forms of transportation in the region with regular consultations with third-party transport agencies, including railway companies.[59]

The "Economic Corridor" includes Mongolian proposals for three auto road corridor projects as well as for the three railway transit corridors in the western and eastern regions of Mongolia. The ADB is providing a $170 million loan for construction of a western regional highway connecting Ulaanbayshint along the Russian border in northwest Mongolia with Yarantay, 743 kilometers south on the Chinese border. This project, cofinanced by the governments of Mongolia and China, will cut travel time from north to south by half, as well as fill a gap in the 6,024-kilometer Asian Highway 4, which runs all the way from the port city of Karachi in southern Pakistan through Mongolia to the Russian city of Novosibirsk in southwestern Siberia.[60]

One month later, in July 2016, a meeting of the joint commission of railway and border delegates of Mongolia, China, and Russia met in Ulaanbaatar to review future plans. The Mongolian side asked the Russians to develop train service en route from Sukhbaatar to Naushki. The Chinese side was concerned about stabilizing daily train services and increasing reciprocal freight transport. All three countries saw the necessity of reducing the time for border transit. Mongolia's National Statistics Office reported the total freight transferred via railway in 2015 increased by 2.2 percent to 197,500 tons of freight, while passenger numbers decreased by 9.4 percent to 134,600 passengers. Since freight transportation is essential for the Mongolian rail system to cover its expenses and generate more profit, the Mongolian side emphasized increasing transit freight transportation. In the first half of 2016, domestic freight transport accounted for around 42 percent of total rail services, a 7.3 percent reduction from the previous year due to a 49 percent decrease in the transportation of construction materials. As for total railway freight transportation over the same period, export products composed 34 percent, imports were 10 percent, and freight transit volume accounted for 13.1 percent.[61] All of this rail connectivity momentum affected Mongolian trade passing through the Chinese port of Tianjin. Freight was able to reach Mongolia or Russia directly without a double transfer to local trucks.[62] A special cross-border pass and frontier office was set up on the China-Mongolia-Russia international road freight route to save clearance time. Additionally, there are plans to create a logistics park located in Tianjin to promote trade between Tianjin and Mongolia.[63]

The trilateral railway consultative meeting proposed in the Tashkent summit took place in mid-September 2016 in Ulaanbaatar. It featured discussions with representatives of private companies such as Northern Railway on the construction of the Erdenet-Ovoot rail spur and a Russian gas fuel station that was operating at the Zamyn-Uud/Erenhot south border checkpoint. Agreements emerging from this consultative meeting were signed during the October 20, 2016, meeting of ministers of road and transport of Mongolia, Russia, and China.[64] In April 2018 Mongolian Prime Minister Ukhnaa Khürelsükh made a state visit to the PRC officials, and reported that the Chinese were willing to move forward on the trilateral economic corridor program. Mongolia proposed to implement the first three projects of the thirty-two proposed within this framework: the Ulaanbaatar Railway Joint Venture reform project, Asia Transport Road AH3 project, and an energy project to be implemented between Mongolia and Russia. A few weeks later, Khürelsükh discussed deepening the Russo-Mongolian bilateral trade relationship by strengthening transit cooperation at the border territories when he met Far Eastern Federal District of the Russian Federation Deputy Prime Minister and presidential envoy Yury Trutnev. At that time he declared, "I see the prospect of trilateral cooperation of Mongolia, Russia and China positively" and expressed his belief that the cooperation will make asignificant contribution not only to the development of the three countries but also to regional development.[65]

Mongolian-Russian-Chinese Northern Railway

In 2013 Mongolia moved to create a new trilateral railroad, the Mongolian-Russian-Chinese Northern Railway, and proposed to build four new accesses to China and another two accesses to Russia—at an estimated investment cost of around $1 billion with over $400 million needed to undertake the first stage. For the Mongols, transit traffic is the most profitable means of transportation, yet their Ulaanbaatar Railway (UR) system is mainly used to move domestic coal to the nation's electric power stations. Despite a capital loss of $14 million for transporting coal in 2013, the railroad was restricted by the government from raising fees. At that point 1.4 million tons of transit was passing through the country. The proposal for a trilateral railroad was a clear indication that Mongolia was frustrated by the GTI project delays but convinced that there must be new rail transit networking inside Mongolia to enable the nation to benefit from the growing Sino-Russian economic rapprochement that BRI and EEU portended.

UR freight turnover grew annually by 2 million tons, and in 2013, its most profitable year, it had reached 20.5 million tons, the highest capacity limit of its technology. UR is 1,800 kilometers long, and there were plans to add an additional 5,600 kilometers to its length. During a November 2013 UR internal meeting, it was announced that the first phase of renovation that had commenced in the fourth quarter required an additional $257 million in expenditures to replace mechanical linkages, widen stations, and lengthen railroad junctions. This renovation would increase UR capacity from 20 million to 34 million tons; however, Mongolia wanted to increase it another 10–20 million tons, since studies had shown that, by 2020, 100 million tons of mining cargo was expected to be exported.[66] Subsequently, the Mongols proposed creating two more transit corridors in addition to the existing one: one transit corridor to connect Russia and China and the other to transport domestic cargo to its neighbors.

That December the Mongolian government's Ministry of Road and Transportation and the Mongolian-Russian shareholding Ulaanbaatar Railway Society organized in Ulaanbaatar the first Consultative Trilateral Transit Conference of the Mongolian-Russian-Chinese Northern Railway. The Northern Railway Corridor is designed to increase rail capacity from Mongolia into Russia at the border site of Naushki, into China at Erenhot, and onto Jining. At that session Deputy Director of Chinese Railways General Authority Chen Lanhua expressed confidence in building upon previously successful cooperation among China, Russia, and Mongolia. The Chinese side reported that it had been working on blueprints for reconstructing the railroads with dual rail beds and electrical power. Discussion included in-depth analysis of railway transport conditions and recommendations for technical innovation along the main routes; trade goods and turnover between China and Russia and China and Europe; the role of railway transportation through Mongolia; tripartite cooperation in the technical reforming of the UR; plans to develop the Erlian-Jinin railway; and the development of modern transportation logistics through Mongolia to connect China via Russia with Europe.[67]

In the 2013 joint statement of the First Consultative Conference,[68] conditions for transit transportation through the Mongolian railway system were introduced. It was proposed that there be two phases of rail investment involving the existing 1,800 kilometers of track. The parties agreed to work out an integrated action plan in the first quarter of 2014 to develop a transit railway in the direction of Ulan Ude-Naushki-Sukhbaatar-Zamyn-Uud-Erlian-Jinin, but the key section for Western investors was the spur from the coal mine at Ukhaa Khudag (near Tavan Tolgoi) to the border at Gashuun Sukhait that connects to the Chinese rail network.[69] Progress had been slow on this 230-kilometer spur due to financing problems and the Mongolian government's desire for majority ownership. The main roadblock was Mongolian reluctance to build the spur with a Chinese, rather than Russian, gauge. The Mongols understood that Russia has enjoyed strategic control over the UR since it was built in the 1950s and that Moscow remains protective of this interest. The Mongolian press reported that the president of Russian Railways, Vladimir Ivanovich Yakunin, wrote directly to Mongolia's prime minister to discourage construction of a Chinese-gauge rail, claiming, "To create a railway with narrow gauge is the wrong decision," and insisting that the present line "represents Russian interests as much as Mongolia's in terms of the railway."[70]

Because of the lack of existing rail freight loading capacity along the Trans-Siberian line, Mongolia invited representatives of Russia and China to launch the Northern Rail Corridor to devise a comprehensive strategy for improving railway efficacy and to establish a joint stock company called RZD, which would be a subsidiary company of Russian Railways Logistics, to construct an east-west transit corridor. In the new venture, the Erdenet to Ovoot railway is specifically included and listed as a priority funding project for the development banks and funds established to support BRI. Although exports to Russia from Mongolia could not be compared in volume to those going to resource-hungry China, Mongolian officials pointed out that, if the Northern Railways line could be extended even further north to the Russian city of Kyzyl and linked to Russia's wider rail network, "Russia and China are looking for 2.5-times expansion of trade. We want to facilitate all this trade."[71]

China would benefit from the improvements on the Trans-Mongolian Railway because up to thirty metric tons of freight a year of Mongolian mineral products could transit China to overseas markets in Japan or South Korea through eight additional seaports. Mongolia had access only to Tianjin's container site, but what it really needed was break bulk shipping[72] for the overseas transport of many tons of minerals, thereby increasing its Sino-Russian transit cargo. Until 2006, Mongolia transported up to six million tons of petroleum a year to China through transit rail, but by 2014 only 1.4 million tons was transited. Much of this transport was one-way freight from Russia to China, returning with empty rail wagons. These two sides agreed to fill the rail containers both ways with Russia's sending mainly mining products to China and China's transporting finished goods to Russia.[73] The attitude of the Chinese toward expanding the rail ties has been linked openly to the BRI by various Chinese officials. Ling Bei Zhang, secretary of China International Freight Forwarders Association, at the Transit Mongolia 2018 forum held April 17–19, 2018, in Moscow, stated, "We will establish a corridor that connect[s] China, Mongolia, Russia and Europe while increasing volume of freight and creating [a] mechanism to coordinate constructions. It is crucial to formulate [an] engineering design of [the] 'Belt and Road' Initiative based on practical need of the three countries and their collaboration and studying market feasibility."[74]

In recent years there was movement on trilateral rail cooperation issues at various bilateral summits between President Elbegdorj with either President Putin or President Xi. At the August 21–22, 2014, Ulaanbaatar summit visit of President Xi, five new transportation agreements were signed that related to Sino-Russo-Mongolian cooperation on regional rail projects: (1) an intergovernmental agreement on "access to the seaport and transit transport"; (2) an intergovernmental general agreement on cooperation on development of railway transit transport; (3) an intergovernmental MOU on development of railway cooperation; (4) an MOU between the Ministry of Road and Transportation of Mongolia and the Railway Authority of the People's Republic of China on renewal of the Mongolia and China Border Railway Agreement; and (5) the Mongolia-China Border Port Management

Cooperation Commission agreement between the National Council of Border Ports of Mongolia and the General Customs Office of the People's Republic of China. The latter document designated six Chinese seaports, including Tianjin, Dalian, and Jinzhou, for the transit of Mongolian exports to overseas markets. A key breakthrough was agreement that two-thirds of Mongolian goods transported on Chinese rails would be destined for the Chinese market, while one-third would be for export via Chinese seaports to third countries. Border-crossing cooperation and access to rail capacity within China were promised, and four new Mongolian port entries (Shiveekhuren, Bichigt, Gashuunsukhait, and Nomrog) were opened for rail transport. New tariffs and additional volume for Mongolian cargo on Chinese railroads also were established, and China gave Mongolia a 40 percent discount on current transportation tariffs.

Mongolia obtained a commitment to support its trilateral rail project from Russian President Putin two weeks later in his Ulaanbaatar bilateral summit. During the press conference held on his Mongolian visit, Putin singled out bilateral transport cooperation:

> This is a very important sector for Mongolia, and it is in our interests too to increase Mongolia's transit potential. Mongolia is located between Russia and China after all. We are big trade and economic partners and have bilateral trade with China that will come to $64 or already $65–67 billion this year. It therefore makes sense to put Mongolia's transport possibilities to greater use than is the case today.[75]

He agreed to help Mongolia upgrade UR Trans-Mongolian rail capacity to 100 metric tons a year by 2020 as part of Moscow's pivot toward Asia: "Developing the railway network will help Mongolia to open up rich but for now hard-to-access deposits, and make broader and more effective use of its potential as a transit country."[76] A strategic partnership agreement for the development of UR was signed on that visit by Russian Railways president Yakunin and Mongolian Minister of Roads and Transportation Amarjargal Gansukh. Yakunin emphasized the importance of using the Russian 1,520 mm gauge for future Mongolian lines since "constructing infrastructure using other standards will lead to the unnecessary duplication of services and an increase in operating costs."[77] The rail projects covered in the Russo-Mongolian agreements potentially could impact Sino-Russian rail cooperation. An example is the electrification and construction of a second track for the 1,100-kilometer (684-mile) rail line from Mongolia's Russian border via the planned Sainshand minerals processing industrial zone in the Gobi to Zamyn-Uud on its Chinese border. Also covered in the agreements were development of a western Mongolian rail line joining Russia and China for Russian exports to China, India, and Pakistan and utilizing the 230-kilometer (143-mile) Choibalsan-Erentsav eastern railway for transiting goods into northeast China.

In October 2014 the Mongolian National Rail Policy was amended to include a new Northern or Steppe Railway extending from the current terminus at Erdenet through to the Mongolian/Russian border at Arts Suuri, and in November the Erdenet-Ovoot section of the Steppe Railway was added to the Mongolian government's Concession List of Approved Projects available for a Public-Private Partnership. At the end of 2014, progress on regional rail interconnectivity was illustrated when Russia and Mongolia tested moving coal along a new rail grid to the North Korean port of Rajin, a possible hub for non-DPRK-bound exports, and 40,500 tons of Russian coal, worth $4 million including transit costs, was delivered to South Korea by rail from the Russian town of Khasan. According to the ROK Unification Ministry, "It [the Khasan-Rajin project] is meaningful . . . to lay the foundation for realizing the Eurasia Initiative, peace in Northeast Asia and the renovation of our economy."[78]

At a December 2014 Mongolia-China-Russia trilateral meeting, Transportation Minister Gansukh explained that Mongolia recognized that more diverse and complex services were required from the international transportation and logistics market:

> The capacity of the transportation corridor, flexibility of nations in communication, smart and swift border customs services, the prices and tariffs competing with other railway transportation corridors, and many other factors are playing a significant role in complex transportation logistics services. We hosted the present consultative meeting with an aim to enhance cooperation with our neighboring nations to develop the capacity of our railways corridor as a first step towards reaching the goal.[79]

Gansukh promised that Mongolia would upgrade transportation facilities to meet all necessary transit requirements for enhancing the transnorthern railway corridor running through Mongolia from Russia's Ulan Ude to Jilin province in China. At the same meeting, RZD deputy chief Igor Mitsuk proclaimed, "The three nations have a common interest to implement the project on freight and goods transportation from China to Europe and from Europe to China through Mongolia,"[80] and he was confident that Chinese, Mongolian, and Russian common interest to improve freight forwarding through this corridor would enable them to find workable solutions. Another test of the new rail network was conducted in early 2015 when Mongolia shipped 20,000 tons of coal from its Sharyn Gol deposit to Rajin port for delivery to South Korea. Afterwards, Tugsuu Batbold, chairman of the Mongolian Railway Authority, said, "There are no technical problems with delivering coal to North Korea, and we are seeking ways to deliver coal through the trans-Siberian railway to Rajin,"[81] and declared that Mongolia was investigating how to deliver other metals, such as copper and gold, via this new rail spur. These comments came at the end of North Korean Foreign Minister Ri Su Yong's February 22–25,

2015, official Mongolian visit, when the two countries finalized several cooperative agreements.

The Mongolian-Russian-Chinese Northern Railway plan has accelerated in implementation during the past three years. On March 1, 2015, the Mongolian Ministry of Transportation and RZD agreed to terms of reference and appointed consultants to prepare financial and technical feasibility studies for modernization and construction rail projects, expected to be completed by 2020, that would be funded from UR's resources and borrowing. The main projects identified were (1) modernization of the 1,100-kilometer north-south route from Sükhbaatar on the Russian border to Zamyn-Uud/Erenhot on the Mongolia/China border, including electrification and/or construction of a second track; (2) construction of the 549-kilometer Northern Railway west from the Erdenet branch to Ovoot to support coal mining developments; (3) construction of a 215-kilometer Ovoot–Arz Sur line, which would connect at Kyzyl in Russia's Tuva Republic with a planned 411-kilometer line to Kuragino and the Trans-Siberian corridor; (4) studying the increasing use of the 239-kilometer Choibalsan-Ereentsav line in the northeast; and (5) planning a western railway line "linking Russia and China through Mongolia to export from Russia to China, India, Pakistan, and other countries in the region."[82] In April, Mongolian Minister of Finance Jargaltulga Erdenebat submitted a draft budget amendment for parliamentary consideration of additional allocations regarding energy and railways.[83] On April 9–10, 2015, in Ulaanbaatar, deputy ministers of railway and transportation from Mongolia, China, and Russia met in the Second Symposium of the Mongolian-Russian-Chinese Northern Railway, organized by the office of Mongolian President Elbegdorj. A protocol for a triparty consultation mechanism on cooperation among the three countries' railway transportation sectors was agreed upon and later finalized in July 2015 in the Ufa, Russia, trilateral summit.[84]

A small private railroad company, Northern Railways, a subsidiary of Australia-based Aspire Mining, had been established in 2010 to build 549 kilometers of track west from Erdenet City to the Nuurstei and Ovoot coal deposits. (See Figure 9.2.) Its final stop would be the Arts Suuri border point in northwest Mongolia across from the Russian Tuva Republic. Recognizing that the Mongolian government would want to own at least 51 percent of the rail line under the Aspire partnership, Aspire's goal was to negotiate a build-operate-transfer contract with Mongolia through Northern Railways under which it would manage the line for at least twenty years. Aspire Mining's interest stemmed from the fact that its discovery at Ovoot, Mongolia's second largest known coal deposit, is far from existing rail lines.[85] In late March 2015, the Mongolian government instructed its Investment Agency to enter into direct negotiations for a concession with Aspire Mining's Northern Railways over the Erdenet to Ovoot section of this new railway. This spur would provide a direct route to the Chinese market for Russian transit freight by reducing by 40 percent the distance

Figure 9.2 Map of Mongolian Railways

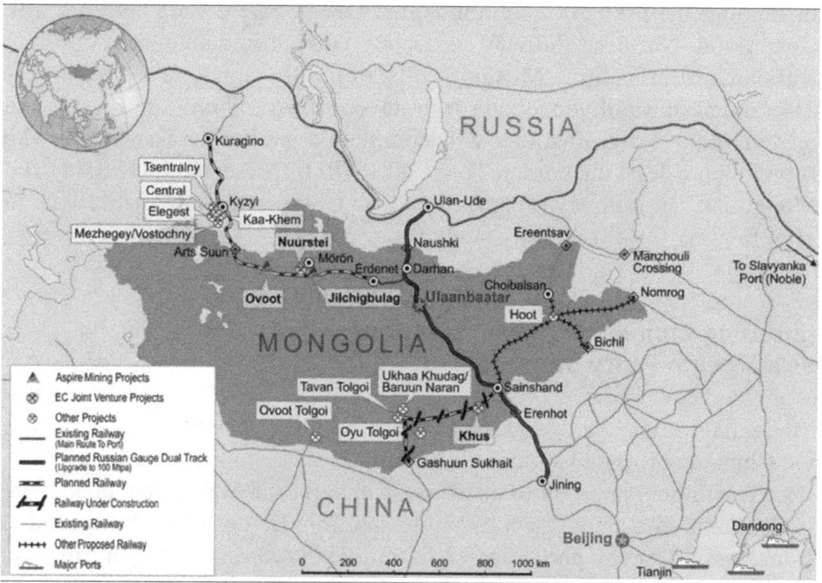

Source: "Mongolian Parliament Backs Rail Expansion," *Railroad Gazette,* October 28, 2014, https://www.railwaygazette.com/news/policy/single-view/view/mongolian-parliament-backs-rail-expansion.html.

traveled from Russia's Elegast coking coal field to Chinese markets and freight to and from Kyzl. In August, Northern Railways was granted the concession in anticipation that this line would be operational in 2017–2018. It was reported that interest from Moscow pushed Mongolia to prioritize the Northern Railways project by adding it to a list of projects for which the country is actively seeking private partners. In September 2016 in Beijing Mongolia sought financing from the AIIB for rail construction of 550 kilometers and to build new routes. Financial blogs also indicated that the China Development Bank expressed interest in providing three-fourths of the financing needed by the Aspire Northern Railway.[86]

To accelerate the construction of this rail spur, which is projected to require five years, Northern Railways now is partnering with Noble Group and two subsidiaries of China Railways Corporation: China Railways 20 Bureau Group Corporation and China Railway First Design Survey and Design Institute.[87] A draft feasibility study for the 549-kilometer Erdenet to Ovoot railway project was delivered for review to Aspire Mining in April 2018 by China Gezhouba Group International Ltd. Aspire said the study "again confirms the financial viability" of the proposed railway, while the estimated costs of construction are comparable to those in a first-stage feasibility study completed in January 2017. At present China Gezhouba is holding discussions with a range of debt and equity providers interested in funding the project, including China Development Bank and the Silk Road Fund. Northern Railway separately entered into an agreement with Russian design institute Mosgiprotrans to jointly complete a preliminary assessment of a rail connection from Ovoot to Arts Suuri and Kyzyl, and a Mongolian design institute will complete a similar assessment for the Mongolian side of the border. The results will be presented by Russian and Mongolian rail ministry representatives to Chinese funding institutions to seek funding for a feasibility study.[88]

Choosing Connectivity over Isolation as a Foreign Policy Strategy

Mongolia's landlocked geographical location makes external transport links via China and Russia key to its international trade. Mongolia currently utilizes Tianjin for almost all of its overseas imports and exports, although there is also some small movement by rail to and from Europe through Russia and from Russian Pacific ports for freight traffic with Japan and North America. Mongolia historically saw its landlocked position as a national security wall and developed political and economic mechanisms to play its two neighbors against each other. These strategies, while in many respects essential to ensure cultural and national independence, locked the government into a reactive foreign policy. During the past decade, Mongolia has recognized that, if it is to attain maximum economic benefit from its rich mineral resources and not be marginalized politically by Russia and China, as happened in past centuries, it needs to proactively take advantage of its geographical position to develop into a significant and cost-effective transit link between its neighbors. Mongolia's UR network, which is the sole rail line linking up with the Trans-Siberian railroad in the north and China's railroad in the south, plays a vital role in export and import transportation of coal, minerals, timber, oil, and animal husbandry–related products, which represent up to 80 percent of all freight transport. The UR also provides passenger service, which is valuable for developing the Sino-Russian tourism industry.

Mongolia now believes that it needs to become part of China's Silk Road Economic Belt and the AIIB in order to avoid becoming isolated from subregional economic integration that would bypass it through the Russian Far East on the east and Kazakhstan on the west.[89] The Mongols finally have accepted the concept of a special cross-border trade zone, and in March 2015 signed an MOU for the establishment of a nine-square-kilometer cross-border trade area with China and a separate FTA. The Inner Mongolian Autonomous Region's local government already has constructed advanced port facilities on the Chinese side in Erenhot.[90] To maximize Mongolia's economic benefits, policymakers have recognized that regional cooperation and integration of transport routes in a Mongolian-oriented Economic Transit Corridor is now a necessary national objective. In order to meet the increasing Chinese demand for the nation's world-class coal and copper deposits and to reach other regional markets such as Japan and Korea, Mongolia understands that obtaining FDI and trade diversification depend upon developing additional transport routes to both Russia and China that allow access to additional seaports. In 2016 the newly elected MPP government developed a government action plan for 2016–2020 that in the next few years "will give the railway transit a priority, including technological renovation of the Ulaanbaatar Railways–Mongolian Russian joint company. Also, putting the New Ulaanbaatar International Airport into operation and becoming a hub connecting Asia with Europe are among the prime concerns of the government's policy."[91]

The Mongolian cabinet in the summer of 2018 again supported a draft resolution on state policy on railway transport to create a new transit transport corridor that connects Europe and Asia and allows Mongolia to reach the third market and seaports using the railway transport networks of China and Russia. It will recommend that the Parliament fund the construction of a southern railroad spur of 281 kilometers from Zuunbayan to Khangi designed to transport iron ore and other raw materials, and a northbound 780-kilometer rail from Erdenet to Arts Suuri.[92] It is expected that the Zuunbayan spur will transport some ten to twenty-one million tons of cargo from 2018 to 2025 and another twenty-one million tons of cargo for the period from 2026 to 2046.[93]

Another aspect of promoting new connectivity is evident in Mongolia's investment in old and new airport infrastructure in the last five years. The major project has been the New Ulaanbaatar International Airport, over 50 kilometers from the capital, with the capacity to receive three million passengers annually and increase present international air cargo capacity ten times. The project includes construction of a six-lane, 30.4 km highway to Ulaanbaatar. Financing for the development of the airport was through Japanese government soft loans totaling 65.6 billion yen ($600 million) to be repaid over forty years.[94] Delayed for several years, it now is scheduled to open in mid-2019. Mongolia also is working to open full-time auto border crossings, introduce a freight and passenger transportation permission-granting system, and expand auto transportation services at the border points. A trilateral pilot transport network from Tianjin, China, to Ulaanbaatar to Ulan Ude, Russia, has been organized, and there is a shift to negotiating road transport agreements to permit Mongolian, Russian, and Chinese trucks to operate in one another's territories.[95] The Mongolian government in 2016 accepted a Chinese soft loan to construct a 250-kilometer highway, and its 2017 budget proposals to the Parliament included 12 percent for projects to be implemented with funding from international financial assistance.[96]

Mongolia over the past ten years has implemented a road building plan known as the Millennium Road to connect all provinces with paved roads, but there have been budgetary problems and documented misuse of funds that have prevented the completion of this major project. Foreign investment in construction projects is vital but inconsistent. The MPP government elected in 2016 believes that new roads as well as new railways must be closely linked to mining operations because their rationale is all about transporting mining products. A bid to construct a new 200-kilometer heavy road from the TT coal mine to the southern border port of Gashuunsukhait alongside the existing road was announced in 2017, and the selection process is under way. Trucks loaded with coal will use the new road while the existing road will be used for empty trucks going back to the coal mines. The heavy road will be built with a build-own-operate-transfer concession agreement. A continuing major problem has been long truck queues at the Gashuunsukhait border crossing that back up hundreds of vehicles for weeks. As of July 2018, Mongolian coal exports had reached twenty-one million tons annually. Some 10,000 out of 14,000 heavy trucks are transporting coal on the Tavan Tolgoi–Gashuunsukhait route, the main gateway of coal export. In April 2018 Mongolian Prime Minister Khürelsükh obtained Chinese agreement to invest 148 billion yuan ($24 million) for the development and passing capacity improvement of the Gashuunsukhait border checkpoint. In the first half of 2018, around 900 vehicles were passing the border loaded with coal, down from the peak of 1,500.[97]

Through the UN, only seven project meetings were devoted to a transit transportation agreement among Mongolia, Russia, and China from 2000 to 2011.[98] It is clear that with the Mongolian-Russian-Chinese Northern Railway plan, momentum since then has shifted and Mongolia's transport ministry finally is committed to developing transportation infrastructure. At present, priority is given to railway facilitation measures, regional rail transport agreements, and rail border-crossing procedures, but at times there is vacillation as when the railway contract with South Korea's Samsung C&T Corporation for a 267-kilometer spur from Ukhaa-Khudag to Gashuunsukhait capable of carrying thirty million tons of TT coal and OT copper was invalidated.

There remain challenges impeding the establishment of the country as a transit corridor: (1) appropriate transit agreements need to be concluded; (2) the domestic railroad and roads system needs to be expanded and modernized; (3) border and port infrastructure and transshipment capacities need to be increased; (4) transit tariffs and regulations must be revised; and (5) more financing and significant investment are required for hard infrastructure development. Moreover, Mongolian transit infrastructure development consistently has been delayed by political factors and corruption.

Notes

1. Embassy of Mongolia website, "Foreign Policy," October 25, 2016, http://mongolianembassy.us/about-mongolia/foreign-relations-of-mongolia/#.W9dIfnpKii4.

2. Dugerjav Gotov, "Northeast Asia and Mongolia: Infrastructure Network Development Issues," *Ritsumeikan Journal of Asia Pacific Studies*, 26 (2009): 77, https://www.apu.ac.jp/rcaps/uploads/fckeditor/publications/journal/RJAPS_V26_Gotov.pdf.

3. Jargalsaikhan Mendee, "Mongolia's Dilemma."

4. Ibid.

5. Indra Overland and Kyrre Elvenes Braekhus, "Chinese Perspectives on Russian Oil and Gas," in *Russian Energy Power and Foreign Relations: Implications for Conflict and Cooperation*, ed. Jeronim Perovic, Robert W. Orttung, and Andreas Wenger, CCS Studies in Security and International Relations series (London: Routledge, 2009), 214.

6. Silk Road Economic Belt agreements were signed with twenty-four cities from eight countries along the Silk Road in November 2013 alone. "China, GCC Set to Walk the New 'Silk Road,'" *Arab News*, February 3, 2014, www.arabnews.com/news/518966, cited in Alexander Kim, "China and the Silk Road: Marching Westward," *Eurasia Daily Monitor* 11, no. 40 (March 3, 2014).

7. Mutual respect for each other's sovereignty and territorial integrity, mutual nonaggression, mutual noninterference in each other's internal affairs, equality and mutual benefit, and peaceful coexistence. See Stephen Perry, "The New Silk Road—OBOR—an Overview," *People's Daily Online,* February 5, 2016, http://en.people.cn/n3/2016/0205/c90883-9014677.html.

8. "Xi'an-Almaty Cargo Train Begins Operation," *Xinhua*, November 28, 2013, cited in Kim, "China and the Silk Road."

9. "Toyota-Motors Will Deliver Its Cars to Kazakhstan Five Times Faster," *Kaz Inform*, November 26, 2013, http://www.inform.kz/rus/article/2608791, cited in Kim, "China and the Silk Road."

10. Neo-Eurasianism was founded by Lev Gumilev (October 1, 1912–June 15, 1992), well known to Mongols because, in contrast to the official idea that Russia had saved Europe and Christianity from the Mongol hordes, Gumilev argued that it was the military prowess of the Mongols that had saved the Eastern Slavs from conquest by the West. In Gumilev's view, there was no Mongol/Tatar yoke, but rather the Mongols handed the imperial torch to the Russians. According to this thinking, the Russian Empire was a type of Orthodox-Mongol Empire. "Prominent Russians: Lev Gumilev," *Russiapedia,* http://russiapedia.rt.com/prominent-russians/science-and-technology/lev-gumilev/.

11. Marlene Laruelle, *The "Russian World": Russia's Soft Power and Geopolitical Imagination* (Washington, DC: Center on Global Interests, May 2015), 18, http://globalinterests.org/wp-content/uploads/2015/05/FINAL-CGI_Russian-World_Marlene-Laruelle.pdf.

12. The Treaty on Increased Integration in the Economic and Humanitarian Fields signed in 1996 laid the first foundation for economic convergence. The treaty was the blueprint for the future common market for goods, services, capital, and labor.

13. According to figures provided by the Interstate Statistics Committee of the CIS in 2015, the EEU's GDP amounted to close to $1.3 trillion (according to end of 2015 exchange rates). Today all EEU members have a trade deficit, comprising about half of Russia's trade surplus of $24 billion. The first integration stage primarily focused on increasing inter–member state trade and created a legal and institutional foundation. The second stage includes the free movement of goods, people, services, and capital. Douglas Green, "EEU Two Years Later: Expansion and Unbalance: The Case of Kyrgyzstan," *Times of Central Asia,* May 21, 2016.

14. "Mongolia Considering Joining Eurasian Economic Union Economy," *Belarus News*, August 30, 2016.

15. "Mongolia Considering Joining Eurasian Economic Union," *Kaz Inform* (Moscow), August 31, 2016.

16. "Park Seeks 'Eurasia Initiative' to Build Energy, Logistics Links," *Korea Herald,* October 18, 2013, www.koreaherald.com/view.php?ud=20131018000620.

17. Sh. Enkhbayar, "Recent Trends in Mongolian Foreign Trade with the Countries of Northeast Asia" (ERINA Report no. 96, Tokyo, November 2010), 43.

18. Khuder, "GTI Consultative Committee Meeting Starts," *Montsame,* October 30, 2013.

19. Wang Weina, "Regional Economic Cooperation in Northeast Asia Under the Greater Tumen Initiative" (PowerPoint presentation prepared for GTI Secretariat), slide 11: "Milestones of the GTI /TRADP," http://www.unescap.org/sites/default/files/Session3_Wang_Regional_Economic_Cooperation_1.pdf.

20. See-Won Byun, "Provincial Impacts of Multilateral Cooperation:. The Greater Tumen Initiative and Environmental Protection in Jilin," China Environment Series (Washington, DC: Woodrow Wilson International Center for Scholars, 2008–2009), 160, https://asiafoundation.org/resources/pdfs/ByunGTICES10.pdf.

21. "Ulaanbaatar Declaration" (Tenth Consultative Commission Meeting of the Greater Tumen Initiative, Ulaanbaatar, Mongolia, March 24, 2009), http://www.tumenprogramme.org/?info-548-1.html.

22. Representatives from the Korea Energy Economics Institute, the Energy Research Institute, NDRC (China), the Energy Balances Forecasting Agency (Russia), the Oxford Institute for Energy Studies (UK), the Energy Authority of Mongolia, the Institute of Energy Economics, Japan, and the Nautilus Institute for Security and Sustainability (USA) and GTI considered projects under a GTI Energy Action Plan, which was drafted as an ongoing framework project for capacity-building on GTI Energy at the regional level. A number of new GTI Energy activities involving the promotion of energy investment projects, an NEA Energy Database, and an Energy Forum for Northeast Asia were discussed. "Inaugural Meeting of the GTI Energy Board Boost Energy Cooperation in Northeast Asia," Greater Tumen Initiative, Ulaanbaatar, September 16, 2009, http://www.tumenprogramme.org/?info-591-1.html.

23. Zhu Shu, "A Perspective on the Greater Tumen Initiative and Northeast Asia Economic Cooperation," Jeju Peace Institute, August 24, 2011, http://www.jpi.or.kr/eng/regular/print_ok.sky?id=4102.

24. "Tumen Development Body Likely to Be Upgraded into Int'l Organization," *Yonhap News,* October 30, 2013.

25. Greater Tumen Initiative, *Integrated Transport Infrastructure and Cross-Border Facilitation Study for the Trans-GTR Transport Corridors* (Greater Tumen Initiative, February 2013), www.tumenprogramme.org/?info-1-115.html.

26. "Regional Development Plans Approved at 14th Greater Tumen Initiative Meeting," UNDP, October 30, 2013, http://www.cn.undp.org/content/china/en/home/presscenter/articles/2013/10/regional-development-plans-approved-at-14th-greater-tumen-initia.html.

27. Khuder, "GTI Consultative Committee."

28. Also attending this meeting was the Association of Development Financing Institutions in Asia and the Pacific, whose mission is to act as the focal point of all development banks and other financial institutions engaged in the financing of development in the Asia Pacific region.

29. The AIIB concept was first suggested by the Center for International Economic Exchanges, a Chinese think tank, at the Bo'ao Forum in April 2009 as a formula to make better use of Chinese foreign currency reserves in the wake of the global financial crisis. See "The Asian Infrastructure Investment Bank: Multilateralism on the Silk Road," *China Economic Journal,* April 4, 2016. Xi indicated that the Chinese government was frustrated with what it believed was the slow pace of reforms and governance in existing global financial institutions like the IMF, World Bank, and Asian Development Bank, which it claims are dominated by US, European, and Japanese interests.

30. Wang Shouwen, China's deputy minister of commerce, quoted in He Na and Liu Mingtai, "Regional Bloc Urges Better Financing Channels," *China Daily,* September 18, 2014, http://www.chinadaily.com.cn/china/2014-09/18/content_18618868.htm.

31. "Railroad Stretch Between Russia's Khasan to N. Korea's Rajin to Be Launched Within Days," *Russia Beyond*, September 7, 2013, https://www.rbth.com/news/2013/09/07/railroad_stretch_between_russias_khasan_to_n_koreas_rajin_to_be_launched_29596.html.

32. "Logistics and energy network in the Eurasian region will not only reduce logistics costs and stimulate global trade, but will also stabilize raw materials costs and con-

tribute to the growth of the world economy. . . . If trade barriers are gradually taken down and Eurasia becomes a free trade zone, Eurasia could be made into a gigantic market like the European Union." President Park quoted in Choi He-suk, "Park Sees 'Eurasia Initiative' to Build Energy, Logistics Links," *Korea Herald,* October 18, 2013, www.koreaherald.com/view.php?ud=20131018000620.

33. Na Hee-Seung, "Integrated International Intermodal Transport of Russia's Far East, Siberia and Korean Peninsula," *The Political Economy of Pacific Russia,* Jing Huang and Alexander Korolev, eds. (Cham, Switzerland: Springer, Palgrave Macmillan, 2017), 203–221, https://link.springer.com/chapter/10.1007/978-3-319-40120-1_9.

34. "2016 Northeast Asia International Conference for Economic Development (NICE) Successfully Held," Greater Tumen Initiative, November 16, 2016, http://www.tumenprogramme.org/?info-641-1.html.

35. "GTI Office Receives MECC Mission," Greater Tumen Initiative, November 11, 2016, http://www.tumenprogramme.org/?info-643-1.html.

36. Joining the Mongols were participants from the PRC Ministry of Agriculture, ROC Food and Rural Affairs Ministry, Russian Ministry of Agriculture, and the Deutsche Gesellschaft für Internationale Zusammenarbeit (GIZ) for discussion of the SAP's coordination with the regional Support for Economic Cooperation in Sub-Regional Initiatives in Asia program. See "Working Meeting on GTI Agriculture Cooperation Strategic Action Plan in Ulaanbaatar, Mongolia [July 5–6, 2016]," Greater Tumen Initiative, November 16, 2016, http://www.tumenprogramme.org/?info-647-1.html.

37. Problems also were identified, including low investment for energy source development, low development of infrastructure for energy transportation, inconsistent electricity demand and supply, and technical barriers. See "GTI Participates in the 1st NEA Energy Forum," Greater Tumen Initiative, November 16, 2016, http://www.tumenprogramme.org/?info-659-1.html.

38. The members were joined by participants from UNESCAP, Korea EXIM Bank, Korea Institute for International Economic Policy, Korea Maritime Institute, GTI Transport Expert Group, JSC Russian Railways, Korea Expressway Corporation, and Korea Rail Network Authority. The GTI Secretariat also took part in the first meeting of the ASEM Eurasia Expert Group on Transport and Logistics. This meeting focused on the specific topics of infrastructure, facilitation, and financing. See "The 6th GTI Transport Board Meeting Held Back to Back with the 1st Meeting of the ASEM Expert Group on Eurasia Transport and Logistics," Greater Tumen Initiative, November 16, 2016, http://www.tumenprogramme.org/?info-648-1.html.

39. "The GTI Secretariat Takes Part in the Eurasia Transport and Logistics Partnership (EuTraLop) Round Table Meeting in Republic of Korea," Greater Tumen Initiative, November 16, 2016, http://www.tumenprogramme.org/?info-656-1.html.

40. Delegations from China and Russia presented their progress priority projects: Cross-Border Self-Driving Tourism, International Tourism Zone of Tea Road Stations, and Touristic Train for Schoolchildren of China.

41. *Integrated Transport Infrastructure and Cross-Border Facilitation Study*, 68.

42. Ibid., 83.

43. Ibid., 84.

44. Ibid.

45. "APTA Welcomes Mongolia as Its Seventh Member," UNESCAP, October 28, 2013, https://www.unescap.org/news-item/apta-welcomes-mongolia-its-seventh-member.

46. President Xi visited Mongolia August 21–22, 2014, and President Putin came for six hours on September 3, 2014.

47. "Mongolia Asks the World Bank's Involvement in the 'Steppe Road' Project," *InfoMongolia.com*, September 18, 2014, http://infomongolia.com/ct/ci/8374. Accessed November 3, 2014.

48. "President Elbegdorj Spoke at the Central European University: 'Mongolian Transition to Democracy and Lessons,'" Embassy of Mongolia, October 18, 2014, http://mongolianembassy.us/2014/10/president-elbegdorj-spoke-at-the-central-european-university-mongolian-transition-to-democracy-and-lessons/#.W9djc3pKii4.

49. "Speech by Tsakiagiin Elbegdorj, President of Mongolia, at the APEC Meeting 'Dialogue on Strengthening Connectivity Partnership,'" November 8, 2014, http://eng.president.mn/newsCenter/viewNews.php?newsId=1353.

50. The expo was held in Hohhot October 23–28, 2015. According to Minister of Industry Dondogdorj Erdenebat, in B. Amarsaikhan, "Mongolia and China Ink Over 100 Commercial and Industrial Deals," October 28, 2015, http://www.montsame.mn/en/read/121166.

51. There was an international symposium in England in December 2015 where Mongolian and international scholars and policymakers assessed the development of such a Steppe Road. The conference was held December 8–9, 2015, at Cambridge University, England. It was the third in a series entitled "Entangled Lines: Railways, Resource Booms, and Transnational Politics in Mongolia"—a British Academy–funded international network and mobility project between the Mongolia and Inner Asia Studies Unit (Cambridge University) and the Institute of International Affairs of the Mongolian Academy of Sciences. The series studied the critical role of the Mongolian railway in relation to the mining sector and Mongol-Chinese-Russian economic and geopolitical relations led by Professor Caroline Humphrey and Dr. U. Bulag.

52. "Ulaanbaatar Railway Modernisation Strategy," *Railway Gazette,* September 4, 2014.

53. "Sustainable Transport Challenges: Strategy of Mongolia," Fourth Regional Environmentally Sustainable Transport Forum (Seoul, Korea, February 24–26, 2009), http://www.uncrd.or.jp/content/documents/4EST-B1G102.pdf.

54. Jargalsaikhan Dambadarjaa, "Mongolia Is the Next Panama," *UB Post,* February 27, 2013.

55. "China Proposes Economic Corridor with Russia and Mongolia," *RT,* April 2, 2015. https://www.rt.com/business/246281-china-russia-mongolia-corridor/.

56. Ibid.

57. "China May Invest $5.2bn in Russia's First High Speed Railway," *RT,* March 30, 2015. https://www.rt.com/business/245125-china-invest-russia-train/.

58. "China, Russia, Mongolia Endorse Development Plan on Economic Corridor," *Xinhua,* June 24, 2016, http://english.cctv.com/2016/06/24/ARTIJkwoLdfFUjK7unWMv0lN160624.shtml.

59. "China Russia, Mongolia Sign Tripartite Economic Partnership Deal," *Dhakha Tribune*, July 5, 2016. https://issuu.com/dhakatribune/docs/160704195333-711b47efde20417495d3197869547193.

60. "New Highway to Open Up Trade, Investment in Western Mongolia," *Asian Development Blog*, December 23, 2015, blogs.adb.org/blog/new-highway-open-trade-investment-western-mongolia.

61. "Railway Delegates of Mongolia, Russia and China Meet in UB," *Mongol Messenger*, August 5, 2016.

62. Jia Kefu, party branch secretary of Tanggu dangerous goods carriage yard of Tianjin Transportation Group Binhai Co. Ltd., quoted in Zhang Min, "New Tianjin Road Cuts Transportation Time, Cost to Mongolia, Russia," *China Daily,* September 28, 2016, http://www.chinadaily.com.cn/bizchina/2016-09/28/content_26922236.htm.

63. Ibid.

64. B. Amarsaikhan, "Transit Transport Might Be 2nd OT for Mongolia," *Montsame,* September 13, 2016.

65. "Prime Minister Meets Presidential Envoy of Russia," American Chamber of Commerce, April 27, 2018, http://mongolia.gogo.mn/r/161599.

66. *Railway Transport Facilitation in Mongolia.*

67. "Mongolia, Russia and China Sign Joint Declaration to Develop Transit Transportation Corridor," *infoMongolia.com,* December 19, 2013, http://covermongolia.blogspot.com/2013/12/mse-top-20-at-9-month-high-imf-urges.html.

68. The statement was signed by Yondon Manlaibayar, chairman of the Ministry of Roads and Transportation's Coordinating Department of Railway and Maritime Policy for Mongolia, RZD Deputy Chairman Igor Mitsuk for Russia, and deputy director of Chinese Railways General Authority Chen Lanhua.

69. Once completed, the capacity of this line south to the border is expected to be around thirty metric tons per year. John Johnson, "Cru Group: Mongolian Prospects on the Up After a Healthy Dose of Reality," CRGroup.com, October 6, 2014, http://covermongolia.blogspot.com/2014/10/mnt-losing-streak-enters-3rd-week-2015.html.

70. Quoted from *Udriin Sonin* in September 2014, see Terrence Edwards, "Ukraine Crisis Sparks Renewed Russian Interest in Aging Trans-Mongolian Railway," *bne IntelliNews,* October 22, 2014, http://www.intellinews.com/ukraine-crisis-sparks-renewed-russian-interest-in-aging-trans-mongolian-railway-500433321/?archive=bne.

71. Yondon Manlaibayar quoted in B. Dulguun, "Yo. Manlaibayar: Mongolia Will Have Three Huge Transit Railroad Corridors," *UB Post,* January 9, 2014.

72. Break bulk shipping is meant to encompass cargo that is transported in bags, boxes, crates, drums, or barrels—or items of extreme length or size. To be considered break bulk, these goods must be loaded individually, not in intermodal containers or in bulk as with liquids or grains. Loading and unloading break bulk cargo can be very labor intensive and requires more resources and coordination—longshoremen, loading and unloading cranes, warehouses, specialized ships, transport vehicles, etc. "What Is Break Bulk Shipping?," Logistics Plus, March 8, 2017, https://www.logisticsplus.net/what-is-break-bulk-shipping/.

73. Dulguun, "Yo. Manlaibayar."

74. B. Batchimeg, "B. Jigjidnyamaa: 'Mongolian Corridor Is Main Supporter Line of Trans-Siberian Transport Corridor,'" *Montsame,* April 20, 2018.

75. "Answers to Journalists' Questions Following a Working Visit to Mongolia," President of Russia website, September 3, 2014, http://en.kremlin.ru/events/president/news/46555, cited in Alicia Campi, "Transforming Mongolia-Russia-China Relations: The Dushanbe Trilateral Summit," *Asia-Pacific Journal* 12, no. 45 (November 3, 2014): http://apjjf.org/2014/12/45/Alicia-Campi/4210.html.

76. President Putin quoted in Edwards, "Ukraine Crisis."

77. "Ulaanbaatar Railway Modernisation Strategy."

78. "'Eurasia Initiative' Gets Boost from Koreas-Russia Cooperation," *North Korea Newsletter* 341, December 4, 2014, https://en.yna.co.kr/view/AEN20141203007200325.

79. D. Myagmasuren, "Talks Held to Develop Continental Railway," *Mongol Messenger,* December 20, 2014.

80. Ibid.

81. "Mongolia, North Korea Sign MoU, North Korean Foreign Minister in Mongolia on Three-Day Visit to Further Cooperation," Nknews.org, February 25, 2015.

82. "Ulaanbaatar Railway Modernisation Strategy."

83. *Mongol Messenger,* April 17, 2015. Accessed September 5, 2015.

84. "Xi Jinping Attends Second Meeting of Heads of State of China, Russia and Mongolia," PRC Ministry of Foreign Affairs, July 10, 2015, https://www.fmprc.gov.cn/mfa_eng/zxxx_662805/t1280848.shtml.

85. "Cabinet Approves Signing Concession Agreement with Aspire Mining to Build Erdenet-Ovoot Railway," CoverMongolia.blogspot, August 12, 2015. http://covermongolia.blogspot.com/2015/08/aspire-rail-deal-approved-modun-sells.html.

86. Mongolian officials claimed their country has already invested $200 million, but the project needs another $800 million. Terrence Edwards, "Mongolia to Pitch Railway Projects to China-Backed AIIB—Govt Adviser," Reuters, September 20, 2016, http://www.reuters.com/article/mongolia-railways-idUSL3N1BW2KQ.

87. A rail pre-feasibility study on the Erdenet to Ovoot railway was completed in February 2012, and a revised rail pre-feasibility study was completed over the western portion of the rail path in April 2013 by SMEC International Limited, which confirmed the cheaper capital cost estimate of $1.2 billion plus contingencies for the entire line.

88. "Mongolian Railway Draft Feasibility Study Completed," *Railway Gazette*, April 10, 2018, https://www.railwaygazette.com/news/news/asia/single-view/view/mongolian-railway-draft-feasibility-study-completed.html.

89. Mendee, "Mongolia's Dilemma."

90. Jeffrey Reeves, "Mongolia's Place in China's Periphery Diplomacy," *Open Forum*, The Asan Forum, April 07, 2016, http://www.theasanforum.org/mongolias-place-in-chinas-periphery-diplomacy/.

91. Minister of Roads and Transportation Development D. Ganbat quoted in "Major Road and Transport Projects Will Be Put into Effect to Promote Economy," *Mongol Messenger,* November 4, 2016.

92. "Cabinet Supports Draft Resolution on State Policy on Railway Transport," *Mongol Messenger,* June 1, 2018; "Proposed Zuunbayan-Khangi and Erdenet-Artssuuri Railway Routes Supported by Cabinet," American Chamber of Commerce in Mongolia, May 31, 2018, http://mongolia.gogo.mn/r/161735.

93. Golomt Capital, http://golomtcapital.com/zuunbayan-khangi-railroad-to-be-constructed/.

94. B. Byambasüren, "ТАНИЛЦ: Онцлох бүтээн байгуулалт буюу ШИНЭ НИСЭХ БУУДЛЫН ажлын явц," [Background: Featured development or progress of a New Life's work], August 21, 2017, https://ikon.mn/n/133b.

95. "Report on Implementation of the Almaty Programme of Action."

96. From a total of 9.54 billion tugriks budget-allocated for the operational cost of the Ministry of Roads and Transportation Development, some 701.2 million is for projects to be implemented with funding from international financial assistance and 8.832 billion is for financing stated-funded projects, programs, and measures. See "Major Road," *Mongol Messenger,* November 4, 2016.

97. "Prime Minister Meets Presidential Envoy of Russia."

98. In Ulaanbaatar: May 15–17, 2005; in Tianjin: January 16–18, 2001; in Irkutsk: October 22–25, 2001; in Ulaanbaatar: November 12–13, 2002; in Qingdao: January 13–14, 2004; in Geneva: December 13–16, 2004; in Ulaanbaatar: November 14–18, 2005; in Beijing January 18–19, 2011. See "Report on Implementation of the Almaty Programme of Action."

10

New Soft-Power Image Making

Soft power is a concept developed originally by Joseph Nye of Harvard University to describe the ability of a government to attract, persuade, and co-opt rather than coerce others to accept the legitimacy of a government's policies and values.[1] This term is applied to large nations that seek to demonstrate their commitment to global or regional peace and stability while pursuing their own specific developmental goals, and it often correlates with a country's growing hard power.[2] In the democratic era, Mongolia, a small nation in population, has been courted through soft-power methods, particularly by wealthy Northeast Asian nations, the United States, and Europe. However, there has been almost no analysis of Mongolia's own plans for raising its regional and global profile through reinvention and reformulation of its national image with new soft-power network-building initiatives. Yet, since 2009 under the activist policies of Mongolian President Tsakhia Elbegdorj, there has been a conscious trend to develop an internationally recognized Mongolian "brand" that can be marketed worldwide. This charm offensive, mainly propagated through the Ministry of Foreign Affairs, explains to foreign investors Mongolia's national foreign policy principles and actions through dissemination of positive information about Mongolia's business and social environment. Its goals are to support the Mongolian economy and, ultimately, bolster national security.

One of the major trends in Mongolian foreign policy in the second decade of the twenty-first century has been a sweeping and imaginative focus on promoting the image of Mongolia globally. This feature of Elbegdorj's presidency may be considered his greatest legacy. As Mongolia has struggled to find economic growth within the overarching parameters of national security and foreign policy requirements, it is promoting its unique nomadic civilization to the world and actively developing new institutional framework mechanisms in the region to raise its national profile. Therefore, Mongolia has "begun articulating policies and implementing programs using soft power and public diplomacy as effective strategies for increasing its cultural and political presence within regional and global politics."[3]

During the early years of democracy, the reaction of most Mongolian national leaders to Western critiques of nomadism was silence or even agreement. Mongolian policymakers did not attach special cultural significance to maintaining nomadism per se or linking Mongolian modern national identity to the nomadic tradition. The exception to this attitude was found among Mongolian historians and some early environmentalists. One Mongolian policymaker who supported nomads was Ts. Adiyasuren, former minister for nature and environment. He wrote of the significance of traditional nomadic civilization to Mongolian political and social issues as well as ecology.[4] Dulguun Batkhishig, a researcher for the British charity CAMDA, also supported nomadism as a sustainable livelihood: "We need to learn from their simplicity of life and also recognize that nomadic herders can embrace development and progress, especially technological. . . . Mongolians ourselves and travelers who visit must all realize that the preservation of this way of life is important."[5] Other Mongolian officials, such as Tungalag Ulambayar of the UNDP, advocated training herders in risk management and new livestock practices: "Of course you [may be] a nomad—but you are a nomad in the 21st century, and you have to adapt to the market to survive."[6]

Prior to Mongolia's mineral boom, Indian researcher Phunchok Stobdan predicted Mongolia would promote its own civilizational experience. He noted that (1) the Mongols, as former leaders of the Turkic world, are reviving their sense of geopolitical responsibilities in the region; (2) Mongolia's geographical position at the junction of Central Asia, Northeast Asia, China, and Russia makes it strategically the most significant country in Asia; (3) the Mongol diaspora across Inner Asia enables it to be a cultural stabilizer in Asia; (4) the Buddhist cultural background of the Mongols has a neutralizing effect on complex Asian cultural and political contradictions; (5) Mongolia will continue its moderating political influence on Sino-Russian relations; (6) with China's rise as a superpower, Mongolia will play a role in moderating US-Chinese conflicts; (7) Mongolia will play a balancing role in South Asia; (8) Mongolia's location near resource-rich Siberia will enhance its strategic importance for the industrialized countries; and (9) Mongolia will assist in stopping the spread of Islamic fundamentalism across Asia.[7]

When Mongolia entered the mineral resource era, the rationale behind nomadism again was questioned. Many foreign environmentalists linked climate warming and increasing desertification of Mongolia's steppes to the nomadic economy. For example, the Swiss Agency for Development wrote,

> The ongoing process of desertification in Mongolia has less to do with natural factors and climate change but more with human activities, such as overgrazing of pastureland, inappropriate management of agriculture land and water resources, destruction of forests and bushes etc. In other words, the existing natural resources are sacrificed for the immediate need to sustain the livelihood of the growing population.[8]

The desertification issue was embraced by the Western media and broadcast around the world. CNN did a story on the connection between increasing cashmere goat herds and desertification.[9] The *New York Times* explored the same theme by criticizing the democratic system for allowing nomads to recklessly increase herd size and "ended a socialist system that tightly controlled the size of the nation's herds to prevent overgrazing. Environmentalists and government officials agree that the two decades of unbridled privatization and a boom in cashmere exports upended the traditional mix of livestock . . . with devastating results for the ecology of the steppe."[10] Akbar Usmani, resident representative for the UNDP, was quoted in the British press as saying, "The key question we have to ask is whether this way of life is sustainable."[11] Other reports claimed that nomadism would be destroyed by the worldwide economic downturn after 2008 or other economic trends beyond the control of individual herder families. Attention paid to poverty, desertification, and overgrazing in the democratic era spurred a very negative view about the legitimacy of nomadism and its practitioners for Mongolia's continued development.

It was in this antagonistic and pessimistic climate that Elbegdorj, during the 2008 presidential campaign, asserted that, while Mongolia's foreign policy had been relatively stable and overcome enormous obstacles during two decades of democracy, the country needed a new international style, which included soft power and branding of its nomadic heritage. Having never been a member of the former communist party and being the first candidate with a Western education, Elbegdorj based his platform on the vision that Mongolia must be recognized definitively as a democratic country, and for Mongolia to develop in a democratic way it was necessary that it be active in the international community. During the election campaign, he criticized his MPRP opponent, the sitting president N. Enkhbayar, for presiding over a fractured economy with a society of haves and have-nots—some benefiting from Mongolia's resource-based modernization and others, especially in the countryside, who appeared to be falling further into poverty. Elbegdorj and his Democratic Party reminded the nearly 40 percent of the population who were nomads that Enkhbayar, while prime minister in 2001, had famously asserted, "It is not my desire to destroy the original Mongolian identity but in order to survive we have to stop being nomads."[12]

For Elbegdorj, the son of a herdsman in the western province of Khovd, the cultural meaning of nomads was embraced as a metaphor for the uniqueness of Mongolia and a symbol of its national identity. In the campaign he chose to discuss, or some might say politicize, the role of nomads in the modern development of the nation, not only because nomadic herdsmen formed a powerful constituency in Parliament, but also because his campaign identified nomadism with the country's very spiritual essence. His recognition of the uniqueness and strength of Mongolia's nomadic heritage was stimulated by domestic political reaction to the loss of "Mongolness" reflected in the modernization of the country as seen in overcrowded Ulaanbaatar, fears of Chinese economic domination, and the polluting impact of foreign mining companies. Domestic concerns also had been raised about the ramifications of a Western version of modernization: "If nomadic pastoralism, the matrix of Mongolian society, is destroyed, what would happen to the community and the individual? What kind of new social structures would replace the old ones?"[13]

In this social climate President Elbegdorj and his new administration promoted a pro-nomadic intellectual trend that was much more than a return to the Mongolian romantic notion captured in the "myth of nomadism." They decisively rejected the old Soviet thesis that the Mongolian traditional nomadic economy could not modernize. Thus, during the heart of Mongolia's economic boom in 2010–2013, the theory was born of Mongolia's returning to "nomadic values" while also experiencing urban modernization and internationalism. Promoting this hybrid conception of democracy with national roots as its basis, not unlike post–World War II Japan, the Mongolian policymaking establishment under Elbegdorj explored the "problem of establishing democratic legal institutions on a rural nomadic society with a socialist legacy."[14]

Although it had been a pawn in the Sino-Russian and Japanese "Great Game" in the twentieth century, policymakers believed that the end of the Cold War fundamentally altered Mongolia's traditional role as a buffer zone in Asian continental politics. Elbegdorj recognized that Mongolia's turn to democracy and the market economy had caused the country to reengage with its Northeast, Southeast, and Central Asian neighbors. At that time Mongolia, despite the worldwide recession, was experiencing double-digit growth,[15] yet it was uneasy with China's monopoly over its economy and FDI. In the complex Eurasian cultural environment, Mongolia, as one of the older nations whose influence penetrated not only Asia but also Europe and Southeast Asia in the premodern period, used the momentum from its modern economic resurgence to play a significant role in shaping the emerging continental geopolitical order as a counterweight to China. Mongolia recognized that its sociohistorical legacy in Central Asia and Russia, together with its newfound mineral wealth, could tie it to Turco-Iranian influenced nations and their elites in ways that could facilitate Mongolian export penetration into the Middle East, Africa, and Europe. Accordingly, Elbegdorj utilized soft power to expand contacts with Eurasian and Southeast Asian nations to reach out to different potential trade partners.

Revised National Security Concept of 2010 and Promotion of Nomadic Values

Recognizing that Mongolia's domestic economic issues were intimately linked to its international profile, Elbegdorj, immediately after assuming the presidency in May 2009, initiated a major reassessment of Mongolia's identity in the globalized world in light of its traditional nomadic culture and then booming mineral-based economy. The question was what concrete steps could Mongolia's democratic government take to strengthen the nomadic economy and glorify nomadic culture in the rapidly changing Eurasian economic environment? Could nomads be a part of Mongolia's modern development rather than just stand apart? In October 2010 the Mongolian government began a public relations campaign to explain the salient points in the National Security Concept through the domestic media and by dispatching well-known Mongolian researchers to embassies around the world to introduce it to both their own embassy officials and host-nation governments. The essential concept element that reflected Elbegdorj's new vision was that, for the first time in the democratic era, Mongolian culture, lifestyle, and traditional nomadic economy were linked in a positive way to the definition of national security. This reevaluation of the importance of Mongolia's nomadic heritage bridged the gap between the traditional and modern economies, refuting the anti-nomadic sentiment espoused by Western aid organizations, including environmentalists, about the "backwardness" of nomadic life.

The key provisions that closely identify nomads and their traditions with the new definition of Mongolia's national identity are found in Article VIII. Section 44 states that the "Security of Mongolian Culture and Way of Life" is "where conditions are ensured for the preservation of the national language, history, culture, customs and traditions that constitute the basis for the existence and development of the Mongolian nation and its statehood, and conditions for the eternal existence of the Mongolian people." The article asserts that different external and internal factors could adversely affect the security of Mongolian culture and way of life. For example, "Emergence of conditions where the blurring of the distinctive features of Mongolian culture and way of life may lead to its eventual assimilation into others' as a result of political, economic and socio-cultural policies of foreign countries and external forces." Regarding internal factors that might adversely affect the continuation of Mongolian culture and way of life, it lists

> 1. Disregard for and belittling of the cultures of other peoples and exaggeration of the values of the historical traditions of Mongolian culture and way of life, which may ultimately lead to the country's self-isolation as a nation; 2. Over estimation and blind imitation of civilizations of other nations or failure to safeguard against the negative side-effects of a market economy and modern science and technology.

The connection of these factors to Mongolia's hereditary culture and pastoral nomadism is made explicit in Article VIII, Section 47, Points 1–6. Point 1 clearly enunciates the necessity of securing the Mongolian civilization by promising that Mongolia shall "formulate and pursue an active policy for reinforcing and enriching the basic characteristics of the nomadic civilization; preserve all valuable and progressive elements of Mongolian culture and traditions in economy statehood, material and intellectual life, and develop them in a harmonious combination with the values of world civilization" [VIII.47.1]. This statement means that Mongolian strategists and policymakers saw the fostering of nomadic culture and pastoral economy as vital to the nation's well-being so the concept pledges to create "an educational system in accordance with the traditions of the Mongolian Enlightenment" [VIII.47.3].[16] National security and national identity are linked openly in Article VIII.47.4 to preserving Mongolia's traditional heritage by advocating

> learning about and perceiving the history, culture and mentality of the people as well as the nature of the homeland, inculcate in every citizen, particularly the younger generation, a strong sense of patriotism and an aspiration to cherish the country's name; make the study, instruction and popularization of Mongolian history, religion and culture the special object of the government's constant care and support.

The vital significance of the traditional nomadic economy is emphasized by the pledge that the Mongolian government will

> carefully preserve and rely on the intrinsic ability of the Mongols to live in harmony with Nature, their traditional abiding respect for statehood, knowledge and talent displayed in thought and in deed, and their keen sense of community; restore and preserve specific types of the traditional economic Mongolian know-how and technology and the heritage of national culture and craftsmanship; and protect their work and masterpieces. [VIII.47.6–7]

Although it is clear that the Mongolian government's national security policy, politically speaking, supports nomads and the country's nomadic heritage, at the same time Mongolian policymakers sought to explicitly define who are and who are not Mongolian people. The concept supports the "Mongolian diaspora" in neighboring countries and emigrant communities around the world, but at the same time it rejects attaching any political meaning to such support. It advocates the expansion of

> relations and ties with Mongols living in other countries, [to] help them maintain and develop Mongolian culture and traditions; Mongolia being the ancestral homeland of the Mongols, while pursuing the policy of encouraging the desire of Mongols living abroad to see Mongolia develop, shall particularly, eschew the injection of any political intent in these relations. [VIII.47.10]

This definition of the relationship between Mongols in the homeland and those historically living in neighboring lands outside the modern borders can be understood as moving the latter from the "brothers" category to that of "cousins." It represents a new calculation of the role of "Mongol blood" in the Concept's definition of national identity found in the "Security of the Population and Its Gene Pool" [IX]. While this whole section deliberately is written to be vague in meaning, it directs national leaders to "formulate and pursue a comprehensive Government policy, aimed at ensuring the gene pool, health and sustained growth of the Mongolian population; revive, on public initiative, the tradition of keeping track and being aware of the family genealogy up to 7–9 generations of one's ancestors" [IX.51.1]. This emphasis on proven bloodlines permits the nation to establish through family genealogy who really is Mongolian, out of concern over the "sharp increase in the number of foreigners and stateless persons resident in Mongolia, and mass emigration of nationally trained personnel and skilled workers" [IX.34.8].

Pastoral nomadism, while in many ways distant from the realities of modern Mongolian city dwellers, captures the national imagination and differentiates Mongols from other Asians. Relevance of the nomadic tradition still remains the key to comprehending the Mongolian psyche. Mongolian policymakers have embraced their unique, but vaguely understood, heritage, codified it in their 2010 National Security Concept, and woven it into a modern definition of national identity, national security, and economic policy planning. The resurgence of this heritage makes it "normal" and "legitimate" and thus a force to be reckoned with in analyzing Mongolia's domestic and international actions. The Mongolian government now incorporates nomadic heritage as a potent representation of Mongolian soft-power image making. It is establishing a national reputation as the native land of nomadic tourism along the Silk Road and anticipates a surge of employment and growth in many spheres of the economy because tourism is one of the fastest growing industries globally.[17] By choosing and maintaining the nomadic brand as an identifying aspect of the tourism sector and endorsing it with frequency and consistency worldwide, Mongolia is positioning its form of tourism as a major contributor to the economy and the lives of its nomadic people. Recognizing that the country has not yet fully realized growth in this sector or in the process of creating a national brand identifier, the Ministry of Environment and Tourism has been making additional efforts by participating in international tourism expos, working to make Mongolia a leading destination for nomadic tours, and promoting tourism services that are competitive in the international market.

The policy directive "Sustainable Development Goals 2030 of Mongolia" outlined the government's decision to connect the Mongolian brand with nomadism and make Mongolia a center of nomadic tourism to diversify the economy and increase employment. Particularly in regard to nomadic tourism along the Silk Road, Mongolia aspires to build its national tourism brand and not let it slip solely into the hands of other nations such as China or the Central Asian states. Thus, the government believed its hosting of the UN World Tourism Organization (UNWTO) Silk Road Conference on Nomadic Tourism and Sustainable Cities in October 2016 further facilitated Mongolia's reputation as the native land of nomadic tourism.

Branding of Mongolia

Some Mongolian economists supported establishing a branding strategy for Mongolian products to break into the world market. In March 2013, respected economic commentator Dambaadarjaa Jargalsaikhan advocated that Mongolia develop a "blue strategy" of inventing a new marketplace and a new demand so that there would be no other global competition, rather than trying to stand out in an existing one. He recommended that the government nurture competition among companies in one sector such as cashmere, tourism, meat, IT, or mining logistics and then set up a shareholding company with most of its shares sold to the public on the stock exchange. Another idea he proposed was for Mongolia to be a railroad transit center, like the Panama Canal, for transportation of mineral resources between Russia and China. He supported a "Go nomadic, experience Mongolia" tourism campaign as a way to "implement the blue strategy in order to develop and diversify our economy."[18]

Mongolia in July 2011 officially established a Mongolian National Marketing Coordination Office (MNMCO) that reports to the Ministry of Foreign Relations, the Mongolian National Chamber of Commerce and Industry, and the National Development and Innovation Committee. MNMCO's strategy for building and sustaining the Mongolian national brand is "to achieve successful, sustainable and profitable international sales of branded goods, agricultural produce and services which promote a common image of Mongolia as a reliable, modern and sophisticated producer." The elements of the strategy are

- To use the reality of new, reliable brands (and government policies) to generate a particular international commercial reputation for Mongolia and Mongolians, as will help those, and other, brands succeed.
- To use coordinated messages in collectively branded exports (including tourism) in several sectors that will spearhead Mongolia's new world reputation. These sectors are based on relevant (i.e., relevant to the end consumers) quality and on production improvements to world-class standards, and selected for their commercial potential and as examples of elements of the international reputation that Mongolia wishes to enjoy.

- To use the developing reputation of Mongolia to underpin the reputation of the sector-branded exports (including tourism) and to enable innovative export products of quality.
- To set up collective marketing boards for each sector based on standards of quality, which ensure that the branding for each sector communicates consistent messages about Mongolia in line with a national strategy developed for the government by the MNMCO.
- To apply proven marketing techniques from successful global business to the national brand (i.e., Mongolia's reputation) and to its exports, and to promote these exports to selected, international, niche target audiences.
- To work with international donors and other NGOs already engaged in projects of supply-side improvement and/or market access so that all such projects contribute to each other's success and work in line with government strategy.[19]

The promotion of nomadism to the Mongolian public and its glorification in tourist promotion were devised for Mongolia to brand its cultural heritage throughout the world through what the government calls Cultural and Humanitarian Foreign Policy. This is defined as

> protecting the culture and the way of life of Mongols, endowing their unique cultural heritage and enriching it with the achievements of world culture, restoring national historical and cultural assets, recovering cultural and art relics from abroad, in using cultural cooperation for the purpose of educating and training skilled personnel capable of working in new conditions, introducing Mongolia to foreign countries, expanding the ranks of well-wishers and supporters of Mongolia, encouraging Mongolian studies in other nations and promoting mutual understanding and trust.[20]

One prime example is utilizing the UNESCO system of registering cultural practices as unique world treasures. Mongolia in 2008 first registered the *morin khuur* or horse-headed fiddle with UNESCO. In 2009 it placed the traditional *biyelgee* folk dance, the Mongolian heroic epic *tuuli* stories, and *tsuur* wooden wind instrumental music on the list in need of urgent safeguarding. In 2010 *khoomei* throat singing and the *naadam* festival were registered on UNESCO's List of Intangible Cultural Heritage. In 2011 *limbe* flute circular breathing and in 2013 the "Ganjuur Sutra" of 1819, Mongolian calligraphy, and Mongolian *ger* were all copyrighted with UNESCO. In 2015 the famous "coaxing camel ritual" was added. Mongols have promoted the marketing value of these traditions to domestic and foreign audiences. For example, in July 2014 Mongolia media called the Naadam Festival's "Three Men's Games" (wrestling, horse racing, and archery) a major contributor to the world's cultural heritage, and President Elbegdorj in the opening ceremonies asserted that the Naadam Festival was Mongolia's "brand" to advertise the country abroad:

> The Great National Festivity, Naadam, is an innate treasure of the Mongol people, which embodies our glorious history, cherished dreams and collective power. The Mongol Naadam attests through time that the accuracy of aiming the arrow, speed and stamina of the horses, and the strength and clout of the fine men of our fathers and forefathers, who upheld good governance, rule of law and order in the world, remain as firm and sustained as ever.[21]

Another major brand for Mongolia both nationally and internationally has been its dinosaur fossils. The Mongolian government in 2016 opened a new museum in Ulaanbaatar solely to house newly discovered or recovered dinosaur bones. It cited Mongolia's 2010 Foreign Policy Concept, which declared that "restoring and protecting Mongolia's historical, cultural and natural heritage and assets and in sharing them with other nations, Mongolia shall cooperate with Asian countries which have similar historical, religious and cultural legacies as well as with other interested countries, UNESCO and other related international organizations."[22] The Elbegdorj government successfully publicized the country's connection with its dinosaur past by working for the repatriation of fossils that had been smuggled outside the country. In 2013–2014, eighteen skeletons were returned to the Mongols at the United Nations in New York and another group of dinosaur eggs and bones in April 2016. It is expected that US and other customs authorities will repatriate additional eight-million-year-old fossil skeletons smuggled out between 2005 and 2012.

Promotion of Mongolian Studies Abroad

Another form of branding is to promulgate Mongolian studies worldwide as part of the Foreign Ministry's mandate to enhance "contacts and cooperation with Mongolian nationals residing abroad and mutual support in preserving and developing the Mongolian language, culture, and traditions as well as securing their contributions to Mongolia's progress and growth."[23] President Elbegdorj originally presented this idea at the tenth International Congress of Mongolists in Ulaanbaatar in 2011 when proposing the establishment of a Mongol Studies Foundation, chaired by the prime minister, to support and finance researchers on Mongolia around the world. In addition, the National Council on Mongol Studies was established to implement numerous projects promoting the study of Mongolian language, culture, and history. The Mongolian government's purpose was "to preserve our national uniqueness, while keeping up with the achievements and discoveries of humanity in the globalization era."[24] A special fund was proposed in 2012 to implement the National Program for Promoting Mongolian Studies, and Parliament voted the funding in 2014. The Council of Mongolians Abroad was founded in 2014 under the auspices of the Foreign Affairs Ministry to coordinate associations and NGOs supporting Mongolian citizens living abroad and to protect the rights of Mongolians residing, working, and studying abroad. The Council aims to implement a comprehensive policy to find solutions for specific difficulties and provide Mongolian citizens with opportunities to contribute to the development and prosperity of their homeland. The Foreign Ministry sponsored a second meeting of the Association of Mongolians Abroad with NGOs in Ulaanbaatar in October 2016 to introduce its new program for 2016–2020 entitled World Mongolians. This ministry will be implementing its activities to protect the rights of 130,000 Mongolian citizens abroad through forty-six diplomatic missions in foreign countries. In collaboration with the Ministry of Education, Culture, Science, and Sports, it will focus on teaching Mongolian language to children living abroad and providing them with textbooks. This program also includes negotiating visa waivers and travel rights for Mongolian citizens.[25]

The promotion of traditional Mongolian culture has a foreign affairs component, as seen in Elbegdorj's policy of returning to the official use of the traditional Mongol *bicig* script. This script was utilized by the early democratic movement protesters as a symbol of nationhood and rejection of the communist-imposed Cyrillic Mongol script. The new democratic government in 1991 had adopted a resolution to reinstitute this script for all official business by 1994, but this goal proved unachievable and was ultimately abandoned.[26] In 2010 on the occasion of the 100th anniversary of the restoration of national freedom with the collapse of the Manchu Qing dynasty, the president issued a decree requiring any official correspondence and letters of the president, speaker, prime minister, and government members to their foreign counterparts to be written in traditional Mongolian script along with a translation in the official language of the country or the UN.[27] He also placed the *bicig* script on his official government website. In February 2015, the Mongolian Parliament passed a law legalizing the use of both Mongolian Cyrillic and traditional Mongol *bicig* as official scripts starting from 2025.

The Foreign Ministry since 2014 has worked together with Mongolia's Ministry of Education, Culture, Science, and Sports to establish Mongolian Cultural Centers throughout the world to project Mongolian soft power internationally.[28] It appears that this concept may have been inspired by the Chinese Confucius Institutes.[29] There was the suggestion in 2016 that the Mongols rename these centers "Genghis Khan" Schools throughout Eurasia in order to highlight Mongolia as a country with "empirical" knowledge from its historical experience as a world empire and to explain to other countries how Mongolia converted its disadvantages to its benefit:

> Looked at from this perspective, if the wisdom buried in Mongolia's historical experience could be brought back into the light, and converted to spiritual and intellectual resources, that could lead to the creation and dissemination of content capable of serving the needs of the world community. In other words it would feed the development of "soft power." . . . Because this will be a cultural rather than a political process, it will not become a cause of friction among currently existing states.[30]

At the same time, it was thought that promotion of a borderless, multicultural Mongolian identity could raise Mongolia's image globally and be useful in helping to establish an international base of support for Mongolia. This concept was described as another dimension of Mongolia's "Third Neighbor" policy wherein shared memories will open the way to a new consciousness, new relationships, and new institutional frameworks, and such "borderless connections" could help create a new mentality for the Eurasian community.

The Elbegdorj government recognized that its efforts to raise the profile of Mongolian civilization and traditional heritage throughout the world needed to be more efficiently organized within the Ministry of Foreign Affairs. Accordingly, the ministry established a new Public Diplomacy and Communications Department in 2015 with responsibility for the promotion of cultural heritage, modern art forms, and people-to-people exchanges. Likely this was modeled on the US Department of State's Bureau of Public Diplomacy and Public Affairs, which combines educational and cultural affairs with a global perspective. The goals of this Mongolian diplomatic top-down strategy are to influence public opinion in foreign countries,

> including increasing foreign direct investment (FDI), promoting tourism, and playing a more substantial role in international politics by emphasizing its strategic position. But for Mongolia to be able to attract FDI, it needs to first demonstrate that investors are making worthwhile investments. In a word, the Mongolian economy would be able to make good returns on the investment. In order to attract tourism, it needs to present its culture as rich and unique. And to play a larger role in world politics, Mongolia would need to showcase itself as a model of good governance as well as successfully persuade other players that Mongolia is in a position to be of strategic importance.[31]

An important objective for the Mongols was to promote the uniqueness of Mongolia's democratization in a potentially unstable region. This reflected Elbegdorj's belief that for Mongolia to continue to attract foreign investment it needs to enhance its reputation for democratic stability and be seen as a reliable investment environment. This image also allows it to claim a role as a diplomatic mediator in the region.

"One-Window" Foreign Relations Policy on Diplomatic Relations

Another image-raising initiative of the Elbegdorj years was to expand official diplomatic relations and increase the country's bilateral footprint. This was a well-conceived concept of the president and his proactive foreign minister, Lu. Bold, to raise the country's profile on the international stage. Therefore, the Ministry of Foreign Affairs announced in its 2012–2013 action plan its intention to establish diplomatic relations with all United Nations member states. As part of the 100th anniversary of the establishment of Mongolia's contemporary diplomatic service, the guiding principle, termed the "One-Window" policy, was initiated to emphasize the coherence of national foreign policy and actions, as well as dissemination of correct information about Mongolia's stable and transparent environment for foreign investors.[32] This was an attempt to counter the 43 percent decline in foreign investment during the first half of 2013. In 2013–2016 bilateral relations were established with twenty-four nations, mainly Caribbean, Pacific Island, and African countries.[33] Most of these bilateral diplomatic communiqués were negotiated and signed in New York City or Beijing. Mongolia now has diplomatic relations with 188 countries, the Holy See, and the European Union and wants to open relations with the remaining UN members.[34] The one-window policy was promoted by both Minister of Foreign Affairs Lundeg Purevsuren[35] and his successor MPP Foreign Minister Mönkh-Orgil, who said,

> Extending relations with many countries means that the country is enforcing its independence and security through diplomatic channels. It is important to support political relations with commercial, economic, cultural and interpersonal ties. . . . Our weight will be increased as we unite voices with many other countries. Solidarity of small countries against big ones is important and more effective in decision making.[36]

As of 2016, there were twenty-four resident embassies in Ulaanbaatar, with the majority of the rest accredited from Beijing, Seoul, New York, or Moscow. Mongolia has thirty-two embassies and twelve consulates abroad. To increase its global visibility, Mongolia in recent years has established new embassies in Brazil and Indonesia, and new consulates-general in Istanbul, Turkey, and Bishkek, Kyrgyzstan. An honorary consulate was opened in 2012 in Edinburgh, Scotland, and in 2013 in Samsun, Turkey. President Elbegdorj on October 4, 2013, personally opened a new honorary consulate in Chicago. In 2014 honorary consulates were opened in Albania and in Blagoevgrad, Bulgaria, and in 2015 in Eskishehir, Turkey.

Another example of welding culture and diplomacy is found in the new policy of appointing cultural envoys and ambassadors, including an Olympic champion wrestler, a ballet artist, and a sumo wrestler, to promote Mongolia abroad. The Elbegdorj government was very creative in using public-to-public interactions and sports to develop a positive reputation for the country. A notable example is utilizing the dominance of Mongolian wrestlers in Japan's sumo circles since 2003 to strengthen the Japanese-Mongolian partnership. Mongolia has had several Yokozuna Grand Champions, and more than thirty Mongolian wrestlers are competing in five different highest divisions. Sumo competitions have become popular broadcasts on Mongolian TV, and Mongolian sumo wrestlers have returned home to invest in private business projects and run for Parliament. Retired professional judo wrestler Battulga, who became Mongolia's president in 2017, is very supportive of sports diplomacy.

Changing the Independence Date of the Nation

In 2011 the Elbegdorj government changed the date of the modern Mongolian state's independence away from the communist-linked July 11 revolution to December 29. There was a much-publicized campaign to celebrate this 100th anniversary of the nation, but at the same time there was little explanation for the new emphasis on 1911 instead of 1921. The calculations behind the move reveal the complexity behind Mongolia's soft-power initiatives. The new independence date de facto includes the legitimizing of the autonomous Lamaist government of the Bogdo Khaan, which assumed political power on that date, and cleverly de-emphasizes the communist revolution of July 1921. The new celebrations were part of a legal process to define Mongolia's twentieth-century national identity from the viewpoint of international law. This particular date confirms that Mongolia declared its modern independence after the official fall of the Manchu Qing dynasty on October 10, 1911, but before the official parliamentary declaration of the Republic of China on January 1, 1912, so it ipso facto invalidates any Chinese legal claim to Mongolian territory. Fundamentally, the new celebration date was a Mongolian reaction to China—a symbolic shot across the bow to say that the Mongols have been independent of their large southern neighbors 100 years and will continue to remain so. But the lack of clarity about the reasons for choosing a new independence date also reflects the Mongolian government's concern about China's reaction. By toning down notification to the world and its own people of the reasons behind the new date, Mongolia gave what Sinologists call "face" to China, in hopes of warning but not insulting its largest trade partner and customer.

This date also is associated with the revival of Buddhism in democratic Mongolia, which was specially mentioned in the 1994 National Security Concept [3.1.4.7]: "Revive and develop Buddhist religion and culture. Encourage activities of monasteries and temples towards enlightenment of societal wisdom, strengthening national unity, alleviating poverty, disaster relief and protection of the natural environment." President Elbegdorj, like his predecessor Enkhbayar, is a strong Buddhist and has not shied away from publicly associating Mongolian culture with Tibetan Buddhist traditions. Nevertheless, Elbegdorj has been sensitive to China's anxiety about Mongolia's ties to the leader of Tibetan Buddhism. He met with the Fourteenth Dalai Lama in November 2011 in Ulaanbaatar, but canceled the Dalai Lama's August 2014 visit due to pressure from China when he arranged a state visit by Chinese President Xi that same month.

Creating New International Organizations

One of the major components of Mongolia's soft-power initiative has been to increase its diplomatic ties beyond its border neighbors and the advanced democracies it emphasized in the first decade of its democracy. In the 2010s the Mongolian government has made it a priority to significantly expand its ties across the continent of Eurasia all the way to the Middle East and Iran. Reengaging with Turco-Iranian culture-dominated nations has meant that Mongolia's "Third Neighbor" policy had to be broadened beyond democratic societies to include those autocratic countries that emerged in Eurasia to become important energy suppliers, rogue states such as North Korea and Iran that have outsized impact on their regions, and nations in Africa and South America with whom it had no previous trade or cultural contacts. Diplomatic outreach increased dramatically with Southeast and South Asian countries, from Vietnam to Indonesia to Myanmar, especially through high-level visits.

Mongolia in the last few years has exhibited its increasingly activist agenda by creating new international organizations to focus on problems that are of concern to the nation and its region. This is explained on the Mongolian Ministry of Foreign Affairs website, which notes that the third direction of the nation's foreign policy activity is

> strengthening its position in Asia and securing a constructive participation in the political and economic integration process in the region. Within the framework of this objective, greater attention shall be given to Asia and the Pacific region, in particular to North-East and Central Asia. Mongolia shall take an active part in the process of initiating dialogues and negotiations on the issues of strengthening regional security and creating a collective security mechanism. It will strive to become a member of the Asia-Pacific Economic Cooperation forum (APEC). Prerequisites for participating in regional integration shall be created primarily through expanding and promoting bilateral relations with the countries of the region.[37]

Foreign policy strategists have suggested that it was "time for Mongolia not to understate itself as a 'small' nation, but become a regional actor."[38] These policymakers called for establishing a multilateral diplomacy platform wherein the country would take new initiatives and propose new strategies so international organizations and foreign countries could conduct dialogues on international issues. This diplomatic activism, generally labeled Karakorum, is expected to increase Mongolia's role and international influence, ensure Mongolian national security in new ways by decreasing its vulnerability, bring economic benefits to the local economy, and strengthen its human resources capacity by training more Mongolian diplomats in the role of international organizations.[39]

Ulaanbaatar Dialogue on Northeast Asia Security

Mongolia's most publicized new initiative is the Ulaanbaatar Dialogue on Northeast Asia Security (UBD), whose objectives are defusing tension on the Korean Peninsula and enhancing NEA security through open dialogue. The brainchild of President Elbegdorj, this new security dialogue mechanism was announced in April 2013 at the VII Ministerial Conference of the Community of Democracies as a part of Mongolia's larger ambition of acting as a third-party mediator in contentious issues such as the question of Korean Peninsular security.[40] At that time Elbegdorj proclaimed that "Mongolia is willing to open up new gateways for the issues at standstill"[41] and that UBD's goal was to assist in and facilitate a peaceful solution to the confrontation on the Korean Peninsula. Mongolia's claim to mediator status is based on its assertion of impartiality in any specific conflict, but also as an interested party to overall regional security. Such a claim is valid, given Mongolia's strategic geographical location as a small democratic nation sandwiched between two large autocratic neighbors. Furthermore, Mongolia has built up an image of a stable and responsible nation that is exercising soft power and cooperative trust-building as an effective agent of diplomatic mediation in international politics.

The Ministry of Foreign Affairs quoted President Elbegdorj as saying, "A duck is calm when the lake is calm," which is an adage indicative of Mongolia's broader foreign policy considerations in Northeast Asia. Mongolia maintains that its own interests are best served when the regional security environment is stable, so it seeks to resolve misunderstandings and disputes through dialogue and discussion. Although Northeast Asia is often labeled as one of the most complex places in the world, it holds a great deal of potential as Asia becomes the engine of the world's economic development. Mongolian policymakers view the regional situation as delicate because North-South Korean issues disrupt regional integration efforts and negatively affect long-term stability, and the nations of the region have unresolved historical and territorial disputes among them: "As an integral part of Northeast Asia, Mongolia prioritizes these regional concerns. It remains one of our top foreign policy objectives not only to develop and strengthen ties with our neighbors but also to constructively contribute our share to the common well-being and security of the region."[42] Mongolian interest in participating in a regional security dialogue in NEA dates back to the early 1980s, when it called for an all-Asian convention prohibiting the use of force to prevent conflicts. In 2000 it began to explore the idea of joining in the Six-Party Talks without achieving any positive feedback from the majority of its participants. In 2008 the Mongolian Institute for Strategic Studies, which is associated with the Ministry of Defense and Mongolian intelligence agencies, hosted a conference on Security Perspectives of Central and Northeast Asia: Ulaanbaatar as a New Helsinki, which was the catalyst for President Elbegdorj's UBD initiative a year later.

When examining why Mongolia promulgated the UBD, it is likely that it had determined it could not solve its own trade and FDI imbalance problems unless there were significant progress on building NEA infrastructure and connectivity through North Korea to the Pacific. Believing that the lack of movement in the Six-Party Talks and Mongolia's continued exclusion from the process could not be overcome by further patience, Elbegdorj's decision to create the UBD was a culmination of years of failed Mongolian back-channel attempts to get the attention of the Six-Party nations, and it also indicates that North Korea was supportive of this initiative. However, Mongolia publicly explained that it created the UBD because it has friendly relations with all countries in Northeast Asia, has no territorial disputes with any of its neighboring countries, and already had a track record of playing an active role in international multilateral mechanisms such as the UN, ASEM, and the Organization for Security and Co-operation in Europe (OSCE). Citing lack of progress in the Six-Party Talks, one Mongolian researcher asserted that "the role of Mongolia can be like Switzerland during WWII—a stable, neutral state serving as a facilitator and mediator of dialogue and conflict resolution."[43] The Foreign Ministry further asserted that because

> Mongolia is uniquely positioned in the region to facilitate the economic integration, development of common infrastructure, use of energy resources, protection of environment, and cooperation in fighting transnational crime, Ulaanbaatar can serve as a neutral meeting ground, literally and metaphorically, as Northeast Asia's Geneva and can be a multilateral venue for regional security dialogue.[44]

The UBD focuses on Track 1.5 and Track 2 efforts[45] so as not to compete with the Six-Party Talks (Track 1). The Mongols choose to utilize Track 1.5 and Track 2 channels so that officials and politicians can meet with academics and talk about security issues under the Chatham House rule.[46] The UBD's objective is to contribute to mutual understanding and greater confidence in order to achieve both "formal and practical security cooperation and consultation."[47] It is organized by the Mongolian Ministry of Foreign Affairs and Mongolia's Institute for Strategic Studies (ISS) around priority areas that are particularly related to NEA problems, to resolve or mitigate challenges affecting regional stability. The fields selected for discussion are (1) traditional security issues; (2) nontraditional security issues; (3) energy connectivity; (4) environmental protection; and (5) infrastructural development.

The first UBD on June 17, 2014, included thirty-five representatives from Mongolia, Russia, China, Japan, North Korea, South Korea, the United States, Germany, and the Netherlands. Conference discussion focused on the present NEA security situation, reasons for the absence of a regional security mechanism, the role of economic and environmental factors in promoting regional cooperation and confidence, and suggestions on how to promote trust and closer regional cooperation.[48] One of the Mongolian keynote speakers, Migeddorj Batchimeg, parliamentarian and a member of the ISS policy council, emphasized that Mongolia believes there is no single formal mechanism for Korean Peninsula discussions and that the UBD could be a useful venue: "Solutions to big problems do not have to start big."[49] Despite the fact that more than 50 percent of conference time was devoted to heated discussion on historical Asian disputes instead of nuclear and militarization issues on the Korean Peninsula, the Mongolian government concluded that the UBD "is not a single action, but a mechanism of trilateral or multilateral dialogues depending on the agenda,"[50] and immediately announced that the conference would be organized annually.

The second UBD international conference took place on June 25–26, 2015, in Ulaanbaatar. Although the number of participants was over 100 and included a representative from India, the North Koreans did not participate. The focus was on energy and transportation connectivity in addition to traditional and nontraditional security trends and opportunities.[51] Mongolian presenters acknowledged that neighboring countries still questioned "Mongolia's potential in this regard, so our efforts to play this role in the region must be more proactive. . . . Going forward, this engagement needs to be upgraded and expanded to continue to promote peace in the region and to impact the future of all countries in Northeast Asia."[52] The third meeting of the UBD was held on June 16–17, 2016. The focus was on "Environmental Protection and Disaster Management in NEA." The DPRK Foreign Ministry sent a delegation headed by a director and a deputy of the Institute for American Studies. North Korean and ROK officials were seen engaging in side discussions. A Mongolian diplomat remarked that the statements of the DPRK representatives were more nuanced and "even thought-provoking. They participated in the discussions and willingly responded to questions raised or comments made. . . . I think that UBD is useful and the two Koreas can make use of such a venue."[53] This positive evaluation was echoed by a Chinese researcher:

> The Ulaanbaatar Dialogue on Northeast Asian Affairs is a worthwhile exploration on the construction of [a] multilateral mechanism in a region which is still [in] lack of any formal forum or dialogue of the same kind.

> It contributes to the solution of security problems and economic integration in the region by means of talks and negotiations, in which Mongolia has been playing an increasingly proactive role.[54]

On June 14–15, 2017, the fourth UBD, financially supported by the German Social Democratic Party–affiliated Friedrich Ebert Foundation, brought a return of the North Koreans to the discussions despite an increasingly tense international situation featuring additional UN sanctions on the DPRK. The DPRK foreign minister also attended and held bilateral meetings on the sidelines with some of the other governments represented, including Canada and Japan. ISS organizer Damba Ganbat explained why Mongolia went forward with the meeting:

> Mongolia is in a unique position to act as an honest broker for peace and security in Northeast Asia, and Ulaanbaatar is the perfect place for a constructive dialogue between otherwise hostile countries. That is why, besides the Ulaanbaatar Dialogue, Mongolia is continuously hosting meetings of parliamentarians, mayors, and researchers from Northeast Asia. We hope that these efforts will ultimately lead to a collective architecture of peace and security in Northeast Asia, comparable to the OSCE [Organization for Security and Co-operation] in Europe.[55]

Mongolian optimism was rewarded in 2018 when, during the fifth round of the UBD on June 14–15, which took place just three days after the Trump-Kim Singapore summit, the over 150 attendees responded positively to the cooperative atmosphere, and there was the suggestion that the UBD could begin a new Helsinki process. The delegates particularly examined NEA security from the perspectives of environment, energy, and humanitarian assistance.[56]

Under the auspices of the UBD, Mongolia has organized other unique initiatives specifically concerned with Northeast Asian issues. On November 25, 2013, the Mongolian government hosted a conference on the "Role of Women Parliamentarians in Promoting Peace and Development Through Education."[57] This was the first meeting expressly for female parliament members and was attended by representatives from Mongolia, Russia, China, DPRK, and ROK. Its objective was to gather regional representatives for discussions about NEA peace and development. A year later in August, the Mongols hosted a "Sustainable and Inclusive Cities" Northeast Asian Mayors Forum. About 120 delegates from cities across the region reviewed existing cooperation among the nations and explored areas for cultural, industrial, economic, and agricultural development. Operating under the framework of the UBD, on March 17–18, 2015, the ISS, Institute of Energy and Economy, and Ministry of Foreign Affairs jointly initiated an international conference attended by delegates from six Northeast Asian countries on Northeast Asian "Energy Connectivity." Also, in 2015 on the sidelines of the UBD, the Northeast Asian Youth Symposium for Regional Cooperation was organized in conjunction with the Mongolian Youth Federation, the Ministry of Foreign Affairs, and ISS. Delegates from Mongolia, Russia, China, Japan, ROK, and the United States discussed UBD confidence-building in NEA. The role of youth in regional cooperation was outlined in its draft declaration, which called for greater NEA governmental engagement with youth to promote regional stability and cooperation.

International Think Tank for LLDCs

The idea to establish a think tank for Landlocked Developing Countries and Transit Countries (LLDCs) originated in the International Ministerial Conference of Landlocked and Transit Developing Countries with donor countries and international financial institutions that was held in Almaty, Kazakhstan, in 2003. This conference specifically addressed the transit and infrastructural problems facing LLDCs. A later interagency meeting endorsed the Almaty Programme of Action to launch a think tank for studying issues surrounding trade in LLDCs. When Mongolian President Enkhbayar addressed a meeting of LLDC heads of state in Havana in 2006, he supported coordinating efforts to establish the international think tank to develop best-practice strategies. The Global Event of Landlocked Developing Countries and Transit Countries on Trade and Trade Facilitation in Ulaanbaatar in 2007 conducted a midterm review of the Almaty Programme. There the LLDCs agreed to consider placing the international think tank in Ulaanbaatar. That same year, the UN General Assembly adopted the Ulaanbaatar declaration, and in 2008 it passed a resolution welcoming

> the proposal to set up an international think tank in Ulaanbaatar to enhance the analytical capability of landlocked developing countries needed to maximize the efficiency of our coordinated efforts for the effective implementations of the international agreed provisions, particularly the Almaty Programme of Action and the Millennium Development Goals. In April 2009 UNESCAP adopted a resolution entitled "Support for the establishment of an international think tank of landlocked developing countries."[58]

In July 2009, immediately after President Elbegdorj assumed office, the International Think Tank for LLDC was officially launched in Ulaanbaatar by UN Secretary-General Ban Ki-moon and Mongolian Minister of Foreign Affairs Sukhbaatar Batbold. The goal of the International Think Tank (ITT) "is to use top-quality research and advocacy to improve the ability of landlocked developing countries to build capacity with a view to benefiting from the international trade including WTO negotiations, with the ultimate aim of raising human development and reducing poverty."[59] ITT objectives are to (1) produce and disseminate research studies on trade-related topics, transport and transit, and databases; (2) promote cooperation between landlocked developing countries to strengthen their analytical capacity in transit transport, infrastructure investment, aid and trade facilitation, trade negotiations, poverty reduction, and economic growth; (3) share information and network among landlocked developing countries; (4) execute analytical studies and research on the effective implementation of the Almaty Programme of Action; (5) foster agreement on approaches to global economic issues facing landlocked developing countries such as effects of the global economic and financial crisis, climate change, and food security; (6) establish long-term relationships with international organizations, the UN, and development partners to mobilize awareness of the special needs of landlocked developing countries and find financial and technical resources for research implementation; and (7) distribute all research results to landlocked developing countries, development partners, and partner research institutions.

Since its inception, the ITT has held numerous international conferences on many topics.[60] One of the key events in 2016 was a joint seminar in Ulaanbaatar with the Economic Research Institute for Northeast Asia (ERINA) of Niigata, Japan, on "Trade Policy Issues of Mongolia." Among the topics discussed were developing and promoting export-oriented high-value-added industries, creating free trade and economic zones along with industrial and technological parks, increasing trade, attracting FDI, and establishing national industrial development policy.[61]

Forum of Asia

Another Eurasia-based soft-power initiative proposed by President Elbegdorj was for a mini-UN-like dialogue platform, which he called Forum of Asia, to build mutual trust and boost regional integration.[62] This is distinct from a similarly titled entity called Forum-Asia, an Asian forum for human rights and development.[63] On May 21, 2015, in Tokyo, Elbegdorj suggested that his Forum of Asia platform should promote equal representation of Asian nations, small or big, to guarantee the independence, integrity, and development models of all members. He likened it to a small UN in Asia, but with all countries' having equal status. Calling Mongolia an honest broker in dealing with promotion of peace and security, Elbegdorj evoked the days of the Mongol Empire when his people "actively engaged with nations near and far in Asia, Europe and the Middle East. It was an era when the Mongols strove to establish a new world order—justice, peace and cooperation in their relations with other states and peoples."[64]

In this speech and another one three weeks later at the European Parliament in Strasbourg, France, he emphasized his nation's commitment to the political and economic integration processes in the Asia Pacific region, which has no single mechanism of regional integration that includes all forty-eight Asian states. He asserted that Mongolia's commitment to international cooperation was strong and the Forum of Asia "will serve as a much-needed mechanism to promote regional integration of all sovereign nations in Asia, promoting equal representation of their diverse interests."[65] However, reaction to this suggestion was tepid and still has not moved beyond the discussion phase.

International Cooperation Fund

The promotion of Mongolia's civilizational experience in adapting its communist economy and society to the free market and democracy is the basis of the new international activism behind the International Cooperation Fund (ICF), which was established March 13, 2013.[66] At the same time, this is a key element of Mongolia's ongoing process of redefining its Third Neighbor Policy, as it shares its experiences in democracy building, human rights, and a market economy with other ex-socialist/communist nations such as Myanmar, Kyrgyzstan, Afghanistan, Nepal, and Kampuchea. President Elbegdorj has explained that "Mongolia does not have an intention to teach others about democracy or path to development. Yet we have lessons to share with others."[67] He has proclaimed that Mongolia's desire is to be a responsible member of the international community and "become more active in tackling broader Asian issues which have impacted Mongolia's regional transportation and communication options."[68]

ICF's activities are supervised by a council that is chaired by the minister of foreign affairs. Other council members include the foreign policy adviser to the prime minister, the foreign policy and national security adviser to the president, and other high-level officials from the Ministry of Foreign Affairs and National Security Council who are appointed by the minister of foreign affairs. The ICF is financed through the state budget, grants, and contributions from various development partners including foreign governments, international organizations, domestic and foreign private enterprises, and individuals. The Mongolian government is utilizing the ICF as an important tool to advance and implement foreign policy objectives in compliance with the Concept of National Security and Foreign Policy Concept to strengthen the nation's role and contributions internationally as a means of projecting soft power. Such a fund is quite unusual since Mongolia, a developing country that is still donor-assistance dependent to some degree, is utilizing its own budget resources to reach out to other developing countries.

It organizes conferences and diplomatic training seminars in Mongolia to share best practices for transition to democracy and the democratic process, to expand bilateral cooperation with countries in the Eurasian continental region, and to provide development and technical support for emerging democracies.[69] In October 2017, ICF hosted an international conference themed "Constitutional Amendment: The Case of Mongolia." More than eighty foreign and domestic government officials participated in a discussion on Mongolian constitutional principles, human rights, freedom, enforcement of the constitution, and improvement of procedures on drafting amendments.[70] The ICF also sends national experts in democracy, human rights, and good governance to relevant international events. Over the last few years the IFC has funded projects in building effective parliamentary democracy and legal reform with Kyrgyzstan and trained Myanmar's public officers in the field of constitutional and election laws,[71] together with hosting media workers, journalists, and civil society members. In Afghanistan it has conducted training for diplomats and public servants. The Fund has been used to engage North Korea in economic and security dialogue and to support children's summer camps, basketball training, and other exchanges in order to promote positive peace and people-to-people development.

The results of Mongolia's new ICF soft-power initiatives are already bearing fruit. The Kyrgyz delegation expressed interest in learning from Mongolia how to better develop Kyrgyzstan's form of parliamentary democracy and market economy.[72] The Kyrgyz prime minister was quoted as saying that "Mongolia's model of democracy is more appropriate to the country as the two countries have many similarities such as traditions, lifestyles, culture and history."[73] In 2016, ICF partnered with Canadian International Resources and Development Institute (CIRDI),[74] a center of expertise in strengthening natural resource governance in the extractive sector, to organize a workshop with the Mongolian Ministry of Foreign Affairs on "The State's Role in Large Resource Projects" to assist the Mongols in sharing their experiences with other developing nations.[75]

Mongolian Activism Within Established International Organizations

Some of Mongolia's new methods of raising its global image and reputation as well as providing temporary stimuli for its capital's economy are to develop a reputation for organizing multilateral events, increase its footprint as a prime international tourism destination, and make its capital of Ulaanbaatar an emerging venue for international conferences. As of 2017, Mongolia was a member of over seventy international and intergovernmental organizations, so it has approached the organizing committees of these organizations to offer Ulaanbaatar as host city.

Mongolia became chair of the Community of Democracies[76] (CD) in July 2011 with the strong support of the United States. This global intergovernmental coalition of democratic countries was established in 2000 with the mandate to promote democracy education and civil society. Every two years participating states of the CD hold a Ministerial Conference, the biggest meeting of democratic countries in the world. Its Governing Council is the core decisionmaking body and is responsible for the activities undertaken on behalf of the CD. During Mongolia's two-year chairmanship, it helped create the Initiative Group on Education for Democracy and the Asian Partnership Initiative for Democracy. At the completion of its term as chair, Mongolia successfully hosted the seventh Ministerial Conference of Community of Democracies on April 27–29, 2013. During this conference it welcomed 800 delegates from 103 nations, including US Deputy Secretary of State William J. Byrnes. The conference concluded with the Ulaanbaatar Declaration,[77] and President Elbegdorj pledged to continue to give an annual contribution of $150,000 to the CD to support the movement as a "moral duty."[78] Spinoffs from the conference included meetings of the Parliamentary Forum for Democracy, the Corporate Democracy Forum, and the Youth Forum. Mongolia continues to be a member of the CD's Governing Council and contributes $150,000 annually to support its activities.

The Mongols have cooperated with the World Economic Forum (WEF) of Davos, Switzerland, since signing a cooperation memorandum with the WEF in 2013 to assist in shaping Mongolia's development strategy. President Elbegdorj realized that this cooperation would enable the country to make great strides in name recognition and economic promotion at the international level. The WEF, the world's biggest brainstorming exercise among world leaders and specialized experts on urgent global issues, has dialogue meetings around the world as well as its annual summit in Davos. On September 14–15, 2013, the WEF coordinated a mini-dialogue in Ulaanbaatar on "Strategic Dialogue on Mongolian Development" to develop potential Mongolian developmental scenarios, which subsequently were discussed in late January 2014 at the annual Davos summit. "The aim of the partnership between Mongolia and the World Economic Forum is for the scenarios to be used as a tool for public discourse, helping Mongolia and its key stakeholders shape the transformation that is under way in this changing and increasingly connected emerging economy."[79] The Mongolian Ministry of Foreign Affairs proclaimed that this first mini-event was very successful in promoting the country internationally and projected an accurate view to foreign countries about Mongolia as an open and democratic nation for new FDI and investments. At the 2014 annual meeting, WEF Executive Chairman Klaus Schwab stated,

> Before, our purpose was to introduce Mongolia to the Annual Meeting of the WEF, but now, Mongolia has become an active partner of the WEF. We are glad to see that Mongolia is strengthening its position in the WEF, actively participating in the session on anticorruption, governance, water, fair mineral development and other important issues.[80]

The WEF has eighty-six Global Agenda Councils. In November 2013, Puntsag Tsagaan, chief of staff of the president of Mongolia, participated in the WEF's sixth summit on the Global Agenda Council in Abu Dhabi as a member of the Global Agenda Council on Responsible Mineral Resources Management.[81] This Council was leading the Responsible Mineral Development Initiative, which examines stakeholder engagement and how the extractive industry can create shared value. Mongolia has attended the annual WEF meetings to elevate its reputation. For example, on the sidelines of the January 2016 Davos Summit, the Mongolian delegates organized a "Mongolia night" event to introduce the nation's economic environment, investment opportunities, and development goals.

United Nations Activities

A major factor in Mongolian soft-power outreach is its active collaboration with the United Nations, its specialized agencies, and other international financial, trade, and economic institutions. Such cooperation has served as a significant engine for the social and economic development of the country for several decades. Mongolia, which celebrated the fiftieth anniversary of its accession to the UN in 2014, believes that its participation in UN activities provides many opportunities to strengthen its world reputation and maintain its independence and national security such as by actively contributing to peacekeeping, or receiving grants and assistance for social and economic projects. Mongolia's UN assessment is measured by factors such as a country's national income and population size. Its 2016 assessment was $124,000 annual membership dues or $800,000 over five years, while over the same five-year period, the UN agreed to implement projects and programs worth $79 million for Mongolia.[82] Over fifty Mongolian citizens work at the UN Secretariat in New York and various associated international organizations' headquarters in Geneva. In June 2016, Oyun Sanjaasuren, Mongolia's minister of environment and green development and a parliamentarian, was elected as the first president of the UN Environment Assembly in Nairobi.[83]

Mongolia increasingly has hosted UN conferences both to boost Ulaanbaatar as an international conference location and to diversify Mongolia's economy. One such event was its hosting on October 13–15, 2016, of the UNWTO Silk Road Conference on Nomadic Tourism and Sustainable Cities, sponsored by the UN World Tourism Organization together with the Ministry of Environment and Tourism of Mongolia and the World Cities Scientific Development Alliance. This conference gathered ministers and high-level officials from nine UNWTO Silk Road member states, official representatives from Silk Road regions, UNESCO, and UNWTO affiliate members to discuss the potential of nomadic and sustainable city tourism, especially along the Silk Road international travel route. Over 350 delegates from twenty-one countries examined not only the growth opportunities of developing nomadic tourism trails and products but also how an increase in tourism brings challenges, such as the protection of the environment and the maintenance of cultural heritage standards. These attendees focused on a Silk Road Action Plan: marketing and promotion, capacity-building and destination management, and travel facilitation.

For Mongolia the conference was a way to reinforce nomadic branding for its tourism industry and to discuss how the brand could be better marketed to obtain more benefits from tourism.[84] Minister of Environment and Tourism of Mongolia Dulamsuren Oyunkhorol noted that this particular conference included more than 150 international guests who stayed in Mongolia for four to five days and was estimated to generate around 1 billion tugriks ($4.35 million) cash inflow to Mongolia.[85] Equally valuable was the political benefit: "We believe that the great and historic Silk Road will be revived as an exciting route full of travelers and adventurers, hereby becoming a symbol for mutual understanding and peace among nations in the new millennium."[86] A few weeks later Minister Oyunkhorol held a press conference at the Government House to reemphasize that Mongolia has set the goal to become a "nomadic tourism center" and that UNWTO had pledged to support Mongolia's plan to become a nomadic tourism hub and regional tourism leader. She announced the government's goals to double the already 50,000 people employed in the sector and to promote tourism in the provincial birthplace of Chinggis Khaan.[87]

Eleventh ASEM Summit

The eleventh Asia-Europe Summit Meeting (ASEM11) was held July 15–16, 2016, in Ulaanbaatar, even though Mongolia had only joined the organization in 2008. The meeting received worldwide media coverage because it opened just after a major terrorist attack in Nice, France, and many of the European heads of state were in Mongolia at the time. ASEM11 brought together heads of state and government from the fifty-three ASEM partners—thirty European and twenty-one Asian countries as well as the ASEAN Secretariat and the European Union—under the overarching theme of "20 Years of ASEM: Partnership for the Future Through Connectivity." Among the participants were German President Angela Merkel, Japanese Prime Minister Shinzo Abe, South Korean President Park Geun-hye, Russian Prime Minister Dmitry Medvedev, Singaporean President Lee Hsien Loong, and Chinese Premier Li Keqiang. In his opening remarks President Elbegdorj took advantage of the high-profile event to promote Mongolia's unique brand and culture: "It is auspicious that the ASEM Summit coincides with the celebration of [the] Mongolian National Festivity Naadam. . . . The Mongol National Festivity Naadam is the supreme assembly of our great history, peace, unique culture, customs and traditions and has manifested our people's national pride, glory and the aspirations of prosperity."[88] This Naadam event was organized to showcase Mongolian traditions through the "Three Manly Games" of wrestling, archery, and horse racing, and to highlight Mongolian customs and lifestyle for foreign delegates of the ASEM Summit.

In the final Summit Declaration and Chair's Statement, the participating leaders expressed their "strong resolve to work together to energize ASEM, promote further connectivity, mutually beneficial partnership and cooperation between Asia and Europe." Specially prepared for the meeting by the government of Mongolia in cooperation with Japan's Economic Research Institute for ASEAN and East Asia was the research document "Asia-Europe Connectivity Vision 2025: Challenges and Opportunities." This study was publicized as an expression of Mongolia's deep belief in developing connectivity between Asia and Europe in the next decade and on the role that ASEM could play in fostering this connectivity.[89] The planning and execution of the ASEM Summit in 2016 from its very outset was seen by the DP-controlled government as a giant exercise in job generation and capacity-building right before the Mongolian 2016 parliamentary elections. The Mongolian economy over the previous two years had dramatically contracted, as FDI dried up over the OT controversy and legislative changes in mining regulations, so that politicians were concerned that poor economic conditions would convince the Mongolian electorate that government policies were moving in the wrong direction. ASEM11 was seen as a way to rapidly inject millions of dollars into the national economy to save the DP from election defeat. Many economists and officials agreed that the fact that Mongolia was chosen to host ASEM was an indication of the nation's ability to host important international events and a sign of trust in Mongolia's foreign policy and reputation.

The government established a national council to prepare for the ASEM Summit chaired by Prime Minister Chimed Saikhanbileg. Subgroups were formed to ensure cybersecurity, define purchasing techniques and facilities for the day-to-day management centers, construct auto roads, renovate street illumination, landscape and renovate Ulaanbaatar streets and sidewalk tiles, create bicycle tracks, and execute financial aspects. Forty hotels were designated conference-affiliated sites, and their staff were trained over several months in all aspects of the hospitality industry, including English language. Foreign funds and Mongolia's domestic budget monies were poured into renovating hospitality-industry facilities to accommodate the more than 4,000 conference guests. By the end of the summit it was claimed that some 4,400 people were trained in various fields, so "all this expertise and vast experience remains with us making it easier for us to hold similar events in our country."[90]

ASEM authorities in Singapore[91] understood that Mongolia would need a great infusion of organizing manpower to coordinate this high-profile meeting, so for months ASEM-participating countries seconded officials, mainly based in Beijing, to an ASEM coordination office in Mongolia's capital. More than sixty officials in advanced teams from nineteen ASEM partner countries were sent to Ulaanbaatar in mid-May to review ASEM11 preparations and examine the security and protocol arrangements for key sites. The ASEM11 Summit and all the attendant publicity the Mongolian government generated around it became controversial in Mongolia. The public and media complained about the high expense of 21 billion tugriks ($9.13 million) from Mongolia's 2016 budget, and this public spending became an election issue. One diplomat, when pressed on this point, opined that the Mongolian Ministry of Foreign Affairs understood that the reputation of Mongolia, the president, and the ministry itself were closely linked:

> People with these thoughts aren't looking at the bigger picture. Hosting a meeting as important as ASEM is tremendously significant for Mongolia. The outcome will not be seen immediately but after a certain amount of time. Heads of states who participated in ASEM11 will make decisions and develop ties and cooperation with Mongolia based on what they've observed, noticed, felt, and seen during their stay in here. The outcome of successfully hosting ASEM with a small population of three million people is that Mongolia will be able to demonstrate its ability and capacity to host any key international event well. This, itself, is a big boost to Mongolia's reputation. Time will make everyone realize how significant ASEM11 was, and the future benefits will be multiple times more than the current expense, as ASEM was the perfect platform for promoting the vast opportunities for cooperation and room for investment in Mongolia. I'm sure that those complaining about ASEM11 will soon realize that it was a historic event, opening incredible opportunities for every sector and, once again, spreading positive news about Mongolia.[92]

In the end, the DP government overwhelmingly lost the 2016 parliamentary elections held six weeks before the ASEM11 Summit, but the event itself was successfully executed, fulfilling many of the economic and soft-power goals of President Elbegdorj. The summit was an indication of the growing international reputation of the Mongolian president who had become the face of Mongolian democracy. It boosted Mongolia's reputation, introduced the country and its civilization to a wider international audience, and upgraded Ulaanbaatar's road, air, and tourism industry infrastructure for the next decade. At the wrap-up news conference, President Elbegdorj said that "over 100 bilateral meetings took place; so global 'music' was playing in Mongolia these days. These two days have added to the reputation of Mongolia. Those who came here knew that Mongolia was a large country. Now they know that it is a big nation."[93]

Soft-Power Initiatives Continue to Evolve

Mongolia's soft-power initiatives likely will evolve in other contexts. Mongolian security strategist Luguusharev Byambakhand has called for Ulaanbaatar, like Vienna, The Hague, and Geneva, to take soft-power steps to sponsor conventions on common international issues by hosting all stakeholders under the rubric of the "Karakorum principle." His suggestions include moving the international think tank for landlocked developing countries to Mongolia, hosting the permanent Secretariat for the UN Convention to Combat Desertification, supporting conferences on improving the situation of rural women in the context of globalization, and transforming the UBD into a permanent mechanism.[94] Mongolian soft power also can be projected through educational exchanges that forge closer professional and interpersonal ties with think tanks and civil society organizations to facilitate capacity-building projects to foster goodwill. The MPP government newly elected in 2016 embraced this form of diplomacy to overcome Mongolia's negative reputation for FDI investment by changing the name of the Ministry of Foreign Affairs to Ministry of Foreign Relations with external economic relations and foreign trade policy in its portfolio. Foreign Minister Tsend Mönkh-Orgil explained that

> A tendency to recognize us as an unreliable partner is noticeable, especially in economy, trade and investment spheres, because we can't keep our word. We fail to take affordable pledge, also say one thing and do another. Our laws are too changeable. As for foreign policy, it should not be dependent upon political parties. Thus, I have realized that I am obliged to correct these negative images.[95]

Therefore, it is probable that the MPP-led government will continue to employ soft-power initiatives to bolster Mongolia's image in the globalized and interconnected world.

Notes

1. Joseph S. Nye Jr., *Soft Power: The Means to Success in World Politics* (New York: PublicAffairs, 2004).
2. In the case of China, see Chin-Hao Huang, *China's Soft Power in East Asia: A Quest for Status and Influence?*, NBR Special Report no. 42 (Seattle: National Bureau of Asian Research, January 2013), 10.
3. Serj Battsetseg, "Winning Hearts and Minds: Mongolia's Soft Power Approaches to Overseas Image Building in the Democratic Era" (paper presented at the Asian Continentalism: Furthering Connections Between East and West conference, Ulaanbaatar, May 31–June 2, 2016), 56.
4. Ts. Borjigd Adiyasuren, *Environment and Development Issues in Mongolia* (Ulaanbaatar: Brain Drain,1998), 11.
5. Batkhishig Dulguun, "Sustainable Living and Mongolian Nomads: Is There Development?," *Consilience: The Journal of Sustainable Development,* no. 2 (2009): 4, https://academiccommons.columbia.edu/doi/10.7916/D8NS0TJZ.
6. Tungalag Ulambayar of the UNDP quoted in Tania Branigan, "Mongolia: How the Winter of 'White Death' Devastated Nomads' Way of Life," *The Guardian,* July 20, 2010.
7. Phunchok Stobdan, "Mongolia and Asian Security," *Mongolian Journal of International Affairs,* no. 7 (2000): 61–62, http://dx.doi.org/10.5564/mjia.v0i7.140.
8. "Facts About Desertification," Swiss Agency for Development and Cooperation, September 30, 2009, http://www.greenmongolia.mn.

9. Dan Sheehy quoted in Kit Gillet, "High Cost of Cashmere on Mongolia Plains," CNN, September 13, 2010, http://www.cnn.com/2010/WORLD/asiapcf/09/12/mongolia.cashmere.herders/index.html?hpt=C2.

10. Andrew Jacobs, "Winter Leaves Mongolians a Harvest of Carcasses," *New York Times,* May 19, 2010.

11. Jonathan Watts, "UN Launches Mongolia $4m Appeal to Clear Up Livestock Killed by Big Freeze," *The Guardian,* February 25, 2010. He quotes Tungalag Ulambayar of the UNDP as saying, "Forty-four million animals was far beyond [Mongolia's] natural capacity" to sustain. Also see David Stanway, "U.N. to Pay Mongolian Nomads to Dispose of Dead Herds," Reuters, February 25, 2010.

12. David Murphy, "No Room for Nomads," *Far Eastern Economic Review*, May 31, 2001.

13. Irina Y. Morozova, *Socialist Revolutions in Asia*, 141.

14. Ibid.

15. In 2011 the growth rate was 17.3 percent; in 2012 it was 12.4 percent; in 2013 it was 11.7 percent. For trade statistics during this period, see Trading Economics, "Mongolia Balance of Trade," www.tradingeconomics.com/mongolia/balance-of-trade. On foreign investment see Justin Li, "Chinese Investment in Mongolia: An Uneasy Courtship Between Goliath and David," East Asia Forum, February 2, 2011, www.eastasiaforum.org/2011/02/02/chinese-investment-in-mongolia-an-uneasy-courtship-between-goliath-and-david/.

16. There is no explanation of what the Mongolian Enlightenment actually is.

17. A report by the UNWTO states that 1.1 billion people traveled in 2015 with industrial growth reaching 5 percent; according to preliminary speculations, the number of global tourists is expected to become 1.8 billion by 2030. Kh. Aminaa, "First International Conference Held on Nomadic Tourism," *Mongol Messenger,* October 14, 2016.

18. Dambaadarjaa Jargalsaikhan, "Blue Strategy," 207–210.

19. The Mongolian National Marketing Office was established July 6, 2011, but its work was discontinued after the presidency of Ts. Elbegdorj. See Stephen Kreppel, "Expert Analysis: Mongolian National Marketing Coordination Office, 'Potential for Profit?—Mongolia's Neglected Non-Mining Economy,'" https://static1.squarespace.com/static/531d6809e4b030d9a208a393/t/54434131e4b0046ddec71d9d/1413693745231/EC_mongolianNationalMarketing.pdf.

20. "Cultural and Humanitarian Foreign Policy," in *Concept of Mongolia's Foreign Policy* 2010. Ministry of Foreign Affairs of Mongolia, http://www.mfa.gov.mn/?page_id=26263&lang=en.

21 S. Batbayar, "Naadam Is Innate Treasure of Mongol People," *Mongol Messenger,* July 18, 2014.

22. "Cultural and Humanitarian Foreign Policy," in *Concept of Mongolia's Foreign Policy* 2010.

23. Ibid.

24. President Elbegdorj, "Speech by President of Mongolia Tsakhiagiin Elbegdorj at the Opening of the 11th International Congress of Mongolists," August 30, 2016, http://www.mfa.gov.mn/?p=35764&lang=en.

25. Ts. Mönkh-Orgil, "Our Weight Depends on How Many Friends We Have Got," *Mongol Messenger,* October 21, 2016.

26. It was taught in the elementary schools but not accepted in government circles or throughout the general society. Christopher Kaplonski, *Truth, History and Politics in Mongolia: Memory of Heroes* (New York: RoutledgeCurzon, 2004), 84–85.

27. The decree also requires birth certificates, marriage certificates, and other certificates, diplomas, and licenses issued by all educational institutions of Mongolia to be written in the traditional Mongolian script as well as present-day Cyrillic Mongolian.

28. Such centers were initially organized in Europe beginning in 2014–2015 in Hungary at the Elte University of Budapest, France with INALCO (National Institute for Oriental Languages and Civilizations) at the University of Paris, Czech Republic at Prague University, Germany at Bonn University and Berlin's Humboldt University, and in Russia. In the United States, Mongolian Studies has been given funds for new cultural pro-

grams at the University of California–Berkeley and at Indiana University, although actual Mongolian Centers have not been organized.

29. Peter Mattis, "Reexamining the Confucian Institutes," *The Diplomat,* August 2, 2012.

30. Norihiko Ikeda, "Mongolians: New Identity? Or Revival? Expanding Mongolia's Options for the 21st Century," *Mongol Messenger,* April 22, 2016, 7.

31. Battsetseg, "Winning Hearts and Minds," 53.

32. "Foreign Relations in 2013," Ministry of Foreign Affairs of Mongolia, www.mfa.gov.mn, accessed December 23, 2013.

33. In 2013: Antigua and Barbuda, Vanuatu, Palau, Micronesia Eritrea, Burundi, Togo, Surinam, Sierra Leone, Uganda, and Rwanda. In 2014: Haiti, Kiribati, Equatorial Guinea, Chad, Mauritius, Gabon, and Santa Lucia. In 2015: Cameroon and the Marshall Islands, In 2016: Djibouti, Niger, St. Kitts and Nevis, and the Bahamas.

34. "FSM Expands Diplomatic Reach in Asia-Pacific," *NEWS Agency*, December 24, 2013, english.news.mn.

35. "In a scope of this policy, the Ministry of Foreign Affairs, the main implementing body of foreign policy, Ambassadors, General Consuls and heads of the diplomatic missions have to be dynamic [to] realize principles of the one-window foreign policy." Foreign Minister Lundeg Purevsuren quoted in B. Khuder, "Consultation of Heads of Diplomatic Missions Launches," *Montsame,* July 7, 2015.

36. Mönkh-Orgil, "Our Weight Depends."

37. "Mongolia's Foreign Policy in the Political Field," Ministry of Foreign Affairs of Mongolia, February 21, 2011, www.mfa.gov.mn.

38. Luguusharav Byambakhand, "Mongolian Initiative to Become a Multilateral Diplomacy Platform," in *Mongolia on the Regional Stage* (Ulaanbaatar: Institute for Strategic Studies, 2015), 21.

39. Ibid., 25.

40. "Ulaanbaatar Dialogue," Permanent Mission of Mongolia to the United Nations, April 2013, https://www.un.int/mongolia/mongolia/ulaanbaatar-dialogue.

41. Ibid.

42. Untitled Ulaanbaatar Dialogue document, Mongolian Ministry of Foreign Affairs, 4, http://www.mfa.gov.mn/wp-content/uploads/2015/12/Ulaanbaatar-Dialogue.pdf.

43. Nanjin Dorjsuren, "Why Mongolia Wants to Be a Part of Traditional Security Framework in NEA" (presented at the Ulaanbaatar Dialogue on Northeast Asian Security 2015, Ulaanbaatar, September 2015), 14.

44. Untitled Ulaanbaatar Dialogue document, 4.

45. Track 2 diplomacy is nongovernmental, informal, and unofficial contacts and activities between private citizens or groups of individuals, sometimes called nonstate actors. It contrasts with Track 1 diplomacy, which can be defined as official, governmental diplomacy that occurs inside official government channels. The Track 1.5 process is defined as either one in which the top leadership of one or both conflict parties are engaged with each other in negotiations or conflict transformation activities in an informal setting and/or in their personal capacity, or as a consultation that attempts to generate new insights and be a source of inspiration for the parties who are involved. The defining element that distinguishes this version of the Track 1.5 process from a classic Track 2 dialogue initiative is the composition of the participants' group, especially the involvement of decisionmakers. The UBD is likely the second version of Track 1.5. See Oliver Wolleh, "Track 1.5 Approaches to Conflict Management: Assessing Good Practice and Areas for Improvement" (Berlin: Berghof Foundation for Peace Support, May 2007), http://peacemaker.un.org/sites/peacemaker.un.org/files/Track1.5ApproachestoConflictManagement_BerghofFoundation2007.pdf.

46. "When a meeting, or part thereof, is held under the Chatham House Rule, participants are free to use the information received, but neither the identity nor the affiliation of the speaker(s), nor that of any other participant, may be revealed." This method aims to provide anonymity to speakers and to encourage openness and the sharing of information. It is now used throughout the world as an aid to free discussion. See https://www.chathamhouse.org/about/chatham-house-rule.

47. Untitled Ulaanbaatar Dialogue document, 5.

48. Ulaanbaatar Dialogue on Northeast Asian Security 2014, Conference Proceedings, Ulaanbaatar, Ministry of Foreign Affairs, September 2014.

49. Migeddorj Batchimeg, ibid.,10.

50. "Nine Countries Participate in the 'Ulaanbaatar Dialogue,'" *Mongol Messenger,* June 20, 2014.

51. Ulaanbaatar Dialogue on Northeast Asian Security 2015, Conference Proceedings, Ulaanbaatar, Ministry of Foreign Affairs, September 2015.

52. Dorjsuren, "Why Mongolia," 16.

53. Jargalsaikhan Enkhsaikhan, who attended the third UBD, expressed private views to the author in Ulaanbaatar, June 17, 2016.

54. Yang Wenjing, associate research professor, chief of American Foreign Policy at the China Institute of Contemporary International Relations, quoted in Untitled Ulaanbaatar Dialogue document, 17.

55. Niels Hegewisch, "Dialogue Is a Powerful Tool if It Leads to Cooperation," Friedrich-Ebert-Stiftung Office for Regional Cooperation in Asia, July 7, 2017, https://www.fes-asia.org/news/dialogue-is-a-powerful-tool-if-it-leads-to-cooperation/.

56. See Mark Goleman, "5th Round of the Ulaanbaatar Dialogues," *New Eastern Outlook*, June 8, 2018, https://journal-neo.org/2018/08/06/5th-round-of-the-ulaanbaatar-dialogues; "Ulaanbaatar Dialogue on Northeast Asian Security Concludes," *UB Post,* June 18, 2018.

57. "The Northeast Asian Women Parliamentarians' Forum in Ulaanbaatar Ends Successfully," www.infomongolia.com, accessed November 25, 2017.

58. "Brief History of the International Think Tank for LLDCs," ITT, http://land-locked.org/history/.

59. "Goals of the International Think Tank," ITT, http://land-locked.org/goals/.

60. See ITT newsletters for 2014 and 2015, http://land-locked.org/wp-content/uploads/2016/02/Newsletter_2014.pdf and http://land-locked.org/wp-content/uploads/2016/02/Newsletter_2015.pdf.

61. "Joint Seminar on 'Mongolia's Trade Policy Issues,'" ITT, June 13, 2016, http://land-locked.org/joint-seminar-on-mongolias-trade-policy-issues/.

62. Tsakhia Elbegdorj, "Asia Beyond 2015: The Quest for Lasting Peace and Prosperity" (keynote speech at the twenty-first International Conference on the Future of Asia, Tokyo, May 21, 2015), http://eng.president.mn/newsCenter/viewNews.php?newsId=1546.

63. The Asian Forum for Human Rights and Development (FORUM-ASIA) was founded in 1991 in Manila, Philippines, and moved to Bangkok, Thailand, in 1994. FORUM-ASIA is a membership-based organization, with fifty-eight member organizations in nineteen countries across South Asia, Southeast Asia, and Northeast Asia. Its mission is to promote and protect all human rights, including the right to development, through collaboration and cooperation among human rights organizations in Asia. Its objective is to strengthen the promotion and protection of human rights and democracy in Asia by consolidating Asian human rights movements through effective collaboration with members and partners on international solidarity action as well as engagement with states and other stakeholders at national, regional, and international levels. See https://www.forum-asia.org/?page_id=7536.

64. Elbegdorj, "Asia Beyond 2015."

65. "Address by H. E. Tsakhiagiin Elbegdorj, President of Mongolia to the European Parliament" (Strasbourg, June 9, 2015), http://president.mn/eng/newsCenter/viewNews.php?newsId=1568.

66. The statute of the ICF was adopted under Government Resolution no. 115 passed on March 30, 2013. According to the statute, the operation of the fund shall be administered by a council consisting of seven members.

67. Elbegdorj, "Asia Beyond 2015."

68. "Remarks by President Ts. Elbegdorj at the Hosting of Diplomatic Corps in Mongolia," January 14, 2015, https://www.un.int/mongolia/news/remarks-president-tselbegdorj-hosting-diplomatic-corps-mongolia.

69. "A Tool to Share Mongolia's Experience in Democracy and Market Economy with Emerging Democracies," Ministry of Foreign Affairs of Mongolia, http://www.mfa.gov.mn/?p=29286.

70. Kh. Aminaa, "International Conference Discussing Constitutional Amendment," *Montsame*, October 19, 2017, http://www.montsame.mn/en/read/11982.

71. "Mongolia's Foreign Minister Highlights Need to Support Democratic Transitions," June 2015, http://www.unesco.org/new/en/member-states/single-view/news/mongolias_foreign_minister_highlights_need_to_support_dem/.

72. "Consulate General of Mongolia to Be Opened in Bishkek," covermongolia.mn, July 9, 2014, http://covermongolia.blogspot.com/2014/07/pm-shifts-blame-to-rio-fitch-warns-of.html.

73. Prime Minister Djoomart Otorbaev quoted in "Kyrgyz to Share Mongolia's Electoral System Experience," *Mongol Messenger,* July 10, 2014.

74. CIRDI is a coalition of the University of British Columbia, Simon Fraser University, and École Polytechnique de Montréal, in partnership with the Canadian government, civil society, and industry.

75. CIRDI program manager Marie-Luise Ermisch quoted in Julian Dierkes, "Small, Unanticipated Impacts," *Mongolia Focus* (blog), June 16, 2016, http://blogs.ubc.ca/mongolia/2016/results-based-workshopping/.

76. Founded in 2000 in Warsaw by former US Secretary of State Madeleine Albright and Professor Bronislaw Geremek, the community strives to promote democratic rules and strengthen democratic norms and institutions around the world. Meloney C. Lindberg, Jeremy Gross, and Tirza Theunissen, "7th Ministerial Conference of the Community of Democracies Showcases Mongolia's Democratic Transition," The Asia Foundation, May 1, 2103, https://asiafoundation.org/2013/05/01/7th-ministerial-conference-of-the-community-of-democracies-showcases-mongolias-democratic-transition/.

77. For full text, see http://www.un.org/en/events/democracyday/pdf/2013-Ulaanbaatar-Declaration.pdf.

78. "Mongolia Pledges USD 150 000 for Community of Democracies," Community of Democracies, April 29, 2013, https://community-democracies.org/?p=3962.

79. *World Economic Forum Strategic Dialogue on the Future of Mongolia* (Ulaanbaatar: World Economic Forum, September 14–15, 2013), http://www3.weforum.org/docs/UB13/WEF_UB13_Report.pdf.

80. "Mongolia Becomes an Active Partner of the World Economic Forum, Notes Professor Klaus Schwab," www.infomongolia.com, accessed on January 25, 2017.

81. "The Chief of Staff of the President of Mongolia Is Participating in the World Economic Forum's Summit on the Global Agenda," President of Mongolia website, November 18, 2013, http://www.president.mn/eng/newsCenter/viewNews.php?newsId=1021.

82. Mönkh-Orgil, "Our Weight Depends."

83. "Mongolia's Environment Minister Elected First President of United Nations Environment Assembly," UN Environment, June 24, 2014, https://www.unenvironment.org/fr/node/6488.

84. Aminaa, "First International Conference."

85. Ibid.

86. "Mongolia Hosts the UNWTO Silk Road Conference on Nomadic Tourism and Sustainable Cities," UN World Tourism Organization, October 18, 2016, http://media.unwto.org/press-release/2016-10-18/mongolia-hosts-unwto-silk-road-conference-nomadic-tourism-and-sustainable-c.

87. "Mongolia Aspires to Become a 'Center of Nomadic Tourism.'"

88. "Opening Statement by H. E. Tsakhiagiin Elbegdorj, President of Mongolia, at the 11th ASEM Summit," *GoGo Mongolia*, July 15, 2016, http://mongolia.gogo.mn/r/153920; see also ASEM 11 official website, http://www.asem11.mn/?p=5954&lang=en.

89. The summit's side events included an Asia-Europe Parliamentary Partnership meeting, Asia-Europe People's Forum, Asia-Europe Business Forum, and Model ASEM for students. For details see "ASEM Senior Official Orgil Luvsantseren Briefs the Press," July 15, 2016, http://www.asem11.mn/?p=5966&lang=en.

90. Lundeg Purevsuren quoted in "Foreign Minister Summarizes ASEM11," *Mongol Messenger,* July 22, 2016.

91. The Asia-Europe Foundation is an intergovernmental nonprofit located in Singapore and is the only permanent institution of the Asia-Europe Meeting (ASEM). It has conducted hundreds of projects in Asia and Europe, mainly conferences, seminars, and workshops.

92. Ambassador Ch. Agvaandamdin quoted in B. Dulguun, "Senior Diplomat Elaborates on Mongolia's Foreign Affairs and ASEM11," *UB Post,* July 19, 2016.

93. President Ts. Elbegdorj quoted in "ASEM Leaders Conclude the Summit," *Mongol Messenger,* July 22, 2016.

94. Byambakhand, "Mongolian Initiative," 25–26.

95. Mönkh-Orgil, "Our Weight."

11

New Strategies for a New Era

Mongolia's twenty-five years of democracy have been described this way: "A democratic anchor in an increasingly undemocratic region, Mongolia is uniquely positioned to be a role model of successful democratic transition as well as a case study in how to address the myriad challenges that a new and consolidating democracy faces."[1] Today, as in the past, Mongols live in a difficult region—climatically, geographically, and politically. Mongolia is totally landlocked with two powerful neighbors that for centuries have been involved in Mongolian internal affairs and that still believe they must maintain special rights and connections to Mongolia in order to ensure their own national security and economic development, as well as to manage peace in the entire North Asian region. The Mongolian people and government may not like the policies of their border neighbors; however, they cannot ignore away this situation but must manage it in the most efficacious way possible.

Mongolia, out of frustration with the status quo of big power dominance in its neighborhood in recent years, has embarked on a much more activist foreign policy that utilizes soft-power mechanisms and embraces political and economic continental integration trends to promote itself. During the past decade it has sought to integrate into the Eurasian market and raise its regional and global profile. A major part of this new strategy is to carve out space to establish new regional institutional frameworks to promote transportation and communication formulas that can be mutually beneficial to all of the parties. Mongolia is not afraid to lead, although its leadership is couched in humble and nonthreatening terms. Professor Norihiko Ikeda has written that Mongolia wishes to strengthen its relationships with the countries around the globe based on the argument that "Mongolia is part of the world community, not merely a buffer nation between China and Russia. The argument is logical, though it is not clear whether other nations will accept it at face value."[2] This chapter will focus on emerging trends in Mongolian foreign policy relations that likely will be a part of its strategy through 2020.

Evolving "Third Neighbor" Policy

After seventy years of socialist isolation as a Soviet satellite, Mongolia successfully reinvented itself during the last twenty-five years as a democratic, free market nation integrated into the global marketplace. The vibrancy of Mongolia's democracy is evidenced in its thirteen national elections (presidential and parliamentary) and seventeen local parliamentary elections since 1990. The overarching concept guiding the country's political and national security has been its "Third Neighbor" policy of balancing its relations with its two border neighbors, Russia and China, by reaching out to other democracies, including the United States, Japan, the European Community, and South Korea, for political and economic support. In recent years, Mongolia has further expanded its "Third Neighbor" definition to a more Eurasian approach emphasizing Turkey, Persian Gulf nations, Vietnam, and Iran in order to diversify trade partners for its minerals and find new sources of energy and consumer goods.

Mongolia's original "Third Neighbor" strategy, devised in the early 1990s when communist Mongolia had to reinvent itself, has been successful politically in allowing the nation to expand ties with democratic nations to both counterbalance Russian and Chinese political influence and increase Mongolia's international profile. However, it failed to prevent China's 90 percent monopoly over its economy or to generate expected Western FDI. Therefore, Mongolian policymakers reexamined this foreign policy pillar and imaginatively "redefined" it in its 2010 National Security Concept. The ongoing process to redefine its "Third Neighbors" is a strong motivation behind Mongolia's new activism on the diplomatic front with its International Cooperation Fund and Ulaanbaatar Dialogue on Northeast Asian Security to discuss North-South Korean issues. Mongolia also is more active in tackling broader Asian issues such as the Mongolian-Russian-Chinese Northern Railway and Asian Super Grid through its Economic Transit Corridor or Steppe Road strategy.

A vibrant "Third Neighbor" policy is the foundation of Mongolia's future—politically and economically—and reflects Mongolia's strong commitment to democracy. However, how the "Third Neighbor" strategy is implemented will determine whether Mongolia "remains a minor, local nation or sets out to become a full member of the global community."[3] At the twenty-fifth anniversary celebrations of the democratic era, President Elbegdorj mentioned three points crucial for Mongolia's future: (1) Development of Mongolia's democracy will depend only on the Mongols. (2) Mongolia should focus on terrorism while never forgetting how communism was formed and spread. (3) Democracy "is a really difficult and torturous process. . . . We should make efforts every day for democracy and take care of it."[4]

Mongolia as a Neutral or Nonaligned State?

President Elbegdorj articulated a new twist to the "Third Neighbor" policy at the UN General Assembly in September 2015 by announcing that Mongolia would seek UN ratification of its "permanent neutrality." He proclaimed that Mongolia's geographic location and unique development path are congruent with the spirit and principles of neutralism and would encourage other states to respect its status quo as a neutral state.[5] Thus, he asked the UN community to ratify his proposal, since "Mongolia's status of permanent neutrality will contribute to the strengthening of peace, security and development in our region and the world at large."[6] He elaborated further a few months later in Davos, Switzerland:

> 1. Since Mongolia adopted its new democratic constitution, Mongolia has actively pursued policies that are neutral in substance. However, we are yet to declare it, in form. The process of shaping and validating this policy is now only a matter of time.
> 2. The history of Mongolia, our geographic location and the uniqueness of our chosen path of development are congruent with the spirit and principles of neutralism. Neutrality enables a country to maintain equal and balanced international relations. Other states and international organizations respect such a status quo of a neutral state.
> 3. The state of international affairs and the international order changes over time. Yet neutral policies and actions can be sustained. The state which upholds neutrality preserves the full power to amend, renew or abandon its neutralist policy.[7]

Noting that the Mongols had declared their nation a nuclear-weapons-free zone, as well as rejected hosting foreign military bases and forming military alliances, Elbegdorj asserted that since the collapse of the Soviet Union in 1992, the country has been de facto neutral along the lines of the Swiss and Turkmenistan models. UN authorities responded to his proposal by requesting he first obtain Mongolian parliamentary approval.

On October 20 a draft law on adopting the status of permanent neutrality was submitted to Parliament. The government emphasized that the adoption of neutrality would not make any change to current foreign policy but would "be fundamental for foreign policy towards having a balanced relationship with other countries."[8] It insisted the law would permit Mongolia to retain its armed forces and to join a military alliance in the event its sovereignty or independence were threatened. Nevertheless, the draft legislation was not approved because its reception was controversial among Mongolia's national security experts. There was a diverse range of opinions from Mongolia's leading foreign policy strategists. Critics pointed out that Russia and China first must accept such a status, and to date both neighbors were noncommittal or somewhat confused about the idea. Ambassador Jargalsaikhan Enkhsaikhan, Mongolia's former representative to the Organization for Security and Co-operation in Europe, disparaged the significance of the exercise, saying that the move would have little value unless China and Russia rein in their diplomatic and economic pressure on Mongolia. He questioned whether Mongols need to "limit our sovereignty voluntarily."[9] His thoughts were echoed by former ambassador to the United States and Australia Ravdan Bold.[10] However, President Jamsran Baysaikh, of the Institute of International Relations at the Mongolian Academy of Sciences, countered, "Our two neighbors are not interested in us getting close to the U.S. So, if our country becomes a permanently neutral country, we will get out of this pressure."[11] Ambassador Jalbuu Choinkhor, director of the Mongolian Geopolitical Institute and former ambassador to the the United States, opined, "In simple words, it is a position that Mongolia will not join any side against any country."[12]

The ambivalence toward the permanent neutrality policy continued after the MPP-controlled government took power in July 2016. Its action plan for the country contained the promise to observe a nonalignment policy and convene a working group under an ambassador inside the Foreign Ministry to study the issue of neutrality. The group, with the understanding that the issue should be solved by Parliament, would examine the reactions of Mongolia's two neighbors and other countries. The government is looking to redirect the neutrality discussion toward Mongolia's long-standing connections to the Non-Alignment Movement (NAM), which Mongolia joined as an observer in 1988 and became a full member of in 1991 (in 2018 NAM has over 120 member countries). In 2016 Foreign Minister Mönkh-Orgil explained,

> For a small country as Mongolia, it is necessary to think over comprehensively, and consider the given issue before introducing important policy changes and making a statement. . . . The foreign policy and external relations of the country, its actions and deeds for many years are linked to the non-alignment policy. . . . There are some connections in the non-aligned and neutral positions.[13]

However, Elbegdorj's successor, Battulga, has not indicated his position on the issue.

North Korean Relations

One of the "Third Neighbor" countries that Mongolia has reached out to in the last few years is in a special category. The DPRK is not a rogue state for the Mongols. Rather, it is a nation with which Mongolia has shared a long history of strong relations during the Cold War that now could be the key to Mongolia's future economic success. Mongolia–North Korea relations date back to the Korean War of 1950–1953. In 1988 the two countries signed a legal assistance agreement for the development of civil society and a criminal justice legal framework. Today Mongolia is seeking political and economic connections with North Korea in order to help Mongolia break away from dependence on its two border neighbors and to allow both nations to solve the isolation they face. Even though Mongolia prides itself on its friendly relations with North Korea, this has not prevented it from vocally opposing Pyongyang's nuclear weapons program. Nevertheless, Mongolia's efforts to diversify its economy through its "Third Neighbor" policy are connected to its efforts to serve as a diplomatic bridge to unlock North Korea so it can become a transit route to the Pacific. For Pyongyang, strengthening its ties with Mongolia could bring measured economic modernization and benefit from Mongolia's growing experience in regional politics.

The new effort to develop connections with the DPRK was evidenced in June 2013 when HBOil JSC, a Mongolian oil trading and refining company, acquired a 20 percent stake in North Korea's not yet fully operational Sungri refinery in the Rason City Special Economic Zone. HBOil will bring Mongolian crude via Russia to Sungri, which will export the refined products back to Mongolia. This investment is part of Mongolia's plan to end its energy dependency on Russia and China and to utilize the DPRK's east coast Rajin port city and Ungsang port to reach Asian customers.[14] The economic bond between Mongolia and the DPRK has been growing. According to the Mongolian Railroad Authority, Mongolia shipped 25,000 tons of coal to North Korea's Rajin port in 2015–2016 as part of a trial export project.[15] Although additional sanctions against North Korea were applied in early 2016 by the world community, Mongolia continued to move forward with cooperation with the DPRK. In July 2013 the two countries signed an agreement in Pyongyang on IT exchanges. Mongolian livestock experts also are working to develop massive stockbreeding grass zones by reclaiming the Sepho tableland in the DPRK's Kangwon province.[16] An agreement since 2008 permits North Korea to provide Mongolia with as many as 5,300 workers over five years.[17] The Mongolian Ministry of Labor reported that, as of April 2013, 1,749 North Koreans worked legally in Mongolia (in textiles and construction), and it was expected that workers would assist in rail and mining projects.[18] Although the exact numbers have never been public, newly released data indicate that the peak may have been 2,123 in 2013,[19] despite other sources' claiming there were 2,500 North Koreans in 2016 who worked in factories producing cashmere garments for export, in road construction, and in restaurants run by the North Korean government. At the end of 2017 the Mongolian government announced that the 1,200 workers in Mongolia would all be leaving in response to the pressure of international sanctions.[20] Two North Korean medical clinics still operate in Ulaanbaatar, offering basic consultations and treatments such as acupuncture and massage with North Korean Health Ministry staff on five-year postings.[21]

Mongolia, in a low-key manner, has provided asylum for North Korean defectors coming through China. Starting in 2004, some South Korean civil society and religious groups offered to construct camps in Mongolia to house North Korean refugees, but the Mongols refused permission. During a 2006 trip to China, Mongolian Prime Minister Miyeegomb Enkhbold denied that there were plans to establish any refugee camps for North Koreans.[22] In 2006 it was estimated that 500 North Korean defectors were entering Mongolia each month,[23] but by June 2007 Mongolia had begun to turn them away. This action reportedly was in response to North Korean pressure and a new South Korean policy to not welcome North Korean refugees coming via Mongolia and Southeast Asia. During the Elbegdorj era, the issue of North Korean refugees publicly was downplayed, although it is known that some of them who do reach Mongolia are repatriated to South Korea.[24]

Diplomatic contacts between Mongolia and North Korea have intensified in recent years. Although their political systems have diverged since Mongolia's peaceful democratic revolution in 1990, President Elbegdorj promoted the view that Mongolia's peaceful democratic transition could be a perfect model for Pyongyang's own eventual political transition. Presidential national security and foreign policy adviser Lundeg Purevsuren went to North Korea in July 2013 to discuss bilateral cooperation and organize the parameters of President Elbegdorj's state visit to Pyongyang. Purevsuren's trip was a continuation of Elbegdorj's policy to deepen connections with the DPRK regime through cooperation in trade, IT, and people-to-people exchanges. Elbegdorj arrived in Pyongyang on October 28, 2013, for a four-day state visit, ostensibly to celebrate the sixty-fifth anniversary of bilateral diplomatic relations and twenty-fifth anniversary of DPRK founder Kim Il-sung's visit to Ulaanbaatar. Despite predictions that he would be the first foreign head of state to meet with the DPRK's new leader, Kim Jong-un, the expected summit with Kim failed to materialize. Nonetheless, several significant cultural agreements, a 2013–2015 cooperation plan between Mongolia's Postal Authority and the North Korean Computer and ICT Centre, and a roads and transportation agreement were concluded, and much publicity was given to Elbegdorj's movements inside the reclusive country by North Korean television. Mongolian Foreign Minister Lu. Bold expressed his government's reaction: "What Mongolia can provide is leverage to improve the situation in the region and pursue the initiative for parties to share dialogue. We see a lot of room to be more active."[25]

Elbegdorj had emphasized this theme at a welcoming banquet hosted by Kim Yong-nam, president of the Presidium of the Supreme People's Assembly, asserting that "Mongolia will cooperate with every country, including the Democratic People's Republic of Korea, for peace and stability in Northeast Asia."[26] Kim responded by lauding the two countries' continuous cooperation in political, economic, military, and sports activities and emphasized that Pyongyang was committed to expanding ties.[27] The visit was full of symbolism that particularly emphasized the long relationship between the two governments and cultures. Elbegdorj visited the tomb of Koryo King Kongmin, who during the Mongolian Empire had a Mongol Queen. The president recalled that Mongolia was the second country to recognize the DPRK and had shared Korean War hardships: "Our two countries are good friends who didn't forsake each other in the times of need and desperation."[28] Elbegdorj became the first head of state to visit the Demilitarized Zone in Panmunjom and was the first foreign leader to deliver a lecture, which emphasized the benefits of democracy, at Kim Il-sung University. He also addressed a Mongolia-DPRK business meeting and promised to expand bilateral economic ties: "We do see ample opportunities of cooperation in railways, air and auto-transport and sea-ports. . . . Mongolia is interested in importing [a] highly qualified and organized workforce."[29] Not long after President Elbegdorj's trip, an MOU to organize a DPRK friendship joint company was signed between the governments in Pyongyang,[30] while another MOU on North Korean workers was signed between the DPRK Ministry of Foreign Trade and Mongolian Ministry of Labor. These agreements may have been instrumental in obtaining DPRK attendance at the first UBD two months later.

The Mongols have established a history of acting as a nonjudgmental active facilitator between North Korea and other nations hostile to the Kim regime such as Japan, South Korea, and the US. While keeping good relations with South Korea, Mongolia has continued to push for international talks with North Korea. In 2014 Ulaanbaatar was the site of discussions about Japanese abductees. The Mongolian Ministry of Foreign Affairs and Mongolia's Institute for Strategic Studies (ISS) organized a secret May 21, 2014, Track 1.5 meeting in Ulaanbaatar between North Korean Deputy Foreign Minister Ri Yong-ho and Robert Einhorn, former Obama administration special adviser for nonproliferation and arms control at the State Department; Joel Wit, an ex–State Department official who was a senior fellow of the US-Korea Institute at the Johns Hopkins University School of Advanced International Studies; and Robert Carlin, a former Central Intelligence Agency analyst.[31] The reasoning behind President Elbegdorj's drive to bring Mongolia to the table for discussions on the Korean Peninsula security situation reflects Mongolia's experience at the end of the Cold War when, as a Soviet satellite, it had to make the difficult simultaneous transition to democracy and a free market economy. Tsedendamba Batbayar, head of the Foreign Ministry's department of policy planning and policy analysis, said that it was only in the past fourteen years that Mongolia "began to recognize its strategic potential in close relations with the DPRK." Batbayar said that his nation strives to "be an honest broker" on the international scene and hopes that it can "open up new channels for dialogue" with North Korea.[32] Mongolia, excluded from the Six-Party Talks, believes that the Korean situation and regional disputes have festered for decades because the region lacks a security dialogue mechanism. Altering this situation would "bring good influence to the world and especially open a new way of development for Mongolia."[33]

In seeking to strengthen its position in Asia, Mongolia raises its international reputation as a mediator nation and secures constructive participation in the political and economic integration process in the region. In mid-November 2016 there was a "Security of Northeast Asia" roundtable meeting co-organized at the Ministry of Foreign Affairs by the Global Partnership for the Prevention of Armed Conflict Northeast Asia and the "Tsenkher Suld" NGO,[34] a nuclear-weapon-free-status supporting group whose president is Punsalmaag Ochirbat, the first democratic-era president of Mongolia. This was the third year of discussions on Northeast Asian nuclear security topics, and attending were peace organizations from North Korea, South Korea, Japan, China, Russia, the United States, and Mongolia.[35]

High-level visits between Mongolia and North Korea have increased in recent years as a result of the UBD. Mongolian Foreign Minister Purevsuren invited his counterpart Ri Su-yong[36] to pay an official visit to Mongolia during February 22–25, 2015. When Ri came, he also met the Mongolian president and prime minister.[37] There is evidence that references to Mongolia in North Korean media have been steadily increasing in recent years, indicating a warming political climate. Numerous high-level exchanges between Mongolia and the DPRK have been linked by South Korean sources to Mongolia's conciliatory stance on North-South relations.[38] Although today many of the world's democracies are at odds with Pyongyang, it is believed that Mongolia can play a unique role as mediator in the North-South Korean dispute, which is why Ulaanbaatar was a finalist as a venue for the first Trump-Kim summit.[39] At a forum examining "Mongolia's Diplomacy with the Two Koreas," which was cohosted by the Global Peace Foundation and the Center for Strategic and International Studies in Washington, DC, former US ambassador to Mongolia Mark C. Minton observed that both nations are seeking leverage and breathing room: "They want to have other partners. They want some traction in regional affairs and in global affairs that allows them to escape the rather vice-like dynamic of just existing and having diplomatic space between two powerful neighbors."[40] Mongolia's mediating role with the DPRK continues to find favor among the public because it reinforces the idea of Mongolia as a problem solver in Asia and as a non-nuclear-weapon state that is positioned to act as a possible peacemaker: "While neighboring countries China, Japan, and South Korea are seeking deterrence, Mongolia may become an integral part of stabilizing the Korean Peninsula with its small country diplomacy."[41]

Intensifying Turkish and Iranian Relations

Turkey considers the Mongolian plateau as its original homeland. Turks and Mongols believe the Xiongnu or Hunnu, a confederation of nomadic peoples who according to ancient Chinese sources inhabited the eastern Asian steppe from the third century BCE to the late first century CE, are their ancestors.[42] Two great Uyghur Turkic empires existed on the Mongolian plateau in the 600s–700s. Gök Türk or Blue Sky Turks left petroglyphs and stone steles throughout the Orkhon Valley in central Mongolia near the site of the Mongolian Empire's capital of Karakorum, 400 kilometers from Ulaanbaatar. In the democratic era, Turkey has become very interested in archaeological excavations in Mongolia, and, because of the historical tie between the nations, the relationship has grown increasingly closer. They established an intergovernmental economic and trade commission in 1994, the same year the Turkish Cooperation and Coordination Agency (TİKA) initiated the Turkish Monuments Project in Mongolia to preserve the Orkhon stone stele monuments outside the old Mongolian capital of Karakorum. The Turks opened an embassy in Ulaanbaatar in 1996, and Mongolia opened its Ankara embassy in 1997.

Turkey has special interest in Mongolia not only due to their common historical roots but also because "Turkey considers Mongolia as a strategically important country with its huge landmass and vast resources."[43] Mongolian foreign policy strategists see Turkey as the key "Third Neighbor" across the Eurasian continent. Since 2004, TİKA has invested in education, health, cultural, and technical cooperation projects worth around $20 million in nonrefundable governmental aid. More than 1,000 Mongolian students today are enrolled in Turkish universities, and Turkology studies have developed in Mongolian universities. When Kadir Topbas, mayor of Istanbul, attended the 2016 Turkish Cultural Days in Mongolia, he said, "We have to support each other in these times when our fate and future depends only upon ourselves. We have to share our achievements and accomplishments."[44]

In June 2014 Turkey's National Assembly speaker Cemil Çiçek agreed to parliamentary cooperation with Mongolia's Parliament while on a visit that included meetings with Mongolia's highest leaders.[45] Mongolia and Turkey went to a visa-free regime in 2013. Trade volume has reached $40 million, and the direct flights between Istanbul and Ulaanbaatar, which began in the middle of 2012, have intensified further collaboration. The governments want to expand cooperation in agriculture, construction, environment, small and medium-sized enterprises (SMEs), tourism, mining, and logistics cooperation. The larger goal is to advance the relationship to a comprehensive partnership level between the two countries at opposite ends of the Eurasian continent. Cooperation between Mongolia and Turkey, particularly in the energy sector, has intensified since 2015. There are training programs for Mongolian engineers and technicians in renewable energy, especially hydropower, and the Mongolian government has accelerated licensing for existing Turkish projects. Two Turkish companies already are operating in Mongolia's energy sector. ZTM, LLC, completed a feasibility study for a hydroelectric power plant in Tavaltain Khavtsal (Tavaltai

Canyon) in Nogoonnuur *sum* of Bayan-Ulgii province in western Mongolia. The company will provide the capital to build an 88.7 MW power plant. ZTM is also interested in developing a second project for the Khovd River hydroelectric power plant on a concession basis. When these power plants come online, Mongolia expects to fully supply its western region with electricity as well as to export electricity. ZTM created a hydropower master plan, based on studies conducted at twenty-nine river basins in Mongolia, which has been submitted to the Ministry of Energy.[46] A second Turkish company, Aidiner Global, LLC, began a wind power plant project in 2009 with two measuring stations to conduct wind capacity studies in Gobisumber province in central Mongolia. It signed an energy supply and purchase agreement in March 2012, which was renewed on January 14, 2014, and is in negotiations with possible funders or partners.

The Turks also have opened a "Made in Turkey" Center in the Altanbulag Free Trade Zone on Mongolia's Selenge provincial border with Russia and are involved in agriculture, transport, education, and food cooperation there. Turkish activity in Mongolia's northern free trade zone has a Eurasian regional integration context. Turkey maintains nineteen free trade zones and has offered Mongolia its expertise to create a favorable environment for foreign investment and logistics. Turkey, which has been watching Sino-Russian transport cooperation plans, announced in Dushanbe, Tajikistan, in September 2014, its intention to develop rail, road, and pipeline infrastructure with Mongolia in order to extend its economic footprint in Northeast Asia. Turkish Ambassador Murat Kartagoz noted in a press interview the special importance of Selenge province's location next to Russia, its demographic setting, and the fact that it hosts key roads, a cross-border rail network, water resources, and a free trade zone: "The Republic of Turkey is willing to cooperate with this strategic locality and to promote Turkish businesses here."[47] Nine hundred kilometers to the south, Turkey is working with Mongolian construction companies in the Gobi city of Dalanzagad, the gateway to both Mongolia's OT copper project with Rio Tinto as well as its giant TT coal mine. Dalanzagad authorities want to utilize Turkish construction technology to build apartments with a small workforce. The techniques of ten Turkish specialists who worked on the construction of a seven-story building for 140 households are to be expanded to a new 10,000-person residential settlement area for completion by 2025.[48]

A significant aspect of the bilateral relationship is deep cooperation on strategic issues. Turkey has been cooperating with Mongolia on military matters since 1999 and annually provides $1 million for defense projects. Seventy-nine Mongolian officers have graduated from the Turkish Military Academy since 2000. In 2014, the forty-fifth anniversary of the 1969 establishment of diplomatic relations, Turkey's Center for Strategic Research met in Ulaanbaatar with ISS, which is under the auspices of Mongolia's National Security Council, to discuss "Third Neighbor" policy cooperation, Turkish regional integration into the EU and SCO, Turkey's strategy to ensure its energy security, Mongolian participation in the regional integration process, and Mongolia's cooperation with NATO as compared with Turkey's NATO experience.[49] Turkish Minister of National Defense İsmet Yılmaz paid an official visit on September 25–26, 2014, met with Mongolian Prime Minister Norov Altankhuyag, and signed an agreement on military financial cooperation with Mongolian Defense Minister Dashdemberel Bat-Erdene.[50] Mongolia and Turkey have signed over a hundred cooperation documents since 1990, and Turkey is willing to upgrade the bilateral comprehensive partnership to a strategic one with increased cooperation in defense and education, as well as trade and economic relations.[51]

Bilateral ties continued to grow under the MPP government led by Prime Minister Khürelsükh, who hosted the state visit of Turkish Prime Minister Binali Yildirim in April 2018. At that time, the two nations discussed how to quickly grow their 2017 $31 million trade turnover to $300 million.[52] A huge complication in the relationship suddenly developed over the summer when a Turkish educator, who was principal of an international school in Ulaanbaatar, was kidnapped from his home by masked Turkish agents who attempted to fly him out of the country. Local Mongols and the Mongolian police stopped the plane from departing and rescued the victim, who is accused by Turkish authorities of supporting antigovernment forces. The Mongolian Foreign Ministry immediately protested the incident as an "unacceptable act of violation of Mongolia's sovereignty and independence and Mongolia will strongly object."[53] The Mongolian ambassador in Ankara was recalled, and ramifications from this peculiar event likely will affect Turko-Mongolian relations for the near future.

Another increasingly key country for Mongolia across the continent is Iran. Since the collapse of communism in the Soviet Union, Iran has aspired to develop closer relations with the entire Eurasian region with which it shares significant historical and cultural ties. While certainly Iran's foreign policy considerations have included spreading Islamic fundamentalism and replacing secular regimes, the expanding regional presence of the United States also has influenced Iran's geopolitical calculations toward Eurasia, including Mongolia. Turkish-Mongolian cooperation and Chinese economic penetration are other factors influencing Iran's calculus about how to use identity politics in Mongolia's western provinces, which are inhabited by Turkic adherents of Islam.[54] While Iran's interest can be comprehended in a geopolitical context, Mongolia's desire to forge closer relations has been ignored or misunderstood. Iran and Mongolia trace their modern political relationship to 1971, when diplomatic relations were first established between the shah's government and communist Mongolia. Two years later, Mongolian leader Yumjaa Tsedenbal paid a state visit to Tehran, which was followed in 1976 by an Iranian prime ministerial visit to Ulaanbaatar to sign economic, trade, and science agreements. In the Islamic

Republic era, Iran has maintained contact via its Beijing embassy and, since 1997, from Moscow. Beginning in 1973, Mongolian ambassadors in Prague were accredited to Tehran, but after Mongolia's democratic revolution, this responsibility moved to Moscow in 1997.

Since the 1990s, the economic relationship has been relatively low key for both countries, although the Iranians did help to draft the first Mongolian law on petroleum, and Iran has hosted Mongolian experts from Mongol Gazriin Tos (Mongolian Oil Ltd.). Additional ambassadorial-level discussions on petroleum took place in 2002 in Ulaanbaatar, and defense and security experts have met on the sidelines of Shanghai Cooperation Organization meetings, where both nations hold observer status. A level of personal rapport was established between Mongolian and Iranian leaders at international forums. In 2003 Mongolian President Bagabandi met his counterpart in a Malaysian conference, and that same year Mongolia contributed 1,000 woolen blankets after the Iranian earthquake. At the 2009 Non-Aligned Summit in Havana, Mongolian President Enkhbayar and Iranian President Mahmoud Ahmadinejad reportedly discussed historical ties and matters related to the Hazara minority people.[55]

The nature of the Mongol-Iranian relationship was recast during the Elbegdorj presidency through meat and uranium. In early December 2010, it was announced that a new Mongolian-Iranian joint venture entitled Bayan Meat, Ltd., had signed a sheep meat export contract with Mongolia's largest meat slaughterhouse, Mahimpex of Ulaanbaatar. Mahimpex is owned by Jenco, whose president, Kh. Battulga, was at the time Mongolian Minister for Road, Transport, Construction, and Urban Development of Mongolia (Battulga became president of Mongolia in July 2017). In January 2010 Iranian direct charter flights from the western Mongolian city of Khovd began to fly out seventy-five metric tons of halal-slaughtered lamb per agreement with Baruun Mongol International, a company that has exported fresh lamb and mutton carcasses to Iran since 2007. Its 2010 target volume from the two western-based slaughterhouses was 2,000 tons.[56] Expanding the meat market to Iran also has been a major goal of President Battulga's government. A slaughterhouse in the eastern Mongolian city of Darkhan now has a halal-slaughter line where 1,000 sheep are prepared under the supervision of experts from Dana Negah Parsian, an Iranian importing company, and the Iranian Veterinary Organization, then frozen and transported by truck through Russia and Kazakhstan, reaching Iran in about two weeks.[57]

Iran also has been exploring its options to purchase Mongolian raw uranium. On October 19, 2010, Mongolian President Elbegdorj received the newly accredited Iranian Ambassador Mehdi Safari, former deputy foreign minister, who was posted to Beijing as part of Iran's plan to shore up Chinese support for its controversial nuclear program. It may not have been a coincidence that Safari made his first appearance in Ulaanbaatar less than one week after France and Mongolia signed a nuclear energy cooperation agreement covering uranium exploration and exploitation by Areva, the French nuclear power company. Areva, which was expanding its presence from Kazakhstan into Asia, had been cooperating with Japan's Mitsubishi Corporation since December 2009 on uranium exploration licenses for more than 14,000 square kilometers in Mongolia's Dornogobi and Sukhbaatar provinces.[58] Not long after Safari's visit, Mongolian Defense Minister Lu. Bold visited Washington to meet with Pentagon officials including US Secretary of Defense Robert Gates, and likely discussed Iranian interest in Mongolian resources.

The major turning point in Mongol-Iranian bilateral relations came in September 2012, when Iran permitted President Elbegdorj to tour one of its nuclear facilities after the sixteenth summit of the Non-Aligned Movement in Tehran. He was the only foreign leader allowed to visit the main uranium enrichment plant in the town of Natanz. A TV broadcast suggested that Elbegdorj endorsed the Iranian claim about the peaceful purposes of its nuclear program: "Maybe in other countries it is not possible to visit such a sensitive place. I found out how the enriched uranium is being used for peaceful energy."[59] In 2015, on the sidelines of the SCO summit, the Iranian president met with President Elbegdorj and stated that "Iranian companies are ready to cooperate with Mongolia energy, road construction and mining sectors."[60] In late December of that year, Mongolian Foreign Minister Purevsuren discussed ways to promote meat sales, energy, and mining ties with Iranian Foreign Minister Mohammad Javad Zarif in Tehran. Purevsuren called on Iran to share with Mongolia its experience in the agriculture and oil sectors.[61]

In mid-September 2018 Mongolian Deputy Foreign Minister Battsetseg Batmunkh visited Tehran to discuss ways to expand trade ties. The Iranians emphasized that at present the high cost of transportation of goods between the two countries is the main factor limiting bilateral trade and called for removing visa restrictions, reducing customs duties, and establishing banking relations to encourage Iranian FDI to enter the Mongolian market.[62] Whether it is meat or uranium, the growth in relations between Mongolia and Iran should continue throughout this decade, even with sanctions imposed on Iran, because both are seeking new trade partners and increasing their participation in regional cooperation and collective security organizations.

Indian "Spiritual" Relations

Mongolia and India even during communist times believed they could have a strong relationship because "of their spiritual connections, shared geopolitical concerns, and ideological compatibility."[63] Nevertheless, these ties were limited by distance and geopolitical realities. Central Asia historically was a zone for India's civilizational influence. Prior to the Arab conquest in the seventh century, Buddhism flourished across the vast Eurasian steppe along the Silk Road, and, during the Mongolian Empire, this religious tradition was introduced to the Mongols via Tibet. From the beginning of the democratic era, Mongolian policymakers saw India as their spiritual inspiration, which was just as much connected to the fact that India was the leader of the G-77 and Non-Aligned Movement as well as the home of the Dalai Lama in exile from Tibet. In 1955 India became the first country outside the Soviet bloc to establish relations with Mongolia. Ratan Kumar Nehru, cousin of then Prime Minister Jawaharlal Nehru, was appointed the first ambassador of India to Mongolia, but it was not until 1970 that India established its embassy in Ulaanbaatar, when Sonam Norbu, a diplomat from Ladakh, became its first resident ambassador. Mongolia's attachment to India in the communist era was characterized by reciprocal high-level visits and early trade agreements. In 1959 and again in 1973, Mongolian Premier Yumjaag Tsedenbal went to Delhi, and former Prime Minister Indira Gandhi, while information and broadcasting minister, visited Mongolia in 1965. Two Indian presidents, R. Venkataraman in 1988 and Pratibha Patil in 2011, have visited Mongolia. Although trade agreements were signed in 1968 and 1978, India's exports throughout the 1980s accounted for less than 0.1 percent, and there were no Mongolian exports during this period.[64]

Recognizing its historical affinity with the region, at the end of the Cold War, India developed a reengaging strategy toward the Central Asian republics, which was known as the "Extended Neighbourhood Policy." This policy was formulated not only to reconnect with the region but also to respond to great power diplomacy in Central Asia.[65] The well-known Indian defense strategist Stobdan recommended in 2010 that India stop viewing Central Asia through a Western prism and redesign its policy goals for the region: "The objective should be to facilitate the revival of civilizational and cultural linkages between India and Central Asia through intellectual and institutional resources available in both regions."[66] Two years later in June 2012, India's Minister of State for External Affairs Shri E. Ahamed announced a new "Connect Central Asia" policy that would continue to build strong political relations through the exchange of high-level visits, work to improve air connectivity to facilitate Indian tourism in the region, and increase exchanges of scholars, academics, civil society, and youth delegations to gain deeper insights into each other's cultures.[67] At that time Stobdan called Mongolia a distant country for India, "but it is the last Asian frontier where Indic cultural imprints continue to thrive."[68] Believing that the Mongolian democratic revolution in the 1990s was inspired by Indian wisdom, he suggested sending Kushok Bakula Rinpoche, a high-ranking Buddhist lama, as India's first ambassador to postcommunist Mongolia. One of the most venerated monks of Ladakh and India's longest-serving ambassador to Mongolia (1990–2000), Bakula Rinpoche funded a monastic school in Ulaanbaatar. "Kushok Bakula Rinpoche's decade-long representation of India in Mongolia, strengthened not only India's position and impression among the people of that country, but also rekindled the civilisational bonds, the bonds of knowledge and spirituality that had existed between the two civilizations and culture."[69]

In Stobdan's analysis, Mongolia's strategic position at the junction of Central Asia, Northeast Asia, and East Asia makes it attractive to the major powers. For example, the US sees Mongolia as an important partner in its pivot to Asia, and a sovereign Mongol state next to China could be the source of Inner Mongolia nationalism with a destabilizing effect on China's unity. Stobdan acknowledges Mongolia's role in thwarting Chinese expansionist designs as a reason for India's continuing interest in the nation, "but to merely relate the partnership with Mongolia from the angle of China's fails to consider Mongolia's own strategic interests. In fact, treating Mongolia only as a hedge against a rising China would be rather simplistic and misleading."[70] He believes that India sees the cultural bond with Mongolia as its biggest strategic asset, which explains why India gifted the construction of the first Mongolian Buddhist monastery in India at Bodh Gaya in 2004.[71]

Mongolia's leading specialist on India, Oidov Nyamdavaa, explains the unique relationship between Mongolia and India in security spatial configuration terms[72] related to the "Third Neighbor" policy. He places India in the middle crescent of "Spiritual Neighbours," bound by the Buddhist culture, and thus it is a source of spiritual and material assistance. President Enkhbayar, a fervent Buddhist, embraced this concept of India as Mongolia's spiritual neighbor. Mongolian presidents Punsalmaag Ochirbat in 1994 (when the Treaty of Friendly Relations and Cooperation was signed), Bagabandi in 2001, and Elbegdorj in 2009, as well as Enkhbayar as prime minister in 2004, all made official visits to Delhi. During the Elbegdorj presidency the bilateral relationship was greatly boosted by the Ulaanbaatar visit on May 16–18, 2015, of Indian Prime Minister Shri Narendra Modi. His trip was organized around the commemoration of the sixtieth anniversary of the establishment of diplomatic relations and the twenty-fifth anniversary of Mongolia's democracy.[73] It was the first visit to Mongolia of an Indian prime minister, and Modi was the second Indian leader after Nehru, who supported Mongolia's entrance into the United Nations in the 1960s, to take cultural ownership of the shared Indo-Mongolian heritage.[74] Modi's trip illustrated India's recognition that "the rhetorical of 'spiritual neighbours' is useful for providing additional justification to efforts at strengthening Indian-Mongolian relations, even if geopolitical calculations might actually carry the day."[75] Modi, who was the first Indian leader to address the Mongolian Parliament, "indicated the shift in India's perception—of actively engaging her civilisational partners in a new paradigm and framework partnership."[76] President Elbegdorj in his meeting with the Indian Prime Minister echoed this message:

> Every word you say and every step you take here in Mongolia will be considered as the historical event and legacy in the mutual relations between

> our two countries. . . . Mongolia regards India as its spiritual neighbor and our two countries connected with a long-historical tie. Secondly, Mongolia and India share common values such as democracy, human rights and rule of law. Thirdly, we have ample opportunities to enhance our bilateral relations and partnership.[77]

Commentators on the visit acknowledged that India and Mongolia, the only two democracies in the region, shared a common strategic concern about Chinese hegemony in the region. India was seen as an economic partner for Mongolia, and it was in India's interest not to cede upper Eurasia to China. On that occasion, India and Mongolia signed thirteen agreements to further strengthen bilateral ties on enhancing cooperation in border guarding, policing and surveillance, air services, cybersecurity, and solar and wind renewable energy. The agreements covered economic relations, development partnership, defense and security, people-to-people contacts, strategic partnership, and a renewed Treaty of Friendly Relations and Cooperation. The two sides agreed to establish an Indian-Mongolian Friendship School in Mongolia, to hold an annual cultural program from 2015 through 2018, to foster connections between Mongolia's Diplomatic Academy and India's Foreign Relations Institute, and to hold regular meetings to discuss national security and defense topics. India extended Mongolia a $1 billion credit line for infrastructure development and expansion of Mongolia's railway system that was extended in April 2016. Both sides agreed to intensify civil nuclear cooperation, especially with regard to cancer treatment applications, and strengthen trade through agreements on shipping and logistics, highways, electric power, energy, dairy products, and taxation.[78] India will establish a Cyber Security Training Centre for the Defense Ministry of Mongolia, and the Indian and Mongolian National Security Councils will hold regular consultations on traditional and nontraditional security issues, counterterrorism, and intelligence cooperation. Modi also visited the India-funded Atal Bihari Vajpayee Centre for Excellence in Information and Communication Technology and a medical center. At a joint press conference with Mongolian Prime Minister Saikhanbileg, he remarked, "Today, Mongolia is also an integral part of India's Act East Policy. The destinies of India and Mongolia are closely linked with the future of [the] Asia Pacific region. We can work together to help advance peace, stability and prosperity in this region."[79]

In India the prime minister's Mongolian visit was seen as particularly significant in that it "reinforced in the national consciousness, the urge to re-invent India's civilisational linkages and create a new grand narrative of cooperation and outreach in the regions where India's culture, knowledge and spirituality had once gained deep acceptance and was eagerly assimilated." It also was interpreted in many quarters as a way for Delhi to strengthen its influence in China's backyard.[80] "This time China will be keeping its fingers crossed when Modi lands in Mongolia."[81] The event was viewed as a win-win situation for the two Asian parliamentary democracies to take their bilateral relationship to the next level. However, other Indian commentators were more reserved in their analysis, citing limits to any Indian power play in Mongolia. They claimed that Modi's cultural diplomacy was a conscious policy of putting shared religious heritage with neighbors at the center of his regional engagement.[82]

Since this trip, the Indian government has organized a milk processing plant and the India-Mongolia Joint Information Technology Education and Outsourcing Centre. In 2016 the Mongolia-India Business Council (MIBC) was established to support the businesses of the two countries and to help in expanding cooperation in developing bilateral e-commerce. The MIBC is studying which Mongolian brands in wool, cashmere, water, and meat products can be introduced to the Indian market.[83] India also is exploring green economic development projects with Mongolia and investing in agroecological farming. The two countries are looking at options to increase trade and investment, building upon the Bilateral Investment Protection and Double Taxation Avoidance Agreements already in place. Mongolian-Indian trade has been small and volatile over the past few years due to lack of Mongolian infrastructure. Indian exports in religious items, which do not represent even 1 percent of total Indian trade, make up the bulk of these products. In 2010, bilateral trade stood at $17.4 million, rising to $46.7 million the following year. In 2012, it increased to $60.2 million, fell to $35 million in 2013, and was only $25 million in 2014. An Indian consortium of engineering consultants was awarded construction contracts for 212 kilometers of the east-west highway known as the Millennium Road in 2002 under the Enkhbayar administration. Although $40 million was to be invested in the project, there was difficulty finding sufficient funds to complete the financing. A major future element in the bilateral economic relationship might be cooperation in the field of uranium. In September 2009 they signed a civil nuclear agreement for supply of uranium, and in January 2010 they renewed their agreement on civil nuclear cooperation and discussed Indian participation in Mongolian uranium mining operations, but India has not yet received any Mongolian uranium.

Bilateral defense cooperation has grown, and the militaries of the two countries have conducted exercises known as "Nomadic Elephant" since 2004. In 2017, the twelfth iteration focused on specialized operations in counterinsurgency and counterterrorism. India is also an active participant in the annual Mongolia-hosted weeklong joint multilateral training exercise called the Khaan Quest. Consultations since 2006 between the national security establishments of the two countries have covered issues such as cybersecurity, and cooperation between the Indian Border Security Force and the Mongol General Authority of Border Protection focuses on upgrading Mongolia's border management capacity. India and Mongolia have the potential to work together in regional and subregional groupings to fight against terrorism and Islamic fundamentalism. Strategically, Indian and Mongolian interests in China and Central Asia often coincide, and the Indian press reports that Mongolia has been consulting India on issues relating to the SCO. The two nations could cooperate in Asian energy transportation development, but Mongolia must recognize that India likely will include its own economic agenda in its calculations vis-à-vis Russia, as Delhi seeks to counterbalance Chinese influence in the Asia Pacific region. As an Indian observer wrote, "India's benign presence in Mongolia is desirable for India's future interest in Russia's resource-rich trans-Siberia and Far East."[84]

Trilateralism

Mongolia's trilateralism strategy is motivated by its overall trade predicament and limited options to find a way forward. Faced with serious economic challenges, Mongolia today is very interested in diversifying its mineral-based economy and participating in Eurasian economic growth through transportation integration. For the Mongols, the question is how to maximize the continental integration trends. The Chinese BRI concept attracted attention in Mongolian policymaking circles, mainly because Mongolia initially appeared to be omitted. Concern was intensified by the rapprochement since 2014 between Chinese President Xi and Russian President Putin, which again seemed to exclude a role for Mongolia. Concerned that a "great game" to create a new version of the Eurasian Silk Road was being played out without any Mongolian input, Mongolian President Elbegdorj in 2014 used the celebrations around the commemoration of different anniversaries in Sino-Mongol and Mongol-Russian relations to make certain that his two powerful neighbors did not proceed with transportation and energy cooperation without taking into account the role of Mongolia. Strategically speaking, this challenge could not be met by the "Third Neighbor" principle. New thinking was needed, and President Elbegdorj's administration provided it under the mantle of a trilateralism policy focused on Mongolian, Russian, and Chinese transnational infrastructure development and economic cooperation stimulated by annual summits at the presidential level.

Sino-Russian-Mongolian Trilateralism

After twenty years of unsuccessful efforts to find significant new trading partners for its minerals and animal by-products other than its two border neighbors, Mongols of all political persuasions have come to recognize that they cannot alter the Chinese monopoly over their economy solely through their own "Wolf Strategy" without careful development of real transport and pipeline alternatives to their present poor infrastructure. The collapse of GDP growth and the instability within their mineral-based economy in recent years finally convinced Mongolian policymakers and average citizens to accept that following World Bank and IMF advice to build new roads and rail spurs south to service the Chinese market was necessary in the short term to keep the economy afloat—even though it would perpetuate their dependence on China. This meant a longer-term strategy was required to revive Russian economic investment in Mongolia, build transport infrastructure northward to link with the Trans-Siberian rail system, and promote Mongolia as a reliable and cheaper alternative within the greater Eurasian transit zone for Sino-Russian transit traffic. Moreover, President Elbegdorj and many other Mongolian strategists recognized that the Chinese-Russian political rapprochement, which is based on economic self-interest, can only profit Mongolia if Mongolia has a seat at the negotiating table and participates in drafting new regional transport and energy growth models. Mongolia's interest in foreign policy trilateralism with Russia and China is understandable in this context, but less comprehensible is why, after many years of refusing to include Mongolia in their bilateral trans-continental economic discussions, China and Russia would change their attitudes. The explanation lies in reviewing what took place in the weeks prior to the first trilateral summit on the sidelines of the September SCO annual meeting in Dushanbe, Tajikistan.

Mongolia utilized the commemoration of different bilateral anniversaries in Sino-Mongol and Mongol-Russian relations to hold separate bilateral summit meetings in the summer of 2014 with Chinese and Russian leaders in Ulaanbaatar. During the summit visit of President Xi over August 21–22, China and Mongolia signed twenty-six agreements covering mining and finance, as well as a significant joint declaration upgrading their relationship to a "comprehensive strategic partnership." They agreed to work to increase bilateral trade to $10 billion by 2020 under a "three-in-one" cooperation model integrating mineral exports, infrastructure construction, and financial cooperation. The Chinese side promised to provide Mongolia 1.3 billion RMB ($260 million) of aid within three years for major economic projects and to possibly grant a soft loan in the amount of 1 billion RMB ($162.7 million). The presidents of Mongol Bank and Chinese National Bank agreed to an increase of the currency swap exchange from 10 billion to 15 billion RMB to provide foreign currency to Mongolia's domestic market.[85]

During the summit visit, President Xi's groundbreaking address to the Mongolian Parliament, which was broadcast live on both Mongolian and Chinese television, included an offer for the Mongols to participate in his "China Dream" initiative. Despite generally positive responses to his speech in the official media of both countries, observers noted the nearly universal grimaces on the faces of the listening Mongolian parliamentarians and high-ranking officials and the lack of applause, all caught by China's CCTV cameras but deliberately not broadcast by Mongol TV. Mongolian blogs the following day resonated with nervous negative chatter about Chinese hegemonic ambitions because Xi had begun his speech by reciting a famous Mongolian nationalist poem, referring to Mongolia as his "native land."[86] As a result, the state visit became tainted with controversy, and blowback overwhelmed Xi's friendly release of a special article to the major Mongolian newspapers timed to coincide with his arrival. In that article he had noted that visiting Mongolia was more like visiting one's relatives, and "China hopes that both countries can push cooperation on building inter-connecting railways and roads, [as well as] the development of mines and processing."[87]

Two weeks later, Putin visited Mongolia, ostensibly to celebrate the seventy-fifth anniversary of the Soviet-Mongol victory over Japan in 1939 at Khalkhin Gol (Nomonhan) but actually aimed to jump-start Russia's moribund economic relations with its former Cold War satellite. When Putin arrived for his one-day summit on September 3, fourteen bilateral agreements were concluded that were even vaguer than those with China. For the Mongolian government the greater importance of the visit was the political message that Russia had not forgotten Mongolia. Seven MOUs were signed on aviation, construction, economic development, financial cooperation, the media, and modernizing the key north-south Ulaanbaatar Railway that accounted for 60 percent of Mongolia's freight traffic in 2013.[88] Russian-Mongolian trade volume in 2013 had fallen to $1.6 billion, and Mongolian exports to Russia reached only $70 million (representing 1.4 percent of total Mongolian exports). As a result, Mongolia proposed increasing Russo-Mongolian trade to $10 billion by 2020 and exempting Mongolian goods from Russian customs duties and quotas for twenty years.[89]

Certainly, the economic results of these two bilateral summits in mid-2014 already were positive signs of Mongolia's close relations with Russia and China, so why would Mongolia's push for a new trilateral mechanism to be accepted by the two neighbors? It is highly likely that Mongolia's political-military relationship with the United States, as represented by the short visit of US Secretary of Defense Chuck Hagel to Ulaanbaatar on April 11, 2014, was one of the key factors. Hagel's appearance in Mongolia was wedged in between his visits to China and South Korea. Both the US and Mongolia used the Hagel visit as much for symbolism as for face-to-face negotiations. The Mongolian government sent the message domestically and to China and Russia that the United States was receptive to Mongolia's assuming a more active voice in regional affairs. Mongolian Prime Minister Norov Altankhuyag had emphasized that the government would continue to further expand defense cooperation with the United States by supporting "an implementation of master goals of the Mongolia-USA defense collaboration."[90] Mongolia's stance was repeated by Minister of Defense Dashdemberel Bat-Erdene in a joint news conference when he explained that the Hagel visit had raised bilateral cooperation "to a new volume," and that "Mongolia is adhering to a policy to take part in international activities as much as possible instead of passively observing them."[91]

The fact that Hagel spent only four hours in Mongolia compared to three days in China was not mentioned in the Mongolian media. The US sought increased military ties because this objective was part of the American policy of rebalance in the Asia Pacific region.[92] Hagel's meetings with Mongolian government and military leaders covered regional security matters and future US-Mongolian cooperation: "We in the United States believe that military-to-military cooperation between Mongolia and the United States is very solid, it is very strong, and we look forward to continuing to deepen and strengthen our military cooperation and relationship."[93] Mongolian reporting did not connect the Hagel visit to the ongoing Russian-Ukrainian situation, even though this issue was raised at the joint press conference. Russian actions in Ukraine were very sensitive for Mongolia, causing the government publicly to remain silent about the Russian takeover of Crimea and to abstain from the subsequent UN vote condemning Russian actions. For the Americans, the main "deliverable" from the visit was the signing by Secretary Hagel and Defense Minister Bat-Erdene of a joint vision statement calling for expanding joint training and assistance with no specific linkage to regional issues. Hagel explained that the joint statement "expresses our shared desire to continue deepening that defense relationship."[94]

Mongolian authorities were conscious that one ramification of Russia's actions in Crimea that could ripple back into Northeast Asia was the threat of reconsidering what were thought to be settled international borders. Prior to the Hagel visit, the Mongols had become concerned about loud chatter on Chinese websites calling for PRC rejection of the 1945 UN plebiscite that recognized formal Mongolian independence from the ROC and urging reincorporation of independent Mongolia to the Chinese homeland. When directly questioned in front of Hagel on this matter and on the possibility of establishing US bases in Mongolia, Defense Minister Bat-Erdene avoided possible severe negative reactions from China and Russia by explaining that the establishment of American bases in Mongolia was not permitted: "We have a law not to establish foreign military bases or to station troops in our country."[95] His statement was prominently featured in Mongolian, including English-language, press accounts; however, Mongolian media did highlight that Hagel's Ulaanbaatar bilateral discussions were friendly and positive, compared to the harsh tone of Hagel's Beijing meetings with the Chinese. It also is apparent that Hagel's references to Mongolia as "a valued partner" and "a growing state in regional and global security"[96] were viewed by Mongolia, China, and Russia as US affirmation of Mongolia's growing importance in Asian security affairs. A few months later, President Elbegdorj successfully leveraged the open discussion of a US military base in Mongolia and the Ukrainian crisis then faced by Russia to convince his neighbors that Mongolia should not be an afterthought in their bilateral Eurasian cooperation plans but rather viewed as a valued partner.

Consequently, the Mongols that same spring publicly sought a trilateral summit meeting in Ulaanbaatar. When the summit finally occurred in Dushanbe, President Elbegdorj hailed the meeting as historically significant for the three countries[97] and asked that it take place every three years in Mongolia. He suggested the three leaders work together on specific projects related to transnational transit infrastructure development, and so he rightly could claim success when they agreed in principle to build a Talyn Zam (Steppe Road) in Mongolia and incorporate it into the Chinese BRI and the Russian EEU to revive a premodern transport network for facilitating trade between China and Russia. President Xi concluded that the first trilateral summit was of "great significance to deepening mutual trust among the three parties, and pushing forward regional cooperation in Northeast Asia."[98] Putin also praised the value of the summit: "Things discussed at this meeting create the appropriate mechanism to discuss and resolve the largest projects to be implemented by us in the future, and we agreed to promote our cooperation in this regard." He asserted that the geographic proximity of Mongolia, Russia, and China facilitated long-term projects in infrastructure, energy, and mining: "We have things to discuss and we find it important, feasible and useful to establish a regular dialogue."[99]

The first tripartite summit was followed by two others, so the continuity of this mechanism became firmly established. On July 9, 2015, at the second trilateral summit in Ufa, Russia, on the sidelines of the BRICS (Brazil, Russia, India, China, South Africa) meeting and fifteenth annual SCO summit, Elbegdorj advocated for trilateral cooperation on railway transportation, logistics, facilitation of agricultural and mineral trade, and infrastructure construction. President Xi responded by urging relevant government departments "to step up the docking of development strategies of each [country] and transform the vision into concrete cooperative projects."[100] The three presidents approved a road map for trilateral cooperation and witnessed the signing of a memorandum guideline for building a trilateral economic corridor, a framework agreement on facilitating trilateral trade, and a framework agreement on cooperation on ports of entry among the three countries.

The third tripartite summit on June 23, 2016, organized on the sidelines of the sixteenth SCO meeting in Tashkent, Uzbekistan, saw the emergence of the breakthrough agreement on establishing an Economic Corridor Plan, the purpose of which is to coordinate specific plans to facilitate economic traffic among the countries, similar to the arrangements among EU members:

> This agreement demonstrates that the infrastructure necessary for the future economic development of Mongolia must be developed not only by Mongolia alone but also by integrating with the plans of its neighbor countries, China and Russia. It is not yet clear whether this decision will be beneficial or harmful to Mongolia. However it represents a significant change in direction beyond the limits of its own national sovereignty for creating a new geo-economic environment.[101]

The presidents also signed an agreement between Russia's Federal Customs Service, China's General Administration of Customs, and Mongolia's General Taxation and Customs Administration calling for mutual recognition of customs control inspections of certain goods. Putin noted, "We have launched a mechanism for political consultations now and this is a good opportunity for coordinating our positions on current regional issues," and he supported intensifying cross-border ties through the launch of over thirty trilateral investment projects.[102]

Elbegdorj secured Russian and Chinese acceptance of his proposal to establish a joint investment planning center to develop new cooperation proposals in transportation and construction of communications infrastructure, electricity transmission lines, and energy transport routes. The investment center would determine funding for projects that could be immediately implemented and develop the required feasibility studies. Elbegdorj underlined the need to select promising avenues of trilateral cooperation beyond economic corridors, transport, and customs issues, suggesting trilateral cooperation be extended to agriculture and emergency prevention. Chinese President Xi expressed satisfaction with the momentum of trilateral cooperation: "We three sides should actively engage in the discussion of building cross-border economic cooperation zones, enhance industrial tie-in, boost sub-regional cooperation in our adjacent areas, and promote the common development of our adjacent areas."[103] He urged building the economic corridor and strengthening cooperation in transportation infrastructure connectivity, port construction, industrial capacity, investment, trade and economy, cultural and people-to-people exchanges, and environmental protection within the framework of the SCO.

Under Mongolian President Battulga, trilateral summitry has continued. On June 9, 2018, a fourth trilateral took place on the sidelines of the SCO meeting in Qingdao, China. President Battulga "underlined that as the Mongolian people are looking for better outcomes from the trilateral cooperation projects, he will cooperate closely with Xi Jinping and Putin to make trilateral collaboration effective and beneficial."[104] He also announced that the government had started a dialogue on the issue of Mongolia's becoming a full member of the SCO with the public and policymakers. The next trilateral summit will be held in June of 2019 during the SCO summit in Kyrgyzstan. These events indicate that it is likely the Sino-Russian-Mongolian trilateral relationship will continue for the next decade, fueled by the necessity for all three countries to focus on modern transport infrastructure construction. Bottlenecks on the Mongolian plateau or in the Greater Tumen River region in the past blocked economic integration in favor of national security concerns. However, with growing stability in the greater Northeast Asian region and, particularly, closer political relations between Russia and China, economic forces now trump these security constraints. As long as this atmosphere between the two neighboring superpowers continues, Mongolia can utilize trilateralism for its benefit. A further factor impacting the trilateral mechanism is the present world financial climate. Limited financial options, especially on the Russian side, mean that economies of scale and executing less-expensive pipe, rail, and road projects cause the Mongolian transit corridor to be seen as economically worth developing.

At the same time, other factors hold the potential to thwart Mongolia's economic rise and the efficacy of trilateralism. Mongolian policymakers have noted that while Putin has been somewhat successful in restoring Russia's economy and projecting outward Russian power through his energy security policies, he has not solved the population crisis Russia faces in Siberia and the Far Eastern maritime provinces. Chinese traders and illegal migrants are pouring into these eastern regions in numbers that could threaten to destabilize Russian control of major cities such as Vladivostok. The ramifications from such migration and possible loss of a great amount of Russian territory to China or regional independence movements would seriously endanger Mongolia's ability to protect its national security.[105] Or, if the relationship between China and Russia turns more hostile, or the huge amount of FDI required to build all the new connective infrastructure does not emerge because of a severe economic downturn in China or greater political instability on the Korean Peninsula or among nations in the Sea of Japan and East China Sea, the trilateral policy will fall apart or be ineffective.

US-Japanese-Mongolian Trilateralism

Many foreign observers see Mongolia's push for trilateralism with China and Russia as a worrisome phenomenon, and there is concern over China and Russia's deepening coordination, especially regarding Mongolia and the greater Eurasian continent. President Elbegdorj's real intentions in promoting trilateralism have been questioned by some of Mongolia's third neighbors, despite the strong democratic record of Elbegdorj from his days in the streets as one of the key protest leaders who brought down Mongolia's communist government in 1990. Although the plethora of agreements with both China and Russia to improve Eurasian transportation connections through Mongolia also would help many other partners such as Turkey, Europe, Japan, and South Korea to become stronger regional trade partners, Mongolia's new trilateralism strategy caught many in the restless foreign investor community off guard. When a Mongolian delegation visited New York and Washington in connection with President Elbegdorj's speech to the UN General Assembly in late September 2014, its members were met with a barrage of questions from US officials about the future of Mongolian allegiance to its "Third Neighbor" policy of reaching beyond its two border neighbors to integrate into the world economy, as if Mongolia were returning to a pre-democratic mentality.

While preservation of democracy in Mongolia has been the single most important achievement of the US-Mongolian partnership over the past two decades, the relationship could become insecure since it was not based on economics but on value-driven partnership. Therefore, the US government, including its embassy in Ulaanbaatar, did not support the concept of a trilateral summit in 2014 in Mongolia among Mongolian President Elbegdorj, Russian President Putin, and Chinese President Xi. This was a nonpublic position held not only by the United States but also by its close allies, especially Japan. US authorities thought that China might receive some special considerations in the lucrative Mongolian market for renewable and traditional power generation to the disadvantage of American companies. Japan was concerned that the fanfare and publicity in the region leading up to the "celebration" of the seventy-fifth anniversary of the joint Soviet-Mongolian victory over the Japanese army at Khalkhin Gol might encourage the Chinese and Koreans to engage in a new round of Japan-bashing.

In response to this unease toward Mongolia's new trilateralism with Russia and China, Mongolian foreign policy strategists called for the formalization of another form of trilateralism, this one among the United States, Japan, and Mongolia. One could argue that this informal trilateralism had already existed since the early 1990s, when the United States encouraged and coordinated Japanese leadership in crafting donor assistance policies for Mongolia to make its transition to democracy and the free market. US-Japanese coordination with Mongolia on the prioritization and funding of this transition was carried out very openly, and a pattern developed whereby the United States took the lead in organizing privatization and democracy-building institutions, while Japan became the prime mentor and guide for establishing the economic mechanisms, including banking, that were necessary for Mongolia's free market to function. Over the years, this informal cooperation morphed into an active policy of US-Mongolian military cooperation paralleling but not competing with Mongol-Japanese joint investment in major domestic construction projects from hospitals to roads to airports and power stations.

Strengthening US-Mongolian ties. During the democratic era, Mongolia and the United States have established effective and dynamic defense cooperation that has been mutually beneficial. In order to promote and maintain Asia Pacific regional security and peace, the United States recognizes the pivotal geographical role Mongolia plays on the Eurasian continent between Russia and China. In the post–Cold War era, Mongolia's willingness to simultaneously embrace democracy and free market principles was much appreciated by the US Congress, so Mongolia became a generously funded poster child for a reformed communist country. A resident US Department of Defense Attaché Office was established at the US embassy in Ulaanbaatar in the late 1990s because American policy wanted

> to see the Mongolians develop their political independence and not again fall under the sway of either of the large neighbors. . . . We had a desire to promote the Mongolian armed forces as a peacekeeping force because Washington and certainly we in Ulaanbaatar correctly perceived that a good way to achieve some degree of Western professionalism and military modernization was through peacekeeping training, improving the capabilities of their personnel, units and so forth.[106]

With the rise of international Islamic terrorism and Mongolia's willingness to participate in international coalitions and peacekeeping operations in the 2000s, the joint military relationship became a useful way for the United States to project power on the Asian continent in a low-key, cost-effective manner. Mongolia's military relationship with the United States has greatly developed over the past fifteen years with Mongolian soldiers deployed on ten rotations to Iraq in support of the US-led international coalition's efforts from 2003 to 2010. Mongolia also has maintained a limited military presence since 2005 with US forces fighting in Afghanistan, and these troops train the Afghan National Armed Forces.

Mongolia's motive for developing efficient defense cooperation with the United States centers around its desire to strengthen its national sovereignty after the collapse of the communist system and the withdrawal of its Soviet protector. The US has been instrumental in modernizing Mongolian military units for UN peacekeeping operations worldwide. The Alaska National Guard was twinned with the Mongolian armed forces, and the two continue to conduct annual exercises. The Mongolian defense establishment quickly understood that such cooperation could have a positive impact on modernizing the Mongolian Armed Forces (MAF). With US assistance, Mongolia increased the MAF's capability to become one of the major contributors to UN peacekeeping operations.[107] The United States has trained high-level Mongolian officers at the Naval Postgraduate School in Monterey, California, and the Defense Legal Institute in Providence, Rhode Island, and in 2003 initiated a noncommissioned officer training program. It provided $3 million in grant foreign military financing (FMF) to install a border communications system that includes cellular phone and satellite capability for border guards. The two countries coordinate military relations via annual Bilateral Consultative Council meetings between the Ministry of Defense of Mongolia and the US Department of Defense (DOD).[108] The DOD provides the MAF with $1 million annually in International Military Education and Training and $2 million annually in FMF for vehicles and communications equipment. The Mongolian military is seeking more sophisticated equipment and even planes, possibly available after the US drawdown in Afghanistan. The two nations already are attempting to define a post-Afghanistan relationship to develop cooperation in areas such as military medical services.

In the second decade of US-Mongolian bilateral relations, annual consultations and visits of high-ranking officials became the most visible mechanism to bolster ties. Secretary of State Madeleine Albright visited Mongolia in May 1998, and Deputy Secretary of State Richard L. Armitage visited in January 2004. Mongolian Prime Minister Enkhbayar visited the United States in November 2001, and in July 2004 Mongolian President Bagabandi came to Washington for a working visit with President George W. Bush. The year 2005 was a busy one for American visits to Mongolia: Speaker of the House Dennis Hastert arrived in August; Defense Secretary Donald Rumsfeld in October; and, most importantly, President Bush, First Lady Laura Bush, and Secretary of State Condoleezza Rice journeyed on November 21. The purpose of the Bush visit, the first by an American president, ostensibly was to thank the Mongols for their military participation in Iraq. Agriculture Secretary Mike Johanns led a US delegation to Mongolia in July 2006 in conjunction with the nation's celebration of its 800th anniversary. The following year, Enkhbayar, this time as president, again visited the Bush White House so the two presidents could sign the first Millennium Challenge Compact for Mongolia.

During the Obama administration, the high-level visits continued. In March 2011 Minister of Defense Lu. Bold made a first-ever visit to the Pentagon to meet Secretary of Defense Robert Gates and then toured US Central Command in Tampa. Bold emphasized that Mongolia considered its joint participation in US-led peace and security military operations as the "supreme form" of bilateral military cooperation. In June 2011 President Elbegdorj visited President Obama in the Oval Office, and two months later on August 22, Vice President Joseph Biden stopped several hours in Ulaanbaatar to support Mongolia as an "emerging power" that was building a secure, prosperous, and democratic Asia.[109] Bilateral political and military ties were further deepened by Secretary of Defense Hagel's Ulaanbaatar visit on April 11, 2014, and Secretary of State John Kerry's trip on June 5, 2016.

Mongolia had a particularly warm relationship with Hillary Clinton. In July 2012 Secretary of State Clinton, who had made her first trip to Mongolia when she was First Lady in 1995, returned to Mongolia to attend the Community of Democracies Opening Council and International Women's Leadership Forum. Lauding Mongolia as an excellent example of how freedom and democracy were not exclusively Western concepts, she recalled her visit to the country seventeen years previous, when she was not only enchanted by the nation's beauty, hospitality, energy, and determination but also "especially inspired by the Mongolian people's commitment to democracy." Noting that the country had powerful neighbors motivated by their own agendas for Mongolia's future, Clinton cited the Mongolian people's courage to transform a one-party communist dictatorship into a pluralistic, democratic political system:

> And here in Asia, let's rededicate ourselves to building a freer region. And as we do that, I can say with the same level of certainty that I felt 17 years

> ago, if you want to see democracy in action, if you want to see progress being shaped by leaders who are more concerned about lifting up their people than fattening their bank accounts, come to Mongolia. If you want to see women assuming more and more positions of responsibility rather than being marginalized and left behind, come to Mongolia.[110]

The US economic relationship with Mongolia has not been growing but declining over the past ten years. The US share of overall trade and investment in Mongolia plunged from 2005 to 2015, even though both nations were aware of the decline and tried various measures to reverse the tide. In 2004 the United States exported to Mongolia only $28.1 million worth of products while importing $239.2 million of mostly textile products. However, by 2010, imports had fallen to a meager $11.6 million—a level comparable to the very early 1990s. In 2010, US exports dramatically rose to nearly $115 million, spurred by President Obama's export initiative. This represented a 180 percent increase over 2009, and this favorable trade balance with Mongolia has continued ever since. The political and military relationship between the two countries is still strong and thriving, but the economic relationship is in trouble, increasing disillusionment. This is a source of great concern for both countries, but so far there has been no progress in reversing this decline. There are several important reasons for this situation: (1) the US is not a market for Mongolian minerals; (2) US companies that were middlemen for trading with China have been replaced by Chinese companies with direct ties; (3) US investors are discouraged by the changeable legal environment; (4) Mongolians feel US investment has led to greater Chinese penetration of and monopoly over Mongolia's economy; and (5) the Mongolian government has chosen other foreign companies over US ones rather than continue the pro-American favoritism policy of the 1990s.

The United States has not been a major player in Mongolian rail and transport development, which is seen as the key to Mongolia's future economy and trade diversification. Because Mongolia had to develop an action plan to refinance or repay its external public debt of $1.08 billion beginning in 2017, the United States recognizes that continuing Mongolian economic weakness plagues the bilateral relationship and encourages the growth of Chinese and Russian influence in the country. During the Obama years, US retrenchment away from Mongolia damaged its public reputation by increasing the sense of abandonment in the minds of the Mongolian citizenry and in some official circles. Mongolia's new president, Battulga, has attempted to energize the US-Mongolian economic relationship with the Trump administration and strengthen the American role in Mongolia-US-Japanese trilateralism. Foreign Minister Damdin Tsogtbaatar visited Washington three times in 2018 to meet with US Secretary of State Mike Pompeo and congressional representatives. He finalized the terms of the $350 million Second Millennium Challenge Compact, which was officially signed by Prime Minister Khürelsükh on his

September 2018 visit to Washington, where he met with US Vice President Mike Pence. The flurry of diplomatic activity has been centered on developing a road map for promoting President Battulga's efforts to increase Mongolian cashmere and textile exports through the Congress-authorized Mongolia Third Neighbor Trade Act.[111]

Accelerating Japanese-Mongolian cooperation. Despite the great bilateral progress between Mongolia and Japan, the Mongols saw the strengthening of the US-Japanese alliance in reaction to China's rise as an opportunity to more effectively capitalize on the strong personal relationship of President Elbegdorj with Japanese Prime Minister Abe to encourage the United States and Japan to act with Mongolia in a more formal counterbalancing triangular relationship to Sino-Russian-Mongolian trilateralism. Japan has promoted the idea of a Mongolian-US-Japanese trilateral relationship as a counterweight to China and Russia, and the Mongols see Japan as the best nation to work in concert with the US to stabilize Mongolia's economy. Japan has great interest in Mongolian minerals, and Mongolia has the potential to be a sizable trade partner, if transportation connectivity within Northeast Asia can be achieved. The need to establish a triangular economic relationship with Russia and China also has convinced Mongolian policymakers that they must be more active in forging bilateral Japanese-Mongolian ties in the mineral and other crucial sectors. This growing relationship with Japan has been welcomed by the United States. John Dinger, US ambassador to Mongolia from 2000 to 2003, commented, "When I got there, my understanding was that when Mongolians spoke of a third neighbor, they meant the United States. However, by the time I left it had broadened into third neighbors, which certainly included Japan and South Korea."[112]

Much of the friendly feeling between Mongolia and Japan has accrued from Japanese generosity in ODA and people-to-people educational assistance. In the last three decades the Japanese government provided hundreds of scholarships for Mongolian students. By 2014, it was estimated that there were about 25,000 Mongols living in Japan, 1,000 of them students.[113] The year 2013 was important in Mongolian-Japanese relations because of the reciprocal state visits of their prime ministers. Their bilateral strategic relationship produced significant contracts in the power and construction fields with Japanese companies' and banks' offering the Mongols very long-term low-interest loans for several big projects such as the new capital airport and Ulaanbaatar's metro system. Three months after assuming office, in March 2013, Japanese Prime Minister Shinzo Abe traveled to Mongolia and stated, "I would like to open a new era in Japan-Mongolia relations."[114] Abe's trip to Mongolia, motivated by the desire to seek greater cooperation in energy and trade relations throughout the Northeast Asian region to offset a rising and increasingly hostile China, was the first by a Japanese prime minister in seven years. It also was spurred by the March 2011 Fukushima Daiichi nuclear power plant accident, which had shut down Japanese nuclear power plants and caused authorities to seek other forms of energy.

In his first visit, Abe stressed his "three spirits" of peace, freedom and democracy, and mutual benefit.[115] He specifically was seeking Japanese involvement in the TT coal project and Mongolian assistance in negotiating with North Korea on the Japanese abductee issue. Although the two nations had established a strategic partnership in 2010, Abe offered to accelerate the bilateral relationship in three main categories: (1) cooperation in politics and security, (2) further development of economic relations, and (3) revitalizing people-to-people and cultural exchanges. He emphasized that the two nations shared "common values not only in terms of bilateral relations, but also with regard to regional and global issues" and called for closer cooperation under the Mongolian concept of "vitality" (*erch* or *erch khuch*). He also offered to assist Mongolia in diversifying its economy beyond natural resources and to strongly advance exchanges between the peoples of Japan and Mongolia.[116] Over the next three years, Prime Minister Abe made three state visits to Ulaanbaatar, and Elbegdorj made nine visits to Abe in Tokyo. Their working relationship, coined "Abe and Ebe," was acknowledged as one of the strongest among Asian leaders.

Mongolian Prime Minister Norov Altankhuyag's September 11–14, 2013, trip to Japan reciprocated his counterpart's and underscored the new vibrancy in Mongolian-Japanese relations. One of the main purposes for the trip was to sign a five-year medium-term program of bilateral cooperation to enhance the bilateral strategic partnership through specific projects. Altankhuyag signed an MOU between Mongolia's Development Bank and Japan's Bank for International Cooperation that gave Mongolia special drawing rights and guaranteed Mongolian bonds for purchase of Japanese equipment. Another significant development was an agreement between the two banks to sell as much as $600 million worth of "Samurai" yen bonds, designed as a mechanism for foreign investors to invest in Mongolia's state-owned TT coal deposit and affiliated rail, power, and water projects. Investors could choose to be repaid in coal. Also discussed were the street project to construct a highway along the capital's Tuul River, a sewage system in Ulaanbaatar's outlying *ger* districts, the Ulaanbaatar metro, a soft loan to implement the New *Sum* (county) Plan, expert training in environment and mining, and cooperation in industrial projects such as establishment of a refinery in Darkhan City and metallurgy and coking coal reprocessing factories in Darkhan and Selenge provinces.[117]

Mongolia has become a conduit between Japan and North Korea because the two nations lack diplomatic ties. In March 2014, the parents of Megumi Yokota, a now-dead Japanese national abducted from Japan in the 1970s by North Korean agents, were allowed by North Korea to meet secretly in Ulaanbaatar with her daughter, Kim Eun Gyong. The Japanese press revealed that Abe discussed such abductions during the mid-September visit of Mongolian

Prime Minister Altankhuyag to Tokyo[118] and likely again during an overnight stay by President Elbegdorj in Abe's private residence on September 29.[119] An unnamed DPRK diplomatic source claimed the agenda for the subsequent Elbegdorj trip to Pyongyang included the abductee issue and then linked the Mongolian President's trip to the mysterious purchase by a Mongolian company of the headquarters of Chongryon, a pro-DPRK organization in Japan. This building also served as Pyongyang's de facto embassy in Tokyo. There was speculation that North Korea was permitted to sell the building at an inflated price to the Mongols in order to pay for the maintenance of Keumsusan Memorial Palace where the bodies of Kim Il-sung and Kim Jong-il are displayed. The entire process was thought to involve money laundering in exchange for North Korean movement on the Japanese abductee issue.[120]

Although the Mongolia government still has not allowed Japanese FDI in the TT coal mine operation, other aspects of their economic relationship have progressed dramatically. In large measure this was due to the persistent hard work of Japan's Ambassador to Mongolia Takenori Shimizu (2011–2016), a fluent Mongolian speaker with in-depth knowledge of the Mongols. The two countries signed the Japan-Mongolia Economic Partnership Agreement in February 2015, which was expected to remove tariffs on about 96 percent of the combined total value of trade, valued at ¥41.8 billion in 2012. Mongolian government statistics for 2012 revealed that 66.4 percent of Japan's exports to Mongolia consisted of automobiles, followed by machinery at 18.5 percent and chemical engineering products at 5.1 percent. Meanwhile, according to the Japanese Finance Ministry, 53 percent of Mongolia's exports to Japan—a total of ¥1.9 billion in 2012—was made up of coal, other mineral products represented 25 percent, and clothing 15.4 percent.[121] Japan also pledged an additional ¥36.85 billion ($307.5 million) in loans beyond the original ¥28.8 billion loan ($284.55 million) of May 2008 to construct a new Ulaanbaatar international airport.[122]

Future bilateral cooperation likely will revolve around railways, coal, and industrial cluster formation. At a July 2016 summit with Abe, Elbegdorj promised to establish closer cooperation in the international arena, support a seat for Japan on the UN Security Council, and promote the Japan-US-Mongolia trilateral dialogue. Abe responded that Japan would continue its economic cooperation and emphasize defense and security collaboration by dispatching a defense attaché to Ulaanbaatar in early 2017. The two nations signed a midterm strategic partnership program (2017–2021) in March 2017 during Mongolian Foreign Minister Mönkh-Orgil's Tokyo visit. At that time, Japan also agreed to an $850 million soft loan for implementing synthetic gas and fuel production projects using Mongolian coal and Japanese technology,[123] and, when Mongolian Parliament Speaker Miyeegomb Enkhbold met with Prime Minister Abe, he noted that "Mongolia is rich in coal and solar and wind energy sources and has [the] possibility to generate energy using those sources, to join [a] unified energy network of the North East

Asia and supply energy to the countries of the region. We would like to implement these projects in collaboration with Japan."[124]

Japanese Prime Minister Abe has started to build a working relationship with President Elbegdorj's successor, Battulga. The two first met in Vladivostok in September 2017, on the sidelines of the third Eastern Economic Forum where Battulga suggested the two countries establish a jointly operated port in the Far East to handle TT coal. Abe pledged Japan's support for Mongolia's policy to secure access to international waters and proposed expanding defense cooperation and working to settle the Korean Peninsula and other Northeast Asian issues.[125] Their second summit, on September 11, 2018, also occurred in Vladivostok while the two were attending the fourth Eastern Economic Forum.[126] At that meeting President Battulga expressed Mongolia's interest in supplying energy to a Northeast Asian super grid and cooperating with Japan in the areas of tourism, agriculture, and the establishment of an eco-city near the new Japanese-built airport.[127]

The public reason given by the Mongols for the US-Japanese-Mongolian trilateral relationship is centered around including Mongolia in a multilateral framework to approach North Korea. The new trilateralism also is justified as nonthreatening toward Mongolia's neighbors because relations would be at the foreign ministerial level rather than the presidential summit level like the Mongolian-Chinese-Russian trilateral relationship. In 2013 the leaders of Japan and Mongolia agreed in principle to pursue a regular trilateral dialogue with the United States,[128] and in September 2015 the United States, Japan, and Mongolia announced that trilateral foreign ministerial talks would be held "to tap into Mongolia's close ties with North Korea and settle a host of issues involving Pyongyang."[129] The inaugural trilateral meeting among Mongolia, the United States, and Japan was held on September 29, 2015, in New York to discuss "some topics of deepening regional security cooperation and expanding economic relations."[130] Mongolian Foreign Minister Purevsuren, US Assistant Secretary of State for the Bureau of East Asian and Pacific Affairs Daniel Russel, and director general for the Asian and Oceanian Affairs Bureau of the Ministry of Foreign Affairs of Japan Junichi Ihara met on the sidelines of the opening of the UN General Assembly. Their joint statement explained that the new framework "laid the foundation for an important dialogue mechanism with our Third Neighbors—the U.S. and Japan—to exchange views on a broad range of regional and global security and economic issues, and on how to coordinate actions at the regional and global levels that reflect shared interest."[131]

The Trump administration has regularized the annual trilateral meeting. In the August 30, 2017, discussion in Ulaanbaatar, the importance of the Mongolia–United States–Japan trilateral meeting was underscored as a foundational mechanism for Mongolia and its two Third Neighbors to exchange views on multilateral cooperation and economic integration. The focus was on the threat posed by North Korea, and the parties agreed to promote trilateral and multilateral security and find ways to increase trade.[132] At the third trilateral meeting in Tokyo on April 26, 2018, they discussed the Indo-Pacific vision of the US and Japan and welcomed Korean Peninsula developments while agreeing to maintain pressure on the DPRK to secure denuclearization.[133]

Notes

1. Mark Green, "Mongolia, 25 Years from Soviet Satellite to Democratic Partner," in IRI Conference on Mongolia's 25 Years of Democracy, *The Hill,* May 1, 2015.

2. Norihiko Ikeda, "Mongolia: Will It Remain a Local Buffer Nation Between China and Russia, or Become a Small Yet Global Nation? A New Perspective on the 'Third Neighbor Policy,'" *Mongol Messenger,* October 28, 2016.

3. Ibid.

4. E. Oyundari, "Mongolia Celebrates the 25th Anniversary of Democratic Parliamentary Elections," *UB Post,* July 30, 2015, http://ubpost.mongolnews.mn/?p=15540.

5. "Mongolia—Neutrality," Former President of Mongolia website, September 9, 2015, http://eng.president.mn/newsCenter/viewNews.php?newsId=1662.

6. Tsakhia Elbegdorj, "Statement by President of Mongolia, at the General Debate of the 70th Session of the United Nations General Assembly," New York, September 29, 2015, http://eng.president.mn/newsCenter/viewNews.php?newsId=1674..

7. Tsakhia Elbegdorj, "Mongolia as a Neutral State" (speech presented at the World Economic Forum, Davos, Switzerland, January 18, 2016), https://www.weforum.org/agenda/2016/01/mongolia-as-a-neutral-state/.

8. Ch. Unurbayar, human rights and legal policy adviser to the president, quoted in B. Erdenechimeg, "Mongolia Submits Draft Law on the Status of Permanent Neutrality," *GoGo Mongolia,* October 21, 2015.

9. Jargalsaikhan Enkhsaikhan quoted in "Sandwiched Between China and Russia, Mongolia Intent on Seeking Permanent Neutrality," Associated Press, November 2, 2015.

10. R. Bold, "Why Ruin Effective Foreign Policy?" (in Mongolian), *Undesnii Shuudan,* no. 272 (October 8, 2015).

11. "Sandwiched Between China and Russia."

12. Ibid.

13. Ts. Mönkh-Orgil quoted in "Our Weight Depends on How Many Friends We Have Got," *Mongol Messenger,* October 21, 2016.

14. Interview with DPRK Ambassador Hong Kyu by Sh. Batbold and N. Gantuya, "DPRK Ambassador Addresses Workforce Issue and Bilateral Relations," *Mongol Messenger,* November 25, 2016.

15. Ha-young Choi, "Mongolia to Send Coal Through N. Korean Port," *NK News,* February 25, 2015.

16. "North Korea, Mongolia Expand Economic Cooperation," Seoul, *Yonhap News Agency,* in Korea Central News Agency, *North Korea Newsletter,* No. 271 (July 18, 2013).

17. "Mongolia: Protect Rights of North Korean Migrant Workers," Human Rights Watch, August 20, 2008. This is second to 5,976 Chinese foreign workers.

18. *North Korea Newsletter,* No. 271 (July 18, 2013).

19. "North Korean Workers to Leave Mongolia as UN Sanctions Bite," *NEWS agency,* December 4, 2017, https://news.mn/en/765907/.

20. Ibid.

21. Gale, "North Korea's Lucrative Labor Exports Come Under Pressure."

22. "Report: Mongolia Could Host North Korean Refugee Camp," *Mongolia Web,* October 2, 2008.

23. "Mongolia Not Planning Camps for N. Koreans," *Gulf Times* (Qatar), November 24, 2006.

24. There were media reports in October 2009 that South Korean president Lee Myung-bak was supportive of opening Mongolian camps, but his successor has not publicly endorsed this policy.

25. "Mongolian President's Visit to North Korea Aimed at Increasing Ties," *South China Morning Post,* October 28, 2013.

26. "Mongolia Will Work with N. Korea to Promote NE Asia Stability: President," *Korea Herald*, October 29, 2013.

27. Ibid.

28. "Ts. Elbegdorj: Our Two Countries Are Good Friends,"*Montsame*, November 5, 2013.

29. "Mongolia's Elbegdorj Sees Trade Boost Through North Korean Ports," *Mongolian Economy and Finance*, October 31, 2013," http://mongoliaeconomy.blogspot.com/2013/10/mongolias-elbegdorj-sees-trade-boost.html.

30. "North Korea Takes First Steps Towards Oil Exploration," *The Guardian*, July 1, 2014, https://www.theguardian.com/world/2014/jul/01/north-korea-oil-gas-exploration.

31. Jee Abbey Lee, "Former US Advisor Meets With N. Korean Officials," *VOA News*, May 28, 2014, https://www.voanews.com/a/former-us-advisor-meets-with-n-korean-officials/1924791.html.

32. J. C. Finley, "Mongolia Leverages Diplomatic Ties with North Korea," United Press International, December 4, 2014, https://www.upi.com/Top_News/World-News/2014/12/04/Mongolia-leverages-diplomatic-ties-with-North-Korea/4921417633447/.

33. Damba Ganbat, "National Security Concept of Mongolia: Basic Principle," in *Security Outlook of the Asia Pacific Countries and Its Implications for the Defense Sector* (Tokyo: National Institute for Defense Studies, 2014), 96.

34. Tsenkher Suld NGO, established in 2005, is a nonprofit organization aimed at promoting Mongolia's nuclear-weapon-free policy and its activities. See "Northeast Asian Delegates Gather in Ulaanbaatar to Discuss Regional Issue," *Mongol Messenger*, November 18, 2016.

35. The Global Partnership for the Prevention of Armed Conflict network, which consists of local, regional, and international civil society organizations and networks involved in conflict prevention and peacebuilding activities, operates in over 100 countries around the globe through its fifteen branches. See ibid.

36. Ri Su-yong has served as ambassador from the DPRK to Lichtenstein, the Netherlands, and Switzerland, as well as DPRK resident representative to the United Nations in Geneva.

37. "North Korean Foreign Affairs Minister to Visit Mongolia," *NK News*, February 23, 2015; "Mongolia, North Korea Sign MoU" and "North Korean Foreign Minister in Mongolia on Three-Day Visit to Further Cooperation," *NK News*, February 24, 2015.

38. According to *NK News,* KCNA Watch data in 2014 and 2015, https://kcnawatch.co/periodicals/dpr-korea/.

39. Adam Taylor, "Why Mongolia Hopes to Host a Trump-Kim Jong Un Meeting," *Washington Post*, April 20, 2018, https://www.washingtonpost.com/news/worldviews/wp/2018/04/20/why-mongolia-hopes-to-host-a-trump-kim-jong-un-meeting/?noredirect=on&utm_term=.235625c456bf.

40. Ambassador Mark Minton quoted in Finley, "Mongolia Leverages Diplomatic Ties."

41. Bolor Lkhaajav, "Mongolia's Small Country Diplomacy and North Korea," *The Diplomat*, September 29, 2016.

42. The Xiongnu ruled the steppes of northeast Central Asia and parts of Siberia, Inner Mongolia, Gansu, and Xinjiang. They were in constant contact with the Chinese kingdoms to the south, particularly the Han dynasty (206 BCE–220 CE) to the south. Times of conflict alternated with exchanges of tribute, trade, and marriage. Scientists have not conclusively identified the ethnicity of the Xiongnu, who may or may not be associated with the Huns of the Roman Empire, but in the minds of Mongolia and Turkey, the connection is widely accepted.

43. "Mongolia Honors Turkey's Deputy Prime Minister," Anadolu Agency, October 28, 2014, https://www.aa.com.tr/en/turkey/mongolia-honors-turkeys-deputy-prime-minister/106698.

44. Kh. Aminaa, "UB Observes Turkish Cultural Days for the 3rd Consecutive Year," *Mongol Messenger*, April 29, 2016.

45. "Mongolia, Turkey Sign Parliamentary Cooperation Agreement," news.mn, in *Mongolia Economy 27.06.2014, Newswire*, Issue 331, June 24, 2014. https://www.slideshare.net/ulziimyagmar/27062014-newswire-issue331.

46. "HPP Development Project on the Khovd River Is Temporarily Suspended," World Wildlife Fund, June 30, 2016, wwf.panda.org/wwf_news/?272256/HPP-development-project-on-the-Khovd-river-is-temporarily-suspended.

47. "Turkish Ambassador Gets au Fait with Altanbulag FTZ," *Mongol Messenger*, March 13, 2015.

48. "Parliament Speaker Visits South Gobi Development Projects," *Mongol Messenger*, March 13, 2015.

49. "Roundtable Meeting: Turkish-Mongolian Relations," Center for Strategic Research, Ministry of Foreign Affairs of Turkey, May 12–15, 2014, http://sam.gov.tr/roundtable-meeting-turkish-mongolian-relations/.

50. "Defense Minister of Turkey Ismet Yilmaz Pays Official Visit to Mongolia," *Montsame*, September 26, 2014, in *Mongolian Economy and Finance*, http://mongolia economy.blogspot.com/2014/10/mongolia-brief-september-26-2014.html.

51. "Mongolia and Turkey Sign Over 100 Cooperation Documents Since 1990," *Montsame*, October 5, 2016.

52. B. Batchimeg, "Mongolia and Turkey Targets to Increase Trade Turnover to USD 300 Million," *Montsame*, April 6, 2018, http://montsame.mn/en/read/14419.

53. Hannah Beech, "Turkish School Leader Abducted, and Released, in Mongolia," *New York Times*, July 28, 2018, https://www.nytimes.com/2018/07/28/world/europe/turkish-school-leader-abducted-and-released-in-mongolia.html.

54. Manochehr Dorraj and Nader Entessar, "Iran's Northern Exposure: Foreign Policy Challenges in Eurasia" (CIRS Occasional Paper no. 13, Center for International and Regional Studies, Georgetown University, School of Foreign Service in Qatar, 2013), 20.

55. Hazara are Shiite Turko-Mongols in Afghanistan who have been repressed by the Taliban and the Afghan majority Sunni population. Continuous war and brutalities resulted in Hazara migration to Iran as well as to Pakistan; however, Hazaras in Iran accuse the Iranians of maltreatment. For the last twenty years, Hazara elements in Iran have appealed for Mongolian sanctuary and support to prevent Iranian forced repatriation to Afghanistan. Mongolia responds cautiously on this issue, because it sees expanding ties to Iran as one partial counterweight to China's economic monopolization.

56. The president of Mongolia's Meat Association, M. Lhachinbaltai, *Montsame*, news.mn, November 13, 2010, accessed March 11, 2011.

57. Davaasharav Munkhchimeg, "Flock On: Mongolia Meat Exporters Turn to Iran's Halal Markets," Reuters, August 22, 2018, https://www.reuters.com/article/us-mongolia-meat-halal/flock-on-mongolia-meat-exporters-turn-to-irans-halal-markets-idUSKCN1L70EU.

58. "AREVA Uranium Exploration and Mining in Mongolia," *nuclear-news.net,* May 4, 2015, https://nuclear-news.net/2015/05/04/areva-uranium-exploration-and-mining-in-mongolia.

59. "Iran Opens Nuclear Site to Mongolia's President," Associated Press, September 3, 2012, http://triblive.com/news/2532074-74/iran-nuclear-site-visit-elbegdorj-iranian-mongolia-president-tehran-uranium.

60. "Iran Ready to Enhance Economic Ties with Mongolia," Mehr News Agency, August 30, 2015, http://en.mehrnews.com/news/109645/Iran-ready-to-enhance-economic-ties-with-Mongolia.

61. "Iran, Mongolia Resolute to Expand Bilateral Ties," Press TV, December 23, 2015, https://theiranproject.com/blog/2015/12/23/iran-mongolia-resolute-to-expand-bilateral-ties.

62. "Iran, Mongolia Discuss Expansion of Trade Ties," *Tehran Times*, September 10, 2018, https://www.tehrantimes.com/news/427378/Iran-Mongolia-discuss-expansion-of-trade-ties.

63. Brandon Miliate, "Modigolia? Indian-Mongolian Relations Post-PM Modi's Trip to Ulaanbaatar," *Mongolia Focus* (blog), "Policy Series: Typical Explanations for Policy Failures (II) Oyu Tolgoi on Track Again," May 18, 2015, http://blogs.ubc.ca/mongolia/2015/modigolia-indian-mongolian-relations/.

64. Oidovyn Nyamdavaa, *Mongolia-India Relations* (Ulaanbaatar: Bhavan Books, 2004), 81–89.

65. It involved signing cooperation agreements and providing substantive development aid and technical support. Beyond military training and transport connectivity

initiatives, New Delhi developed programs to support capacity-building and human resource development. P. Stobdan, "India, Buddhism and Geopolitics in Central Asia: Regaining Centrality," *IDSA Policy Brief*, June 25, 2010, 3, https://idsa.in/system/files/PB_IndiaBuddhismandGeopoliticsinCentralAsia.pdf.

66. Ibid., 4.

67. At the First India–Central Asia Dialogue, a Track II initiative. See "Keynote Address by MOS Shri E. Ahamed at First India-Central Asia Dialogue," *Media Center*, Ministry of External Affairs (India), June 12, 2012, http://www.mea.gov.in/Speeches-Statements.htm?dtl/19791/Keynote+address+by+MOS+Shri+E+Ahamed+at+First+IndiaCentral+Asia+Dialogue#.

68. Stobdan, "India, Buddhism and Geopolitics in Central Asia," 4.

69. Anirban Ganguly, "Modi in Mongolia: Rekindling a Civilisational Link," *Focus News* (New Delhi), May 18, 2015.

70. P. Stobdan, "In Modi's Mongolia Pivot, a Test of Indian Soft Power."

71. India and Mongolia signed an agreement to construct a Mongolian-run Buddhist monastery in Bodh Gaya, Bihar, where according to Buddhist tradition Gautama Buddha attained enlightenment. The Bihar government gave a free grant of land on which to build the monastery; Prime Minister of Mongolia Nambar Enkhbayar personally laid the foundation stone. See "Mongolian PM Lays Monastery Stone," *Times of India*, January 19, 2004; Azera Rahman, "From Land of Chinggis Khan, a Buddhist Monastery for India," *India News Post*, December 13, 2009.

72. From a Mongolian strategic point of view of special security, Russia and China are in the inner crescent; India, Japan, and South Korea in the middle (spiritual) crescent; and the United States and European Union in the outer crescent. See Nyamdavaa, *Mongolia-India Relations*, 75–76.

73. Phunchok Stobdan, "India and Mongolia."

74. Monish Gulati, "Modi in Mongolia: India Looking to Play Larger Asia-Pacific Role?," *South Asia Monitor*, May 16, 2015, http://southasiamonitor.org/detail.php?type=sl&nid=11828.

75. Miliate, "Modigolia."

76. Ganguly, "Modi in Mongolia."

77. "Prime Minister of the Republic of India Shri Narendra Modi Pays Courtesy Call on President Elbegdorj," *GoGo Mongolia*, May 18, 2015, http://mongolia.gogo.mn/r/146096.

78. Miliate, "Modigolia."

79. "Text of the PM's press statement after the Signing of Agreements in Ulaanbaatar, Mongolia," PMINDIA, May 17, 2015, http://www.pmindia.gov.in/en/news_updates/text-of-the-pms-press-statement-after-the-signing-of-agreements-in-ulaanbaatar-mongolia/.

80. "Modi Holds Talks in Mongolia, Seeks Stronger Ties," *Gulf Times*, May 17, 2015. Mongolia was seen as a new opportunity and strategic leverage for India in dealing with China: "If China spends so much political energy in cultivating India's neighbours in the subcontinent and the Indian Ocean, it has been argued, Delhi should be doing the same on China's periphery." See C. Raja Mohan, "Chinese Takeaway: PM Modi in Mongolia," *Indian Express,* May 12, 2015, http://carnegieendowment.org/2015/05/12/chinese-takeaway-pm-modi-in-mongolia/i8gf.

81. Rajeev Sharma, "Forget Uranium: Real Reason Behind PM Modi's Mongolia Visit Is China," *Firstpost*, May 9, 2015.

82. Mohan, "Chinese Takeaway."

83. Ch. Khaliun, "Mongolia India Business Council Opens to Support Businesses," *UB Post*, April 18, 2016.

84. Mohan, "Chinese Takeaway."

85. "Currency Swap," *Investopedia*, https://www.investopedia.com/terms/c/currencyswap.asp.

86. From the Natsagdorj poem, "My Native Land." Xi read this poem to open his August 21, 2014, speech to the Mongolian Parliament.

87. Terrence Edwards, David Stanway, "Mongolia Eyes Economic Boost from China President's Visit," Reuters, August 21, 2014, https://www.reuters.com/article/us-mongolia-china-idUSKBN0GL0HG20140821.

88. Ulaanbaatar Railway currently manages 50 percent of Mongolia's freight transport and one-fourth of passenger transport. However, they do not pay any taxes to the government and run huge deficits every year. Khash-Erdene Bayarsaikhan, "Ulaanbaatar Railway's Bear Service," *UB Post*, September 26, 2016.

89. "Russia's Putin in Mongolia for 5-Hour Visit," Associated Press, September 3, 2014, http://www.dailymail.co.uk/wires/ap/article-2741432/Putin-traveling-Mongolia-5-hour-visit.html.

90. *Mongol Messenger*, April 11, 2014, accessed April 23, 2014.

91. B. Khuder, "Hagel: It Is Important for Our Countries to Keep Friendly Cooperation," *Montsame,* April 10, 2014.

92. E. Dari, "U.S. Defense Minister Chuck Hagel Seeks Increased Ties with Mongolia," *UB Post*, April 11, 2014, http://ubpost.mongolnews.mn/?p=8691.

93. Cheryl Pellerin, "Hagel, Mongolian Defense Minister Agree to Deepen Ties," American Forces Press Service (Ulaanbaatar), April 11, 2014, http://archive.defense.gov/news/newsarticle.aspx?id=122044.

94. Ibid.

95. "US Defence Secretary Chuck Hagel Boosts Mongolia Ties As Asia Trip Ends," *South China Morning Post*, April 10, 2014, https://www.scmp.com/news/asia/article/1474493/us-defence-secterary-chuck-hagel-boosts-mongolia-ties-asia-trip-ends.

96. Pellerin, "Hagel, Mongolian Defense Minister Agree to Deepen Ties."

97. With the exception of a tripartite meeting held almost a century ago at the level of vice foreign ministers. G. Purevsambuu, "First-Ever Summit Held Between Presidents of Mongolia, Russia, and China," *Mongol Messenger*, September 19, 2014.

98. "China, Russia, Mongolia to Create Economic Corridor," *BRICS Post,* September 12, 2014, http://thebricspost.com/china-russia-mongolia-to-create-economic-corridor/#.VEqSQDHD-po4.

99. Purevsambuu, "First-Ever Summit Held Between Presidents of Mongolia, Russia, and China."

100. "Xi Assents to Trilateral Summit with Russia, Mongolia," *BRICS Post,* August 22, 2014, http://thebricspost.com/xi-assent-to-trilateral-summit-with-russia-mongolia/#.WBy6EoWcF9A.

101. Ikeda, "Mongolia."

102. Khaliun Chimeddorj, "Mongolia, Russia and China Agree to Establish Economic Corridor," *UB Post,* June 27, 2016.

103. "China, Russia, Mongolia Endorse Development Plan on Economic Corridor," *Xinhua*, June 24, 2016, http://english.cctv.com/2016/06/24/ARTIJkwoLdfFUjK7unWMv0lN160624.shtml.

104. T. Bayarbat, "Mongolian, Russian and Chinese Presidents Meet at SCO Summit," *UB Post*, June 11, 2018.

105. While the Russian population in 2000–2010 saw a total decrease of 3.4 percent, in the Far East the decrease was 6.8 percent because of unemployment and quality of life issues. See Jeffrey Reeves, "Mongolia's Place in China's Periphery Diplomacy," *Open Forum*, The Asan Forum, April 7, 2016, http://www.theasanforum.org/mongolias-place-in-chinas-periphery-diplomacy/.

106. "Ambassador Alphonse F. La Porta," interview by Charles Stuart Kennedy, Association for Diplomatic Studies and Training Foreign Affairs Oral History Project, February 11, 2004, 166–167, http://www.adst.org/OH%20TOCs/La%20Porta,%20Alphonse%20F.toc.pdf.

107. Mongolia has deployed a battalion with 850 peacekeepers in support of the UN mission in South Sudan and provided field hospitals to the UN mission in Darfur, and numerous individual military officers from Mongolia serve at other UN peacekeeping missions in Africa and worldwide.

108. "Ambassador Talks to the Mongolian Observer," Embassy of Mongolia website, June 1, 2016, http://mongolianembassy.us/2016/06/ambassador-talks-to-the-mongolian-observer/#.WCZfrIWcF9A.

109. "Conference Call with Reporters to Discuss Vice President Biden Trip to China, Mongolia, and Japan," The White House Office of the Vice President, August 15, 2011, https://obamawhitehouse.archives.gov/the-press-office/2011/08/15/conference-call-reporters-discuss-vice-president-biden-trip-china-mongol.

110. "Hillary Clinton at the International Women's Leadership Forum Ulaanbaatar Mongolia," *Still4Hill.com*, July 9, 2012, https://still4hill.com/2012/07/09/hillary-clinton-at-the-the-international-womens-leadership-forum-ulaanbaatar-mongolia/.

111. "U.S., Mongolia Celebrate Signing of $350 Million MCC Compact to Address Impending Water Crisis," Millennium Challenge Corporation, September 20, 2018, https://www.mcc.gov/news-and-events/release/release-092018-us-mongolia-joint-declaration.

112. "Ambassador John R. Dinger," interview by Charles Stuart Kennedy, Association for Diplomatic Studies and Training Foreign Affairs Oral History Project, March 4, 2013, 59, http://adst.org/wp-content/uploads/2013/12/Dinger-John-R.pdf.

113. The numbers differ according to Jargalsaikhan Mendee, "Beyond the Quagmire: The Future of Mongolia's United States and Japan Partnerships," video, East-West Center, August 20, 2014, https://www.eastwestcenter.org/events/beyond-the-quagmire-the-future-mongolia%E2%80%99s-united-states-and-japan-partnerships.

114. William Sposato, "Japan Seeks Stronger Mongolia Ties," *Wall Street Journal*, March 30, 2013, http://www.wsj.com/articles/SB10001424127887324685104578392123216653156.

115. "Prime Minister Abe's Article Contributed to Four Mongolian Newspapers," *Speeches and Statements by the Prime Minister*, Prime Minister of Japan, March 29, 2013, http://japan.kantei.go.jp/96_abe/statement/201303/29_mongol_e.html.

116. Ibid.

117. *Mongol Messenger*, September 20, 2013, accessed October 1, 2013.

118. *Asahi shimbun*, October 29, 2013.

119. This is the first time that the prime minister of Japan, Shinzo Abe, had invited a leader of a foreign country to his home. "Shinzo Abe Invites President Ts. Elbegdorj to His Home," *Montsame,* September 30, 2013.

120. "Chongryon Hq Sale Decision Delayed," Japan Property Central, October 24, 2013, http://japanpropertycentral.com/2013/10/chongryon-hq-sale-decision-delayed/.

121. Masaaki Kameda, "Japan, Mongolia Sign Economic Partnership Agreement," *Japan Times*, February 15, 2015.

122. Loan provided by the Japan Bank for International Cooperation. See "New Ulaanbaatar International Airport, Mongolia," Airport Technology, http://www.airport-technology.com/projects/new-ulaanbaatar-international-airport/.

123. The thirty-year loan has a 1 to 1.5 percent interest rate. Turmunkh Bayarbat, "Japan to Grant an 850 Million USD Soft Loan to Mongolia," *UB Post*, March 31, 2017.

124. B. Ooluun, "Midterm Program on Strategic Partnership Signed," *Mongol Messenger*, March 31, 2017.

125. "Prime Minister of Japan Shinzo Abe Pays Courtesy Call on President of Mongolia Kh. Battulga," President of Mongolia website, September 6, 2017, https://president.mn/en/2017/09/06/prime-minister-of-japan-shinzo-abe-pays-courtesy-call-on-president-of-mongolia-kh-battulga/.

126. "Japan-Mongolia Summit Meeting," Ministry of Foreign Affairs of Japan, September 11, 2018, https://www.mofa.go.jp/a_o/c_m1/mn/page3e_000919.html.

127. "Meeting with Shinzo Abe, Prime Minister of Japan," President of Mongolia website, September 11, 2018, https://president.mn/en/2018/09/11/meeting-with-shinzo-abe-prime-minister-of-japan-eef2018/.

128. Sposato, "Japan Seeks Stronger Mongolia Ties."

129. "Japan, U.S., Mongolia Mull First Trilateral Foreign Ministerial Talks," *Japan Times,* August 14, 2015.

130. "Ambassador Talks to the Mongolian Observer."

131. "The First Mongolia-U.S.-Japan Trilateral Meeting Was Held in New York," Mongolian National Broadcasting, September 15, 2015, http://www.mnb.mn/i/64855.

132. "Joint Statement from Mongolia-U.S.-Japan Trilateral Meeting," Ministry of Foreign Affairs of Mongolia, August 30, 2017, http://www.mfa.gov.mn/?p=41580&lang=en.

133. "Joint Statement of the 2018 U.S.-Japan-Mongolia Trilateral Meeting," US Department of State, April 27, 2018, https://www.state.gov/r/pa/prs/ps/2018/04/281266.htm.

12

Future Options

In the early decades of the twenty-first century, world demand for energy resource minerals has put a spotlight on Mongolia's boom-bust economy. However, because these natural resources have posed demanding hurdles for sustainable and effective management, many Mongolians have come to believe that development of these vast resources has not resulted in the promised broad-based, inclusive growth and benefits to the population. Rather, it has led to corruption within government and in the mining sector and foreign, specifically Chinese, control over trade and economic relations. Mongolia distinguishes itself from other countries in its region and even in the world because of its strong links to its traditional nomadic heritage, so different from the sedentary, agricultural societies that dominate the Asian region. Many inside and outside Mongolia are firmly committed to preserving and extending the country's pristine natural habitats. We should not expect conditions to be static, because the nomadic lifestyle over the millennia constantly has been evolving, like all lifestyles and economies, and does not exist in a vacuum. Rather, it is dependent upon and a supplier of the sedentary economies that surround it.

A modern dilemma is that there are millions more herded animals on the Mongolian plateau than ever in Mongolian history, some seventy-three million as of July 2016,[1] yet the animal types and pasturing system are not the same as centuries ago. This is the situation facing today's Mongolian nomads and the rest of their countrymen as they attempt to modernize and adapt themselves and their nation to the globalized world. During the last twenty-five years of democracy building and the creation of a free market economy, Mongolian policymakers have faced the challenge of development and poverty alleviation while managing delicate foreign relations.

Although economic growth has helped to reduce poverty by more than 11 percent in recent years, rising income inequality remains a problem. Poverty is higher in rural areas (35.5 percent) compared to urban areas (23.2 percent), as herders in the countryside struggle to survive as their traditional livelihood dissolves.[2]

Mongolia at the end of the socialist era had an economy with three distinct sectors: industrial and mining, with the main national income source being the giant copper mine at Erdenet; collectivized agriculture, which included animal husbandry; and tourism. Yet, the Soviets during that period had to subsidize about one-third of Mongolia's budget. Nearly three decades later, the same three major sectors still are promoted as the most important economic drivers. State-owned industries may have collapsed and the proportion of private mining operations funded all or partially by FDI greatly expanded, but mining revenues and taxes continue to provide the largest income to a state budget that operates with great shortfalls, which are sustained today by assuming large amounts of debt from foreign lenders. The privatization of the herding economy and the dismantling of cereal crop and vegetable collectives in the early 1990s led to an explosion of animals on the land and the return of people to the countryside. Although welcomed as a rational return to the traditional Mongolian way to utilize the harsh steppe environment of the Mongolian plateau, the meat, animal by-product, and animal hair processing industries that should have emerged to maximize profits and greatly increase export trade did not develop. Rather, Mongolia put its hopes in developing its minerals with huge FDI inflows and mortgaged the nation's future to Western and Chinese investors.

It is problematic now to call for Mongolia to diversify its economy and rebalance away from the profitable, but more environmentally damaging, mining sector, which alone can fund the domestic infrastructure, finance better health and welfare systems, and pay down foreign loans. Nearly ten years ago, Mongolian foreign policy strategist Dorjjugder Munkh-Ochir noted that Mongolia's national security strategy was moving into a more complicated stage, as it shifted from prioritizing economic strategy over politics. He believed that Mongolia's core concern remained the same: it should pursue a strategy of diversifying its trade and political partners—"more partners result in greater balancing opportunities and hence, a more guaranteed external security environment."[3] In October 2016 Foreign Minister Ts. Mönkh-Orgil was asked, "What would be the role and contribution of your Ministry in involving foreign relations in the economic sector or improving the country's economy?" In his reply Mönkh-Orgil pointed out that the ministry's participation and contribution are significant in implementing bilateral and multilateral measures to expand foreign trade and economics, creating a favorable environment for investors, and inspiring their confidence in Mongolia's legal regime. He noted that Mongolia's top foreign policy priorities are continuing dialogue on the creation of an "Economic Corridor," actively participating in regional integration, joining the US-Asia Trans-Pacific Partnership and the WTO's Trade Facilitation Agreement, promoting business, and improving the investment environment for investors.[4] Thus, it is apparent that the future of Mongolian foreign economic policy lies in implementing strong measures to diversify the economy and more aggressively developing new energy resources.

Development of Non-Mineral Sectors

One of the biggest stories about Mongolia's economy in the democratic era has been the rise of its mineral-based economy. Mining in Mongolia currently contributes about a third of GDP and accounts for 89.2 percent of the country's total exports. Although this is the main trend that attracts the attention of international financial and development experts, other approaches can be employed to enhance prosperity while also accommodating Mongolian tradition and culture. In 2016, nineteen companies were carrying out mining activities in twenty-two areas under a product sharing agreement.[5] In November 2016, the Ministry of Mining and Heavy Industry reported a total of 2,142 exploration licenses and 1,564 exploitation permits granted for private mining companies, and the area covered by the licenses totaled 14.7 million hectares or some 9.4 percent of Mongolia. It announced a bid for exploration and exploitation licenses on another 20.9 million hectares, which would make a total of 63.44 percent of Mongolia's territory available for either private or public mining licenses. This plan, to be presented to Parliament, will double the land available for exploration, capitalize on the mining industry's improved appetite for new resources, and help shore up the country's finances while still excluding ecologically sensitive areas.[6] However, a major problem is that the mineral sector is not generating sufficient job creation. In 2015, 87 percent of Mongolian exports were mining commodities, which represented only 4 percent of the nation's jobs, while animal husbandry employs nearly 30 percent of the total workforce. This livestock sector provides subsistence, income, and wealth for nearly half of Mongolia's population.

Diversification of the economy has been attempted throughout the entire democratic era, but results have ranged from uneven to failure. Nevertheless, Mongolian policymakers, in response to the appeals of their constituents, are seriously exploring options beyond mining and trading with Mongolia's two giant neighbors. Better exploitation of the abundant livestock resources and tourism promotion are still the major alternatives, but there are other opportunities that increasing transport connectivity and easing tensions in the Northeast Asian region could offer Mongolia. Such topics are addressed by the Economic Policy and Competitiveness Research Center (EPCRC), a think tank established in 2012 under the auspices of the

President's Office. Its vision is to enhance Mongolia's national economic competitiveness to enable a strong, sustainable business environment and socioeconomic framework to improve the quality of life of all citizens. In collaboration with the Asia Foundation and local chapters of the Mongolian National Chamber of Commerce and Industry in each province, EPCRC conducts the Mongolia Provincial Competitiveness Survey to inform the decisions and strategies of policymakers and businesses using 180 criteria to rank Mongolia's provinces in four categories: economic performance, governance efficiency, business efficiency, and infrastructure.[7]

On March 24, 2017, the Ministry of Finance of Mongolia and the World Bank launched an Export Development Project, funded with a credit of $20 million from the World Bank's International Development Association. Over the next five years, the project aims to help small and medium-sized enterprises in non-mineral sectors to strengthen their export capabilities and boost access to export markets by providing firms with training, matching grants, and access to export credit-insurance products. James Anderson, World Bank country manager for Mongolia, explained, "In an economy where exports are heavily dominated by mining commodities, export diversification will boost productivity, overall entrepreneurship, and employment. This project also complements other efforts by the World Bank to support inclusive economic growth and livelihoods in Mongolia."[8] Mongolian Minister of Finance Battogtokh Choijilsuren noted that this project would enable the agricultural Reinsurance Joint Stock Company, private insurance companies, and other financial institutions to learn how to provide export-oriented financial products and services for Mongolian SMEs.[9]

The tourist sector has grown significantly from 12,000 visitors in 1990 to over 400,000 in 2014. Nevertheless, this represents only about 2–3 percent of the nation's GDP[10] because the tourist industry's development is stymied by lack of hotel and *ger* camp facilities, poor domestic transport infrastructure, and a shortage of passenger air and train capacity. While a new international capital airport will be fully functional by 2020, domestic air travel is not being exploited, and the national road network does not reach many places and is paved only in and around the capital and a handful of other semi-urban areas. Successive Mongolian administrations have failed to adopt strategies for promoting tourism that include concrete plans with a proper budget: "No systematic set of policies has been developed to maintain the flow of tourists from Third Neighbor Countries throughout the year, overcoming seasonal constraints."[11]

Development of New Economic, Energy, and Industrial Zones

To maximize its economic and mineral resources, Mongolia in the future must increase the value of its abundant raw materials and sell them as processed products. Otherwise, Mongolia's development will be linked tightly with vacillations in the Chinese economy. This became very clear with the Chinese economic slowdown since 2015, when Mongolia's coking coal exports to China decreased to 12.7 million tons from 14.7 million tons in 2014 and continued to fall in 2016. One way to reduce dependence on China is for Mongolia to create economic free trade zones to incubate new forms of industrial production to produce higher-value exports. Mongolia's Parliament in 2007 approved the Law on Economic Zones. Two special free economic zones (FEZs) were to be established in the cities of Altanbulag on the Russian-Mongolian border and Zamyn-Uud on the Chinese-Mongolian border. Although this legislation envisioned a virtually tax-free business environment and minimum bureaucratic obstacles for foreign and domestic companies, the southern border zone never moved beyond two controversial and compromised international tenders, which ultimately were rejected by the government. The southern Zamyn-Uud FEZ, an area of 900 hectares, was planned in three major sections—industrial, commercial, and tourism/service. The industrial section would emphasize environmentally friendly industrial production, including assembly factories for foreign audio and video equipment, home appliances, and electronic goods, and the production of textiles, clothing, furniture, and souvenirs. The commercial section would include warehouses, businesses, exhibition centers, and commodity exchanges; parceling, bottling, and packaging plants; and banking, financial services, information, and communication centers. In the third tourism/services section, tourist camps, hotels, restaurants, cafes, fast food shops and entertainment, golf courses, horse racing, camel polo, and a casino with cross-border Chinese as clientele would be located.

This FEZ is still a goal, but the Elbegdorj government, after the failed tenders, instead turned its attention to creating an industrial park at Sainshand, 230 kilometers to the north in the Gobi. Sainshand, a city of 20,000 people, is an old caravan city not far from OT and TT. It could be the site of coking coal plants, a copper smelter, and electric and other processing facilities to develop food, clothes, iron pellets, and cement—all financed by public-private foreign and domestic investment and employing Mongol workers. The tourism/casino idea is not part of the Sainshand plan. The government approved a plan to sell 66 percent of the Sainshand Industrial Complex, worth about $4 billion, to build infrastructure such as a power distribution network and a wastewater facility. Potential investments in the park, designed by US civil engineering company Bechtel Group, Inc., may exceed $10 billion. Feasibility studies have proceeded, but water problems were discovered that delayed development. The MPP government convened a working group in May 2018 under the prime minister's office to explore establishing a dry port in Sainshand. It will examine the feasibility of a cement plant, coke plant, iron pellets plant, coal gasification plant, oil refinery, copper smelter, and power plant.[12]

The Altanbulag FEZ northern border zone, which was expected to be less lucrative, began operations slowly because Mongolian-Russian trade volume was small. Its size of 500 hectares, 335 kilometers away from Ulaanbaatar and adjacent to the Siberian Russian Khiagt border port, is planned for 15,000–20,000 inhabitants. After two decades, the official launch of the Altanbulag FEZ was on June 24, 2014. Most of the export goods now are hauled by trucks, but plans call for it to be developed into a modern industrial site to serve as a direct rail link to Russian markets and out to the Pacific for international trade, import and export processing, and warehousing.[13] In the first stage, construction materials and auto parts will be the focus, so a trade center will be built. Proposals to build a twenty-five-kilometer road from Altanbulag FEZ to the closest railway station at Sukhbaatar City, a thermal power plant, residential areas, hotel complexes, and recycling plants are now under discussion.[14] The Korean company Kyeryong will construct a 365-kilometer highway between Ulaanbaatar and Altanbulag.[15]

Within the UNDP's Tumen River project, a Tumen River FEZ is to be established and developed under the auspices of the UN plan to transform the Tumen River delta into a hub of economic growth and international cooperation. The plan includes a huge duty-free shipping and processing zone; a processing site for eastern Mongolia (bordering China's Jilin province) also has been discussed. If this were to develop, Mongolia would have access to Pacific seaports, airports, and telecommunications facilities.

Nationalizing of Workforce

According to the World Bank, in spite of rapid economic growth in recent years, more than a quarter of the Mongolian people, 27.4 percent in 2012, remain below the national poverty line. It has identified that the economic imperative for Mongolia is to create alternative employment sources, especially for young adults. The overall unemployment rate in the mid-2010s was around 10 percent, but nearly one in four youths from fifteen to twenty-four years old was unemployed. According to the UNDP, "A key limitation is the low skill base of the youth."[16] This was a major reason why there were so many foreigners in the workforce during the early decades of democracy, especially in construction and mining. The Mongolian government since the early 2000s recognized the skills deficit and foreign worker employment connection. In 2005, a total of 8,173 foreigners from sixty-eight countries were permitted to work in Mongolia. In that year the number of foreign employees equaled 0.3 percent of the total population of Mongolia and 0.9 percent of the total workforce. In 2006 the proportion of foreign workforce and specialists was fixed by cabinet resolution. Thirty percent of the total foreign workforce was permitted in educational organizations and 40 percent in educational and scientific organizations that deal with foreign languages training. In October 2016, there were 11,072 foreign workers in Mongolia;[17] by June 2018 that number had fallen to 9,600 foreign workers from ninety-two countries.[18]

The ministries were ordered to conclude intergovernmental agreements, announce tenders, and execute projects in accordance with these regulations.[19] But with the onset of the mineral boom, this regulation was criticized harshly by foreign governments and companies. The Canadian government publicly reported that Mongolia's "rapidly growing mining sector relies to a significant degree on foreign workers because Mongolia's workforce lacks relevant skills."[20] The Ivanhoe–Rio Tinto OT contract specifically called for 90 percent of the workforce to be Mongolian to Mongolize the mining workforce and defuse local complaints about lack of on-site jobs. About 14,600 people were employed at OT during phase one of development, but during the 2013–2015 slowdown over phase two, 3,000 Mongols lost their jobs as total employment shrank to fewer than 7,000. This caused a substantial reduction in revenue of some $200–$300 million per year from the state budget and meant that Mongolian employees and contractors did not develop the skills needed to run mining operations.[21] To respond to the changing economic and unemployment situation and to domestic pressure, the cabinet annually reviews and modifies the percentage rate of the foreign workforce and specialists. Since 2013, the allowance for the agriculture, forestry, and fishing/hunting sector has been completely eliminated. In 2015 it was ruled that the foreign labor force should not exceed 5 percent of a company's total employees, and legal entities that hire up to twenty Mongolian employees can employ only one foreigner.[22] These same parameters continued in 2017 but Parliament dropped the cap for foreign residents in 2018, although the quota system for businesses continues.[23]

Major Energy Infrastructure Projects and Green Energy

Mining is the backbone of Mongolia's economy and has been since the 1960s. In the last decade Mongolia has enjoyed rapid economic growth fueled by large mining investments. Yet over the past few years, falling commodity prices, conflicts with local communities, cost overruns, a nontransparent legal environment, and vacillating foreign investment laws have squeezed FDI for mining projects in Mongolia. After cresting in 2011–2012, FDI fell by almost half in 2013. Since Mongolia is sending 90 percent of its mineral exports to China, China's economic slowdown has led to falling demand for Mongolian coal exports. Nomads in rural areas have not suffered as much from the downturn because they rely on meat or cashmere for income, but people in urban areas, rural communities surrounding the large mining deposits, and private enterprises that support the mining industry have suffered substantial loss of income. The unemployed often move to provincial centers or to crowded *ger* settlements in Ulaanbaatar, which accelerates income inequality and pollution. Mongolia sees its own future over the next thirty years, as well as that of the North Asia region, as closely connected to implementing major energy infrastructure projects. Despite potential environmental challenges, new power plants are the key to solving Mongolia's electricity problems and economic development. The country must replace the Soviet-era coal-fired plants that provide most of the country's limited electricity and diversify to other less-polluting sources that will reduce dependence on expensive Russian electricity, which in 2015 Mongolia imported at a cost of about $24 million a year.[24]

To fund expensive power stations, the Mongolian government decided to accept even more Chinese FDI. The Chinese in 2015 promised to provide a $1 billion soft loan to double the capacity of Shivee-Ovoo power station for the coal mine outside Ulaanbaatar.[25] The Ulaanbaatar Amgalan thermopower plant, which can produce 116 megawatts (MW) of electricity, began operations in December 2015 for 50,000–60,000 of the capital's residents. This plant, built under a concession agreement between the Mongolian government and China Machinery Engineering Corporation, is the basis for other major projects to be implemented.[26]

Mongolia's present 700 MW generation capacity falls short of demand by about 200 MW. It has set its hopes for becoming energy independent on the construction in northern Mongolia of a 315 MW facility on the Eg River, a tributary of the Selenge River, as part of the Egiin Gol Hydropower Plant Project. The project, which includes a dam, is estimated to cost $1 billion and was scheduled to begin construction in 2016. However, this dam project is connected to the more controversial 300 MW World Bank–supported Shuren hydroelectric project on the Selenge River that would divert water via a 1,000-kilometer-long pipeline to the Gobi region. The idea of damming the Eg River dates back to 1964, when Russian scientists first researched the possibility. Further studies were conducted intermittently from 1991 to 2013 when Mongolia's Ministry of Energy formally approved the project. If this plant is built, it could save 200,000 metric tons of coal and 709,000 tons of carbon dioxide, according to the company's prospectus.[27] The Export-Import Bank of China agreed to provide the majority of the financing for an $827.6 million concession loan.[28] Tractebel Engineering, SA, a subsidiary of France's GDF Suez, SA, was contracted to update the feasibility study, and a $100 million concession was awarded to the state-owned China Gezhouba Group Company, Ltd. to build access roads and bridges for the site.[29]

In recent years Russian environmental scientists and some Mongolian NGOs have labeled plans for hydroelectric plants on rivers that feed downstream into Lake Baikal[30] as hazardous, and Russian President Vladimir Putin promised to personally monitor the situation. In June 2016 Putin pressured the Chinese government not to fund the Eg hydroelectric project.

China's National Development and Reform Commission, the China EXIM Bank, and the Mongolian government announced a temporary hold on construction, citing concerns over transboundary issues and "due diligence" related to downstream environmental concerns. The issue is not dead and has become embroiled in domestic politics. As one official put it, "It's rather rude to treat Mongolia in this way when nothing has been done. . . . Truthfully, Mongolians are people without water. Therefore, our people shouldn't die of thirst to keep intact and ensure the integrity of another country's lake."[31]

There are other major deals with foreigners for new power plants that are proceeding. To replace imported Chinese power for the OT copper-gold mine, the Rio Tinto venture has agreed to purchase power from a planned 450 MW TT power station, whose contract was awarded to Japan's Marubeni earlier in March 2016.[32] The Ulaanbaatar Thermal Plant No. 5 in July 2015 signed a power purchase agreement to finance, construct, and operate for twenty-five years with Posco Energy of South Korea and partners Engie (formerly GDF Suez, SA) of France, Sojitz Corp. of Japan, and Mongolia's Newcom Group, the first public-private partnership in the energy sector.[33] In March 2016 China's Hunan Industrial Equipment Installation and the Mongolian Ministry of Energy broke ground for the $53.8 million Erdenet Thermal Power Plant to supply the giant Mongol-Russian copper mine, a project funded by a concessional loan from the Government of China, Development Bank of Mongolia, and government-backed Chinggis bonds.[34] Expanding the plant's capacity could double or triple energy production at the mine for twenty-five to thirty years, compensate for shortages in electric power supply in Mongolia's central region, and reduce the overall import of electricity.[35] Additionally, heating pipelines in nine Mongolian provinces will be funded through a South Korean soft loan.

Mongols also see their energy future as tied closely to innovation from green energy. Most believe they have a "green" mentality because they are nomadic and so assume their "nomadic civilization is based on a non-materialistic, efficient, re-cycling, and waste-free lifestyle."[36] T. Chuluun, director of the Institute for Sustainable Development at the National University of Mongolia, has spoken about Mongolia's "green civilization" concept: "That's why Mongolia could shift to green civilization by supporting production with highly-efficient, modern technology on the basis of its traditional nomadic civilization."[37] Yet many foreigners, having seen the destruction emanating from ninja mining and abandoned countryside community wells, would disagree with this viewpoint. It is true that an antipollution environmental movement has emerged in the Mongolian countryside, usually tied to anti-mining activism and supported financially by foreign nonprofits. In the past ten years the drive to find alternative technologies to boost employment in manufacturing has merged with the environmental movement to produce a government-led green energy policy in a country that is rich in cheaper fossil fuel minerals.

> Central Asian nomadic civilization is kept in Mongolia. We have lost some land to mining licenses but we should keep the rest of the territory to develop towns of many ethnicities and cultures with modern technological innovations. We should never lose our nomadic culture. We have to use education, science, technology, standard and innovation as accelerators of green development.[38]

Mongolia adopted a Renewable Energy Law in 2007. The Ministry of Energy over the years has announced a number of short- and mid-term domestic priorities, including creation of a safe, reliable, and integrated energy system; developing public-private partnerships to build new power plants; conserving energy and expanding renewable energy; and transitioning to a more market-oriented system of prices and regulation. These job creation and export diversification factors have prompted Mongolian policymakers to explore the potential for energy exports via construction of high-voltage transmission capacity integrated to serve international partners in the region and by exploitation of wind and large-scale Gobi solar power for energy exports.[39]

A variety of international groups have developed green technology studies for Mongolia. They recognize that to greatly expand renewable energy and energy efficiency, and in order to overcome the financial, technical, and administrative obstacles, political leadership and partnerships with the international community are fundamental.[40] Mongolia has determined its sustainable development goals in a document on green development policy. It calls for 20 percent of total domestic energy to derive from renewable energy sources by 2020 and 30 percent by 2030. Many new technologies are being financed by donor assistance rather than the market, so it will be interesting to see if Mongolia can continue to find funds for the green revolution as donor assistance disappears. The country does have wind and solar renewable sources to exploit, which presently provide 7 percent of its power. It opened its first wind park in 2013, and now, near its new airport fifty kilometers from Ulaanbaatar, it is developing a science park and university green campus to focus on developing scientific, educational, and private sector clusters to nurture the future leaders of Mongolia's sustainable development.

Mongolia's Place in a Northeast Asian Super Grid

Power grid interconnection has been discussed for two decades in Northeast Asia as a means to build an economically efficient, renewable power system. Although research studies[41] indicated only modest benefits in lowering total cost because of the large initial investments required to develop the renewables and the transmission lines, grid interconnections are projected to become more economically attractive in higher-fuel-price or lower-initial-cost situations. The European Bank for Development and Reconstruction remains supportive of such large-scale renewable power investment. In addition to its rich and cheap fossil fuel mineral reserves, Mongolia has exceptional renewable energy resources, but as of 2012 also had the third highest greenhouse gas emissions per capita in Northeast Asia. Thus, it is committed to exploitation of its renewable resources. Mongolia has been increasingly active in researching the establishment of a regional energy super grid called the Strategy for Northeast Asia Power System Interconnection (NAPSI). The NAPSI project is looking at different cost-benefit scenarios benchmarked at 2026, which will require $5.55 billion of investment; by 2036, another $4.2 billion; and by 2051, after a total of $57.33 billion in investment, which is projected to represent 60 percent of the country's GDP.

The Mongolian government obtained $1.75 million in ADB technical assistance funding for a two-year study through May 2019 to explore how the country might more effectively utilize its abundant renewable wind and solar resources in the Gobi Desert, together with Mongolian and Russian hydropower sources, to reduce the carbon footprint in the NEA (PRC, East Russia, Japan, ROK, Mongolia) power sector, the largest source (40 percent) of greenhouse emissions in the region. This new NAPSI study was undertaken by the Mongolian Ministry of Energy, Électricité de France, China Electric Power Research Institute, and NovaTerra, LLC, a Mongolian investment and advisory firm with extensive renewable energy project experience that in 2013 developed the 50 MW Salkhit Wind Farm, the first utility-scale renewable power plant in Mongolia. NovaTerra just began a joint venture with Symbior Solar Limited, a leading Asian company engaged in developing solar photovoltaic installations in emerging markets, for the development of a 50 MW photovoltaic project in the South Gobi region of Mongolia for $100 million.[42] Advisers on the NAPSI research project include the State Grid of China and/or GEIDCO, Korea Electric Power Corporation, Japan's Renewable Energy Institute, Russia's PAO Rosseti, Energy Charter of Belgium, and International Renewable Energy Agency in the UAE. Energy Charter has advanced the Gobitec concept to produce clean energy from renewable energy sources in the Gobi Desert and to deliver the produced energy to high-demand power corridors via the planned Asian Super Grid, connecting Russia, Mongolia, China, South Korea, and Japan.[43]

Driven by a projected 9 percent annual increase of electricity demand to feed its growing mining sector, Mongolian imports of electricity have increased from less than 5 percent in 2010 to over 20 percent in 2015, even though the cabinet determines pricing and regulates licensing and technology.[44] This trend likely will continue, since in January 2018, the Mongolian Parliament exempted imported electricity from Russia and China in its Western Energy System, one of the four national systems, from taxes until January 2021.[45] On September 12, 2018, at the fourth Eastern Economic Forum, Mongolian President Khaltmaa Battulga strongly supported going forward on the region-wide energy grid: "I call upon the urgent and prompt commencement of the 'North East Asian Super Grid' project which can share the load during the peak hours and will be a resource-efficient and optimal solution for supplying Northeast Asian countries with energy." He announced that Mongolia and China will begin a joint project for an energy complex and high-voltage transmission lines. The complex will be comprised of stations with an installed capacity of 5,350 MW from solar, wind, and coal sources, as well as a 1,500-kilometer-long high-voltage direct current. Noting that Mongolian solar and wind energy production could help supply peak-hour electricity loads in Japan and Korea and be a backup energy source, Battulga called for establishing an organization consisting of Mongolia, Russia, China, Japan, the ROK, and North Korea to implement the Northeast Asian Super Grid project; offered to host and support this organization in Mongolia; and lobbied with the other Northeast Asian leaders for the immediate creation of a joint working group. It appears that recent political developments on the Korean Peninsula have raised hopes for substantive progress on integration of North Korea into NEA's regional economy. These could change the dynamics of the Northeast Asian Super Grid concept and permit the NAPSI project to begin steps toward implementation.

Final Comments

Mongolian foreign policy and foreign economic relations in the democratic era since 1990 have undergone waves of development. These stages have proceeded under peaceful and constitutional mechanisms, despite serious economic crises and national security pressures. One Mongolian foreign policy strategist has said, "Mongolia has learned a single indelible lesson in terms of national sovereignty and security—that the nation should seek balanced, equidistant relations with its two neighbors while seeking wider recognition and global interaction to the utmost possible degree."[46] Its 1992 constitution created a solid legal framework for genuine democratic and free market reforms. Domestically, the country developed political pluralism and a multiparty system, while internationally, its membership in the IMF, World Bank, ADB, and WTO have stimulated integration into the global marketplace.

In 2011 the Mongols celebrated 100 years of independence, with their ongoing struggle to redefine and legitimate their identity as a nation-state in today's world. That year saw two important anniversaries connected to the nation's modern quest for sovereignty and independence: the 100th anniversary of Mongolia's modern independence after the fall of the Manchu Qing dynasty and the 90th anniversary of the 1921 communist "people's" revolution. These anniversaries, celebrated two decades into Mongolia's democratic era, are part of an ongoing desire to develop a modern definition of Mongolian culture and identity that will guide the nation in the twenty-first century. Fundamentally, the 100th anniversary celebration was a Mongolian reaction to China—a symbolic shout that the Mongols have been independent and will continue to remain so. But the lack of clarity about the reasons for inaugurating its grand celebration was a reflection of the Mongolian government's concern over China's reaction. Another aspect behind this new celebration is its impact on the legal issues swirling around Chinese-Tibetan relations. In 1913 Mongolia and Tibet signed a treaty declaring themselves free from Manchu Chinese rule and recognizing each other as independent states. This same line of reasoning also can be employed to establish the date of Tibetan independence from the ROC, and thus remains extremely sensitive for Chinese authorities.

Preserving Mongolia's heritage is a key consideration in the exercise of Mongolia's national security policy and an explosive element of domestic politics. Sustaining Mongolian cultural traditions, including pastoralism, is intertwined with the ideology of present-day Mongolian nationalism, which roils FDI and immigration policies. Mongolians of all political parties, nomads, and city dwellers, from all socioeconomic classes, believe that the country is at a critical—even dangerous—crossroads, at a time when its extensive \$1.3 trillion mineral resources are expected to generate much wealth. Another complication is that Mongolian-blooded people outside the country want to be a part of the definition of Mongol. The majority Khalkha Mongolian population inside independent Mongolia is conflicted by feelings of pride in this rising pan-Mongolist spirit coupled with genuine fear of this trend washing over it to the point of destruction. Mongolia started celebrating National Pride Day in 2012, marking the birthdate of Chinggis Khaan on the first day of winter on the lunar calendar, which usually falls in mid-November. In 2017 President Battulga remarked, "This day is of utmost significance to not only Mongolians, but also Mongol ethnicities spread around the globe, who are united by Chinggis Khaan's greatness, mighty honor and the wish to protect the Mongolian state rather than his own life."[47]

With the dismantling of the socialist economy's public sector in the first decade of the democratic era in the 1990s, the country's artificial and fragile industrial economy collapsed, which forced a rapid return to the traditional nomadic economic lifestyle for tens of thousands of Mongols. Western economists, full of widespread confidence in globalization and free market expansion, advised the Mongolian government to utilize development models that did not include the retention of the traditional style of nomadic herding economic production. Nevertheless, during this decade of not-so-benign neglect, the numbers of countryside residents nomadizing to various degrees with their livestock increased to nearly 50 percent, although this number has stabilized nowadays to around 40 percent.

The economic and political turmoil of the twenty-five years of the democratic era has highly influenced the views on national identity of both

Mongolian policymakers and the Mongolian people. During this period, many Mongolian researchers and development planners have become concerned about the appearance of two distinct societies—one traditional and nomadic and the other sedentary and urban. The divide between the two societies strains Mongolian political cohesion and contributes to rural poverty. Nomadic groups in the countryside have demonstrated against national government decisionmaking, especially regarding internationally funded mining and its effects upon the environment.[48] Holding hunger strikes and burning effigies in Ulaanbaatar's main square, as well as protesting at the countryside mining camps and even firing bullets at mining equipment, are all examples of the rising political activism of nomads who are demanding that Mongolian leaders listen to their opinions about economic development and about the role of FDI in the country's future.[49] The herding segment of Mongolian society has not stayed silent and thus has increasingly had an impact on how Mongolia has developed its foreign economic policies in its third decade of democracy.

Mongolia today is a postcommunist society and often, mistakenly, has been compartmentalized as very similar to Eastern European and Central Asian countries. While the bureaucratic structures and central planning aspects are in fact copied from the Soviet model, these elements alone do not adequately explain Mongolia's attitude toward its socialist past or its present policies. Understanding the relevance of the nomadic tradition is still the key to comprehending the Mongolian psyche and Mongolia's deeply held principles about national security. Pastoral nomadism, while in many ways distant from the realities of modern Mongolian city dwellers, continues to capture the national imagination and differentiates Mongols from other Asians. Mongolian political and economic strategists see their nation, region, and continent as being at a "critical juncture," which stimulates openness to institution-building to reduce tensions and the rise of regional networks to overcome energy and transportation challenges. From the "critical juncture" theory perspective, the major factors of a changing geostrategic context, political leadership, and crises, real or perceived, are all present. As part of its national security strategy, Mongolia has learned to adopt a more proactive foreign policy, including soft power and other initiatives within the Eurasian region, to enhance its global image, and to seek a more stable regional security framework. Mongolia's nuclear-weapons-free policy remains a significant component of its multipillar foreign policy that has contributed to maintaining peace and stability in the Northeast Asian region. This strategy, together with international support for the consolidation of Mongolia's democracy via the "Third Neighbor" principle, is the mainstay of modern Mongolian foreign relations. Mongolia has declared its territory a nuclear-free zone and maintains strong relations with the two Korean states, its two border neighbors, Japan, the European Community, and the United States. All of this has been pursued under the rubric of its own multipillared foreign policy vision. It also has developed and modernized its military through active participation in international peacekeeping.

Mongolia's vast mineral resources have been viewed as the stimulus to economic growth and wealth for the nation. However, the twenty-first century already has seen boom and bust as Mongols have struggled with managing world mineral prices, foreign monopoly of the economy, and endemic corruption. The capacity of the government to wisely manage exploitation of its natural resources in ways that result in greater value-added industrial production remains an open question. It still must resolve the environmental pollution, health, income inequality, poverty, and crime issues that its mineral-based, highly FDI-reliant economy engenders, while constantly seeking to strengthen its greater national security not only from regional powers but also from transnational foreign investors. Yet, Mongolia and those who wish it well can be optimistic. The Mongols and their policymakers during the last quarter century have reacted with much flexibility and resiliency to the complicated internal and external environment they have faced. Despite the many challenges, Mongolia's democratic political and economic institutions have grown stronger. There is good reason to hope that the future of Mongolia will be bright and that the nation will continue its development into an Asian powerhouse in the succeeding decades.

Notes

1. According to the Ministry of Food and Agriculture, this livestock is managed by 153,000 livestock herder families, which represents 28 percent of the country's labor force—the same percentage as during the communist era that herded eighteen million head. Oscar Rosseau, "Mongolia Reports Highest Ever Livestock Count," *GlobalMeatNews.com*, July 4, 2016.

2. Tirza Theunissen, "Poverty, Inequality, and the Negative Effects of Mongolia's Economic Downturn," *InAsia*, Asia Foundation, June 25, 2014, http://asiafoundation.org/in-asia/2014/06/25/poverty-inequality-and-the-negative-effects-of-mongolias-economic-downturn/.

3. Dorjjugder Munkh-Ochir, "Same Rules, New Dimensions for Mongolia's National Security: Adapting to the New Geo-Economic Environment" (Washington, DC: Brookings East Asia Commentary, October 20, 2009), https://www.brookings.edu/opinions/same-rules-new-dimensions-for-mongolias-national-security-adapting-to-the-new-geo-economic-environment/.

4. "Our Weight Depends on How Many Friends We Have Got," *Mongol Messenger,* October 21, 2016.

5. "9.4 Percent of Mongolian Land Being Used for Mining Activity," *Mongol Messenger,* November 11, 2016.

6. According to mining and heavy industry minister Dashdorj Tsedev, reported in "Mongolia Ups Mining Land," *Mining Journal,* March 9, 2017.

7. Economic Policy and Competitiveness Research Center, https://ecrc.mn/about-research/.

8. "World Bank Project Aims to Help Mongolia Diversify Exports," *Mongol Messenger,* March 31, 2017.

9. Ibid.

10. "Mongolia's Tourism Sector Looks to Its Natural Assets to Secure Its Future," Oxford Business Group, http://www.oxfordbusinessgroup.com/overview/mongolias-tourism-sector-looks-its-natural-assets-secure-its-future.

11. Norihiko Ikeda, "Mongolia: Will It Remain a Local Buffer Nation Between China and Russia, or Become a Small Yet Global Nation? A New Perspective on the 'Third Neighbor Policy,'" *Mongol Messenger,* October 28, 2016.

12. P. Solongo, "Current Status and Future Development of Dry Ports in Mongolia" (PowerPoint presentation for Asian Way, LLC, Almaty, Kazakhstan, May 30, 2018), https://www.unescap.org/sites/default/files/6.%20%20Mongolia%20resource%20person%20presentation.pdf.

13. "Law on Economic Zones," *Invest Mongolia* (blog), May 11, 2007, https://invest-mongolia.wordpress.com/.

14. M. Zoljargal, "Altanbulag Free Trade Zone to Improve Cross Border Trade," *UB Post,* June 19, 2014.

15. Zoljargal, "Tsast Group Partners with Kyeryong Group for Redevelopment."

16. "About Mongolia," UNDP Mongolia, http://www.mn.undp.org/content/mongolia/en/home/countryinfo.html.

17. B. Amarsaikhan, "5 Percent Quota Set for Foreign Employees," *Montsame,* November 11, 2016, http://www.montsame.mn/en/read/7521.

18. B. Batchimeg, "9.6 Thousand Foreign Workers from 92 Countries Employing in Mongolia," *Montsame*, July 19, 2018, http://montsame.mn/en/read/16018.

19. The percentage of foreigners employed in the educational field was not broken out. "Mongolia to Regulate Workfield of Foreigners to Boost Education," *Montsame,* April 9, 2006, http://www.mongolia-web.com/education/347-mongolia-to-regulate-workfield-of-foreigners-to-boost-education/.

20. "Canadian International Assistance in Mongolia," Government of Canada, June 9, 2017, http://international.gc.ca/world-monde/issues_development-enjeux_developpement/priorities-priorites/where-ou/mongolia-mongolie.aspx?lang=eng.

21. US Department of State, *2014 Investment Climate Statement: Mongolia* (Washington, DC: Bureau of Economic and Business Affairs, 2014), 8, https://www.state.gov/documents/organization/231251.pdf.

22. "Resolution of the Government of Mongolia, No. 2 Approving the Percentage of Foreign Labor Force and Specialists for the Year 2015" (Ulaanbaatar: Government of Mongolia, January 7, 2015), https://www.scribd.com/document/261221108/.

23. "Resource-Rich Mongolia Rejects Cap on Foreign Workers for 2018," *Reuters*, February 13, 2018, https://www.reuters.com/article/us-mongolia-immigration/resource-rich-mongolia-rejects-cap-on-foreign-workers-for-2018-idUSKBN1FX0PV.

24. Egiin Goliin Hydropower Plant director Odkhuu Durzee quoted in Michael Kohn, "Mongolia Seeks $828 Million from China for Largest Hydro Project," *Bloomberg,* March 23, 2015.

25. "Mongolia and China Sign Cooperation Agreements," Info Mongolia, November 11, 2015, https://www.sourcewatch.org/index.php/Shivee_Ovoo_power_station.

26. "Mongolian Energy Sector Anticipates A Productive Year Ahead," *UB Post,* January 8, 2016, http://ubpost.mongolnews.mn/?p=17722.

27. Kohn, "Mongolia Seeks $828 Million."

28. A projected $172.4 million of the loan would be spent on a fifty-kilometer highway from Ulaanbaatar to its new international airport.

29. Gregory B. Poindexter, "US$1 Billion Proposed 315-MW Egiin Gol Hydroelectric Project in Mongolia, on Hold," *Hydro Review*, June 24, 2016, http://www.hydroworld.com/articles/2016/06/us-1-billion-proposed-315-mw-egiin-hydroelectric-project-in-mongolia-on-hold.html.

30. According to the United Nations Educational, Scientific, and Cultural Organization, Lake Baikal is the oldest (twenty-five million years) and deepest (1,700 m) lake in the world and has a capacity of 25.6 million acre-feet. It contains 20 percent of the world's total unfrozen freshwater reserve and affects the regional climate of North Asia and the Arctic Basin.

31. Interview with the head of the Policy Implementation Department of the Ministry of Energy of Mongolia in Ts. Bayarbaatar, "Mongolia's Nationalistic Officials Present Clear Threat to Their Own Country and Its Neighbors," *Rivers Without Boundaries,* April 24, 2015, www.transrivers.org/2015/1511/.

32. "Japan's 'Marubeni' Wins Tavan Tolgoi Power Plant Tender," *UB Post,* March 2, 2016.

33. Michael Kohn, "Accord for $1.4 Billion Mongolia Power Plant Could Reduce Pollution," *Bloomberg*, July 29, 2015, https://www.bloomberg.com/news/articles/2015-07-29/engie-led-group-in-accord-for-1-4-billion-mongolia-power-plant.

34. Chimeddorj Khaliun, "Groundbreaking Ceremony for Erdenet Thermal Power Plant Expansion Takes Place," *UB Post*, March 31, 2016.

35. Ch. Khaliun, "Energy Ministry Signs Erdenet Power Plant Expansion Agreement with China," *UB Post,* December 11, 2015, http://ubpost.mongolnews.mn/?p=17381.

36. B. Oyundelger, "Nomadic Culture Simplifies the Shift to Green Development," *Mongol Messenger,* November 11, 2016.

37. Ibid.

38. Professor Chuluun quoted in ibid.

39. P. Tovuudorj, "Mongolian National Energy Agenda and Policy Measures: Scope for Subregion Cooperation" (Presentation to Senior Officials Committee on Energy Cooperation in Northeast Asia Eighth Session, Ulaanbaatar, April 10–11, 2013) cited in *Strategies for Development of Green Energy Systems in Mongolia* (Stockholm: Global Green Growth Institute, March 2014), 25, https://www.sei.org/mediamanager/documents/Publications/Climate/GGGI-SEI-2014-Mongolia-green-energy-systems.pdf.

40. Ibid., 8.

41. "Third Workshop on Power Grid Interconnection in Northeast Asia," Nautilus Institute for Security and Sustainability (Vladivostok, September 30–October 3, 2003), https://nautilus.org/projects/by-name/asian-energy-security/workshop-on-power-grid-interconnection-in-northeast-asia/third-workshop-on-power-grid-interconnection-in-northeast-asia/; Takashi Otsuki, "Electric Power Grid Interconnections in Northeast Asia: A Quantitative Analysis of Opportunities and Challenges," *SSRN Electronic Journal* (January 2015), www.researchgate.net/publication/314525572; "Asia International Grid Connection Study Group Second Report," Tokyo, Renewable Energy Institute (July 23, 2018), https://www.renewable-ei.org/en/activities/reports/20180614.html.

42. "Symbior Solar and NovaTerra Enter into Shareholders' Agreement for Joint Venture Development of 50MW Solar PV Project in Mongolia," *NovaTerra*, January 18, 2017, http://novaterra.mn/press-release.html.

43. Alicia Campi, "Mongolia's Place in Northeast Asia's Renewable Power Grid," *Eurasia Daily Monitor*, June 28, 2018.

44. "Mongolia: Strategy for Northeast Asia Power System Interconnection," Renewable Energy Institute, May 25, 2016.

45. O. Onon, "Tax Exempt on Imported Energy from China and Russia," *Montsame,* December 22, 2017, http://montsame.mn/en/read/12862.

46. Munkh-Ochir, "Same Rules." He divides the stages into early 1990s: "Security Through Democratization"; mid- to late-1990s: "Security Through Proactive Diplomacy"; the twenty-first century: "Security Through Peacekeeping Commitments; the new era: "Security Through Vested Interests."

47. Kh. Aminaa, "President: We Should Be Reminded of Chinggis Khaan's Wisdom," *Montsame*, November 20, 2017, http://montsame.mn/en/read/12452.

48. Goldbeck, US embassy cable, "Protests Against Mongolian Government Grow," April 12, 2006, https://wikileaks.org/plusd/cables/06ULAANBAATAR261_a.html.

49. In April 2006, the chairman of the Canadian Ivanhoe mining company, Robert Friedland, was burned in effigy at a protest against Ivanhoe Mines in the Mongolian capital, one of the largest protests in the nation's history. See "Ivanhoe's Controversial Mongolian Mine Boosted by Canadian State Support," *Unuudur,* July 23, 2010, http://www.unuudur.com/?p=9753. In later demonstrations that month, President N. Enkhbayar was burned in effigy. Some 200 demonstrators, including ten hunger-strikers, ended their

protests over alleged government corruption and the mishandling of mineral wealth in Mongolia after the country's leaders agreed to investigate their complaints. Namjil Ganbat, "Mongolians End Protests Demanding Resignation of Government, President," *Mines and Communities,* April 24, 2006, http://www.minesandcommunities.org/article.php?a=5534.

Acronyms

ADB	Asian Development Bank
ADRA	Adventist Development and Relief Agency
AIIB	Asian Infrastructure Investment Bank
APEC	Asia-Pacific Economic Cooperation
APTA	Asia-Pacific Trade Agreement
ARF	ASEAN Regional Forum
ARMZ	Atomredmetzoloto of Russia
ASEAN	Association of Southeast Asian Nations
ASEM	Asia-Europe Meeting
BRI	Belt and Road Initiative (see also OBOR)
BRICS	Brazil, Russia, India, China, South Africa
CAMDA	Cambridge Mongolia Disaster Appeal
CAUC	Central Asian Uranium Co. Ltd
CD	Community of Democracies
Chalco	Aluminum Corp. of China Ltd.
CHRD	Centre for Human Rights and Development
CIS	Commonwealth of Independent States (Central Asia)
CMEA	Council for Mutual Economic Assistance
CNNC	China National Nuclear Corporation
CNPC	China National Petroleum Corporation
COMECON	(aka CMEA)
CSTO	Collective Security Treaty Organization
DOD	Department of Defense
DP	Democratic Party
DSM	Democratic Socialist Movement
EBRD	European Bank for Reconstruction and Development

ECPAT	End Child Prostitution, Pornography, and Trafficking of Children for Sexual Purposes
EEU	Eurasian Economic Union
ERINA	Economic Research Institute for Northeast Asia
ESCAP	United Nations Economic and Social Commission for Asia and the Pacific
ETT	Erdenes Tavan Tolgoi
EXIM	Export-Import (bank)
FAO	Food and Agriculture Organization (UN)
FDI	foreign direct investment
FEZ	free economic zone
FIFTA	Foreign Investment and Foreign Trade Agency
FMF	foreign military financing
FTA	free trade agreement
FTO	Free Trade Organization
GNI	gross national income
GPPAC	Global Partnership for the Prevention of Armed Conflict
GTI	Greater Tumen Initiative
IAAC	Independent Authority Against Corruption
ICF	International Cooperation Fund
IFAD	International Fund for Agricultural Development
IFC	International Finance Corporation
IMF	International Monetary Fund
INGO	international nongovernmental organization
IPO	initial public offering
IRI	International Republican Institute
ISS	Institute for Strategic Studies
ITT	International Think Tank
JCS	Joint Christian Services
KOTRA	Trade-Investment Promotion Agency South Korea
LLDCs	Landlocked Developing Countries and Transit Countries
LNG	liquefied natural gas
LPG	liquefied petroleum gas
MAF	Mongolian Armed Forces
MCC	Millennium Challenge Corporation
MDGs	Millennium Development Goals
MDU	Mongolian Democratic Union
MEC	Mongolia Energy Corporation Limited (Chinese: 蒙古能源有限公司, i.e. *menggu nengyuan youxian gongsi*)
MECC	Mongolian Economic Cooperation Confederation
MFT	most favored trade
MGEC	Mongolian Gender Equality Center
MIBC	Mongolia-India Business Council
MMC	Mongolian Mining Corporation

MNMCO	Mongolian National Marketing Coordination Office
MNT	Mongolian tugriks
MOU	memorandum of understanding
MPP	Mongolian People's Party
MPR	Mongolian People's Republic
MPRP	Mongolian People's Revolutionary Party
MSE	Mongolian Stock Exchange
MWLA	Mongolian Women Lawyers Association
NAM	Non-Alignment Movement
NAPSI	Northeast Asia Power System Interconnection
NEA	Northeast Asia
NED	National Endowment for Democracy
NGO	nongovernmental organization
NPAP	National Poverty Alleviation Programme
NPU	New Progressive Union
NRA	Nuclear Regulatory Authority of Mongolia
OBOR	One Belt, One Road (aka BRI)
ODA	official development assistance
OPIC	Overseas Private Investment Corporation
OSCE	Organization for Security and Co-operation in Europe
OT	Oyu Tolgoi
PAM	Petroleum Authority of Mongolia
PRC	People's Republic of China
PSC	production sharing contract
ROC	Republic of China
RZD	Russian Railways
SCO	Shanghai Cooperation Organisation
SEFIL	Strategic Entities Foreign Investment Law
SIDA	Swedish International Development Cooperation Agency
SMEs	small and medium-sized enterprises
SOE	state-owned enterprise
SOTAMO	SOCO Tamtsag Mongolia
SPC	State Privatization Commission
TACIS	Technical Assistance to the Commonwealth of Independent States
TİKA	Turkish Cooperation and Coordination Agency
TT	Tavan Tolgoi
UBD	Ulaanbaatar Dialogue on Northeast Asia Security
UNCAC	United Nations Convention Against Corruption
UNDP	United Nations Development Programme
UNESCAP	UN Economic and Social Commission for Asia and the Pacific
UNESCO	United Nations Educational, Scientific, and Cultural Organization

UR	Ulaanbaatar Railway
USAID	United States Agency for International Development
USGS	US Geological Survey
USSR	Soviet Union
WEF	World Economic Forum
WTO	World Trade Organization

Bibliography

Abilgal. *Monkhuun Uzegdel bish* [Bribery: No perception of money]. Ulaanbaatar, 2002.

Abimbola, Olumide. "Press Release: Mongolian Government Unlikely to Receive Dividends from Oyu Tolgoi Until 2035." OpenOil. October 26, 2016. http://openoil.net/2016/10/26/press-release-mongolian-government-unlikely-to-receive-dividends-from-oyu-tolgoi-until-2035/.

"About MCC." Millenium Challenge Corporation. https://www.mcc.gov/about.

"About Mongolia." UNDP Mongolia. http://www.mn.undp.org/content/mongolia/en/home/countryinfo.html.

"About Us." http://en.tavantolgoi.mn/.

ADB. "Executive Summary." [Program Performance Audit of its 1995–1998 $35 million agricultural loan project] *Audit Report* (2002).

———. "Program Performance Audit Report on the Agricultural Sector Program (Loan 1409-MON[SF]) in Mongolia. PPA:MON 27536. November 2002.

Addleton, Jonathan S. *Mongolia and the United States: A Diplomatic History.* Hong Kong: Hong Kong University Press, 2013.

———. "The United States and Mongolia: A Diplomatic Perspective." Speech to the East-West Center Washington Office, Washington, DC, October 23, 2013. https://www.eastwestcenter.org/events/the-united-states-and-mongolia-diplomatic-perspective.

Adiyasuren, Ts. Borjigd. *Environment and Development Issues in Mongolia.* Ulaanbaatar: Brain Drain, 1998.

Aldrich, Michael. *The Report: Mongolia 2012.* London: Oxford Business Group, 2012.

Altantsetseg, N. "Russian-Mongolian and Sino-Mongolia Relations Since the Nineties." In *The Geopolitical Relations Between Contemporary Mongolia and Neighboring Asian Countries: Democracy, Economy and Security.* Taipei: Mongolian and Tibetan Affairs, 2003.

Amarsaikhan, B. "5 Percent Quota Set for Foreign Employees." *Montsame,* November 11, 2016. http://www.montsame.mn/en/read/7521.

———. "Mongolia and China ink over 100 commercial and industrial deals." October 28, 2015. http://www.montsame.mn/en/read/121166.

———. "Transit Transport Might Be 2nd OT for Mongolia." *Montsame,* September 13, 2016.

"Ambassador Alphonse F. La Porta." Interview by Charles Stuart Kennedy, Association for Diplomatic Studies and Training Foreign Affairs Oral History Project. February 11, 2004, 166–167. http://www.adst.org/OH%20TOCs/La%20Porta,%20Alphonse%20F.toc.pdf.

"Ambassador John R. Dinger." Interview by Charles Stuart Kennedy. Association for Diplomatic Studies and Training Foreign Affairs Oral History Project, March 4, 2013. http://adst.org/wp-content/uploads/2013/12/Dinger-John-R.pdf.

"Ambassador Talks to the Mongolian Observer." Embassy of Mongolia, June 1, 2016. http://mongolianembassy.us/2016/06/ambassador-talks-to-the-mongolian-observer/#.WCZfrIWcF9A.

Aminaa, Kh. "First International Conference Held on Nomadic Tourism." *Mongol Messenger,* October 14, 2016.

———. "International Conference Discussing Constitutional Amendment." *Montsame*, October 19, 2017. http://www.montsame.mn/en/read/11982.

———. "President: We Should Be Reminded of Chinggis Khaan's Wisdom." *Montsame*, November 20, 2017. http://montsame.mn/en/read/12452.

———. "UB Observes Turkish Cultural Days for the 3rd Consecutive Year." *Mongol Messenger*, April 29, 2016.

Amnesty International. "Mongolia: Amnesty International Submission to the UN Universal Periodic Review." Ninth session of the UPR Working Group, November–December 2010, lib.ohchr.org/HRBodies/UPR/Documents/session9/MN/AI_Amnesty%20International_Revised.pdf.

Amsel, Peter. "Mongolia Casinos to Target Chinese, Russian and Japanese Gamblers." CalvinAyre.com, February 18, 2015.

"APTA Welcomes Mongolia as Its Seventh Member." UNESCAP, October 28, 2013. https://www.unescap.org/news-item/apta-welcomes-mongolia-its-seventh-member.

Area Handbook for Mongolia. Washington, DC: Foreign Area Studies, 1970.

"AREVA Uranium Exploration and Mining in Mongolia." *nuclear-news.net,* May 4, 2015. https://nuclear-news.net/2015/05/04/areva-uranium-exploration-and-mining-in-mongolia/.

Ariuntuya, N. "Strategy on Strategic Mineral Missing." *Mongolian Mining Journal*, August 8, 2012.

Armitage, Richard L. "Contract Signing Ceremony Between SOCO International and the Petroleum Authority of Mongolia." US Department of State Archive, January 31, 2004. http://2001-2009.state.gov/s/d/former/armitage/remarks/29141.htm.

"ASEM Leaders Conclude the Summit." *Mongol Messenger,* July 22, 2016.

"ASEM Senior Official Orgil Luvsantseren Briefs the Press." July 15, 2016. http://www.asem11.mn/?p=5966&lang=en.

The Asia Foundation. "Mongolia Highlights." June 2007. https://asiafoundation.org/resources/pdfs/1-MGMultistakeholderIV.pdf.

The Asia Foundation Conference on Mongolia's Political and Economic Transition: Challenges and Opportunities, Ulaanbaatar, September 11–13, 2000. https://asiafoundation.org/resources/pdfs/MongloiaPolEconTransition.pdf.

"Asia International Grid Connection Study Group Second Report." Tokyo: Renewable Energy Institute, July 23, 2018. https://www.renewable-ei.org/en/activities/reports/20180614.html.

Asian Development Bank. "Audit Report on Mongolia." Mandaluyong, Philippines: ADB, November 2002.

———. *Country Strategy and Program Update (2004–2006): Mongolia*. Mandaluyong, Philippines: ADB, August 2003. https://www.adb.org/sites/default/files/institutional-document/32345/files/csp-mon-2003.pdf.

———. *Governance: Progress and Challenges in Mongolia* (2004). http://journals.sfu.ca/ipmr/index.php/ipmr/article/viewFile/151/151.

"The Asian Infrastructure Investment Bank: Multilateralism on the Silk Road." *China Economic Journal,* April 4, 2016.

Baabar, B. "The Central Asian Security Zone." *Mongolian Journal of International Affairs*, no. 2 (1995): 18–32.

Baev, Pavel K. *Russian Energy Policy and Military Power: Putin's Quest for Greatness.* London: Routledge, 2008.

Baker, James A., III. *The Politics of Diplomacy.* New York: G. P. Putnam's Sons, 1995.

Batbayar, Ts. Or Tsedendamba. "The Development of Mongolia's External Relations in the 1990s." In *Renovation of Mongolia on the Eve of the XXI Century and Future*

Development Patterns, edited by Ts. Batbayar. Ulaanbaatar: Mongolian Development Research Center, 2000.

———. "Geopolitics and Mongolia's Search for Post-Soviet Identity." *Journal of Eurasian Geography and Economics* 43, no. 4 (June 2002): 323–335.

———. "Mongolia and the New Central Asia." *Mongolian Journal of International Affairs*, no. 3 (1996): 3–11.

———. "Mongolian-Chinese Economic Cooperation as an Important Factor in Northeast Asian Economic Regionalism." ERINA Report no. 64. Niigata, Japan: Economic Research Institute for Northeast Asia, July 2005.

———. "Mongolian Perspectives on Northeast Asian Regional Development." In *Politics and Economics in Northeast Asia*, edited by Tsuneo Akaha, 207–224. New York: St. Martin's Press, 1999.

———. *Mongolia's Foreign Policy in the 1990s: New Identity and New Challenges*. Regional Security Issues and Mongolia series, no. 17. Ulaanbaatar: Institute for Strategic Studies, 2002.

Batbayar, Ts., and K. Demberel. "Contemporary Mongolian-Russian Relations: Problems and Perspectives." In *The Geopolitical Relations Between Contemporary Mongolia and Neighboring Asian Countries: Democracy, Economy and Security*, 329–343. Taipei: Mongolian and Tibetan Affairs Commission Conference, September 2003.

Batbold, Sh., and N. Gantuya, "DPRK Ambassador Addresses Workforce Issue and Bilateral Relations." *Mongol Messenger,* November 25, 2016.

Batchimeg, B. "B. Jigjidnyamaa: 'Mongolian Corridor Is Main Supporter Line of Trans-Siberian Transport Corridor,'" *Montsame,* April 20, 2018.

———. "Mongolia and Turkey Targets to Increase Trade Turnover to USD 300 Million." *Montsame*, April 6, 2018. http://montsame.mn/en/read/14419.

Batchimeg, Migeddorj. "National Security of Mongolia: Past, Present and Future." Speech presented at Indiana University, November 17, 2010. Reprinted in *Mongolian Journal of International Affairs*, no. 10 (2011).

Batkin, Andy, Ts. Bumhorol, Robin Mearns, and Jeremy Swift. *Independent Evaluation of the National Poverty Alleviation Programme and Options Post-2000*. Ulaanbaatar: Government of Mongolia and World Bank, October 1999. http://www.forum.mn/res_mat/Independent%20Evaluation%20of%20the%20Natinoal%20Poverty%20Alleviation.pdf.

Batmunkh, Jambyn. *There Will Be No Use of Force Under Any Circumstances.* Compiled by D. Tsedev, translated by R. Baasan. Ulaanbaatar: The Mongolia Society, 2001.

Batsaikhan, Ookhnoin. *Mongolin Suulchiin Ezen Xaan VIII Bogd Jabzandamba, 1911 Oni Yndesnii Xuvisgal* [The last king of Mongolia Bogdo Jebtsundamba Khutukhtu]. Ulaanbaatar: Admon, 2008.

Batsukh, Zagdin. *Khergiin Gazraas Survaljilsan Temdeglel* [The struggle to identify criminal sites]. Ulaanbaatar: Mongolian Police, 2006.

Battsetseg, Serj. "Winning Hearts and Minds: Mongolia's Soft Power Approaches to Overseas Image Building in the Democratic Era." Paper presented at Asian Continentalism: Furthering Connections Between East and West, Ulaanbaatar, May 31–June 2, 2016.

Bawden, C. R. *The Jebtsun Damba Khutukhtus of Urga.* Wiesbaden: O. Harrassowitz, 1961.

———. *The Modern History of Mongolia.* New York: Frederick A. Praeger, 1968.

Bayantur, Gerelt-Od. "Democratic Transition and the Electoral Process." Master's thesis, University of Saskatchewan, Saskatoon, April 2008. http://www.collectionscanada.gc.ca/obj/s4/f2/dsk3/SSU/TC-SSU-04082008161438.pdf.

Bayarbaatar, Ts. "Mongolia's Nationalistic Officials Present Clear Threat to Their Own Country and Its Neighbors." *Rivers Without Boundaries,* April 24, 2015. www.transrivers.org/2015/1511/.

Bayarbat, Turmunkh. "Are Casinos the Right Path to Riches?" *UB Post,* November 23, 2016.

———. "Japan to Grant an 850 Million USD Soft Loan to Mongolia." *UB Post*, March 31, 2017.

———. "Mongolian, Russian and Chinese Presidents Meet at SCO Summit." *UB Post*, June 11, 2018.

Bayarsaikhan, Khash-Erdene. "Ulaanbaatar Railway's Bear Service." *UB Post*, September 26, 2016.

Beech, Hannah. "Turkish School Leader Abducted, and Released, in Mongolia." *New York Times*, July 28, 2018. https://www.nytimes.com/2018/07/28/world/europe/turkish-school-leader-abducted-and-released-in-mongolia.html.

Benson, Charlotte. "*Dzud* Disaster Financing and Response in Mongolia." Paper prepared for World Bank study on Structuring Dzud Disaster Preparation, Financing and Response to Increase Resilience of Herder Households to Climatic Risk in Mongolia, Washington, DC, May 2011.

"Bibliography of Materials Related to Poverty in Mongolia" (2004). http://pdc.ceu.hu/archive/00002470/01/Poverty_Eng_0002.pdf.

Bideleux, Robert, and Ian Jeffries. *A History of Eastern Europe: Crisis and Change.* London: Routledge, 1998.

"Board of Directors." https://www.socointernational.com/board-of-directors.

Bold, R. "Why Ruin Effective Foreign Policy?" (in Mongolian). *Undesnii Shuudan,* no. 272 (October 8, 2015).

Bolormaa, L. "At Tide's Ebb." *Mongolian Mining Journal,* October 25, 2013.

———. "Tavan Tolgoi Gets Ready for New Suitor, at Long Last." *Mongolian Mining Journal,* December 2, 2014. http://en.mongolianminingjournal.com/content/58189.shtml.

Bradshaw, Michael. "Russian Energy Dilemmas: Energy Security, Globalization and Climate Change." In *Russia's Energy Policies: National, Interregional and Global Levels*, edited by Pami Aalto. Cheltenham, UK: Edward Elgar, 2012.

Branigan, T. "Mongolia: How the Winter of 'White Death' Devastated Nomads' Way of Life." *The Guardian,* July 20, 2010.

"Brief Introduction." www.soros.org.mn, 2004.

Brooke, James. "Down and Almost Out in Mongolia." *New York Times,* December 29, 2004. http://www.nytimes.com/2004/12/29/business/worldbusiness/down-and-almost-out-in-mongolia.html?_r=0.

Bruun, Ole. "Nomadic Herders and the Urban Attraction." In *Mongols from Country to City: Floating Boundaries, Pastoralism and City Life in the Mongol Lands*, edited by Ole Bruun and Li Narangoa. Copenhagen: NIAS Press, 2006.

———. *Precious Steppe: Mongolian Nomadic Pastoralists in Pursuit of the Market.* Lanham, MD: Lexington Books, 2006.

Bruun, Ole, and Ole Odgaard. "A Society and Economy in Transition." In *Mongolia in Transition: Old Patterns, New Challenges*, edited by Ole Bruun and Ole Odgaard, 23–41. Richmond, UK: Curzon, 1999.

Bryce, Robert. "The Man at Their Side." *The Nation,* September 28, 2004. http://www.alternet.org/story/20012/the_man_at_their_side.

Bulag, Uradyn E. *Nationalism and Hybridity in Mongolia.* London: Oxford Press, 1998.

Buyantogs, A. "Foreign Investment, Loans and Assistance in Mongolian Development." *Mongolian Journal of International Affairs*, no. 7 (2000): 43–50.

Byambajav, D. "NGOs in Mongolia: A Crucial Factor in Mongolian Society and Politics." *Mongolian Journal of International Affairs*, no. 13 (2006): 132–146.

Byambakhand, Luguusharav. "Mongolian Initiative to Become a Multilateral Diplomacy Platform." In *Mongolia on the Regional Stage.* Ulaanbaatar: Institute for Strategic Studies, 2015.

Byambasüren, B. "ТАНИЛЦ: Онцлох бүтээн байгуулалт буюу ШИНЭ НИСЭХ БУУДЛЫН ажлын явц." ["Background: Featured development or progress of a new life's work"]. August 21, 2017. https://ikon.mn/n/133b.

Byun, See-Won. "Provincial Impacts of Multilateral Cooperation: The Greater Tumen Initiative and Environmental Protection in Jilin." China Environment Series. Washington, DC: Woodrow Wilson International Center for Scholars, 2008–2009. https://asiafoundation.org/resources/pdfs/ByunGTICES10.pdf.

"Cabinet Approves Signing Concession Agreement with Aspire Mining to Build Erdenet-Ovoot Railway." CoverMongolia.blogspot, August 12, 2015. http://covermongolia.blogspot.com/2015/08/aspire-rail-deal-approved-modun-sells.html.

"Cabinet Supports Draft Resolution on State Policy on Railway Transport." *Mongol Messenger,* June 1, 2018; "Proposed Zuunbayan-Khangi and Erdenet-Artssuuri Railway Routes Supported by Cabinet." American Chamber of Commerce in Mongolia, May 31, 2018. http://mongolia.gogo.mn/r/161735.

Calder, Kent E. *The New Continentalism: Energy and Twenty-First-Century Eurasian Geopolitics.* New Haven, CT: Yale University Press, 2012.

Campbell, Kurt. "Testimony Before the U.S. House of Representatives' Committee on Foreign Affairs Subcommittee on Asia and the Pacific." Washington, DC, March 9, 2011.

Campi, Alicia. "Definition of Mongolian Heritage and Its Connection to National Identity, National Security, and Economic Development in Today's Mongolia." Sydney, Australia, Public Interest Advocacy Centre, forthcoming.

———. "Developing U.S.-Mongolian Relations." *Asia-Pacific Bulletin*, no. 113 (May 26, 2011).

———. "Evolution of Governance in Mongolia: From Autocracy to Decentralization: How to Give an Historical Perspective." Paper presented at the New Trends in Mongol Studies II conference, Ulaanbaatar, March 20–23, 2014.

———. *The Impact of China and Mongolia on United States–Mongolian Political Relations in the Twentieth Century.* Lewiston, NY: Edwin Mellen Press, 2009.

———. *Modern Mongolia-Chinese Strategic Relations Challenges for the New Century.* Regional Security Issues and Mongolia series, no. 21. Ulaanbaatar: Institute for Strategic Studies, 2004.

———. "Mongolia Confronts Transnational Crime Issues in Its New Democracy." In *East Asian Intelligence and Organised Crime*, edited by Stephan Blancke, 399–437. Berlin: Verlag Dr. Koster, September 2015.

———. "Mongolia's Place in Northeast Asia's Renewable Power Grid." *Eurasia Daily Monitor*, June 28, 2018.

———. "Mongolia's Quest to Balance Human Development in Its Booming Mineral-Based Economy." *Brookings East Asia Commentary,* January 10, 2012.

———. "The Rise of Cities in Nomadic Mongolia." In *Mongols from Country to City: Floating Boundaries, Pastoralism and City Life in the Mongol Lands*, edited by Ole Bruun and Li Narangoa, 21–55. Copenhagen: NIAS Press, 2006.

———. "Significance of Mongolia's 100th Anniversary Celebration of Independence from the Manchus." Paper presented at the fifty-fourth PIAC conference, Bloomington, Indiana, July 2011.

———. "Transforming Mongolia-Russia-China Relations: The Dushanbe Trilateral Summit." *Asian Pacific Journal* 12, no. 45 (November 3, 2014). http://apjjf.org/2014/12/45/Alicia-Campi/4210.html.

———. "Xi and Putin in Ulaanbaatar: Mongolia's Balancing Act." *China Brief* 14, no. 18 (September 25, 2014). https://jamestown.org/program/xi-and-putin-in-ulaanbaatar-mongolias-balancing-act/#sthash.2q2Aet8M.dpuf.

"Canadian International Assistance in Mongolia." Government of Canada, June 9, 2017. http://international.gc.ca/world-monde/issues_development-enjeux_developpement/priorities-priorites/where-ou/mongolia-mongolie.aspx?lang=eng.

"Canadian Miner Buys $50 Million Mongolian Debt." *New York Times,* January 1, 2005. http://www.nytimes.com/2004/01/01/business/canadian-miner-buys-50-million-mongolian-debt.html?_r=0.

Capoccia, Giovanni, and R. Daniel Kelemen. "The Study of Critical Junctures: Theory, Narrative, and Counterfactuals in Historical Institutionalism." *World Politics* 59 (April 2007): 341–369.

"Casino Resort Part of Mongolia Project." Cash at Casinos, April 29, 2006. http://www.cashatcasinos.com/casino_news/3863.php.

"Chalco to Buy Coal Miner SouthGobi." *South China Morning Post,* April 3, 2012. http://www.scmp.com/article/997345/chalco-buy-coal-miner-southgobi.

Chen, Oswald. "Chalco to Buy SouthGobi's Majority Stake." *China Daily Asia,* April 3, 2012. http://www.chinadailyasia.com/news/2012-04/03/content_112879.html.

Cheng, Kevin C. "Growth and Recovery in Mongolia During Transition." IMF Working Paper no. 03/217. Washington, DC, November 2003.
"The Chief of Staff of the President of Mongolia Is Participating in the World Economic Forum's Summit on the Global Agenda." President of Mongolia, November 18, 2013. http://www.president.mn/eng/newsCenter/viewNews.php?newsId=1021.
"China May Invest $5.2bn in Russia's First High Speed Railway." *RT,* March 30, 2015. https://www.rt.com/business/245125-china-invest-russia-train/.
"China-Mongolia Relations." *China Daily*, May 27, 2010. http://www.chinadaily.com.cn/china/2010wentour/2010-05/27/content_9899648.htm.
"China Proposes Economic Corridor with Russia and Mongolia." *RT,* April 2, 2015. https://www.rt.com/business/246281-china-russia-mongolia-corridor/.
"China, Russia, Mongolia Endorse Development Plan on Economic Corridor." *Xinhua,* June 24, 2016. http://english.cctv.com/2016/06/24/ARTIJkwoLdfFUjK7unWMv0lN160624.shtml.
"China, Russia, Mongolia Sign Tripartite Economic Partnership Deal." *Dhakha Tribune*, July 5, 2016. https://issuu.com/dhakatribune/docs.
"China, Russia, Mongolia to Create Economic Corridor." *BRICS Post,* September 12, 2014. http://thebricspost.com/china-russia-mongolia-to-create-economic-corridor/#.VEqSQDHD-po4.
Choi, Ha-young. "Mongolia to Send Coal Through N. Korean Port." *NK News*, February 25, 2015.
Choi, He-suk. "Park Sees 'Eurasia Initiative' to Build Energy, Logistics Links." *Korea Herald,* October 18, 2013. www.koreaherald.com/view.php?ud=20131018000620.
Choi, Kyung-soo. "The Mining Industry of North Korea." *Korean Journal of Defense Analysis* 23, no. 2 (June 2011).
"Chongryon Hq Sale Decision Delayed." Japan Property Central, October 24, 2013. http://japanpropertycentral.com/2013/10/chongryon-hq-sale-decision-delayed/.
Chuluunbaatar, Gelegpil. *Problems of the Contemporary Socio-Political Transformation in Mongolia.* Ulaanbaatar: Institute of Philosophy, Sociology and Law, Mongolian Academy of Sciences, 2009.
———. "Renewal of Mongolia's Political System and Its Democratic Development." In *Renovation of Mongolia on the Eve of the XXI Century and Future Development Patterns*, edited by Tsedendamba Batbayar, 5–27. Ulaanbaatar: Mongolian Development Research Center, 2000.
CIA World Factbook. http://www.indexmundi.com/g/g.aspx?c=mg&v=66.
Concept of Mongolia's Foreign Policy 2010. Ministry of Foreign Affairs of Mongolia. http://www.mfa.gov.mn/?page_id=26263&lang=en.
"Conference Call with Reporters to Discuss Vice President Biden Trip to China, Mongolia, and Japan." The White House Office of the Vice President, August 15, 2011. https://obamawhitehouse.archives.gov/the-press-office/2011/08/15/conference-call-reporters-discuss-vice-president-biden-trip-china-mongol.
Conference Proceedings: Ulaanbaatar Dialogue on Northeast Asian Security 2014. Ulaanbaatar: Ministry of Foreign Affairs of Mongolia, September 2014.
Conference Proceedings: Ulaanbaatar Dialogue on Northeast Asian Security 2015. Ulaanbaatar: Ministry of Foreign Affairs of Mongolia, September 2015.
"Consulate General of Mongolia to Be Opened in Bishkek." covermongolia.mn, July 9, 2014. http://covermongolia.blogspot.com/2014/07/pm-shifts-blame-to-rio-fitch-warns-of.html.
Country Assistance Program for Mongolia. Tokyo: Ministry of Foreign Affairs of Japan, November 2004. http://www.mofa.go.jp/policy/oda/assistance/pdfs/e_mongolia2004.pdf.
"Country Profile—Mongolia." *New Agriculturalist,* May 2009. http://www.new-ag.info/en/country/profile.php?a=732.
"Currency Swap." *Investopedia*. https://www.investopedia.com/terms/c/currencyswap.asp.
Dan. "Mongolia and Ivanhoe to sign Tuesday Oct. 6 the $3.6 Billion Oyu Tolgoi Copper-Gold mine agreement." *To Mongolia* (blog), October 3, 2009. https://tomongolia.blogspot.com/2009/10/oyu-tolgoi.html.
Dari, E. "U.S. Defense Minister Chuck Hagel seeks increased ties with Mongolia." *UB Post*, April 11, 2014. http://ubpost.mongolnews.mn/?p=8691.

Dashpurev, D., and S. K. Soni. *Reign of Terror in Mongolia, 1920–1990.* New Delhi: South Asian Publishers, 1992.

David, Grainger. "The Great Mongolian Gold Rush: The land of Genghis Khan has the biggest mining find in a very long time. A visit to the core of a frenzy in the middle of nowhere." *Fortune Magazine,* December 22, 2003. http://archive.fortune.com/magazines/fortune/fortune_archive/2003/12/22/356094/index.htm.

"Defense Minister of Turkey Ismet Yilmaz Pays Official Visit to Mongolia." *Montsame,* September 26, 2014, in *Mongolian Economy and Finance.* http://mongoliaeconomy.blogspot.com/2014/10/mongolia-brief-september-26-2014.html.

DeHaemer, Christian. "With Erdenes-Tavan Tolgoi's IPO, Mongolians 'Will Suddenly Be Rich,'" *Asia Journal of Mining,* June 9, 2011. http://www.asianmining.com/2011/06/with-erdenes-tavan-tolgois-ipo.html.

Dellecker, Adrian, and Thomas Gomart, eds. *Russian Energy Security and Foreign Policy.* New York: Routledge, 2011.

"'Democratic Revolution in Mongolia—25' Conference Held." *Montsame,* December 5, 2014.

Denizer, Cevdet, and Alan Gelb. "Mongolia—Privatization and System Transformation in an Isolated Economy." Working Paper no. 1063, World Bank, Country Economics Department, Washington, DC, December 1992. https://www.researchgate.net/publication/23721596_Mongolia_-_Privatization_and_system_transformation_in_an_isolated_economy.

Dierkes, Julian. "Contract Transparency in Mongolian Mining: Unbundling Contract Transparency in the Extractive Industry: The Case of Mongolia—Part I." *Mongolian Focus* (blog), December 11, 2015. http://blogs.ubc.ca/mongolia/2015/contract-transparency-in-mongolian-mining/.

———. "Small, Unanticipated Impacts." *Mongolia Focus* (blog), June 16, 2016. http://blogs.ubc.ca/mongolia/2016/results-based-workshopping/.

Distelhorst, Luke. "Civil Movements Burn Effigies, Start Hunger Strike." *UB Post,* April 20, 2006.

Dorjdari, Namkhaijantsan. "EITI in Mongolia 2006–2011: Lessons and Prospects." PowerPoint presentation for seminar on promoting EITI in Tajikistan, Dushanbe, July 12, 2011. http://siteresources.worldbank.org/EXTEXTINDTRAINI/Resources/3634714-1315498215486/Mongolia.pdf.

Dorjsuren, Nanjin. "Why Mongolia Wants to Be a Part of Traditional Security Framework in NEA." Presented at Ulaanbaatar Dialogue on Northeast Asian Security 2015, Ulaanbaatar, September 2015.

Dorraj, Manochehr, and Nader Entessar. "Iran's Northern Exposure: Foreign Policy Challenges in Eurasia." CIRS Occasional Paper no. 13, Center for International and Regional Studies, Georgetown University, School of Foreign Service in Qatar, 2013.

Dügersüren, M. "Changing Mongolia in a New Environment." *Mongolian Journal of International Affairs,* no. 1 (1994): 15–22.

Dulguun, Batkhishig. "Sustainable Living and Mongolian Nomads: Is There Development?" *Consilience: The Journal of Sustainable Development,* no. 2 (2009). https://academiccommons.columbia.edu/doi/10.7916/D8NS0TJZ.

Dulguun, Bayarsaikhan. "Former PM Speaks About Mongolia's Financial Woes and Forgotten Promises of Politicians." *UB Post,* November 21, 2016.

———. "Senior Diplomat Elaborates on Mongolia's Foreign Affairs and ASEM11." *UB Post,* July 19, 2016.

———. "Yo. Manlaibayar: Mongolia Will Have Three Huge Transit Railroad Corridors." *UB Post,* January 9, 2014.

Ebel, Robert E. *The Geopolitics of Russian Energy: Looking Back, Looking Forward.* Washington, DC: Center for Strategic and International Studies, 2009.

Economic Policy and Competitiveness Research Center. https://ecrc.mn/about-research/.

Edwards, Terrence. "Mongolia to Pitch Railway Projects to China-Backed AIIB—Govt Adviser." Reuters, September 20, 2016. http://www.reuters.com/article/mongolia-railways-idUSL3N1BW2KQ.

———. "Mongolia's Giant Tavan Tolgoi Coalmine Soon to Be Under New Management." *IntelliNews,* January 14, 2015. http://www.intellinews.com/mongolia-s-giant-tavan-tolgoi-coalmine-soon-to-be-under-new-management-500442965/?archive=bne.

———. "Ukraine Crisis Sparks Renewed Russian Interest in Aging Trans-Mongolian Railway." *bne IntelliNews,* October 22, 2014. http://www.intellinews.com/ukraine-crisis-sparks-renewed-russian-interest-in-aging-trans-mongolian-railway-500433321/?archive=bne.

Edwards, Terrence, and David Stanway. "Mongolia Eyes Economic Boost from China President's Visit." Reuters, August 21, 2014. https://www.reuters.com/article/us-mongolia-china-idUSKBN0GL0HG20140821.

Elbegdorj, Tsakhia. "Address by H. E. Tsakhiagiin Elbegdorj, President of Mongolia to the European Parliament." Strasbourg, June 9, 2015. http://eng.president.mn/newsCenter/viewNews.php?newsId=1568.

———. "Asia Beyond 2015: The Quest for Lasting Peace and Prosperity" (keynote speech at the twenty-first International Conference on the Future of Asia, Tokyo, May 21, 2015). http://eng.president.mn/newsCenter/viewNews.php?newsId=1546.

———. "Mongolia as a Neutral State." Speech to the World Economic Forum, Davos, Switzerland, January 18, 2016. https://www.weforum.org/agenda/2016/01/mongolia-as-a-neutral-state/.

———. "Mongolia—Neutrality." Former President of Mongolia website, September 9, 2015. http://eng.president.mn/newsCenter/viewNews.php?newsId=1662.

———. "Opening Statement by H. E. Tsakhiagiin Elbegdorj, President of Mongolia, at the 11th ASEM Summit." July 15, 2016. http://mongolia.gogo.mn/r/153920.

———. "Remarks by President Ts. Elbegdorj at the Hosting of Diplomatic Corps in Mongolia." Ulaanbaatar, January 14, 2015. https://www.un.int/mongolia/news/remarks-president-tselbegdorj-hosting-diplomatic-corps-mongolia.

———. "Speech by President of Mongolia Tsakhiagiin Elbegdorj at the Opening of the 11th International Congress of Mongolists." Ulaanbaatar, August 30, 2016. http://www.mfa.gov.mn/?p=35764&lang=en.

———. "Statement by President of Mongolia, at the General Debate of the 70th Session of the United Nations General Assembly." New York, September 29, 2015. www.president.mn/eng/newsCenter/viewNews.php?newsId=1674.

Els, Frik. "Oyu Tolgoi Copper, Gold Production Drops." *mining.com*, August 2, 2016.

Emailnews Daily, no. 236 (Ulaanbaatar), December 5, 2001.

Empson, Rebecca. "An Interview with Bill Bikales." *Emerging Suspects* (blog), University College London, October 31, 2016. https://blogs.ucl.ac.uk/mongolian-economy/2016/10/31/an-interview-with-bill-bikales/.

Enkhbat, B. "More Local Companies to Benefit from OT Underground Development." GoGo Mongolia, November 4, 2015. http://mongolia.gogo.mn/r/149498.

Enkhbayar, Shagdar. *Mongolia's Economic Transition and Development Challenges: An Evidence of Poorly Managed Neo-Liberal, Shock Therapy Transition and Economic Destitution.* Riga, Latvia: Lambert Academic Publishing, 2012.

———. "Neo-Liberal 'Shock Therapy' Policy During the Mongolian Economic Transition" (ERINA Discussion Paper no. 0703e, Niigata, Japan, April 2007), "Recent Trends in Mongolian Foreign Trade with the Countries of Northeast Asia" (ERINA Report no. 96, Tokyo, November 2010).

———. "Unemployment and Impoverishment in Mongolia: A Close Look at the Reality." ERINA paper, 2003, 2. http://www.academia.edu/6718735/Unemployment_and_Impoverishment_in_Mongolia_A_Close_Look_at_the_Reality.

Enkhsaikhan, J. "Developing Nuclear Landscape in the Asian Heartland: Role of Nuclear-Weapon States." *Mongolian Journal of International Affairs*, no. 11, 2004: 22–45.

Enkhtuul, B. and R. Oyun. "Ж.Батмөнх агсны гэргий А. Даариймаа: Хань минь багшийнхаа ажлыг хийж байсан бол өнөөдөр амьд сэрүүн байх байлаа" ["Batmunkh's widow A. Daariimaa: If my husband was working as a professor, he would have been alive today"]. *Zuunii Medee* [Century News], April 18, 2011. http://www.bolod.mn/modules.php?name=News&nID=54864.

Erdene, Lkhagva, and Sergey Radchenko. "The Mysterious Sale of Mongolia's Erdenet Mine." *The Diplomat,* July 9, 2016. http://thediplomat.com/2016/07/the-mysterious-sale-of-mongolias-erdenet-mine/.

Erdenebat, Mungunzul, and Taikoo Chang. "Foreign Direct Investment in the Mongolian Mining Sector." *International Journal of u- and e- Service, Science and Technology* 9, no. 3 (2016): 254. http://dx.doi.org/10.14257/ijunesst.2016.9.3.24.

Erdenechimeg, B. "Mongolia Submits Draft Law on the Status of Permanent Neutrality." *GoGo Mongolia,* October 21, 2015.

Erdenechuluun, Luvsangiin. "Mongolia's Strategic Options." In *Northeast Asia Towards 2000: Interdependence and Conflict?*, edited by Kyongsoo Lho and Kay Möller. Baden-Baden, Germany: Nomos, 1999.

———. "The Principal Document of the Friendly Relations." Ulaanbaatar: Ministry of Foreign Affairs, 2003.

"'Eurasia Initiative' Gets Boost from Koreas-Russia Cooperation." *North Korea Newsletter* 341 (December 4, 2014). https://en.yna.co.kr/view/AEN20141203007200325.

Fernández-Gimenez, María E., Batbuyan Batjav, and Batkhishig Baival. *Lessons from the Dzud: Adaptation and Resilience in Mongolian Pastoral Social-Ecological Systems.* Colorado State University and the World Bank, June 2012. http://documents.worldbank.org/curated/en/986161468053662281/pdf/718440WP0P12770201208-01-120revised.pdf.

"FIFTA." *Invest Mongolia.* https://investmongolia.wordpress.com/category/fifta/.

Finley, J. C. "Mongolia Leverages Diplomatic Ties with North Korea." United Press International, December 4, 2014. https://www.upi.com/Top_News/World-News/2014/12/04/Mongolia-leverages-diplomatic-ties-with-North-Korea/4921417633447/.

"The First Mongolia-U.S.-Japan Trilateral Meeting Was Held in New York." Mongolian National Broadcasting, September 15, 2015. http://www.mnb.mn/i/64855.

Fish, M. Steven. "Mongolia: Democracy Without Prerequisites." *Journal of Democracy,* no. 9 (1999).

FlorCruz, Jaime. "Mining Fuels Mongolia's 'Wolf Economy,'" CNN, May 20, 2011. http://www.cnn.com/2011/WORLD/asiapcf/05/19/mongolia.mining.economy/index.html.

"Foreign Minister Summarizes ASEM11." *Mongol Messenger,* July 22, 2016.

"Foreign Relations in 2013." Ministry of Foreign Affairs of Mongolia. www.mfa.gov.mn. Accessed December 23, 2013.

"Former US Secretary of State Puts Pressure on Mongolian Government." *Shards of Mongolia* (blog), March 27, 2006. http://shardsofmongolia.blogspot.com/2006/03/former-us-secretary-of-state-puts.html.

"14th Meeting on Greater Tumen Development Initiative." Sejong: ROK Ministry of Economy and Finance, October 30, 2013. http://english.moef.go.kr/pc/selectTbPressCenterDtl.do?boardCd=N0001&seq=3422.

Friedman, Josh. "Mongolia Marks Passage of Landmark Anti-Trafficking and Corruption Legislation." Asia Foundation, February 15, 2012. http://asiafoundation.org/2012/02/15/mongolia-marks-passage-of-landmark-anti-trafficking-and-corruption-legislation/.

"Frontier Capital Drops Deal for Lottery Licence in Mongolia." GGRAsia, February 23, 2016.

"FSM Expands Diplomatic Reach in Asia-Pacific." *NEWS Agency*, December 24, 2013. english.news.mn.

Gale, Alastair. "North Korea's Lucrative Labor Exports Come Under Pressure." *Wall Street Journal,* July 7, 2016.

Ganbat, Damba. "National Security Concept of Mongolia: Basic Principle." In *Security Outlook of the Asia Pacific Countries and Its Implications for the Defense Sector*. Tokyo: National Institute for Defense Studies, 2014.

Ganguly, Anirban. "Modi in Mongolia: Rekindling a Civilisational Link." *Focus News* (New Delhi), May 18, 2015.

Gellman, Barton. "'Impressed' Albright Gets a Taste of the New Mongolia." *Washington Post,* May 3, 1998, A28.

Gillet, Kit. "High Cost of Cashmere on Mongolia Plains." CNN, September 13, 2010. http://www.cnn.com/2010/WORLD/asiapcf/09/12/mongolia.cashmere.herders/index.html?hpt=C2.

Ginsburg, Tom. "Nationalism, Elites, and Mongolia's Rapid Transformation." In *Mongolia in the Twentieth Century: Landlocked Cosmopolitan*, edited by Stephen Kotkin and Bruce A. Elleman, 247–276. Armonk, NY: M. E. Sharpe, 1999.

Glover, Maury. "Minnesota Native Pardoned, Released from Mongolian Prison." Fox9.com, February 26, 2015. http://www.fox9.com/news/1564143-story.

"GNI per Capita, Atlas Method (Current US$)." World Bank. https://data.worldbank.org/indicator/NY.GNP.PCAP.CD?end=2017&start=1962.

Goldbeck. US embassy cable. "Protests Against Mongolian Government Grow." April 12, 2006. https://wikileaks.org/plusd/cables/06ULAANBAATAR261_a.html.

Goleman, Mark. "5th Round of the Ulaanbaatar Dialogues." *New Eastern Outlook*, June 8, 2018. https://journal-neo.org/2018/08/06/5th-round-of-the-ulaanbaatar-dialogues/.

———. "Mongolia and the US: From Acquaintance to Strategic Cooperation." *New Eastern Outlook,* May 5, 2015. http://journal-neo.org/2015/05/31/rus-mongoliya-i-ssha-ot-znakomstva-k-strategicheskomu-sotrudnichestvu/.

Golomt Capital. http://golomtcapital.com/zuunbayan-khangi-railroad-to-be-constructed/.

Gotov, Dugerjav. "Northeast Asia and Mongolia: Infrastructure Network Development Issues." *Ritsumeikan Journal of Asia Pacific Studies*, 26 (2009): 73-82. https://www.apu.ac.jp/rcaps/uploads/fckeditor/publications/journal/RJAPS_V26_Gotov.pdf.

Government of Mongolia. *Human Development Report Mongolia 2003: Urban-Rural Disparities in Mongolia.* Ulaanbaatar: Government of Mongolia, 2003. http://hdr.undp.org/sites/default/files/mongolia_2003_en.pdf.

———. *Managing the Transition from the Millennium Development Goals to the Sustainable Development Goals.* Ulaanbaatar: Government of Mongolia, 2015.

———. "Mongolian Government Paper on Social Sector Issues and Strategies, Medium-Term Economic and Social Development Strategy 1999–2000." Ulaanbaatar: Government of Mongolia, 1999.

———. "Resolution of the Government of Mongolia, No. 2 Approving the Percentage of Foreign Labor Force and Specialists for the Year 2015." Ulaanbaatar: Government of Mongolia, January 7, 2015.

Government of Mongolia, UNDP and World Bank. Independent Evaluation of the National Poverty Alleviation Programme and Options Post-2000, mimeo, Ulaanbaatar, 1999.

Government of Mongolia/USAID. "Mongolia Country Strategic Plan, 1999–2003." Ulaanbaatar: Government of Mongolia, 1998.

Greater Tumen Initiative. *Integrated Transport Infrastructure and Cross-Border Facilitation Study for the Trans-GTR Transport Corridors*. Beijing: Greater Tumen Initiative Secretariat, February 2013. www.tumenprogramme.org/?info-1-115.html.

Green, Douglas. "EEU Two Years Later: Expansion and Unbalance. The Case of Kyrgyzstan." *Times of Central Asia,* May 21, 2016.

Green, Mark. "Mongolia, 25 Years from Soviet Satellite to Democratic Partner." *The Hill* (blog), May 1, 2015. https://thehill.com/blogs/pundits-blog/international/240747-mongolia-25-years-from-soviet-satellite-to-democratic.

Griffin, Keith. "Agricultural Involution and Urban-to-Rural Migration in Mongolia." Department of Economics Working Paper, University of California Riverside, February 2, 2000. http://economics.ucr.edu/papers/papers02/02-02.pdf.

———. *Poverty and the Transition to a Market Economy in Mongolia.* London: Macmillan, 1995.

———, ed. *Poverty Reduction in Mongolia.* Canberra: Asia Pacific Press, 2003.

"GTI Office Receives MECC Mission." Greater Tumen Initiative, November 11, 2016. http://www.tumenprogramme.org/?info-643-1.html.

"GTI Participates in the 1st NEA Energy Forum." Greater Tumen Initiative, November 16, 2016. http://www.tumenprogramme.org/?info-659-1.html.

"The GTI Secretariat Takes Part in the Eurasia Transport and Logistics Partnership (EuTraLop) Round Table Meeting in Republic of Korea." Greater Tumen Initiative, November 16, 2016. http://www.tumenprogramme.org/?info-656-1.html.

Guanghui, Que. *China's Energy Sector: A Sustainable Strategy.* Beijing: Foreign Language Press, 2007.

Gulati, Monish. "Modi in Mongolia: India Looking to Play Larger Asia-Pacific Role?." *South Asia Monitor*, May 16, 2015. http://southasiamonitor.org/detail.php?type=sl&nid=11828.
Gumilev, L. N. *People and Nature of the Great Steppe.* Moscow: Voprosy Istorii, 1987.
Gutin, John, and Robin Young, eds. "Khan Bank: The Agricultural Bank of Mongolia." January 2005. https://www.marketlinks.org/sites/marketlinks.org/files/resource/files/ML1790_mr_11_khan_bank_the_agricultural_bank_of_mongolia_1_04.pdf.
Hanson, Jennifer L. *Nations in Transition: Mongolia.* New York: Facts on File, 2003.
Hanson, Philip. "The Sustainability of Russia's Energy Power: Implications for the Russian Economy." In *Russian Energy Power and Foreign Relations: Implications for Conflict and Cooperation*, edited by Jeronim Perovic, Robert W. Orttung, and Andreas Wenger, 23–50. CCS Studies in Security and International Relations series. London: Routledge, 2009.
He Na and Liu Mingtai. "Regional Bloc Urges Better Financing Channels." *China Daily,* September 18, 2014. http://www.chinadaily.com.cn/china/2014-09/18/content_18618868.htm.
Hegewisch, Niels. "Dialogue Is a Powerful Tool if It Leads to Cooperation." Friedrich-Ebert-Stiftung Office for Regional Cooperation in Asia, July 7, 2017. https://www.fes-asia.org/news/dialogue-is-a-powerful-tool-if-it-leads-to-cooperation/.
Hibbert, Reginald, and Ann Hibbert. *Letters from Mongolia.* London: Radcliffe Press, 2005.
Hill, Matthew. "Mongolia Reaffirms Oyu Tolgoi Investment Agreement." *Mining Weekly*, October 6, 2011.
"Hillary Clinton at the International Women's Leadership Forum Ulaanbaatar Mongolia." *Still4Hill.com*, July 9, 2012. https://still4hill.com/2012/07/09/hillary-clinton-at-the-the-international-womens-leadership-forum-ulaanbaatar-mongolia/.
Hoare, Jim, and Susan Pares. "Ochirbat." In *A Political and Economic Dictionary of East Asia.* London: Routledge, 2005.
"HPP Development Project on the Khovd River Is Temporarily Suspended." World Wildlife Fund, June 30, 2016. http://wwf.panda.org/wwf_news/?272256/HPP-development-project-on-the-Khovd-river-is-temporarily-suspended.
Huang, Chin-Hao. *China's Soft Power in East Asia: A Quest for Status and Influence?* NBR Special Report no. 42. Seattle: National Bureau of Asian Research, January 2013.
Human Development Report Mongolia 2003: Urban-Rural Disparities in Mongolia. Ulaanbaatar: Government of Mongolia, UNDP, 2003. http://hdr.undp.org/sites/default/files/mongolia_2003_en.pdf.
Human Rights Development Center. "Combating Human Trafficking in Mongolia: Issues and Opportunities." Ulaanbaatar: ME Consulting, 2005.
Humber, Yuriy. "Mongolia Bars SouthGobi's U.S. Chief from Leaving Country." Bloomberg, February 1, 2013. http://www.bloomberg.com/news/articles/2013-02-01/mongolia-bars-southgobi-s-u-s-chief-from-leaving-country.
Humphrey, Caroline, and David Sneath. *The End of Nomadism? Society, State and the Environment in Inner Asia.* Durham, NC: Duke University Press, 1999.
Hynes, Phill. "The Uranium Shakedown: How Mongolia and Russia Conspired Against Western Investors (Part 2)." *Frontera,* March 29, 2016. https://frontera.net/news/uranium-shakedown-mongolia-russia-conspired-western-investors-part-2/.
Ikeda, Norihiko. "Mongolia: Will It Remain a Local Buffer Nation Between China and Russia, or Become a Small Yet Global Nation? A New Perspective on the 'Third Neighbor Policy,'" *Mongol Messenger,* October 28, 2016.
———. "Mongolians: New Identity? Or Revival? Expanding Mongolia's Options for the 21st Century." *Mongol Messenger,* April 22, 2016, 7.
IMF (International Monetary Fund). *Economic Growth Support and Poverty Reduction Strategy*. Washington, DC: IMF, July 3, 2003.
———. "Mongolia: Poverty Reduction Strategy Paper of Government of Mongolia." *Economic Growth Support and Poverty Reduction Strategy.* Washington, DC: IMF, July 3, 2003.
———. *Mongolia Selected Issues and Statistical Appendix.* Washington, DC: IMF, September 7, 2005.

———. "Mongolia, Staff Report for the 2005 Article IV Consultation." Washington, DC: September 1, 2005. https://www.imf.org/external/pubs/ft/scr/2005/cr05396."Inaugural Meeting of the GTI Energy Board Boost Energy Cooperation in Northeast Asia." Greater Tumen Initiative, Ulaanbaatar, September 16, 2009. http://www.tumenprogramme.org/?info-591-1.html.

Infomongolia.com, December 12, 2014.

Infomongolia.com, December 23, 2014.

Infomongolia.com, December 15, 2014. Accessed January 20, 2015.

International Energy Agency. *Russia Energy Survey 2002*. Paris: IEA, 2002.

———. *World Energy Outlook*. Paris: IEA, 2010.

International Federation of Red Cross and Red Crescent Societies. *Annual Report: Mongolia*. Geneva: IFRC, 2002. http://www.ifrc.org/docs/appeals/annual02/013902annrep.pdf.

"International Support Measures: The Case of Mongolia." Draft UN discussion paper, Vientiane, Lao People's Democratic Republic, February 27, 2013. http://www.unescap.org/sites/default/files/DP3-B.pdf.

International Think Tank for Landlocked Developing Countries. http://land-locked.org.

"Iran, Mongolia Discuss Expansion of Trade Ties." *Tehran Times*, September 10, 2018. https://www.tehrantimes.com/news/427378/Iran-Mongolia-discuss-expansion-of-trade-ties.

"Iran, Mongolia Resolute to Expand Bilateral Ties." Press TV, December 23, 2015. https://theiranproject.com/blog/2015/12/23/iran-mongolia-resolute-to-expand-bilateral-ties/.

"Iran Opens Nuclear Site to Mongolia's President." Associated Press, September 3, 2012. http://triblive.com/news/2532074-74/iran-nuclear-site-visit-elbegdorj-iranian-mongolia-president-tehran-uranium.

"Iran Ready to Enhance Economic Ties with Mongolia." Mehr News Agency, August 30, 2015. http://en.mehrnews.com/news/109645/Iran-ready-to-enhance-economic-ties-with-Mongolia.

"Ivanhoe Welcomes Mongolian Government's Acceptance of New Initiatives to Facilitate the Completion of a Stability Agreement for Development of Oyu Tolgoi Copper-Gold Project." Ivanhoe press statement, March 23, 2006.

"Ivanhoe's Controversial Mongolian Mine Boosted by Canadian State Support." *Unuudur,* July 23, 2010. http://www.unuudur.com/?p=9753.

Jacobs, Andrew. "Winter Leaves Mongolians a Harvest of Carcasses." *New York Times,* May 19, 2010.

Jamasmie, Cecilia. "Mongolia Halts Landmark Deal with Foreign Firms over Massive Coal Mine." *mining.com*, April 7, 2015.

Japan International Cooperation Agency (JICA). "Major Projects in Mongolia." http://www.jica.go.jp/mongolia/english/activities/activity16.html.

"Japan-Mongolia Summit Meeting." Ministry of Foreign Affairs of Japan, September 11, 2018. https://www.mofa.go.jp/a_o/c_m1/mn/page3e_000919.html.

"Japan, U.S., Mongolia Mull First Trilateral Foreign Ministerial Talks." *Japan Times,* August 14, 2015.

"Japan's 'Marubeni' Wins Tavan Tolgoi Power Plant Tender." *UB Post,* March 2, 2016.

Jargalsaikhan, Dambaadarjaa. "Blue Strategy." In *Creation of New Wealth,* 207–210. Ulaanbaatar: MGL Design Group LLC, 2014.

———. "Mongolia Is the Next Panama." *UB Post,* February 27, 2013.

Jeffries, Ian. *Mongolia: A Guide to Economic and Political Developments*. New York: Routledge, 2007.

Joel. "Mongolia Wins Debt Relief (and Russia Does Well, Too)." *Far Outliers* (blog), January 25, 2004. http://faroutliers.blogspot.com/2004/01/.

Johnson, John. "Cru Group: Mongolian Prospects on the Up After a Healthy Dose of Reality." CRGroup.com, October 6, 2014. http://covermongolia.blogspot.com/2014/10/mnt-losing-streak-enters-3rd-week-2015.html.

"Joint Declaration, the People's Republic of China, France, the Russian Federation, the United Kingdom of Great Britain and Northern Ireland, and the United States of America on Mongolia's Nuclear-Weapon-Free Status." Ulaanbaatar, Ministry of Foreign Affairs of Mongolia, September 17, 2012.

"Joint Statement Between Mongolia and the United States of America." Washington, DC: White House Office of the Press Secretary, November 21, 2005. https://georgewbush-whitehouse.archives.gov/news/releases/2005/11/20051121-1.html.

"Joint Statement from Mongolia-U.S.-Japan Trilateral Meeting." Ulaanbaatar: Ministry of Foreign Affairs of Mongolia, August 30, 2017. http://www.mfa.gov.mn/?p=41580&lang=en.

"Joint Statement of the 2018 U.S.-Japan-Mongolia Trilateral Meeting." Washington, DC: US Department of State, April 27, 2018. https://www.state.gov/r/pa/prs/ps/2018/04/281266.htm.

Kameda, Masaaki. "Japan, Mongolia Sign Economic Partnership Agreement." *Japan Times*, February 15, 2015.

Kaplonski, Christopher. *Truth, History and Politics in Mongolia: Memory of Heroes.* New York: RoutledgeCurzon, 2004.

Kaye, Lincoln. "Two Mongolias: Faltering Steppes." *Far Eastern Economic Review,* April 9, 1992.

"Keynote Address by MOS Shri E. Ahamed at First India-Central Asia Dialogue." *Media Center*, Ministry of External Affairs (India), June 12, 2012. http://www.mea.gov.in/Speeches-Statements.htm?dtl/19791/Keynote+address+by+MOS+Shri+E+Ahamed+at+First+IndiaCentral+Asia+Dialogue#.

Khaliun, Chimeddorj. "Energy Ministry Signs Erdenet Power Plant Expansion Agreement with China." *UB Post,* December 11, 2015. http://ubpost.mongolnews.mn/?p=17381.

———. "Groundbreaking Ceremony for Erdenet Thermal Power Plant Expansion Takes Place." *UB Post*, March 31, 2016.

———. "Mongolia India Business Council Opens to Support Businesses." *UB Post*, April 18, 2016.

———. "Mongolia, Russia and China Agree to Establish Economic Corridor." *UB Post,* June 27, 2016.

Khazanov, Anatoly M., and André Wink, eds. *Nomads in the Sedentary World.* London: Routledge, 2001.

Khuder, B. "Consultation of Heads of Diplomatic Missions Launches." *Montsame,* July 7, 2015.

———. "GTI Consultative Committee Meeting Starts." *Montsame,* October 30, 2013.

———. "Hagel: It Is Important for Our Countries to Keep Friendly Cooperation." *Montsame,* April 10, 2014.

———. "Minister of Mining Reports." *Montsame,* December 18, 2015. http://en.montsame.mn/mining/minister-mining-reports.

King, John. "Bush Appoints Baker Envoy on Iraqi Debt." CNN, December 3, 2003.

Kingsley, Patrick. "Nomads No More: Why Mongolian Herders Are Moving to the City." *The Guardian,* January 5, 2017.

Klein, Naomi. "James Baker's Double Life." *The Nation,* October 12, 2004. https://www.thenation.com/article/james-bakers-double-life/.

Kohn, Michael. "Accord for $1.4 Billion Mongolia Power Plant Could Reduce Pollution." *Bloomberg*, July 29, 2015. https://www.bloomberg.com/news/articles/2015-07-29/engie-led-group-in-accord-for-1-4-billion-mongolia-power-plant.

———. "Mongolia Seeks $828 Million from China for Largest Hydro Project." *Bloomberg,* March 23, 2015.

Kojima, Shuhei. *Stable Supply of Mineral Resources.* Tokyo: Ministry of Economy, Trade and Industry, Mineral and Natural Resources Division, July 12, 2002.

Kosich, Dorothy. "Russian Disinformation Campaign Aimed at Oyu Tolgoi, Mongolian Debt." Mineweb.com, October 15, 2009.

Kreppel, Stephen. "Expert Analysis: Mongolian National Marketing Coordination Office. 'Potential for Profit?—Mongolia's Neglected Non-Mining Economy.'" https://static1.squarespace.com/static/531d6809e4b030d9a208a393/t/54434131e4b0046ddec71d9d/1413693745231/EC_mongolianNationalMarketing.pdf.

Krishna, Vaishali. "Mongolian Foreign Policy Implications for Russia and China." *Mongolian Journal of International Affairs* 19 (2015): 67–81. http://www.mongoliajol.info/index.php/MJIA/article/viewFile/406/427.

Kuribayashi, Sumio. "Structural Change and Economic Performance in Mongolia." In *The Geopolitical Relations Between Contemporary Mongolia and Neighboring Asian Countries: Democracy, Economy and Security.* Taipei: Mongolian and Tibetan Affairs, 2003.

"Kyrgyz to Share Mongolia's Electoral System Experience." *Mongol Messenger,* July 10, 2014.

Kyung-soo, Choi. "The Mining Industry of North Korea." *Korean Journal of Defense Analysis* 23, no. 2 (June 2011).

Lake, Joseph E. "Ambassador Joseph E. Lake." Interview by Charles Stuart Kennedy. Association for Diplomatic Studies and Training Foreign Affairs Oral History Project, September 5, 1994, 8. http://www.adst.org/OH%20TOCs/Lake,%20Joseph%20E.toc.pdf.

———. "Frontier Embassy." *Foreign Service Journal,* December 1992: 35–38.

———. "Perspectives on Early Political Change." Remarks at the Asia Foundation conference on Mongolia's Political and Economic Transition: Challenges and Opportunities, Ulaanbaatar, September 11, 2000: 3–10. https://asiafoundation.org/resources/pdfs/MongloiaPolEconTransition.pdf.

La Porta, Alphonse F. "Ambassador Alphonse F. La Porta." Interview by Charles Stuart Kennedy. Association for Diplomatic Studies and Training Foreign Affairs Oral History Project, February 11, 2004. http://www.adst.org/OH%20TOCs/La%20Porta,%20Alphonse%20F.toc.pdf.

Laruelle, Marlene. *The "Russian World": Russia's Soft Power and Geopolitical Imagination*. Washington, DC: Center on Global Interests, May 2015. http://globalinterests.org/wp-content/uploads/2015/05/FINAL- CGI_Russian-World_Marlene-Laruelle.pdf.

Law of Mongolia on Minerals Revised (Ulaanbaatar: July 8, 2006). https://s3.amazonaws.com/rgi-documents/2c242a91b27ecc449f3040515c517d7c1e20c21a.pdf.

"Law on Economic Zones." *Invest Mongolia* (blog), May 11, 2007. https://investmongolia.wordpress.com/.

Lee, Jee Abbey. "Former US Advisor Meets with N. Korean Officials." *VOA News*, May 28, 2014. https://www.voanews.com/a/former-us-advisor-meets-with-n-korean-officials/1924791.html.

Legrand, Jacques. "The Mongolia 'Zud': Facts and Concepts from the Description of a Disaster to the Understanding of the Nomadic Pastoral System." In *International Symposium on Dialogue Among Civilizations: Interactions Between Nomadic and Other Cultures of Central Asia*, 14–30. Ulaanbaatar: International Institute of the Study of Nomadic Civilizations, 2001.

———. "Nomadic Pastoral Societies: The Importance of Compromise in Dealing with Tension, Conflict and Security." In *Mongols et Nomades: Société, Historie, Culture.* Ulaanbaatar: Admon, 2011.

Li, Justin. "Chinese Investment in Mongolia: An Uneasy Courtship Between Goliath and David." East Asia Forum, February 2, 2011. www.eastasiaforum.org/2011/02/02/chinese-investment-in-mongolia-an-uneasy-courtship-between-goliath-and-david/.

Lindberg, Meloney C., Jeremy Gross, and Tirza Theunissen. "7th Ministerial Conference of the Community of Democracies Showcases Mongolia's Democratic Transition." The Asia Foundation, May 1, 2103. https://asiafoundation.org/2013/05/01/7th-ministerial-conference-of-the-community-of-democracies-showcases-mongolias-democratic-transition/.

Lindenberg, Marc, and Coralie Bryant. *Going Global: Transforming Relief and Development NGOs.* Boulder, CO: Kumarian Press, 2001.

"Local Company Head Arrested As Foreign Executives Pardoned." *The Economist,* March 3, 2015.

Luxbacher, Kirsten, and Andrew Goodland. "Building Resilience to Extreme Weather: Index-Based Livestock Insurance in Mongolia." Washington, DC: World Resources Report, 2011.

MacDonald, Alistair, and Carolyn King. "Ivanhoe Mines CEO Quits in Deal with Rio Tinto." *Wall Street Journal*, April 18, 2012. http://www.wsj.com/articles/SB10001424052702303513404577351572187687512.

Maire, Antoine. "Mongolia at War: Economic Warfare Under Blue Sky." Paper presented at the Tenth International Congress of Mongolists, Ulaanbaatar, August 9–13, 2011.

"Major Road and Transport Projects Will Be Put into Effect to Promote Economy." *Mongol Messenger,* November 4, 2016.

Man, John. *Kublai Khan.* New York: Bantam Press, 2007.

Managing the Transition from the Millennium Development Goals to the Sustainable Development Goals. Ulaanbaatar: Government of Mongolia, 2015.

Marfenin, N. *Rossiâ v okruzausem mire: 2000.* Moscow: MNEPY, 2000.

Mattis, Peter. "Reexamining the Confucian Institutes." *The Diplomat,* August 2, 2012.

McKinley, Terry. "The National Development Strategy and Aid Coordination." In *Poverty Reduction in Mongolia,* edited by Keith Griffin. Canberra: Asia Pacific Press, 2003.

"Meeting with Shinzo Abe, Prime Minister of Japan." President of Mongolia website, September 11, 2018. https://president.mn/en/2018/09/11/meeting-with-shinzo-abe-prime-minister-of-japan-eef2018/.

Mellor, John W. *Mongolia Food Sector Study*. Washington, DC: International Science and Technology Institute, November 1992. http://pdf.usaid.gov/pdf_docs/pnacb064.pdf.

"Memorandum from Mongolia Regarding the Consolidation of Its International Security and Nuclear-Weapon-Free Status." In 2015 Review Conference of the Parties to the Treaty on the Non-Proliferation of Nuclear Weapons, New York, April 27–May 22, 2015. http://www.un.org/en/ga/search/view_doc.asp?symbol=NPT/CONF.2015/8.

Mendee, Jargalsaikhan. "Beyond the Quagmire: The Future of Mongolia's United States and Japan Partnerships" (video). East-West Center, August 20, 2014. https://www.eastwestcenter.org/events/beyond-the-quagmire-the-future-mongolia%E2%80%99s-united-states-and-japan-partnerships.

———. "Permanent Neutrality Debate in Mongolia." *Asia Pacific Memo* #355, Institute of Asian Research, Vancouver, December 7, 2015.

———. "What's Next for American and Japanese Partnerships with Mongolia?" August 20, 2014, unpublished paper presented at the East West Center. https://www.eastwestcenter.org/events/beyond-the-quagmire-the-future-mongolia's-united-states-and-japan-partnerships.

Menon. "Integrating Poverty Reduction Study." UNDP, November 26, 2002.

Miliate, Brandon. "Modigolia? Indian-Mongolian Relations Post-PM Modi's Trip to Ulaanbaatar." *Mongolia Focus* (blog), Policy Series: Typical Explanations for Policy Failures (II) Oyu Tolgoi on Track Again, May 18, 2015. http://blogs.ubc.ca/mongolia/2015/modigolia-indian-mongolian-relations/.

"Millennium Challenge Compact Between the United States of America Acting Through the Millennium Challenge Corporation and the Government of Mongolia, Annex." October 22, 2007, 2–4. https://www.state.gov/documents/organization/111590.pdf.

Milne, Elizabeth. "The Mongolian People's Republic: Toward a Market Economy." International Monetary Fund occasional paper, Washington, DC, March 15, 1991.

Ministry of External Relations of Mongolia. *Foreign Policy Blue Book.* Ulaanbaatar: Admon, 2000.

Ministry of Foreign Affairs of Japan. *Country Assistance Program for Mongolia.* Tokyo: Ministry of Foreign Affairs of Japan, November 2004. http://www.mofa.go.jp/policy/oda/assistance/pdfs/e_mongolia2004.pdf.

———. "Regional Situations and Relations with Japan." In *Japanese Bluebook.* Tokyo: MOFA, 1992–1993. http://www.mofa.go.jp/policy/other/bluebook/1992/1992-3-1.htm.

Ministry of Foreign Affairs of Mongolia. "Cultural and Humanitarian Foreign Policy." Ulaanbaatar: Ministry of Foreign Affairs of Mongolia, February 21, 2011. http://www.mfa.gov.mn/?lang=en.

"Modi Holds Talks in Mongolia, Seeks Stronger Ties." *Gulf Times*, May 17, 2015.

Mohan, C. Raja. "Chinese Takeaway: PM Modi in Mongolia." *Indian Express,* May 12, 2015. http://carnegieendowment.org/2015/05/12/chinese-takeaway-pm-modi-in-mongolia/i8gf.

Mongol Messenger, December 16, 1998.

Mongol Messenger, March 3, 1999.

Mongol Messenger, January 21, 2004.

Mongol Messenger, December 19, 2014.

Mongol Messenger, December 18, 2015.

"Mongolia: A Case Study in Foreign Direct Investment." *Steppe Dispatches,* March 23, 2015. https://steppedispatches.com/2015/03/23/mongolia-a-case-study-in-foreign-direct-investment/.
"Mongolia: Amnesty International Submission to the UN Universal Periodic Review." Ninth Session of the UPR Working Group, November–December 2010. lib.ohchr.org/HRBodies/UPR/Documents/session9/MN/AI_Amnesty%20International_Revised.pdf.
"Mongolia and China to Sign Oil for Petroleum Deal." *Montsame,* March 19, 2013. http://covermongolia.blogspot.com/2013/03/southgobi-restarting-production.html.
"Mongolia and Coal." *SourceWatch*. https://www.sourcewatch.org/index.php/Mongolia_and_coal.
"Mongolia and Turkey Sign Over 100 Cooperation Documents Since 1990." *Montsame,* October 5, 2016.
"Mongolia Asks the World Bank's Involvement in the 'Steppe Road' Project." *infoMongolia.com,* September 18, 2014. http://infomongolia.com/ct/ci/8374.
"Mongolia Becomes an Active Partner of the World Economic Forum, Notes Professor Klaus Schwab." *www.infomongolia.com,* accessed on January 25, 2017.
"Mongolia Compact." Millennium Challenge Corporation. https://www.mcc.gov/where-we-work/program/mongolia-compact.
"Mongolia Considering Joining Eurasian Economic Union Economy." *Belarus News,* August 30, 2016.
"Mongolia Fully Repays Big Debt to Russia." *Montsame,* March 2, 2016. http://en.montsame.mn/video/politics/mongolia-fully-repays-big-debt-russia.
"Mongolia Has 163.2 Billion Tons of Coal Reserve." *Business Mongolia,* September 5, 2011. http://www.businessmongolia.com/mongolia/2011/05/09/mongolia-has-163-2-billion-tons-of-coal-reserve/.
"Mongolia Honors Turkey's Deputy Prime Minister." Anadolu Agency, October 28, 2014. https://www.aa.com.tr/en/turkey/mongolia-honors-turkeys-deputy-prime-minister/106698.
"Mongolia Hosts the UNWTO Silk Road Conference on Nomadic Tourism and Sustainable Cities." UN World Tourism Organization, October 18, 2016. http://media.unwto.org/press-release/2016-10-18/mongolia-hosts-unwto-silk-road-conference-nomadic-tourism-and-sustainable-c.
"Mongolia Launches Construction of First Oil Refinery with Indian Aid." Reuters, June 22, 2018. https://www.reuters.com/article/mongolia-refinery/mongolia-launches-construction-of-first-oil-refinery-with-indian-aid-idUSL4N1TO1TO.
Mongolian Mining Journal, September 20, 2012. mongolianminingjournal.com.
"Mongolia Monument Honors Prisoners." *Japan Times,* December 11, 2001. http://www.japantimes.co.jp/news/2001/12/11/national/mongolia-monument-honors-prisoners/#.U-kw_PldWCl.
"Mongolia, North Korea Sign MoU, North Korean Foreign Minister in Mongolia on Three-Day Visit to Further Cooperation." Nknews.org, February 25, 2015.
"Mongolia Not Planning Camps for N. Koreans." *Gulf Times* (Qatar), November 24, 2006.
"Mongolia Pledges USD 150 000 for Community of Democracies." Community of Democracies, April 29, 2013. https://community-democracies.org/?p=3962.
"Mongolia: Protect Rights of North Korean Migrant Workers." Human Rights Watch, August 20, 2008.
"Mongolia, Russia and China Sign Joint Declaration to Develop Transit Transportation Corridor." *infoMongolia.com,* December 19, 2013. http://covermongolia.blogspot.com/2013/12/mse-top-20-at-9-month-high-imf-urges.html.
"Mongolia: Strategy for Northeast Asia Power System Interconnection." Renewable Energy Institute, May 25, 2016.
"Mongolia to Approve Draft Law on Casino." February 24, 2015. business-mongolia.com.
"Mongolia to Regulate Workfield of Foreigners to Boost Education." *Montsame,* April 9, 2006. http://www.mongolia-web.com/education/347-mongolia-to-regulate-workfield-of-foreigners-to-boost-education/.

"Mongolia, Turkey Sign Parliamentary Cooperation Agreement." news.mn, in *Mongolia Economy 27.06.2014, Newswire*, Issue 331, June 24, 2014. https://www.slideshare.net/ulziimyagmar/27062014-newswire-issue331.
"Mongolia Ups Mining Land." *Mining Journal,* March 9, 2017.
"Mongolia Water Compact." Millennium Challenge Corporation. https://www.mcc.gov/where-we-work/program/mongolia-water-compact.
"Mongolian and Chinese Joint Communique." Ulaanbaatar: Ministry of Foreign Affairs, 1999.
"Mongolian Authorities Must Respect the Human Rights of Former Mongolian President Following His Arrest." Amnesty International, May 2012. www.amnesty.mn/en/aim-news/amnesty-international-public-statement.
"Mongolian Energy Sector Anticipates a Productive Year Ahead." *UB Post,* January 8, 2016. http://ubpost.mongolnews.mn/?p=17722.
"Mongolian Government Paper on Social Sector Issues and Strategies, Medium-Term Economic and Social Development Strategy 1999–2000." Unpublished paper, 1999.
Mongolian Mining Corporation. *Interim Report 2016.* Ulaanbaatar: MMC, 2016. http://www.mmc.mn/uploads/MMC_Interim%20report_2016_Eng.pdf.
Mongolian Ministry of External Relations. *Foreign Policy Blue Book* (Ulaanbaatar: Admon, 2000).
"Mongolian PM Lays Monastery Stone." *Times of India*, January 19, 2004.
"Mongolian President's Visit to North Korea Aimed at Increasing Ties." *South China Morning Post,* October 28, 2013.
"Mongolian Railway Draft Feasibility Study Completed." *Railway Gazette*, April 10, 2018. https://www.railwaygazette.com/news/news/asia/single-view/view/mongolian-railway-draft-feasibility-study-completed.html.
Mongolian Statistical Yearbook 2000. Ulaanbaatar: National Statistics Office of Mongolia, 2001.
"Mongolia's Elbegdorj Sees Trade Boost Through North Korean Ports." *Mongolian Economy and Finance*, October 31, 2013." http://mongoliaeconomy.blogspot.com/2013/10/mongolias-elbegdorj-sees-trade-boost.html.
"Mongolia's Foreign Direct Investment at a Crossroads." *Unuudur.com.* http://www.unuudur.com/?p=26969.
"Mongolia's Foreign Minister Highlights Need to Support Democratic Transitions." June 2015. http://www.unesco.org/new/en/member-states/single-view/news/mongolias_foreign_minister_highlights_need_to_support_dem/.
"Mongolia's Foreign Policy in the Political Field." Ministry of Foreign Affairs of Mongolia, February 21, 2011. www.mfa.gov.mn.
"Mongolia's 'Third Neighbor' Foreign Policy." Asia Society, June 23, 2013. http://asiasociety.org/korea/mongolias-third-neighbor-foreign-policy.
"Mongolia's Tourism Sector Looks to Its Natural Assets to Secure Its Future." Oxford Business Group. http://www.oxfordbusinessgroup.com/overview/mongolias-tourism-sector-looks-its-natural-assets-secure-its-future.
Montsame (Ulaanbaatar), March 26, 2001.
Montsame, September 19, 2002.
Montsame, October 3 and 7, 2002.
Montsame, March 19, 2013.
Montsame News Agency, *Mongolia* (Ulaanbaatar: 2006).
"Moody's Assigns B1 Rating to Mongolia." Moody's, October 4, 2005.
Morozova, Irina Y. *Socialist Revolutions in Asia.* London: Routledge, 2009.
Morris, Elizabeth, and Ole Bruun. *Promoting Employment Opportunities in Rural Mongolia: Past Experience and ILO Approaches*. Bangkok: International Labour Office, 2004.
Morton, John. "A Note on Comparing International Experiences of Drought Management in the Pastoral and Agro-Pastoral Livestock Sectors." Chatham, UK: Natural Resources Institute, University of Greenwich, 2002.

Munkhchimeg, Davaasharav. "Flock On: Mongolia Meat Exporters Turn to Iran's Halal Markets." Reuters, August 22, 2018. https://www.reuters.com/article/us-mongolia-meat-halal/flock-on-mongolia-meat-exporters-turn-to-irans-halal-markets-idUSKCN1L70EU.

Munkh-Ochir, D. Khirghis. "Adrift or Advance? Socioeconomic Aspects of Mongolia-Russia Relations at the Onset of the 21st Century." In *Neighbors Through the Centuries: History and Contemporary Aspects of Bilateral Relations Between Mongolia and Russia*, no. 27. Ulaanbaatar: Institute for Strategic Studies, 2005.

Munkh-Ochir, Dorjjugder. "Same Rules, New Dimensions for Mongolia's National Security: Adapting to the New Geo-Economic Environment." Washington, DC: Brookings East Asia Commentary, October 20, 2009. https://www.brookings.edu/opinions/same-rules-new-dimensions-for-mongolias-national-security-adapting-to-the-new-geo-economic-environment/.

Murphy, David. "No Room for Nomads." *Far Eastern Economic Review,* May 31, 2001.

Myagmasuren, D. "Talks held to develop continental railway." *Mongol Messenger,* December 20, 2014.

Na Hee-Seung, "Integrated International Intermodal Transport of Russia's Far East, Siberia and Korean Peninsula." In *The Political Economy of Pacific Russia,* edited by Jing Huang and Alexander Korolev, 203–221. Cham, Switzerland: Springer, Palgrave Macmillan, 2017. https://link.springer.com/chapter/10.1007/978-3-319-40120-1_9.

Namjil, Ganbat, "Mongolians End Protests Demanding Resignation of Government, President." *Mines and Communities,* April 24, 2006. http://www.minesandcommunities.org/article.php?a=5534.

———. "Mongolians Protest Over Canadian Firm." Associated Press, April 12, 2006. http://www.globalgoodnews.com/government-news-a.html?art=1144798812117613.

Naranhuu L., D. Shombodon, B. Jandagsuren, S. Amgaa, and Ts. Altanbat. "An Examination of the Effectiveness of Herd Restocking Strategies in Building and Securing the Incomes and the Livelihoods of Herder Households." Ulaanbaatar: Ministry of Finance and Economy of Mongolia and UNDP/SIDA, 2003. https://www.openforum.mn/res_mat/PRG%20Maljuulalt%20Eng.pdf.

Nath, Caroline, and Ros Armitage. "A Way of Life Imperiled: Mongolia's Uncertain Future." *In Action* (blog), 2000. http://www.redcross.int/EN/mag/magazine2000_2/Mongolia.html.

The National Committee on North Korea, "Special Economic Zones in the DPRK." *NCNK Issue Brief*, January 14, 2014. https://www.ncnk.org/sites/default/files/issue-briefs/NCNK_Issue_Brief_DPRK_SEZ.pdf.

National Foreign Policy Concept 2011 (of Mongolia).

"Neutral Mongolia Looks to Be Economic Link." *Global Times,* November 11, 2015.

"New Highway to Open Up Trade, Investment in Western Mongolia." *Asian Development Blog*, December 23, 2015, blogs.adb.org/blog/new-highway-open-trade-investment-western-mongolia.

New Straits Times, Kuala Lumpur, February 27, 1997.

"New Ulaanbaatar International Airport, Mongolia." Airport Technology. http://www.airport-technology.com/projects/new-ulaanbaatar-international-airport/.

"NGOs in Mongolia." Open Society Forum, 2005. www.forum.mn/res_mat/NGOS_Survey20060314_en.pdf.

"Nine Countries Participate in the 'Ulaanbaatar Dialogue.'" *Mongol Messenger,* June 20, 2014.

"9.4 Percent of Mongolian Land Being Used for Mining Activity." *Mongol Messenger,* November 11, 2016.

Nixson, Frederick, and Bernard Walters. "The Transition to a Market Economy: Mongolia, 1990–1998." *International Journal of Economic Development* 2, no. 1 (January 2000): 35–66.

"North Korean Foreign Affairs Minister to Visit Mongolia." *NK News*, February 23, 2015.

"North Korean Foreign Minister in Mongolia on Three-Day Visit to Further Cooperation." *NK News*, February 24, 2015.

"North Korean Workers to Leave Mongolia as UN Sanctions Bite." *NEWS agency*, December 4, 2017. https://news.mn/en/765907/.

"Northeast Asian Delegates Gather in Ulaanbaatar to Discuss Regional Issue." *Mongol Messenger*, November 18, 2016.

"The Northeast Asian Women Parliamentarians' Forum in Ulaanbaatar Ends Successfully." *www.infomongolia.com,* accessed November 25, 2017.

Nyamdavaa, Oidovyn. *Mongolia-India Relations.* Ulaanbaatar: Bhavan Books, 2004.

Nye, Joseph S., Jr. *Soft Power: The Means to Success in World Politics.* New York: PublicAffairs, 2004.

"O. Tsendsuren: Mongolian and Russian Consortium Doesn't Exist." *Business Mongolia,* July 5, 2011.

Och, Maya. "Privatization of SOE in Mongolia" (slide presentation, December 6, 2012). https://prezi.com/_a8a1_swa3vh/privatization-of-soe-in-mongolia/.

Och, Od. "Declaration by Mongolia Regarding Its Nuclear-Weapon-Free Status." New York, September 17, 2012. http://nautilus.org/wp-content/uploads/2012/09/signed-Mongolian-declaration.pdf.

Ochirbat, Punsalmaalagiin. *The Time of Heaven*, edited by Peter K. Marsh. Bloomington, IN: The Mongolia Society, 2018.

O'Clery, Conor. *May You Live in Interesting Times.* Dublin: Poolbeg Press, 2008.

Odgaard, Ole. "Living Standards and Poverty." In *Mongolia in Transition: Old Patterns, New Challenges*, edited by Ole Bruun and Ole Odgaard. Richmond, UK: Curzon, 1999.

Odgerel, Tseveen, and Battsetseg Ganbold. "The Mongolian Legal System and Laws: A Brief Overview." *GlobaLex,* NYU Hauser Global Law School (January 2006). http://www.nyulawglobal.org/globalex/Mongolia.html.

Office of Inspector General. "Audit of the Millennium Challenge Corporation's Funding of Activities in Mongolia," audit report no. M-000-12-001-P, Washington, DC, March 22, 2012. https://oig.usaid.gov/sites/default/files/audit-reports/m-000-12-001-p.pdf.

Office of the Press Secretary. "President Bush and President Enkhbayar of Mongolia Sign the Millennium Challenge Corporation Compact." October 22, 2007. https://georgewbush-whitehouse.archives.gov/news/releases/2007/10/20071022-.html.

Office of the US Trade Representative. *Mongolia.* 2013. https://ustr.gov/countries-regions/china-mongolia-taiwan/Mongolia.

"Oil in Mongolia." https://www.petromatadgroup.com/mongolia/oil-in-mongolia/.

Olzvoy, Khumbayn. "J. Beikeriin Ailchlal xiigeed 'guravdaxi tunsh'—uun asuudald." *Olon Ulsin Xariltsaa, World Affairs* 184 (5), no. 1 (2002).

———. "A Mongol's View of Economic Development and Cooperation in Northeast Asia." *Mongolian Journal of International Affairs*, no. 3 (1996): 50–55.

———. "Political and Economic Aspects of Mongolia's Transition into a Market Economy." In *Regional Economic Cooperation in Northeast Asia: Proceedings of the Yongpyeong Conference, September 26–28, 1993.* Honolulu: Northeast Asia Economic Forum, Hawaii Asia-Pacific Institute, April 1994.

Ono Kotaro. "Abe Strikes Energy Deal with Mongolia in a Bid to Curb China's Clout." *Asahi Shimbun,* March 31, 2013. http://livedrifting23.blogspot.com/2013/04/abe-strikes-energy-deal-with-mongolia.html.

Onon, O. "Tax Exempt on Imported Energy from China and Russia." *Montsame,* December 22, 2017. http://montsame.mn/en/read/12862.

Ooluun, B. "Dependence on Foreign Oil Products to Be Reduced." *Mongol Messenger*, March 22, 2013.

———. "Midterm Program on Strategic Partnership Signed." *Mongol Messenger*, March 31, 2017.

"Opposition Questions Hoopla Around Forgiveness of Soviet-Era Debt." *UB Post,* January 8, 2004.

Orban, Anita. *Power, Energy and the New Russian Imperialism.* Westport, CT: Praeger Security International, 2008.

Otgonsaikhan, N. "The Current Situation for Mongolian Foreign Trade and Cooperation with Northeast Asian Countries." ERINA Report no. 127. Niigata, Japan, December 2015. http://www.erina.or.jp/en/wp-content/uploads/2015/02/se12712_tssc.pdf.

"OT's Underground Development Slows as Talks Continue." *Montsame,* April 18, 2014.

Otsuki, Takashi. "Electric Power Grid Interconnections in Northeast Asia: A Quantitative Analysis of Opportunities and Challenges." *SSRN Electronic Journal* (January 2015). www.researchgate.net/publication/314525572.

"Our Weight Depends on How Many Friends We Have Got." *Mongol Messenger,* October 21, 2016.

Overland, Indra, and Kyrre Elvenes Braekhus. "Chinese Perspectives on Russian Oil and Gas." In *Russian Energy Power and Foreign Relations: Implications for Conflict and Cooperation,* edited by Jeronim Perovic, Robert W. Orttung, and Andreas Wenger, 201–220. CCS Studies in Security and International Relations series. London: Routledge, 2009.

Oyundari, E. "Mongolia Celebrates the 25th Anniversary of Democratic Parliamentary Elections." *UB Post,* July 30, 2015. http://ubpost.mongolnews.mn/?p=15540.

Oyundelger, B. "Nomadic Culture Simplifies the Shift to Green Development." *Mongol Messenger,* November 11, 2016.

"Park Seeks 'Eurasia Initiative' to Build Energy, Logistics Links." *Korea Herald,* October 18, 2013. www.koreaherald.com/view.php?ud=20131018000620.

"Parliament Speaker Visits South Gobi Development Projects." *Mongol Messenger,* March 13, 2015.

"Pastoral Risk Management Strategy." FAO project number TCP.MON/0066A.

"Peace Corps Director Visits Mongolia to Celebrate 25th Anniversary." Peace Corps Mongolia, August 15, 2016. https://www.peacecorps.gov/news/library/peace-corps-director-visits-mongolia-celebrate-25th-anniversary/.

Pellerin, Cheryl. "Hagel, Mongolian Defense Minister Agree to Deepen Ties." American Forces Press Service (Ulaanbaatar), April 11, 2014. http://archive.defense.gov/news/newsarticle.aspx?id=122044.

Permanent Mission of Mongolia to the United Nations. Ulaanbaatar Dialogue. April 2013. https://www.un.int/mongolia/mongolia/ulaanbaatar-dialogue.

Perry, Stephen. "The New Silk Road—OBOR—an Overview." *People's Daily Online,* February 5, 2016. http://en.people.cn/n3/2016/0205/c90883-9014677.html.

Petroleum Authority of Mongolia. http://english.pam.gov.mn/home.shtml.

Poindexter, Gregory B. "US$1 Billion Proposed 315-MW Egiin Gol Hydroelectric Project in Mongolia on Hold." *Hydro Review*, June 24, 2016. http://www.hydroworld.com/articles/2016/06/us-1-billion-proposed-315-mw-egiin-hydroelectric-project-in-mongolia-on-hold.html.

Pomfret, Richard. "Transition and Democracy in Mongolia." CIES Discussion Paper 99/07. Adelaide, Australia, April 1999.

Poussenkova, Nina. "'They Went East, They Went West . . .': The Global Expansion of Russian Oil Companies." In *Russia's Energy Policies: National, Interregional and Global Levels*, edited by Pami Aalto, 185–205. Cheltenham, UK: Edward Elgar, 2012.

Pozdneyev, A. M. *Mongolia and the Mongols*, edited and translated by John R. Krueger. Bloomington: Indiana University Press and The Hague: Mouton and Company, 1971 [1896].

"Preliminary Results for the Year Ended 31 December 2003." SOCO International, March 11, 2004. https://www.socointernational.com/news_33.

"President Bush and President Enkhbayar of Mongolia Sign the Millennium Challenge Corporation Compact." Washington, DC: White House Office of the Press Secretary, October 22, 2007. https://georgewbush-whitehouse.archives.gov/news/releases/2007/10/20071022-3.html.

"President Elbegdorj Spoke at the Central European University: 'Mongolian Transition to Democracy and Lessons,'" Embassy of Mongolia, October 18, 2014. http://mongolianembassy.us/2014/10/president-elbegdorj-spoke-at-the-central-european-university-mongolian-transition-to-democracy-and-lessons/#.W9djc3pKii4.

"Prime Minister Abe's Article Contributed to Four Mongolian Newspapers." *Speeches and Statements by the Prime Minister.* Tokyo: Prime Minister of Japan, March 29, 2013. http://japan.kantei.go.jp/96_abe/statement/201303/29_mongol_e.html.

"Prime Minister Meets Presidential Envoy of Russia." American Chamber of Commerce, April 27, 2018. http://mongolia.gogo.mn/r/161599.

"Prime Minister of Japan Shinzo Abe Pays Courtesy Call on President of Mongolia Kh. Battulga." President of Mongolia website, September 6, 2017. https://president.mn/en/2017/09/06/prime-minister-of-japan-shinzo-abe-pays-courtesy-call-on-president-of-mongolia-kh-battulga/.

"Prime Minister of the Republic of India Shri Narendra Modi Pays Courtesy Call on President Elbegdorj." *GoGo Mongolia*, May 18, 2015. http://mongolia.gogo.mn/r/146096.

"Prominent Russians: Lev Gumilev." *Russiapedia*. http://russiapedia.rt.com/prominent-russians/science-and-technology/lev-gumilev/.

"Provision of Animal Health Inputs and Animal Feed to Assist the Restoring of Severely-Affected Households in Snowstorm-Affected Areas." FAO project number TCP/MON/00067 E.

Purevsambuu, G. "First-Ever Summit Held Between Presidents of Mongolia, Russia, and China." *Mongol Messenger*, September 19, 2014.

Quah, Jon S. T. *Curbing Corruption in Asian Countries: An Impossible Dream?* Research in Public Policy Analysis and Management, vol. 20. Bingley, UK: Emerald Group Publishing Limited, 2011.

Radchenko, Sergey. "Soviet Withdrawal from Mongolia, 1986–1992: A Reassessment." *Journal of Slavic Military Studies* 25, no. 2 (2012): 183–203.

Rahman, Azera. "From Land of Chinggis Khan, a Buddhist Monastery for India." *India News Post*, December 13, 2009.

"Railroad Stretch Between Russia's Khasan to N. Korea's Rajin to Be Launched Within Days." *Russia Beyond*, September 7, 2013. https://www.rbth.com/news/2013/09/07/railroad_stretch_between_russias_khasan_to_n_koreas_rajin_to_be_launched_29596.html.

"Railway Delegates of Mongolia, Russia and China Meet in UB." *Mongol Messenger*, August 5, 2016.

Railway Transport Facilitation in Mongolia. Ulaanbaatar: Ministry of Roads and Transportation of Mongolia, 2014.

Reeves, Jeffrey. *Development Planning in Mongolia: Failure and Potential*. Honolulu: Daniel K. Inouye Asia-Pacific Center for Security Studies, January 21, 2014. http://apcss.org/development-planning-in-mongolia-failure-and-potential/.

———. "Mongolia's Place in China's Periphery Diplomacy." *Open Forum*, The Asan Forum, April 7, 2016. http://www.theasanforum.org/mongolias-place-in-chinas-periphery-diplomacy/.

"Regional Development Plans Approved at 14th Greater Tumen Initiative Meeting." UNDP, October 30, 2013. http://www.cn.undp.org/content/china/en/home/presscenter/articles/2013/10/regional-development-plans-approved-at-14th-greater-tumen-initia.html.

"Regional Situations and Relations with Japan." In *Japanese Bluebook*, chap. III, section 3-3. Tokyo: Ministry of Foreign Affairs of Japan, 1992–1993. http://www.mofa.go.jp/policy/other/bluebook/1992/1992-3-1.htm.

"Remarks by Secretary Shultz at US-Mongolian Normalization Ceremony, January 27, 1987." *Mongolia Society Newsletter* (Bloomington, IN), no. 3, February 1987.

"Report: Mongolia Could Host North Korean Refugee Camp." *Mongolia Web*, October 2, 2008.

"Report on Implementation of the Almaty Programme of Action." Paper presented at the Second United Nations Conference on Landlocked Developing Countries, Vienna, Austria, November 3–5, 2014. http://www.lldc2conference.org/custom-content/uploads/2013/07/Mongolia-National-report.pdf.

"Resolution of the Government of Mongolia, No. 2 Approving the Percentage of Foreign Labor Force and Specialists for the Year 2015" (Ulaanbaatar: Government of Mongolia, January 7, 2015). https://www.scribd.com/document/261221108/.

"Resource-Rich Mongolia Rejects Cap on Foreign Workers for 2018." *Reuters*, February 13, 2018. https://www.reuters.com/article/us-mongolia-immigration/resource-rich-mongolia-rejects-cap-on-foreign-workers-for-2018-idUSKBN1FX0PV.

Riseborough, Jesse. "Rio CEO Says Mongolia Won't Receive Mine Dividend for 10 Years." *Bloomberg*, October 6, 2016. https://www.bloomberg.com/news/articles/2016-10-06/rio-ceo-says-mongolia-won-t-receive-mine-dividend-for-10-years.

"Robert Friedland." *New Internationalist,* August 2, 2006. https://newint.org/columns/worldbeaters/2006/08/01/.

Roberts, Dexter. "Mineral-Rich, People-Poor Mongolia Prepares for Flood of Money Next Decade." *Bloomberg News,* July 21, 2011. http://www.bloomberg.com/news/2011-07-21/mineral-rich-people-poor-mongolia-prepares-for-flood-of-money.h.

Rosenberg, Daniel. "The Collectivization of Mongolia's Pastoral Production." *Nomadic Peoples,* no. 9 (September 1981): 23–39.

———. "Leaders and Leadership Roles in a Mongolian Collective: Two Case Studies." *Mongolian Studies, Journal of the Mongolia Society* 7 (1981–1982): 17–51.

Rossabi, Morris. *China and Inner Asia.* London: Thames and Hudson, 1975.

———. *Khubilai Khan: His Life and Times.* Berkeley: University of California Press, 1990.

———. *Modern Mongolia: From Khans to Commissars to Capitalists.* Berkeley: University of California Press, 2005.

Rosseau, Oscar. "Mongolia Reports Highest Ever Livestock Count." *GlobalMeatNews.com*, July 4, 2016.

"Roundtable Meeting: Turkish-Mongolian Relations." Center for Strategic Research, Ministry of Foreign Affairs of Turkey, May 12–15, 2014. http://sam.gov.tr/roundtable-meeting-turkish-mongolian-relations/.

Rowland, Jonathan. "Mongolia: The Slow and Bumpy Road." *World Coal* special report, March 7, 2016.

Rupen, Robert. *How Mongolia Is Really Ruled.* Stanford, CA: Hoover Institution Press, 1979.

"Russia Writes Off Mongolian Debt." January 13, 2004, accessed January 3, 2005. http://www.russiajournal.com/node/17010.

"Russia's External Debt Grew by $25Bln in 2004." *MosNews,* April 04, 2005. http://cbonds.com/news/item/310381.

"Russia's Putin in Mongolia for 5-Hour Visit." Associated Press, September 3, 2014. http://www.dailymail.co.uk/wires/ap/article-2741432/Putin-traveling-Mongolia-5-hour-visit.html.

"Sale of Mongolian Assets." SOCO International, April 1, 2005. https://www.socointernational.com/news_24.

Sandag, Shagdariin, and Harry H. Kendall. *Poisoned Arrows: The Stalin-Choibalsan Mongolian Massacres, 1921–1941.* Boulder, CO: Westview Press, 2000.

Sanders, Alan J. K. "Foreign Relations and Foreign Policy." In *Mongolia in Transition: Old Patterns, New Challenges,* edited by Ole Bruun and Ole Odgaard. Surrey, England: Curzon Press, Nordic Institute of Asian Studies, 1996.

———. *Historical Dictionary of Mongolia.* 3rd ed. Lanham, MD: Scarecrow Press, 2010.

———. "Mongolia's New Constitution: Blueprint for Democracy." *Asian Survey* 32, no. 6 (June 1992): 506–520.

"Sandwiched Between China and Russia, Mongolia Intent on Seeking Permanent Neutrality." Associated Press, November 2, 2015.

Scalapino, Robert. "The Political Process in Northeast Asia and Mongolia's Challenge." Paper presented at Mongolia-US Bilateral Conference, Mongolia-US Comprehensive Partnership in the Context of North East Asia: Challenges and Opportunities, Washington, DC, February 28, 2005.

Schatz, Thomas A. "CAGW Expresses Concern with Millennium Challenge Corporation." Citizens Against Government Waste, March 28, 2008. https://www.cagw.org/media/press-releases/cagw-expresses-concern-millennium-challenge-corporation.

Schmidt, Sabine M. "Pastoral Community Organization, Livelihoods and Biodiversity Conservation in Mongolia's Southern Gobi Region." In *Rangelands of Central Asia: Proceedings of the Conference on Transformations, Issues, and Future Challenges.* Fort Collins, CO: USDA Forest Service, 2006.

Schwarz, Henry G. "The Security of Mongolia." *Mongolian Journal of International Affairs*, no. 3 (1996): 63–72. http://www.mongoliajol.info/index.php/MJIA/article/view/431/452.

"Senate Confirmation Hearings for Ambassador-Designate Joseph Lake." Committee on Foreign Relations, May 4, 1990.

Shafaie, Amir. "Rio Tinto, Mongolia, and the Art of Negotiating Amidst Price Volatility." Natural Resource Governance Institute blog, June 24, 2015. https://resourcegovernance.org/blog/rio-tinto-mongolia-and-art-negotiating-amidst-price-volatility.

Shagdar, Enkhbayar. *Mongolia's Economic Transition and Development Challenges: An Evidence of Poorly Managed Neoliberal, Shock Therapy Transition and Economic Destitution.* Riga, Latvia: Lambert Academic Publishing, 2012.

———. "Neo-Liberal 'Shock Therapy' Policy During the Mongolian Economic Transition." ERINA Discussion Paper no. 0703e. Niigata, Japan, April 2007.

———. "Recent Trends in Mongolian Foreign Trade with the Countries of Northeast Asia." ERINA Report no. 96. Niigata, Japan, November 2010.

———. "Unemployment and Impoverishment in Mongolia: A Close Look at the Reality." ERINA research paper, Niigata, Japan, 2003. http://www.academia.edu/6718735/Unemployment_and_Impoverishment_in_Mongolia_A_Close_Look_at_the_Reality.

Shapiro, Fred. "Starting from Scratch." *The New Yorker,* January 20, 1992.

Sharma, Rajeev. "Forget Uranium: Real Reason Behind PM Modi's Mongolia Visit Is China." *Firstpost*, May 9, 2015.

"Shinzo Abe Invites President Ts. Elbegdorj to His Home." *Montsame,* September 30, 2013.

Shirendev, B. *The History of the Mongolian People's Republic.* Translated by William A. Brown and Urgunge Onon. Cambridge, MA: East Asian Research Center and Harvard University Press, 1976.

"The 6th GTI Transport Board Meeting Held Back to Back with the 1st Meeting of the ASEM Expert Group on Eurasia Transport and Logistics." Greater Tumen Initiative, November 16, 2016. http://www.tumenprogramme.org/?info-648-1.html.

Sneath, David. "The Rural and the Urban in Pastoral Mongolia." In *Mongols from Country to City: Floating Boundaries, Pastoralism and City Life in the Mongol Lands*, edited by Ole Bruun and Li Narangoa, 140–161. Copenhagen: NIAS Press, 2006.

Snow, Keith Harmon. "Goldman Prizewinner Gets 21 Years for Resistance to Genocide." *Dissident Voice,* February 6, 2014.

Solongo, P. "Current Status and Future Development of Dry Ports in Mongolia." PowerPoint presentation for Asian Way, LLC, Almaty, Kazakhstan, May 30, 2018. https://www.unescap.org/sites/default/files/6.%20%20Mongolia%20resource%20person%20presentation.pdf.

Soni, Sharad K. *Mongolia-Russia Relations: Kiakhta to Vladisvostok.* New Delhi: Shipra Publications, 2002.

"SouthGobi Says Chalco Abandons Bid, Unveils Board Changes." Proactive Investors, September 4, 2012. https://www.proactiveinvestors.com/companies/news/89246/southgobi-says-chalco-abandons-bid-unveils-board-changes-34213.html.

"Speech by Tsakiagiin Elbegdorj, President of Mongolia, at the APEC Meeting 'Dialogue on Strengthening Connectivity Partnership,'" November 8, 2014. http://eng.president.mn/newsCenter/viewNews.php?newsId=1353.

Sposato, William. "Japan Seeks Stronger Mongolia Ties." *Wall Street Journal*, March 30, 2013. http://www.wsj.com/articles/SB10001424127887324685104578392123216653156.

Stanway, David. "Mongolian Court Orders Govt to Enforce Mining Ban." Reuters, October 21, 2011.

———. "U.N. to Pay Mongolian Nomads to Dispose of Dead Herds." Reuters, February 25, 2010.

Stobdan, Phunchok. "In Modi's Mongolia Pivot, a Test of Indian Soft Power." *The Wire* (New Delhi), May 16, 2015.

———. "India, Buddhism and Geopolitics in Central Asia: Regaining Centrality." *IDSA Policy Brief*, June 25, 2010. https://idsa.in/system/files/PB_IndiaBuddhismandGeopoliticsinCentralAsia.pdf.

———. "India and Mongolia: Modi on Ashoka's Path." *IDSA Comment,* Institute for Defence Studies and Analyses, May 13, 2015. https://idsa.in/idsacomments/IndiaandMongolia_pstobdan_130515.

———. "Mongolia and Asian Security." *Mongolian Journal of International Affairs*, no. 7 (2000): 51–62. http://www.mongoliajol.info/index.php/MJIA/article/view/140/141.

Strategies for Development of Green Energy Systems in Mongolia. Stockholm: Global Green Growth Institute, March 2014. https://www.sei.org/mediamanager/documents/Publications/Climate/GGGI-SEI-2014-Mongolia-green-energy-systems.pdf.

"Strengthening Human Rights and Fostering Democratic Governance." http://www.indexmundi.com/mongolia/millennium-development-goals.html.

Sturgess, Brian. "Investing in Mongolia." *World Economics,* September 2012. http://www.worldeconomics.com-Papers/Investing%20in%20Mongolia_c93dbdb0-1a04-4e33-b331-51c25d21d47a.paper#_ftn5.

Sumiya, B. "Globalization and Mongolian Nomadics Cultural Heritage." In *Dialogue Among Civilizations: Interaction Between Nomadic and Other Cultures of Central Asia.* Ulaanbaatar: International Institute for the Study of Nomadic Civilizations, 2001.

Sundaram, K. "Human Resource Development and Training in Mongolia: Issues and Options." Unpublished report. Bangkok: International Labour Office East Asia Multidisciplinary Advisory Team, August 2000.

"Sustainable Transport: Challenges, Strategy of Mongolia." Presented at the Fourth Regional Environmentally Sustainable Transport Forum, Seoul, Korea, February 24–26, 2009. http://www.uncrd.or.jp/content/documents/4EST-B1G102.pdf.

Swiss Agency for Development and Cooperation. "Supporting Mongolia's Civil Society Organisations." December 16, 2013. www.swiss-cooperation.admin.ch/mongolia/en/Home/State_Reform_Local_Governance_and_Civic_Participation/Mongolia_s_Civil_Society_NGO_Capacity_Building_Project or http://www.loginasia.org/ga2-assets/files/KnowledgeProducts/Political-Economy-Mapping-of-LOGIN-Member-Countries.pdf.

"Symbior Solar and NovaTerra Enter into Shareholders' Agreement for Joint Venture Development of 50MW Solar PV Project in Mongolia." *NovaTerra,* January 18, 2017. http://novaterra.mn/press-release.html.

Tabata, Shinichiro, and Xu Liu. "Russia's Energy Policy in the Far East and East Siberia." In *Russia's Energy Policies: National, Interregional and Global Levels*, edited by Pami Aalto, 156–182. Cheltenham, UK: Edward Elgar, 2012.

Tajima, Hiroshi. "Japan in Depth: Abe's Mongolia Visit Strategic Move." *The Daily Yomiuri,* March 31, 2013. https://www.questia.com/newspaper/1P3-2931677501/japan-in-depth-abe-s-mongolia-visit-strategic-move.

"Tapping Offshore: Issuing and Floating Abroad to Finance Growth." Oxford Business Group, 2012.

Tarnoff, Curt. Millennium Challenge Corporation. Congressional Research Service, April 5, 2016, 17. https://fas.org/sgp/crs/row/RL32427.pdf.

Taylor, Adam. "Why Mongolia Hopes to Host a Trump–Kim Jong Un Meeting." *Washington Post*, April 20, 2018. https://www.washingtonpost.com/news/worldviews/wp/2018/04/20/why-mongolia-hopes-to-host-a-trump-kim-jong-un-meeting/?noredirect=on&utm_term=.235625c456bf.

"Tenth Anniversary of First Major Gold and Copper Discovery at Oyu Tolgoi by Ivanhoe Mines Coincides with Period of Peak Construction on Mongolia's Largest Mining Complex." *Yahoo! Marketwire*, July 17, 2011. https://www.yahoo.com/news/Tenth-Anniversary-of-First-ccn-1681354512.html.

"Text of the PM's press statement after the Signing of Agreements in Ulaanbaatar, Mongolia." PMINDIA website, May 17, 2015. http://www.pmindia.gov.in/en/news_updates/text-of-the-pms-press-statement-after-the-signing-of-agreements-in-ulaanbaatar-mongolia/.

Theunissen, Tirza. "Poverty, Inequality, and the Negative Effects of Mongolia's Economic Downturn." *InAsia*, Asia Foundation, June 25, 2014. http://asiafoundation

.org/in-asia/2014/06/25/poverty-inequality-and-the-negative-effects-of-mongolias-economic-downturn/.
"Third Workshop on Power Grid Interconnection in Northeast Asia." Nautilus Institute for Security and Sustainability, Vladivostok, September 30–October 3, 2003. https://nautilus.org/projects/by-name/asian-energy-security/workshop-on-power-grid-interconnection-in-northeast-asia/third-workshop-on-power-grid-interconnection-in-northeast-asia/.
"A Tool to Share Mongolia's Experience in Democracy and Market Economy with Emerging Democracies." Ulaanbaatar: Mongolian Ministry of Foreign Relations, November 21, 2015. http://www.mfa.gov.mn/?p=29286&lang=en.
Tovuudorj, P. "Mongolian National Energy Agenda and Policy Measures: Scope for Sub-region Cooperation." Presentation to Senior Officials Committee on Energy Cooperation in Northeast Asia Eighth Session, Ulaanbaatar, April 10–11, 2013.
"Transparency Matters: Disclosure Payments to Governments by Chinese Extractive Companies." Global Witness, January 15, 2013. https://www.globalwitness.org/en/archive/transparencymatters/.
"Ts. Elbegdorj: Our Two Countries Are Good Friends." *Montsame*, November 5, 2013.
Tse, Pui-Kwan. "The Mineral Industry of Mongolia." In *2006 Minerals Yearbook: Mongolia.* Washington, DC: US Geological Survey, October 2007. http://minerals.usgs.gov/minerals/pubs/country/2006/myb3-2006-mg.pdf.
Tseveen, Odgerel, and Battsetseg Ganbold. "The Mongolian Legal System and Laws: A Brief Overview." New York: Hauser Global Law School, January 2006. http://www.nyulawglobal.org/globalex/Mongolia.html.
"Tumen Development Body Likely to Be Upgraded into Int'l Organization." *Yonhap News,* October 30, 2013.
"Turkish Ambassador Gets au Fait with Altanbulag FTZ." *Mongol Messenger*, March 13, 2015.
Tuvshintugs, A. "National Perspectives on Linkage Strategy: Mongolian Perspective." In *Political Economy of the Northeast Asian Regionalism: Linkages Between Economic and Security Cooperation.* Seoul: Korea Institute for National Unification, 2006.
Tuya, N. "Dimensions of Mongolia's National Security." Remarks at the Asia Foundation Conference on Mongolia's Political and Economic Transition: Challenges and Opportunities, Ulaanbaatar, September 13, 2000. https://asiafoundation.org/resources/pdfs/MongoliaPolEcon Transition.pdf.
"2016 Northeast Asia International Conference for Economic Development (NICE) Successfully Held." Greater Tumen Initiative, November 16, 2016. http://www.tumenprogramme.org/?info-641-1.html.
UB Post, December 15, 1998.
UB Post, October 13, 2009.
"Ulaanbaatar Declaration." Tenth Consultative Commission Meeting of the Greater Tumen Initiative, Ulaanbaatar, Mongolia, March 24, 2009. http://www.tumenprogramme.org/?info-548-1.html.
"Ulaanbaatar Dialogue." Permanent Mission of Mongolia to the United Nations, April 2013. https://www.un.int/mongolia/mongolia/ulaanbaatar-dialogue.
Ulaanbaatar Dialogue on Northeast Asian Security 2014, Conference Proceedings. Ulaanbaatar: Ministry of Foreign Affairs, September 2014.
"Ulaanbaatar Dialogue on Northeast Asian Security Concludes." *UB Post,* June 18, 2018.
"Ulaanbaatar Railway Modernisation Strategy." *Railway Gazette,* September 4, 2014.
UN Conference on Trade and Development. *World Investment Report 2006: FDI from Developing and Transition Economies: Implications for Development.* New York: UNCTAD, 2006. http://unctad.org/en/Docs/wir2006_en.pdf.
UNDP/SIDA. "Poverty Research, Options." 2004.
UNDP/Swedish International Development Agency (SIDA). "Poverty Research, Examination of Effectiveness." 2003.
United Nations Development Programme. *Human Development Report Mongolia 2003: Urban Rural Disparities in Mongolia.* Ulaanbaatar: Government of Mongolia and UNDP, 2003. http://hdr.undp.org/sites/default/files/mongolia_2003_en.pdf.

United Nations Economic and Social Council. "Annex to the Letter Dated 9 April 2015 from the Permanent Representative of Mongolia to the United Nations Addressed to the President of the Economic and Social Council, Executive Summary." New York: Mongolian Mission to the UN, April 10, 2015.

Untitled Ulaanbaatar Dialogue document. Ulaanbaatar: Ministry of Foreign Affairs of Mongolia. http://www.mfa.gov.mn/wp-content/uploads/2015/12/Ulaanbaaţar-Dialogue.pdf.

"Update 3: Two Japan-Led Groups to Bid for Tavan Tolgoi Coal Mine." Reuters, January 31, 2011. http://www.reuters.com/article/mongolia-tavan-tolgoi-idUSTOE70U02Q20110131.

"Uranium in Mongolia." World Nuclear Association, April 2016. http://www.world-nuclear.org/information-library/country-profiles/countries-g-n/mongolia.aspx.

USAID and Asia Foundation. *Assessment of Corruption in Mongolia: Final Report.* Alexandria, VA: Casals and Associates, August 31, 2005. http://pdf.usaid.gov/pdf_docs/Pnade136.pdf.

US-China Economic and Security Review Commission. *China's Energy Needs and Strategies*. Washington, DC: US Government Printing Office, 2003. https://babel.hathitrust.org/cgi/pt?id=umn.31951d02062349n.

"US Defence Secretary Chuck Hagel Boosts Mongolia Ties As Asia Trip Ends." *South China Morning Post*, April 10, 2014. https://www.scmp.com/news/asia/article/1474493/us-defence-secretary-chuck-hagel-boosts-mongolia-ties-asia-trip-ends.

US Department of State. *Investment Climate Statements for 2016: Mongolia.* Washington, DC: Bureau of Economic and Business Affairs, 2016. https://www.state.gov/e/eb/rls/othr/ics/2016investmentclimatestatements/index.htm?year=2016&dlid=254299#wrapper.

———. *Mongolia 2013 Human Rights Report*. Washington, DC, 2013. https://www.state.gov/documents/organization/220425.pdf.

———. *2010 Investment Climate Statement: Mongolia.* Washington, DC: Bureau of Economic and Business Affairs, 2010. www.state.gov/e/eb/rls/othr/ics/2010/138766.htm.

———. *2014 Investment Climate Statement: Mongolia.* Washington, DC: Bureau of Economic and Business Affairs, 2014. https://www.state.gov/e/eb/rls/othr/ics/2014/231041.htm.

"U.S., Mongolia Celebrate Signing of $350 Million MCC Compact to Address Impending Water Crisis." Millennium Challenge Corporation, September 20, 2018. https://www.mcc.gov/news-and-events/release/release-092018-us-mongolia-joint-declaration.

"U.S.-Mongolia Relations: History and Future Prospects." Roundtable Unpublished Proceedings (Washington, DC: October 31, 2005).

Vandangombo, Danaasuren. "NGOs as Accountability Promoters: In the Mongolian Case." Paper presented at the Sixth Asia Pacific Interdisciplinary Research in Accounting Conference, Sydney, Australia, July 12, 2010. http://apira2010.econ.usyd.edu.au/conference_proceedings/APIRA-2010-166-vanDanGombo-NGOS-as-accountability-promoters-Mongolia.pdf.

Wang, Weina. "Regional Economic Cooperation in Northeast Asia Under the Greater Tumen Initiative." PowerPoint presentation. Beijing: Greater Tumen Initiative Secretariat, n.d. https://www.unescap.org/sites/default/files/Session3_Wang_Regional_Economic_Cooperation_1.pdf.

Watts, Jonathan. "UN Launches Mongolia $4m Appeal to Clear Up Livestock Killed by Big Freeze." *The Guardian,* February 25, 2010.

"What Is Break Bulk Shipping?." Logistics Plus, March 8, 2017. https://www.logisticsplus.net/what-is-break-bulk-shipping/.

Williams, Martin John. "Australian Miner Set to Run Mongolia's Lottery." GamblingCompliance, July 15, 2015. https://gamblingcompliance.com/premium-content/insights_analysis/australian-miner-set-run-mongolia%E2%80%99s-lottery.

Wink, André. *Nomads in the Sedentary World*, edited by Anatoly M. Ikhazanov and André Wink. London: RoutledgeCurzon, 2001, 285–295.

Wolleh, Oliver. "Track 1.5 Approaches to Conflict Management: Assessing Good Practice and Areas for Improvement." Berlin: Berghof Foundation for Peace Support, May

2007." https://peacemaker.un.org/sites/peacemaker.un.org/files/Track1.5Approaches toConflictManagement_BerghofFoundation2007.pdf.

Worden, Robert L., ed. *Mongolia: A Country Study.* Washington, DC: US Government Printing Office, 1991.

"Working Meeting on GTI Agriculture Cooperation Strategic Action Plan in Ulaanbaatar, Mongolia [July 5–6, 2016]." Greater Tumen Initiative, November 16, 2016. http://www.tumenprogramme.org/?info-647-1.html.

"World: Asia-Pacific Mongolian MPs Face Corruption Probe." BBC News, April 12, 1999. http://news.bbc.co.uk/2/hi/asia-pacific/317344.stm.

World Bank. "Mongolia Energy Sector Review." World Bank Report no. 14586-MOG. Washington, DC: World Bank, November 3, 1995. http://documents.worldbank.org/curated/en/483911468773986690/pdf/multi-page.pdf.

"The World Bank in Mongolia: Overview." 2012. http://www.worldbank.org/en/country/mongolia/overview.

"World Bank Project Aims to Help Mongolia Diversify Exports." *Mongol Messenger,* March 31, 2017.

World Economic Forum Strategic Dialogue on the Future of Mongolia. Ulaanbaatar: World Economic Forum, 2013. http://www3.weforum.org/docs/UB13/WEF_UB13_Report.pdf.

Wu, John C. "The Mineral Industry of Mongolia." Washington, DC: US Geological Survey, July 30, 2010. https://minerals.usgs.gov/minerals/pubs/country/1995/9319095.pdf.

"Xi Assents to Trilateral Summit with Russia, Mongolia." *BRICS Post,* August 22, 2014. http://thebricspost.com/xi-assent-to-trilateral-summit-with-russia-mongolia/#.WBy6EoWcF9A.

"Xi Jinping Attends Second Meeting of Heads of State of China, Russia and Mongolia." PRC Ministry of Foreign Affairs, July 10, 2015. https://www.fmprc.gov.cn/mfa_eng/zxxx_662805/t1280848.shtml.

Yun, Michelle. "Chalco Agrees to Buy SouthGobi Stake to Gain Coal Mines." *Bloomberg,* April 2, 2012.

Zhang Min, "New Tianjin Road Cuts Transportation Time, Cost to Mongolia, Russia." *China Daily,* September 28, 2016. http://www.chinadaily.com.cn/bizchina/2016-09/28/content_26922236.htm.

Zhang Yunbi, and Wu Jiao. "China, Mongolia to Boost Ties." *China Daily,* January 13, 2012. www.chinadaily.com.cn/cndy/2012-01/13/content_14436254.htm.

Zhu Shu. "A Perspective on the Greater Tumen Initiative and Northeast Asia Economic Cooperation." Jeju Peace Institute, August 24, 2011. http://www.jpi.or.kr/eng/regular/print_ok.sky?id=4102.

Zoljargal, M. "Altanbulag Free Trade Zone to Improve Cross Border Trade." *UB Post,* June 19, 2014.

———. "Tsast Group Partners with Kyeryong Group for Redevelopment." *UB Post,* July 7, 2013. http://ubpost.mongolnews.mn/?p=4732.

Index

About the Book

Strategically located at the crossroads of Central Asia, China, and Russia, Mongolia has long attracted the attention of major world powers. How has this traditionally nomadic, but resource rich, country used a "Wolf Strategy" to establish its own place in the modern world? What challenges does it now face? Answering these questions, Alicia Campi provides a multifaceted examination of the context, formulation, and execution of contemporary Mongolian foreign policy.

Alicia Campi, president emeritus of the Mongolia Society, is research fellow in the Edwin O. Reischauer Center for East Asian Studies at the Johns Hopkins University School of Advanced International Studies (SAIS) and adjunct professor in SAIS's Asia Programs. She also lectures at the Northeast Asia regional studies course at the Foreign Service Institute.

